AF588488

Cybersecurity Auditing

Cybersecurity Auditing

Principles, Practices, and Frameworks

Jason Edwards

This edition first published 2026

© 2026 by John Wiley & Sons Ltd

All rights reserved, including rights for text and data mining and training of artificial intelligence technologies or similar technologies. No part of this publication may be reproduced, stored in a retrieval system, or transmitted, in any form or by any means, electronic, mechanical, photocopying, recording or otherwise, except as permitted by law. Advice on how to obtain permission to reuse material from this title is available at http://www.wiley.com/go/permissions.

The right of Jason Edwards to be identified as the author of this work has been asserted in accordance with law.

Registered Offices
John Wiley & Sons, Inc., 111 River Street, Hoboken, NJ 07030, USA
John Wiley & Sons Ltd. New Era House, 8 Oldlands Way, Bognor Regis, West Sussex, PO22 9NQ, UK

For details of our global editorial offices, customer services, and more information about Wiley products visit us at www.wiley.com.

The manufacturer's authorized representative according to the EU General Product Safety Regulation is Wiley-VCH GmbH, Boschstr. 12, 69469 Weinheim, Germany, e-mail: Product_Safety@wiley.com.

Wiley also publishes its books in a variety of electronic formats and by print-on-demand. Some content that appears in standard print versions of this book may not be available in other formats.

Trademarks: Wiley and the Wiley logo are trademarks or registered trademarks of John Wiley & Sons, Inc. and/or its affiliates in the United States and other countries and may not be used without written permission. All other trademarks are the property of their respective owners. John Wiley & Sons, Inc. is not associated with any product or vendor mentioned in this book.

Limit of Liability/Disclaimer of Warranty: In view of ongoing research, equipment modifications, changes in governmental regulations, and the constant flow of information relating to the use of experimental reagents, equipment, and devices, the reader is urged to review and evaluate the information provided in the package insert or instructions for each chemical, piece of equipment, reagent, or device for, among other things, any changes in the instructions or indication of usage and for added warnings and precautions. While the publisher and the authors have used their best efforts in preparing this work, including a review of the content of the work, neither the publisher nor the authors make any representations or warranties with respect to the accuracy or completeness of the contents of this work and specifically disclaim all warranties, including without limitation any implied warranties of merchantability or fitness for a particular purpose. No warranty may be created or extended by sales representatives, written sales materials or promotional statements for this work. The fact that an organization, website, or product is referred to in this work as a citation and/or potential source of further information does not mean that the publisher and authors endorse the information or services the organization, website, or product may provide or recommendations it may make. This work is sold with the understanding that the publisher is not engaged in rendering professional services. The advice and strategies contained herein may not be suitable for your situation. You should consult with a specialist where appropriate. Further, readers should be aware that websites listed in this work may have changed or disappeared between when this work was written and when it is read. Neither the publisher nor authors shall be liable for any loss of profit or any other commercial damages, including but not limited to special, incidental, consequential, or other damages.

Library of Congress Cataloging-in-Publication Data has been applied for:

Hardback: 9781394423040
ePDF: 9781394423071
epub: 9781394423057
obook: 9781394423088

Cover Design: Wiley
Cover Image: © olmax1975/stock.adobe.com

Set in 9.5/12.5pt STIX Two Text by Lumina Datamatics

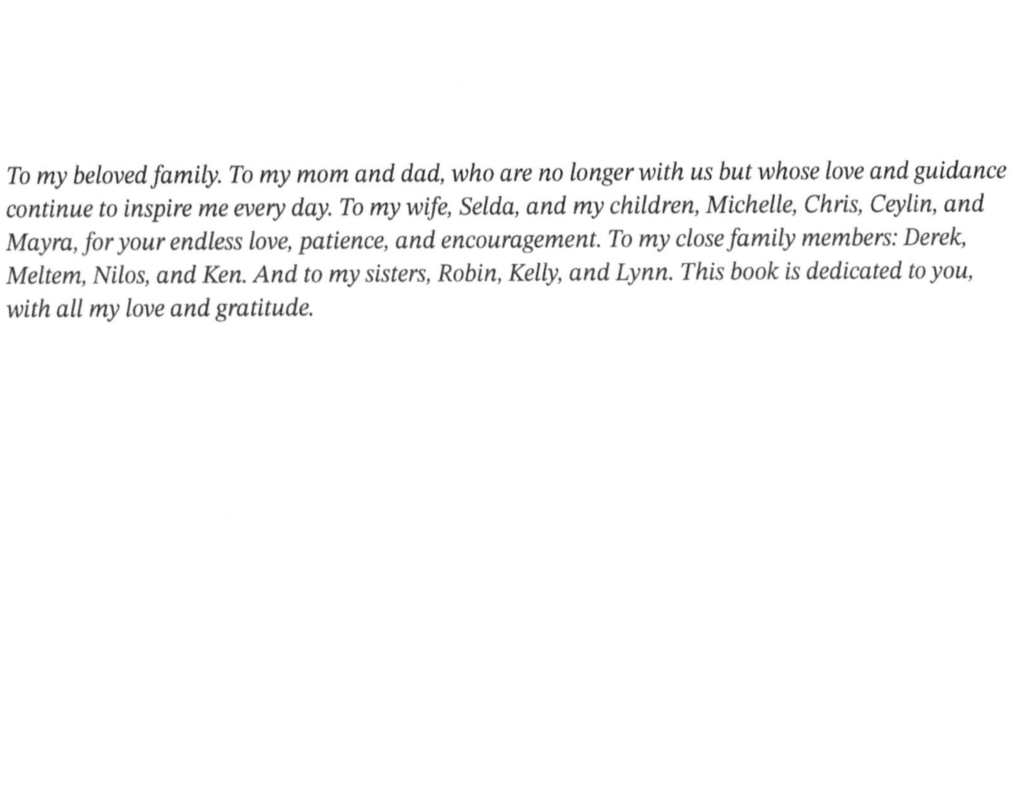

To my beloved family. To my mom and dad, who are no longer with us but whose love and guidance continue to inspire me every day. To my wife, Selda, and my children, Michelle, Chris, Ceylin, and Mayra, for your endless love, patience, and encouragement. To my close family members: Derek, Meltem, Nilos, and Ken. And to my sisters, Robin, Kelly, and Lynn. This book is dedicated to you, with all my love and gratitude.

Contents

Preface

Cybersecurity has matured from a niche technical discipline into a core business function that shapes strategy, protects revenue, and sustains trust. As that transition has unfolded, the role of internal audit has evolved with it. Today's cyber auditor is expected to evaluate complex control environments, translate technical risks into business terms, and provide assurance that withstands scrutiny from boards, regulators, and customers. This book was written to help auditors meet that mandate with clarity, rigor, and practicality.

Cyber risk moves quickly, but assurance must remain durable. Many resources explain how to implement security; far fewer show how to independently test it, document it, and communicate conclusions that drive action. The focus here is the auditor's work: scoping with purpose, selecting appropriate criteria, gathering defensible evidence, applying sound sampling and testing methods, and issuing findings that are both technically accurate and operationally useful. The aim is to be actionable in real environments—hybrid networks, multi-cloud estates, SaaS portfolios, modern application pipelines, and AI-enabled workflows—without losing sight of independence and professional judgment.

This book is intended for internal auditors, IT and security audit specialists, second-line risk and compliance leaders, and security managers who want to anticipate how assurance will be performed. It assumes familiarity with foundational security concepts and concentrates on how those concepts are assessed through clear criteria, reliable evidence, and disciplined testing. Practitioners will find it useful as a guide to preparing for audits; auditors will find it a framework for producing workpapers that are complete, accurate, and reviewable.

Across the chapters, the emphasis is consistent: define scope and criteria up front; collect evidence that proves what it purports to prove; use testing methods that align with control frequency and materiality; and report in a way that motivates remediation while preserving independence. The material avoids vendor-specific prescriptions unless they illustrate generalizable assurance principles. Wherever judgment is required—on materiality thresholds, reliance on others' work, or conclusions under uncertainty—the discussion explains what should be considered and how that judgment should be documented.

The early chapters establish the assurance foundation with governance, ethics, standards, risk translation, evidence quality, sampling, and testing techniques. Subsequent chapters move through domain-specific audits, including identity and access management, networks and perimeter defenses, applications and APIs, cloud and SaaS, data protection, logging and detection, incident response, vulnerabilities and penetration testing oversight, third-party risk, and operational technology. Later sections address sector overlays and continuous assurance, then turn to AI-centric risks, secure MLOps practices, and monitoring, before concluding with reporting, issues management, stakeholder communication, and program maturity.

Readers can use the content in several ways. Audit leaders can plan risk-based engagements and set expectations for evidence and testing. Field auditors can execute procedures with confidence, knowing what "good" looks like and where evidence typically resides. Security leaders can align control design and operating practices with how auditors evaluate effectiveness. Program owners can adopt the maturity and continuous assurance guidance to evolve from periodic projects to data-driven, ongoing assurance.

Conventions are kept simple to promote usability. Terms are defined on first use. Design effectiveness is clearly distinguished from operating effectiveness, advisory work from assurance, and evidence sources are identified with attention to completeness, provenance, and integrity. Examples favor clarity over exhaustiveness so they can be adapted to varied technology stacks and organizational contexts.

This book does not prescribe a single framework or toolset. It shows how to map and compare criteria, assemble a defensible basis for conclusions, and communicate results that stand up to review. It also does not replace organizational policies or regulatory obligations; rather, it provides practical methods for testing against them and reporting results in a manner that aids decision-making.

Finally, a note on change. Threats, technologies, and regulations evolve, but the assurance principles presented here—clear criteria, reliable evidence, appropriate testing, transparent reporting, and disciplined professional judgment—remain stable. Apply them with curiosity and humility. When the environment shifts, revisit your scoping, refresh your criteria, and verify that the evidence you collect still supports the conclusions you reach.

This work reflects the contributions of auditors, engineers, risk leaders, and executives who share a common goal: better decisions through trustworthy assurance. Their candor, rigor, and willingness to challenge assumptions have shaped the practices described in these pages. Whether you are planning your first cybersecurity audit or refining a mature program, I hope this preface sets the tone for a resource that is firm in principle, flexible in execution, and focused on clarity, evidence, and impact.

Dr. Jason Edwards

Acknowledgments

I am deeply grateful to all those who have contributed to the creation of this book. First and foremost, I would like to express my heartfelt appreciation to my family for their unwavering support and understanding throughout the writing process. To my wife, Selda, and my children, Michelle, Chris, Ceylin, and Mayra, your patience and encouragement have been my anchor. I am also thankful for the love and support from my extended family: Derek, Meltem, Nilos, Ken, and my sisters Robin, Kelly, and Lynn.

I am indebted to the organizations and the many fellow educators who have been pivotal in my professional development and the success of this book: Hallmark University, Moravian University, IronCircle, Cybrary, and the more than 100 K LinkedIn subscribers who follow me.

To the millions of readers and listeners who follow my cybersecurity content each year on BareMetalCyber.com & DailyCyber.News, your trust and engagement are the fuel that keeps this work moving forward. Thank you for making this journey possible.

I also encourage everyone reading this to support a cause close to my heart—the Beagle Freedom Project, which fights for the rights and rescue of animals used in laboratory testing. You can learn more about their work and my children's cybersecurity book series, starring Darwin the Cyber Beagle, at CyberBeagle.kids.

To find more of my books, check out CyberAuthor.Me

And please Connect/Follow me on LinkedIn: Jason-edwards.me

About the Companion Website

This book is accompanied by a companion website for BCS Standard: Student

www.wiley.com\go\edwards\cybersecurityauditing1

1

The Role of Audit in Security Governance, Risk, and Compliance

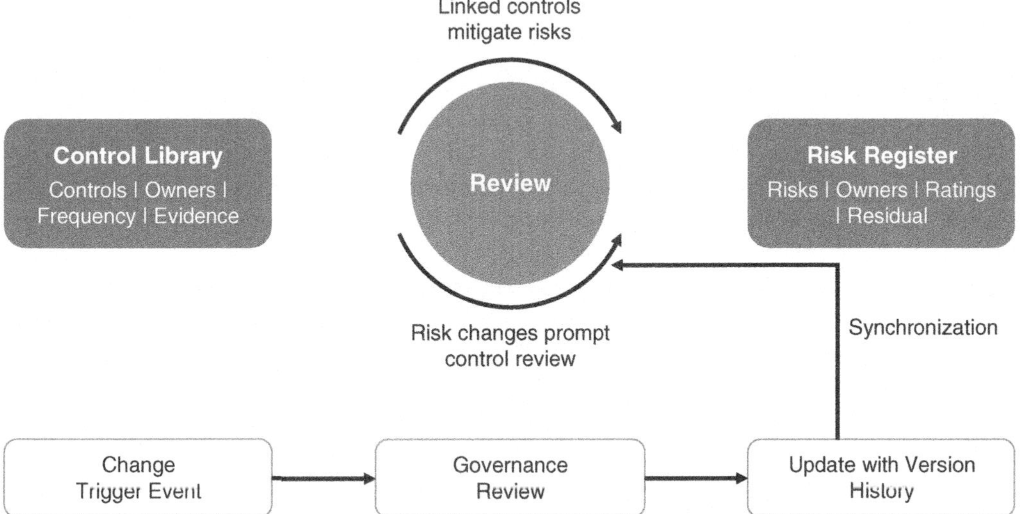

Audit exists at the intersection of governance and trust—the discipline that verifies whether risk management is more than a promise. In cybersecurity, that trust depends on how well assurance functions are defined, empowered, and executed. This chapter examines the structures that make independence real: from the authority granted in an audit charter to the flow of information between the board, the CISO, legal, and privacy leaders. It explores how policies, standards, and procedures become auditable systems rather than documents, and how control libraries and risk registers anchor those systems in measurable accountability.

Understanding these governance foundations is essential in an era when digital ecosystems evolve faster than oversight frameworks. Artificial intelligence, automation, and continuous delivery reshape how organizations identify and mitigate risk, but they also amplify the cost of weak governance. Effective auditors must therefore trace assurance from principle to proof—linking intent, control design, and evidence stored across cloud, CI/CD, and monitoring platforms. The result is not only regulatory compliance but operational confidence in how security decisions are made, justified, and sustained.

From independence boundaries to exception management, this chapter highlights how a modern cybersecurity audit function preserves objectivity while staying relevant in a dynamic threat landscape. It emphasizes that true assurance is not achieved through endless testing, but through disciplined architecture—policies aligned to risks, controls mapped to evidence, and exceptions constrained by time and transparency. In a world increasingly governed by data and algorithms, these mechanisms ensure that oversight remains both human in judgment and machine-verifiable in fact.

Assurance Mandate Within the Three Lines Model

In modern enterprises, cybersecurity auditing lives in the third line of defense—the line that doesn't build, doesn't enforce, and doesn't approve, but instead shines light on whether all those functions truly work as intended. It is the organization's independent conscience, separate from the teams that manage daily risks and the ones that design policies. While the first line owns and operates the controls, and the second line oversees and guides them, the third line stands apart to answer a single, profound question: can our leaders, regulators, and customers trust that our security program actually does what it claims?

The essence of cyber audit's role is assurance—an evidence-based opinion about how well the organization's security controls are designed and operating. Design effectiveness examines whether a control, on paper, could prevent or detect a risk if performed correctly. Operating effectiveness tests whether it actually does so in practice. When auditors conclude that controls are both sound in concept and reliable in execution, they provide the kind of confidence that executives can act on, directors can endorse, and regulators can respect. That's the currency of assurance: trust, but verified.

Assurance in cybersecurity is different from advice, though the two often coexist. Assurance looks backward and inward—it measures what *is*. Advice looks forward—it suggests what *could be*. An auditor can highlight weak encryption key management as a risk, but if that same auditor designs the new key management system, independence dissolves. Once you help build the engine, you can't fairly test how it runs. Advisory input is valuable when bounded by clear safeguards, but it must never bleed into ownership of the control environment itself.

The Three Lines model exists precisely to preserve that separation of roles. The first line—the operational and security teams—owns risk and controls. They patch servers, configure firewalls, and enforce access rules. The second line—the risk and compliance functions—translates organizational risk appetite into policies, standards, and monitoring. They advise, interpret, and escalate. The third line—the audit function—sits above both, accountable only to the board or audit committee, not to the management chain it reviews. This independence is the foundation that allows assurance to carry weight.

When an audit team is truly independent, its work transcends box-checking. Its findings become a mirror that reflects reality as it is, not as management hopes it to be. That mirror might reveal a control framework that looks strong on paper but falters in daily execution—incident response plans that never get tested, access reviews rubber-stamped without real scrutiny, or vulnerability scans performed but never triaged. The assurance mandate requires not just identifying those gaps but linking them back to the risk they represent, so decision-makers can see the full picture of exposure and resilience.

For boards and audit committees, assurance is the instrument of accountability. It verifies that management's claims about cybersecurity readiness aren't built on optimism or assumption. In an era when regulators and customers expect transparency, the independent audit report becomes a symbol of organizational maturity. It tells external stakeholders, "Our security has been measured, not merely promised." Within the enterprise, it tells management, "You are responsible for managing risk, and we are responsible for verifying how well you've done it."

The boundary between assurance and advice often tests an auditor's discipline. There's a natural temptation, especially in cybersecurity, to roll up one's sleeves and "fix" a problem once it's spotted. But an auditor who builds a control forfeits the right to later opine on its effectiveness. The audit function must remain the referee, not the player. That doesn't mean auditors can't guide or educate—offering perspective, suggesting frameworks, or sharing lessons from other organizations—but it means the final design and execution must remain firmly in management's hands.

In practice, maintaining that line is both an art and a principle. Cyber auditors walk a tightrope between being useful and being independent. Too detached, and they become irrelevant; too involved, and they lose credibility. The best audit teams manage this balance by framing their insights as questions that provoke better decisions: "What risk does this exception introduce?" or "How will this control sustain under load?" In this way, assurance still teaches, but through challenge rather than direction.

The independence of the third line is not merely structural—it is ethical. Reporting to the board or audit committee is a formal safeguard, but real independence lives in the auditor's mindset: professional skepticism, intellectual honesty, and courage to publish uncomfortable truths. A compromised auditor who softens findings to protect relationships erodes not only the audit function's credibility but also the organization's entire governance foundation. Independence, once traded away, is almost impossible to regain.

Cyber assurance, at its heart, is a trust mechanism. The board trusts the auditors to tell the truth, the auditors trust management to provide complete and accurate information, and management trusts that audit opinions are fair, objective, and free from bias. This trust triangle only works when the roles stay distinct and the promise of the third line—to deliver independent, evidence-based assurance—remains unbroken. The minute that promise blurs, assurance becomes advice, advice becomes influence, and the line of defense collapses into the very system it was meant to test.

Audit Charter, Authority, and Independence Boundaries

An effective audit charter grants unimpeded access to people, information, and technology environments necessary to form an opinion on control design and operating effectiveness. Access must explicitly include production systems, cloud consoles, logs, tickets, change records, incident files, physical facilities, and third-party deliverables held by vendors on the organization's behalf. The charter should authorize the collection and secure retention of copies of evidence, including datasets and configurations, with appropriate confidentiality protections. Without this breadth of access, audits devolve into declarations of faith rather than evidence-based conclusions.

Scope authority in the charter must extend across legal entities, business units, shared services, and outsourced or cloud-hosted operations that influence the organization's risk posture. It should allow the audit function to define engagement objectives and criteria, determine sampling approaches, and adjust scope dynamically when emerging facts indicate a material risk. The charter should permit the use of specialists—internal or external—when expertise in cryptography, cloud architecture, identity governance, or threat detection is required. Clear scope language prevents management from narrowing reviews to low-risk corners while leaving systemic exposure unexamined.

Escalation rights are a core element of authority and must be unambiguous. The charter should establish that unresolved access restrictions, scope limitations, intimidation, or retaliation will be escalated by the chief audit executive to the executive sponsor and, if not promptly remedied, directly to the audit committee. Time-bound escalation ladders reduce the chance that delays or negotiation fatigue will erode audit effectiveness. The ability to brief the board without management preapproval is the practical guarantee that independence can be exercised when pressure mounts.

Independence is protected through organizational placement and decision rights that separate audit from the management chain it evaluates. The chief audit executive should have a functional reporting line to the audit committee, with administrative support from management that does not compromise engagement planning or conclusions. Budget, staffing, and the audit plan must be approved by the board-level committee to insulate priorities from operational preferences. This structure ensures that the incentive to "make the program look good" never outranks the obligation to tell the truth.

Functional safeguards complement structure by defining what auditors may and may not do. The charter should prohibit auditors from owning controls, authorizing transactions, or making management decisions about tool selection, security configurations, or risk acceptance. It should set boundaries for advisory services, permitting pre-implementation reviews, training, and benchmarking that stop short of design or operation. When advisory work is performed, the charter must require documentation of safeguards and, where necessary, separation of personnel for any subsequent assurance over the same subject.

Threats to independence generally fall into self-review, management participation, advocacy, familiarity, and intimidation. Self-review arises when prior design or implementation work becomes the object of audit; management participation occurs when auditors help run a control or approve an exception; advocacy appears when auditors champion a solution or vendor; familiarity grows from long standing relationships that dull skepticism; intimidation shows up as implied consequences for adverse findings. The charter should call for explicit evaluation of these threats during planning and require mitigation before fieldwork begins. Naming the threats in policy makes it harder for them to masquerade as efficiency.

Safeguards must be practical and documented, not aspirational. Typical mitigations include rotating engagement teams, assigning independent reviewers, imposing cooling-off periods between advisory and assurance work, and bringing in external specialists when internal separation is not feasible. The charter should require an independence declaration for each engagement, a conflicts register maintained centrally, and a safeguards log embedded in the workpapers. Documentation turns professional judgment into an auditable trail of how independence was preserved. Table 1.1 maps common independence threats to practical safeguards and the artifacts auditors should maintain to evidence objectivity.

Prior design work is a recurring hazard in cyber, where auditors often possess deep technical expertise. The boundary is crossed when advice becomes specification, configuration, or acceptance of a control. Where prior involvement exists, the charter should mandate either recusal from the

Table 1.1 Independence threats and safeguards mapping.

Threat type	Description	Typical safeguard	Documentation artifact
Self-review	Prior design or build involvement	Recusal or team rotation	Independence declaration
Management participation	Auditor helps operate a control	Segregation of duties with cooling off	Safeguards log
Advocacy	Auditor champions a solution or vendor	Independent reviewer for conclusions	Conflicts register

Threat type	Description	Typical safeguard	Documentation artifact
Familiarity	Long standing relationships dull skepticism	Periodic rotation and external quality review	Annual independence attestations
Intimidation	Pressure to soften or delay findings	Escalation to audit committee within set timeline	Escalation record
Scope limitation	Management blocks access to evidence	Board level escalation and direct chair briefing	Access limitation memo
Ownership creep	Advisory input drifts into decision making	Boundaries for advice and no management decisions	Engagement scope letter

assurance engagement or demonstrable safeguards, such as a complete re-performance of critical procedures by an uninvolved auditor. If safeguards cannot reduce the threat to an acceptable level, the charter should direct the chief audit executive to engage an external firm or defer the engagement.

Third-party and cloud considerations require the charter to reach beyond the corporate perimeter. Contract and procurement clauses should be standardized to guarantee audit and access rights to service providers, sub-processors, and relevant facilities, including the right to rely on and evaluate independent attestations. The charter should authorize the use of alternative evidence when direct inspection is impractical, provided auditors assess the independence, period, scope, and criteria of the external report. Without these provisions, the move to outsourced and cloud models can quietly hollow out audit's authority.

Confidentiality and legal privilege guardrails protect independence by ensuring candor does not create undue legal exposure. The charter should require auditors to safeguard sensitive data, minimize the collection of personal information, and coordinate with legal counsel when work product may intersect with attorney–client privilege or litigation holds. Clear handling rules allow auditors to request what they need without triggering defensive gatekeeping. Independence thrives when the rules of evidence handling are known, lawful, and consistently applied.

The charter should also define ownership and retention of audit workpapers, which are the formal record of the opinion's basis. Workpapers must belong to the audit function, remain unaltered by management, and be retained under a schedule that meets regulatory and organizational requirements. Access by management should be read-only, with any disagreements captured through formal management responses rather than edits to the record. Control of the record is a quiet but decisive element of independence.

Personnel conduct provisions convert independence into daily behavior. The charter should require annual and per-engagement disclosures of conflicts, limitations on gifts and entertainment from audited areas, and immediate reporting of attempted interference. Training in professional skepticism and independence scenarios helps auditors recognize subtle pressure, such as "friendly previews" of conclusions or requests to delay reports for optics. Independence is not only a structure; it is a habit reinforced by policy and culture.

The charter must be a living instrument reviewed at least annually by the audit committee. As the organization's technology stack, sourcing model, and regulatory landscape evolve, access rights, scope definitions, and escalation paths need recalibration. Periodic external quality assessments should test whether independence safeguards operate as intended and whether any advisory work crept into ownership. A current, specific, and enforced charter is the strongest line of defense for the assurance mandate.

Governance Interfaces: Board/Audit Committee, CISO, Legal, Privacy

Cybersecurity audit functions as both a mirror and a messenger within the governance ecosystem, and its credibility depends on clear, structured interfaces with senior stakeholders. These interfaces—particularly with the board or audit committee, the Chief Information Security Officer (CISO), the legal department, and privacy leadership—form the circulatory system through which assurance insights flow. The quality of that flow determines whether findings lead to informed action or vanish into bureaucratic silence. The charter defines access, but governance defines rhythm—who hears what, when, and with what authority to act.

The audit committee is the primary customer of cybersecurity assurance. It requires independent, periodic updates that distill the state of cyber control effectiveness, residual risk, and management responsiveness. Most organizations anchor this relationship through quarterly briefings where the chief audit executive delivers a formal report summarizing completed engagements, major control themes, unresolved findings, and significant risk trends. Emerging issues that signal material exposure—such as systemic identity weaknesses or third-party dependency failures—warrant immediate, off-cycle notification. These reports must be concise but evidence-based, enabling the committee to probe, challenge, and direct management without stepping into operational detail.

Between board meetings, the chief audit executive maintains direct access to the committee chair, ensuring urgent matters bypass managerial filters. This access right is more than procedural—it protects independence by guaranteeing that material risk or obstruction is never buried under hierarchy. The committee's decision rights include approving the audit plan, endorsing the budget and staffing model, and ratifying changes to audit scope prompted by emerging threats. Audit may recommend priority adjustments, but final approval of risk appetite and remediation ownership remains with management. The relationship thrives on transparency and disciplined cadence, not surprise.

The CISO is the operational counterpart most deeply intertwined with audit. Where the committee seeks assurance, the CISO delivers accountability. Regular coordination—often monthly—ensures that audit's planned work aligns with current threat conditions and technology changes without preclearing conclusions. The CISO provides control documentation, evidence, and contextual briefings, while audit provides preliminary observations to validate understanding before formal issuance. This relationship should be collegial yet carefully bounded: collaboration cannot become co-authorship. The CISO cannot dictate what is tested or when a finding is closed, just as audit cannot direct how controls are implemented.

Information exchange between audit and security operations must be deliberate and time-aware. Cybersecurity controls often produce live data—logs, alerts, configuration snapshots—that change by the hour. Audit teams must agree with the CISO on evidence capture timing to avoid disrupting production or interfering with incident investigations. Read-only access, cloned datasets, or controlled observation windows are standard mechanisms. When real-time data includes sensitive content—such as threat intelligence feeds, active forensics, or confidential investigation notes—audit relies on metadata, sampling, or attestations to respect containment boundaries while still obtaining reasonable assurance.

Legal counsel operates as both shield and interpreter in the audit interface. The general counsel or designated legal representative reviews audit plans for potential privilege, regulatory, or litigation exposure. If audit work intersects with matters under attorney–client privilege—such as breach response analysis or ongoing regulatory inquiries—legal determines whether portions of the engagement fall within privilege protection or require separate handling. Counsel may direct how audit workpapers referencing legal assessments are stored, labeled, or distributed. Privilege does not preclude assurance, but it may delay or compartmentalize the flow of certain evidence to protect the organization's legal position.

The relationship with legal also governs escalation of compliance or ethics concerns. If auditors encounter potential violations of law or policy—such as improper data collection, noncompliance with breach notification timelines, or falsified evidence—protocol requires immediate consultation with legal before communicating externally. Legal's decision rights here focus on containment, regulatory disclosure, and privilege preservation, while audit retains the duty to report factually to the audit committee. This dual channel ensures that oversight continues without compromising ongoing legal strategies.

Privacy officers form a parallel governance interface centered on the lawful and ethical handling of personal data. Privacy leadership provides guidance on what categories of information can be reviewed, anonymized, or redacted during audit sampling. Where audit requires evidence that includes personal data—such as access logs, HR records, or user communications—privacy ensures that data minimization and retention requirements are met. Joint protocols should define secure transfer mechanisms, role-based access within audit systems, and destruction timelines once the engagement concludes. These safeguards protect not only individuals but also the integrity of the audit function by demonstrating respect for data protection laws.

Decision rights between audit and privacy must be complementary, not competitive. Audit determines whether privacy controls are designed and functioning effectively; privacy defines the lawful boundaries within which those tests occur. When privacy identifies a potential legal constraint that limits audit's evidence collection, the chief audit executive informs the audit committee of the limitation and any compensating assurance obtained through alternate procedures. This transparency prevents management from invoking "privacy" as a shield against scrutiny while still upholding legitimate legal protections.

Cross-functional coordination between audit, legal, and privacy also ensures consistent messaging to regulators and external assessors. When a regulatory examination or certification review requests evidence overlapping with audit workpapers, legal and privacy review what can be shared externally without breaching privilege or confidentiality. The chief audit executive controls release of audit materials, while legal determines disclosure boundaries and privacy ensures compliance with jurisdictional transfer laws. A harmonized governance interface reduces confusion, duplication, and the risk of inconsistent statements across the enterprise.

Timing and cadence of communication are central to these interfaces. The board receives quarterly assurance summaries; the CISO and audit maintain continuous collaboration through scheduled checkpoints; legal and privacy engagement occurs at defined milestones—planning, fieldwork, and reporting—to validate scope and evidence handling. Ad hoc interactions occur when emerging legal issues, regulatory requests, or new privacy legislation affect audit scope. These interfaces must be documented in governance policies or a combined assurance framework so that roles and escalation paths are understood across leadership transitions.

Maintaining confidentiality while ensuring transparency is the final balancing act. The audit function must communicate enough detail for governance bodies to act while withholding sensitive operational or personal data from broad circulation. Legal and privacy play gatekeeper roles here, reviewing draft reports for unintended disclosures without altering factual conclusions. When this balance works, information flows efficiently upward for oversight, laterally for coordination, and downward only as needed for remediation tracking—each movement governed by purpose, necessity, and respect for independence.

Policy–Standards–Procedures Architecture (Audit View)

From an auditor's perspective, the architecture of policies, standards, and procedures is not just a documentation exercise—it is the control system's blueprint. Each layer serves a distinct governance purpose: policy establishes intent and accountability, standards translate that intent into measurable requirements, and procedures operationalize those requirements into repeatable actions. When these layers align, they create a traceable, testable hierarchy that connects executive commitment to verifiable control evidence. When they drift apart, governance decays into good intentions without proof.

A cybersecurity policy expresses the organization's risk philosophy and assigns ownership for safeguarding information assets. It is the "constitution" of the security program—approved by the board or senior executives, published enterprise-wide, and version-controlled with a clear effective date. From an assurance standpoint, a strong policy document demonstrates endorsement at the highest level and explicit mapping to legal, regulatory, and contractual obligations. Auditors look for evidence of that endorsement—board minutes, approval signatures, or formal memos—because such artifacts prove that the organization's leadership not only issued the policy but accepted accountability for its enforcement.

Beneath the policy sit standards: the measurable criteria by which compliance and assurance are judged. Standards translate policy principles into specific control expectations—such as encryption strength, password composition, patch time frames, or data retention limits. Good standards are written in objective terms that can be verified or falsified; vague statements like "systems should be adequately protected" offer no assurance value. From an audit lens, effective standards are versioned, reviewed at regular intervals, and traceable to the parent policy and risk domain they support. Version history provides evidence of continuous governance—an audit trail of how the organization adapts its security expectations to evolving threats and technology.

Procedures form the tactical playbook for implementing standards. They describe how specific teams perform control activities in consistent, repeatable ways—configuring a firewall rule, provisioning an identity, or reviewing a vulnerability report. For assurance purposes, procedures should identify responsible roles, inputs, expected outputs, and validation points. Auditors examine whether procedures are accessible, current, and aligned with both the standard they implement and the system of record that proves performance. A well-documented procedure reduces reliance on tribal knowledge and enables auditors to evaluate process execution without guesswork or personality dependency.

The relationship among these documents is hierarchical but also traceable—a vertical chain of logic that links intent to evidence. An auditor should be able to start at a policy clause, follow its reference to one or more standards, and trace those standards to specific procedures and system records that prove compliance. This traceability transforms documentation from static text into a living control system. It also allows assurance teams to sample at any layer: reviewing design at the policy level, sufficiency at the standard level, and performance at the procedural level, with clear line-of-sight among them.

From a governance standpoint, document management is itself a control domain. Each policy, standard, and procedure must have a defined owner, version number, last review date, and formal approval record. These attributes allow auditors to test whether the organization follows a disciplined life cycle—drafting, reviewing, approving, distributing, and retiring documents according to schedule. Outdated or orphaned documents signal a lapse in governance maturity. In high-performing organizations, document control is automated through governance, risk, and compliance (GRC) platforms, providing auditors with a consolidated view of change history and review cadence. Table 1.2 shows how policy intent links to standards procedures and the exact systems where proof of performance resides.

Approval pathways must reflect authority levels proportional to impact. Policies require executive or board approval; standards are endorsed by security governance or risk councils; procedures are approved by operational managers. The hierarchy ensures that the right people accept responsibility for the right level of decision. From an audit standpoint, this distribution of authority prevents concentration of power and aligns accountability with organizational structure. Auditors verify that approvals occur at the designated level and that any delegated authority is documented and traceable.

Control traceability extends beyond paper. Every statement within a standard or procedure should point toward where its proof resides in the organization's systems. For example, a standard requiring "critical vulnerabilities remediated within 15 days" links to ticketing system data, patch management dashboards, and CI/CD pipeline configurations. Audit does not merely confirm the presence of these systems—it tests whether the linkage between standard and evidence is explicit and retrievable. The same principle applies to access management standards traced to identity governance systems, or logging standards tied to SIEM retention configurations. The health of this mapping is a leading indicator of governance maturity.

Auditors also assess whether the documentation hierarchy accounts for the velocity of change in modern technology environments. Cloud infrastructure, DevOps pipelines, and software-defined networks evolve faster than traditional policy cycles. "Good" from an assurance view means the organization's standards and procedures can adapt rapidly without undermining policy intent. Auditors review whether policy updates are risk-triggered, whether standards reference dynamic configuration baselines rather than static documents, and whether procedures incorporate automation or version-controlled code repositories to maintain alignment.

Versioning discipline is another hallmark of audit fitness. Each document should record what changed, when, and why, along with the approver's identity. Change logs demonstrate continuous improvement and allow auditors to reconstruct governance decisions during post-incident

Table 1.2 Traceability across policy standards procedures and evidence.

Policy clause	Standard requirement	Procedure artifact	System of record
Identity governance	Joiner mover leaver actions within 24 hours	Access provisioning runbook	Identity governance platform
Vulnerability management	Critical findings remediated within 15 days	Patch change workflow	Ticketing system
Cryptography	Approved algorithms and key rotation intervals	Key rotation checklist	Key management service
Logging and monitoring	Security events retained 365 days	SIEM onboarding steps	SIEM platform
Change management	Production changes require peer review	Change approval steps	Change management tool
Data protection	Sensitive data encrypted at rest and in transit	Storage and TLS configuration steps	Cloud console
Incident readiness	Playbooks reviewed and tested semiannual	Exercise execution guide	Document repository

reviews or regulatory inquiries. Versioning also guards against "shadow documents"—informal updates circulating outside official repositories. During audit, discrepancies between published and actual procedures often reveal cultural weaknesses where staff rely on personal copies or outdated instructions. Strong version control systems, ideally with audit trails and read-only publication rights, prevent this drift.

Ownership is both a structural and cultural signal. A document with no clear owner reflects a control with no steward. Auditors expect every policy, standard, and procedure to name a role—not just a department—as accountable for its maintenance. Ownership clarity allows audit follow-up when inconsistencies arise, ensures review cycles are met, and provides a line of defense when regulators inquire who approved a particular requirement. High-functioning organizations maintain an ownership matrix linking each control domain to accountable roles and escalation points, which auditors can verify against organizational charts.

Traceability to controls closes the assurance loop. Every control in the audit universe should map to one or more requirements in standards or procedures, ensuring coverage across the risk landscape. When auditors find controls that lack such mapping, it signals either undocumented practices or ungoverned risk mitigation. Conversely, if a standard contains requirements unsupported by any implemented control, it points to policy debt—expectations that exist only on paper. By assessing both directions of traceability, auditors gauge not only compliance but coherence: whether the governance architecture reflects how the organization actually manages risk.

The connection between documentation and the systems where proof lives is where theory meets evidence. Policies and standards define "what must happen," but assurance depends on "what did happen." Ticketing systems, CI/CD pipelines, vulnerability scanners, and cloud configuration managers hold that proof. The auditor's task is to determine whether those systems capture the right evidence automatically, timestamp it reliably, and retain it long enough to support independent verification. A well-architected governance stack makes that linkage transparent, so every control statement leads naturally to data that proves—or disproves—its operation.

GRC Architecture: Control Library and Risk Register

The control library and the risk register form the backbone of an organization's governance, risk, and compliance (GRC) architecture. They are not static repositories of information but living, interdependent systems that translate risk awareness into actionable control assurance. From an auditor's viewpoint, these two artifacts must be complete enough to support traceability, yet structured enough to allow consistent evaluation of control design and operation. The quality of a cyber audit depends heavily on whether the control library and risk register are mature, current, and synchronized—because together, they define what the organization is defending, how it is defending it, and why those defenses matter.

A control library is a structured inventory of all preventive, detective, and corrective measures the organization relies on to manage security, compliance, and operational risk. Each control entry should answer five questions: what the control is intended to achieve, who owns it, how it operates, how often it operates, and where its evidence resides. From an assurance perspective, a usable control library is more than a spreadsheet of control statements—it's a normalized data model that supports linkage between frameworks, policies, systems, and risks. Without that structure, controls become isolated actions without context or accountability.

At a minimum, each control record should contain metadata fields for unique identifier, title, objective or purpose statement, control owner, control operator (if different), frequency, evidence location or system of record, last test date, and mapping to one or more risks. Additional attributes—such as control category (preventive, detective, corrective), control type (manual, automated, hybrid), and status (active, retired, superseded)—enhance transparency. Auditors use this metadata to understand coverage and completeness: whether critical risks have adequate controls, whether ownership is assigned, and whether any controls lack supporting evidence.

The control owner field is essential because it defines accountability. Ownership does not necessarily imply daily operation; rather, it identifies the person or role responsible for ensuring the control remains designed and functioning as intended. The control operator may be an engineer, administrator, or process lead who executes the activity, but the owner ensures its adequacy, documentation, and remediation. From an audit lens, clear ownership eliminates ambiguity during evidence requests and management responses. Controls without owners are effectively unmanaged risks waiting to surface.

Frequency is another key element of assurance metadata. Whether a control runs continuously, daily, monthly, or annually determines how auditors evaluate timeliness and sufficiency. A log correlation control that operates hourly demands different evidence than an access review that occurs quarterly. Auditors confirm that the stated frequency matches both policy expectations and observed execution in system logs or tickets. In mature environments, frequency metadata feeds into automated control monitoring, alerting control owners when a required activity is missed or delayed.

Evidence location provides the traceability that connects the control library to operational systems. Each control should reference where proof of execution is stored—such as a ticketing system, configuration management database, cloud console, or code repository. The metadata must specify not only the system name but also the evidence type and retention duration. For example, a control might record "SIEM: log of weekly correlation rule execution, retained 90 days." This transparency allows auditors to locate, sample, and verify evidence efficiently without guesswork or dependence on tribal knowledge.

Control-to-risk mapping is where the library intersects with the risk register. Each control must link to one or more risk statements that articulate the underlying threat or vulnerability it mitigates. Conversely, each risk in the register should map back to one or more controls providing mitigation coverage. This bidirectional linkage is the foundation of risk-based assurance: it allows auditors to test whether significant risks are sufficiently controlled and whether controls still serve a valid purpose as the threat landscape changes. A missing link in either direction signals a potential blind spot in the governance model.

The risk register itself is the authoritative record of the organization's known risks, their assessed likelihood and impact, current treatment strategies, and residual exposure. From a minimum viable perspective, each risk entry must include a unique identifier, risk statement, owner, impact area, likelihood rating, inherent risk score, residual risk score, control linkage, and last review date. Some organizations extend this with additional metadata such as treatment plan, target residual risk, key risk indicators, or associated frameworks. For audit purposes, completeness and consistency matter more than quantity; a smaller, current register is more useful than a sprawling one filled with stale or duplicative entries.

Ownership of risks parallels ownership of controls but with a broader mandate. A risk owner is typically an executive or process leader accountable for managing that risk category, ensuring mitigation strategies are funded, and accepting any residual exposure. The auditor evaluates whether risk ownership aligns with authority—that is, whether the person named actually has the power to reduce or accept the risk. Misaligned ownership, such as assigning "ransomware resilience" to a mid-level analyst, signals a governance weakness even if the register looks populated.

Synchronization between the control library and risk register is the test of GRC maturity. As new risks emerge—cloud misconfigurations, vendor breaches, regulatory changes—the risk register must evolve, and the control library must adapt alongside it. Likewise, when controls are added, automated, or retired, corresponding risks must be reevaluated to confirm that residual exposure remains within appetite. This synchronization should not rely on ad hoc updates; it should be governed by a defined change process that triggers reviews of linked records whenever one side changes materially. Auditors assess whether such change triggers exist and whether updates are timely, documented, and reviewed by governance forums.

In practice, synchronization often occurs through GRC platforms that integrate both artifacts. These systems allow risk and control owners to link objects dynamically, propagate updates, and generate dashboards showing residual risk by control domain. Auditors reviewing such systems focus on the integrity of those linkages: whether changes to risk ratings automatically prompt reassessment of related controls, whether retired controls deactivate risk mappings, and whether version histories preserve traceability over time. A well-implemented GRC platform provides not only visibility but auditability—a history of how the organization's defensive posture has evolved in response to changing conditions.

As the environment changes, so too must the architecture. Emerging technologies like infrastructure as code, containerization, and AI-driven automation introduce new risks and controls that don't fit traditional frameworks. A flexible control library accounts for these by allowing categorization beyond classic IT domains, while the risk register evolves to capture novel exposure types such as model bias or data poisoning. Auditors examine whether the architecture accommodates these innovations or remains locked in legacy structures that blind the organization to modern risks.

The cadence of review is what keeps the GRC architecture alive. Both the control library and risk register should undergo formal review at least annually, with interim updates triggered by significant events—mergers, incidents, audits, or regulatory changes. The audit function does not manage these reviews but validates that they occur as scheduled, that changes are approved by authorized governance bodies, and that historical versions remain archived for reference. This disciplined rhythm of review ensures that assurance work is built on current, reliable data rather than outdated assumptions.

Exception and Waiver Governance

In any mature security governance model, exceptions and waivers act as the pressure valves that keep control frameworks practical. They acknowledge that perfect compliance is not always immediately achievable—and sometimes not economically rational—but they do so within a structure that preserves visibility, accountability, and time-bound risk acceptance. From an auditor's perspective, exception governance reveals more about an organization's culture than its control library does. A disciplined exception process signals maturity; a sprawling, undocumented set of "temporary" allowances signals quiet erosion of the very controls designed to protect the enterprise.

An exception, in governance terms, is a formally approved deviation from a control requirement, standard, or policy for a defined purpose and duration. Exceptions differ from control failures, which occur without authorization, and from risk acceptances, which acknowledge inherent exposure without breaking policy. A waiver typically refers to a broader or more enduring exemption—often policy-level—granted under executive authority when remediation is infeasible or strategic. The distinction lies in scope and duration: exceptions are tactical and time-limited; waivers are strategic and exceptional in themselves. Auditors expect both to exist within the same governance framework, subject to documented criteria and review.

Approval criteria must be explicit and risk-based. A valid exception request should document the control requirement being bypassed, the reason for noncompliance, the potential risk introduced, the duration requested, the compensating controls in place, and the responsible owner. The approval authority should correspond to the residual risk level after compensating controls are considered—low-risk exceptions may be approved by operational managers, while high-risk or enterprise-level waivers require CISO or even board-level approval. This hierarchy ensures proportional scrutiny and prevents normalization of high-risk deviations through procedural convenience.

Compensating controls are the safety net that allows risk to be temporarily tolerated. They must be specific, measurable, and demonstrably effective in reducing the exposure created by the exception. For example, if multifactor authentication cannot be enforced on a legacy application, the compensating control might include network segmentation, enhanced monitoring, and restricted access windows. Auditors examine whether compensating controls truly address the same risk vector as the original requirement or merely provide adjacent comfort. Documentation should include how these alternate safeguards are validated, who monitors them, and what triggers their reevaluation. Table 1.3 defines actionable exception metrics with thresholds and governance responses to prevent exception sprawl and hidden risk.

Mandatory expiry and renewal mechanics are the heart of exception governance. Every approved deviation must carry an explicit expiration date, typically no longer than one year, after which it automatically lapses or requires formal re-approval. Renewal must never be automatic; it should require updated justification, risk reassessment, and evidence that remediation remains infeasible. The expiry mechanism transforms exceptions from lingering liabilities into actively managed risk

Table 1.3 Exception governance metrics and actions.

Metric	Purpose	Typical threshold	Governance action
Total active exceptions	Visibility of aggregate exposure	Trend increase quarter over quarter	Review at risk committee
High risk exceptions	Focus leadership attention	Any count greater than zero	Board notification with owner plan
Aging over 180 days	Detect lingering deviations	More than 10% of total	Escalate and require remediation timeline
Expiring in 30 days	Prevent silent lapse or auto renewal	Any with upcoming expiry	Trigger renewal workflow with reassessment
Clusters by control	Spot systemic design issues	Three or more similar exceptions	Initiate control redesign review
Auto renewal attempts	Enforce time bound accountability	Any occurrence	Reject and require fresh justification
Compensating control health	Validate temporary safeguards	Missing validation evidence	Increase monitoring and schedule retest

decisions. During audit, reviewers verify that expired exceptions are either closed or reapproved and that controls listed as "temporarily deferred" are not effectively permanent by neglect.

Effective exception management relies on robust metadata to ensure transparency and accountability. Each record should include a unique identifier, exception type, associated control or policy reference, business owner, approving authority, risk rating, compensating controls, start and expiry dates, and evidence of periodic review. Mature organizations maintain these records in an integrated GRC system rather than in spreadsheets or emails. Such systems allow real-time reporting on total active exceptions, distribution by risk level, average age, and upcoming expirations—metrics auditors use to assess governance discipline and responsiveness.

Exception sprawl occurs when deviations accumulate faster than they are resolved. It often begins innocently—one urgent production fix, one vendor integration—but grows into a shadow governance system where entire domains operate outside approved standards. As exception counts rise, aggregate residual risk exceeds management's line of sight, and the illusion of control persists only because the exceptions are fragmented across systems or owners. From an assurance standpoint, exception sprawl represents governance debt. Auditors look for indicators such as rising exception volumes, missing closure documentation, and large clusters of similar justifications that hint at structural design flaws in the control framework itself.

Tracking exception aging is critical to preventing sprawl. A governance dashboard should show the number of exceptions by age bracket—less than 90 days, 90–180 days, 181–365 days, and over one year—along with trend lines. Aging exceptions without remediation plans signal management fatigue or lack of accountability. Similarly, exceptions should be categorized by severity of risk exposure and business impact, allowing prioritization of oversight. Auditors review whether escalation occurs automatically when exceptions exceed age or severity thresholds, ensuring that risk appetite boundaries remain visible to leadership.

Coverage mapping provides another layer of insight by showing which controls, systems, or business units are most frequently subject to exceptions. When multiple exceptions cluster around a single control requirement—say, endpoint encryption or privileged access monitoring—it suggests either that the control is poorly designed, infeasible in certain contexts, or under-resourced. Audit's role is not to fix the control but to highlight the pattern, prompting governance bodies to examine root causes. Concentrated exception coverage can expose systemic weaknesses more effectively than individual audit findings.

Governance visibility depends on routine reporting to risk and audit committees. Summary dashboards should display total active exceptions, categorized by risk tier, business function, and expiration horizon. High-risk or long-standing exceptions warrant explicit discussion in quarterly assurance reports, including management's remediation timelines and any compensating control performance metrics. The goal is not to shame operational teams but to maintain the board's situational awareness of risk levels that deviate from approved policy. When the board understands the cumulative exposure, it can determine whether to adjust risk appetite, allocate resources, or demand accelerated closure.

Auditors evaluate not only the existence of exception governance but also its consistency and transparency. A strong framework exhibits standardized templates, centralized tracking, tiered approval, and automated reminders for renewal or closure. Weak frameworks rely on ad hoc approvals buried in email threads, with no central inventory or evidence of review. During assurance engagements, auditors trace a sample of exceptions from approval through expiry, confirming whether compensating controls were monitored and whether closure documentation exists. While testing procedures belong elsewhere, design adequacy is judged by the presence of reliable processes that enforce accountability.

Conclusion

Mastering the governance foundations of cybersecurity auditing is critical for any organization that aspires to sustain trust in complex, technology-driven environments. The chapter's core themes—independence, structure, traceability, and disciplined exception management—define the scaffolding that supports credible assurance. When these foundations are weak, audits become procedural checklists; when they are strong, they become instruments of truth. In a landscape where artificial intelligence and automation accelerate both control execution and potential failure, this discipline ensures that oversight evolves as quickly as the systems it monitors.

For AI security professionals, the concepts explored here extend beyond compliance—they define how assurance adapts to intelligent, adaptive systems. Risk and control registers must reflect algorithmic behavior and data dependencies, while policies and standards must anticipate self-modifying or opaque processes. The same principles that govern cloud or infrastructure controls—clear ownership, evidence lineage, and version integrity—now apply to machine learning models, pipelines, and decision logic. The auditor's role remains constant: to confirm that what was intended, built, and operated aligns with defined risk tolerance and ethical boundaries.

With these foundations in place, professionals are better equipped to balance innovation with accountability. A well-governed audit function provides the connective tissue between strategy and security, transforming abstract frameworks into measurable confidence. While tools and technologies will continue to evolve, the principles of transparency, independence, and disciplined governance endure as the constants of trustworthy assurance. These are not merely administrative practices—they are the architecture of integrity in cybersecurity and AI risk management alike.

Auditor Recommendations

1. **Codify the Audit Charter:** Establish an annually reviewed charter that grants unimpeded access, enterprise-wide scope, and time-bound escalation to the audit committee. Specify inclusion of production environments, cloud consoles, logs, tickets, and third-party evidence held on the organization's behalf. Document approval authority, effective dates, and version history so the charter's legitimacy is never in doubt. Confirm that functional reporting to the committee and administrative support from management are both clearly stated.
2. **Enforce Independence Safeguards:** Require per-engagement independence declarations and evaluate self-review, management participation, advocacy, familiarity, and intimidation threats before fieldwork begins. Apply rotation, cooling-off periods, or external reviewers when prior design work or close relationships exist. Record the safeguards in a centralized register and reference them in engagement workpapers. Escalate unresolved threats through the chartered ladder to preserve objectivity.
3. **Structure Governance Cadence with Decision Rights:** Schedule concise quarterly briefings for the board or audit committee and maintain direct chair access for urgent matters. Agree on monthly checkpoints with the CISO to coordinate evidence windows without pre-clearing conclusions. Involve legal and privacy at planning, fieldwork, and reporting milestones to manage privilege and lawful data handling. Keep these interfaces documented so leadership transitions do not disrupt information flow.
4. **Make Standards Testable and Traceable:** Rewrite ambiguous requirements into objective criteria that can be verified or falsified against evidence. Map each standard upward to policy clauses and downward to procedures with named roles, inputs, outputs, and system-of-record

locations. Require versioning, effective dates, and approvals appropriate to the document tier. Use this traceability to design risk-based audit steps without rewriting policy.

5. **Align Procedures to Where Proof Lives:** Ensure procedures explicitly point to the ticketing system, CI CD pipelines, cloud configuration baselines, SIEM, or identity platforms that hold evidence. Verify that evidence is captured automatically where possible, timestamped, and retained long enough for independent review. Confirm that operators know the expected artifacts and reviewers know how to retrieve them read-only. Flag any reliance on tribal knowledge as a governance gap.
6. **Normalize the Control Library Metadata:** Maintain a single repository where each control has a unique ID, objective, owner and operator, frequency, category and type, status, evidence location with retention, last test date, and linked risks. Verify that ownership aligns to authority and that every active control has a current entry. Use the library to identify coverage gaps and orphaned controls with no evidence path. Require documented retirement or supersession to prevent shadow controls.
7. **Keep the Risk Register Decision-ready:** Record a clear risk statement, owner, impact area, likelihood, inherent and residual ratings, linked controls, treatment approach, and last review date for each entry. Validate that owners have authority to fund mitigation and accept residual exposure. Retire duplicates and stale items so the register reflects present exposure, not historical inventory. Use review cadence to ensure ratings keep pace with technology and sourcing changes.
8. **Synchronize Risks and Controls with Change Triggers:** Define triggers—such as new services, vendor changes, control automation, or retirements—that force reassessment of linked records in both artifacts. Require version history that shows what changed, when, why, and who approved it. Report misalignments where a significant risk lacks mitigating controls or a control lacks a current risk link. Use governance forums to resolve gaps and confirm residual risk remains within appetite.
9. **Discipline Exception and Waiver Governance:** Mandate standardized requests that specify the bypassed requirement, justification, residual risk, compensating controls, owner, approver, and explicit expiry. Prohibit auto-renewals and require fresh justification and feasibility evidence for extensions. Track volume, age brackets, severity, and clusters by control or unit to detect exception sprawl. Present high-risk or aging items to the committee with owner remediation timelines.
10. **Respect Privilege and Privacy While Preserving Assurance:** Plan read-only or cloned evidence windows that do not disrupt operations or incident handling. When legal privilege or privacy constraints apply, employ metadata, sampling, or attestations to maintain sufficient appropriate evidence. Label workpapers that reference privileged material per counsel's guidance and control distribution accordingly. Document any scope limitations and compensating procedures to keep the opinion defensible.

Chapter Questions

1. In the Three Lines model, what is the primary role of the cybersecurity audit function?
   - **A.** To design and implement security controls
   - **B.** To set policy and monitor adherence as a management function
   - **C.** To provide independent assurance on control design and operating effectiveness
   - **D.** To approve risk exceptions and manage remediation plans

2. Which element must an effective audit charter explicitly grant to ensure credible assurance work?
   - A. Unimpeded access to systems, records, personnel, and time-bound escalation to the audit committee
   - B. Exclusive authority over security tool selection and configuration
   - C. Sole approval power for the organization's risk appetite statement
   - D. Operational ownership of incident response playbooks

3. Which statement best differentiates assurance from advice in preserving independence?
   - A. Assurance is hypothetical and advice is evidence-based
   - B. Advice must be retrospective while assurance is prospective
   - C. Assurance allows auditors to co-design controls they later test
   - D. Advisory input cannot later be self-reviewed by those who designed the control

4. What reporting cadence most appropriately supports the board/audit committee's oversight of cybersecurity assurance?
   - A. Annual summaries bundled with financial audit results
   - B. Concise quarterly updates with off-cycle notification for material issues
   - C. Monthly deep dives into ticket-level evidence
   - D. Ad hoc briefings only after major incidents conclude

5. From an audit perspective, what characterizes a "good" security standard within the policy–standards–procedures hierarchy?
   - A. Broad principles that encourage flexible interpretation by teams
   - B. Embedded step-by-step runbooks for every control operator
   - C. Objective, verifiable criteria traceable to policy and mapped to procedures
   - D. One-time approvals with no version history to reduce overhead

6. Which metadata set is most essential for a usable control library entry?
   - A. Unique ID, objective, owner/operator, frequency, evidence location, and linked risks
   - B. Business slogan, preferred tool, historical vendor, and budget code
   - C. Informal notes, email threads, and screenshots saved by operators
   - D. Only the policy reference, with testing details deferred indefinitely

7. What minimum elements should appear in a well-governed risk register entry?
   - A. Marketing impact, press strategy, and brand tone
   - B. Tool inventory, patch counts, and server hostnames
   - C. Sprint number, backlog rank, and developer assignment
   - D. Unique ID, risk statement, owner, likelihood/impact, inherent/residual ratings, linked controls, last review date

8. How should organizations keep the control library and risk register synchronized as conditions change?
   - A. Rely on ad hoc updates during annual audits
   - B. Use defined change triggers so risk or control updates prompt reassessment of linked records
   - C. Lock both artifacts for stability and avoid midyear edits
   - D. Defer alignment until after external certification reviews

9. Which practice is central to disciplined exception and waiver governance?
   A. Open-ended approvals to minimize administrative burden
   B. Auto-renewals for recurring operational constraints
   C. Explicit expiry dates with renewals requiring fresh justification and risk reassessment
   D. Informal approvals documented only in email

10. When legal privilege or privacy constraints limit direct evidence access, how should assurance be maintained?
   A. Plan read-only or cloned data access and use metadata, sampling, or attestations to preserve evidence sufficiency
   B. Cease testing until all constraints are lifted and restart later
   C. Replace evidence with verbal confirmations from control owners
   D. Publish full raw datasets to the board for transparency

2

Security Standards and Regulations

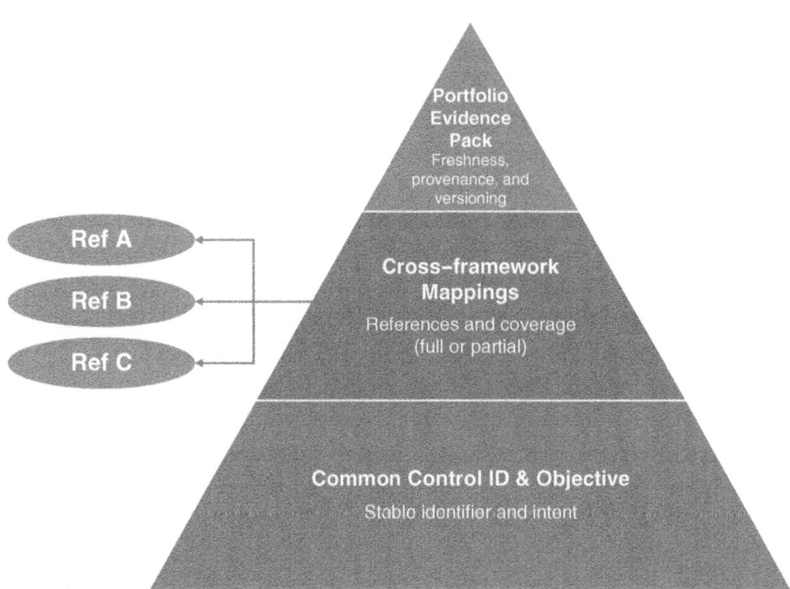

Security standards and regulations form the foundation upon which every cybersecurity assurance program is built. They transform abstract expectations of "good security" into measurable, auditable requirements that define how systems, data, and organizations must behave under scrutiny. Understanding how auditors apply these frameworks is essential to building programs that withstand both regulatory review and operational reality. In an era where organizations operate across multiple jurisdictions, cloud providers, and data protection regimes, the ability to interpret and align these standards determines whether governance remains coherent or collapses into duplication and confusion.

Effective auditors must see beyond the letter of a standard to the intent of its control objectives. Evaluating security through the lens of frameworks, assertions, and evidence requires more than checklist compliance—it demands judgment about sufficiency, traceability, and scope. This chapter examines how auditors define assurance criteria, harmonize control sets across regimes, and evaluate equivalency without sacrificing rigor. It also explains how scoping, mapping, and reliance decisions affect the credibility of assurance, especially when responsibilities are distributed across third parties, cloud providers, and shared infrastructures.

The importance of these disciplines grows as organizations integrate AI, automation, and global service models into their security architecture. Each new system layer introduces regulatory complexity, overlapping obligations, and increased dependency on inherited and shared controls. Establishing common control frameworks, maintaining reusable evidence packs, and documenting deviations transparently enable consistent assurance across diverse operating environments. By mastering these practices, security leaders and auditors create a foundation of trust—one capable of supporting resilient governance in the face of evolving technology and expanding compliance expectations.

Auditor's Use of Frameworks

Auditors rely on frameworks not as optional guidance but as the foundation for credible assurance. A security framework defines the criteria against which an auditor evaluates whether management's stated controls, processes, and outcomes are fairly represented. Without this anchor, the audit devolves into opinion rather than assessment—findings would depend on personal interpretation rather than objective benchmarks. Frameworks such as ISO/IEC 27001, NIST SP 800-53, or SOC 2 Trust Services Criteria give both auditor and management a shared language for defining expectations and judging evidence. The framework transforms vague questions like "Is our security good enough?" into measurable inquiries: "Do our controls satisfy the required objectives of confidentiality, integrity, and availability according to defined criteria?" Table 2.1 clarifies how criteria assertions and conclusions interact to anchor defensible assurance.

The concept of *criteria* lies at the heart of every assurance engagement. Criteria are the standards or rules against which the subject matter—such as a control environment or risk management program—is evaluated. They must be suitable, meaning relevant, complete, reliable, neutral, and understandable to users of the report. For example, ISO 27001 Annex A controls or NIST CSF subcategories can serve as criteria because they represent accepted definitions of good practice and can be objectively tested. Criteria must also be stable; auditors cannot form consistent conclusions if the rules shift during the engagement. The framework's published control requirements therefore serve as a fixed measuring stick against which evidence is examined and judgments are formed.

Table 2.1 Core assurance elements and roles.

Element	Definition	Purpose	Illustrative phrase
Criteria	Rules used to evaluate subject matter	Provide objective yardstick	Defined requirements anchor testing
Management assertion	What leaders claim about controls	State scope and truth of control posture	Controls operated effectively over period
Auditor conclusion	Independent judgment against criteria	Communicate assurance outcome	Fairly stated in all material respects
Suitability of criteria	Quality of chosen requirements	Ensure relevance and measurability	Relevant complete measurable neutral
Scope boundary	Defined entities systems data classes	Prevent unintended coverage	Only in scope components are opined

Management's assertions represent what leadership claims to be true about their system or environment when evaluated against the chosen criteria. In effect, they are management's side of the assurance equation. A SOC 2 report, for instance, begins with management asserting that controls were suitably designed and operated effectively to meet the service commitments described. Similarly, a company pursuing ISO 27001 certification asserts that its information security management system conforms to the standard's requirements. These assertions are not ceremonial—they define the audit's scope and boundaries. An auditor's task is not to create or modify the assertion but to test whether the assertion is accurate, complete, and fairly stated.

The *auditor's conclusion* is the independent judgment rendered after testing evidence against the established criteria and within the scope of management's assertion. This conclusion must directly reference both elements, stating whether the auditor believes the assertion is fairly presented in all material respects. The conclusion's strength depends on the quality of the criteria and the clarity of the assertion. If either is vague or unsuitable, the conclusion's reliability collapses. For this reason, auditors evaluate suitability before fieldwork begins, ensuring that the chosen framework is capable of supporting meaningful assurance for the intended users of the report.

A well-structured framework also establishes consistency and comparability between engagements. Two auditors evaluating different organizations under the same framework can reach conclusions that are interpretable in a similar way, even if the control implementations differ. This consistency benefits regulators, boards, and customers who rely on audit results to make decisions. Framework alignment prevents "scope drift," where an audit gradually expands into unrelated territory or overlooks essential control domains. By explicitly linking each test procedure to the criteria, auditors preserve coherence between purpose, evidence, and outcome.

Frameworks further strengthen audit defensibility. When conclusions are challenged—by management, regulators, or external stakeholders—the auditor can point to defined requirements and evidence mappings that show how conclusions were derived. This traceability is the hallmark of professional assurance. It transforms an auditor's opinion from a narrative judgment into a conclusion grounded in repeatable logic. In regulated environments such as healthcare, finance, or government, that defensibility is not optional; it is a condition of trust.

The relationship between management's assertion and the auditor's conclusion mirrors a contract: management promises that the system meets the agreed-upon criteria, and the auditor verifies whether that promise holds under scrutiny. If management overstates control effectiveness or omits key systems from scope, the assertion itself becomes misleading, and the auditor must qualify or disclaim the conclusion. Conversely, when criteria and assertions are clear and supported by strong evidence, the audit report becomes a credible instrument for accountability. This clarity of roles—management asserts, auditor tests, and criteria define the standard—ensures that assurance remains disciplined rather than interpretive.

Common Control Set and Cross-framework Traceability

A common control set allows an organization to manage its cybersecurity and compliance obligations without duplicating work for every framework. Instead of maintaining separate control libraries for ISO 27001, NIST SP 800-53, SOC 2, and others, the organization creates a single catalog of "common controls." Each control in that catalog represents one security objective that can satisfy multiple external requirements. This approach replaces the chaos of overlapping spreadsheets and redundant testing with a unified structure that aligns all frameworks to the same set of implemented safeguards. The purpose is simple: design, operate, and test each control once, then reuse the results wherever applicable.

Creating a common control set begins with harmonization. Security and compliance teams review all applicable frameworks and group together controls that share the same intent—for example, access control, change management, or vulnerability remediation. From these clusters, they write one standardized control statement that captures the shared goal without repeating the exact language of any single framework. That control becomes the "source of truth." It receives a permanent identifier and clear control objective text that will not change even if external frameworks update their numbering or terminology. Table 2.2 shows the minimal metadata needed to trace one common control across multiple regimes.

Each common control is supported by metadata that keeps it traceable and auditable. At a minimum, this includes the control ID, title, objective statement, owner, testing method, and evidence references. The most critical metadata, however, is the *mapping information*. For every external framework, the common control must show which specific requirement it covers—for example, "NIST SP 800-53 AC-2" or "ISO 27001 Annex A.9.2.1." These mappings are stored in structured form so auditors can generate reports by framework or by control without manually remapping requirements each time.

Traceability depends on precision. Each mapping should specify the *source framework name and version*, the *original control reference ID*, and the *text of the control objective* as published by that framework. It should also describe the *coverage type*: whether the common control fully satisfies, partially satisfies, or does not address the external requirement. When only partial coverage exists, a note points to the related common control that completes it. This transparent linkage prevents gaps and double counting, allowing auditors to confirm at a glance which frameworks are fully covered by implemented controls.

Table 2.2 Common control set mapping metadata.

ID	Objective text	Source	Coverage type	Evidence location	Owner role
CC AC 01	Restrict and review privileged access	NIST SP 800 53 AC 2	Full	Ticket system path Access Reviews	Identity manager
CC AC 02	Authenticate users with strong factors	SOC 2 CC6 1	Partial	Auth dashboard export MFA Status	Security engineering lead
CC LG 01	Log security events with integrity	ISO 27001 Annex A 8 16	Full	SIEM index reference and query ID	Security operations manager
CC VM 01	Remediate vulnerabilities by severity	NIST SP 800 53 RA 5	Partial	Vulnerability console report ID	Platform owner
CC CH 01	Control and approve changes	SOC 2 CC7 2	Full	Change tool query and record set	Change management owner
CC EN 01	Protect data at rest	ISO 27001 Annex A 8 24	Full	Storage baseline hash and config export	Infrastructure lead

Evidence metadata ties the control to tangible proof of operation. Instead of scattering screenshots, tickets, and reports across shared drives, the catalog includes evidence references for each control—such as URLs to ticketing systems, paths to configuration exports, or identifiers for compliance dashboards. Each entry notes the evidence type, source system, frequency of collection, and last update date. This makes it possible for auditors to verify that the evidence is current and sufficient without manually chasing files across departments.

Ownership fields identify who is responsible for each control. The catalog should clearly state the control owner (typically a process or system manager), the control operator (the person or team that performs it), and the reviewer (often a compliance or internal audit role). Including these roles ensures accountability and enables escalation when evidence or remediation is delayed. Some organizations also record the business unit or system that inherits the control to show how centrally managed safeguards extend across the enterprise.

Testing metadata connects the control set to assurance activities. Each common control includes information about how it will be tested, what evidence supports the test, and what frequency or sample size applies. For example, the metadata might show that the control is tested annually by inspection of configuration baselines or quarterly through automated reporting. Having this data in one place allows both internal and external auditors to reuse test results across frameworks, reducing redundant work and minimizing audit fatigue across teams.

Multi-regime Scoping: Entities, Systems, and Data Classes

When an organization operates under multiple regulatory or assurance regimes, defining scope becomes one of the most critical and complex steps in the audit process. Each standard or framework—whether ISO 27001, SOC 2, HIPAA, or NIST—defines its own boundary of responsibility, yet most organizations function as interconnected ecosystems of shared systems and services. Multi-regime scoping determines which legal entities, business processes, systems, and data classes fall within each obligation and how those overlaps are managed. The goal is to make boundaries explicit so that every control, test, and assertion aligns with the right portion of the environment.

Scoping starts at the legal-entity level because accountability flows through corporate structure. In some organizations, a single legal entity operates all systems and services, making the boundary straightforward. In others—especially multinational enterprises or holding groups—different entities own assets, employ personnel, or host data on behalf of others. Each regime may recognize only certain entities within its jurisdiction; for instance, a U.S. subsidiary may fall under SOX and HIPAA, while the parent company's European division faces GDPR. Auditors must ensure that management's assertion clearly identifies which entities are included and whether any intercompany arrangements or service-level agreements affect those boundaries.

The next layer is business processes—the activities through which data and systems are actually used. Processes such as onboarding, incident response, procurement, and change management may cross multiple legal entities or operate from centralized functions. When defining scope, auditors identify which processes materially contribute to meeting control objectives and whether they are shared, outsourced, or locally executed. Centralized processes, such as enterprise identity management, can serve multiple frameworks at once, but only if their controls and evidence are traceable to each participating entity. Omitting or vaguely describing shared processes is a common source of misalignment during multi-regime audits.

Systems are the operational heart of scope definition. They include infrastructure, applications, networks, and data repositories that support in-scope processes or handle in-scope data. Multi-regime scoping distinguishes between *shared systems* (for example, a common HR or ERP platform) and *dedicated systems* that support a specific service or line of business. Centralized systems simplify control management but complicate evidence collection, since the same system must demonstrate compliance for several frameworks simultaneously. When systems are hosted externally—through SaaS providers or cloud platforms—the organization must determine whether those environments are considered part of its control boundary or treated as subservice providers with their own assurance reports.

Shadow IT and unsanctioned SaaS use complicate these boundaries further. Unregistered tools may process regulated data without formal approval or monitoring, creating gaps that span multiple frameworks at once. During scoping, both auditors and management must identify where such systems exist, determine whether they handle data or perform functions relevant to the control environment, and either bring them into scope or explicitly exclude them with documented risk acceptance. A control cannot be considered effective if significant data flows occur through unscoped systems.

Data classification provides the connective tissue between entities, processes, and systems. Different frameworks emphasize distinct data categories—personally identifiable information for privacy regimes, cardholder data for PCI DSS, protected health information for HIPAA—but they often coexist within the same infrastructure. A single database may store multiple data classes, each triggering different obligations. Scoping therefore requires clear data maps showing what types of information exist, where they reside, and which regimes govern them. When boundaries are defined by data class rather than system, auditors must ensure that controls like encryption, retention, and access restriction align with the strictest applicable requirement.

Centralized services such as network security monitoring, identity management, and incident response further blur scoping lines. These services may be operated by a parent organization or managed service provider supporting multiple subsidiaries or cloud tenants. In such cases, the scoping statement must explain how the shared service meets obligations for each framework, how control ownership is divided, and which entity provides evidence. If one centralized service supports all frameworks, auditors will rely heavily on that service's documentation and change management to avoid redundant testing across entities.

Equivalency and Mapping Rules: Sufficiency and Residual Gaps

Equivalency in cybersecurity auditing refers to achieving the same security objective or assurance outcome, even if the wording, structure, or format of requirements differ between frameworks. It is not a word-for-word match but an alignment of intent. For example, ISO 27001, SOC 2, and NIST SP 800-53 all require some form of logical access control, yet each phrases it differently. What matters to the auditor is whether the implemented control accomplishes the same risk mitigation purpose. This concept allows organizations to leverage a single, well-designed safeguard to satisfy multiple regulatory and assurance regimes without reinventing their control environment for each one.

The foundation of equivalency is *objective-level alignment*. Auditors and control owners compare what each framework is trying to achieve, not how it says to achieve it. This means mapping controls at the level of "prevent unauthorized access to systems and data" rather than at the procedural level of "review accounts every 90 days." By focusing on the underlying objective, the auditor determines whether the control achieves the required outcome. This distinction is crucial, because frameworks vary in tone and specificity. Some emphasize policy formalization; others stress operational measurement. Equivalency requires understanding both and confirming that the implemented control satisfies the most demanding interpretation.

Sufficiency determines whether equivalency is acceptable in practice. Even if two controls share the same objective, they may not provide the same assurance strength. To claim equivalency, the mapped control must meet or exceed the rigor expected by all frameworks it supports. Sufficiency considers factors such as control design quality, operating frequency, documentation depth, and the reliability of supporting evidence. For example, a manual quarterly access review may meet ISO expectations but not SOC 2's need for continuous monitoring. In that case, the control would be equivalent in intent but insufficient in strength, and the mapping must reflect that gap.

Organizations establish *mapping rules* to ensure these judgments are made consistently. Mapping rules specify how equivalency is evaluated, what documentation is required, and who approves mappings before they are adopted. They define criteria for acceptable evidence, frequency, and assurance coverage, ensuring that equivalency decisions are reasoned and defensible. For instance, a mapping rule may state that equivalency can only be claimed if the control's objective, evidence type, and review frequency match or exceed the strictest requirement among the mapped frameworks. This formalization keeps mapping decisions from becoming subjective or opportunistic.

Every mapping decision should include written justification that links the implemented control to each referenced requirement. The justification describes how the control satisfies the external objective, identifies any deviations in scope or rigor, and provides references to evidence or test results. This rationale acts as an audit trail, allowing independent reviewers to understand why equivalency was accepted. Without such documentation, mappings become opaque and difficult to defend during external reviews. Over time, organizations may store these rationales in a centralized mapping repository so they can be reused and versioned across audits.

Residual gaps emerge when a control satisfies one framework but does not fully meet another's expectation. These differences can result from varying depth of prescription, differing definitions of control ownership, or divergent assurance periods. For example, ISO 27001 may require the existence of a process for incident response, while another framework like NIST SP 800-53 specifies metrics for incident closure times. If the implemented process lacks those metrics, a residual gap exists. The purpose of identifying these gaps is not to expose weaknesses but to make control coverage transparent, allowing management and auditors to see where further work or compensating measures are needed.

Each residual gap should be recorded in a *mapping gap log* that includes the control identifier, affected frameworks, unmet requirement reference, and the reason equivalency could not be achieved. The log should also describe any planned remediation, compensating control, or risk acceptance decision. This record creates accountability and enables risk owners to track progress toward full coverage. Auditors rely on this log to validate that management's assertions are accurate and that no framework has been overstated in its level of compliance. Properly maintained, the gap log becomes an important governance artifact showing continuous improvement over time.

Residual gaps are often prioritized by risk and business impact. Gaps that expose high-risk control areas—such as encryption, logging, or change management—should receive remediation plans with defined owners and timelines. Others may be accepted if they fall outside legal or contractual obligations. When management chooses risk acceptance, the decision must be documented with rationale, approval authority, and the specific frameworks affected. Transparency in this process preserves the integrity of cross-framework mapping and prevents organizations from unintentionally misrepresenting their compliance posture.

Maintaining equivalency and gap documentation is an ongoing process. Frameworks evolve, and mappings that were sufficient one year may become outdated the next. Organizations should periodically revalidate equivalency by reviewing changes to frameworks, control objectives, and operational practices. This ensures that mappings remain defensible and that residual gaps do not expand unnoticed. A mature governance program treats mapping updates as part of continuous control improvement rather than a one-time exercise at audit preparation.

Portfolio Evidence Packs and Evidence Reuse

Portfolio evidence packs are curated collections of artifacts designed for reuse across multiple obligations, frameworks, and entities within the enterprise. Rather than assembling bespoke folders for every audit, the organization maintains canonical packs that prove a control's design and operation at the portfolio level, then references them wherever that control appears in scope. Each pack is organized around a single common control or a tightly related control family, and it contains only authoritative, reproducible artifacts. The result is a durable evidence layer that can be cited by many engagements without duplicating document gathering or risking inconsistent versions.

Composition is deliberate and standardized so that reviewers immediately understand what they are looking at and why it matters. A typical pack includes the governing policy or standard, configuration baselines or IaC excerpts, architecture diagrams, procedural records, and machine-produced exports such as logs, tickets, and dashboards. Every artifact is tagged with the system of record, collection parameters, and the period of coverage to prevent ambiguity about what was captured. Narrative context within the pack explains the control objective and identifies where each artifact demonstrates design or operation, without describing how tests are executed.

Freshness is governed by explicit currency rules that reflect how often the underlying control changes or produces new outputs. Each pack declares a validity window—for example, "quarterly refresh required" or "rolling 90-day dataset"—and the repository enforces these windows with alerts when artifacts approach staleness. Timestamping is accompanied by source-generated metadata such as report run dates, query IDs, export filters, and environment labels to establish that the content represents the correct time and scope. Artifacts that cannot be auto-refreshed include a renewal schedule and named owner accountable for timely updates.

Provenance is documented to make lineage indisputable and reproducible. For machine-generated evidence, the pack preserves the exact job definition, query text, API route, or export configuration used to produce the artifact, along with the producing system's version and identity. Hashes or content-addressable IDs provide tamper-evident integrity markers so auditors can verify that the artifact presented during a walkthrough is the artifact that was originally captured. When evidence is derived—such as a dashboard that aggregates multiple data sources—the pack includes a short dataflow description and references to the upstream artifacts to maintain end-to-end traceability.

Versioning treats evidence as a controlled configuration item rather than a disposable file. Each pack carries a semantic version and a change log that records what changed, why, who approved it, and which engagements consumed which version. Superseded versions are retained for the statutory or contractual retention period so prior audits remain reproducible even after improvements. Where evidence is sensitive, access controls and classification labels travel with the pack, and retrieval is logged so access to regulated data elements is defensible. Versioning discipline prevents "evidence drift," where different audiences unknowingly review different snapshots of the environment.

Linkage to the common control set is explicit and machine-readable. The pack header records the common control identifier, title, and objective text, along with the mapping table that lists the source framework references and coverage type for each (full or partial). Cross-references point to companion packs when partial mappings must be combined to achieve full coverage of a framework requirement. This alignment allows auditors to navigate from requirement to control to evidence without reinterpreting scope or chasing artifacts across silos. The same linkage enables portfolio-level dashboards that show which obligations are satisfied by current packs and where refresh or remediation is pending.

Evidence reuse across entities and services is handled through scoped overlays rather than duplicating core artifacts. A shared-service pack—for example, enterprise identity or network security monitoring—provides the canonical artifacts and portfolio-level narrative, while entity-specific annexes add local parameters such as tenant IDs, OU paths, or subscription scopes. The overlay records any entity-level variations in configuration, noting whether they are within policy tolerance or require compensating measures. This structure preserves a single source of truth for shared controls while honoring differences that matter for assurance.

Exceptions and limitations are documented inside the pack so that they travel with the evidence rather than living in a separate register that can be overlooked. Each declared limitation states the affected systems or data classes, the reason the artifact does not fully cover them, and the time period impacted. Where reliance is placed on a subservice organization or a third-party attestation, the pack includes the reference report and the carve-out or inclusive method used, tying the reliance back to the common control mapping. If a limitation persists, the pack links to the approved risk acceptance or remediation plan with the current status.

Operational governance ensures that packs remain trustworthy assets rather than stale archives. A named evidence owner maintains the pack, a governance reviewer approves material changes, and automation captures fresh artifacts on the defined cadence wherever feasible. Periodic portfolio reviews reconcile pack coverage against the current scope statement and common control library, retiring or merging packs when controls are redesigned. Integration with the control change-management process guarantees that when a control's design, ownership, or tooling changes, its evidence pack and mappings are updated in lockstep.

Consumption is streamlined but controlled to avoid misinterpretation. Auditors receive read-only access to the pack with its metadata, lineage, and limitations intact, along with pointers back to the common control entry that frames purpose and scope. Control owners and compliance staff reference the same pack during readiness activities, ensuring that what is previewed internally matches what is provided during external assessment. By anchoring reusable artifacts to clear governance for freshness, provenance, and versioning—and by binding them to the common control set and explicit exceptions—the organization turns evidence reuse into a reliable capability that reduces audit friction while preserving assurance quality.

Inherited/Shared Controls and Third-party Reliance (SOC, Certifications)

Auditors often rely on third-party assurance to avoid re-testing controls that are designed and operated by external providers, but that reliance is never blind. Acceptable reliance begins with determining whether the third party's report or certification directly addresses the control objectives in scope, covers the correct services and locations, and spans the relevant period. A SOC 2 Type II opinion or an ISO/IEC 27001 certificate with an explicit statement of applicability carries more weight than marketing attestations or point-in-time letters. The objective is to reuse reliable assurance where appropriate while preserving accountability for the parts of the control environment that remain the organization's responsibility.

Inherited controls are safeguards operated entirely by another party where the consuming organization has no practical ability to design or operate the control. Typical examples include physical data center security run by a hosting provider or hypervisor hardening managed by an IaaS platform. When a control is truly inherited, the auditor evaluates the sufficiency of the provider's assurance and confirms that the inherited control aligns with the consuming organization's control objective as defined in the common control set. No retesting of the provider's operation is performed by the consuming auditor; the reliance is placed on the provider's attestation within its stated scope.

Shared controls are safeguards where responsibility is split between the provider and the customer, often along a "responsibility model" boundary. Identity and access management in a SaaS platform, for instance, may be shared: the provider enforces authentication pipelines, while the customer defines authorization models and role assignments. For shared controls, third-party assurance may confirm the provider's portion, but the customer's portion remains subject to the organization's assertion and the auditor's procedures. Clarity on this split prevents gaps where each party assumes the other has fulfilled a requirement that no one actually owns.

Third-party SOC reports require careful reading beyond the opinion page. Auditors review the system description to verify which services, components, and regions are included, and they reconcile those details with what the organization actually uses. Carve-out versus inclusive subservice methods matter: a carve out indicates that a critical subservice organization's controls are outside the report's testing, which may create residual risk for any inherited claim. Complementary subservice organization controls identified as necessary for the provider to meet its objectives also signal dependencies that must be satisfied elsewhere in the environment. Table 2.3 provides a reusable checklist to document reliance on external attestations and inherited controls.

Complementary user-entity controls (CUECs) appear in most SOC reports and specify what the customer must do for the provider's controls to be effective. Auditors trace each applicable CUEC to a corresponding control in the organization's common control set and confirm that management has asserted and implemented it. Where CUECs are absent, incorrectly interpreted,

Table 2.3 Third-party reliance documentation fields.

Third-party type	Attestation type	Period covered	Scope notes	CUECs implemented	Carve out or inclusive
IaaS platform	SOC 2 Type II	Full year stated	Compute storage network regions listed	Yes	Inclusive
SaaS identity service	SOC 2 Type II	Full year stated	Auth pipeline and admin portal in scope	Yes	Carve out
Colocation facility	ISO 27001 Certificate	Current cycle	Physical security and site list defined	N A	Inclusive
Managed security provider	SOC 2 Type II plus bridge letter	Year plus subsequent events	Monitoring and alerting service only	Yes	Carve out
Subservice organization	SOC 2 Type II	Prior year	Dependent logging component excluded	N A	Carve out

or not implemented, reliance on the third-party report becomes conditional at best, because the end-to-end objective is not achieved. Documenting this linkage is essential so that reliance decisions are transparent and defensible.

Certifications such as ISO/IEC 27001, PCI DSS, or equivalents can also support reliance, but scope precision is critical. Certificates that reference a specific statement of applicability, site list, or service catalog provide a usable boundary; generic certificates without these details are weak evidence for inherited control claims. Surveillance and recertification cycles introduce cadence considerations, so auditors verify issue and expiry dates, any nonconformities, and whether corrective actions have been closed. When certifications and SOC reports overlap, the stricter or more relevant attestation should anchor the reliance decision for that control objective.

Temporal coverage must be reconciled so that the period of the third-party attestation aligns with the audit period. If a SOC report ends before the organization's coverage window, a bridge letter addressing subsequent events may be acceptable, provided it clearly states whether control operation continued without material change. Significant architectural changes, service migrations, or incident disclosures during the gap may invalidate simple reliance and require updated evidence. The same logic applies when providers add regions or features that were not included in the original attestation.

Reliance documentation belongs in the control record, not scattered among email threads. Each inherited or shared control entry should identify the provider, the attestation type and period, the exact services and regions relied upon, the mapping to the organization's control objective, and any applicable CUECs or complementary subservice controls. Carve-outs, limitations, and excluded components are listed explicitly, along with the rationale for why reliance remains sufficient despite those limits. This record becomes the single source of truth for how external assurance supports the organization's assertions.

Residual gaps arise when third-party assurance covers only part of the objective or omits a critical subservice. In these cases, the organization logs the gap, ties it to the affected frameworks, and records the compensating approach, such as operational monitoring of provider SLAs, additional configuration controls, or contractual amendments. Where no practical compensating measure exists and the obligation is non-negotiable, risk acceptance must be formally approved and traceable to the relevant business owner. Reliance that masks unresolved gaps is a governance failure, not an efficiency gain.

Deviations and Compensating Controls: Carve-outs and Documentation

Deviations occur when a required control cannot be implemented as prescribed, whether due to technical constraints, business necessity, or inherited system limitations. In cybersecurity auditing, these deviations are not treated as immediate failures but as exceptions that must be formally justified, documented, and governed. Proper handling of deviations ensures that the organization remains transparent about its compliance posture while preserving flexibility to manage risk pragmatically. Each deviation must be traceable to the specific requirement or control objective it departs from and supported by evidence that management has consciously evaluated and accepted the resulting exposure.

A compensating control may be introduced when a prescribed control cannot be implemented as written but an alternative measure achieves an equivalent level of protection. This equivalency must be demonstrable, not assumed. The alternative control should address the same risk vector, operate with comparable rigor and frequency, and produce verifiable evidence of effectiveness. For instance, if a legacy system cannot support full disk encryption, compensating measures such as physical access restrictions, segmented storage, and continuous data-loss monitoring may together achieve the same risk reduction. Auditors assess whether such substitutes preserve the intent of the original requirement and maintain the same assurance strength.

The documentation of a deviation begins with the *exception record*, which captures the essential metadata needed for traceability and review. Each record identifies the control ID, framework or requirement reference, affected systems or processes, description of the deviation, reason for nonconformance, and proposed compensating measures if any. It must also include a concise risk statement outlining the potential impact on confidentiality, integrity, or availability, along with the likelihood of occurrence. The entry is not considered complete until both the risk owner and the relevant governance authority (such as the Chief Information Security Officer, Compliance Officer, or Audit Committee delegate) have reviewed and approved it.

Approval of compensating controls requires careful evaluation of sufficiency and duration. Governance bodies assess whether the proposed measure truly mitigates the same risk and whether it introduces new dependencies or monitoring needs. They also confirm that the deviation is temporary and tied to a remediation plan, or if permanent, that it represents a deliberate and accepted design choice within the organization's risk appetite. Each approved deviation must carry an explicit expiration or review date to prevent exceptions from becoming indefinite workarounds. When the review date passes, the control owner must either demonstrate remediation or revalidate the compensating control's continued adequacy.

Carve-outs differ slightly from general deviations in that they define a formal exclusion from scope rather than a variation in implementation. A carve-out may apply when a system, region, or business unit cannot be feasibly audited or included in a particular certification period. These carve-outs are disclosed in scope statements and audit reports so that readers understand the exact coverage boundary. The auditor does not opine on carved-out components, but management must still document the reason for exclusion, assess any residual risk, and disclose whether alternate assurance mechanisms exist—such as separate audits, third-party certifications, or inherited control coverage.

Deviations and compensating controls must feed into the organization's overall assurance reporting. When compiling management's assertion or preparing audit-ready documentation, the list of approved exceptions is referenced to ensure transparency about the environment's control posture. Each deviation record links back to the common control set so that mappings to affected frameworks remain accurate. During external audits, the deviation register allows the auditor to reconcile reported exceptions against known control objectives, confirming that management's assertion does not overstate compliance. This linkage also enables portfolio-level metrics on the number and severity of deviations, helping governance committees understand systemic weaknesses.

Risk impact statements are central to this documentation process. Each must describe not only the technical effect of the deviation but also the potential business and regulatory implications. For example, an unpatched legacy system may carry low operational impact but high compliance risk if it stores regulated data. Risk scoring models, whether qualitative or quantitative, can be used to prioritize deviations for remediation. High-risk exceptions generally require more frequent review and senior-level sign-off, while low-risk or temporary deviations may be handled by operational management. Consistency in risk language ensures comparability across reporting periods and frameworks.

The audit trail for deviations should also capture the sequence of approvals and rationale for decisions. Each record includes the initiator, reviewers, approvers, and timestamps for every action, along with supporting commentary or evidence. This governance chain protects against informal or undocumented exceptions that bypass risk evaluation. It also provides the historical context necessary for future audits—showing when and why decisions were made, whether compensating controls were maintained, and how the organization managed the associated risk exposure over time.

Integration with planning processes ensures that deviations are not isolated administrative artifacts. Approved deviations inform control testing scopes, internal audit priorities, and risk remediation roadmaps. When recurring deviations appear in similar control areas—such as access management or change control—they signal systemic design issues that may require broader remediation or process redesign. By feeding this information into governance cycles, the organization turns deviation documentation into a continuous improvement mechanism rather than a static record of exceptions.

Conclusion

Mastering the principles of regulatory alignment and control assurance is critical for any organization seeking credible cybersecurity governance. Frameworks, assertions, and evidence are not abstract constructs—they are the mechanisms through which accountability is proven and trust is earned. By understanding how criteria are defined, how scope is bounded, and how equivalency and deviations are managed, professionals can translate complex regulatory demands into coherent control architectures. These competencies form the bridge between compliance documentation and operational security resilience.

For AI-driven and cloud-distributed enterprises, this discipline becomes even more consequential. Automated decision systems, shared infrastructures, and data-rich analytics environments amplify both risk exposure and regulatory scrutiny. The ability to trace every control to its framework origin, validate inherited assurances, and maintain reusable evidence packs ensures that compliance keeps pace with innovation. In this context, auditors and security architects serve as translators—converting assurance language into the engineering realities that underpin trustworthy AI systems.

With these foundations in place, cybersecurity and audit teams are better equipped to maintain integrity across overlapping obligations and rapidly evolving technologies. Whether verifying control sufficiency, documenting exceptions, or reconciling shared responsibilities, their work sustains the credibility of the enterprise in the eyes of regulators, partners, and customers alike. The outcome is more than compliance—it is an operational model of transparency and consistency that strengthens both human oversight and automated security assurance at scale.

Auditor Recommendations

1. **Anchor Assurance to Criteria and Assertions:** Define explicit assurance criteria and require management to state a precise assertion with period and system boundaries. Validate the suitability of the criteria for relevance, completeness, measurability, and neutrality. Document the linkage so every procedure and conclusion traces cleanly to the chosen criteria and the assertion.

2. **Harmonize Controls into a Common Control Set:** Consolidate overlapping requirements into canonical controls with stable identifiers and clear objective text. Map each control to all applicable framework references and record whether coverage is full or partial. Use this library as the authoritative source for ownership and evidence references during planning and reporting.
3. **Enforce Traceability Metadata for Every Control:** Capture framework name and version, exact source reference ID, control objective text, evidence locations, owner roles, and coverage type. Maintain bidirectional mapping so auditors can roll up by framework or drill down by control without rework. Treat metadata quality as an auditable requirement with periodic review.
4. **State Scope Boundaries with Operational Precision:** Specify included entities, business processes, systems, and data classes, and identify shared services and known shadow IT or SaaS explicitly. Tie inclusions and exclusions to the assertion and document rationale to prevent unintended opining. Reconcile scope when new workloads or data classes appear in the environment.
5. **Evaluate Equivalency by Objective and Test for Sufficiency:** Focus mapping decisions on whether the safeguard achieves the same risk outcome rather than matching wording. Compare rigor, frequency, and evidence expectations and adopt the strictest applicable threshold. Record written justification so each equivalency decision is defensible to external assessors.
6. **Log Residual Gaps and Assign Accountable Ownership:** Document unmet elements when coverage is only partial, including affected requirements and frameworks. Link each entry to the relevant common control and specify remediation or risk acceptance with target dates. Review the register on a defined cadence and escalate high-impact gaps to governance bodies.
7. **Build Reusable Portfolio Evidence Packs with Governance:** Curate canonical artifacts around each common control and govern them for freshness, provenance, and versioning. Preserve lineage details such as query IDs, export parameters, and timestamps to ensure reproducibility. Provide scoped overlays for entities or tenants while keeping the core pack authoritative.
8. **Document Third-party Reliance with CUECs and Carve-outs:** Reconcile SOC reports or certifications to actual services, regions, and coverage periods in use. Trace complementary user-entity controls into the common control set and verify implementation. Record carve-outs or subservice methods and describe any limitations that condition reliance.
9. **Formalize Deviations and Compensating Controls:** Require exception records that include rationale, risk impact, compensating measures, governance approval, and an expiration or review date. Ensure the compensating control addresses the same risk with comparable rigor and produces verifiable evidence. Link deviations to mappings so report users see accurate coverage and limitations.
10. **Integrate Mapping, Gaps, and Reliance into Reporting and Plans:** Feed equivalency decisions, residual gaps, and third-party reliance records into readiness reviews and improvement roadmaps. Align conclusions explicitly to criteria, assertions, scope, and documented limitations in the final reporting. Use these artifacts to sustain transparent, reproducible assurance as AI-enabled environments evolve.

Chapter Questions

1. What is the primary reason auditors use formal security frameworks in assurance engagements?
   - **A.** To anchor conclusions to explicit criteria and align with management's assertions
   - **B.** To replace management's responsibilities with auditor-defined policies
   - **C.** To standardize tool choices across all engagements
   - **D.** To minimize report length regardless of scope

2. After management selects the criteria for an engagement, what is the auditor's first key judgment?
   - **A.** Determining the sampling method to be used
   - **B.** Evaluating whether the chosen criteria are suitable for the subject matter
   - **C.** Selecting which business units to exclude from scope
   - **D.** Writing the final opinion wording in advance

3. What is the chief purpose of a common control set in multi-regime environments?
   - **A.** To mirror each external framework word-for-word in separate libraries
   - **B.** To prioritize one framework and ignore the rest
   - **C.** To harmonize overlapping requirements into single canonical controls mapped across regimes
   - **D.** To defer all control ownership to third parties

4. Which metadata element is most critical for demonstrating cross-framework traceability for a control?
   - **A.** The control owner's job title history
   - **B.** The number of audit hours spent testing the control
   - **C.** The color-coding used in evidence folders
   - **D.** The framework name and version with the exact source control reference ID

5. Why must scope boundaries explicitly identify entities, processes, systems, and data classes in multi-regime audits?
   - **A.** To prevent auditors from opining on components not intended to be in scope
   - **B.** To reduce the number of control objectives required by half
   - **C.** To remove the need to review shared services or SaaS usage
   - **D.** To allow informal evidence collection from any available source

6. What defines equivalency when mapping controls across different frameworks?
   - **A.** Using identical wording to the strictest requirement
   - **B.** Demonstrating objective-level alignment that achieves the same risk outcome
   - **C.** Matching the same vendor tools used in reference implementations
   - **D.** Ensuring the same number of artifacts is produced for each framework

7. How should residual gaps be handled when a control satisfies one regime but only partially meets another?
   - **A.** Ignore them if the stricter regime is voluntary
   - **B.** Replace the control entirely in all frameworks
   - **C.** Log the gap with justification, identify affected requirements, and plan remediation or risk acceptance
   - **D.** Rephrase the mapping to claim full coverage

8. Which governance elements make portfolio evidence packs reliable for reuse?
   - **A.** Informal attestations from control owners
   - **B.** Ad hoc screenshots gathered at audit time
   - **C.** Annual deletion of all prior artifacts
   - **D.** Freshness rules, provenance documentation, and versioning with change history

9. In the context of third-party reliance, what is the role of complementary user-entity controls (CUECs) in a SOC report?
   - **A.** They specify customer responsibilities that must be implemented for the provider's controls to be effective
   - **B.** They authorize the auditor to re-perform provider controls
   - **C.** They list optional enhancements with no bearing on assurance
   - **D.** They replace the need to reconcile carve-outs or subservice methods

10. What is required when approving a deviation supported by compensating controls?
    - **A.** Permanent acceptance with no review date
    - **B.** Formal exception documentation with rationale, risk impact, governance approval, and an expiration or review date
    - **C.** A verbal acknowledgement by the system administrator
    - **D.** Consolidation of all deviations into a single generic statement

3

Risk Assessment and Control Design for Modern Systems

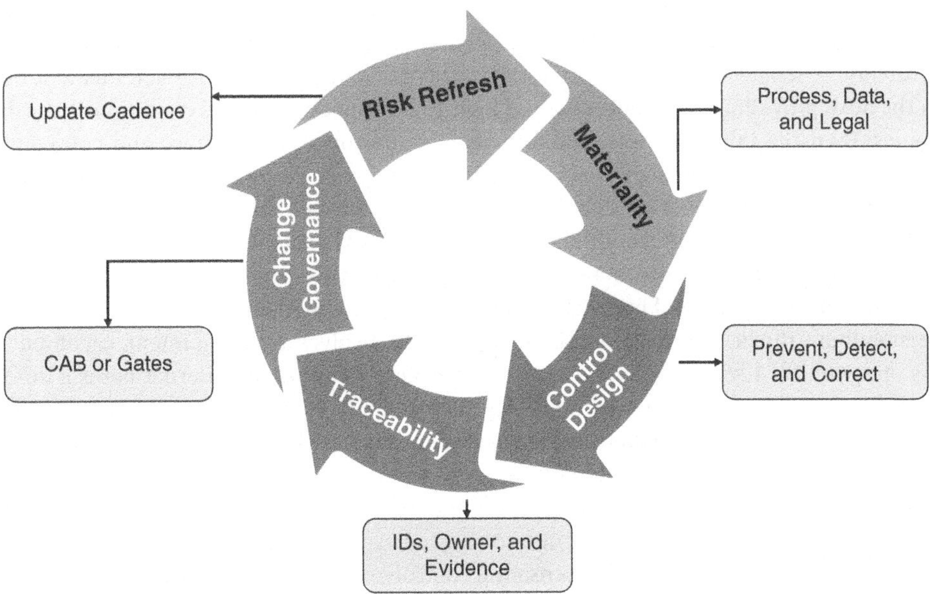

Modern cybersecurity auditing begins long before a test script runs or evidence is collected—it starts at the design table, where risk, architecture, and control intent intersect. The ability to trace a threat through to its corresponding control, owner, and assurance evidence defines whether an organization manages risk deliberately or by accident. This chapter establishes that linkage, showing how effective audit oversight depends on structured taxonomies, materiality thresholds, and design choices that align preventive, detective, and corrective safeguards with business priorities. Understanding these foundations is essential to ensure that assurance activities measure not just compliance, but the integrity of the organization's entire security architecture.

Design quality determines audit quality. Preventive versus detective controls, manual versus automated enforcement, and the documentation that connects them form the practical core of governance assurance. Auditors must be able to evaluate control sufficiency without becoming part of the design process, maintaining independence while still contributing to secure-by-design outcomes. Through structured documentation, clear ownership, and disciplined change governance, control design becomes testable, traceable, and sustainable—qualities that allow future audits to re-perform conclusions confidently and defend them under scrutiny.

In the age of continuous delivery, AI integration, and adaptive cloud infrastructure, the lines between design, operation, and audit are thinner than ever. Modern systems evolve daily, and with them the risks that auditors must understand and measure. Integrating audit perspectives into enterprise architecture and change governance ensures that security intent endures through automation, reconfiguration, and machine-driven decision-making. From risk taxonomy to evidence traceability, this chapter reinforces a single principle: durable assurance depends on designs that can withstand both technological change and the test of time.

Cyber Risk Taxonomy and Materiality

A structured cyber risk taxonomy provides auditors with a consistent method to deconstruct complex security issues into manageable, analyzable components. The framework of *threat → vulnerability → scenario → impact* forms the backbone of this approach. Each element builds upon the next, providing a traceable chain of logic that connects technical conditions to business outcomes. By using this taxonomy, auditors avoid confusion between cause and consequence, ensuring that each risk statement describes a clear path from exposure to effect. The goal is to enable disciplined analysis rather than intuition-driven risk assessment.

A *threat* represents an actor, condition, or event that could exploit a weakness in an organization's systems. Threats encompass a spectrum that includes external adversaries, insiders, suppliers, and even environmental factors that could degrade confidentiality, integrity, or availability. Understanding a threat requires more than naming it; it involves assessing intent, capability, and access opportunity. A script-driven ransomware operator scanning the internet poses a different level of risk than a trusted insider with privileged credentials. Auditors must characterize threats based on verifiable evidence—what exists in the environment, who is capable of acting against it, and how often that vector is relevant to the business sector under review.

A *vulnerability* is the condition that allows a threat to succeed. It is not the threat itself but the weak link that transforms potential harm into realized exposure. These can manifest as software flaws, misconfigurations, missing compensating controls, or process design failures. For example, unencrypted object storage in a public cloud, a lack of access reviews for privileged accounts, or an outdated cryptographic library each create exploitable conditions. Auditors document vulnerabilities in precise terms: where they exist, what control is missing or degraded, and which policy or standard they violate. This level of specificity allows for consistent testing and meaningful remediation tracking.

A *scenario* describes the credible sequence of actions connecting a threat and a vulnerability. It transforms technical weaknesses into operational risk narratives that make sense within the organization's context. A scenario might detail how an attacker could escalate privileges from a compromised web service account to exfiltrate sensitive data through an unmonitored outbound API. The value of the scenario lies in its plausibility and traceability—it is neither a theoretical imagination exercise nor a repetition of past incidents, but a grounded representation of how real-world actors could interact with actual system conditions. Effective auditors craft scenarios that reflect production architectures, data flows, and identity relationships rather than generic "what-if" statements.

The *impact* represents the measurable consequence if the scenario were realized. Impacts are categorized in business-relevant dimensions such as financial loss, regulatory exposure, customer trust erosion, or operational downtime. Auditors must be able to explain impacts in terms decision-makers understand, translating technical breaches into enterprise-scale consequences.

A denial-of-service event against an internal collaboration tool may be operationally inconvenient but not materially significant, whereas unauthorized access to a customer billing database could invoke breach notification laws and substantial regulatory penalties. The clarity with which impacts are defined determines how well risk discussions integrate with broader governance frameworks.

Setting *materiality thresholds* is what converts this taxonomy from analysis into audit prioritization. In cybersecurity, materiality cannot rely solely on financial quantification because the consequences of loss often include intangible effects such as compliance violations or strategic disruption. Instead, materiality is determined by combining process criticality, data sensitivity, and legal exposure. Each dimension provides a different lens for evaluating when a risk moves from tolerable to significant. The auditor's responsibility is to define and document these thresholds clearly so that audit scope, testing depth, and reporting all align with the organization's risk appetite.

Process criticality refers to how essential a system or function is to the organization's ability to operate or meet regulatory obligations. Systems supporting revenue recognition, financial reporting, or safety operations typically receive higher weighting. The interdependencies between these systems also affect criticality; a seemingly minor outage in a directory service could cascade into loss of authentication across multiple critical applications. By mapping these relationships, auditors can trace how localized failures scale into broader operational disruptions and adjust their focus accordingly.

Data sensitivity further shapes materiality by emphasizing the confidentiality and regulatory requirements associated with the information a system handles. Personally identifiable information, trade secrets, and regulated data categories such as protected health information elevate risk severity because of their potential for reputational or legal consequences. Auditors evaluate how data is classified, encrypted, transmitted, and retained to determine whether existing controls match the declared sensitivity. When these safeguards are inconsistent or poorly enforced, it signals not just control weakness but also governance misalignment that may amplify downstream risks.

Legal and regulatory exposure provides the boundary conditions for what constitutes an unacceptable level of risk. Compliance mandates such as GDPR, HIPAA, or sector-specific regulations impose explicit requirements for control operation and breach notification. The presence of contractual security obligations—such as those in vendor agreements or service-level commitments—can also raise materiality. Auditors must interpret these obligations in the context of actual system behavior, ensuring that control failures are evaluated not only for likelihood but also for their potential to trigger statutory or contractual consequences. Table 3.1 links each risk from threat to impact and highlights the business driver that determines materiality.

Table 3.1 Risk taxonomy with materiality drivers.

ID	Threat	Vulnerability	Scenario	Impact	Driver
RSK-001	External ransomware operator	Missing phishing resistant MFA on admin portal	Compromise of admin portal leading to privilege escalation	Service outage and data encryption	Process criticality
RSK-002	Insider with privileged access	Lack of segregation of duties in identity governance	Unauthorized change to access policy expands entitlements	Excessive access to regulated data	Legal exposure

(Continued)

Table 3.1 (Continued)

ID	Threat	Vulnerability	Scenario	Impact	Driver
RSK-003	Automated botnet scanning	Public storage with misconfigured policy	Direct read of sensitive data from storage	Confidentiality breach of customer data	Data sensitivity
RSK-004	Supplier integration risk	Unmonitored outbound API	Data exfiltration via partner API	Loss of customer trust and disclosure obligations	Legal exposure
RSK-005	Cloud tenant escape scenario	Unpatched platform flaw	Lateral access to adjacent workload	Cross tenant data exposure	Data sensitivity

Control Design Choices

Preventive, detective, and corrective controls represent different points along the timeline of risk, and the design choice sets the auditor's expectations for failure modes and residual risk. Preventive controls block or constrain an action before it can cause harm, so their operating effectiveness is judged by their ability to be applied universally and consistently under load. Detective controls surface deviations after the fact and therefore carry latency and reliance on response processes; their value depends on coverage, signal quality, and the speed with which escalation occurs. Corrective controls restore a secure state or service level after an adverse event and are evaluated on recovery time, recovery point, and the risk of recurrence. The earlier the control sits in the timeline, the lower the expected residual risk but the higher the bar for completeness and false-negative avoidance.

Assurance expectations should track the control's intent and enforceability. For preventive designs, auditors expect strong evidence that enforcement cannot be trivially bypassed and that exceptions are governed, time-bound, and visible. For detective designs, auditors expect demonstrable ability to distinguish true events from noise, documented thresholds for alerts, and a defined response workflow that routinely closes the loop. Corrective designs invite scrutiny on playbook quality, rehearsals, and the durability of lessons learned that reduce reoccurrence, such as post-incident hardening. Across all three, the auditor calibrates testing to the expected error rate and blast radius if the control misses.

Evidence durability is shaped by the control's source of truth and mutability. Automated preventive controls that execute within policy engines, identity platforms, or deployment pipelines typically emit system-generated logs that are time-stamped, tamper-evident, and reproducible—providing durable evidence without human memory. Manual controls often rely on tickets, emails, or sign-offs that can lack context, be inconsistently captured, or be altered after the fact; durability improves when these artifacts are produced by systems that preserve metadata and retain history. Detective controls should produce artifacts that link detection to disposition, including alert content, triage notes, and closure rationales, so an auditor can re-perform the decision path. Corrective controls need records that tie restoration steps to specific affected assets and data, capturing when normalcy was achieved and whether compensating safeguards were introduced.

Table 3.2 contrasts assurance implications of preventive detective and corrective designs including evidence durability and cadence.

Control frequency and execution cadence must reflect the speed of risk creation. High-velocity environments—continuous deployment, ephemeral infrastructure, and federated SaaS—demand controls that operate per transaction or continuously rather than on periodic schedules. Preventive guardrails in code repositories, infrastructure-as-code validators, or identity provisioning flows should trigger on every change, not just at release gates. Detective analytics for authentication anomalies or data egress should evaluate near-real time streams rather than daily batches when the exposure window matters. Where processes are slow-moving or low volume, periodic detective reviews can be sufficient if their interval does not allow risks to compound silently.

Automation changes the assurance profile by improving consistency and sample size while introducing dependencies on configuration management and software quality. Automated preventive controls reduce variance across users and time, enabling auditors to rely more on configuration inspection and re-performance at scale than on small-sample walkthroughs. Automated detective controls enable population-level coverage, but auditors will probe for model drift, logic accuracy, and alert fatigue that can suppress response quality. Automated corrective steps, such as gold-image redeployments or key rotations, are powerful but must be safeguarded against cascading failures and must produce verifiable state evidence, not just success messages. In each case, change control and monitoring of the control itself become part of the assurance scope.

Criteria for preferring automated, continuously enforced controls start with repeatability and authoritative data. If the decision can be expressed as deterministic policy using attributes available at decision time, automation should be the default because it scales enforcement and eliminates discretion where discretion adds risk. If the affected population is large, the transaction rate is high, or the exposure window from a miss is material, continuous enforcement is warranted to minimize residual risk. Where the control point is close to the asset boundary—such as identity, network boundaries, deployment pipelines, or data access gates—automation generally delivers better coverage with lower operational burden. Feasibility improves when the platform natively supports policy-as-code or control hooks and when exceptions can be transparently governed with expiration and independent approval.

Automated controls should also be preferred when evidence integrity is a priority or when external obligations require demonstrable, consistent enforcement. Systems that emit immutable

Table 3.2 Control design tradeoffs across prevent detect correct.

Type	Intent	Durability	Frequency	Emphasis	Automation
Preventive	Block unsafe action before harm	High via system logs and policy states	Per transaction or continuous	Bypass resistance and completeness	Strong when policy is deterministic
Detective	Surface deviations after they occur	Medium to high with alert and case records	Near real time or periodic	Signal quality and response timeliness	Strong for streaming analytics
Corrective	Restore secure state after adverse event	Medium with recovery artifacts	On demand per incident	Recovery time and recurrence risk	Strong for scripted remediation with safeguards

logs, attach cryptographic proofs, or align to standardized event schemas simplify auditability and reduce disputes about what happened. Automation allows precise scoping of exceptions, recording who approved them, for what purpose, and for how long, while automatically restoring baseline at expiry. In regulated contexts that mandate continuous conformance—such as encryption at rest, least privilege, or segregation of duties—automated enforcement provides a defensible posture that manual processes rarely match. Cost-benefit analyses should include the avoided cost of periodic review, rework, and incident response attributable to control misses.

Manual controls remain acceptable—and sometimes preferable—when the decision requires nuanced human judgment or context unavailable to systems at enforcement time. Complex vendor risk reviews, legal interpretations of novel data use, and architectural risk sign-offs for new patterns often require subject-matter deliberation that cannot be reduced to deterministic rules. Manual detective reviews are also reasonable when population size is small, event frequency is low, and the potential impact is bounded, provided that reviewer competency, independence, and documentation standards are strong. Temporary manual controls can bridge gaps during transformations or tool migrations, but they should have explicit sunset dates and monitoring for backlog growth, which signals that automation is overdue.

Designing manual controls for auditability requires more than a checklist; it requires verifiable trails and repeatable criteria. Decision templates, required evidence attachments, and standardized rationales reduce variance and allow re-performance by the auditor. Segregation of duties and supervisory review add assurance that critical judgments are not made unilaterally, while periodic calibration sessions keep reviewers aligned on thresholds. Sampling strategies should be risk-based and dynamic, expanding when error rates rise or when process changes are introduced. Where a manual control rejects items at a gate, the disposition of rejects should be tracked to confirm that rework resolves the underlying issues rather than merely deferring them.

Hybrid patterns often yield the best balance: use preventive automation to enforce nonnegotiables and pair it with detective human review for edge cases and continuous improvement. For example, automatically block deployments lacking required security tests while having architects periodically review exceptions to refine policies and reduce friction. Automated detectors can surface outliers and suspected policy circumventions for human adjudication, turning manual effort into targeted, high-value analysis rather than broad, low-yield inspection. Corrective playbooks can be machine-executed for common events but require human confirmation for actions with irreversible consequences, such as data purges or key revocations. Auditors evaluate how clearly these handoffs are defined and whether ownership and escalation are unambiguous.

Traceability

A minimum traceability chain begins with a uniquely identified risk and proceeds through a defined control objective, an accountable control owner, and a resolvable evidence location. Each link must be explicit, queryable, and durable over time so that an auditor can reconstruct why a control exists and how its effectiveness is substantiated. The aim is not ornamental documentation but a living map that ties enterprise risk to the specific people and systems responsible for managing it. Without this chain, findings devolve into isolated defects that cannot be prioritized or sustainably remediated.

The risk anchor requires a stable identifier, a concise statement of the risk scenario, and the business context that makes it material. The identifier should be immutable and human-readable, such as RSK-2025-017, and the statement should describe the cause, event, and consequence in one sentence. Business context captures affected processes, data classifications, and legal obligations so that downstream control decisions can be evaluated against the right stakes. A system of record for risks, whether a GRC platform or a lightweight register, must be designated to prevent divergence across spreadsheets and project trackers.

The control objective translates risk into a verifiable intent that can be assessed independent of specific tools. A good objective describes the safeguarded asset, the enforced property, and the expected condition or threshold. It should have its own identifier, such as CTR-OBJ-142, and a status that reflects whether the objective is in force, deprecated, or superseded. The system of record for control objectives should maintain version history so auditors can see when wording or scope changed and why.

Ownership is the accountability fulcrum that turns a control objective into consistent action. The control owner must be a named role or person with decision authority over the control's design and operation, not merely an implementer. Ownership metadata should include an authoritative directory key, such as an enterprise identity or group ID, a defined delegate model, and an escalation path if the owner is unavailable. An update cadence indicating how frequently the owner must attest to the control objective's status helps ensure that ownership is not a one-time assignment but an active responsibility.

Evidence location links the abstract objective to the tangible artifacts that demonstrate operation. Each evidence pointer should resolve to a system, dataset, or report that is stable across reporting cycles and accessible to authorized reviewers. Pointers benefit from URI-like formats that can be validated programmatically, along with metadata such as the generating system, retention period, and integrity guarantees. When evidence is generated on a schedule or per event, the cadence should be recorded so auditors can align the expected artifact dates to the period under review.

Durable traceability depends on consistent metadata conventions across the chain. Every record should carry a unique ID, a life cycle state, a last-updated timestamp, and a steward distinct from the owner when necessary. Systems of record must implement role-based access, audit logs for changes, and change rationales so that edits are attributable and explainable. Cross-references should be stored as hard links using the target IDs rather than free text so that linkage remains intact even when titles change. Table 3.3 enumerates the metadata that keeps the risk to control to owner to evidence chain durable and auditable over time.

Table 3.3 Minimum traceability chain and metadata requirements.

Element	Metadata	Record	Cadence	Format
Risk	Statement and context and life cycle state	GRC risk registry	Monthly or quarterly or continuous	RSK-YYYY-NNN
Control objective	Asset property threshold and status	GRC control library	Monthly or quarterly	CTR-OBJ-NNN
Control owner	Role and directory id and delegate and escalation	HR or Identity directory	Quarterly attestation	DIR-UID or Group-ID
Evidence location	Pointer and source system and retention and integrity	SIEM or Data lake or Platform logs	Per event or daily or weekly	EVD-NNN
Exception record	Rationale and approver and expiry	Exception register	Time bound with reminders	EXC-NNN
Change record	Rationale and impact assessment and approval	Change management portal	Per change	CHG-NNN

The update cadence for each link should be calibrated to the rate of change of the underlying risk and control environment. High-velocity risks tied to cloud entitlements or external interfaces warrant monthly or even continuous updates, while slower-moving risks tied to physical assets may justify quarterly review. Cadence should not be uniform across the portfolio; it should be a property of the item recorded in the system of record, visible to auditors, and enforced through reminders and escalation. Staleness rules—such as auto-flagging any record that exceeds its cadence by more than one cycle—keep the chain credible.

The distinction between owner and system of record is critical when organizations rely on federated tooling. Ownership denotes accountability for design and operation, while the system of record denotes where truth resides for audit and reporting. When tools change, the owner remains constant but the evidence pointer must be migrated with documented equivalence criteria to preserve continuity. Mapping tables that capture "old pointer → new pointer" with cutover dates protect against gaps that would otherwise undermine reliance on historical evidence.

Dependencies within the chain should be explicit so auditors can detect blast-radius effects. A single control objective may mitigate multiple risks, and a single evidence location may support multiple objectives; these many-to-many relationships must be recorded rather than implied. When a control objective is retired or a data source is decommissioned, dependent risks should be auto-flagged for reassessment. This dependency awareness prevents silent erosion of assurance due to architectural changes elsewhere in the estate.

Design Reviews and Auditor Boundaries

Design reviews occupy a delicate intersection between governance and assurance. When performed correctly, they provide early visibility into control design quality before systems are built or deployed, reducing the cost of future remediation. However, they also introduce a risk that auditors may become participants in design decisions, creating a self-review threat that later undermines audit independence. The challenge is to engage constructively—helping the organization interpret control objectives—without assuming responsibility for the resulting design choices. Maintaining this boundary requires clear scoping, transparent documentation, and consistent language in all communications.

The auditor's role in a design review is to evaluate the sufficiency of control design against defined objectives, not to engineer or approve the solution itself. The distinction is subtle but critical. Auditors can ask probing questions, highlight unaddressed risks, and point out where design assumptions appear inconsistent with policy or regulation. What they cannot do is prescribe configurations, dictate vendor selections, or author control logic. If an auditor drafts or approves such technical content, they become a designer, and any later assurance activity on that same system would constitute a self-review. The principle to follow is that auditors assess adequacy, not implementation.

Permissible feedback focuses on criteria, not conclusions. For example, an auditor might state, "The proposed control does not appear to enforce least privilege for all access paths; please document how residual access will be monitored," rather than "Reconfigure the IAM role to deny all except X and Y permissions." The first comment tests alignment with a control objective; the second alters design ownership. This type of phrasing helps preserve independence while still adding value to the development team. The same principle applies when commenting on vendor controls, encryption strength, or architectural patterns—auditors should surface questions and implications, not specific fixes.

All advisory input must be explicitly recorded as *advisory* to ensure future audit teams can distinguish between informal guidance and tested assurance evidence. A common practice is to produce a "Design Review Memo" that identifies the reviewed system, lists participants, outlines the control objectives discussed, and summarizes the auditor's observations. Each observation should be tagged either *advisory (nonbinding feedback)* or *deficiency (requires remediation before go-live).* Only deficiencies tied directly to mandatory policies or control failures become part of the audit record; advisory comments remain outside the formal assurance boundary. This separation maintains transparency while allowing designers to benefit from auditor insights.

To reinforce independence, auditors should avoid language that conveys approval or endorsement. Phrases such as "approved," "validated," or "authorized" imply ownership and should be replaced with neutral wording like "reviewed," "observed," or "noted." A suitable example might read: "Control design reviewed for alignment with access governance policy; design appears consistent with stated objectives pending implementation verification." This phrasing signals that the auditor evaluated the concept but reserves the right to test and conclude later. Every document or meeting outcome should include a disclaimer that the review was advisory in nature and that subsequent assurance work may yield different conclusions once controls are implemented.

Artifacts generated during the review should include a sign-off section that distinguishes participants by role—designer, risk owner, and reviewer. The auditor's signature or electronic acknowledgment should appear in a distinct area labeled *Reviewer (Advisory Capacity).* The corresponding statement might read, "Reviewed for completeness of control intent; no assurance testing performed." This simple convention provides an evidentiary boundary, allowing future audit teams to rely on the document for context without inheriting a conflict of interest. It also clarifies to management that audit input does not equate to approval.

When design reviews occur within integrated governance workflows, such as agile sprint ceremonies or architecture boards, the auditor's participation must be framed in observer or consultative capacity. The record should note attendance and summarize high-level risk observations without attributing design decisions to the auditor. For example, meeting notes might include: "Audit function observed security design session; noted absence of key rotation strategy; management to address in subsequent design iteration." This language provides traceability without assuming accountability for the eventual control configuration. The goal is to remain part of the conversation but not part of the implementation.

Documentation discipline is what protects independence months later when the same auditor—or another within the same function—returns to test controls in production. Each advisory artifact should contain metadata indicating its type (e.g., "design review memo"), date, participants, and systems covered. These documents must be stored separately from formal audit working papers and clearly labeled as *non-assurance materials.* If a subsequent audit references these artifacts, the file must demonstrate that design reviews influenced scope or context but not the audit opinion. This recordkeeping practice prevents future disputes over whether the auditor "helped design" what they later tested.

Auditors must also remain alert to *scope creep*—the gradual shift from evaluating risk coverage to optimizing control performance. For instance, suggesting that a developer reduce logging verbosity to save cost might seem helpful but crosses into operational advice. Similarly, proposing a new identity role structure or cloud service configuration exceeds the mandate of assurance review. The safe boundary is to ask "Does the proposed control achieve its stated purpose?" not "How can we make it better?" That distinction keeps the audit function focused on adequacy and risk alignment, leaving efficiency and optimization to management.

Integration with Enterprise Architecture and Change Governance

Enterprise architecture serves as the blueprint where control design becomes institutionalized. It translates abstract security principles into enforceable standards and reusable patterns that shape how technology is selected, configured, and interconnected. When controls are designed well, they are embedded not as exceptions or add-ons but as structural elements of the architecture itself. Reference models—such as data flow topologies, identity trust boundaries, and shared service baselines—act as the first line of defense in ensuring consistency. These artifacts define where controls must exist, what interfaces they protect, and which technologies are sanctioned for use. Auditors examining an organization's security posture look for these architecture artifacts to verify that security intent is systematically reflected in the design ecosystem, not individually reinvented for each project.

Architecture patterns serve as the practical expression of these reference models. They encapsulate proven control configurations for recurring design problems, such as enforcing encryption at rest, implementing multifactor authentication, or segmenting workloads across network tiers. A mature enterprise architecture repository will version these patterns, assign ownership, and mark which controls are mandatory versus optional. From an audit perspective, this traceability ensures that each system's implementation can be mapped back to a vetted pattern, providing inherent assurance that control objectives were considered during design. When projects deviate from established patterns, auditors expect a documented exception review describing the rationale, compensating safeguards, and expiration timeline for that deviation.

Standards and baselines reinforce these patterns by defining measurable configuration criteria. They specify control thresholds—minimum key lengths, required logging formats, or retention durations—and they link each criterion to a governing policy or framework reference. This allows the auditor to test compliance objectively by comparing current configurations to the authoritative baseline. The presence of an architecture standards catalog signals that security design has moved beyond individual heroics toward repeatable, policy-driven engineering. In this context, the audit function evaluates whether those standards are updated in step with technology evolution, whether exceptions are tracked, and whether ownership for each standard is explicitly assigned.

Change governance extends this architectural discipline into the operational life cycle. Every technology environment evolves, and the function of change control—whether through a formal Change Advisory Board (CAB) or embedded DevOps change gates—is to ensure that those evolutions preserve control intent. Control intent refers to the purpose and design rationale behind each safeguard, not merely its implementation state. A change request to replatform an application, modify an API gateway, or decommission a shared service may all appear routine, but from an assurance perspective, each one potentially alters the control landscape. Auditors examine whether change governance processes require proposers to assess and document the impact of such changes on control coverage and risk exposure before approval.

In environments where DevOps pipelines manage deployment, change governance is often enforced programmatically through policy checks, approval workflows, and automated validations. These gates ensure that the same architectural rules—encryption, access, segregation—are continuously applied even when releases occur at high velocity. Auditors do not need to review the mechanics of the pipelines themselves but expect to see documented mapping between change gates and corresponding control objectives. For example, an automated check that validates infrastructure-as-code templates against a configuration baseline is a control in support of the same objective as a CAB review in a traditional environment: verifying that implemented changes do not violate approved security design. This demonstrates continuity of governance despite differing technical delivery methods.

Effective change governance captures four essential data points that auditors scrutinize: change rationale, risk impact assessment, approval evidence, and rollback or contingency plans. The rationale describes what is changing and why; the risk impact assessment identifies which controls or assets might be affected; the approval evidence demonstrates that responsible authorities reviewed the proposal; and the contingency plan confirms that recovery paths exist if the change degrades control performance. Each element supports auditability by linking a single change to the broader assurance framework. When any of these components are missing, auditors interpret it as a gap in governance discipline rather than an isolated documentation failure.

Architectural governance bodies—such as enterprise design councils or security architecture review boards—play a complementary role to CABs by assessing structural impacts before operational deployment. Their review outcomes should flow into the same system of record that tracks change approvals. Auditors expect this linkage to be visible: when a new architecture pattern is introduced or a foundational service is modified, the associated control mapping should be updated in both repositories. This synchronization ensures that risk assessments, standards, and change control data all describe the same reality. Discrepancies—such as a retired control pattern still listed as active in the change portal—signal breakdowns in alignment and weaken the reliability of assurance conclusions.

When architecture or service changes alter risk or control coverage, auditors expect a structured response process. First, the affected risk and control registers should be updated with revised ownership, scope, or status. Second, any retired or superseded controls should have documented sunset plans, including compensating measures until replacements are fully operational. Third, the change record should reference these updates explicitly, creating traceability from the architectural modification to the adjusted risk entries. This end-to-end linkage assures auditors that control evolution is deliberate, not incidental, and that governance processes remain anchored in risk-based rationale.

Material changes—those that shift data classification boundaries, introduce new technologies, or externalize critical services—warrant formal re-assessment of both design and control adequacy. Auditors reviewing such transitions expect to see design artifacts demonstrating that new risks were analyzed and mapped to updated control objectives before go-live. For example, migrating from an on-premise database to a managed cloud service should trigger a documented evaluation of data residency, encryption, and monitoring controls under the new model. If that documentation is missing, the audit cannot reasonably conclude that control intent was preserved through the transition, regardless of the system's operational success.

Sustained control assurance depends on architectural hygiene—keeping reference models, standards, and governance processes synchronized. Auditors assess whether the architecture repository, risk register, and change management records are integrated or at least cross-referenced. The minimum expectation is that every approved change can be traced to a control objective in the architecture baseline and that each control in the baseline has evidence of having passed through governance review at least once. When these systems operate cohesively, they form a durable chain connecting strategic design to day-to-day operations. That traceability is what allows auditors to evaluate not only whether controls exist but whether they continue to embody the intent for which they were originally designed.

Design Documentation: Approvals, RACI, and Version Control

Design documentation must read like a definitive ledger of control intent, not a collection of screenshots. At minimum, it should identify the control objective with a stable identifier, the systems and data classes in scope, and the authoritative policy line it implements. The document needs a clearly designated system of record so readers are not chasing copies across wikis and shared drives. Every reference to risks, standards, assets, and evidence should resolve to canonical IDs rather than mutable titles to survive reorganizations and naming changes.

Approval history is the spine that shows who accepted what risk, when, and under which authority. Each approval entry should capture the approver's role bound to an enterprise identity, the decision type, the timestamp with time zone, and a succinct rationale that cites the driving policy or risk entry. Conditional approvals require explicit conditions and expiry, along with the party accountable for verifying closure; without this, "approve with conditions" becomes a silent risk acceptance. Avoid verbs that imply operational endorsement; an auditor-friendly sentence reads, "Reviewed for alignment with Encryption Standard v3.2; approval granted by Data Protection Officer contingent on KMS rotation evidence by 2025-11-30."

RACI must be unambiguous and resistant to personnel churn. The accountable owner should have budget and policy authority to sustain the control, while the responsible role operates it day to day; these are often different functions and the document should make that separation visible. Consulted stakeholders such as legal or privacy should be tied to durable group identities rather than individuals, and informed parties should include the downstream services that rely on the control's guarantees. When ownership changes, the record needs a dated transfer entry that states the trigger for the change and the effective date so later reviewers can re-perform decisions against the right accountable party.

Effective dates anchor the version of truth that applied at any point in time. The document should show an effective-from date for the current design, a review-by date calibrated to risk velocity, and a life cycle state of active, deprecated, or superseded. Supersession entries should point to the successor control ID and briefly describe scope deltas to prevent quiet erosion of coverage. If a control is retired, keep the final configuration reference and last-known evidence pointer to support incident reconstruction and historical audits.

Version control transforms the artifact from a snapshot into a trustworthy timeline. Every change should carry a unique version identifier, author, change summary, and a link to the triggering ticket or architecture decision record. Semantic cues help readers gauge impact: use major versions for scope or objective changes, minor for design adjustments that preserve intent, and patch for editorial fixes. A stable permalink to each version allows auditors to cite the exact text that governed a specific period without arguing over "which copy" is authoritative.

Consistency and retrievability depend on a common schema and controlled vocabulary across the portfolio. Field names, identifier formats, and life cycle states should be standardized and validated by the system of record rather than left to author discretion. Required fields—approval history, RACI, effective dates, and version—should be enforced at save time, and records that reference unknown IDs should be rejected. Routine data quality scans ought to flag stale records, broken links, orphaned controls with no owner, and controls with expired conditional approvals, driving remediation before an audit does.

Design documentation must link outward to the procedures that operationalize control intent, and those links need to be durable and verifiable. For runbooks and operating procedures, reference the repository path and commit hash rather than a PDF export, and record the procedure version that was effective on the control's effective date. Where the control is expressed as policy-as-code or platform configuration, point to the source file and commit, along with the environment it applies to, so a reviewer can rehydrate the state. If operational procedures change independently, the design record should state whether the change affects intent and whether a design review was required.

Evidence systems require resolvable pointers with enough metadata to support re-performance. Each pointer should include the generating system, the expected cadence of evidence generation, the retention policy, and any integrity guarantees such as immutability or access-log enforcement. Where evidence is event-driven, define the event types the control is expected to emit and the index or dataset where those events land, so reviewers can pull the correct time window. If an evidence location changes due to tool migration, the document should carry a migration log mapping old locations to new ones, with cutover dates and equivalence notes to protect longitudinal analyses.

Approval and attestation cadence should be explicit, measurable, and recorded in the same artifact. Owners ought to attest on a defined schedule that the design remains accurate, dependencies are still valid, and exceptions are tracked with current expiry dates. The attestation entry should include the attester's identity, timestamp, and a short assertion such as, "Design and links verified against Control Library and SIEM index; no scope changes since v2.1." This practice prevents slow drift from turning a once-accurate design into historical fiction.

Security and retention of the design artifact are themselves part of audit readiness. Access should be role-based with change logging, and significant edits should require a second-party review to deter unilateral rewrites of risk-bearing text. Retention policies must outlive the systems the control protects, since investigations and audits regularly revisit prior periods after decommissions or migrations. When mergers, divestitures, or platform changes occur, a controlled archival process should freeze the artifact alongside a manifest of dependent links, ensuring that future reviewers can reconstruct the chain without depending on now-retired tooling.

Traceability improves when the document explicitly models dependencies to upstream architecture patterns and downstream services. If the control implements Pattern PAT-018 and mitigates risks RSK-101 and RSK-233, those links should be first-class fields rather than prose. When the pattern or risk entries change, the system of record should prompt a review of this control and require a dated outcome: "No change to design intent" or "Scope adjustment to include partner-managed data plane." This keeps design, risk, and architecture repositories synchronized so later audits can follow the thread from policy to evidence without guesswork.

Clarity of language matters as much as structure. Use phrasing that expresses intent and boundary conditions, not step-by-step operation or tool minutiae. An approval might say, "Design aligns with Access Governance Objective CTR-OBJ-042; exception E-119 authorized for break-glass accounts with quarterly review and expiry 2026-03-31," while the version note reads, "v3.0—expanded scope to SaaS tenants; no change to least-privilege thresholds." These sentences give a future reviewer everything needed to re-perform conclusions: who decided, what changed, when it took effect, and where to verify the outcome.

Conclusion

Mastering the principles of risk-based control design and traceability is critical for transforming cybersecurity auditing from a reactive checklist exercise into a disciplined governance function. The practices explored throughout this chapter establish how assurance begins at design time—when risks are defined, control intent is documented, and ownership is made explicit. By embedding traceable links between risk, control objective, and evidence, auditors move beyond testing outcomes to evaluating the integrity of entire control ecosystems. This mindset elevates auditing from compliance validation to strategic oversight, ensuring that security investments align with enterprise risk tolerance.

These principles carry particular weight in environments shaped by automation, AI, and continuous delivery. Machine-driven systems operate at speeds that human oversight alone cannot match, making durable control design and clear accountability essential for sustained assurance. Automated enforcement, structured metadata, and consistent version control enable auditors to validate compliance and resilience even as systems evolve autonomously. While tools and platforms may change, the requirement for verifiable lineage—from risk identification to control operation—remains the constant safeguard against drift and uncertainty.

Auditor Recommendations

1. **Establish a Risk Taxonomy that Links Threat to Vulnerability to Scenario to Impact:** Use this chain to craft specific, testable risk statements tied to named assets and data classes. Require each statement to include why it is material based on process criticality, data sensitivity, or legal exposure. Record the entry with a stable risk ID in a single system of record to enable later re-performance.
2. **Define Materiality Thresholds Driven by Business Context Rather than Raw Technical Severity:** Calibrate thresholds using the expected blast radius on critical processes, the sensitivity of affected data, and applicable regulatory or contractual obligations. Document the rationale and a review cadence so thresholds evolve with architectural change and AI adoption. Apply these thresholds to determine audit depth and reporting priority.
3. **Balance Preventive, Detective, and Corrective Control Intent Deliberately and Document the Rationale:** Specify the purpose of each layer, the expected miss rate, and how gaps are detected and remediated. Align assurance expectations accordingly, emphasizing bypass resistance for preventive controls and signal quality plus escalation speed for detective controls. Capture dependencies so weaknesses in one layer automatically increase scrutiny in the others.
4. **Prefer Automated, Continuously Enforced Controls Where the Decision Can Be Expressed as Deterministic Policy at the Enforcement Point:** Verify that these controls emit time-stamped tamper-evident logs and that exceptions are approved, time-bound, and visible. Include monitoring and change control for the control itself to detect configuration drift. Re-perform logic at population scale instead of relying on small samples.
5. **Use Manual Detective Controls Only Where Event Frequency Is Low and Human Judgment Materially Improves Accuracy:** Define reviewer competency, independence, and documentation standards so decisions can be re-performed. Set execution cadence to match risk velocity and expand sampling when error rates rise. Track rejected items to confirm that rework addresses root causes rather than deferring issues.
6. **Preserve Auditor Independence During Design Engagements by Keeping Feedback Advisory and Criteria-focused:** Avoid prescriptive configuration guidance and refrain from language that implies approval or authorization. Label artifacts as advisory, record participants

and scope, and include a statement reserving the right to test post-implementation. Store these memos separately from assurance workpapers to prevent self-review threats.

7. **Integrate Security Design with Enterprise Architecture and Change Governance to Protect Control Intent over Time:** Map systems to approved reference models, patterns, and standards, and require change records to identify affected control objectives. Demand documented impact assessments and links to updated risk and control registers for material changes. Ensure that CAB or DevOps gates enforce these expectations consistently across delivery paths.
8. **Maintain End-to-end Traceability from Risk to Control Objective to Control Owner to Evidence Location:** Assign unique IDs, life cycle states, systems of record, and update cadences to each link in the chain. Use resolvable pointers for evidence sources with metadata on cadence, retention, and integrity guarantees. Auto-flag stale links and orphaned records so traceability cannot silently decay.
9. **Enforce Rigorous Design Documentation with Approvals, RACI, Effective Dates, and Version Control:** Capture approver roles, decisions, timestamps, and rationales tied to authoritative policy or risk entries. Record accountable and responsible parties using durable directory identities, along with review-by or sunset dates. Version every change with author and change summary, and preserve stable links to dependent procedures and configurations.
10. **Tighten Exception and Waiver Governance so Temporary Risk Decisions Do Not Become Permanent Weaknesses:** Require explicit rationale, approver identity, compensating safeguards, and expiry for each exception. Monitor approaching expirations and verify that baseline controls are restored or formally replaced. Report aging or recurrent exceptions as indicators of control design debt that warrants remediation or redesign.

Chapter Questions

1. Which sequence best represents a practical cyber risk taxonomy used in audits?
   - **A.** Vulnerability → Threat → Impact → Scenario
   - **B.** Impact → Scenario → Threat → Vulnerability
   - **C.** Threat → Vulnerability → Scenario → Impact
   - **D.** Scenario → Impact → Vulnerability → Threat

2. What should primarily drive materiality thresholds for security risks?
   - **A.** The number of identified vulnerabilities in a scan
   - **B.** The age of the systems in the environment
   - **C.** The volume of security alerts generated daily
   - **D.** Business context including process criticality, data sensitivity, and legal exposure

3. Which statement most accurately characterizes preventive controls?
   - **A.** They are primarily valuable for documenting incidents after they occur.
   - **B.** They block or constrain actions before harm and are judged by universal, consistent enforcement.
   - **C.** They rely on human triage to separate true events from noise after an incident.
   - **D.** They restore service levels following an adverse event and focus on recovery time.

4. Which evidence source provides the greatest durability for assurance purposes?
   A. System-generated logs that are time-stamped, tamper-evident, and reproducible
   B. Ad hoc emails confirming that a control ran successfully
   C. Meeting notes taken by a system owner during deployment
   D. A screenshot pasted into a slide deck after a release

5. Under which condition should automated, continuously enforced controls be the default choice?
   A. When decisions require nuanced legal interpretation not available at runtime
   B. When events are rare and the affected population is very small
   C. When the decision can be expressed as deterministic policy using attributes available at enforcement time
   D. When exception handling cannot be recorded or limited by duration

6. When are manual detective controls acceptable in modern environments?
   A. When population size is large and transaction velocity is high
   B. When event frequency is low, potential impact is bounded, and human judgment adds value
   C. When evidence integrity requires cryptographic proofs and immutable logs
   D. When the control point is at an identity or data-access gateway with native policy hooks

7. Which chain reflects the minimum traceability auditors require?
   A. Risk → Control Objective → Control Owner → Evidence Location
   B. Control Owner → Evidence Location → Control Objective → Risk
   C. Evidence Location → Risk → Control Owner → Control Objective
   D. Control Objective → Risk → Evidence Location → Control Owner

8. Which phrasing best preserves auditor independence during a design review?
   A. "Approved: configure the IAM role to allow only listed permissions X and Y."
   B. "Validated: vendor Z should be selected; alternative proposals are rejected."
   C. "Authorized: encryption must be AES-256 and keys rotated every 30 days as directed."
   D. "Reviewed for alignment with access governance policy; design appears consistent pending implementation verification."

9. What do auditors expect when architecture or service changes may alter control coverage?
   A. A verbal confirmation that no new risks were introduced
   B. A new tool deployment with no documentation updates
   C. Documented impact assessment linking the change to affected control objectives and updates to relevant registers
   D. Immediate rollback of the change regardless of business need

10. Which documentation elements most enable later re-performance of conclusions?
    A. Approval history, RACI, effective dates, versioning, and resolvable links to procedures and evidence with stable IDs
    B. A high-level diagram and an owner's informal notes stored in email threads
    C. A single PDF export of settings taken at go-live with no version history
    D. A meeting recording summarizing the intended control behavior without identifiers

4

Evidence, Sampling, and Testing Techniques

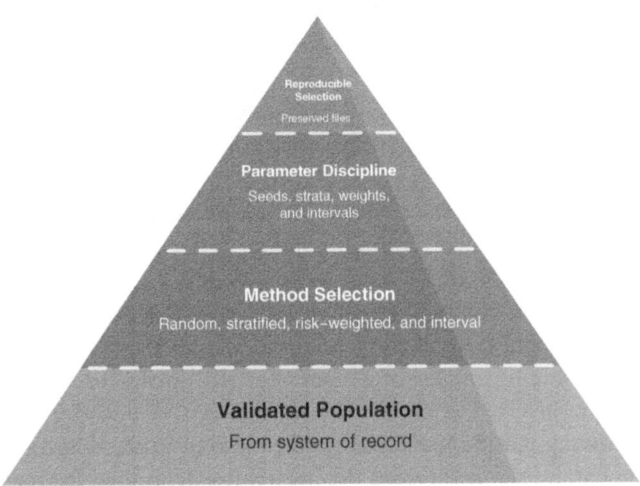

Evidence and testing form the heartbeat of cybersecurity auditing, transforming abstract control statements into measurable assurance. Without disciplined evidence evaluation, sampling strategy, and procedural rigor, even the most advanced audit program risks collapsing under scrutiny. This chapter examines how auditors convert vast, complex data into defensible conclusions—through principles of evidence quality, chain of custody, sampling methodology, and testing precision. Understanding these foundations is essential to establishing credibility in assurance work, where every finding must withstand both technical and legal review.

Modern digital environments generate more data than any auditor can inspect manually, yet the expectation of accuracy and completeness has never been higher. From verifying control design to testing operational performance across automated and human processes, the auditor must apply structured reasoning and analytic rigor. Techniques such as inspection, re-performance, and analytics-assisted testing extend audit coverage while preserving reproducibility and integrity. The result is not just compliance evidence but operational insight—showing how effectively an organization's security controls function in practice over time.

In the age of AI-driven systems and continuous monitoring, the ability to validate evidence objectively and test controls across dynamic, data-rich environments defines the maturity of an enterprise's security governance. Precision in timing, sampling, and documentation transforms auditing from procedural validation into a strategic discipline that informs risk decisions.

By mastering these evidence-based techniques, auditors strengthen the trust architecture that underpins regulatory assurance, incident response validation, and AI system accountability alike.

Evidence Quality and Chain of Custody

Evidence quality begins with a clear definition of what makes evidence suitable for audit purposes and ends with explicit acceptance criteria that determine whether it can be relied upon. Completeness, accuracy, authenticity, provenance, and period coverage are the attributes that matter most, and they translate into sufficiency (enough of the right kind) and appropriateness (relevant and reliable) of evidence. Acceptance criteria should be stated up front in the work program to minimize dispute later, such as what level of reconciliation is required or which sources are considered authoritative. The goal is not perfection but defensibility: a reasonable, documented basis for concluding that the evidence supports or contradicts management's assertions. When quality attributes are defined with measurable thresholds, evidence review becomes repeatable and resistant to bias. Table 4.1 links core evidence attributes to concrete acceptance criteria and validation steps.

Completeness addresses whether the evidence set covers the full scope and population under review, not merely a convenient subset. Auditors should define the universe precisely, verify that population boundaries match the engagement scope, and test for omissions through techniques such as control totals, record counts, and gap analysis across sequential identifiers or timestamps. Acceptance criteria often require reconciling delivered records to system-of-record totals within a small variance and explaining any missing sequences, late entries, or suppressed fields. Where continuous processes are involved, completeness checks may include sampling across the entire time horizon and verifying that no periods are absent due to batch failures, retention limits, or export filters. Documentation should record the population definition, the method of extraction, and the results of any gap analysis that demonstrate the evidence set is whole.

Accuracy concerns whether the evidence faithfully reflects the underlying events or states without transcription, calculation, or transformation error. Reperformance and recomputation are primary tools here: independently deriving totals, balances, or counts from raw records and

Table 4.1 Evidence quality attributes to acceptance criteria mapping.

Attribute	Definition focus	Acceptance criterion example	Primary verification method
Completeness	All eligible items are present	Population equals system total within small variance	Reconciliation to control totals
Accuracy	Records reflect true facts without error	Independent totals match derived calculations	Reperformance and cross footing
Authenticity	Artifact is from the stated source and unaltered	File hash validates at receipt and archive	Hash validation and trusted timestamp
Provenance	Lineage from original capture through transformations	Original and derived artifacts are linked with steps recorded	Documented lineage with tool and version
Period coverage	Evidence aligns to the audit window	Entries fall within stated bounds with time normalized	Boundary tests with normalized time

comparing results to those provided. Cross-footing, control totals, and constraint checks (for example, verifying that status transitions follow allowed states) can reveal internal inconsistencies. Acceptance criteria should specify tolerances for rounding, derived-field calculations, and unit conversions so that differences are interpreted consistently. When multiple sources represent the same facts, auditors should reconcile discrepancies and escalate unresolved differences as potential exceptions rather than averaging them away.

Authenticity is the assurance that the evidence originated from the claimed source and has not been tampered with, substituted, or altered outside of documented processes. Reliable evidence is obtained directly from an authoritative system or custodian, with contextual metadata intact, rather than through ad hoc screenshots or manually curated spreadsheets. Cryptographic measures strengthen authenticity: generating file-level hashes (for example, SHA-256), verifying digital signatures where available, and recording trusted timestamps provide tamper-evident controls. Acceptance criteria should require that any evidence entering the file validates against its recorded checksum upon receipt and again upon archival or transfer. Where intermediary handling is unavoidable, custodial attestations and system-generated logs should corroborate the chain of events around collection and access.

Provenance describes the lineage of evidence from original capture through any transformations that yield the version under review. Auditors should require a data-flow narrative or mapping that names each source, extraction method, transformation step, and storage location, including the tools and versions used. This lineage documentation should distinguish between lossless normalization (such as column reordering or format conversions) and lossy operations (such as redaction or aggregation) that change the granularity or semantics of the data. Acceptance criteria typically require retaining both the original artifact and the derived artifact, with step-by-step transformation notes sufficient to reproduce the result. If the evidence passes through third-party processors, the provenance record should include contractual or procedural assurances that those processors preserve integrity and confidentiality.

Period coverage ensures that the evidence relates to the exact time window relevant to audit procedures, expressed in absolute dates and times with clear time zone and clock-source assumptions. Auditors should test for boundary effects—late-posted entries, backdated corrections, and system clock drift—that can shift records just inside or outside the audit period. Acceptance criteria often require a defined buffer on either side of the engagement window and a documented approach for handling retroactive adjustments, such as extracting both the as-of snapshot and the change history. When multiple systems contribute evidence, time normalization must be applied so comparisons and joins are valid; this should be recorded as a reversible transformation in the provenance notes. Evidence that lacks reliable timestamps or clock references should be downgraded in reliability or corroborated with independent sources.

Translating quality attributes into acceptance criteria requires a reliability hierarchy that distinguishes stronger, system-generated evidence from weaker, manual, or testimonial forms. Criteria should specify the number and type of corroborating artifacts needed when relying on lower-reliability evidence, as well as escalation paths when contradictions emerge. Sufficiency is reached when the combination of completeness and coverage provides adequate basis for testing, while appropriateness is met when authenticity and provenance indicate the artifacts are trustworthy for the purpose at hand. The engagement file should show how each attribute was evaluated and whether the evidence met, exceeded, or failed the stated thresholds. Where criteria are not met but testing proceeds under constraint, the file should include an impact assessment and any compensating procedures performed.

Chain of custody is the formal record of possession, control, transfer, and storage for evidence from the moment of collection through archival or disposition. Each custody event should be time-stamped, identify the handler, describe the action taken (collection, verification, transformation, transfer, and storage), and reference the storage location or medium. Integrity controls should be embedded in each handoff: generating or revalidating a cryptographic hash, using read-only media or write-once storage when feasible, and sealing physical media with tamper-evident methods if physical transfer is required. Access must be controlled with least privilege, and all accesses—including reads—should be logged to provide an audit trail. Acceptance criteria for custody are met when the record demonstrates unbroken control, verifiable integrity at each step, and documented authorization for every access.

Collection practices should prefer direct exports from systems of record using documented procedures that preserve metadata and ensure repeatability. When intermediated by administrators or custodians, requests should specify the exact query or report definition, including filters, time bounds, and output format, and require that those definitions be included with the delivered evidence. Immediately upon receipt, the evidence should be placed under version control in an evidence repository, hashed, and labeled with a unique identifier that ties it to the work program step and population definition. Any delay between request and collection should be recorded, especially for volatile data with short retention cycles. Where real-time capture is impractical, attestations of system configuration and retention settings can supplement, but not replace, primary evidence.

Storage and preservation practices should maintain both integrity and readability over the retention period. Write-once-read-many (WORM) storage or immutable retention controls reduce the risk of inadvertent or malicious alteration; periodic hash revalidation detects bit rot or corruption. The repository should store originals and derivatives in separate locations with clear naming conventions, with strict controls preventing overwrite of originals. If encryption is used for confidentiality, key management procedures must ensure the evidence remains decryptable for as long as retention requires, including during personnel turnover. Acceptance criteria should require periodic restore tests to prove that archived evidence remains accessible and intact.

Documenting transformations is essential to preserving evidentiary value while enabling analysis. Each transformation should include the purpose, tool and version, exact steps taken or scripts executed, input and output file identifiers, and pre- and post-transformation hashes. Redactions for privacy or confidentiality should be applied in a way that is consistent, reversible only under strict authorization, and annotated so reviewers understand what was removed and why. Normalization and standardization steps, such as date reformatting or column renaming, should be described as lossless unless aggregation or filtering changed the content, in which case the impact on testing should be explicitly stated. Acceptance criteria should require that a competent practitioner could reproduce the transformation pipeline from the record and obtain the same output.

The evidence register ties these practices together by providing a single, indexed catalog of every artifact, its quality assessments, and its custody history. Each entry should link to the associated procedures, population definitions, and acceptance criteria, and record the outcomes of completeness, accuracy, authenticity, provenance, and period coverage checks. Exceptions—such as late-discovered gaps, unverifiable sources, or custody discontinuities—should be logged with resolution steps and residual risk statements. Retention periods and destruction eligibility should be calculated per artifact, with holds applied when matters remain open or litigation is reasonably anticipated. A well-maintained register not only accelerates peer review and external scrutiny but also demonstrates disciplined, repeatable assurance practice suitable for complex security engagements.

Building Populations and Defensible Sampling Strategies

Building a population begins with defining what "in scope" truly means in the context of the audit objective. The auditor must identify the system or systems of record that contain authoritative evidence for the process being examined and ensure that population boundaries align precisely with the control or risk statement under review. For example, if the control concerns privileged account reviews, the population should encompass every account with elevated rights across relevant systems, not merely those in a single directory. Scoping decisions must be documented in terms of inclusion and exclusion criteria, supported by queries, exports, or reports that show how the population was constructed. A defensible population is one that any competent reviewer could regenerate independently using the same criteria and obtain identical results.

Completeness of the population is the foundation upon which all sampling validity rests. The auditor must be able to demonstrate that no qualifying records were omitted, intentionally or otherwise. This is achieved through reconciliation to authoritative totals, such as comparing the count of extracted entries to system dashboards, configuration management databases, or transaction ledgers. Gap testing ensures continuity—for instance, confirming that log sequence numbers are unbroken or that all calendar months within the period of review are represented. Where multiple systems feed the process, cross-system matching and duplicate elimination are required to avoid double counting. The completeness validation, including query parameters, data sources, and reconciliation results, should be included in the audit documentation as proof that the population represents the true universe of items subject to testing.

The definition of "system of record" must be anchored in governance evidence, not convenience. Many organizations maintain multiple reporting tools, but only one system is formally designated as the authoritative source for each dataset. The auditor should confirm this designation through policy, data ownership documentation, or attestation from system stewards. Populations built from non-authoritative sources risk challenge because the data could differ from the official record due to synchronization delays or data enrichment processes. Once the system of record is confirmed, population extracts must capture sufficient identifiers—such as transaction IDs, timestamps, or account names—to enable traceability back to the original source during testing. The inclusion of these identifiers makes it possible to revalidate sampled items later and demonstrates transparency in how the population was derived.

When building populations that involve time-bound data, auditors must verify that the extract covers the entire audit period without spillover or omission. This requires defining start and end boundaries explicitly, expressed in absolute timestamps rather than relative phrases like "last quarter." Time drift between systems can create off-by-one errors, so normalization of time zones and formats is essential. If records are cumulative or rolling (as in configuration histories or cumulative metrics), auditors must take care to isolate entries that correspond to the defined review period only. Documenting the extraction logic, including filters, joins, and time-based criteria, ensures that another reviewer could recreate the same population independently—an essential attribute of defensibility.

Once a complete and validated population has been established, sampling strategies determine how evidence is selected for testing in a way that balances efficiency with assurance strength. The most fundamental method is random sampling, in which every item in the population has an equal probability of selection. Random sampling provides unbiased representation when the population is homogeneous and the auditor's goal is generalization of results. Its defensibility rests on transparency of the randomization method—using a reproducible seed value or tool output that

Table 4.2 Sampling strategy selection guide.

Scenario	Preferred method	Why appropriate	Key documentation
Homogeneous population	Random sampling	Ensures unbiased selection across similar items	Random seed and selection file
Distinct subgroups present	Stratified sampling	Guarantees coverage of each meaningful segment	Strata definition and allocation basis
High impact risk zones	Risk weighted sampling	Directs effort where failure would matter most	Weighting rationale and risk factors
Large sequential stream with no periodicity	Interval sampling	Simplifies selection while keeping broad spread	Random start point and fixed interval
Digital evidence for all items	Full population test	Eliminates sampling risk and expands coverage	Query logic parameters and data validation

can be independently verified. The audit file should include both the algorithm and random seed used so that sample selection can be reproduced exactly if questioned. Table 4.2 maps common audit scenarios to defensible sampling choices with required documentation.

Stratified sampling becomes necessary when the population contains distinct subgroups with differing characteristics or risk profiles. By dividing the population into strata—such as by transaction type, value, or system criticality—the auditor ensures that each relevant segment is adequately represented. The number of samples per stratum can be proportionate to size or adjusted based on perceived risk. For instance, higher-value transactions or high-privilege accounts may warrant denser sampling. The rationale for each stratum's sample size should be clearly tied to its contribution to overall audit risk, preventing accusations of bias or neglect. Proper stratification enhances coverage without requiring full enumeration, achieving efficiency without compromising reliability.

Risk-weighted sampling adds analytical depth by aligning selection density with inherent or residual risk. Here, the auditor considers both quantitative and qualitative risk factors—such as control criticality, past incident frequency, and exposure magnitude—to assign weights to population elements. Sampling probabilities are then adjusted accordingly, concentrating testing where failure would have the most significant impact. The documentation must specify how these weights were derived, whether from risk assessments, materiality thresholds, or auditor judgment, and include a justification for each decision. This approach demonstrates professional skepticism in action and provides a rational, traceable link between risk evaluation and testing effort.

Interval or systematic sampling offers a practical compromise when the population is large, sequential, and relatively uniform. After randomly selecting a starting point, items are chosen at fixed intervals—say, every hundredth transaction or every tenth configuration change. This method is easy to execute and to explain, making it defensible in operational audits with high-volume data. However, auditors must ensure that the population has no hidden periodic patterns that could align with the interval, such as batch jobs or maintenance cycles, which would introduce bias. The audit documentation should record both the starting point and the interval used, along with tests performed to confirm absence of cyclical structures in the population.

Sample size determination is both statistical and practical. While formal sampling tables exist for quantitative audits, cybersecurity audits often rely on professional judgment informed by risk and control frequency. As a rule of thumb, more heterogeneous populations require larger samples to capture variation, while well-controlled, low-variance processes may justify smaller samples. The auditor should record the rationale for chosen sample sizes in terms of confidence level, expected error rate, and acceptable deviation. If smaller-than-normal samples are used due to time or data constraints, compensating procedures—such as targeted re-testing or secondary corroboration—must be documented to sustain defensibility.

Defensibility also depends on traceability. Each sampled item should retain a unique reference to its position within the population, enabling anyone to re-identify and re-test it later. This can be achieved through population indexes or unique record identifiers stored alongside the sample list. The sample selection file should be version-controlled, with cryptographic hashes to prevent alteration. Such rigor ensures that the auditor can prove not only which items were selected but also that the selection was made impartially and preserved without modification. These controls transform the sampling process from a black box into a transparent, reproducible sequence of steps.

Test Types: Design vs. Operating Effectiveness

Design effectiveness asks whether a control, as conceived and implemented, is capable of preventing or detecting the error it targets. The focus is on intent, structure, placement in the process, and clarity of criteria—does the control address the stated risk, at the right point in the workflow, with defined inputs, decision rules, and outcomes. Evidence for design typically includes policies, procedures, configuration settings, approvals, and a walkthrough that traces a realistic transaction or event through the control. A well-designed control has unambiguous ownership, triggers, tolerances, and escalation paths that align to the risk statement and control objective.

Operating effectiveness evaluates whether that control actually functioned as intended throughout a defined period. The question shifts from capability to consistency: given the frequency of the control, was it performed when required, by the right role, with evidence of review and resolution where exceptions occurred. Persuasive evidence includes dated performance artifacts and traceable records that cover the period, not a single point in time. A control can be perfectly designed yet ineffective in operation if it is skipped, performed late, or executed without the required scrutiny.

Selecting whether to test design, operating effectiveness, or both begins with the control's role and materiality. Key controls that directly address significant risks generally warrant testing of both design and operation to support reliance. Non-key or compensating controls that backstop a primary mechanism may justify design-only testing when reliance is not planned and the objective is limited to understanding architecture and coverage. The decision should be documented as a rationale tied to risk, control criticality, and intended reliance in downstream conclusions.

Control frequency strongly influences test selection and sample strategy. Point-in-time controls, such as one-off approvals tied to infrequent events, may be sufficiently addressed by a rigorous design evaluation plus targeted testing of the specific occurrence. Recurring controls—daily reconciliations, weekly reviews, monthly certifications—require operating effectiveness procedures over the stated period, because consistency over time is intrinsic to their value. Continuous or event-driven controls need evidence that the triggering logic and response executed consistently across representative intervals within the period.

Automation changes the balance between design and operating testing, but it does not eliminate the need for either. Highly automated controls with stable configurations and robust change governance may allow for heavier reliance on design verification—confirming rule logic, parameterization, and authoritative data sources—supplemented by targeted evidence that the automation executed over the period. Where automation is partial or dependent on human judgment, operating testing must verify both the machine step and the human review step, including timing, thresholds, and documented decisions. If automation depends on upstream data quality or clock synchronization, those dependencies must be considered in the test plan and documented as assumptions or preconditions.

The nature of the control—preventive versus detective—also guides emphasis. Preventive controls often lend themselves to deep design scrutiny, because their effectiveness depends on correct placement and accurate decision criteria before an error can occur. Detective controls, by definition, rely on recurring execution and follow-up; operating effectiveness testing must therefore validate not only detection but the timeliness and completeness of remediation. Where a detective control feeds a secondary oversight control, reliance on the second layer should be conditioned on evidence that the first layer operated or that the second layer compensates for known gaps.

Reliance on other controls and dependencies should be explicit in the decision logic. If a control's effectiveness presumes the integrity of underlying system access, data interfaces, or time sources, the plan should either test those dependencies or reference independent assurance over them. When reliance is placed on upstream, complementary, or entity-level controls, the documentation must describe how that reliance reduces, but does not remove, the need for direct testing. Where reliance is weak or unproven, expand operating effectiveness procedures to compensate for the uncertainty introduced by the dependency.

Maturity and change history are practical determinants for test scope. Newly implemented or significantly changed controls typically require a full design evaluation followed by operating testing over the period available, with the documentation acknowledging any shortened coverage. Stable controls with no material changes and a strong history of performance may, in some engagements, justify a lighter operating sample if supported by evidence of continuous execution and effective monitoring. Any reduction from a standard approach must be justified in the workpapers with reference to risk, stability, and corroborating oversight mechanisms.

Documentation is the backbone of defensibility across both test types. For design effectiveness, record the control objective, risk addressed, process point, inputs, decision rules, ownership, escalation, and the walkthrough artefacts that prove the control could work. For operating effectiveness, define the period, frequency, population, selection criteria, attributes tested, and the evidence that demonstrates performance and resolution of deviations. Each conclusion should state whether reliance is supported, conditions or assumptions applied, and any residual risk that remains.

A useful way to frame the decision is to ask three questions and capture the answers verbatim in the file: Is the control capable, is it consistent, and what dependencies must hold for it to matter. "Capable" maps to design effectiveness, "consistent" to operating effectiveness, and "dependencies" to reliance considerations that may expand or contract procedures. When these answers are explicit, the selection of test type follows logically: test design to establish capability, test operation to demonstrate consistency, and address dependencies to sustain reliance. This clarity allows reviewers and stakeholders to see the line from risk to control to evidence to conclusion without guessing at the auditor's judgment.

Inspection and Re-performance Procedures

Inspection provides assurance by examining artifacts for evidence that a control exists and is being applied as described, while re-performance provides assurance by independently executing the same steps or logic to see whether the stated outcome can be reproduced. Adequate inspection is not a quick glance at a screenshot or a cursory read of a ticket; it is a structured evaluation against defined attributes that tie directly to the control objective. The procedure narrative should state which attributes are being verified and why each attribute matters to the risk being addressed. When inspection cannot resolve doubt about capability or consistency, the auditor escalates to re-performance to obtain a direct, independent result.

Document inspection begins with verifying authenticity, scope, and timing. Policies, procedures, approvals, and attestation memos must be current for the period under review, reflect proper authorization, and align with the described control steps without contradiction. Version identifiers, effective dates, and ownership metadata should be visible, with any superseded versions either archived or referenced to demonstrate continuity. The narrative should record the specific passages or clauses that articulate trigger conditions, decision criteria, and escalation paths, because those are the parts that translate policy into control behavior.

Configuration inspection focuses on whether the parameters that drive control behavior are present, correctly set, and effective for the intended population. The auditor looks for explicit values, inheritance or override behavior, and the scope to which a setting applies, along with evidence of last change, approver, and effective timestamp. Ambiguity—such as undocumented defaults or values that differ across environments—must be identified and explained within the procedure narrative. To preserve evidential weight, the inspection should capture the configuration in a durable form and document how the snapshot was obtained, including any read-only context that limits alteration risk.

Work ticket and workflow inspection tests whether process steps were initiated, authorized, executed, and closed in accordance with stated criteria. Adequacy requires traceability from initiation to resolution, including timestamps, status transitions, and the identities of requestors, performers, and approvers. The narrative should confirm that the performer and approver roles are segregated where required and that deviation comments, attachments, or remediation notes are present and substantive. Where tickets reference external artifacts, the inspection must follow those references to confirm that they exist, are contemporaneous, and support the recorded decisions.

Log and event record inspection aims to validate occurrence, timing, and sequence integrity. The auditor examines whether entries are complete for the period, whether timestamps are synchronized, and whether identifiers allow correlation across systems when necessary. Indicators of sufficiency include continuous sequence numbers, absence of unexplained gaps, and error or exception codes that are understood and accounted for in the procedure. The narrative should explicitly reconcile observed event counts or rates with expectations implied by the control design, explaining any variance and its impact on assurance.

Re-performance is required when inspection cannot answer whether the control would reach the correct decision given the same inputs and rules. It is particularly important for controls that depend on algorithmic logic, quantitative thresholds, or human judgment that could vary across performers or time. The auditor should obtain or reconstruct the inputs that triggered the control, apply the documented rules without alteration, and record the resulting outcome, preserving intermediate calculations where applicable. The narrative must compare the re-performed outcome to the recorded outcome, explain any differences, and state whether those differences are attributable to documented exceptions, data quality, or control failure.

Corroboration strengthens assurance by triangulating independent sources that speak to the same fact pattern. A coherent procedure names the primary source used for the conclusion, identifies secondary sources used to confirm or challenge it, and explains the reliability hierarchy among them. Consistency across sources suggests sufficiency; inconsistency triggers deeper inquiry, expanded sampling, or re-performance until the conflict is resolved or its impact is explicitly bounded. The narrative should connect the dots, describing how each source reinforces or limits the others so that a reviewer can follow the chain from evidence to inference.

Procedure clarity is achieved when another qualified practitioner could replicate the steps and obtain the same evidentiary view. The narrative should articulate the objective being tested, the population and time window, the attributes inspected, and the criteria that determine pass or deviation. It must specify the exact artifacts examined, how they were obtained, and any transformations applied, using stable identifiers so that items can be re-located. Dates of performance, the identity of the auditor, and any supervision or review notes complete the record and anchor accountability.

Exceptions and anomalies should be handled within the procedure, not as afterthoughts. The narrative should define what constitutes a deviation, capture the first point at which it was detected, and describe additional steps taken to distinguish documentation gaps from true control failures. If an anomaly suggests a systemic issue—such as recurring timing slippage or role conflicts—the procedure should expand in scope or depth, and that expansion must be recorded with its rationale. Management explanations may inform the analysis, but the file must reflect the corroborating evidence that either substantiates or refutes those explanations.

Analytics-assisted Testing and Tooling Considerations

Data analytics extends the reach and precision of audit testing by allowing the auditor to analyze entire populations or complex relationships that traditional sampling cannot easily capture. The goal is not to replace professional judgment but to enhance it—enabling deeper visibility into process consistency, exceptions, and correlations that manual inspection would likely miss. Analytics-assisted testing becomes appropriate when the population is large, the data is structured and accessible, and the risk of hidden anomalies is material. In such cases, the audit objective shifts from evaluating a sample to evaluating the population itself, turning what was once probabilistic assurance into near-deterministic insight.

Full-population testing is the most powerful use of analytics in an audit context. Instead of selecting a subset of records for inspection, the auditor designs queries or algorithms that apply control criteria to every item in scope. This approach is suitable for controls with digital evidence, such as approvals, logs, or configurations that can be programmatically evaluated. The benefit lies in comprehensive coverage—no reliance on sampling tolerances and no missed exceptions due to chance. However, completeness and accuracy of input data remain critical; a full-population test based on incomplete extracts provides false confidence. The procedure narrative should therefore document not only the logic of the analytic but also the validation of the underlying dataset before execution.

Outlier and variance analysis is another key use of analytics in auditing. These techniques identify patterns or items that diverge from expected norms, suggesting control gaps, data errors, or potential fraud indicators. For example, the auditor may compute distributions of transaction values, response times, or frequency counts and highlight those beyond statistical or business thresholds. The interpretation of such results demands care—an outlier is not automatically a control failure, but an invitation to investigate why the deviation occurred. The testing narrative should describe the metric used, the expected range, the rationale for threshold selection, and the follow-up performed on detected anomalies. Documenting both detection and disposition of outliers ensures the analysis remains traceable and reproducible.

Analytics can also reveal inconsistencies between systems by performing joins or reconciliations across datasets. When controls depend on accurate data flow—such as synchronization between an asset inventory and an access management system—cross-system analysis confirms whether records align as expected. The auditor designs joins on unique identifiers, timestamps, or key attributes and reports discrepancies for follow-up. To maintain defensibility, the join logic, matching rules, and tolerance levels must be documented explicitly. This form of testing is especially valuable when systems have independent governance boundaries, because it identifies control blind spots where reconciliations or ownership delineations fail.

Reproducibility of analytics is a core expectation in audit practice. Every query, script, or analytic process must be preserved in a manner that allows another auditor to re-run it and obtain identical results using the same inputs. This requires version control for code, explicit documentation of parameters and filters, and immutable storage of both the scripts and raw outputs. Queries should be time-stamped, labeled with the responsible auditor's identifier, and accompanied by metadata indicating the data source, extract date, and record count. Where visual analytics tools are used, screenshots alone are insufficient; the underlying query definitions or exportable logic must be retained in the workpapers.

Parameter management ensures that analytics remain objective and consistent across runs. Each parameter—such as date range, threshold value, inclusion filter, or exclusion rule—should be recorded with justification and tied to the audit scope or control objective. Parameter values must not be adjusted after seeing results unless a formal rationale is added explaining the adjustment. Re-running an analysis with altered parameters without preserving the original constitutes an undocumented transformation and undermines evidential integrity. Auditors should use a structured template or parameter log to record each value, its source, and the reason it was selected.

Evidence persistence encompasses the retention of both the analytic artifacts and their outputs. Raw data extracts, query scripts, intermediate files, and result sets must be stored in a controlled repository with unique identifiers and cryptographic hashes to verify integrity over time. Outputs should be frozen once reviewed, with any re-runs treated as new versions rather than overwrites. Versioning provides transparency into analytical evolution—showing what changed, when, and why. For large datasets, storing derived metrics or sample records rather than full outputs may be acceptable, provided that re-execution against the preserved query and input data can regenerate identical results.

Interpretation and corroboration remain essential even when analytics cover the full population. Automated results can identify anomalies, but they cannot explain them. The auditor must review patterns in context—validating whether flagged records represent genuine control failures, system nuances, or acceptable exceptions. Triangulating analytics results with other evidence, such as logs, approvals, or communications, ensures that conclusions are grounded in fact rather than pattern recognition alone. The testing narrative should therefore bridge analytic findings to manual inspection and re-performance where needed, forming a chain of reasoning from data to assurance conclusion.

The reliability of analytics-assisted testing also depends on the auditor's control over the data environment. Queries should be executed in a read-only context to prevent accidental modification of production data, and audit copies should be isolated to preserve integrity. The environment's access controls, logging, and change management must support evidence defensibility, but this remains a procedural concern rather than a governance one. The emphasis is on ensuring that what the auditor saw and analyzed is exactly what existed in the system at the time of collection.

Analytic outputs should be expressed in forms that preserve audit meaning—counts, exceptions lists, summaries, or visualizations that directly map to the control objective. The narrative should describe how results were interpreted, how anomalies were followed up, and how conclusions were derived. When results show no exceptions, the workpapers must still contain enough information to demonstrate that the analysis executed correctly and covered the defined population. When exceptions appear, the file must trace their investigation and resolution, including whether they represent true control failures or explainable data conditions.

Period Coverage, Timing, and Frequency of Tests

The credibility of audit conclusions depends heavily on the alignment between the testing window and the period during which the control was expected to operate. Each control functions according to its own frequency and timing—some act once at a specific event, while others recur continuously or at set intervals. The auditor's test design must mirror that rhythm precisely. A point-in-time control, such as system configuration or policy approval, can be evaluated through inspection and re-performance of that single instance. In contrast, a recurring control demands sampling or evidence across the full operating period to confirm sustained performance. The testing plan must explicitly state the control's frequency, define the corresponding period under review, and justify how the selected evidence window provides a reliable basis for assurance.

For point-in-time controls, the test period aligns with the date or event on which the control should have been executed. The auditor verifies that the control's conditions were in place at that specific moment, supported by time-stamped evidence such as configurations, approvals, or signed attestations. These tests are inherently limited in scope—they can confirm whether the control existed and was effective on that date, but not whether it persisted or recurred later. To preserve transparency, the workpapers should label such results as "point-in-time assurance" and specify the exact timestamp or event context used. This distinction prevents misinterpretation of instantaneous checks as period-wide conclusions.

Controls executed daily, weekly, or monthly require broader coverage that reflects their operational cadence. The auditor must ensure that sample selections represent the entire review period and that no significant intervals are omitted. For example, a weekly reconciliation control operating over a year requires evidence from multiple, well-distributed weeks to confirm consistency. Where analytics permit, the entire population may be analyzed to confirm completeness. The frequency of occurrence also affects the number of samples required for operating effectiveness testing: the higher the repetition rate, the greater the expectation of consistency, and therefore, the more evidence points available for verification. Each test file should document how many cycles occurred, how many were tested, and why that ratio is sufficient for reasonable assurance.

Quarterly, semiannual, and annual controls introduce distinct timing challenges because fewer data points exist, and execution timing may vary slightly between cycles. The auditor must confirm not only that the control occurred but also that it occurred within the intended window. Evidence such as timestamps, meeting minutes, or report generation dates should be cross-checked against the defined cadence. When controls are event-triggered but expected at least once per quarter—such as management reviews or access certifications—the narrative should specify how coverage was determined and whether any quarters lacked performance evidence. If execution slipped outside the intended window, the impact on assurance should be explicitly noted, distinguishing between delay and omission.

Partial-period operations require particular care, as they can distort the perception of control maturity and reliability. New controls introduced mid-period must be tested only from their effective date forward. The auditor should verify the implementation date, supporting approvals, and any pilot or transition evidence that demonstrates when the control began producing reliable output. Conversely, controls retired or replaced during the period must be tested only up to their decommission date. Where gaps exist between decommissioning one control and enabling its successor, the auditor should assess whether compensating controls or manual oversight bridged that interval. The documentation should clearly delineate these temporal boundaries so that assurance conclusions apply only to the time frame during which the control was active.

Cut-over testing addresses the moment when a process or system transitions—whether due to migration, tool change, or reorganization. The objective is to ensure that control coverage was continuous and that neither the old nor new environment introduced a blind spot. The auditor should perform dual verification: confirm that the legacy control operated up to the migration date and that the successor control became effective immediately thereafter. Evidence may include pre- and post-cut-over logs, approval chains, and validation results confirming data integrity and configuration transfer. The workpapers must highlight the exact cut-over date, describe the verification steps, and state any residual risk arising from untested overlap or downtime.

Look-back procedures serve as a retrospective validation technique, often used when evidence from earlier periods is needed to assess consistency or completeness. They are appropriate when a control's operation before the formal audit period influences conclusions—for example, when testing a newly adopted process with prior pilot activity or when verifying remediation of a prior deficiency. Look-back periods should be explicitly limited and justified, showing how they contribute context without overstating assurance for periods outside the official scope. The auditor should ensure that evidence from look-back testing is clearly marked as supplemental and that any results inconsistent with the current period are analyzed for potential residual risk.

Timing constraints frequently arise from practical factors such as data availability, system retention settings, or delays in evidence collection. When such constraints prevent full alignment with the intended period, the auditor must disclose them transparently in the workpapers. The narrative should describe what evidence was accessible, what portion of the period it covers, and how the limitation was mitigated—for example, by increasing sample depth in available months or by performing targeted re-performance on adjacent periods. Documenting these timing limitations ensures that readers of the audit file understand the boundary conditions under which assurance was achieved.

In some cases, controls may not operate uniformly throughout a period due to business seasonality or operational pauses, such as during maintenance or organizational transitions. The auditor should identify these inactive intervals and assess whether they are inherent to the process or indicative of a lapse. When inactivity is planned and documented, it does not weaken assurance; when unexplained, it warrants further inquiry and notation. Each exception should be evaluated for its impact on risk coverage and, if necessary, addressed with additional testing once operations resume. Table 4.3 provides timing rules that align test coverage with control frequency and transitional states.

Table 4.3 Aligning control frequency to test coverage.

Control frequency	Required coverage window	Minimum evidence units	Assurance notes
Point in time	On stated effective date	One validated instance	Label as point in time assurance
Daily	Representative days across period or full population	Multiple days or full population	Confirm absence of unexplained gaps
Weekly	Evenly distributed weeks across period	Several weeks	Note planned downtime where applicable
Monthly	Each month in scope	Twelve months or in scope months	Verify completion within allowed window
Quarterly	Each quarter in scope	Four quarters or in scope quarters	Confirm performance within quarter bounds
New control mid period	From effective date to period end	Evidence from activation onward	Record implementation approval and date
Cut over migration	Legacy to cut over then successor after	Evidence on both sides	Demonstrate continuous coverage
Look back supplemental	Limited prior window for context	Defined prior cycles	Mark as supplemental not primary

Workpaper Standards and Reviewability

Workpapers are the backbone of audit defensibility. They document not only what was tested and found, but how, why, and under what assumptions. A complete workpaper serves as both a record of evidence and a procedural blueprint that another qualified auditor could follow to replicate the test and reach the same conclusion. This standard of *reviewability*—the ability for an independent reviewer to understand, re-perform, and validate the test—is the defining measure of documentation quality. Every workpaper should tell a self-contained story: what risk or control was evaluated, how the evidence was gathered and tested, what was found, and why the conclusion is reasonable.

Each workpaper must begin with a clearly stated purpose that explains the control or assertion being tested and the objective of the procedure. The purpose connects the specific test to the broader audit scope, but it should remain concise and technical, identifying the control statement, associated risk, and assurance question being answered. The reader should understand immediately what the test intends to prove or refute. Without a clear purpose, even a well-executed procedure loses its context and cannot be independently interpreted.

The criteria section defines what "good" looks like—the standards or thresholds against which evidence is evaluated. Criteria may derive from policies, control descriptions, regulatory requirements, or management-defined expectations, but they must be explicit. This section anchors the auditor's judgments, ensuring that findings are not subjective impressions but reasoned comparisons to agreed benchmarks. Each test should specify both qualitative criteria (e.g., proper authorization present, segregation of duties maintained) and quantitative criteria (e.g., review must occur within seven days, variance below 5%). When criteria are ambiguous, the auditor must document any interpretive assumptions and obtain agreement before testing begins.

A defensible workpaper also requires a precise population definition, describing the full set of items eligible for testing and how that set was derived from authoritative systems. The definition must identify the data sources, extraction methods, and filters used to isolate the relevant population. If the population was constructed from multiple systems, the join logic and reconciliation results should be summarized or referenced to supporting extracts. The completeness validation—how the auditor confirmed that the population matches the control's operational scope—must be evident. This clarity allows reviewers to determine whether the test truly covers the risk universe intended.

The sample selection section explains how items were chosen for testing from the population. It should specify the sampling method (random, stratified, risk-weighted, or systematic), the total population size, the number of samples selected, and the rationale for that number. The random seed, interval, or weighting criteria should be preserved so that another auditor could regenerate the same selection. If full-population analytics were used instead of sampling, the workpaper should clearly state that and describe the query logic and data validation performed. The principle is reproducibility: a reviewer should be able to recreate the sample exactly as it was drawn.

The heart of the workpaper is the procedure steps, a chronological narrative of what the auditor did and observed. Each step should describe the action taken, the evidence examined, the attributes tested, and the results obtained. The language should be factual and neutral—describing observations, not conclusions—and reference specific evidence identifiers or filenames rather than generic descriptions. The level of detail should allow another auditor to follow the same steps, access the same artifacts, and see what was seen. Screenshots, data extracts, or configuration captures should be properly labeled and linked to their step numbers for cross-referencing.

The results section distills the factual outcomes of testing—what passed, what failed, and what was inconclusive. This is not yet the conclusion, but a summary of empirical findings. Results should reference the relevant evidence items, include record counts or metrics where applicable, and distinguish between expected outcomes and deviations. If quantitative analysis was performed, the calculations or queries should be preserved so that numeric results can be replicated. The results section forms the factual foundation upon which the conclusion rests, so clarity and precision are paramount.

All exceptions and anomalies discovered during testing must be fully described in their own subsection, with enough context for reviewers to understand their nature and significance. Each exception should state the condition observed, the expected condition based on criteria, the number of instances affected, and any management explanation obtained. The workpaper should then document how the auditor evaluated that explanation, whether corroborating evidence was found, and what conclusion was reached regarding impact. Exceptions should not be buried within results; isolating them ensures they receive proper analysis and allows reviewers to trace how deviations were handled.

The conclusion synthesizes the evidence and results into a professional judgment: did the control meet its objective for the period tested. Conclusions should directly address the criteria and purpose stated earlier, stating clearly whether the control is effective, partially effective, or ineffective based on evidence. Any scope limitations, timing constraints, or residual risks must be noted so that conclusions are properly bounded. The tone should be objective and supported by the evidence presented—no speculation, no implied findings beyond what was tested.

A well-constructed workpaper also includes cross-references that connect it to related tests, evidence repositories, and summary documentation. Cross-references allow reviewers to trace a logical path from the control description to supporting analytics, population files, and any follow-up remediation work. Each link should identify where supplementary evidence resides and under what identifier it can be retrieved. This interconnected structure creates transparency across the audit file, allowing reviewers to navigate seamlessly between planning, testing, and conclusion phases.

Reviewability depends on presentation as much as content. A reviewer must be able to pick up the workpaper with no prior context and understand the test's intent, method, and outcome without additional explanation. The documentation should use consistent terminology, structured labeling (e.g., "Step 1," "Step 2"), and clear references to evidence filenames or IDs. Ambiguity is the enemy of reviewability; every statement should be verifiable. Workpapers should read like precise technical documentation, not personal notes. Formatting consistency—dates, versioning, pagination, and sign-offs—helps ensure that each file stands on its own and supports quality assurance or external inspection.

Ultimately, the standard for a complete and reviewable workpaper is simple yet demanding: could a qualified, independent auditor re-perform the test using the same materials and reach the same conclusion. If the answer is yes, the workpaper meets professional sufficiency. If not, no amount of retrospective clarification can fix what was undocumented. By adhering to these standards—clear purpose, defined criteria, complete population, defensible sampling, transparent procedures, factual results, analyzed exceptions, supported conclusions, and precise cross-referencing—the auditor produces documentation that withstands both technical scrutiny and time.

Conclusion

Mastering evidence and testing principles is critical for any cybersecurity auditor seeking to transform raw data into defensible assurance. The ability to define complete populations, apply appropriate sampling, and evaluate evidence quality determines whether findings withstand professional and regulatory scrutiny. These practices ensure that audit conclusions are not merely opinions but structured, reproducible results rooted in sound methodology. In the evolving landscape of AI and automation, such methodological rigor is the safeguard against bias, error, and overconfidence in data-driven assurance.

This chapter reinforces the role of disciplined testing, documentation, and analytical reasoning in securing AI-enabled environments at scale. As systems grow more autonomous and interconnected, auditors must rely on strong procedural controls—chain of custody, reproducible analytics, and period-aligned testing—to maintain trust in what the data reveals. Evidence handling becomes not just a technical task but an ethical one, preserving objectivity and transparency when evaluating systems that may themselves make probabilistic or opaque decisions. The rigor with which evidence is tested directly reflects the credibility of the organization's overall governance posture.

With these foundations in place, professionals are better equipped to provide assurance that is both technically sound and strategically relevant. Whether assessing traditional infrastructure or machine learning pipelines, the same principles—completeness, consistency, and verifiability—anchor the auditor's work. By internalizing these disciplines, cybersecurity and AI auditors strengthen the connective tissue between control execution and enterprise accountability. The outcome is a more resilient assurance function—capable of testing not only compliance but also confidence itself, in a digital era defined by speed, automation, and complexity.

Auditor Recommendations

1. **Define Evidence Standards Early:** Establish clear, measurable acceptance criteria for completeness, accuracy, authenticity, provenance, and period coverage before testing begins. Specify tolerances, authoritative sources, and reconciliation expectations so judgments are objective rather than interpretive. Document these criteria in the work program and reference them verbatim in each conclusion.
2. **Construct Populations from Systems of Record:** Build the testing universe using authoritative sources and prove completeness with reconciliations and gap checks. Preserve extraction logic, filters, and unique identifiers so another auditor can regenerate the same population. Record any de-duplication or joins across sources to maintain traceability.
3. **Select Sampling Methods Proportionate to Risk:** Choose random, stratified, risk-weighted, or interval sampling based on population characteristics and exposure. Document the rationale, population size, sample size, and parameters such as random seed, strata rules, weights, or interval. Preserve the selection file to enable exact re-creation under review.
4. **Separate Design from Operating Effectiveness:** Evaluate whether the control is capable before testing whether it worked consistently over the period. Tie design conclusions to placement, decision rules, ownership, and escalation; tie operating conclusions to frequency, timing, and evidence of performance. Record dependencies that must hold for reliance and expand procedures when those are weak.
5. **Execute Structured Inspection and Re-performance:** Inspect documents, configurations, tickets, and logs against defined attributes and escalate to re-performance when inspection cannot validate decision logic. Capture how inputs were obtained, rules applied, and outcomes compared to recorded results. Describe any deviations and the steps taken to distinguish documentation gaps from true failures.
6. **Apply Analytics to Expand Coverage Responsibly:** Use full-population tests, outlier analysis, and cross-system joins when digital evidence allows programmatic evaluation. Validate dataset completeness and accuracy before execution, and preserve all queries, parameters, and outputs for reproducibility. Corroborate analytic flags with independent evidence before reaching conclusions.
7. **Align Testing Windows to Control Cadence:** Match procedures to point-in-time, daily, weekly, monthly, or quarterly operation and disclose any timing limitations. For partial-period operations, restrict conclusions to the effective dates and note any compensating oversight. During migrations, perform cut-over testing that verifies continuous coverage across legacy and successor controls.
8. **Maintain an Unbroken Chain of Custody:** Record timestamps, handlers, storage locations, and integrity checks for every evidence handoff. Use immutable or read-only repositories where feasible and re-validate hashes at key milestones. Log all transformations with tool versions and before-after identifiers to preserve provenance.
9. **Document Workpapers for Independent Re-performance:** Write purpose, criteria, population, sample selection, procedure steps, results, exceptions, and conclusion with precise references to artifacts. Use consistent labels, version control, and cross-references so a qualified reviewer can replicate the test. Avoid ambiguous language and capture assumptions explicitly.
10. **Corroborate Findings and Bound Residual Risk:** Triangulate conclusions across logs, tickets, configurations, and analytic outputs to confirm facts and resolve conflicts. Record how inconsistencies were investigated and whether any unresolved issues remain immaterial to the assertion tested. State residual risk conditions and any reliance on complementary controls.

Chapter Questions

1. Which evidence quality attribute establishes the lineage of an artifact from original capture through transformations?
   A. Completeness
   B. Accuracy
   C. Provenance
   D. Period coverage

2. During a chain-of-custody handoff, which action most directly demonstrates integrity preservation of the evidence?
   A. Capturing an annotated screenshot of the artifact
   B. Obtaining a verbal attestation from the custodian
   C. Generating and validating a cryptographic hash at transfer
   D. Placing the file on a shared network drive

3. What is the most defensible method for constructing an audit population?
   A. Export from the system of record using documented queries and reconcile counts to authoritative totals
   B. Pull a convenience sample from an analyst's report and expand if needed
   C. Request screenshots of representative items from process owners
   D. Use a manually curated spreadsheet compiled by administrators

4. When is stratified sampling the most appropriate choice?
   A. When the population is small and highly homogeneous
   B. When distinct subgroups exhibit different characteristics or risk profiles
   C. When every item must have an equal chance of selection
   D. When items occur in a uniform sequence suitable for fixed-interval picks

5. Which statement best describes risk-weighted sampling?
   A. Selecting items at equal probability across the entire population
   B. Choosing items at fixed intervals after a random start
   C. Dividing the population into mutually exclusive strata and sampling each
   D. Adjusting selection probabilities based on inherent or residual risk

6. What does testing operating effectiveness primarily evaluate?
   A. Whether the control is conceptually capable of addressing the risk
   B. Whether the control functioned consistently over the defined period
   C. Whether the auditor maintained independence during testing
   D. Whether the related policy document is comprehensive

7. When should an auditor escalate from inspection to re-performance?
   A. When the control owner is unavailable for interview
   B. When the evidence contains minor formatting differences
   C. When the policy references an outdated template
   D. When inspection cannot determine if the control would reach the correct decision from the same inputs

8. What prerequisite must be met for full-population analytics to provide reliable assurance?
- **A.** Presenting results through interactive visualizations
- **B.** Encrypting all analytic outputs before review
- **C.** Validating that input datasets are complete and accurate
- **D.** Using a random seed to generate the exception list

9. What approach best characterizes cut-over testing during a migration?
- **A.** Verify the legacy control up to the cut-over date and the successor control immediately after, confirming continuous coverage
- **B.** Focus only on the successor control because legacy operations are out of scope
- **C.** Review a single point-in-time configuration from the new system
- **D.** Rely on management's attestation that no gaps occurred

10. Which condition most strongly evidences workpaper reviewability?
- **A.** Extensive screenshots without underlying artifacts or scripts
- **B.** Documented, reproducible steps and preserved artifacts that enable an independent reviewer to re-perform the test and reach the same conclusion
- **C.** A concise narrative summary with no references to evidence identifiers
- **D.** Management sign-off indicating the control is effective

5

Auditor Ethics, Independence, and Professional Judgment

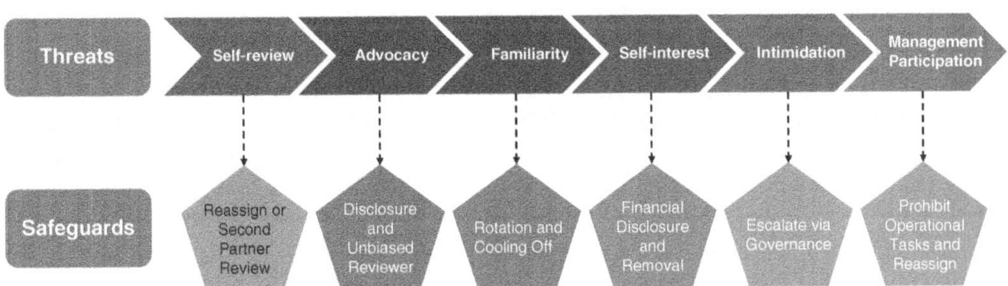

Ethics and independence define the credibility of every cybersecurity audit. In a field where technical findings can influence investment, regulation, and reputation, professional judgment must be exercised with discipline and transparency. This chapter examines how auditors preserve objectivity under organizational pressure, navigate conflicts of interest, and apply skepticism to evidence that is often incomplete or ambiguous. By grounding every conclusion in integrity and due care, the auditor transforms complex technical evaluation into a trustworthy form of assurance.

Modern cybersecurity operations blur traditional lines between builder, defender, and reviewer—creating new challenges to impartiality. Auditors now evaluate environments shaped by their own prior design input, automated systems that produce evidence at scale, and leadership teams accustomed to negotiating risk rather than disclosing it. Maintaining independence in this context requires clear ethical boundaries, documented rationale for decisions, and safeguards that make impartiality observable. These practices ensure that the audit process not only withstands scrutiny but also reinforces governance confidence in an era of accelerating digital accountability.

From managing sensitive evidence to confronting bias and pressure, this chapter underscores that professional ethics are not abstractions but operational controls in their own right. Transparent documentation of reasoning, respectful handling of disagreement, and formalized sign-offs together create an audit record that others can trust. In AI-driven and cloud-native enterprises, where data and decision-making are increasingly opaque, these ethical disciplines are the anchor that keeps assurance credible. The auditor's independence is therefore both a professional duty and a strategic safeguard for organizational integrity.

Code of Ethics and Objectivity in Cyber Audits

Integrity, objectivity, and due professional care are not slogans in cybersecurity auditing; they are the guardrails that keep technical judgment from drifting under pressure. Integrity requires that every conclusion be anchored to evidence rather than preference, convenience, or institutional politics—especially when control assessments touch high-stakes areas like identity governance or incident response readiness. Objectivity demands that the auditor's lens remain unclouded by prior involvement with the systems under review, vendor loyalties, or career incentives that might unconsciously steer severity ratings. Due care compels competent scoping, disciplined evidence handling, and measured interpretation so that findings neither exaggerate nor trivialize risk. These principles are foundational to credible assurance and professional trust.

Ethical integrity shapes how an auditor approaches control reasonableness when the facts are messy or incomplete. When access reviews reveal lingering privileged accounts, integrity rejects the temptation to "explain away" exceptions as operational necessities and instead frames the residual risk and ownership with precision. When detection rules miss a real incident, integrity avoids retrofitting narratives to protect reputations and records the precise gap between intended and observed control behavior. When management invokes risk tolerance to soften an issue, integrity requires explicit articulation of the tradeoff, who owns it, and what will verify that the risk remains acceptable. In each case, the ethical question is whether the reader can trust that risk is being described rather than negotiated.

Objectivity governs independence in both fact and appearance, and it is frequently tested in modern DevSecOps and cloud environments where roles blur. An auditor who built a detection pipeline last year may understand it deeply but is ethically constrained from opining on its effectiveness without safeguards such as reassignment or independent review. Familiarity and advocacy threats arise when auditors repeatedly cover the same product teams or feel responsible for outcomes; rotation and peer review mitigate those biases. Self-interest and intimidation threats surface when budgets, performance ratings, or leadership favor hinge on "good news." Objectivity demands transparent escalation paths and the willingness to issue uncomfortable conclusions. The ethical standard is not perfection but a demonstrable posture that would convince a reasonable outsider the work was impartial.

Due professional care translates competence into disciplined choices before a single log is collected. It guides the selection of criteria that actually measure the risk in play rather than what is easiest to check, such as validating encryption key management where sensitive data resides instead of defaulting to network perimeter controls. It calls for scoping that reflects materiality, ensuring ephemeral container workloads and control plane configurations receive attention proportionate to their potential impact. It demands the use of techniques and tools the auditor is qualified to apply, along with consultation or referral when the engagement crosses into areas that exceed current expertise. Care also covers timing and resource allocation, resisting compressed schedules that could undermine the sufficiency of evidence.

Ethical constraints are most visible during planning, where early choices can predetermine outcomes. Objectivity resists anchoring bias—starting from last year's findings or a public breach narrative—and instead centers the plan on current risk posture, architectural changes, and threat-driven priorities. Integrity requires that exclusions, such as omitting SaaS tenants or disaster recovery environments, be justified by risk, not convenience, and clearly documented. Due care favors criteria transparency up front, clarifying what "effective" means for zero trust controls, endpoint detection capabilities, or secrets-management practices. These decisions demonstrate that the audit seeks truth, not theatrics.

During fieldwork, ethics determines how evidence is obtained, handled, and interpreted. Integrity keeps collection nondisruptive and purposeful, avoiding intrusive actions that could degrade production systems or violate change control, while still obtaining what is necessary to reach a conclusion. Objectivity insists on least-privilege access for auditors, use of dedicated credentials, and segregation of duties to prevent the perception that the auditor is administering the environment. Due care governs data minimization, redaction of personally identifiable information when log detail suffices, and secure handling of artifacts with traceable chain-of-custody. When anomalies appear, skepticism demands follow-up that seeks disconfirming evidence rather than confirmation of initial assumptions.

Tool selection and use are also ethical decisions, because tools can amplify bias or introduce risk. Objectivity discourages reliance on a single vendor's dashboards as the sole measure of control health, favoring corroboration through independent telemetry or configuration sampling. Due care limits the use of proof-of-concept exploits to controlled test ranges or explicitly authorized conditions, protecting operational integrity and legal boundaries. Integrity governs the handling of discovered secrets or vulnerabilities, ensuring immediate containment and communication without transforming the audit into an unsanctioned penetration test. Where automated analytics or AI summarize findings, due care requires understanding model limitations and validating outputs against raw evidence before forming conclusions.

Professional skepticism is where ethics meets analysis. It treats management assertions—such as "MFA is enforced everywhere" or "S3 buckets are private by default"—as claims to be tested, not accepted. It weighs contradictory indicators, like clean configuration baselines alongside incident tickets showing repeated policy exceptions, and determines which evidence is more probative. It calibrates severity to likelihood and impact supported by fact, avoiding both understatement to maintain relationships and overstatement to dramatize the audit. The auditor's ethical compass ensures that each finding withstands scrutiny and that every recommendation is rooted in verifiable reality.

Independence Threats and Safeguards

Independence is the foundation of credible audit judgment, yet it is also the most fragile quality an auditor possesses. In cybersecurity contexts—where auditors often have deep technical histories with the systems they assess—the boundary between expertise and involvement can easily blur. Independence threats arise whenever personal, professional, or organizational interests could reasonably be perceived to influence the auditor's objectivity. These threats are not theoretical; they occur in subtle, everyday ways, such as participating in prior design decisions, recommending tools now under evaluation, or maintaining collegial ties with operations staff whose performance the audit might affect. The auditor's obligation is to identify these risks early, evaluate their significance, and apply safeguards that restore confidence in impartiality.

The self-review threat occurs when an auditor is asked to assess work in which they previously had a design, implementation, or configuration role. In cybersecurity audits, this might involve evaluating a vulnerability management workflow the auditor once helped script or a SIEM rule set they tuned in a prior operational role. The conflict is clear: the auditor would be reviewing their own judgment, consciously or not. Even if the technical work was years ago, the perception of bias can persist. Safeguards include assigning a different auditor or team to perform the evaluation, having the prior contributor act only in an advisory capacity, or conducting an independent second-partner review to validate findings. When separation cannot be achieved—such as in a small organization where the same personnel built and now monitor the control—the ethical course is to disclose the relationship and decline or re-scope the engagement.

The advocacy threat arises when the auditor becomes a champion for a particular outcome, technology, or vendor solution. In cybersecurity audits, this may occur after the auditor has publicly endorsed a product, contributed to a vendor white paper, or advised management to adopt a specific framework that now forms part of the audit scope. Once advocacy enters the equation, the auditor's conclusions risk appearing as defense of a prior position rather than a neutral assessment. Appropriate safeguards include formal disclosure of past advocacy, assigning another reviewer without that association, and ensuring that engagement acceptance decisions are made by someone uninvolved in the original recommendation. The auditor must be willing to step back when personal endorsement would call the independence of the report into question.

Familiarity threats develop gradually through repeated engagement with the same teams, systems, or executives. Over time, professional distance erodes, and skepticism is replaced by comfort. In cyber programs, this might mean overlooking weak logging configurations because "the team is reliable" or hesitating to challenge a long-standing process owner. Familiarity can also emerge from shared social circles, mentorships, or even informal collaboration on community projects. The key indicator is when professional skepticism gives way to assumption. Safeguards include rotating audit assignments, imposing "cooling-off" periods between operational and audit roles, and introducing independent reviewers unfamiliar with the environment. Where such rotation is impossible, enhanced supervision and documentation of decision rationale become essential to demonstrate continuing objectivity. Table 5.1 maps common independence threats to observable indicators and concrete safeguards aligned to the chapter guidance.

The self-interest threat occurs when personal or organizational gain could derive from the audit outcome. In cybersecurity, this might include future consulting opportunities tied to remediation work, bonuses linked to favorable audit ratings, or ownership interests in vendors

Table 5.1 Independence threats indicators and safeguards.

Threat	Primary indicator	Example cyber context	Safeguard
Self-review	Auditor previously designed or configured the control	Prior tuning of SIEM rules now under evaluation	Reassign evaluator or require independent second partner review
Advocacy	Public endorsement of a tool or framework now in scope	Authored vendor white paper on the selected EDR	Disclose advocacy and assign unbiased reviewer with approval
Familiarity	Longstanding coverage of the same team reduces skepticism	Repeated audits of the same cloud platform team	Rotate assignments and apply cooling off period
Self interest	Personal or organizational gain tied to outcome	Bonus or consulting opportunity linked to favorable rating	Full financial disclosure and remove conflicted staff
Intimidation	Pressure to alter severity or narrative without evidence	Executive request to soften rating due to optics	Escalate through audit leadership and committee oversight
Management participation	Dual role in operations during engagement	Temporary help configuring security tooling during audit	Prohibit operational tasks and immediately reassign role

supplying assessed controls. Even a perception of such interests can compromise trust in the report. Effective safeguards require complete financial disclosure, exclusion from engagement acceptance decisions, and independent oversight of final report issuance. Where financial entanglements are significant or cannot be mitigated through transparency and oversight, the audit must be declined. No amount of technical competence can offset compromised independence.

Intimidation threats arise when auditors face pressure—explicit or implicit—to alter conclusions or tone. This pressure might come from senior executives concerned about regulatory exposure, program managers seeking to maintain funding, or peers who fear reputational damage. In cyber audits, where findings can implicate leadership accountability for breaches or compliance failures, the potential for intimidation is real. Safeguards include escalation to an audit committee or governance body, maintaining written records of communications, and ensuring the auditor's reporting line allows direct access to independent oversight. Where intimidation cannot be neutralized, withdrawal from the engagement is ethically required.

Management participation threats occur when auditors take on operational tasks during or between engagements, such as temporarily assisting with incident response, drafting policy content, or configuring security tools. While this may seem helpful, it creates dual roles that compromise independence. Once an auditor participates in decision-making or implementation, they lose the ability to objectively evaluate those choices later. Safeguards include formal engagement boundaries prohibiting operational assistance, explicit documentation of role limitations, and immediate reassignment if boundaries are crossed. Auditors must remember that independence is not only a matter of mindset but of documented structure.

Effective management of independence threats depends on early recognition and structured response. Indicators such as role overlap, prior design input, tool selection influence, and personal relationships should trigger a formal independence evaluation before fieldwork begins. Organizations with mature audit functions establish independence checklists, mandatory disclosure forms, and periodic peer reviews to verify that safeguards remain adequate. The discipline of documenting potential conflicts—no matter how minor—creates transparency that protects both the auditor and the integrity of the assurance process. Table 5.2 summarizes minimum access storage transmission and disposal controls for sensitive audit evidence types.

Table 5.2 Sensitive evidence handling controls summary.

Evidence type	Access control minimum	Storage requirement	Transmission method	Disposal requirement
PII or PHI dataset	Individual accounts with MFA and time bound rights	Encrypted repository with managed keys	Managed file transfer over TLS or approved VPN	Cryptographic wipe after retention window
Export controlled data	Preapproved personnel only with documented authorization	Segregated encrypted repository with jurisdiction control	Authorized channel with out of band key verification	Documented destruction with certificate
Production credentials	Need to know access during testing only	No plaintext storage and vault if transient capture occurs	Out of band exchange with immediate reset on completion	Immediate invalidation and purge of artifacts

(Continued)

Table 5.2 (Continued)

Evidence type	Access control minimum	Storage requirement	Transmission method	Disposal requirement
Forensic images	Tightly scoped lab access with chain of custody	Sealed tamper evident storage in authorized lab	No email use secured transfer only within lab boundary	Destruction per policy after hold release
Configuration exports with identifiers	Role based read only rights for assigned staff	Encrypted working area separate from raw evidence	Secure portal with access logging	Secure delete after report issuance and QA
Centralized log extracts with PII	Least privilege per dataset with approved purpose	Encrypted repository with version tracking	TLS protected portal with owner approval	Redacted copies retained raw deleted per schedule

Confidentiality, Data Handling, and Sensitive Evidence

Confidentiality is the cornerstone of ethical auditing, especially in cybersecurity engagements where the auditor's access often exceeds that of most system administrators. The nature of audit evidence—configuration exports, access logs, identity records, or forensic images—means it may contain data subject to privacy, regulatory, or national security controls. The obligation to protect this information extends beyond policy compliance; it defines professional trust. An auditor's mishandling of sensitive material can cause more harm than the control weakness under review. For that reason, data protection must be treated as an operational discipline embedded in every stage of audit planning, execution, and closure.

Handling regulated or secret evidence requires awareness of classification boundaries and governing laws. Personally identifiable information (PII), protected health information (PHI), and export-controlled data each carry distinct legal obligations that dictate where and how data may reside. For example, evidence containing PHI from a healthcare system must remain within HIPAA-compliant repositories; export-controlled material may not be transferred outside approved jurisdictions or accessible by non-authorized personnel. Auditors are responsible for verifying that their evidence repositories, collaboration platforms, and backup systems meet the same or higher security requirements as the environment being audited. Compliance cannot be assumed simply because the data belongs to the auditee—it must be revalidated for the audit context.

Access to sensitive evidence must follow the principle of least privilege. Only those team members whose specific tasks require interaction with particular datasets should be granted access, and those rights must be time-bound and auditable. Shared credentials, convenience copies, or informal data exchanges violate this standard and introduce accountability gaps. Role-based permissions and individual authentication are mandatory, ideally using multifactor authentication and explicit approval workflows. Access logs should be retained for the duration of the engagement and through any subsequent quality assurance review to confirm adherence to established controls. Independence and confidentiality are mutually reinforcing—each prevents the other from being compromised.

Secure storage is equally critical. Evidence should be held in encrypted repositories that meet enterprise or regulatory encryption standards, using managed keys and hardware-backed security modules where possible. Local drives, removable media, and unsecured cloud folders are categorically unacceptable for storing audit data, no matter how temporary the use. The storage environment must include version control to track file modifications and must segregate working papers from sensitive raw evidence to prevent unintentional exposure. Auditors should assume that every artifact—whether a screenshot, packet capture, or exported log—may contain latent identifiers or metadata linking back to live systems, and they must handle it accordingly.

Transmission controls govern how evidence moves between systems or personnel. All transfers must be performed using encrypted channels such as TLS-protected file portals, secure VPN tunnels, or enterprise-grade managed file transfer solutions. Email attachments, even when encrypted, should be avoided due to the risk of persistence in multiple mailboxes and backups. When evidence must cross organizational boundaries, written authorization from data owners is required, and encryption keys must be exchanged through out-of-band verification methods. In high-sensitivity cases—such as defense or critical infrastructure audits—transmission may require dedicated networks or air-gapped devices to satisfy classification restrictions.

Redaction is both a confidentiality safeguard and an ethical necessity. Auditors should remove or obfuscate unnecessary identifiers before storing, sharing, or reporting evidence. IP addresses, hostnames, employee names, ticket numbers, and internal asset tags can often be masked without impairing the substance of the audit finding. Redaction must be irreversible and performed on copies, never the originals, to preserve the integrity of source evidence. The rule is simple: redact everything not essential to substantiating the control conclusion. Reports and appendices must reflect this same discipline, ensuring that no confidential or regulated data leaves the secure boundary of the audit repository.

For highly sensitive materials such as production credentials, cryptographic keys, or forensic images, additional safeguards apply. Credentials obtained during testing or observation must never be reused, stored in plain text, or retained beyond the point of necessity. If passwords or tokens are viewed as part of the audit, they must be immediately reset or invalidated by system owners once testing concludes. Forensic images and memory captures must be stored in sealed, tamper-evident containers—digital or physical—and accompanied by a documented chain of custody. Auditors must not mount or analyze these images outside authorized lab environments, even for benign inspection, as doing so risks data alteration and legal exposure.

Disposal procedures are the final act of confidentiality. Once audit retention periods expire, all copies of sensitive evidence must be irreversibly destroyed, including redundant backups, temporary cache files, and transfer logs. Destruction should follow verifiable processes such as cryptographic wiping, shredding of physical media, or deletion from immutable repositories with certificate of destruction documentation. Disposal is not optional cleanup; it is part of the life cycle control that demonstrates ongoing accountability for entrusted data. Premature deletion, however, is equally unacceptable when legal holds or regulatory retention mandates are in effect.

Legal holds represent a special intersection between confidentiality and compliance. When an organization places an audit under legal hold—typically in anticipation of litigation or regulatory inquiry—the auditor must preserve all relevant evidence in its current state, suspending disposal and change operations. The existence of a legal hold does not relax confidentiality obligations; in fact, it intensifies them. During the hold, evidence must remain segregated, access must be frozen except to authorized counsel or regulators, and any transfer or review must be logged and approved in writing. Once the hold is lifted, normal retention and destruction cycles can resume.

Professional Skepticism and Cognitive Bias Awareness

Professional skepticism is a disciplined mindset that treats every assertion as a claim to be examined and every absence of evidence as data about the control environment. It is not cynicism or distrust of people; it is neutrality toward claims until sufficient, appropriate evidence accumulates. The skeptical auditor resists quick closure, asks what would falsify a conclusion, and actively considers alternative explanations for the same observation. Applied well, this stance slows snap judgments, surfaces hidden assumptions, and keeps conclusions tethered to verifiable facts rather than narratives or expectations.

Confirmation bias is the most common hazard to skeptical practice because it masquerades as efficiency. After hearing that "MFA is enforced across all admin accounts," an auditor may unconsciously sample the obvious directories or the best-managed business units, accumulating evidence that fits the story while overlooking edge cases in service accounts or legacy consoles. In log analysis, it can show up as building queries that prove a hypothesis rather than testing for counterexamples. Effective countermeasures include deliberately seeking disconfirming evidence, documenting a competing hypothesis alongside the primary one, and requiring that any conclusion state what evidence would have changed the rating but did not appear.

Anchoring bias takes hold when first impressions—last year's report, a dashboard's default severity scale, or a persuasive scoping call—set a mental benchmark that subsequent evidence struggles to dislodge. A team might anchor on a prior "effective" rating and unconsciously treat new gaps as exceptions rather than indicators of drift, or fixate on an initial estimate of coverage and rationalize missing segments as immaterial. To counter anchoring, auditors should recalibrate after initial fieldwork by restating criteria in plain terms and reestimating severity from scratch using only the collected evidence. Structured pauses at predetermined points in the engagement to "reanchor" on current facts, not historical expectations, help keep judgment current.

Availability bias distorts risk perception by overweighting what is vivid, recent, or easily recalled. A fresh breach headline or a noisy alert type can dominate attention, leading to undue focus on controls associated with memorable events while quiet, high-impact exposures remain under-examined. Evidence selection can also skew when rare, dramatic log entries feel more probative than routine but telling patterns. Auditors can temper this bias by consulting base rates and population characteristics before weighing any single observation, ensuring that visibility is earned by systemic relevance rather than memorability.

Authority bias emerges when deference to senior leaders, celebrated architects, or renowned vendors tilts judgment. Statements such as "the platform enforces this by design" or "the provider guarantees encryption at rest" can prematurely close inquiry, particularly when the messenger carries organizational prestige. Professional skepticism treats authority as a source of information, not a substitute for corroboration, and records assertions as testable claims with traceable evidence. Clear escalation paths and the freedom to disagree respectfully are necessary so that expertise informs conclusions without dictating them.

Independent corroboration is the practical backbone of bias resistance. Rather than relying on a single tool's dashboard or a single interview, the auditor should triangulate conclusions across configuration states, operational records, and outcome indicators that are independently generated. When feasible, blind sampling reduces cherry-picking risk by selecting items through predefined rules or automation without auditor discretion, and anonymized artifacts limit halo effects from team reputation or system name recognition. Corroboration is not about volume; it is about diversity and independence of sources that converge on the same conclusion.

Structured challenge from a reviewer converts skepticism into a team sport. A second-partner or peer reviewer who did not participate in fieldwork should probe the reasoning chain, ask for alternative interpretations, and request to see the strongest contradictory evidence encountered. Formal challenge sessions work best when they follow a predictable script: restate criteria, summarize evidence by source, articulate the counter-hypothesis, and explain why it was rejected. Checklists that explicitly call out confirmation, anchoring, availability, and authority bias serve as cognitive speed bumps, forcing auditors to document how each risk was addressed before sign-off.

Decision hygiene—how judgments are recorded and communicated—matters as much as the judgments themselves. Writing down the criteria, the evidence-to-assertion mapping, and the rationale for severity forces clarity that exposes hidden assumptions. Calibration meetings across concurrent audits help align severity scales and reduce idiosyncratic drift driven by local experiences or personalities. Maintaining a concise decision log that captures pivotal moments, evidence additions, and changes in position creates an audit trail of reasoning that can be independently reviewed for bias leakage.

Forming Conclusions Under Uncertainty and Incomplete Evidence

Auditors rarely enjoy perfect visibility, and competent judgment begins by acknowledging that reality rather than obscuring it. When evidence is partial, conflicting, or constrained by time, the objective is to reach a conclusion that is proportionate to the evidence while making its limits explicit. Sufficiency concerns the quantity of evidence, appropriateness concerns its quality and independence, and both are evaluated relative to materiality and risk. A conclusion is defensible when the record shows how these factors were weighed, which alternatives were considered, and why the chosen path best fits the engagement's objectives given the constraints. The discipline is not to eliminate uncertainty, but to manage it transparently.

Conflicts in evidence should be treated as a signal to widen the lens before moving toward resolution. A clean configuration baseline alongside recurring incident tickets is not a contradiction to be averaged away; it is an invitation to examine whether the criteria measure outcomes or paperwork. The auditor should map each piece of evidence to the specific assertion it supports, identify which items are independent, and assess which is more probative in the context of control objectives. If conflicts persist, the conclusion should reflect the dominant evidence while documenting the unresolved discrepancy and its potential effect on assurance. A defensible position shows the path taken and the forks left unexplored.

Time-boxed engagements demand explicit tradeoffs between breadth and depth. When schedule limits prevent full population coverage, the auditor should prefer procedures that maximize inferential value per unit effort, such as selecting transactions across risk-relevant strata rather than concentrating on a single system. Where depth is chosen, the rationale should tie to materiality and the likelihood of discovering systemic issues, not convenience. When unavoidable gaps remain, the conclusion may be qualified to reflect reduced confidence, and the workpapers must specify which areas were not examined and why. Transparency about the cost of speed prevents false impressions of completeness.

Qualifications are appropriate when scope limitations or evidence defects could reasonably affect a reader's reliance on the conclusion. A qualification is not a rhetorical flourish; it is a boundary marker that delineates where the auditor's assurance applies and where it does not. Use a qualification when access to critical environments was denied, when data integrity could not be established, or when contradictory evidence could not be resolved within the engagement window. If the effect of the limitation is pervasive or the missing area is central to the control objective, the auditor should consider expanding scope or declining to conclude on that objective. The decision turns on whether the residual uncertainty is tolerable for the intended use of the conclusion.

Alternative procedures serve as bridges when primary evidence is unavailable or unreliable. If centralized logs are incomplete, the auditor might corroborate activity through endpoint artifacts, change tickets, or identity provider records that reflect the same control outcome. If interviews are necessary but potentially biased, the auditor can seek independent artifacts that reflect actions rather than intentions, such as automation run histories or immutable configuration states. The key is to ensure that alternatives test the same assertion, not a nearby convenience proxy. Documenting why an alternative is relevant and how it mitigates specific uncertainties strengthens the chain of reasoning.

Assumptions are inevitable and must be documented as first-class elements of the conclusion, not buried in workpaper commentary. An assumption should be stated in testable terms, tied to a source or rationale, and accompanied by an explanation of how the conclusion would change if the assumption proves false. Examples include assuming that a synchronization job ran successfully because a checksum matched, or that an allow-list is exhaustive because it is generated by policy code. Each assumption carries a residual risk that should be articulated in terms of exposure, not merely probability. Clear assumptions convert hidden guesswork into explicit, reviewable premises.

Residual risk should be described as what remains credible after the concluded control posture, not as a generic warning label. If evidence supports that access reviews occur but sampling revealed stale service accounts, the residual risk is not "access management issues" but "persistence of unreviewed nonhuman identities with elevated permissions." Tying residual risk to specific failure modes clarifies why certain monitoring or compensating activities matter post-audit. Where feasible, note whether the residual risk is expected to shrink with routine control operation or requires structural change to address. Framing residual risk this way avoids both minimization and alarmism.

Scope expansion is warranted when the unanswered question is central to the control objective or when early results suggest systemic drift beyond the initial boundary. Expansion is not a default response; it is a remedy for a material uncertainty that cannot be mitigated by alternative procedures. Before expanding, the auditor should assess stakeholder tolerance for delay, the added evidence needed to resolve the uncertainty, and whether independence or resourcing constraints would compromise additional work. If expansion is impractical, a qualified conclusion with a statement of the unresolved issue and its potential magnitude is preferable to silent omission. The record should show that expansion was considered and why the chosen path best preserved assurance quality.

Management representations can fill context gaps but cannot substitute for missing probative evidence. When representations are used, they should address specific facts, identify the signatory with decision rights, and be cross-referenced to the evidence they contextualize. Representations are most useful to explain intent, timing, or planned remediation sequencing; they are least useful to prove effectiveness. Treat them as auxiliary inputs that guide where to look next or how to interpret ambiguous artifacts, not as anchors for conclusions. Overreliance on representation invites overconfidence unsupported by the record.

Managing Management Pressure and Disagreement

Professional independence is tested not only by technical complexity but by interpersonal and organizational dynamics. Auditors operate in environments where findings can influence funding, leadership credibility, and regulatory exposure, creating strong incentives for management to shape outcomes. Pressure may present as subtle requests to "revisit tone," overt attempts to delay access, or persistent questioning of sampling choices intended to fatigue the audit team into concessions. Recognizing and managing these pressures is part of the auditor's ethical duty to preserve objectivity and public trust. The goal is not confrontation but disciplined adherence to process—ensuring that every engagement remains transparent, documented, and defensible.

Pressure to narrow scope is among the most common forms of influence. It can appear as a claim that certain systems fall outside audit authority, that a new acquisition is "too immature" for review, or that particular control families "belong to compliance, not audit." While some exclusions may be legitimate due to timing, materiality, or jurisdiction, auditors must evaluate each claim against the approved engagement objectives and risk assessment. Any change to scope must be justified in writing, approved by audit leadership, and supported by evidence that the exclusion will not materially weaken assurance. When a limitation is imposed unilaterally by management, the auditor should issue a formal scope restriction notice and, if unresolved, escalate through the audit committee or governing oversight body. Documentation, not debate, is the primary safeguard.

Delays in access represent another form of pressure that can erode independence under the guise of logistics. Requests to "wait until next sprint," "hold off until after the migration," or "circle back once documentation is updated" can cumulatively compress testing time and reduce coverage. Legitimate scheduling conflicts may occur, but auditors must distinguish these from strategic delays meant to control narrative or evidence availability. The protocol is to record each delay, its stated reason, and its impact on the audit timeline, then escalate when repeated or unexplained postponements begin to impair evidence sufficiency. Clear communication that the engagement clock does not stop for internal convenience reinforces professional boundaries without resorting to confrontation.

Attempts to dilute findings often surface during draft review, when management seeks rewording that downplays risk severity or reframes responsibility. The distinction between legitimate factual dispute and pressure to alter conclusions lies in the nature of the feedback. Fact-based disagreement provides new evidence, contradictory data, or alternative interpretations of criteria; influence-based pressure focuses on tone, optics, or downstream impact. Auditors should welcome factual clarifications and incorporate them where they strengthen accuracy. However, requests that aim to change ratings or remove findings without new evidence must be declined and logged as management comments, preserving the original conclusion. Every version of the finding narrative should remain traceable to demonstrate that edits were evidence-driven, not politically negotiated.

Escalation paths must be predefined and known to all parties. The first level of resolution lies with the engagement lead and auditee management. If disagreement persists or pressure becomes coercive, the issue escalates to audit leadership, then to the audit committee or board-level oversight as appropriate. Each escalation should be supported by contemporaneous documentation—meeting summaries, emails, or memoranda capturing what was discussed, who was present, and what decisions were made. The presence of a structured escalation path reassures management that their concerns will be heard while also protecting auditors from isolation or improvised decision-making.

Auditors should maintain contemporaneous notes throughout any interaction involving contested scope, access, or findings. These notes should be factual, free of opinion, and time-stamped to establish an evidentiary record. Entries might include the date and participants of a meeting, topics discussed, specific statements or requests made, and the auditor's responsive action. These records serve as a defense against retrospective revisionism—where parties later reinterpret events to fit a preferred outcome. Detailed notes also help audit committees assess patterns of management interference and determine when corrective governance action is needed.

Professionalism is paramount when disagreements arise. The auditor's demeanor must remain calm, factual, and consistent regardless of provocation. Engaging emotionally or adopting a defensive posture undermines credibility and can escalate tension. The focus should remain on evidence and criteria, not personalities or perceived motives. When management raises concerns, auditors should respond by clarifying how conclusions were reached, what evidence supports them, and what additional information could reasonably alter the outcome. Transparency and technical precision defuse most disputes without compromising integrity.

Legitimate disagreement over evidence interpretation deserves respect and methodical resolution. Differences in risk appetite, control maturity models, or terminology often explain divergent views more than bad faith. Where feasible, auditors can schedule joint evidence reviews, provide clarifying references to authoritative standards, or consult independent technical specialists. These steps demonstrate openness to factual refinement while maintaining the independence of judgment. A disagreement resolved through evidence strengthens credibility; one resolved through concession weakens it.

The line between collaboration and compromise is defined by documentation. Collaboration means integrating valid corrections or context that improve accuracy; compromise means altering substance to appease stakeholders. The former is integral to quality assurance; the latter corrodes independence. Audit teams should use version-controlled working papers, ensuring that every change to findings or scope has a documented rationale and reviewer approval. This transparency transforms potential conflict into traceable governance, shifting the discussion from influence to accountability.

Audit leadership has a parallel responsibility to protect teams from undue pressure. This includes reinforcing escalation protocols, reviewing contentious cases promptly, and providing direct communication channels to the board or audit committee when management behavior threatens independence. Training sessions should prepare auditors to recognize early signs of coercion, such as repeated informal "off-the-record" requests or conditional access offers. Proactive support ensures that individual auditors are never forced to negotiate independence alone.

Documenting Judgment

Sound professional judgment is not self-evident—it must be documented in a way that allows others to see how it was exercised. Every audit conclusion represents a chain of reasoning that connects evidence, criteria, and professional interpretation. Documenting that reasoning ensures transparency, enables quality review, and protects the credibility of the engagement when challenged. The standard for documentation is that a qualified, independent auditor should be able to reconstruct the logic of each key decision without relying on verbal explanation from the original team. This standard applies equally to technical and ethical judgments throughout the audit life cycle.

The foundation of documented judgment is the explicit statement of the criteria applied. Whether drawn from a regulatory framework, internal control standard, or risk-based threshold, the criteria define what "effective" or "deficient" means in context. Each criterion must be referenced by authoritative source—such as a NIST control, ISO clause, or company policy—and tied to the specific objective tested. Where criteria have been interpreted or adapted, the rationale for interpretation must be described, including how materiality, relevance, and context informed that choice. This prevents later confusion about whether the finding reflects the control's design, its operation, or the auditor's assumptions.

Auditors must also capture the alternative courses of action considered when forming a conclusion. These alternatives might involve different interpretations of evidence, optional testing procedures, or varied severity ratings based on risk. Documenting them demonstrates that judgment was the product of deliberation rather than instinct. For example, when conflicting logs suggest inconsistent control operation, the record should show whether the team considered expanding the sample, performing corroborating tests, or qualifying the conclusion. Each option rejected should be accompanied by a concise justification—such as insufficient time, immaterial impact, or redundant coverage elsewhere. This practice not only enhances transparency but also strengthens the defensibility of the chosen approach.

The rationale for the final decision must integrate the evidence, criteria, and alternatives into a coherent narrative. It should explain why the selected conclusion best reflects the balance of facts and professional assessment. This includes identifying the relative weight given to each evidence source, how reliability was determined, and how residual uncertainty was managed. The rationale should be explicit about whether the conclusion is based on direct observation, indirect inference, or corroboration across multiple sources. Avoiding generic phrasing like "based on evidence reviewed" is essential; specificity allows later reviewers to trace reasoning to actual records and judgments. Table 5.3 outlines the core elements that must be recorded so another auditor can reconstruct the reasoning path from evidence to conclusion.

Table 5.3 Documenting professional judgment elements and cross references.

Decision point	Required documentation	Alternatives considered example	Cross reference location
Scope exclusion	Written rationale tied to risk and materiality	Expand scope to include SaaS tenant or defer with qualification	Decision log entry ID and scope memo page
Severity rating	Criteria mapping and weight of evidence by source	Rate as high due to systemic drift or medium with monitoring	Finding worksheet section and evidence file path
Qualification decision	Statement of limitation and residual risk impact	Expand scope versus issue qualified conclusion	Conclusion memo paragraph and approval record
Use of alternative procedures	Why primary evidence was unavailable and relevance of substitute	Corroborate via endpoint artifacts or change records	Test plan addendum and artifact index
Assumption accepted	Explicit assumption source and sensitivity of conclusion	Treat sync job as successful based on checksum or seek further proof	Assumption register entry and evidence reference
Escalation for pressure	Summary of interaction and governance escalation outcome	Continue negotiation or elevate to audit committee	Meeting notes timestamp and escalation ticket

Every documented rationale must link back to the supporting workpapers and decision logs that underpin it. These cross-references form the evidentiary map of the engagement. Each reference should point to the precise location—such as section, page, or file path—where the supporting material resides. Decision logs should chronologically record significant points of judgment, including the date, participants, key evidence cited, and the resulting decision. This allows reviewers to reconstruct the sequence of reasoning and verify that conclusions evolved logically as new information emerged. An audit file without clear cross-references may appear complete but will fail to demonstrate professional reasoning under scrutiny.

When professional judgment involves the use of estimates, assumptions, or probability-based reasoning, these must be explicitly stated and justified. The documentation should describe why the assumption was necessary, what source informed it, and how sensitive the conclusion is to its validity. For instance, assuming that a vulnerability scan was comprehensive because its coverage aligned with asset inventory must be supported by evidence of inventory completeness and tool configuration. Each assumption should be testable and subject to reviewer challenge, ensuring that the conclusion is not built on invisible foundations.

Reviewer and approver sign-offs formalize accountability for judgment. Each significant decision point—such as risk rating adjustments, scope changes, or conclusion finalization—must be reviewed by a senior auditor or engagement lead who did not make the original call. The reviewer's sign-off should include a date, the scope of the review, and any conditions or reservations noted. Where differences in opinion arise, both perspectives and their resolution must be documented in the decision log. This dual-layer documentation demonstrates that professional skepticism was applied not only by individuals but by the audit team collectively.

Temporal integrity is another vital element of judgment documentation. All rationale, alternatives, and sign-offs must be recorded contemporaneously with the decisions themselves, not reconstructed afterward. Retrospective documentation invites revisionism and undermines credibility. Version control within the audit repository should show when entries were added or modified, by whom, and under what authorization. The integrity of the audit file depends as much on its metadata as on its contents; an undated rationale carries less evidentiary weight than one tied to a verifiable decision timestamp.

Audit leaders must establish conventions for how judgment documentation integrates with existing records without duplicating them. For example, while workpapers contain raw evidence and test results, a dedicated "judgment memorandum" or decision log can summarize key interpretations, cross-referencing underlying data. This keeps narrative reasoning distinct yet connected, ensuring that reviewers can navigate seamlessly between fact and interpretation. Clear separation between evidence and judgment protects both—the former from subjective influence and the latter from becoming lost in data.

When documentation of judgment is complete, the audit file becomes more than a record of what was tested—it becomes a record of how the team thought. It demonstrates that conclusions emerged through disciplined reasoning, competing perspectives were weighed, and oversight was applied in real time. This transparency transforms professional judgment from a private mental process into an auditable artifact. In cybersecurity auditing, where control assessments often rest on nuanced interpretation rather than binary outcomes, such documentation is the ultimate defense of integrity and the clearest proof that assurance was earned, not asserted.

Conclusion

Mastering ethical independence and disciplined judgment is critical for any cybersecurity auditor operating in today's complex, AI-driven landscape. The ability to separate professional reasoning from operational bias defines whether audit results can be trusted by regulators, executives, and the public. Ethical principles such as integrity, objectivity, and due care are not abstractions; they are practical mechanisms for ensuring that audit conclusions reflect truth rather than convenience. In environments shaped by automation, continuous deployment, and adaptive controls, these human-centered standards remain the final safeguard for assurance credibility.

This chapter reinforces the role of professional skepticism and transparency as active controls within the audit process. Documented rationale, disclosure of assumptions, and structured peer review transform individual insight into organizational reliability. By anticipating bias, managing evidence responsibly, and recording the path of reasoning, auditors make their conclusions reproducible and defensible even under legal or regulatory challenge. Such rigor is indispensable when assessing systems whose decisions—and potential failures—are increasingly shaped by machine learning and complex data flows.

With these foundations in place, professionals are better equipped to operate within a governance model that demands both speed and integrity. Ethical consistency ensures that assurance functions scale alongside emerging technologies without diluting accountability. Whether evaluating a traditional network control or an AI risk management process, the disciplined application of ethics, independence, and skepticism preserves the trust on which all cybersecurity auditing depends.

Auditor Recommendations

1. **Establish a Clear Process for Maintaining Auditor Independence:** Define boundaries that prevent self-review, advocacy, familiarity, self-interest, intimidation, and management participation threats. Require preengagement disclosures, assignment rotation, and second-partner review where risks are identified. Document all safeguards so independence is demonstrable in fact and appearance.
2. **Apply Professional Skepticism as a Default Stance:** Treat all assertions as claims to be tested and actively seek disconfirming evidence before forming conclusions. Write down what would falsify your hypothesis and look for it in the data. Reassess early impressions after initial fieldwork to ensure conclusions remain anchored to current facts.
3. **Implement Bias Countermeasures in Every Engagement:** Guard against confirmation, anchoring, availability, and authority bias through independent corroboration and blind selection where feasible. Schedule structured challenge sessions with a reviewer not involved in fieldwork. Use a simple bias checklist at planning and sign-off to verify that countermeasures were actually used.
4. **Protect Sensitive Evidence with Rigorous Controls End-to-end:** Enforce least-privilege access with individual accounts, time-bound rights, and multifactor authentication. Store artifacts only in encrypted, approved repositories and transmit them via secured channels with owner authorization. Redact nonessential identifiers and document chain-of-custody and destruction steps per retention requirements.

5. **Qualify Conclusions when Limitations Are Material:** State scope restrictions, evidence defects, or access denials that reduce assurance, and describe the residual risk that remains. Consider alternative procedures first, then expand scope if the uncertainty is central and resolvable. When expansion is impractical, issue a qualified conclusion rather than implying full coverage.
6. **Document Professional Judgment so Another Auditor Can Reconstruct It:** Record the criteria applied, alternatives considered and rejected, and the rationale for the decision with dated reviewer sign-offs. Cross-reference each judgment to specific workpapers and entries in the decision log. Capture assumptions explicitly and note how the conclusion would change if an assumption proves false.
7. **Escalate and Record Management Pressure Systematically:** Log attempts to narrow scope, delay access, or dilute findings with timestamps, participants, and stated reasons. Maintain the original conclusion unless new probative evidence emerges, and elevate persistent issues through governance channels. Preserve a clear trail showing that outcomes were evidence-driven, not negotiated.
8. **Use Alternative Procedures to Bridge Gaps in Primary Evidence:** When centralized logs or standard artifacts are incomplete, corroborate the same assertion via independent sources such as endpoint artifacts, change records, or immutable configurations. Explain why the substitute is relevant and how it mitigates the specific uncertainty. Update the decision log to reflect the change in approach and its effect on confidence.
9. **Reanchor Judgments After Initial Evidence Is Gathered:** Restate the evaluation criteria in plain terms and rate severity from scratch using only the current record, not last year's outcomes. Calibrate with a peer reviewer to test for hidden influence from prior ratings or reputational cues. Document the recalibration point to show how prior anchors were neutralized.
10. **Treat Transparency and Timing as Quality Controls, Not Paperwork:** Enter reasoning, assumptions, escalations, and sign-offs contemporaneously rather than retrospectively. Maintain version history for key decisions and ensure reviewers attest to the scope of their review on specific dates. Make the audit file tell a coherent story from criteria to conclusion so assurance remains defensible under scrutiny.

Chapter Questions

1. Which statement best captures the auditor's stance of professional skepticism?
   - **A.** A neutral posture that withholds judgment until sufficient, appropriate evidence is gathered
   - **B.** A default distrust of management representations in all cases
   - **C.** Deference to domain experts to accelerate agreement on findings
   - **D.** Rapid closure on the most likely hypothesis to maintain schedule

2. An auditor is assigned to evaluate SIEM rules they previously tuned while in an operations role. Which independence threat is most relevant?
   - **A.** Advocacy threat
   - **B.** Familiarity threat
   - **C.** Self-review threat
   - **D.** Intimidation threat

3. What is the most appropriate control for handling highly sensitive artifacts such as forensic images?
   A. Storing images on encrypted personal laptops for convenience
   B. Sending images as encrypted email attachments to the team
   C. Preserving images with tamper-evident controls and documented chain of custody in an authorized lab
   D. Hosting images in a broadly shared cloud folder to speed collaboration

4. During draft review, management requests lowering a severity rating because "the optics are bad," but offers no new evidence. How should this request be characterized?
   A. A legitimate factual dispute that warrants retesting
   B. Pressure to alter conclusions without evidence
   C. A calibration issue requiring industry benchmarking
   D. An anchoring check based on prior audit ratings

5. When should an auditor issue a qualified conclusion to reflect uncertainty?
   A. Whenever stakeholders disagree with a finding's tone
   B. Whenever any conflicting data is identified, regardless of materiality
   C. Whenever time is limited, even if evidence is sufficient
   D. When access is restricted or evidence defects are material to reliance and scope expansion is impractical

6. Which documentation approach best evidences sound professional judgment?
   A. Recording applied criteria, alternatives considered and rejected, rationale for the decision, and reviewer sign-offs with dated cross-references
   B. Capturing only raw evidence and final ratings to avoid biasing reviewers
   C. Relying on informal notes and memory, then drafting rationale at the end of fieldwork
   D. Documenting disagreements verbally to keep files concise

7. What is an effective countermeasure to anchoring on last year's "effective" rating?
   A. Restate criteria and reestimate severity from scratch after initial fieldwork using only current evidence
   B. Accept prior ratings unless disproved by a major incident
   C. Prioritize the most memorable alerts to confirm current performance
   D. Defer to senior architects who designed the control set

8. Which practice aligns with least-privilege access for auditors handling sensitive evidence?
   A. Using shared read-only credentials to simplify access
   B. Granting broad read-only rights to all audit artifacts for the engagement duration
   C. Using dedicated individual accounts with multifactor authentication and time-bound, task-specific permissions
   D. Allowing auditors temporary administrative rights to speed evidence collection

9. How should auditors respond when repeated access delays begin to impair evidence sufficiency?
   A. Accept delays as routine logistics if the team remains cooperative
   B. Pause the engagement without documenting the impact to avoid conflict
   C. Remove delayed systems from scope and proceed silently
   D. Record each delay with its impact and escalate through governance when patterns persist

10. If centralized logs are incomplete but a control outcome must still be assessed, what is the appropriate next step?
    A. Accept management representation that the logs "usually capture everything"
    B. Perform alternative procedures that corroborate the same assertion via independent sources such as endpoint artifacts or change records
    C. Automatically lower the severity due to uncertainty
    D. Wait for a future audit cycle when logging has improved

6

Identity and Access Management

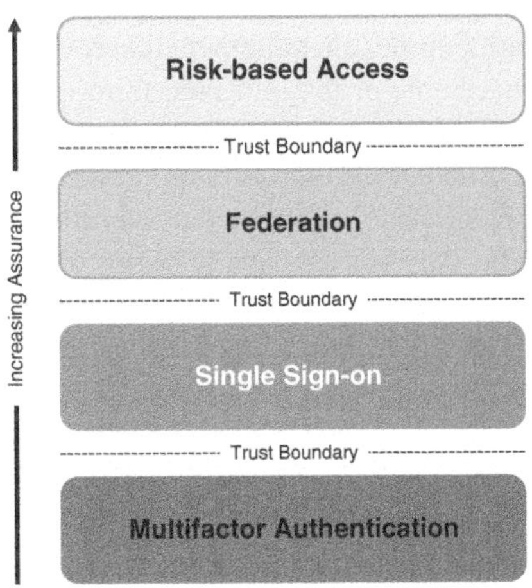

Identity and access management (IAM) sits at the center of cybersecurity assurance. It defines how trust is established, maintained, and revoked across every layer of an organization's technology ecosystem. From onboarding new users to managing privileged credentials and machine identities, the effectiveness of these controls determines whether the enterprise can enforce least privilege and maintain accountability in a complex digital environment. As threat actors increasingly exploit identity weaknesses rather than technical vulnerabilities, understanding and auditing this domain has become one of the most critical elements of enterprise security governance.

Modern identity systems extend far beyond usernames and passwords. They integrate with cloud directories, federated partners, and automated workflows that grant and revoke access across thousands of systems in real time. This chapter examines the full life cycle of identity assurance—from how user and service identities are created and governed to how authentication, elevation, and emergency access are controlled and monitored. It also addresses how evidence from disparate systems such as HR platforms, identity providers, and privileged access management (PAM) tools must align to demonstrate compliance and operational integrity.

For organizations building AI-driven or cloud-native architectures, the integrity of identity controls underpins every other layer of security. Algorithms, automation, and data pipelines operate through nonhuman identities that require the same rigor once reserved for administrators. A single misconfigured token or stale privilege can undermine even the most advanced detection systems. Effective auditing of IAM therefore strengthens not only compliance but also the resilience of the organization's entire AI and digital infrastructure—ensuring that every trusted connection, whether human or machine, remains verifiable, accountable, and governed.

Identity Life cycle: Joiner–Mover–Leaver and Sources of Truth

Every identity within an organization follows a predictable path—joining, moving, and leaving. Managing this life cycle effectively ensures that people have the right level of access at the right time and that unnecessary privileges are removed promptly. The foundation of this process lies in using authoritative sources of truth—systems that define who is part of the organization and in what capacity. Typically, a Human Resources Information System (HRIS) governs employee data, while vendor or contractor management systems track nonemployee records. These systems serve as the origin point for all identity events, dictating when accounts should be created, modified, or removed. When they are inaccurate or disconnected from identity systems, access decisions become inconsistent and potentially dangerous. Table 6.1 aligns joiner mover leaver events to required attributes actions and evidence locations to support life cycle assurance.

During the joiner phase, the goal is to create digital identities that accurately represent real people entering the organization. This process usually begins when the HRIS records a new hire or contract start. The record contains critical details such as start date, role, department, and manager—information that identity governance tools use to automatically assign access based

Table 6.1 Life cycle events and evidence anchors.

Life cycle event	Authoritative source	Required attributes	Access provisioning action	Deprovisioning action	Primary evidence
Joiner employee	HRIS	start date unique id job code manager department	Provision baseline access via role mapping effective start date	n a	HR hire record IdP account creation log
Joiner contractor	Contractor system	start date sponsor company end date role	Provision time bound access with expiry	n a	Vendor record IdP account creation log
Mover role change	HRIS	new job code new manager effective date	Grant new role entitlements	Revoke prior role access	HR change record IdP group diff
Mover department transfer	HRIS	new department location effective date	Update app access per new department	Remove prior department access	HR change record IdP group removal log
Leaver termination	HRIS	term date status inactive	Disable accounts and revoke tokens same day	Deprovision apps and remove memberships	HR term record IdP disable log
Leaver contract end	Contractor system	end date sponsor confirmation	Disable accounts at end date	Rotate any shared secrets and remove access	Vendor end record IdP disable log

on predefined rules. Accounts should not be activated until the start date to prevent premature access, and privileges should align strictly with job requirements. Failure to link account creation to an authoritative source often results in manual provisioning, inconsistent naming conventions, and the creation of unauthorized accounts.

The mover phase occurs when an individual changes positions, departments, or responsibilities. This transition is often the weakest link in the identity life cycle because systems may fail to remove outdated permissions when new ones are added. For example, when an employee transfers from finance to marketing, their finance system privileges may remain active if not automatically revoked. These leftover rights—often called "permission residue"—can accumulate over time, creating compliance issues and enabling privilege escalation. A sound mover process includes both the addition of new entitlements and the removal of old ones, ensuring that access always reflects current responsibilities.

The leaver phase is where timing becomes critical. When an employee resigns or a contractor's engagement ends, their access should be revoked immediately upon termination. The HRIS or contractor system must signal this event in real time to the identity provider (IdP), which, in turn, disables accounts, revokes tokens, and terminates active sessions. Delays in processing offboarding events can leave "ghost accounts" active—identities that still exist in systems even though the person is no longer associated with the organization. Ghost accounts are one of the most common audit findings and represent a serious risk, as they can be exploited by insiders or external attackers.

Across all three phases, synchronization between authoritative sources and directories is essential. The HRIS may be the system of record for personnel data, but directories like Active Directory or cloud-based identity providers are responsible for enforcing access controls. Any mismatch between these systems—such as an employee marked as inactive in HR but still active in the directory—must be reconciled promptly. Periodic automated reconciliation ensures that identity records remain aligned, closing gaps before they turn into security incidents or audit deficiencies.

A common cause of life cycle failure is the existence of shadow or duplicate sources of truth. Departments sometimes maintain local spreadsheets or independent databases for contractors, interns, or temporary workers. When these systems are not integrated into the central identity architecture, they create blind spots where access cannot be easily tracked or revoked. Centralizing identity data under a small number of validated sources helps eliminate these inconsistencies and enforces a single authoritative view of each person's access status.

Identity life cycle management also depends on the granularity and accuracy of metadata flowing from the source systems. Job codes, cost centers, and role attributes should follow consistent naming and formatting standards, allowing automated systems to interpret and enforce policy decisions correctly. If HR data is incomplete or ambiguous—for example, missing a department code—access rules may fail to trigger properly, forcing manual workarounds that erode governance quality. Data quality in the authoritative source directly translates to access accuracy in downstream systems.

Strong life cycle governance doesn't end with automation—it includes verification. Audit teams must periodically compare HRIS, IdP, and directory data to ensure alignment. This process, known as reconciliation, validates that every active account corresponds to an active individual and that no terminated users retain access. Such reviews often reveal misalignments due to late HR updates, integration errors, or manual account creations that bypassed standard workflows. Automating this validation process strengthens the organization's overall identity assurance posture.

A mature Joiner–Mover–Leaver model reflects not only technology integration but also organizational discipline. When HR, IT, and security teams coordinate their data and timing, access changes happen seamlessly and safely. When they operate in silos, timing gaps and manual errors creep in, allowing dormant accounts and excessive permissions to accumulate. Effective identity life cycle management is therefore less about software and more about orchestration—aligning the people, processes, and systems that define who truly belongs in your digital environment.

Authentication Controls: MFA, SSO, Federation, and Risk-based Access

Authentication controls form the backbone of any IAM program. They ensure that only verified individuals gain entry to systems, applications, and data. Modern enterprises no longer rely on a single password prompt; instead, they implement multiple, reinforcing layers of authentication that build confidence in a user's identity while minimizing friction for legitimate users. The four pillars of this structure—multifactor authentication (MFA), single sign-on (SSO), federation, and risk-based access—work together to create a balanced mix of assurance, consistency, and adaptability. An effective authentication strategy integrates all four to form a coherent, auditable system of control rather than a patchwork of separate mechanisms.

MFA is now a fundamental expectation across nearly all industries. By requiring two or more distinct forms of verification, MFA drastically reduces the likelihood of a single compromised credential leading to unauthorized access. The most common factors are knowledge-based (something you know), possession-based (something you have), and inherence-based (something you are). While older systems relied heavily on passwords and one-time codes, contemporary designs increasingly use phishing-resistant methods such as FIDO2 keys or device-bound passkeys. These hardware- or platform-backed factors protect against interception, credential stuffing, and replay attacks. The effectiveness of MFA depends on its breadth of coverage across the user base and the strength of the factors employed. A well-governed program enforces MFA universally—administrators, developers, third-party users, and remote workers alike—while minimizing reliance on weaker methods like SMS codes or email links.

However, strong MFA coverage is only meaningful when exceptions are managed carefully. Legacy systems, service accounts, and certain technical integrations may not support modern MFA mechanisms, creating unavoidable gaps. Each exception should be justified, documented, and mitigated through compensating controls such as network segmentation, restricted access hours, or additional logging. Emergency "break-glass" accounts must be strictly limited, named distinctly, and secured in password vaults. Their usage should trigger alerts and be reviewed immediately afterward. Auditors often uncover bypass risks in poorly controlled MFA resets or recovery paths—particularly help desk workflows that send password resets to the same mailbox being unlocked. Effective programs eliminate such circular logic and enforce re-proofing before reactivation. Table 6.2 summarizes authentication patterns their relative assurance coverage goals typical gaps and the evidence an auditor should expect.

Single sign-on (SSO) simplifies the user experience while tightening security oversight. Through an identity provider (IdP), users authenticate once and gain access to multiple applications under a unified session. This model improves both compliance and operational efficiency. Policies such as MFA enforcement, password rotation, and device posture checks can be applied centrally rather than at each application. From an audit perspective, SSO reduces complexity by consolidating authentication logs, creating a single authoritative record of user access activity. However, it also concentrates risk. If the SSO service itself is compromised, the attacker may inherit wide-ranging access. Therefore, organizations should enforce strong administrative controls, separate duties for

Table 6.2 Authentication controls and assurance indicators.

Control	Assurance level	Coverage goal	Common gaps	Auditor evidence
MFA SMS code	Low	Avoid for admins aim phase out	Sim swap risk legacy telephony	IdP factor usage report
MFA app OTP	Medium	Near universal for workforce	Push fatigue or seed reuse	IdP challenge logs
MFA FIDO2 passkey	High	All admins all developers	Lack of compatible devices	IdP webauthn registration logs
SSO centralized	Medium high	All SaaS and internal apps	Direct logins that bypass IdP	IdP app federation list and app logs
Federation token validation	High	All partner and cloud relying parties	Long refresh tokens weak signing	Token validation settings and certificate records
Risk based access step up	Adaptive	Sensitive apps privileged actions	Noisy policies or blind spots	Decision logs with risk reason codes

IdP management, and implement conditional access policies that continually assess session risk. High-value administrative portals or financial systems should still require reauthentication or step-up MFA, even when accessed through SSO.

Federation extends authentication trust beyond organizational boundaries. Using standards such as SAML, OAuth 2.0, or OpenID Connect, a user from one domain can access resources in another without creating a new account. Federation is essential in cloud and hybrid environments, where employees routinely access Software-as-a-Service (SaaS) platforms and partner systems. The key to secure federation lies in well-defined trust boundaries—knowing precisely which systems issue tokens, how those tokens are validated, and what conditions govern their lifespan. Auditors should review token signing configurations, certificate management, and logout synchronization. Common weaknesses include lingering legacy protocols like basic authentication or NTLM, misconfigured redirect URIs, and unmonitored refresh tokens that never expire. When federation boundaries are unclear, an attacker can exploit the trust relationship to impersonate legitimate users across systems.

Risk-based access introduces adaptive intelligence into authentication decisions. Instead of treating every login attempt equally, the system analyzes contextual signals to gauge the likelihood of compromise. These signals include device fingerprinting, IP address reputation, geolocation, time of day, and user behavior patterns. For example, a login from a recognized laptop in a normal location might proceed silently, while one from an unfamiliar device in another country would trigger step-up MFA or temporary denial. This approach balances security with usability, reserving friction for higher-risk situations. Mature implementations integrate with security analytics and threat intelligence platforms, allowing real-time updates to risk scores based on active attack campaigns. From an audit standpoint, risk-based access controls must be transparent—decision logs should clearly document why certain logins were allowed, challenged, or blocked, enabling retrospective review and continuous improvement.

While each of these mechanisms serves a distinct purpose, their true strength emerges when they operate as a unified control framework. MFA provides proof of identity, SSO centralizes enforcement, federation extends trust securely, and risk-based systems inject adaptability.

When properly integrated, they deliver an authentication model that is both resilient and user-friendly—reducing the attack surface without impeding productivity. However, success depends on more than technology. Policies must define clear enrollment procedures, exception criteria, and periodic reviews of control effectiveness. Logging, monitoring, and correlation across all authentication layers enable early detection of anomalies such as brute-force attempts, token abuse, or unusual login patterns.

In practice, auditors evaluating authentication controls focus on three qualities: coverage, consistency, and assurance. Coverage measures how completely the control set applies to all user categories and systems. Consistency ensures that policies are enforced uniformly across environments, including legacy and third-party integrations. Assurance reflects the strength and reliability of the mechanisms themselves—whether factors are resistant to phishing, whether tokens are signed with strong cryptography, and whether fallback options meet the same security bar as primary methods. Weak fallback factors, excessive bypass paths, or inconsistent federation boundaries erode assurance, even when the surface implementation appears sound.

Ultimately, effective authentication is a balance between user convenience and control rigor. Organizations that achieve this balance move beyond passwords toward identity-driven trust—where every access request is verified, contextual, and enforceable. For the auditor, the question is not merely "Is MFA enabled?" but "Is authentication managed as a living control system that adapts, enforces, and protects every identity every time?"

Privileged Access: PAM, Break-glass, Session Monitoring

Privileged access sits at the heart of cybersecurity assurance because it defines who can make changes that affect the security posture of an entire organization. These accounts—system administrators, database owners, domain controllers, network engineers, and cloud tenant admins—operate with elevated authority that bypasses many normal safeguards. Privileged access also includes nonhuman identities such as service accounts, application credentials, and automation tokens that carry out essential system tasks. Because these accounts have the ability to alter configurations, extract sensitive data, or disable controls, they represent the single highest-value target for attackers and must be treated with a level of scrutiny far above standard user access. Auditors assess not just the existence of controls but also how effectively they enforce accountability, traceability, and timely revocation.

A mature PAM program begins with classification. Privileged identities are categorized according to risk and scope—interactive administrators, service accounts, and machine or application credentials. Each category has unique management requirements. Human administrators require authentication controls, multifactor enforcement, and clear separation between personal and administrative sessions. Service accounts demand life cycle tracking and credential rotation, while automation identities should use nonpersistent tokens or certificates. By maintaining an accurate inventory and risk classification, organizations can align technical controls with the operational behavior of each privileged identity type, ensuring that the most powerful accounts receive the strongest protection.

At the center of any PAM system is the vault, a secure, centralized repository that stores and manages sensitive credentials. Instead of memorizing or sharing passwords, administrators request access through the vault, which authenticates them and issues temporary credentials. These credentials can be single-use passwords, ephemeral tokens, or time-bound session keys. Each issuance is logged with the requestor's identity, purpose, and time of access. When the task is complete, the credential is automatically rotated or expired, ensuring that any previous value becomes invalid. Vaults should enforce encryption at rest, integrate with the organization's directory services for authentication, and require multifactor verification before release. From an audit standpoint, the vault's log data—combined with approvals and session records—forms the definitive evidence trail of privileged activity.

Check-in and check-out workflows provide traceability and accountability for every privileged access event. A user "checks out" a credential for a specific purpose, often referencing a change ticket or incident number. The PAM system validates the request against policy, records an approval, and issues access for a defined window. Once the window expires or the task is complete, the credential is "checked in," at which point the password is rotated, the account is disabled, or a new key pair is generated. This process eliminates shared credentials and ensures that no single person maintains continuous access to privileged systems. Auditors should confirm that the vault enforces automatic rotation and that check-in events are verified before credentials are reissued to another user.

Elevation workflows manage the transition between standard and administrative access. Instead of granting users permanent membership in privileged groups, organizations can employ just-in-time (JIT) elevation models that provide temporary rights on demand. The elevation request must be tied to a valid business purpose—such as applying a system patch, updating firewall rules, or resolving an incident—and approved through a structured workflow. Once granted, privileges exist only for a limited time and are automatically revoked afterward. This approach sharply reduces the risk of "standing privilege," where users retain unnecessary rights indefinitely. From an assurance perspective, effective JIT systems maintain detailed logs of requests, approvals, and expirations, which should align with supporting evidence in ticketing and change management systems.

Emergency or break-glass accounts exist to maintain control during identity system outages or other critical failures. These accounts should be created sparingly, stored offline or in an isolated vault, and known to as few individuals as possible. They must use long, complex passwords that are changed immediately after any use. When a break-glass account is activated, automated alerts should notify security operations teams, and the entire session must be monitored or recorded. Afterward, administrators must perform a post-event review to verify that all actions were legitimate, rotate the account's credentials, and document the justification in the incident record. Periodic testing of break-glass procedures ensures that they remain functional without compromising the integrity of normal access workflows.

Session monitoring is a critical layer of visibility that transforms privileged activity into verifiable evidence. When administrators access systems through a PAM gateway or proxy, the platform can record the entire session—including keystrokes, commands, file transfers, and configuration changes. For graphical sessions, screen recordings may be captured; for command-line access, text transcripts are sufficient. These recordings deter misuse, support investigations, and allow organizations to demonstrate compliance with audit and regulatory requirements. Mature implementations store recordings in tamper-resistant repositories with access controls, retention policies, and cryptographic integrity checks to ensure authenticity. Auditors typically review these recordings to confirm that high-risk changes were authorized and executed appropriately.

Privileged access controls also extend to nonhuman identities such as service accounts and application credentials. These accounts frequently operate without user interaction, running background processes or enabling system-to-system communication. Because they cannot use MFA, assurance depends on strong credential management—vaulting, automatic rotation, and least-privilege assignment. Each service account should have a documented owner, clear purpose, and restricted scope. Credentials should never be embedded in scripts or configuration files, and interactive logins should be disabled. Rotations should occur automatically on a fixed schedule or at every deployment cycle, ensuring that credentials remain short-lived and difficult to reuse.

The evidence that demonstrates control over privileged access lives in multiple systems and must be consistent. The identity provider maintains group memberships and role assignments; the vault retains credential issuance and rotation logs; the PAM gateway captures session recordings; and the change management system holds approvals and justifications. Cross-referencing these data sources allows auditors to verify that every privileged session was requested, approved, executed, and terminated correctly. Discrepancies—such as vault access without a corresponding ticket, or sessions without check-in confirmation—indicate control failures that require investigation.

Common weaknesses in privileged access programs include overuse of shared administrator credentials, standing membership in privileged groups, and reliance on manual processes for access revocation. Some organizations treat PAM as a technical deployment rather than a governance function, failing to enforce consistent request and approval workflows. Others deploy vaults but never enable automatic password rotation, leaving secrets static for months or years. These gaps undermine the intent of the control set. Strengthening assurance requires enforcing expiration dates on elevated access, linking every request to a business ticket, validating periodic reauthorization, and ensuring that session recordings and vault logs remain intact and reviewed regularly.

An effective privileged access program integrates vaulting, elevation control, emergency access, and session monitoring into a single continuous process. Each mechanism reinforces the others: vaults protect credentials, JIT workflows limit exposure, break-glass controls preserve continuity, and session monitoring provides transparency. When these pieces work together, privileged access becomes both manageable and auditable. Every privileged action—from the moment a user requests elevation to the point credentials are revoked—is documented, reviewable, and reversible. For auditors, this end-to-end traceability provides the strongest possible assurance that the organization's most powerful accounts are governed, not guessed at.

Service Accounts, Nonhuman Identities, and Secrets Handling

Service accounts and other nonhuman identities form the invisible machinery of enterprise systems. Unlike human users, these identities do not log in interactively or use passwords in the traditional sense—they authenticate programmatically to enable applications, automation, and infrastructure to function. Common examples include service principals in cloud platforms, workload identities for containers or microservices, API tokens used for integration, and cryptographic keys used for system-to-system trust. These identities often operate continuously and with elevated privilege, making them essential to uptime but also a major source of risk if left unmanaged. Effective governance over nonhuman access is therefore as critical as managing human users, yet it often receives less attention.

Service accounts are traditionally operating system or application-level accounts that allow background services to run without user intervention. They may start and stop services, connect to databases, or perform scheduled maintenance tasks. Cloud and DevOps environments expand this concept through service principals and workload identities—digital entities assigned to applications, containers, or functions that need to authenticate to other services. Each of these represents a potential attack vector if their credentials are exposed or reused. The guiding principle is that every nonhuman identity should have a defined purpose, minimal necessary privileges, and a full life cycle that mirrors human account management—creation, use, rotation, and decommissioning.

Nonhuman credentials come in various forms: static passwords, SSH keys, API tokens, client certificates, and cryptographic keys. These secrets are often stored in code repositories, configuration files, or orchestration pipelines, where they are easily forgotten or inadvertently exposed. Public breaches have repeatedly shown attackers exploiting hard-coded credentials to pivot deeper into cloud or enterprise environments. Unlike human passwords, these secrets rarely expire on their own and may remain valid for years unless rotated intentionally. From an assurance standpoint, the persistence and invisibility of these secrets make them particularly dangerous, which is why auditors view static, untracked credentials as critical findings.

A mature secrets-handling strategy begins with governance—assigning clear ownership to every service account and nonhuman identity. Each identity should have a designated business owner responsible for ensuring that its credentials are stored securely, rotated regularly, and scoped appropriately. Ownership must be documented in the identity repository or configuration management database (CMDB) to prevent "orphaned" accounts that remain active after the associated service is retired. Automated reconciliation between directories, configuration management, and deployment pipelines can help identify unmanaged identities before they become long-term liabilities.

Credential rotation and expiration policies are the second pillar of control. Static credentials must be replaced by short-lived or automatically renewable tokens wherever possible. In modern environments, service accounts can authenticate through brokered workflows that issue temporary credentials on demand, valid only for a single session or limited duration. Rotation should be enforced at the system level, not reliant on developer memory or manual scripts. When static secrets are unavoidable—such as in legacy systems—they should be vaulted, versioned, and rotated frequently, with audit logs capturing each change. Expiration enforcement ensures that no key, certificate, or token remains valid beyond its expected lifespan.

Usage monitoring bridges governance and detection by providing visibility into how nonhuman identities behave over time. Each credential or token should be traceable in system logs, revealing which services used it, when, and for what purpose. Deviations from expected patterns—such as a service account accessing unfamiliar systems or executing commands outside its role—should generate alerts. Integration with security information and event management (SIEM) platforms allows this telemetry to be correlated with other activity, helping to detect misuse or compromise early. Mature programs extend monitoring into continuous behavior analytics, flagging overuse, failed authentications, or credential anomalies that suggest leakage or automation error.

Segregation between human and nonhuman credentials is another essential practice. Service accounts should never share authentication stores with user accounts, nor should they rely on human-interactive mechanisms like password resets via email. Administrative teams must resist the temptation to use personal credentials for automated tasks, even temporarily, as this breaks auditability. In a healthy identity ecosystem, human accounts authenticate through directories or identity providers with MFA and session policies, while nonhuman identities authenticate through secure service principals or workload tokens managed by automated brokers. Each authentication type should have distinct paths, logs, and policies to prevent overlap and confusion.

Integration with secret stores provides the operational foundation for secure automation. Secret stores—or vaults—act as centralized, encrypted repositories that issue credentials to workloads as needed without embedding them in code. Modern vault systems can inject secrets into containers, cloud functions, or CI/CD pipelines at runtime, then revoke or rotate them after use. This approach ensures that developers never handle plaintext credentials directly and that secrets remain short-lived. From an audit perspective, the presence of secret store integration demonstrates that the organization has replaced static credential distribution with dynamic, traceable management—a key indicator of maturity in identity security.

Risk also extends to cryptographic keys, which are often used to sign, encrypt, or authenticate communications between systems. These keys must be treated as sensitive secrets, with generation, storage, and destruction processes governed by policy. Keys should be stored in hardware security modules (HSMs) or cloud key management services that enforce role-based access, logging, and periodic rotation. Auditors should verify that key material is never exported in plaintext, that life cycle events are logged, and that expired or compromised keys are revoked immediately. Failure to control key management undermines the entire authentication chain for service and application identities.

Common failure modes for nonhuman identities include excessive privileges, uncontrolled sprawl, and static credentials that outlive their services. Over time, organizations accumulate hundreds or thousands of forgotten service accounts, each a potential entry point for attackers. To counter this, regular reviews must reconcile all active nonhuman identities against a current inventory of applications and workloads. Any unused accounts should be disabled or deleted, and any credentials older than their rotation threshold should be replaced. These reviews also validate ownership, ensuring that no active credential exists without a responsible manager.

Strong governance over service accounts and secrets transforms what is often an operational blind spot into a defensible control domain. When every nonhuman identity is owned, vaulted, monitored, and time-bounded, it becomes far less likely to serve as an attacker's foothold. Integration between vaulting systems, identity providers, and monitoring platforms creates a closed loop of control—one that issues credentials only when needed, observes every use, and invalidates them promptly afterward. For auditors, the assurance outcome is clear: nonhuman access must be governed with the same rigor as human access, supported by evidence that secrets are managed, not merely stored.

Evidence Locations: IdP, PAM, HRIS, Ticketing, and Logs

IAM evidence does not live in a single location. It spans multiple interconnected systems that record who someone is, what they can access, how that access was approved, and what they did once granted. Each of these systems has a distinct role in the assurance chain, and together they form the audit trail that proves the organization's identity governance processes are working as intended. The most common repositories for IAM evidence are the HRIS, the Identity Provider (IdP), the PAM platform, the ticketing or change management system, and the various operational and security logs that capture activity within target systems.

The HRIS acts as the authoritative source for workforce identity. It establishes the initial record for each employee or contractor, containing key attributes such as name, role, department, manager, and employment status. These attributes flow downstream into directories and identity platforms, dictating when a person should be onboarded, transferred, or terminated. From an evidence standpoint, the HRIS provides proof of when employment began and ended, who approved the hire, and what classification the individual held at any given time. Its records form the baseline against which all downstream identity data should reconcile. If an account remains active in the IdP after the HRIS marks a termination, that discrepancy signals a control failure.

The IdP is the operational core of authentication and authorization. It enforces who can log in, through what methods, and under which policies. The IdP maintains records of identity attributes, group memberships, and role assignments, as well as authentication events, multifactor challenges, and federation token issuance. These logs demonstrate whether users were properly authenticated, whether policies such as MFA were enforced, and whether any bypass conditions existed. When examining evidence, auditors correlate IdP records with HRIS data to confirm that only active personnel possess active accounts and that their assigned roles align with their employment function.

PAM systems extend identity controls to the most sensitive accounts. PAM records contain check-in and checkout logs for privileged credentials, approval workflows for elevated access, and session recordings of administrator activity. These data points are essential for demonstrating that privileged actions—such as changes to infrastructure, directory configurations, or security settings—occurred within authorized windows and under controlled conditions. Auditors reviewing PAM evidence look for consistency between the vault's transaction logs, the approvals recorded in the ticketing system, and the execution activity captured in infrastructure logs. Each record must align to tell a single coherent story of how and why a privileged action took place. Table 6.3 maps common assurance questions to primary and secondary evidence sources with identifiers required for reliable reconciliation.

Ticketing and change management systems link business justification to technical action. Every access request, modification, or removal should have a corresponding ticket that documents who requested the change, who approved it, and for what purpose. These systems serve as the connective tissue between people, policy, and technology, providing context for otherwise raw technical evidence. For example, a PAM session that changes firewall rules should reference a ticket authorizing that task. During audits, the presence of matching ticket identifiers in IdP, PAM, and log data demonstrates traceability and accountability throughout the access life cycle.

Operational and security logs from target systems form the final layer of IAM evidence. These logs record the actual events that occurred once access was granted—such as logins, file modifications, configuration changes, or data exports. They confirm that actions taken by an identity in the IdP or PAM system correspond to real activity in the environment. When correlated with ticketing and identity data, these logs allow auditors to verify that access was not only granted appropriately but also used responsibly. Logs should include timestamps, source IPs, and user identifiers to support reliable cross-system matching. Gaps or inconsistencies between identity systems and operational logs often reveal where monitoring or integration is incomplete.

Table 6.3 Cross-system evidence reconciliation map.

Evidence question	Primary source	Secondary source	Identifier used	Expected match
Is person employed	HRIS	IdP	HR employee ID	Active status equals active account
Who approved elevation	Ticketing	PAM	Ticket ID	Approval record matches vault checkout
What actions occurred in session	PAM	Target system logs	Session ID user ID	Commands and changes align
Was break glass used	PAM or isolated vault	SIEM alert log	Account name distinct	Alert and session record present
Are service accounts rotated	Secrets vault	Deployment pipeline logs	Secret ID or version	Rotation events within policy window
Do federation tokens validate	IdP	Relying party logs	Token ID or jti	Signature and lifetime accepted

Reconciling data across these systems requires careful handling of identifiers. Usernames, employee IDs, and account names may differ slightly between HRIS, IdP, and target systems due to naming conventions, domain prefixes, or legacy migrations. A robust audit process maps these identifiers explicitly, maintaining a translation table that links the canonical HRIS identity to each system account. This mapping allows auditors to follow the full chain of evidence from hire to access to action, regardless of how systems label the identity internally. Where automation assists this process, its results must still be manually verified for accuracy to ensure that no mismatched accounts distort findings.

Provenance and versioning of evidence exports are also vital for audit integrity. When data is pulled from systems such as the IdP or PAM, it must include metadata that identifies when the export was generated, by whom, and from which source version. Exports should be time-stamped and, where possible, cryptographically hashed to prevent tampering or accidental overwriting. Storing these exports in a controlled repository with version tracking allows auditors to reproduce findings months or years later, even if the live systems have changed. Provenance documentation establishes that the evidence being reviewed is authentic and corresponds to the period under examination.

Each evidence source contributes to a different layer of assurance. The HRIS confirms legitimacy of the identity, the IdP enforces authentication and authorization, the PAM system controls privileged actions, the ticketing platform links approvals and purpose, and the logs provide behavioral proof of execution. When these layers are reconciled, they collectively demonstrate that access was granted appropriately, used within scope, and terminated on time. Effective IAM auditing therefore depends not on any single system but on the consistency and completeness of evidence across all of them.

In practice, the strongest IAM assurance comes from systems that are both integrated and independently verifiable. Automated provisioning ensures data consistency, but manual reviews validate trust boundaries and reveal exceptions. Each evidence source—whether a vault record, HR export, or log archive—must stand on its own and align with the others to form a verifiable chain of custody. When properly documented, this chain proves that the organization not only enforces access controls but can also demonstrate, through durable evidence, exactly how those controls operated in practice.

Conclusion

IAM represents the living core of cybersecurity governance—the point where human accountability, machine automation, and organizational control converge. The concepts explored throughout this chapter illustrate that secure access is not a static configuration but an ongoing process of validation, adjustment, and oversight. Mastering these principles is critical for auditors and practitioners alike, as they define how risk is measured, enforced, and proven across systems that now span on-premises networks, cloud platforms, and AI-driven automation. A mature IAM program provides the evidence trail that transforms security claims into verifiable assurance.

The discipline of auditing identity controls extends beyond compliance checklists. It requires an understanding of how technology and policy interact to sustain least privilege and traceability under constant operational change. While the tools may differ—whether human directories, privileged vaults, or federated tokens—the strategic intent remains the same: to ensure that every access event can be justified and every identity can be trusted. This assurance forms the backbone of security resilience, enabling organizations to respond confidently to incidents and satisfy regulatory obligations with data, not assumptions.

As AI systems and automated workloads take on greater decision-making authority, the precision of identity governance becomes inseparable from overall system integrity. Auditors who can evaluate both human and nonhuman access controls bring a unique capability to safeguard algorithmic trust, data lineage, and operational accountability. With these foundations in place, professionals are better equipped to audit complex digital ecosystems, ensuring that every action—whether initiated by a user, a service, or an intelligent agent—remains visible, authorized, and governed within the organization's security fabric.

Auditor Recommendations

1. **Evaluate Identity Life cycle Controls:** Audit the full joiner–mover–leaver process to confirm that identity events originate from authoritative systems such as HRIS or contractor management platforms. Examine a sample of life cycle events and verify that access provisioning and deprovisioning occurred within approved timelines. Identify delays, missed terminations, or duplicate accounts and trace them to control weaknesses in automation or oversight. Document the reliability of the HRIS–IdP relationship as a foundation for identity assurance.
2. **Verify Authentication Control Effectiveness:** Review MFA configurations, enforcement coverage, and exception handling across user classes. Confirm that high-risk users and administrators use phishing-resistant factors and that fallback options like SMS are phased out. Assess the adequacy of exception tracking, ensuring each exemption has a defined expiry and compensating control. Collect system evidence such as factor enrollment data and challenge logs to substantiate enforcement claims.
3. **Audit Federation and Trust Relationships:** Inspect federation configurations to determine whether token lifetimes, signature validation, and logout synchronization align with policy. Review metadata and certificates exchanged with external providers to ensure authenticity and expiry management. Identify any residual legacy protocols or direct login methods that bypass centralized control. Evaluate whether trust boundaries are clearly documented and periodically revalidated.
4. **Review Risk-based Access Decisioning:** Confirm that risk-based access mechanisms evaluate contextual factors such as device health, location, and behavioral anomalies. Obtain decision logs and verify that risky logins trigger step-up authentication or denial events. Ensure that risk policies are not overly permissive and that thresholds are tuned based on threat intelligence and historical misuse patterns. Verify that outcomes are logged, reviewable, and mapped to policy criteria.
5. **Examine Privileged Access Management Evidence:** Audit PAM systems for traceable checkout and check-in activity linked to approved tickets. Confirm that credentials are rotated after use and that vault policies enforce least privilege and time-bounded access. Evaluate whether session monitoring is operational and whether recordings are preserved according to retention requirements. Review a sample of privileged sessions to confirm alignment with approved change requests.
6. **Assess Just-in-time Elevation Controls:** Review JIT workflows to verify that elevation requests require approval and are tied to business-justified tickets. Confirm that elevated

privileges are time-limited and automatically revoked at session end. Inspect audit logs for evidence of elevation events and corresponding revocation entries. Determine whether exceptions or manual overrides exist and document their risk implications.

7. **Evaluate Break-glass Governance:** Review documentation and control evidence for emergency account management. Verify that break-glass credentials are stored securely, rotated after use, and restricted to true emergencies. Examine monitoring and alerting mechanisms that detect activation and require post-use review. Confirm that testing of break-glass procedures is conducted periodically without compromising secrecy or oversight.
8. **Review Session Monitoring and Retention:** Confirm that privileged sessions are recorded with sufficient detail to reconstruct activity. Evaluate whether recording mechanisms are tamper-resistant and accessible only to authorized auditors or investigators. Test retrieval of session data to ensure logs can be produced within a reasonable time frame. Assess whether review processes exist to analyze anomalous or policy-violating actions.
9. **Audit Nonhuman Identity Management:** Identify all service accounts, workload identities, and automation credentials, verifying that each has an assigned owner and defined purpose. Confirm that nonhuman secrets are vaulted, rotated, and segregated from human authentication stores. Evaluate monitoring for unusual use patterns or excessive privileges. Ensure that all nonhuman identities are linked to life cycle governance with periodic attestation by owners.
10. **Reconcile Cross-system Evidence:** Verify that identifiers align across HRIS, IdP, PAM, and ticketing systems to enable traceable audits. Reproduce a complete evidence chain—from access request to approval to execution and revocation—to test consistency. Review how exports are time-stamped, versioned, and stored to preserve provenance. Ensure that evidence sources can independently substantiate one another, providing auditors with defensible assurance over identity governance.

Chapter Questions

1. What drives the timing and scope of access changes in a mature identity life cycle?
   A. Manual provisioning by application owners
   B. Ad hoc requests from line managers
   C. Authoritative events from HRIS and contractor systems
   D. Quarterly user access reviews

2. Which MFA method provides the highest assurance against phishing for interactive logins?
   A. SMS one-time passcodes
   B. FIDO2/WebAuthn security keys or platform passkeys
   C. Email-based magic links
   D. Voice call verification

3. In a federated authentication model, which element most directly defines the trust boundary between parties?
   A. Password complexity configured in the relying application
   B. Color scheme and branding of the login page
   C. Token lifetimes and signature validation parameters
   D. Size of the user directory in the identity provider

4. Which practice best characterizes well-governed break-glass access?
  A. Sharing emergency credentials among senior admins for convenience
  B. Allowing permanent MFA exemptions for emergency accounts
  C. Storing break-glass passwords in a team wiki for quick retrieval
  D. Triggering real-time alerts on use, conducting immediate post-use review, and rotating credentials

5. What is the primary objective of just-in-time elevation workflows?
  A. Reduce standing privilege by granting time-bound rights tied to an approved purpose
  B. Improve password complexity requirements for administrators
  C. Consolidate all admin accounts under a single shared credential
  D. Replace privileged access with local caching to reduce latency

6. Which control is most appropriate for service accounts and other nonhuman identities?
  A. Enabling interactive logins with MFA for convenience
  B. Vaulting credentials and enforcing rotation or short-lived tokens
  C. Allowing developers to embed static passwords in configuration files
  D. Managing service accounts with personal administrator credentials

7. What evidence most strongly demonstrates accountability for privileged activity?
  A. A monthly report of total admin logins per system
  B. A list of users assigned to administrator groups
  C. Session recordings or command transcripts linked to approved tickets
  D. An email from the change manager approving weekend work

8. When reconciling cross-system IAM evidence, what technique best avoids mismatches?
  A. Relying solely on display names for all joins
  B. Ignoring legacy accounts during mapping
  C. Using the primary email address as the only identifier
  D. Maintaining an explicit mapping of canonical HRIS IDs to each system's account identifiers

9. What is the core purpose of risk-based access in authentication controls?
  A. Adjust challenges based on contextual risk while minimizing user friction
  B. Replace MFA completely for trusted devices
  C. Speed up login performance during peak hours
  D. Allow bypasses for executives to reduce delays

10. In a PAM check-in/checkout model, what should occur when a privileged credential is checked back in?
  A. Nothing; reuse is acceptable if logs are kept
  B. Automatic rotation or invalidation of the credential before any future issuance
  C. Manual note-taking by the administrator who used it
  D. Deletion of the account to ensure it cannot be reused

7

Network and Perimeter Security

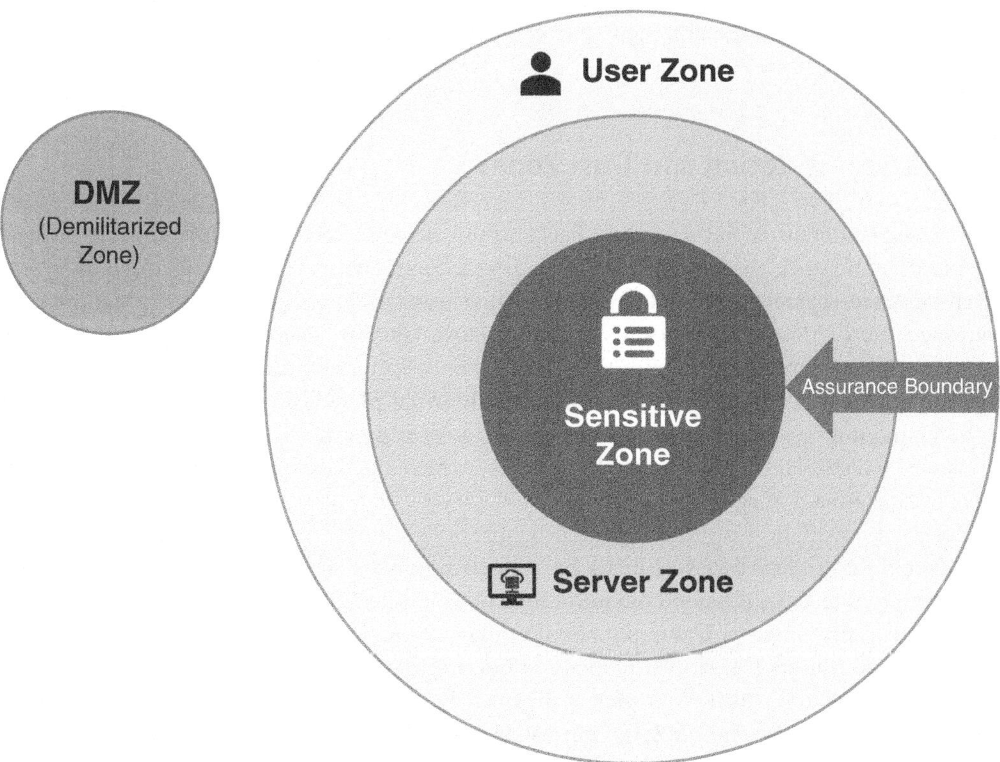

Network and perimeter security define the boundaries of organizational trust, shaping how systems communicate and how threats are contained. As enterprise architectures evolve toward hybrid cloud and distributed access, these boundaries have become more fluid and complex, requiring precision in both design and oversight. Understanding how segmentation, edge enforcement, and outbound control interact allows auditors to verify not just the existence of defenses, but their actual effectiveness in practice. The modern perimeter is no longer a static wall—it is a dynamic fabric of gateways, inspection points, and policy engines that must work in harmony to sustain resilience.

Effective auditing of this fabric depends on visibility into intent, implementation, and operation. From firewall governance and egress controls to DNS enforcement, intrusion prevention, and secure access edge frameworks, each control represents a contract between business purpose and technical reality. Auditors must validate that these contracts are upheld—ensuring configurations match approved design, that rulebases and trust zones remain current, and that automation does not introduce silent risk. In an era of AI-driven threats and rapid infrastructure change, these assurance activities provide the foundation for measurable, evidence-based confidence in network security posture.

This chapter reinforces the idea that strong network security is as much about disciplined management as it is about technology. Baselines, backups, and drift detection define whether devices remain hardened; telemetry, configuration archives, and change records prove whether governance processes are working as intended. By connecting architectural principles to auditable evidence, cybersecurity auditors can bridge the gap between control theory and operational truth. The result is a perimeter strategy capable of adapting to evolving attack surfaces—one that supports AI-era risk management, regulatory compliance, and the broader mission of trustworthy digital operations.

Network Segmentation and Trust Zones

Network segmentation is the structural backbone of network security architecture. It divides the enterprise network into smaller, purpose-driven zones that reflect varying levels of trust. A well-designed segmentation strategy ensures that users, systems, and services only interact where necessary, limiting an attacker's ability to move laterally. These zones typically include user networks for employees and endpoints, server networks for application workloads, sensitive zones for regulated or high-value systems, and demilitarized zones (DMZs) that manage inbound and outbound internet-facing traffic. Each zone has a defined purpose, enforced through routing boundaries, VLANs, and access control lists (ACLs), which together form the operational expression of organizational trust.

In design, segmentation is guided by the principle of least privilege. Every connection between zones should be justified by a legitimate business requirement. For instance, users may access application front ends, but they should never directly connect to database servers. Similarly, DMZ systems can receive internet traffic but should only communicate internally through restricted ports to approved hosts. These restrictions are not arbitrary—they form a trust hierarchy. The sensitive zone, holding critical assets such as financial data or intellectual property, must operate as the most controlled layer. The DMZ, by contrast, is treated as semi-trusted and heavily monitored. The intent is to contain threats within lower-trust areas and protect core assets from exposure.

Network architects often capture this intent through formal design documents and diagrams. These artifacts show the logical relationships among zones and detail how firewalls, routers, and VLANs enforce boundaries. The visual representations are complemented by written policies that define acceptable communications, such as "traffic from the user zone to the server zone must be proxied through the application gateway." In mature organizations, these diagrams are version-controlled and approved through governance processes, ensuring that any design change receives proper review. The documented design becomes the "gold standard" against which implementation is measured during audits.

For auditors, the challenge lies in determining whether the implemented network truly reflects the documented design. Audit testing begins by gathering the network topology, configuration backups, and access control exports. Routing tables reveal how traffic is actually forwarded, while firewall and switch ACLs show what is truly permitted or denied. The auditor maps these real configurations to the intended trust zones, comparing actual traffic paths with documented expectations. In some cases, tools such as network discovery scans or flow monitoring utilities can help visualize current state and detect unauthorized connections between zones. The goal is to validate whether segmentation is not just designed but actively enforced.

In nearly every large organization, some level of "trust drift" occurs over time. This drift happens as IT teams make ad hoc changes to meet operational demands, troubleshoot issues, or enable new applications. A firewall rule meant to be temporary might remain indefinitely. VLANs that were once isolated can become interconnected through shared switches or trunk ports. Over time, these incremental changes flatten what was once a carefully segmented environment. The auditor's task is to identify and quantify this drift, recognizing that many such deviations arise not from negligence but from a lack of sustained configuration governance. Table 7.1 links each trust zone to its intended flows enforcement points and evidence so auditors can detect drift quickly.

Certain patterns of drift appear repeatedly across audits. Flat VLANs are among the most common—where network segmentation exists in name only, and all systems effectively reside within the same broadcast domain. "Any-any" firewall rules are another frequent red flag, allowing unrestricted communication between zones. Orphaned subnets, which are network ranges not clearly associated with active systems or documented functions, suggest poor inventory management and oversight. These artifacts collectively indicate that segmentation has eroded, increasing both lateral movement risk and the organization's attack surface. Each pattern tells a story about how daily operations have slowly undermined the intended design.

Table 7.1 Zone intent vs. implemented controls checklist.

Zone	Intended flows	Enforcement points	Evidence artifacts	Common drift indicator
User zone	To app front ends only via approved ports	Access lists and firewalls and NAC	Routing tables and ACL exports and zone diagram	Flat VLAN or any rule
Server zone	To database tier and management jump hosts	Firewalls and jump host policy and segmentation	Rulebase export and hit counts and change tickets	Overbroad subnet objects
Sensitive zone	To specific app tiers and no direct admin access	Isolation controls and strict ACLs	Data flow map and firewall rules and recertification log	Shadow rules or orphan subnets
DMZ	To reverse proxy or API gateway only	Edge firewall and proxy policy	Firewall export and proxy policy snapshot	Direct inside access from DMZ
Contractor zone	To designated apps with time bound access	ZTNA policy and identity based segmentation	Access policy export and session logs	Legacy VPN full access
Management zone	To device control planes via jump hosts only	Out of band network and control plane ACLs	Device config and management ACL snapshot	Open management from user networks
Backup zone	To backup targets and vault only	Network segmentation and egress deny	Routing and ACL evidence and job logs	Any to any egress from backup hosts

To accurately document findings, auditors rely on specific technical evidence. Exports from routers and firewalls show ACL configurations, while VLAN and routing tables illustrate traffic segmentation at Layer 2 and Layer 3. Network diagrams, often outdated, serve as a reference for what should exist but must be reconciled with live configurations or discovery scans. Supporting artifacts such as change tickets, firewall review logs, and exception approvals help determine whether deviations were authorized or accidental. Comparing these evidence sources gives the auditor a complete picture of design intent versus operational reality—a critical step before issuing formal recommendations.

Segmentation auditing is not purely technical; it also tests governance maturity. A technically perfect network can still fail from a compliance standpoint if change control, documentation, and review processes are weak. For example, if firewall rules are added without documented justification or periodic review, the organization has lost control of its segmentation posture. The auditor evaluates whether network and security teams follow established workflows for approving, reviewing, and expiring access rules. Controls like NIST SP 800-53 AC-4 (Information Flow Enforcement) and ISO/IEC 27001 Annex A.13 (Network Security Management) emphasize these processes because segmentation is only as strong as its ongoing management.

A mature organization enforces segmentation dynamically, using automation and continuous monitoring to detect deviations in near real time. Network Access Control (NAC) systems, microsegmentation technologies, and Zero Trust Network Access (ZTNA) solutions can complement traditional firewalls by enforcing identity-based policies. For auditors, the existence of these advanced controls introduces a new layer of complexity—they must verify that these tools operate according to policy and are not bypassed by legacy routes or misconfigurations. The audit must therefore cover both traditional perimeter segmentation and modern, software-defined trust boundaries.

Firewall and Egress Controls (Allowlists, Rule Hygiene, Change History)

Firewalls serve as the primary enforcement point of network trust boundaries, controlling what traffic is allowed or denied across segments. Their effectiveness depends not only on their presence but on the precision of their configuration and maintenance. A secure firewall policy begins with the principle of "deny by default," meaning all traffic is blocked unless explicitly permitted by an approved rule. This establishes a defensive baseline, ensuring that every communication path between systems must be intentional and documented. From there, access is granted under the principle of least privilege, allowing only the minimum protocols, ports, and destinations required for legitimate business functions. Anything beyond this scope introduces unnecessary exposure that can be exploited by adversaries.

Rule hygiene refers to the ongoing discipline of creating, maintaining, and reviewing firewall rules to ensure they continue to reflect business needs and risk appetite. Each rule should carry a clear justification, linked to an approved change request or documented business case. Over time, network environments evolve, and without structured review cycles, outdated or redundant rules can accumulate—often referred to as "rule bloat." This clutter not only reduces visibility but can also mask risky or overly permissive access paths. A well-governed firewall policy enforces routine recertification, where administrators and auditors validate that every active rule remains necessary, properly scoped, and aligned with organizational policy. Table 7.2 metrics translate firewall hygiene and egress intent into reviewable evidence and cadences for assurance.

Table 7.2 Firewall hygiene and egress review metrics.

Control area	Expected practice	Evidence source	Review frequency	Typical risk if weak
Default deny	Block by default with narrow allows	Rulebase export and policy	Quarterly or semiannual	Unintended lateral movement
Rule justification	Document business need and owner	Change ticket and rule comment	Per change and during recertification	Untracked exposure growth
Rule recertification	Expire and reapprove rules on schedule	Recertification records and attestations	Semiannual or annual	Policy bloat and stale access
Egress allow list	Restrict destinations and ports to known services	Outbound rulebase and proxy profile	Quarterly	Exfiltration and C2 channels
Split tunnel policy	Use selective split for approved services only	Remote access profile and gateway config	Quarterly and after changes	Uninspected traffic paths
Logging and hits	Enable logging and review hits and unused rules	Firewall logs and hit counts and SIEM	Monthly	Blind spots and noisy rules
Change control	Peer review and approval before deploy	Change system records and diffs	Per change	Unauthorized or unsafe edits
Shadow rule scan	Detect superseded or never hit rules	Analysis report and hit data	Quarterly	Hidden misconfigurations

Auditors evaluating firewall hygiene look for four core indicators of maturity: justification, review frequency, scope control, and traceability. Justification ensures that each rule was purpose-built for a known need, not added haphazardly. Review frequency indicates whether the organization performs scheduled validations—commonly every six or twelve months—to retire stale entries. Scope control means rules are written with precision, using specific source and destination addresses rather than broad subnets or "any" objects. Traceability is demonstrated when each rule can be mapped to a corresponding change ticket, work order, or request number. When these indicators are missing, it suggests that firewall governance has weakened, and the organization's risk tolerance may have drifted without explicit acknowledgment.

Change management history plays a vital role in assessing the integrity of firewall controls. Every modification—whether adding, deleting, or adjusting a rule—should pass through a formal approval process that evaluates both technical and business implications. Auditors often request change logs and ticketing system exports to confirm that all rule changes were authorized, peer-reviewed, and tested before deployment. In some environments, automated compliance systems track change deltas, highlighting configuration drift and ensuring rollback capabilities. A strong audit trail provides confidence that the firewall rulebase evolves in a controlled manner rather than as a collection of emergency fixes or undocumented exceptions.

Egress control, often underappreciated compared to inbound protection, is critical for preventing data exfiltration and command-and-control traffic. Firewalls should restrict outbound connections so that internal hosts cannot freely communicate with arbitrary internet destinations. Allowlists are central to this control philosophy: only known, approved domains or IP ranges should be reachable, while all others are blocked by default. This ensures that malware or rogue applications cannot exfiltrate data or establish persistent channels without triggering alerts. In a mature security architecture, outbound traffic is not merely limited but also inspected through proxies, secure web gateways, or data loss prevention (DLP) solutions to verify compliance with data handling policies.

Auditors test the effectiveness of egress controls by analyzing the outbound rulebase and confirming that default-deny logic is implemented. They also examine whether the organization distinguishes between user-initiated internet access (e.g., browsing) and system-initiated access (e.g., software updates, API calls). For instance, a firewall that allows all outbound HTTPS traffic from any host may meet short-term functionality goals but leaves significant blind spots for exfiltration risk. Evidence such as firewall hit counts, proxy logs, and egress monitoring reports can demonstrate whether rules operate as intended or if permissive configurations are being overused to bypass operational friction.

The most reliable evidence of firewall control intent and operation includes rulebase exports, configuration snapshots, hit count statistics, and recertification records. Rulebase exports allow auditors to verify adherence to least-privilege and deny-by-default principles. Hit counts show which rules are actively used, highlighting candidates for cleanup when activity is absent. Recertification records demonstrate that ongoing reviews occur and that owners confirm continued need for each rule. Change tickets and approval logs complete the picture, proving that control modifications follow a structured, traceable process. Together, these artifacts form a chain of evidence linking design intent, operational practice, and control assurance.

Common gaps frequently emerge when auditors compare policy documentation to actual configurations. Shadow rules—entries that never trigger because a higher-order rule supersedes them—are a sign of poor policy organization and can obscure visibility into which controls truly matter. Disabled logging is another recurring issue, as it prevents administrators and auditors from verifying that controls are working or identifying potential misuse. Similarly, overly broad service definitions or "any" objects make it difficult to determine whether segmentation and egress restrictions are genuinely enforced. These gaps represent governance weaknesses rather than purely technical flaws, revealing that the organization may lack sufficient oversight or tool support for rule analysis.

Rule hygiene also extends to the structure and readability of the firewall policy itself. A clean, well-documented rulebase should follow consistent naming conventions, logical grouping by zone or application, and standardized comments indicating purpose, owner, and expiration date. Auditors often view disorganized or cryptically labeled policies as a red flag—if administrators cannot easily interpret the rulebase, the likelihood of misconfiguration increases. Maintaining clarity in firewall configurations is not merely an administrative convenience; it is a control in itself, reducing the risk of human error during troubleshooting or change implementation.

Secure Edge/SASE and Remote Access (VPN/ZTNA Posture)

The modern enterprise perimeter no longer ends at the office wall. As organizations embrace remote work, cloud migration, and hybrid infrastructures, network access has shifted from static VPN tunnels to dynamic edge architectures. Secure Access Service Edge (SASE) and Zero Trust Network Access (ZTNA) represent the evolution of this model. Instead of routing all traffic through a centralized VPN gateway, these frameworks push enforcement closer to the user and the data. A "secure edge" integrates identity, device health, and context into every access decision, verifying not just who is connecting, but what they are connecting from and why. This approach replaces the implicit trust of legacy VPNs with continuous validation at every step.

Traditional VPNs were designed for a world of fixed offices and predictable user patterns. They extend the corporate network to remote devices, often granting broad network-level access once authentication succeeds. While functional, this model creates unnecessary exposure—if a user's device is compromised, the attacker inherits the same trusted connection. VPNs also struggle to scale under heavy load or multicloud architectures, as they depend on central concentrators and static routes. These limitations highlight why many organizations are moving toward cloud-based access models that enforce policies at the application level rather than the network layer.

SASE and ZTNA reverse the traditional VPN trust model. Instead of connecting users to the entire network, they connect users only to the applications and services they are authorized to use. SASE combines several cloud-delivered components—secure web gateways, cloud access security brokers (CASB), data loss prevention (DLP), and ZTNA—into a unified platform. ZTNA specifically focuses on replacing implicit network trust with identity-aware access. Each session is brokered through a control plane that continuously validates credentials, device health, and contextual risk before granting access. In this way, access is dynamic and conditional rather than static and assumed.

Good posture for secure edge and remote access begins with strong authentication. Multifactor authentication (MFA) should be mandatory for all remote sessions, combining user credentials with a second factor such as a hardware token, mobile app approval, or biometric verification. Beyond identity, device posture validation ensures that only managed, compliant, and secure endpoints connect. This includes checks for up-to-date antivirus software, disk encryption, OS patch levels, and configuration baselines. When devices fail posture assessment, connections should be quarantined or denied. These mechanisms turn the edge platform into a real-time gatekeeper rather than a simple tunnel.

Segmentation on connect is another hallmark of strong SASE or ZTNA posture. Instead of granting network-wide visibility, users are placed into microsegments—isolated access zones scoped to their specific role or application need. For example, a contractor accessing a ticketing system should have no visibility into file shares or administrative portals. This segmentation is enforced dynamically by the access broker, based on identity attributes and policy definitions. Auditors often assess this capability by reviewing configuration exports, access policies, and test accounts to ensure that segmentation is not only documented but actively applied during sessions.

Split-tunnel policies are an important assurance consideration in remote access configurations. A split-tunnel allows a user's device to send some traffic through the corporate network and the rest directly to the internet. While this can improve performance, it introduces risk if sensitive data bypasses inspection or if malicious traffic reaches the device unmonitored. A mature edge security posture applies split-tunneling selectively, often routing only trusted cloud services directly while keeping all other traffic under policy enforcement. Auditors verify this by reviewing configuration settings, endpoint VPN profiles, and DNS resolution paths to ensure compliance with the organization's intended design.

Per-application access policies further reduce exposure by defining which specific apps or services each user can reach. Rather than broad subnet permissions, rules are tied to user identity, device state, and application classification. Access decisions are reevaluated continuously—if a device drifts out of compliance or the user's risk score increases, the session can be limited or terminated. This "always verify, never trust" approach aligns with zero trust principles and allows for far more granular control than legacy VPN implementations. Auditors often examine access logs, policy sets, and session records to confirm that these conditional checks are functioning as intended.

Idle and session timeouts also play a critical role in secure edge assurance. Remote sessions should terminate automatically after defined periods of inactivity or total connection duration. These limits minimize risk from unattended sessions or stolen tokens. Effective configurations balance user convenience with security by setting timeouts appropriate to sensitivity—for example, administrative sessions may have shorter limits than general access. Auditors assess these controls by reviewing system configuration settings, authentication policies, and timeout enforcement records, confirming that session governance aligns with risk classifications.

Edge policy governance ensures that these controls evolve under proper oversight. Because SASE and ZTNA platforms are highly configurable, unauthorized changes can quickly undermine security. Mature organizations manage edge policy through structured change control, requiring peer review, justification, and approval for every modification. Logs of policy changes, access control adjustments, and exception handling form the audit trail for this process. Auditors look for alignment between change records and configuration states, verifying that policy updates were tested, documented, and deployed intentionally.

DNS, Web Proxies, and URL Filtering (Policy Alignment)

Outbound name resolution and web access controls form a critical line of defense in any organization's security posture. They determine not only what users can access on the internet but also what destinations systems can contact behind the scenes. DNS (Domain Name System) translates human-friendly names into IP addresses, and when that translation process is centrally controlled, it becomes a powerful security control point. Similarly, web proxies and URL filtering solutions evaluate the intent of outbound traffic at a higher layer—inspecting, categorizing, and often blocking requests that violate corporate policy or pose security risk. For auditors, assurance depends on whether these controls are consistent, enforced organization-wide, and aligned with written acceptable-use and egress policies.

A secure DNS architecture channels all resolution requests from managed devices to authorized internal resolvers or trusted third-party filtering services. These resolvers apply rules that prevent connections to known-malicious or inappropriate domains, using curated block lists, commercial threat feeds, or internal intelligence sources. When a domain is identified as risky, the resolver may respond with an empty record or redirect the query to a "sinkhole," a controlled internal address that allows security teams to detect and analyze attempts to reach that destination. Auditors typically validate this by reviewing resolver configurations, DNS forwarder settings, and DHCP scope options to confirm that endpoints receive correct DNS assignments. They also examine egress firewall rules to ensure public DNS services—like 8.8.8.8 or 1.1.1.1—are blocked, preventing users or malware from bypassing enterprise DNS controls.

Web proxies and secure web gateways extend this governance from the network layer to the application layer. These systems mediate all HTTP and HTTPS traffic, comparing outbound requests to policy definitions that reflect business requirements. They can block access to malicious or noncompliant sites, inspect downloads for malware, and apply data loss prevention (DLP) scans to outbound uploads. Some organizations use explicit proxies requiring browser configuration; others deploy transparent or cloud-based gateways that automatically capture outbound web traffic. Regardless of form, the assurance objective remains the same: every managed user and device must traverse the proxy path so that all web activity is visible, filterable, and logged. Auditors verify this through configuration exports, endpoint profiles, and evidence of forced routing such as Proxy Auto-Config (PAC) files or secure web gateway enforcement rules.

URL filtering is the mechanism that translates acceptable-use policy into enforceable categories. Sites are organized into thematic groups such as "social media," "malware," "file sharing," "streaming media," or "finance." Administrators then decide which categories to allow, warn, or block based on organizational values and risk tolerance. For instance, financial institutions might block cloud storage services to prevent data leakage, while creative agencies may allow them but monitor file transfers. Allowlists fine-tune legitimate business tools, while block lists address newly discovered threats. An auditor reviewing this control expects to find a formal acceptable-use policy, the corresponding proxy category configuration, and documented update cycles for category data feeds—typically daily or weekly, depending on vendor integration.

Alignment between DNS, proxy, and egress firewall policies is essential for layered defense. DNS filtering prevents domain resolution; web proxies inspect and categorize permitted traffic; and firewalls enforce the final boundary by restricting which IPs and ports can be reached. If these controls are misaligned, risk gaps appear. For example, if the DNS resolver blocks "malwaredomain.com" but the firewall allows unrestricted outbound IP connections, a compromised host could connect directly to the site's IP address. Conversely, a firewall that denies outbound web access loses effectiveness if users can resolve and tunnel traffic through public DNS-over-HTTPS (DoH) services. Auditors cross-check policy consistency across these layers, ensuring that control intent is mirrored by configuration reality.

Monitoring and logging provide the proof that these controls operate continuously and effectively. DNS servers should log query results, blocked lookups, and sinkhole events in a centralized repository. Web proxies must retain detailed access logs that identify users, timestamps, requested URLs, and the category-based decisions applied. TLS interception records, where lawful and approved, should show when and why encryption inspection occurred. These data sources help detect policy violations, trace potential breaches, and demonstrate compliance with legal or regulatory requirements. Auditors examine sample logs, retention policies, and SIEM integration to ensure data is not only captured but retained for an appropriate period—often 90 days for operations and up to a year or more for compliance.

Exception governance is another area that distinguishes mature control environments from ad hoc ones. When legitimate business needs require access to blocked sites or when TLS inspection must be bypassed for specific applications, the organization should document these deviations in an exception register. Each entry should record the requester, business justification, technical scope, expiration date, and any compensating monitoring applied. Exceptions should not be permanent; periodic recertification ensures they remain valid and limited in scope. Auditors test these records against live configurations, checking whether expired exceptions were removed and whether open-ended allowances exist without formal review.

Common weaknesses surface in most DNS and proxy audits. Some endpoints use public DNS resolvers—either manually configured or embedded in applications—bypassing internal controls. Split-DNS configurations, if not properly documented, may allow sensitive internal names to leak or external names to resolve differently depending on location. Disabled or incomplete logging is another recurring issue, as administrators may turn off verbose logging to improve performance, sacrificing auditability. A more subtle gap occurs when multiple filtering systems operate independently, leading to inconsistent rule enforcement or conflicting block lists. The auditor's role is to identify these inconsistencies and recommend tighter integration across control points.

TLS interception requires special attention both for technical accuracy and privacy considerations. Because interception involves decrypting user traffic, organizations must clearly define where and why it occurs and ensure that private keys and trusted certificates are securely managed. Some categories—such as banking, healthcare, or government services—should be exempt from interception due to privacy or compliance requirements. Auditors review documentation of these exceptions, examine proxy certificate configurations, and confirm that interception scope aligns with approved policy boundaries. Transparent governance in this area demonstrates ethical security management and respect for user trust.

Intrusion Prevention/Threat Intel at the Edge

Intrusion Prevention System (IPS) and threat-intelligence-driven controls at the network edge are the active defenders of perimeter security, stopping malicious traffic before it can enter or leave the trusted network. Unlike passive monitoring tools, an IPS sits inline—analyzing packets, flows, and session patterns in real time and blocking or resetting connections that match signatures of known attacks. These systems detect exploits targeting operating systems, applications, and network services, while also identifying behavioral patterns such as port scans, brute-force attempts, or command-and-control (C2) traffic. Their strength lies in combining precise signature-based detection with broader reputation and context data, transforming the network perimeter into a responsive, adaptive shield that evolves as new threats appear.

The foundation of any effective IPS program is consistent and timely signature or pattern updates. Because attacker techniques change rapidly, signature accuracy has a limited shelf life. Vendors release daily or even hourly updates that reflect the latest vulnerabilities and exploit patterns seen in the wild. Mature organizations integrate these updates through automated synchronization or change-management pipelines that verify successful application and test for stability. Missed or delayed updates are a serious finding during audits because they indicate potential blind spots where new attack methods could pass undetected. Auditors therefore look for update schedules, logs confirming recent signature imports, and procedures ensuring failed updates are caught and corrected immediately.

Reputation-based and threat-intelligence feeds augment IPS rules by scoring external entities—IPs, domains, and autonomous systems—based on observed malicious behavior. Instead of matching payloads, the system can make proactive decisions about who it communicates with, blocking or flagging connections to known bad or suspicious destinations. These feeds typically aggregate global telemetry from multiple sources, correlating spam origins, botnet controllers, malware distribution points, and phishing hosts. For auditors, evidence of active use includes subscription records, feed update timestamps, and configuration exports showing how reputation scores map to policy actions. A key assurance test is verifying that multiple feeds are blended effectively and that stale or redundant lists are pruned to avoid unnecessary performance impact.

Geo and IP-based policies provide an additional control layer by limiting communication with regions, providers, or network ranges that have no legitimate business purpose. A healthcare provider operating solely in North America, for example, may block inbound administrative connections from other continents or prevent outbound traffic to data centers in high-risk jurisdictions. These restrictions reduce the "background noise" of global scanning activity and help contain exposure during early-stage reconnaissance. Auditors expect to see documentation explaining the rationale for each geo restriction, exceptions for legitimate third parties, and log data showing that such policies are enforced and reviewed periodically to prevent unintended disruption of legitimate partners.

The real test of an IPS or threat-intelligence control is not only how many attacks it detects but how the organization handles those detections. Effective security operations treat IPS alerts as actionable signals rather than background noise. Hit counts and alert metrics provide initial insight, but deeper assurance comes from analyzing disposition records—how many alerts were verified, tuned, or dismissed, and why. Mature teams integrate IPS alerts into their incident management system, linking each event to a ticket that records investigation results and remediation steps. Auditors review these linkages to confirm that the control produces measurable outcomes and contributes to faster containment of genuine threats rather than overwhelming analysts with noise.

Ongoing tuning ensures that IPS protection remains both strong and sustainable. Overly aggressive rules can block legitimate traffic, disrupting business operations, while overly broad exclusions can leave critical systems exposed. Tuning involves testing new signatures in "monitor-only" mode before enabling blocking, refining overly chatty rules, and applying suppressions that are precise in scope—targeting a specific subnet or application instead of an entire rule category. Properly managed tuning activities are documented in change tickets or tuning registers, including the rationale for each adjustment and evidence that compensating monitoring is in place. Auditors look for before-and-after hit statistics, peer review approvals, and recurring rule validation to verify that tuning supports security without silently eroding protection.

Encryption and evolving network protocols have introduced new challenges for intrusion prevention. As more traffic moves over TLS or encrypted DNS, traditional payload inspection becomes limited. Some IPS devices integrate with SSL/TLS interception systems to inspect decrypted flows, while others rely on metadata—such as certificate attributes, domain reputation, and traffic behavior—to infer risk. Similarly, the growing adoption of UDP-based protocols like QUIC complicates stateful inspection and logging. A thorough audit should document what percentage of traffic the IPS can inspect, what portions are excluded, and how the organization compensates with endpoint or proxy-layer visibility. Without this clarity, there is a risk that attackers could hide within uninspected channels.

Performance and reliability are practical aspects often overlooked but critical to control assurance. Deep packet inspection consumes significant processing power, and an overloaded IPS can introduce latency, packet drops, or fail-open conditions that negate its purpose. A mature edge design uses clustering or high-availability pairs to maintain throughput and resilience. Capacity planning documents, performance baselines, and stress-test results serve as evidence that the system can enforce protection under load. Auditors also review whether fail-open or fail-close behavior is explicitly defined and whether decisions about availability versus security were risk-assessed and approved by management.

Several recurring pitfalls reduce IPS and threat-intelligence effectiveness across industries. The most common is outdated or poorly maintained rule and feed content, which gives the illusion of security while failing to detect new exploits. Equally damaging are broad suppressions made during emergency troubleshooting that are never revisited, leaving permanent blind spots. Other weaknesses include leaving signatures in "alert-only" mode indefinitely, not integrating alerts into ticketing systems, and inconsistent review of reputation feeds. Each issue reflects not a technical flaw but a lapse in operational discipline and governance—the true differentiator between organizations that merely deploy security tools and those that manage them effectively.

Device/Config Management: Baselines, Backups, and Drift

Network and perimeter devices—routers, switches, firewalls, VPN concentrators, and wireless controllers—form the skeleton of enterprise connectivity and security. Their configurations define how data moves, which systems can talk, and what protections are enforced. For that reason, device and configuration management is both an operational necessity and a governance requirement. Hardened baselines, golden configurations, systematic backups, and drift detection together ensure that these devices remain trustworthy over time. The auditor's focus is not simply whether these controls exist, but whether they are applied consistently, reviewed regularly, and recoverable in the event of a failure or breach.

Hardened baselines represent the minimum secure starting point for every device type. They incorporate vendor best practices, hardening guides from standards like CIS Benchmarks, DISA STIGs, or NIST 800-53, and organization-specific security settings. Baselines define required configurations for authentication methods, logging destinations, password complexity, management interface restrictions, SNMP versions, and default service disablement. Auditors expect to see a documented baseline for each device class, approved by both network engineering and security teams, with version control to track changes. A mature program applies these baselines automatically during provisioning, using configuration management tools or templates that enforce consistency and reduce human error.

Golden configurations extend the baseline concept to include site- or role-specific details. While the baseline defines what *must* exist everywhere, the golden configuration represents a validated, known-good instance for a specific deployment—such as a branch firewall, data center router, or core switch pair. This file serves as the reference point for compliance checks and drift detection. Auditors will ask whether these golden configurations are stored securely, versioned, and accessible to authorized personnel only. The presence of digital signatures, checksums, or configuration hash comparisons strengthens assurance that the golden copy has not been tampered with.

Change control governs how these configurations evolve. Network devices are not static; firmware updates, topology changes, and new security policies all require adjustments. The key is that each change must be intentional, reviewed, and documented. Mature organizations use integrated change-management systems that link proposed configuration edits to work orders, approval workflows, and risk assessments. Auditors assess whether configuration changes align with approved tickets and whether emergency changes are followed by retrospective reviews. They also check for segregation of duties—ensuring that no single engineer can both approve and deploy significant configuration changes without oversight.

Automated backups are the safety net that ensures configuration integrity over time. Every device should have scheduled exports of its running and startup configurations to a secure, centralized repository. These backups allow restoration after hardware failures, corruption, or unauthorized changes. A robust program encrypts stored backups, protects access with multifactor authentication, and retains multiple historical versions for audit and troubleshooting. Auditors validate backup automation by reviewing schedules, transfer logs, and restoration scripts. They may also sample backup files to verify completeness and ensure sensitive information—like private keys or plaintext passwords—is stored safely or redacted according to policy.

Configuration drift occurs when a device's active settings deviate from the approved baseline or golden configuration. Drift can result from emergency changes, manual fixes, or unrecorded updates performed under pressure. Left unchecked, these discrepancies erode both security and reliability. Auditors identify drift by comparing current device configurations against baseline templates or prior versions using automated diff tools. The output highlights unauthorized or unexplained deviations—such as new access lists, changed routing statements, or modified administrative accounts. Regular drift reports should feed into change-management reviews so that deviations can be reconciled, approved, or rolled back promptly.

Unauthorized changes represent a significant operational and security risk because they often bypass peer review or formal testing. In some cases, attackers exploit misconfigurations or compromised credentials to modify device settings for persistence or data exfiltration. Auditors therefore examine access control mechanisms around configuration interfaces, such as TACACS+, RADIUS, or centralized SSH key management, to confirm that administrative sessions are logged and accountable. Audit trails showing who made each change, when it occurred, and what commands were executed provide assurance that configuration integrity is continuously monitored.

Disaster readiness is another critical lens through which auditors evaluate configuration management maturity. The ability to restore a device quickly and accurately after hardware failure or security incident is a direct measure of resilience. Routine restore tests, either in lab environments or controlled production simulations, verify that backups are not only available but usable. Successful restoration should include reloading configurations, reestablishing certificates or keys, and validating connectivity. Auditors expect evidence of such tests, including test logs, restoration time metrics, and posttest validation results demonstrating full operational recovery.

Secrets and cryptographic material used in device configurations—such as VPN keys, shared secrets, and private certificates—must also be escrowed securely. These assets enable decryption, authentication, and trusted communications, and losing them can render recovery impossible. Best practice involves storing keys in dedicated secret-management systems or hardware security modules (HSMs) rather than embedding them directly in configuration files. The audit trail should demonstrate key life cycle controls: generation, distribution, rotation, and retirement. Auditors will ask where secrets are kept, who can access them, and whether procedures exist to reissue or revoke them during a disaster scenario.

Evidence Locations

Auditing network and perimeter security controls depends on tangible proof—artifacts that demonstrate what is configured, what has changed, and how those changes are monitored. This proof is rarely found in one place. Instead, it resides across several interlocking systems, each offering a different perspective on the same infrastructure. Understanding where this evidence lives—and how these sources connect—is essential for both effective auditing and sustainable governance. The main data sources are configuration management systems, change control records, device consoles, and network telemetry repositories, all anchored by a comprehensive Configuration Management Database (CMDB) or asset inventory that serves as the master reference.

The CMDB or asset inventory is the foundation upon which all other evidence rests. It provides the authoritative list of network devices—firewalls, routers, switches, intrusion prevention systems, and edge gateways—along with identifying details such as hostname, management IP, location, serial number, firmware version, and responsible owner. A well-maintained CMDB allows auditors to determine whether every active device is represented and whether its attributes align with observed configurations. For example, if firewall logs show traffic from a device not listed in the CMDB, that discrepancy signals potential shadow infrastructure or a governance gap. Auditors typically request export reports from the CMDB and compare them to discovery scans, network diagrams, or configuration manager outputs to verify completeness and accuracy. Table 7.3 shows how inventory configuration consoles and telemetry link to provide complete and verifiable audit evidence.

Configuration management systems act as the operational bridge between the CMDB and the devices themselves. Tools such as Ansible, SolarWinds Network Configuration Manager, or Cisco

Table 7.3 Evidence source crosswalk for network assurance.

Source system	Primary content	Device identity fields	Proof of completeness	Versioning provenance
CMDB	Authoritative asset list and owners	Hostname and mgmt IP and serial	Inventory export matched to discovery scan	Report timestamp and approver
Config manager	Backups and golden configs and diffs	Hostname and device ID and mgmt IP	Backup roster compared to CMDB	Repo commit id and collector log
Firewall console	Access rules and hit counts and change log	Hostname and cluster name and interface	All firewalls present and exporting	Export time and rule count
IPS console	Signatures and feed status and alert history	Sensor name and device ID	All sensors reporting and healthy	Feed update time and policy version
DNS resolver	Query logs and block events and sinkhole hits	Resolver name and IP	Endpoints pointed to enterprise resolvers	Log retention record
Web proxy	URL categories and actions and TLS outcomes	Gateway name and node id	Coverage for managed users and devices	Policy version and change id
SIEM NetFlow	Correlated events and flows and alerts	Device name and IP and parser type	All sources onboarded and sending	Ingest checksum and parser version
Change system	Approvals and justifications and testing notes	Ticket id and requester and owner	All config changes mapped to tickets	Ticket history and status

DNA Center maintain golden configurations, push updates, and capture running configurations directly from devices. These systems often hold the most direct evidence of what is deployed in production at a given time. Configuration archives show version histories and diffs that reveal when and how devices changed—critical for identifying configuration drift or unauthorized edits. Auditors verify that configuration backups are tied to the CMDB asset records and that version metadata includes timestamps, device identifiers, and user accounts responsible for each change. The chain of custody for these exports should be clearly documented so configuration files can serve as reliable evidence.

Rulebase exports from firewall, intrusion detection, and intrusion prevention consoles provide the clearest view of edge enforcement. These exports show what access controls exist, in what order they are processed, and when they were last modified. Auditors use them to confirm that deny-by-default, least-privilege, and segregation principles are actually implemented. When collected regularly, these exports also serve as an evidence trail of operational change over time. To preserve integrity, organizations should export in a consistent, automated manner and store each version in a secured repository with version tagging. Metadata—such as rule count, export date, and associated change ticket number—should accompany each file so auditors can confirm provenance and verify that the data has not been manually altered.

Change management systems contain the narrative that explains *why* configurations changed. Each ticket or request describes the business reason, risk assessment, testing steps, approval status, and final outcome of a modification. During an audit, these records tie directly to technical evidence from configuration exports or rulebase updates. For example, if a firewall rule allowing new outbound traffic appears in a recent export, auditors trace that rule to a corresponding change ticket to confirm it was authorized. Missing or unlinked tickets are red flags indicating that governance controls over changes may be weak. Best practice is to enforce mandatory ticket identifiers within configuration management tools, ensuring traceability between technical and procedural records.

Telemetry sources—such as system logs, NetFlow, or SIEM dashboards—demonstrate how configurations behave in real operation. While a rulebase shows *intent*, telemetry shows *activity*. NetFlow or sFlow data reveals which rules are hit, which routes are active, and which devices generate anomalous traffic. SIEM platforms aggregate this telemetry, correlating events from multiple network segments to identify security-relevant trends. Auditors evaluate these logs to verify that rules are not just defined but exercised as expected, and that alerts or anomalies are properly logged and reviewed. For example, unused firewall rules evident in telemetry suggest policy bloat, while unexpected flows might indicate a configuration drift. Evidence here consists of report exports, log retention policies, and SIEM correlation rules that confirm monitoring completeness.

Reconciling device identities across these systems is often one of the most time-consuming parts of an audit. Hostnames may differ from inventory labels; IP addresses may change due to DHCP or redesigns; and serial numbers may not always appear in logs. To achieve a unified view, auditors correlate multiple identifiers—hostname, management IP, MAC address, or device ID—and document a reconciliation map. This cross-reference ensures that each device in configuration managers and SIEM telemetry aligns with an asset record in the CMDB. A good practice is to automate reconciliation through scripts or asset-discovery tools, flagging discrepancies for human review. Evidence of this reconciliation, such as cross-system mapping tables, demonstrates both coverage and governance maturity.

Population completeness is another key assurance factor. The auditor must confirm that every in-scope device contributes data to each relevant system. A complete inventory should appear in the CMDB, with matching configuration data in management tools, and corresponding logs visible in the SIEM or NetFlow collector. Sampling a subset of devices—such as all edge firewalls or a random 10% of access switches—and tracing them through all systems helps validate end-to-end coverage. Missing telemetry, absent backups, or unregistered devices signal blind spots in monitoring and control, which could conceal both operational failures and security events.

Provenance and versioning are critical to the evidentiary reliability of configuration data. Each export or log file should be traceable to its source system, collection method, and time of capture. Version control platforms—such as Git or secured network configuration archives—help maintain this integrity by automatically recording timestamps, commit hashes, and user attribution for each update. Auditors review whether these controls are applied consistently and whether data is protected from alteration after collection. Proper versioning not only supports current assessments but also enables forensic reconstruction if a configuration-related incident occurs months later.

When assembled correctly, these evidence sources form a coherent web of validation: the CMDB defines what should exist, the configuration manager shows what is actually configured, the firewall and IDS consoles reveal what is enforced, the change management system explains why modifications occurred, and the telemetry or SIEM confirms how everything behaves in practice. Each source reinforces the others, closing gaps and exposing inconsistencies. Auditors document this chain of evidence meticulously, noting where exports originated, who collected them, and when they were verified. The ability to connect intent, implementation, and operation through verifiable artifacts is the hallmark of a mature, audit-ready network governance environment.

Conclusion

Mastering network and perimeter auditing principles is critical for maintaining control in environments where trust is increasingly distributed and automated. The boundaries that once defined the enterprise have dissolved into complex ecosystems of cloud edges, remote access gateways, and software-defined overlays. In this context, the auditor's role is not limited to confirming device hardening or firewall policy compliance—it is to ensure that every enforcement point collectively upholds the organization's intended security posture. Precision, evidence, and traceability are what convert network defense from a series of controls into a governed system of trust.

This chapter reinforces the role of disciplined configuration management, segmentation validation, and continuous monitoring in securing AI-enabled infrastructures at scale. As machine learning and automation accelerate network operations, they also amplify the consequences of drift and misalignment. Ensuring that policies, telemetry, and change records remain synchronized protects not just data in transit, but the integrity of the systems that process and analyze it. The auditor's capacity to connect architectural design with operational behavior provides an essential counterbalance to the speed and complexity introduced by AI-driven automation.

With these foundations in place, cybersecurity professionals are better equipped to evaluate the resilience of modern perimeters and detect weaknesses before adversaries exploit them. Effective auditing transforms reactive defense into proactive assurance, enabling organizations to prove—not merely claim—that their controls function as designed. While tools and platforms will continue to evolve, the underlying principle remains constant: governance must extend wherever trust is granted. By maintaining that alignment between policy, configuration, and evidence, auditors ensure that network security remains a verifiable, measurable, and dependable cornerstone of enterprise defense.

Auditor Recommendations

1. **Validate Segmentation Against Design Intent:** Conduct independent verification of network segmentation to ensure that logical trust zones align with approved architecture diagrams. Compare routing tables, VLAN maps, and ACL exports against documented boundaries to confirm enforcement of least-privilege and deny-by-default principles. This validation allows auditors to identify configuration drift and highlight gaps between intended design and operational reality.
2. **Assess Firewall Governance Discipline:** Evaluate the organization's adherence to firewall rule hygiene practices, including justification, review cycles, and expiration processes. Require that every active rule has a linked change ticket and documented business rationale to maintain traceability. Regular rule recertification ensures that security controls evolve responsibly without accumulating unnecessary or risky access.
3. **Examine Egress Control Coverage:** Review how outbound traffic is restricted through DNS, proxy, and firewall policies to prevent data exfiltration and command-and-control activity. Confirm that allowlists are specific, documented, and reviewed periodically for business justification. Testing these egress restrictions helps auditors verify that outbound pathways are controlled and monitored as effectively as inbound traffic.
4. **Evaluate the Strength of Remote Access Posture:** Verify that remote connectivity follows SASE or ZTNA principles by enforcing identity verification, device posture assessment, and

session segmentation. Ensure that split-tunnel policies are approved, limited to defined use cases, and reviewed for compliance with monitoring requirements. An auditor's assurance over remote access confirms that access boundaries remain secure even when traditional perimeters do not exist.

5. **Correlate DNS, Proxy, and Firewall Policies:** Assess whether outbound filtering mechanisms reinforce one another instead of operating in silos. Confirm that DNS requests are forced through enterprise resolvers, proxies apply category filtering, and egress firewalls block unsanctioned direct IP traffic. This integrated review ensures layered controls provide unified enforcement and reduce opportunities for policy bypass.
6. **Verify Intrusion Prevention and Threat Intelligence Management:** Review update and feed synchronization logs to ensure that IPS and reputation databases are refreshed on schedule. Examine tuning records and alert disposition workflows to confirm that detections are acted upon rather than ignored. Auditors should look for evidence that these controls are maintained as living systems—continuously adapting to current threat intelligence.
7. **Review Configuration Baselines and Drift Controls:** Confirm that hardened baselines exist for all network device types and that deviations from golden configurations are automatically detected. Assess how unauthorized changes are identified, reviewed, and reconciled through the change management process. This assurance step ensures the network remains consistent with the organization's approved security posture.
8. **Test Backup Integrity and Restoration Readiness:** Examine whether device configuration backups are performed automatically, securely stored, and regularly tested for restoration accuracy. Require documentation of restore drills that verify recovery speed and the validity of stored keys or secrets. Effective audit validation of backup and restore processes demonstrates operational resilience under adverse conditions.
9. **Cross-verify Evidence Sources for Completeness:** Map asset data across CMDB, configuration managers, firewall consoles, and SIEM telemetry to ensure all devices are represented and producing data. Evaluate how device identities are reconciled using multiple identifiers such as hostname, IP, and serial number. This cross-verification gives auditors confidence that the organization's control environment is fully covered and evidence chains are intact.
10. **Scrutinize Exception and Change Documentation:** Review exception registers and change tickets to confirm that all deviations from policy—such as firewall or proxy exceptions—are justified, approved, and time-limited. Ensure that each exception includes a defined owner, risk assessment, and expiration date to prevent permanent erosion of control strength. This governance practice helps auditors demonstrate accountability and maturity in managing controlled flexibility within security operations.

Chapter Questions

1. Which activity best validates that network segmentation matches the intended trust boundaries?
   - **A.** Reviewing vendor hardening guides for each firewall model
   - **B.** Running an external vulnerability scan of internet-facing hosts
   - **C.** Comparing routing tables and ACL exports to approved zone diagrams
   - **D.** Checking that all VLAN names follow a standardized naming convention

2. Which firewall policy principle most directly prevents unauthorized lateral movement across zones?
   A. Deny-by-default on inter-zone traffic with narrowly scoped allow rules
   B. Allow-by-default with alerting on unusual port and protocol combinations
   C. Time-based rules that open all ports during maintenance windows
   D. Geo-blocking all traffic from regions outside the company's footprint

3. What is the primary security objective of outbound egress controls?
   A. Increasing user bandwidth for web browsing and streaming
   B. Reducing the complexity of firewall rulebases by consolidating rules
   C. Preventing data exfiltration and command-and-control communications
   D. Enabling direct access to public DNS resolvers for faster lookups

4. Which capability most distinguishes ZTNA/SASE approaches from legacy VPNs?
   A. Static tunnels that grant full network access once authenticated
   B. Per-application access decisions based on identity and device posture
   C. Split tunneling that sends all SaaS traffic directly to the internet
   D. Shared local admin accounts for simplified remote troubleshooting

5. How should split-tunnel policy be applied to balance performance and assurance?
   A. Permit all HTTPS traffic to bypass inspection for user convenience
   B. Allow only explicitly approved cloud services to go direct, with the rest enforced through inspection
   C. Force all traffic through the corporate data center regardless of destination
   D. Use end-user discretion to decide which traffic should be split

6. Which action best aligns DNS, proxy, and egress firewall controls to avoid bypass paths?
   A. Constrain outbound IP/port rules to match approved domains and services enforced by DNS/proxy
   B. Disable TLS interception to reduce proxy complexity and latency
   C. Allow public DNS-over-HTTPS so endpoints can resolve SaaS more reliably
   D. Rely solely on URL category filtering without changing firewall rules

7. What does a DNS sinkhole accomplish in an enterprise control design?
   A. It accelerates recursive resolution for performance testing
   B. It replaces the need for web proxy logging on encrypted sessions
   C. It automates certificate issuance for HTTPS inspection
   D. It returns a harmless internal address for blocked domains to expose and monitor attempted misuse

8. Which evidence most convincingly demonstrates an effective IPS/threat-intel program?
   A. A large number of blocked events reported each week
   B. A quarterly presentation listing new rule families enabled
   C. Timely signature and feed updates with alert disposition and tuning records
   D. A policy statement that commits to best-effort prevention

9. What is the primary purpose of a golden configuration in device management?
   - **A.** Serving as a validated, known-good reference for a specific deployment to support compliance checks and drift detection
   - **B.** Providing a generic vendor baseline that applies to all device types equally
   - **C.** Enabling emergency access by embedding shared credentials for administrators
   - **D.** Replacing the need for automated backups by storing the latest running config

10. Which practice most reliably reconciles device identities across CMDB, configuration tools, and SIEM telemetry?
    - **A.** Trusting hostnames as the single source of identity across all systems
    - **B.** Mapping MAC addresses only, since they never change
    - **C.** Using dynamic IP addresses to ensure coverage in cloud environments
    - **D.** Correlating multiple identifiers (hostname, management IP, serial/device ID) and maintaining a cross-system mapping

8

Application and API Security/CI-CD

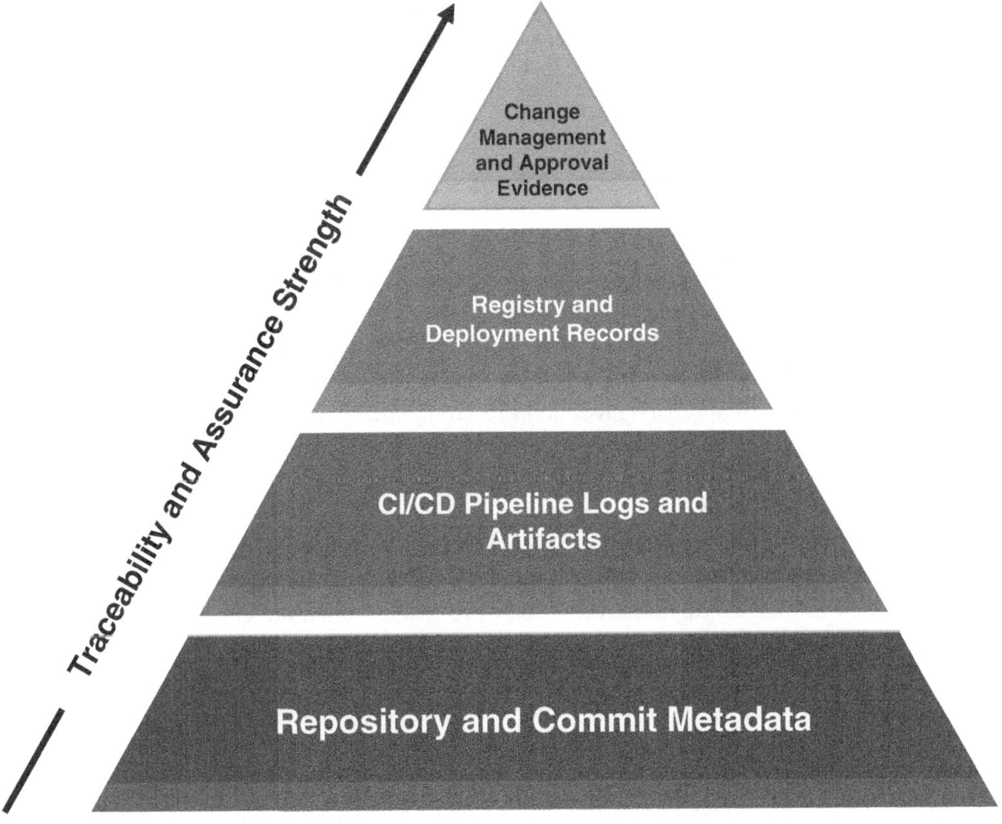

Software today is assembled and delivered at a speed and scale that outpaces traditional security oversight, making governance within the software development life cycle a central concern for auditors and risk professionals. Application and API ecosystems form the connective tissue of modern digital operations, and their security posture directly influences enterprise resilience. Understanding how development pipelines, code repositories, and runtime controls interlock is essential to validating whether an organization's assurance claims are credible. This chapter examines the mechanisms that make software delivery verifiable, measurable, and enforceable from an audit perspective.

Modern cloud environments demand that policies, configurations, and reviews are embedded directly into the tools that create and deploy software. Automated controls—ranging from static and dynamic testing to dependency analysis and policy-as-code enforcement—replace informal approvals with machine-enforced evidence. By focusing on governed software pipelines, hardened environments, and structured release processes, this chapter illustrates how security becomes a built-in property of engineering rather than an afterthought. These practices allow auditors to trace accountability from the developer's keyboard to the production endpoint, ensuring transparency across the entire DevSecOps chain.

From code scanning and environment hardening to release gates and artifact traceability, the ideas explored here form the foundation of audit-ready software assurance. They demonstrate how strong governance not only prevents defects but also provides defensible evidence of compliance, risk control, and operational maturity. In the era of AI-driven development and continuous deployment, such rigor is indispensable. It ensures that automation enhances, rather than erodes, accountability—preserving trust in the integrity of systems that increasingly make autonomous decisions and safeguard critical data.

SDLC Governance and "Policy as Code"

In a governed software development life cycle (SDLC), the same discipline applied to financial or operational controls is applied to how code moves through development, testing, and deployment. Governance in this context means that every rule, approval, and exception is clearly defined, consistently enforced, and automatically auditable. Instead of relying on human memory or manual enforcement, the process itself—through the tools developers already use—applies security and compliance standards. This approach gives auditors confidence that security controls are not just written down, but actually built into the system. A governed SDLC provides transparency into who can make changes, what rules are in place to guide those changes, and how exceptions are recorded for accountability.

"Policy as code" is the operational form of that governance. It means that policies once written in documents or spreadsheets—such as who can approve code merges or when tests must run—are now expressed in code or configuration that the development environment enforces. Examples include GitHub branch protection rules that require pull request reviews, code scanning jobs that run before merges, and automated security checks in the continuous integration/continuous deployment (CI/CD) pipeline. By turning policy into code, organizations gain the ability to test, version, and review their governance controls the same way they do with application code. This ensures that no rule is silently changed and that all policy updates are tracked with timestamps and approvals. Table 8.1 maps key governed SDLC controls to their enforcement points and the artifacts that prove they were active.

In a governed SDLC, authority is distributed but controlled. Developers can propose changes, but they cannot bypass established review gates. Typically, pull requests must be approved by designated code owners or reviewers, and builds must pass automated checks before deployment. Each approval or rejection creates a record—complete with who performed the action and when. This history provides auditors with a clear sequence of decisions that demonstrate compliance with change control policies. In this model, "who approves changes" is not a vague procedural note—it is an enforced setting within the repository, backed by automation that ensures rules are followed every time.

Table 8.1 Governed SDLC controls and evidence artifacts.

Control surface	Enforcement location	Example rule	Durable evidence
Branch protection	Repository	Require pull request reviews	Repository settings export
Code ownership	Repository	Require CODEOWNERS approval	Pull request approval record
Commit integrity	Repository	Require signed commits	Commit signature verification log
Mandatory checks	CI pipeline	Require status checks to pass	Pipeline run report
Security gates	CI pipeline	Block merge on scan fail	Stored scan artifact
Admin restrictions	Repository	Disallow force push to main	Audit log entry
Separation of duties	Repository	Prohibit self-approval	Merge rule configuration
Change approval	CI pipeline	Require manual approval step	Approval record with timestamp

Security gates form another key layer of governance. These are automated controls placed at specific points in the pipeline that evaluate code for security and quality issues. They may include static code analysis, dependency vulnerability scans, or configuration checks against policy baselines. If a gate fails, the pipeline stops until the issue is resolved or an approved exception is granted. This structure ensures that releases cannot proceed without passing the defined security checks, reducing the risk of introducing vulnerabilities through haste or oversight. Importantly, these gates are not optional—they are integrated and version-controlled just like the code itself.

The location of rules in a governed SDLC is intentional and layered. Repository-level configurations handle developer-facing policies such as branch protection, review requirements, and commit signatures. Pipeline configurations handle process-level controls such as test coverage thresholds and security scans. Finally, organization-wide settings govern overarching requirements such as who can create repositories, who can modify security settings, and what integrations are approved. Together, these form a hierarchy of enforceable rules that prevent drift and maintain consistency across teams and projects.

Exception handling within a governed SDLC is also formalized. When a rule must be bypassed—for instance, to address a production emergency—the exception is requested, reviewed, and approved within the same version-controlled environment. The request is logged, given an expiry date, and tied to the specific commit or release it affects. This eliminates "temporary" workarounds that never get reversed and provides an audit trail for any deviation from policy. By embedding exception workflows directly into the SDLC tools, teams can move quickly without sacrificing traceability or compliance.

The benefits of this approach extend beyond compliance. Engineers work within a predictable structure that reduces friction and misunderstanding. Security teams can see at a glance which controls are in place and how they operate. Auditors can verify not only that rules exist, but that they are being consistently applied. In effect, governance becomes part of the engineering fabric rather than an external audit exercise. This integration reduces manual oversight while increasing confidence in the security and reliability of every deployment.

Code and Dependency Scanning: SAST, SCA, and Secrets Detection

Static Application Security Testing (SAST), Software Composition Analysis (SCA), and secrets detection form the triad of code-level assurance within a governed DevSecOps pipeline. Each has a distinct focus—SAST examines custom source code for insecure constructs, SCA inspects dependencies for known vulnerabilities, and secrets detection searches for credentials or tokens inadvertently committed to repositories. Together, they provide a comprehensive defense against the introduction of weaknesses before code ever executes. A mature SDLC treats these scans not as optional hygiene, but as enforceable quality gates built into every merge, build, and deployment pipeline.

SAST tools operate directly on the source code, parsing syntax, and control flows to identify patterns that could lead to vulnerabilities such as injection, unsafe deserialization, or insecure API calls. Unlike dynamic testing, which requires a running application, SAST finds issues early in the development cycle—often at commit or pull request time. Its coverage extends across all in-scope repositories, languages, and frameworks used by the organization. For auditors, the scope of SAST is typically documented through an inventory of codebases and the corresponding rulesets applied. Coverage is verified when each repository or build target is associated with an automated SAST job that runs as part of the CI/CD process, producing a report that can be traced back to the exact code revision scanned.

SCA complements SAST by addressing the growing security risks in third-party components. Modern applications rely heavily on open-source libraries, container images, and package dependencies—each a potential source of inherited vulnerabilities. SCA tools analyze dependency manifests, lock files, and container layers to map all included components and cross-reference them against vulnerability databases such as the National Vulnerability Database (NVD). The purpose is to identify outdated or vulnerable libraries before deployment, ensuring that developers are alerted to risks introduced through indirect dependencies. For complete auditability, organizations maintain both the tool's configuration files and the resulting reports as build artifacts, showing which versions were evaluated and what remediation actions followed.

Secrets detection targets a different class of risk—accidental exposure of sensitive data within code repositories. These may include API keys, database passwords, cloud access tokens, or encryption keys embedded in source files. Once pushed to a public or even internal repository, secrets can persist indefinitely and may be harvested by attackers. Automated secret scanners integrate into the commit or push workflow, flagging any matches against known credential patterns or entropy-based rules. When a secret is detected, the workflow typically blocks the merge until it is revoked and replaced. Auditability here depends on retention of detection logs and confirmation that remediation occurred, creating a traceable record of secret management.

To remain effective, SAST, SCA, and secrets detection must be maintained as living systems, not static configurations. Rule sets and signatures require regular updates—often daily or weekly—to reflect new vulnerability patterns and emerging threat intelligence. Auditors expect documentation of update cadences, along with evidence that update processes are automated and monitored for failure. Version control for tool configurations is equally important; any rule customizations, exclusions, or suppressions should be captured in the same repository as the code, ensuring traceability over time. This approach prevents "configuration drift" and enables auditors to reconstruct exactly which rules were active for any historical scan.

Exception management is a critical element of audit readiness in these scanning programs. False positives and non-exploitable findings are inevitable, but they must be handled systematically. Mature organizations track suppressions and waivers through formal approval workflows that record the justification, reviewer, and expiration date. Each suppression entry links back to a specific finding, ensuring visibility into which issues are deferred and why. Automatic reminders or dashboards highlight expiring waivers so they do not silently persist. This structured handling of exceptions demonstrates that risk acceptance decisions are deliberate and reversible, not ad hoc.

Artifact retention underpins the auditability of all scanning activities. For each build or release, the resulting SAST, SCA, and secret-scan reports are stored as immutable artifacts—often in centralized storage or within the CI/CD platform itself. These artifacts should include metadata such as the tool version, rule set identifier, timestamp, and commit hash, enabling auditors to verify the lineage of results. Retention periods typically align with organizational policy or regulatory requirements, often ranging from one to seven years depending on the system's criticality. Without these artifacts, it becomes impossible to demonstrate consistent execution of security scans over time.

Language and platform diversity add further complexity to coverage. A governed DevSecOps pipeline ensures that appropriate tools exist for every major language and build target in use—Java, Python, JavaScript, C#, Go, and more. Each tool's capabilities and limitations are documented to avoid false assumptions of full coverage. When specialized frameworks or compiled components are introduced, the security team extends or replaces scanning tools accordingly. This ensures that no part of the codebase—whether source, dependency, or configuration—falls outside the reach of automated inspection.

Ultimately, code and dependency scanning are not one-time checks but continuous validation mechanisms embedded in the fabric of software delivery. When properly implemented, they offer real-time visibility into the security posture of every build. Their outputs feed into risk dashboards, vulnerability management systems, and audit evidence repositories, ensuring that the organization can demonstrate not only detection but also response and remediation. For auditors, the hallmark of maturity is consistency—scans that run predictably, produce reproducible results, and leave behind an immutable trail of who approved what, when, and why. Table 8.2 summarizes how SAST SCA and secrets detection are scoped triggered and evidenced for audit purposes.

Table 8.2 Scanning coverage and audit readiness matrix.

Scan type	Primary scope	Trigger	Required artifact	Exception tracking field
SAST	Custom source code	On pull request	Static scan report	Suppression justification
SCA	Dependencies and images	On build	Dependency scan report	Waiver expiry date
Secrets detection	Repository history and diffs	On commit	Secrets finding log	Revocation confirmation
Coverage mapping	Repos and build targets	On schedule	Coverage inventory	Owner and review link
Rule updates	Tool rules and signatures	On update cadence	Ruleset version record	Change ticket reference

Dynamic Testing and API Security: DAST, AuthN/AuthZ, and Rate Limits

Dynamic Application Security Testing (DAST) is the runtime counterpart to static analysis. Instead of reading source code, DAST interacts directly with a running web application or API to find weaknesses that only appear during execution. These include input validation flaws, broken authentication logic, and misconfigured headers. By simulating real requests, DAST exposes how the system behaves under live conditions. It checks for vulnerabilities such as cross-site scripting, injection flaws, and insecure redirects that static scans might miss. In a mature DevSecOps process, DAST is integrated into the CI/CD pipeline, generating reports tied to specific builds or releases so that auditors can see which environment was tested, when it was scanned, and what was found.

Dynamic testing is especially important for APIs, where the security model depends on how endpoints handle authentication, authorization, and data validation. Many APIs fail not because of bad code, but because their runtime configuration is inconsistent with design intentions. For example, an API might properly validate user input in code, but fail to enforce rate limits or token expiration at runtime. DAST complements SAST and SCA by confirming that deployed services actually enforce controls as intended. It also provides measurable coverage, showing which endpoints and authentication paths were tested. For auditors, the key question is not just "Did you scan?" but "Can you prove the scan exercised the real service configuration?"

Authentication (AuthN) is the first enforcement layer for any API. It confirms that each request is tied to a known identity before allowing access. This enforcement typically happens at the API gateway or service mesh, where tokens or credentials are validated before traffic reaches the backend code. Common mechanisms include OAuth 2.0 bearer tokens, JSON Web Tokens (JWT), and mutual TLS between services. Logs from the gateway or authentication service serve as durable evidence, showing that invalid tokens were rejected and expired sessions were blocked. If authentication checks occur only in application code, they must be version-controlled, reviewed, and verified by tests that confirm all entry points require valid credentials.

Authorization (AuthZ) follows authentication and determines what an authenticated user or service is allowed to do. Authorization logic can live in several places—inside the API gateway, in a service mesh sidecar, or directly within the application code. Most organizations use a layered approach: the gateway enforces high-level rules (such as which roles can access which paths), while the application enforces business-specific decisions (such as which records a user owns). Mature implementations externalize these rules through policy engines or configuration files rather than hard-coding them. For audit purposes, version-controlled authorization policies, change logs, and test results that show "allow" and "deny" outcomes are the primary evidence of proper access control.

Schema validation acts as the contract between the client and the API. Every request and response should follow an agreed structure—defined in an OpenAPI or JSON schema. When a client sends data that doesn't match the schema, the system should reject it before it reaches application logic. Enforcement can occur at the API gateway, which validates requests automatically, or within the service code if the gateway does not handle this function. Evidence of effective schema validation includes versioned schema files, pipeline logs showing validation steps, and consistent 400-series responses to malformed requests during DAST testing. These artifacts demonstrate that input validation is enforced in practice, not just documented in design.

Rate limiting and quotas protect APIs from abuse and accidental overload. They define how many requests a user or system can make in a given time window. This control typically resides in the API gateway or load balancer, which monitors traffic volume per user or token and automatically returns HTTP 429 ("Too Many Requests") responses when thresholds are exceeded. For auditors, the evidence includes configuration files showing the defined limits, operational metrics demonstrating throttling behavior, and change logs documenting approved adjustments to those limits. Rate limits are especially important for public-facing APIs where a denial-of-service condition could result from either attack or misconfiguration.

Enforcement location determines both strength and auditability. API gateways provide centralized enforcement for authentication, rate limiting, and input validation. Sidecars in service meshes extend enforcement into internal service-to-service communication. Application code provides the final layer for fine-grained authorization and context-aware rules. Each enforcement point should be clearly documented in architecture diagrams and configuration repositories. Version-controlled gateway configurations, sidecar policy files, and application middleware code give auditors tangible proof that controls exist and are consistently deployed. Consistency across environments is critical—rules enforced in one layer must not be silently disabled or overridden in another.

For audit evidence, change control is just as important as enforcement. All gateway, mesh, and service configurations should be managed as code, reviewed before deployment, and deployed through the same CI/CD pipeline that builds the applications themselves. This ensures every security rule—whether a rate limit, token validation rule, or schema file—has a tracked history of who changed it and when. Durable artifacts include configuration files, approval records, deployment manifests, and scan reports. Together, these show not only that controls are configured, but that they are reviewed, versioned, and verified in a controlled process.

DAST validates that these protections actually work in runtime conditions. Automated tests attempt to bypass authentication, exceed rate limits, send malformed payloads, or access restricted resources. Successful defenses produce consistent error codes—401 for unauthenticated, 403 for unauthorized, 400 for schema violations, and 429 for throttling. DAST results, combined with runtime logs from gateways and applications, provide concrete proof that security policies are both enforced and effective. In a well-governed environment, this evidence is archived with each release, giving auditors a complete picture of API security from configuration to behavior.

Infrastructure as Code and Environment Hardening

Infrastructure as Code (IaC) is the foundation for maintaining consistent and secure environments across development, staging, and production. Instead of manually configuring servers, networks, and services, engineers define the entire environment in version-controlled templates—such as Terraform, AWS CloudFormation, or Azure Resource Manager files. These templates describe everything from virtual machines and networks to IAM policies, encryption settings, and logging configurations. By defining infrastructure this way, the organization ensures that each environment is built from a known, repeatable baseline. This makes every change traceable, reviewable, and reversible, which is essential for both operational reliability and audit assurance.

A hardened baseline represents the secure default configuration for each type of resource—such as enforcing encryption at rest, disabling public access to storage, or limiting SSH to approved management networks. These baselines are codified within IaC templates and stored in a controlled repository that only designated administrators can modify. When new environments are created, they inherit these secure defaults automatically. This eliminates configuration drift caused by ad hoc manual changes. For example, if every EC2 instance or Kubernetes node is provisioned from an approved template, auditors can verify that the correct security controls are applied by simply reviewing the template source and confirming it matches the deployed configuration.

Environment drift occurs when deployed infrastructure deviates from the approved baseline, often due to emergency changes, manual updates, or external dependencies. Detecting drift is critical for maintaining assurance. Automated compliance tools—such as Terraform plan checks, AWS Config, or Azure Policy—continuously compare live configurations to their IaC definitions. When differences appear, alerts are generated, and remediation workflows are triggered to restore alignment. Each drift detection event is logged, timestamped, and retained, creating an auditable history of what changed, when, and who approved any exceptions. In a governed DevSecOps model, drift detection reports are reviewed alongside code and vulnerability scans to ensure environmental integrity is maintained.

Separation of duties is central to preventing conflicts of interest in IaC workflows. Developers may author or propose template changes, but only designated reviewers—often from a security or cloud governance team—can approve and merge them into production branches. The CI/CD pipeline enforces this separation by requiring pull request approvals and successful automated checks before deployment. Deployment privileges are typically restricted so that no single individual can both approve and release a change. This structure mirrors traditional audit controls but applies them in a modern, automated context. For auditors, version history and approval logs within the repository provide clear evidence of compliance with change control policies.

Peer review is an equally important safeguard. Every change to IaC templates must pass through code review, automated validation, and security scanning stages. Reviewers examine proposed changes for deviations from hardened baselines—such as new network exposures, relaxed IAM roles, or missing encryption requirements. Automated policy-as-code tools, like Open Policy Agent or Checkov, help enforce these standards by blocking merges that would weaken the security posture. This ensures that all changes are both human-reviewed and machine-validated before they can be deployed. The review process itself becomes part of the audit record, demonstrating due diligence in protecting critical environments.

Hardened baselines and their associated controls are maintained in dedicated version-controlled repositories, often under the stewardship of the security architecture or platform engineering team. These repositories serve as the "source of truth" for environment configuration. Each baseline version is tagged and documented with the specific controls it enforces—such as CIS benchmark compliance or organizational security standards. Exception records, when needed, are stored alongside these templates, detailing the justification, reviewer approval, and expiration date. This proximity ensures that any deviation from policy is transparent, documented, and time-bound rather than hidden in external systems or informal notes.

Different environments—development, staging, and production—are often derived from the same IaC templates but parameterized for their specific purposes. Development may allow broader access or test data sources, while production enforces stricter controls and monitoring. The key is that differences are intentional and documented, not accidental. Parameter files or environment-specific modules define what varies, while the underlying security controls remain consistent. For auditors, this demonstrates that lower environments are not neglected or insecure; instead, they follow the same baseline patterns with controlled relaxations appropriate to their purpose.

Artifact retention ties the entire process together. Every deployment of infrastructure code produces logs, manifests, and state files that show exactly what was built and when. These outputs are stored centrally, often in secure artifact repositories or object storage with immutable retention settings. During audits, these records provide direct evidence of compliance—showing that environments were created from approved templates, that changes followed formal review, and that drift detection mechanisms continuously validated integrity. By combining IaC discipline with hardened baselines and transparent change tracking, organizations achieve both operational agility and defensible assurance across all environments.

Release Governance: Change Approval Gates and Rollback Paths

A controlled release is one in which every deployment follows a documented, verifiable path from code commit to production deployment. Nothing moves to production by accident or convenience; each change is intentional, reviewed, tested, and approved before it goes live. Release governance ensures that development speed does not come at the cost of reliability or compliance. In a well-governed CI/CD pipeline, every step—build, test, approval, and deploy—is automatically recorded, time-stamped, and traceable back to the originating commit or tag. This creates a transparent chain of custody that auditors and operations teams can both rely on to confirm that what was deployed is exactly what was reviewed and approved.

Pre-deployment checks form the first layer of release control. These automated gates validate build integrity, run security scans, execute test suites, and ensure all dependencies are approved and up to date. They may include static analysis, software composition checks, secret detection, and infrastructure validation. Each check must pass before the deployment job can proceed. In modern pipelines, these validations are enforced through configuration as code—meaning that no one can manually bypass a failed gate without documented approval. Logs from these checks, along with their results and timestamps, serve as durable audit evidence showing that due diligence was performed prior to release.

Approvals are the human complement to automated gates. They reflect organizational accountability by requiring explicit consent from designated reviewers before a deployment can proceed. Typically, the approval process includes peer review by technical leads, security review for high-risk changes, and change management acknowledgment for production deployments. Approvers must operate within defined roles—developers cannot approve their own changes, and production approvers must belong to a distinct operations or governance group. Each approval is logged in the version control and deployment system, preserving a clear record of who authorized what and when. This approval trail is one of the most important forms of compliance evidence in a DevSecOps workflow.

Controlled release patterns such as canary and blue-green deployments further reduce operational risk. In a canary deployment, a small percentage of users or systems receive the new release first, allowing teams to monitor performance and security indicators before expanding rollout. Blue-green deployments take a different approach by running two identical environments—one live ("blue") and one idle ("green"). New code is deployed to the idle environment, and traffic is switched only when validation is complete. If issues arise, traffic can be redirected instantly to the previous version. These strategies ensure that deployment risk is minimized, recovery is fast, and rollback can occur without unplanned downtime.

Rollback procedures are a critical part of release governance and must be tested, documented, and automated wherever possible. Rollbacks should not depend on improvisation or manual intervention; they should be built into the deployment pipeline itself. For example, each deployment artifact should include a version identifier and be stored in a central repository, allowing the pipeline to redeploy a prior version automatically if a failure or anomaly occurs. Auditors expect to see evidence that rollback paths have been tested under controlled conditions—not just theoretically planned. Logs showing a successful rollback during a scheduled test demonstrate readiness and resilience in production operations.

Traceability is the thread that ties release governance together. Every release must be linked to its originating commit or tag, its build artifact, and its deployment ticket. This linkage allows auditors to move from a production system back to the specific code change and approval that produced it. Common tools achieve this by embedding commit hashes and build numbers into deployment manifests, containers, or image metadata. The CI/CD pipeline then records this lineage automatically, mapping each production release to the associated version control records. This traceability not only supports compliance but also accelerates incident response, since teams can immediately identify which code introduced a given behavior.

Change approval gates combine both human and automated validation. A typical release pipeline includes several stages: pre-deployment checks, required sign-offs, staging deployment, performance validation, and production promotion. Between each stage, approval gates enforce pause points where required reviewers must sign off before promotion can continue. These gates are defined in code, stored with the pipeline configuration, and protected against modification without peer review. Approvals may be tied to change tickets in systems such as Jira or ServiceNow, ensuring that governance workflows align with enterprise change management. For every promotion event, the pipeline records who approved it, when it occurred, and which artifacts were deployed.

Evidence of release control comes from multiple sources: signed build artifacts, deployment logs, version control histories, and approval records. Together, they form an auditable record that demonstrates governance in action. Each build artifact carries a cryptographic signature or checksum verifying its integrity. Deployment logs show environment details, timestamps, and success or failure outcomes. Version control histories document review and approval events, while ticketing systems provide context around the business purpose of the change. When combined, these artifacts prove that releases were conducted through approved channels, under controlled conditions, and with proper oversight.

Evidence Locations: Repos, Pipelines, Registries, and API Gateways

In a well-governed DevSecOps environment, every change—whether a line of code, a configuration adjustment, or a policy update—must be traceable through a continuous chain of evidence. This evidence spans multiple systems that work together to create an auditable narrative of how software moves from development to production. Each system must reference the one before it, forming a connected chain that links the initial code commit to the deployed artifact, configuration, and approval record. The goal is not just to collect logs, but to provide verifiable proof of accountability, integrity, and compliance at every stage of the release process. Table 8.3 shows the standard identifiers that link each system to the next to create an unbroken chain of custody.

Table 8.3 Canonical evidence chain for release traceability.

System	Primary identifier	Links to next by	Immutable snapshot
Repository	Commit hash	Build pipeline run ID	Signed tag or commit
CI pipeline	Run ID	Artifact digest and build number	Archived job logs
Artifact registry	Image digest	Deployment record reference	Registry retention record
Deployment pipeline	Release ID	Ticket ID and approval record	Promotion log
API gateway and policy repo	Policy version	Change ticket and commit link	Exported config snapshot
Change system	Ticket ID	PR link and deployment link	Closed ticket with approvals

The version control system (VCS) serves as the first and most important source of truth. Systems such as GitHub, GitLab, or Bitbucket store not only the code itself but also its complete history—who made changes, when they were made, and what approvals occurred. Each commit should carry a verified author identity and timestamp, and ideally, a cryptographic signature to prevent tampering. Pull or merge requests capture peer reviews, required status checks, and security scan results. Branch protection rules and approval workflows enforce that only authorized reviewers can approve changes to main branches. For auditors, repository metadata such as commit history, tags, and approval records provides direct evidence that changes were peer-reviewed and passed through established governance gates before being merged.

Once the code is merged, it flows into the continuous integration (CI) pipeline, which is responsible for building, testing, and packaging the application. The CI pipeline logs every stage of this process, from the initial build to unit testing, vulnerability scanning, and artifact generation. Each run is tied back to a specific commit hash from the VCS, creating a one-to-one relationship between the code and the resulting build. The pipeline produces immutable artifacts—such as compiled binaries, test reports, and scan results—that serve as evidence of what was tested and approved. These logs and artifacts must be retained with timestamps, build identifiers, and the identity of the service account or user who triggered the build. They demonstrate that the release was created through a controlled, automated process, not manual intervention.

The next link in the evidence chain is the artifact or container registry. This is where final build outputs—such as container images, infrastructure templates, and application binaries—are stored. Each item in the registry should include metadata linking it back to the pipeline run, commit hash, and build number that produced it. Cryptographic digests, such as SHA-256 image hashes, ensure that what is deployed in production exactly matches what was built and tested. Access controls and logging on the registry confirm that only authorized systems can push or pull production images. During an audit, these logs serve as proof that build integrity was maintained and that no unverified artifacts entered the release process.

Deployment records and CI/CD release logs provide the next layer of evidence, connecting what was built to what is actually running. Each deployment should reference the artifact digest or image tag, ensuring that the production environment uses verified and approved builds. Deployment pipelines also capture environment variables, configurations, and approval steps required for promotion between stages. These logs show who approved the release, when it occurred, and whether post-deployment verification checks passed. For traceability, the deployment record must link back to both the originating commit and the corresponding change ticket or service request, proving that each production change followed formal review and authorization.

API gateways and policy repositories add another dimension of runtime evidence. These systems define and enforce how services communicate, authenticate, and protect data. Every configuration—such as authentication rules, rate limits, and access policies—should be version-controlled and reviewed like code. Changes to these configurations are logged with commit histories, reviewer approvals, and timestamps, providing a record of what policies were active at any point in time. Exported snapshots or backups of gateway configurations offer additional assurance, allowing auditors to verify that the policies enforced in production match the approved configurations stored in source control.

Change management and ticketing systems, such as Jira or ServiceNow, complete the governance chain by documenting the business context and approvals that drive each release. Every change request should be linked directly to a corresponding repository commit, pull request, and pipeline execution. Tickets record the rationale for the change, its risk classification, and its approval before deployment. By connecting ticketing systems to pipelines and repositories, organizations can demonstrate that all production changes were properly justified, reviewed, and tracked from start to finish.

Reconciling identities across these systems is essential for a trustworthy audit trail. All human users and automated service accounts should authenticate through a centralized identity provider using single sign-on (SSO) or federated credentials. This ensures that a single identity can be traced consistently across repositories, pipelines, registries, and ticketing tools. Service accounts should have clearly defined scopes and ownership, with logs showing which system or person used them to perform an action. These identity records—paired with timestamps and digital signatures—ensure accountability and prevent ambiguity about who approved or executed a given change.

To preserve evidence for reviewability, each system should capture immutable snapshots at key milestones. Repositories should retain signed commits and pull request metadata; pipelines should archive build logs and security reports; registries should store images with immutable digests; and gateways should export configuration states at deployment. These snapshots are stored in read-only archives with defined retention periods aligned to compliance requirements. When auditors review these records, they can reconstruct the exact state of the system at any moment in time, verifying both compliance and operational control.

When repositories, pipelines, registries, policy configurations, and ticketing systems are all connected through consistent identifiers and verified identities, they form a complete chain of custody for every change. The repository proves who wrote and approved the code, the pipeline shows how it was built and tested, the registry confirms what was deployed, the gateway records how it was protected, and the ticket explains why it happened. This integrated evidence model not only satisfies audit and compliance requirements—it also strengthens trust, improves accountability, and provides long-term visibility into how secure software delivery is achieved in practice.

Conclusion

Mastering the principles of governed software delivery is critical for any organization that builds, deploys, or audits digital systems at scale. The disciplines covered in this chapter—ranging from policy-as-code enforcement to secure release pipelines—demonstrate how assurance can be engineered into every stage of the software life cycle. When properly implemented, these mechanisms transform compliance from a static reporting exercise into a living control system that continuously validates integrity, accountability, and security. This shift represents the maturation of DevSecOps into a true governance function rather than a development convenience.

For AI security professionals, the implications extend beyond traditional application assurance. Automated systems and intelligent agents rely on the same underlying delivery infrastructure, and weaknesses in that pipeline can undermine the trustworthiness of AI outputs. Embedding auditability into code repositories, pipelines, and runtime policies ensures that model updates, training data, and API integrations are deployed under the same disciplined oversight as any other production software. The result is not only technical consistency but also demonstrable control over the systems that increasingly influence business decisions and regulatory obligations.

With these foundations in place, auditors and engineers are better equipped to evaluate how securely software evolves—from concept to production and from automation to autonomy. While tools and platforms will continue to change, the strategic intent remains consistent across all environments: to make every code change accountable, every deployment reversible, and every control verifiable. By treating infrastructure, code, and policy as unified audit subjects, professionals reinforce the transparency and resilience required to maintain trust in a world where digital systems, and the AI that powers them, operate at unprecedented speed and scale.

Auditor Recommendations

1. **Embed Governance into Code:** Establish a clear process for validating that governance controls are defined and enforced directly within repositories and CI/CD pipelines. Auditors should verify that approval gates, review requirements, and branch protections are configured as policy-as-code rather than informal practices. This approach ensures traceable evidence of compliance and eliminates reliance on undocumented team habits.
2. **Evaluate Scanning Coverage and Reporting:** Prioritize consistent review of SAST, SCA, and secrets detection reports across all relevant repositories and build targets. Confirm that scan configurations, rule updates, and suppression records are version-controlled and auditable. This ensures that automated scanning provides trustworthy assurance rather than inconsistent or incomplete testing.
3. **Assess Exception Governance:** Require every exception, waiver, or policy deviation to have a documented justification, approval, and expiration date. Auditors should confirm that exception records are stored with the same rigor as baseline policies and linked to the specific code or configuration they affect. This structure provides visibility into accepted risks and prevents temporary allowances from becoming permanent exposures.
4. **Verify Runtime Controls Through Testing:** Evaluate whether DAST and related runtime validation methods are being used to confirm that authentication, authorization, schema validation, and rate limits operate as intended. Auditors should look for stored DAST reports and environment details that tie results to specific builds or configurations. This evidence demonstrates that runtime protections are not just configured but actively validated under real operating conditions.
5. **Inspect Infrastructure Baselines for Consistency:** Ensure that hardened baseline templates for infrastructure as code are versioned, reviewed, and consistently applied across

development, staging, and production. Auditors should examine drift detection reports and change records to confirm that live environments match approved configurations. Consistency across environments reduces risk and proves control over infrastructure evolution.

6. **Review Separation of Duties in Deployment Workflows:** Validate that roles for code authorship, review, and deployment are distinct and enforced through system configuration, not manual discipline. Auditors should confirm that production deployment credentials are scoped, short-lived, and not shared among development teams. This maintains accountability while preventing unilateral or unauthorized production changes.
7. **Trace Change Approval and Rollback Evidence:** Examine release pipelines to ensure that every deployment can be linked back to its originating commit, build artifact, and approval ticket. Verify that rollback paths have been tested and logged as part of regular release exercises. Such traceability provides auditors with verifiable proof that every production change followed a controlled, reversible process.
8. **Audit Evidence Retention Across Systems:** Confirm that repositories, pipelines, registries, and gateways each retain immutable records of their respective actions, outputs, and approvals. Auditors should verify that retention periods meet policy requirements and that evidence is stored in read-only or tamper-evident locations. Reliable evidence retention supports defensible assurance during compliance reviews or incident investigations.
9. **Reconcile Identities Across All Toolchains:** Ensure that both human and service accounts are uniquely identifiable and consistently represented across repositories, pipelines, registries, and ticketing systems. Auditors should check that authentication is integrated with centralized identity providers and that logs can map any action to a verified entity. This consistency eliminates ambiguity when reconstructing change history or investigating anomalies.
10. **Evaluate Continuous Assurance Practices:** Encourage organizations to treat auditability as an ongoing activity rather than a periodic exercise. Review how policy-as-code enforcement, drift detection, and automated tests contribute to continuous compliance visibility. By emphasizing continuous assurance, auditors can measure not only control design but also operational effectiveness over time.

Chapter Questions

1. What is the primary benefit of expressing governance as policy in code repositories and pipelines?
   - **A.** Automatic, versioned enforcement of rules and approvals
   - **B.** Faster build times regardless of controls
   - **C.** Eliminating the need for code reviews
   - **D.** Replacing CI/CD with manual change windows

2. Which scanning approach focuses on identifying vulnerabilities in third-party libraries, packages, and images included by the application?
   - **A.** Static Application Security Testing (SAST)
   - **B.** Software Composition Analysis (SCA)
   - **C.** Dynamic Application Security Testing (DAST)
   - **D.** Secrets detection

3. What does dynamic testing uniquely validate in an API-centric system?
   - **A.** Whether dependencies are up to date
   - **B.** Whether branch protection rules are configured
   - **C.** Whether runtime behavior and controls work under real request–response conditions
   - **D.** Whether unit tests exist for all endpoints

4. Where should coarse-grained API authentication and initial authorization checks be enforced to ensure uniform control?
   - **A.** Exclusively in application business logic
   - **B.** Inside database stored procedures
   - **C.** In client-side JavaScript before requests are sent
   - **D.** At the API gateway or service mesh before requests reach services

5. What is the principal purpose of request and response schema validation for APIs?
   - **A.** Ensuring payloads conform to defined contracts and rejecting malformed data early
   - **B.** Eliminating the need for rate limiting
   - **C.** Guaranteeing no injection flaws ever occur
   - **D.** Removing the need for authorization checks

6. What is the main objective of rate limiting and quotas in API security?
   - **A.** Improving search engine optimization
   - **B.** Encrypting data at rest automatically
   - **C.** Controlling request volume per identity and returning HTTP 429 when thresholds are exceeded
   - **D.** Reducing cold-start times for serverless functions

7. Which evidence best demonstrates infrastructure drift detection in a governed environment?
   - **A.** Authentication logs showing user sign-ins
   - **B.** "Plan"/diff outputs comparing desired IaC state to live resources, plus policy evaluation reports
   - **C.** Increased unit test coverage numbers
   - **D.** CPU utilization charts during peak hours

8. Which arrangement best upholds separation of duties for production infrastructure changes?
   - **A.** The same engineer authors and applies all production changes
   - **B.** Break-glass access is used for routine deployments
   - **C.** Developers approve their own pull requests to expedite releases
   - **D.** Authors propose changes; designated code owners approve; limited deployment identities apply to production

9. What linkage establishes traceability for a controlled release?
   - **A.** Commit or tag → build artifact digest → deployment ticket and approval records
   - **B.** Team calendar event → stand-up notes → chat acknowledgments
   - **C.** Marketing request → blog post → social metrics
   - **D.** Endpoint alert → SIEM correlation → dashboard widget

10. Which sequence represents the canonical evidence chain across systems in DevSecOps?

A. SIEM → EDR → NDR → SOAR

B. HR system → payroll → procurement

C. VCS/repo metadata → CI logs/artifacts → artifact registry digests → gateway/policy repos → change tickets

D. Email threads → spreadsheets → chat logs

9

Cloud and SaaS Security

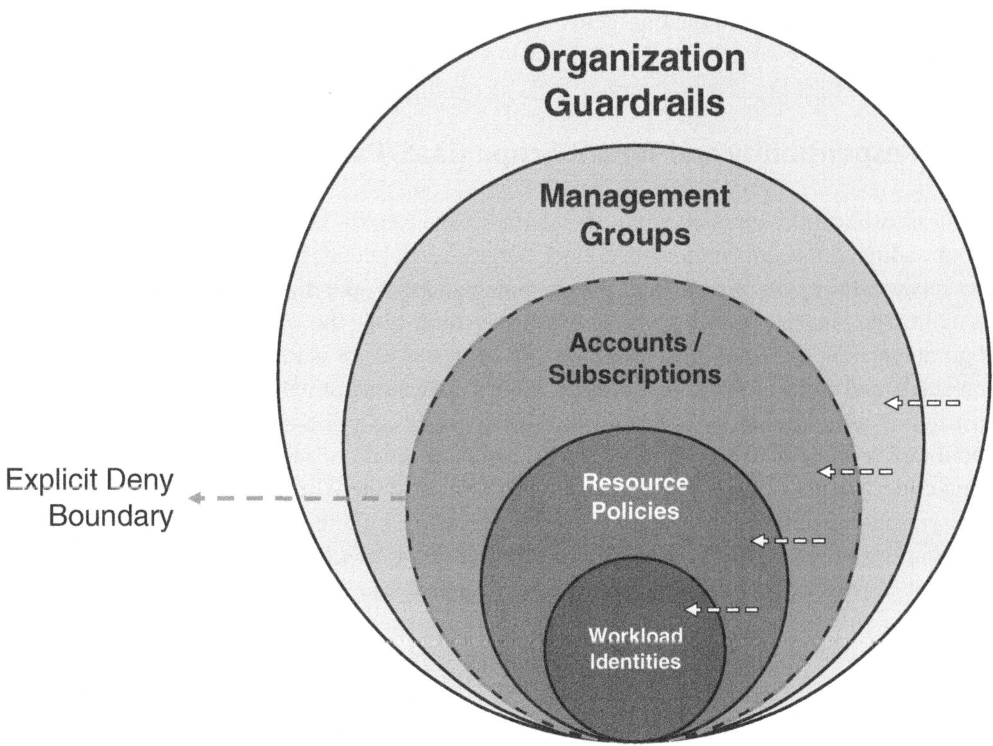

Modern cloud ecosystems have reshaped how organizations think about control, accountability, and assurance. As enterprises shift workloads to Infrastructure, Platform, and Software as a Service environments, traditional audit boundaries dissolve into shared responsibility models that demand precision and technical fluency. Understanding where provider obligations end and tenant accountability begins is essential to establishing credible audit scope and defensible evidence chains. The complexity of distributed identity systems, ephemeral infrastructure, and automated orchestration means that assurance now depends less on physical controls and more on verifiable configuration states, governance policies, and telemetry coverage.

Effective cybersecurity auditing in the cloud requires the ability to evaluate not just policy, but posture. This chapter examines how identity boundaries, baseline configurations, and logging coverage converge to define what can be tested and trusted. It explores how keys and secrets are governed at the data plane, how segmentation prevents lateral movement, and how evidence is gathered across multi-tenant architectures. By emphasizing exportable, machine-verifiable states rather than screenshots or manual attestations, this chapter reinforces the principle that cloud assurance must be repeatable, transparent, and data-driven.

In the broader context of security and compliance strategy, these concepts bridge the gap between governance frameworks and operational reality. Cloud auditability underpins regulatory confidence, incident response readiness, and AI-driven risk analytics, all of which rely on clean, structured telemetry and consistent control implementation. From defining shared responsibilities to verifying configuration provenance, the practices outlined here equip auditors and security leaders to evaluate cloud environments with the same rigor once reserved for on-premises systems—while recognizing the unique dynamism and scale that define the modern cloud.

Shared Responsibility and Tenant Scope (IaaS/PaaS/SaaS)

In cloud environments, understanding the shared responsibility model is essential to defining what an auditor can—and cannot—test. Each service model defines a different split of security duties between the cloud provider and the customer, and that split directly determines the scope of an audit. The provider owns the physical infrastructure, while the customer owns the data and configurations built on top of it. But the layers in between—such as the operating system, application stack, and identity plane—shift responsibility depending on whether the environment is Infrastructure as a Service (IaaS), Platform as a Service (PaaS), or Software as a Service (SaaS). Without clarity on these divisions, auditors risk assessing areas outside the customer's control or missing critical responsibilities that fall squarely within it. Table 9.1 clarifies how service models shift responsibilities and define what can be tested directly within the tenant.

In an IaaS model, the provider manages the physical data centers, power, cooling, and the virtualization platform itself. The customer, however, is responsible for everything above the hypervisor, including the virtual machines, operating systems, storage configurations, identity controls, and data protection. For auditors, this means that IaaS assessments resemble traditional IT audits—there is still a need to verify system hardening, patch management, and access controls—but the

Table 9.1 Shared responsibility vs. auditable tenant scope.

Service model	Provider responsibilities	Tenant responsibilities	Auditable in tenant
IaaS	Physical security and hypervisor and core networking	OS hardening and identity and network rules and keys and data life cycle	Yes
PaaS	Managed runtime and patching and platform hardening	Identity and secrets and configuration and encryption and network exposure	Yes
SaaS	Full application stack and service operations	Admin config and identity federation and access governance and data retention	Yes limited to tenant config

auditor must rely on the provider's assurance reports (such as SOC 2 or ISO 27001) to confirm the integrity of the underlying infrastructure. What remains fully in scope is the tenant's virtual environment, which is entirely under the customer's operational control.

With PaaS, the cloud provider assumes a larger share of the workload, managing the underlying servers, operating systems, and runtime environments. The tenant is responsible for configuring identity access, database schemas, application settings, and security features like encryption, logging, and API restrictions. For the auditor, the focus shifts toward configuration reviews, key management, and role-based access enforcement within the provided platform. The line of accountability becomes narrower, but it remains vital that the auditor confirm the organization's use of available security options—such as enforcing TLS, enabling audit logs, and restricting network access—since these are still within the customer's control.

In a SaaS model, the provider delivers the full application stack, including the infrastructure, platform, and software. The tenant only manages the configuration and use of the service itself. This may appear to minimize audit complexity, but it introduces a different challenge: verifying that the tenant's configuration, data management, and user access policies align with internal security requirements. The auditor's emphasis here is on administrative setup—such as single sign-on (SSO), multifactor authentication, least privilege roles, and data retention settings. The customer must also verify that contractual assurances, data residency commitments, and compliance reports from the provider are up to date and sufficient for the organization's regulatory context.

The concept of the "tenant boundary" defines where an organization's authority begins and ends within a cloud environment. A tenant may correspond to a single subscription, account, or organizational unit, depending on the platform. In AWS, a tenant might be represented by one or more accounts under an AWS Organization; in Microsoft Azure, by subscriptions under an Azure Active Directory tenant; and in Google Cloud, by projects within an organization. Understanding this boundary is critical, because it dictates which controls, configurations, and logs are owned and auditable by the customer. Anything beyond that boundary falls under provider control and must be validated indirectly through assurance artifacts or third-party reports.

Auditors must also consider how regions and services interact within that boundary. A multiregion deployment or multicloud strategy may fragment responsibility, particularly if data replication or cross-region backups are involved. Each region may introduce its own regulatory or contractual considerations, such as differing data sovereignty laws or encryption key requirements. The audit scope should clearly document which regions, accounts, and services are in scope, ensuring that the review remains aligned with both organizational policy and legal obligations.

The shared responsibility model is not static—it evolves as new features, services, and integration layers emerge. Providers frequently expand their managed offerings, shifting once-tenant-controlled responsibilities to provider-managed capabilities. For example, automated patching, managed firewalls, and container orchestration security can transfer operational responsibility away from the customer. Auditors must therefore stay current with provider documentation and architecture updates to correctly interpret where control responsibilities now reside.

When auditing within a tenant boundary, evidence collection depends on what the customer can access. Configuration baselines, identity management logs, encryption policies, and data life cycle controls form the backbone of tenant-level audit evidence. Where the provider's responsibilities begin, auditors should rely on independent audit reports, compliance certifications, and shared assurance portals offered by major cloud vendors. These sources, when properly mapped to control requirements, allow auditors to verify that provider-managed areas meet industry standards without breaching contractual or technical boundaries.

Identity Boundaries in Cloud: Roles, Policies, and SCPs/Guardrails

Identity in the cloud is the foundation of every access decision, defining who can act, on what resources, and under what conditions. Unlike traditional on-premises systems where access control is centralized within a directory service, cloud platforms distribute identity constructs across accounts, subscriptions, and services. Each provider uses its own terminology—principals, roles, and policies—but the principle is universal: every action in the cloud must be explicitly authorized. The auditor's role is to understand how these constructs form boundaries of control, how permissions flow through inheritance, and how guardrails at the organizational level prevent privilege escalation or cross-tenant abuse.

In most cloud platforms, a *principal* represents an identity capable of making requests. This may be a human user, a service account, an application identity, or even another cloud service acting on behalf of the tenant. These principals assume *roles* that define sets of allowed actions on specific resources. In AWS, for instance, roles and policies are attached to IAM users, groups, or service accounts, while in Azure, roles bind to identities through role assignments within management groups, subscriptions, or resource groups. Google Cloud follows a similar model, where members (users, groups, or service accounts) are granted IAM roles at various resource levels. Across all providers, these role constructs determine the effective permissions that a principal inherits at runtime.

Policies serve as the granular mechanism that defines what those roles can actually do. A policy describes the specific actions, resources, and conditions that determine whether an access request is allowed or denied. Most clouds evaluate these policies through a logic engine that resolves multiple layers of inheritance—from organization down to service or resource level. When conflicting statements exist, explicit denies override allows. This structure is vital to enforce least privilege, ensuring that users and services receive only the permissions they require to perform their function and nothing more. Auditors should verify that policies are scoped narrowly, referencing only the minimum set of actions and resources necessary.

Least privilege in the cloud is not a single setting but a design pattern woven through every identity construct. It is expressed through tightly scoped roles, minimized policy inheritance, and condition-based constraints such as time, location, or multifactor requirements. A well-designed environment leverages role-based access control (RBAC) or attribute-based access control (ABAC) to restrict access dynamically. For example, an auditor might review a policy that grants write access to a storage bucket only when the request originates from a specific subnet and uses an approved encryption key. These conditional expressions are where modern cloud IAM systems excel, but they can also introduce hidden complexity if not documented and tested regularly.

The hierarchy of inheritance is another crucial area for auditors to understand. Cloud identity systems evaluate access by traversing this hierarchy, aggregating permissions from higher-level entities like organizations or management groups down to individual projects or resources. A permissive policy applied at the top level can unintentionally cascade downward, expanding access across environments. Therefore, auditors should confirm that higher-level roles and inherited permissions are intentionally scoped, and that sensitive environments—such as production workloads—are isolated from inherited developer permissions. The goal is to ensure that the access structure supports segregation of duties and does not allow implicit privilege sharing between unrelated environments. Table 9.2 maps identity constructs and guardrails to where they operate and what auditors should verify at each layer.

Table 9.2 Identity boundaries and guardrails across organizational layers.

Layer	Construct	Primary function	Example enforcement	Auditor focus
Organization	Service Control Policies or Organization Policies	Permission ceiling across accounts	Block disallowed services and restrict regions	Confirm guardrails applied and effective denies present
Management group or org unit	Blueprints or landing zones	Preapproved defaults and inheritance	Auto enable logging and tagging and private endpoints	Verify inheritance and deviation handling
Account or subscription	IAM roles or role assignments	Grant scoped permissions to principals	Least privilege roles bound to resources	Review role scope and explicit denies
Resource scope	Resource policies or access rules	Constrain access at service boundary	Bucket policy blocks public access and enforces TLS	Validate resource level segmentation
Workload identity	Service accounts or workload identities	Just in time credentialing for runtime	Short lived tokens bound to runtime identity	Check binding and absence of hard coded secrets

To prevent misconfiguration at scale, cloud providers offer organization-level guardrails that constrain what accounts and projects can do. In AWS, Service Control Policies (SCPs) define permission boundaries at the organizational unit or account level, ensuring that even administrators within those accounts cannot exceed centrally defined limits. Azure enforces similar constraints using Azure Policy and management group hierarchies, allowing governance teams to restrict configurations, enforce resource tagging, or block the use of noncompliant services. Google Cloud uses Organization Policies and constraints to serve the same purpose, dictating which APIs can be enabled, where resources can be deployed, and what configurations are permitted. These mechanisms collectively establish a top-down enforcement model that limits deviation from organizational standards.

SCPs and organization policies do not grant permissions; they filter them. This distinction is vital in audit work. While identity policies define what *can* be done, guardrails define what *may never* be done, regardless of local policy. In practice, this means that even if an IAM user or role grants a powerful action, an SCP at the organization level can deny it before the request is executed. This layered approach allows centralized governance teams to manage risk consistently across multiple business units or cloud accounts. An auditor should verify that these global guardrails exist, are applied to all accounts in scope, and are reviewed periodically for completeness.

Blueprints and landing zones extend these guardrails into deployment automation. They define preapproved configurations for identity, networking, and monitoring controls, ensuring that any new project or account inherits compliant defaults. From an audit perspective, this reduces the surface area of misconfiguration and simplifies control validation. However, these templates are only as strong as their enforcement mechanisms. Auditors should confirm that deviations from blueprints require formal exception processes and that monitoring systems alert when resources drift from approved baselines.

Baseline Configurations

A secure cloud environment begins with a consistent, auditable baseline configuration. Without a defined baseline, every account, region, and service risks drifting into unique configurations that are difficult to monitor or compare. For auditors, the baseline serves as a benchmark—a known good state against which deviations can be measured. It defines what "secure by default" means across the organization's cloud environments. The objective is not to create identical infrastructures but to establish minimum configuration standards for networking, storage, compute, and service-level controls that can be verified, exported, and compared across accounts or projects.

Network segmentation is the first line of defense in any cloud baseline. Virtual Private Clouds (VPCs) and Virtual Networks (VNets) define logical isolation boundaries, much like traditional subnets, but with far greater flexibility and risk of misconfiguration. Each network should be segmented according to function—such as separating development, testing, and production environments—and access between these segments must be explicitly defined through routing rules and network access control lists. Security groups or firewall rules should follow a "default deny" posture, allowing inbound and outbound traffic only when explicitly required. Cross-account or cross-region connectivity should pass through controlled endpoints, ideally using private links or peering rather than public IP exposure. The auditor's concern is not whether the organization uses one provider's networking tools or another's, but whether network segmentation and isolation principles are consistently enforced and documented.

Baseline storage configuration is equally critical, as data exposure in cloud storage services remains one of the most frequent causes of breaches. The standard expectation is that all storage—whether object, block, or database—is encrypted at rest using managed or customer-controlled keys. Default encryption should be mandatory, and unencrypted storage creation should be disabled. Public access to storage buckets, file shares, or databases must be blocked by policy unless explicitly approved and documented. Versioning and deletion protection should be enabled to defend against accidental loss or malicious tampering. From an audit perspective, configuration states for storage should be exportable as policy snapshots or configuration manifests, allowing an auditor to compare them across accounts to verify consistent enforcement of encryption and access restrictions.

Compute resources form another cornerstone of the baseline. Virtual machines, containers, and serverless functions should launch from hardened images or templates that align with organizational standards. For traditional compute instances, this includes operating system patching, minimal installed software, and restricted administrative access. For container-based workloads, base images should originate from trusted registries and be regularly scanned for vulnerabilities. Serverless environments, though abstracted from the host layer, must still enforce least privilege through function-level permissions and network restrictions. Every compute environment should log administrative and runtime events to a central audit trail, ensuring that execution traces can be reconstructed if necessary. The baseline must define these expectations clearly so they can be programmatically validated and compared across deployments.

Hardening in the cloud does not end at the operating system. Service-level defaults—such as enforcing encryption in transit, enabling logging, and restricting external sharing—must be part of the baseline itself. Many cloud services allow insecure defaults to simplify setup; disabling those defaults is part of responsible governance. Examples include ensuring databases require authentication, API gateways use TLS 1.2 or higher, and management consoles enforce multifactor authentication. The key for auditors is that these configurations are centrally defined and measurable. A mature organization maintains baseline templates or configuration frameworks that encode these settings, making them exportable and comparable across accounts.

An auditable baseline also supports drift detection and continuous compliance. When configuration states are exportable in formats such as JSON, YAML, or policy manifests, they can be automatically compared against approved baselines. This allows teams to identify changes that introduce new exposure or violate policy. From an audit standpoint, this capability is crucial: it demonstrates not only that the baseline exists, but that it is actively monitored and enforced. The baseline's value is diminished if it cannot be measured or verified in practice. Therefore, configuration data must remain accessible for independent validation, even when the environment scales across multiple regions or accounts.

Baseline networking expectations often extend beyond segmentation to include visibility and monitoring. Flow logs, packet capture points, and security event telemetry must be enabled by default wherever possible. Auditors should expect to see network-level logging as a standard part of the baseline, with retention policies that align with the organization's data governance standards. Similarly, storage and compute services should produce audit logs detailing administrative actions and access patterns. Without this visibility, even the strongest configuration controls are difficult to verify after deployment.

Consistency across accounts is the real test of a baseline's effectiveness. It is not enough for one team or region to be compliant while others drift. A sound configuration framework enforces the same expectations everywhere, regardless of deployment scale or automation method. This can be achieved through infrastructure-as-code templates, organizational policies, or central governance services, but the auditor's interest lies in the outcome: that exported configuration states from different accounts show alignment with the defined baseline. Such comparability supports both internal assurance and external compliance, demonstrating maturity in configuration management practices.

Logging/Telemetry in Cloud and SaaS

In cloud and SaaS environments, logging is not just a record of past activity—it is the audit trail that proves accountability and enables forensic reconstruction. Every action, whether administrative or operational, should leave a trace in one or more logging planes. Because these environments are dynamic and distributed, the auditor's challenge is to confirm that logging coverage is complete across tenants, that retention aligns with organizational and regulatory requirements, and that logs are actually being preserved in a consistent, reviewable manner. Logging cannot be an afterthought; it must be a core element of the cloud baseline.

A complete logging strategy covers multiple planes of activity: the control plane, the data plane, the network plane, and the authentication plane. The control plane records management actions—such as provisioning new services, changing configurations, or modifying IAM roles—and it is the most directly tied to accountability. The data plane captures operational interactions with resources, such as reading from a storage bucket or executing a database query. Network plane telemetry records traffic flow, connections, and routing decisions, while the authentication plane provides logs for identity events like logins, token usage, and access grants. Together, these planes create a multilayered visibility fabric that allows auditors to trace an event from the initial user action through to its effect on resources.

Control plane logging is often the foundation of cloud auditing. It captures the "who did what, when, and from where" of configuration changes. Every major cloud provider offers this capability—AWS CloudTrail, Azure Activity Logs, and Google Cloud Audit Logs are the canonical examples—but enabling them does not guarantee complete coverage. Auditors must confirm that all accounts, subscriptions, or projects are enrolled and that no tenant or region has been omitted. Because control plane logs are typically stored regionally, cross-region replication or centralized aggregation must be configured to prevent gaps when accounts span multiple geographies. The auditor's focus is not on the tool but on ensuring that control plane logging is consistently enabled, stored securely, and retained for a defined period.

Data plane logs, by contrast, record the interactions that occur once resources are active. These include read and write operations to storage objects, API invocations, and runtime executions. Data plane telemetry is often optional and must be explicitly enabled at the service level. Auditors should verify that data plane logging is turned on for high-value assets, such as storage buckets, databases, and compute runtimes, and that access events are directed to a unified log sink. Without this layer, investigators can see who configured a resource but not who used it, leaving a blind spot that undermines accountability. Data plane logs are also essential for demonstrating compliance with privacy and data-handling obligations, since they establish evidence of access to sensitive information.

The network plane adds context to these actions by showing how systems communicate. Cloud network logs—such as VPC Flow Logs in AWS or Network Watcher in Azure—provide metadata about traffic flows, sources, destinations, and protocols. These records do not reveal payloads, but they are invaluable for identifying unexpected external connections or lateral movement. Network telemetry should be enabled for every VPC or VNet, with logs centralized and correlated against identity and resource logs. Auditors should ensure that network logging adheres to retention requirements consistent with other log types and that it is stored in immutable or version-controlled storage to prevent tampering. Table 9.3 highlights the mandatory logging planes and the specific checks needed to verify complete coverage and adequate retention.

Authentication and authorization logs form the fourth critical plane. They capture events like sign-ins, failed logins, token refreshes, and changes to access credentials. In many SaaS and cloud systems, these logs reside in separate identity services such as Azure AD, AWS IAM Identity Center, or Google Workspace. Because authentication often spans multiple tenants or providers, auditors

Table 9.3 Logging planes with coverage and retention validation.

Logging plane	Key events	Coverage check	Retention check
Control plane	Provisioning and configuration changes	Enabled in all accounts and regions and centralized	Meets policy and archived in immutable storage
Data plane	Reads and writes and API calls	Enabled for high value resources and unified sink	Meets policy with life cycle rules verified
Network plane	Flow records and connections	Enabled for all VPC or VNet segments	Aligned with policy and tamper resistant
Authentication plane	Sign ins and token use and access grants	Collected from all identity sources and correlated	Meets policy with exportable history

must confirm that logs from all identity sources are collected and correlated. A common audit gap arises when SaaS providers manage authentication separately and tenants fail to export or retain their identity logs. Without these records, investigators lose the ability to link resource actions to verified user identities.

Retention and coverage are equally important to collection. Logs are only as valuable as their availability when needed, and many cloud services default to short retention—often 30 or 90 days. Auditors should verify that log retention settings meet or exceed the organization's recordkeeping requirements, which may be defined by internal policy or regulation. This includes ensuring that logs are archived in secure, long-term storage and that rotation or life cycle rules do not delete them prematurely. Cloud-native retention controls must be validated for each log type and tenant, as these settings can vary widely between providers and even between services within the same provider.

A recurring audit finding in cloud environments is inconsistent or incomplete log aggregation. Unified log sinks or centralized logging accounts are designed to collect telemetry from multiple tenants, but they are frequently misconfigured or disabled. When that happens, individual accounts may hold their logs locally, making cross-tenant correlation nearly impossible. Auditors should confirm that a central aggregation point exists and that log delivery from all tenants, regions, and services is verified periodically. Automated compliance checks or configuration exports can help confirm that logging configurations match approved baselines across accounts.

Another common issue is per-account drift, where logging configurations slowly diverge as new accounts or projects are created. Over time, older accounts may retain compliant settings while newer ones lack full coverage or extended retention. To mitigate this, mature organizations enforce logging through organization-level policies, infrastructure templates, or landing zones that automatically enable logging when a new account is provisioned. Auditors should examine these mechanisms and confirm that they apply globally. If configuration state can be exported, auditors can compare it across tenants to confirm uniform coverage.

Data-plane Protections: Keys, Secrets, and Segmentation

In cloud environments, the data plane encompasses the resources that actually hold or process information—object stores, file shares, databases, message queues, containers, and serverless functions—and the controls that govern how data is read, written, and transformed. Keys and secrets are the gatekeepers of this plane: encryption keys protect data at rest and in transit, while secrets such as passwords, API tokens, and database credentials authorize access to the services themselves. Practically, keys reside in cloud-native Key Management Services backed by hardware security modules, and secrets belong in managed secret stores designed for secure retrieval at runtime. The audit question is straightforward: does every workload retrieve its credentials from an approved vault and use keys provisioned through a controlled KMS, or do credentials still live in source code, images, or configuration files where they can be copied undetected? A defensible environment treats key and secret management as the first-class boundary of the data plane, not a convenience feature that teams can opt in or out of.

A well-governed KMS provides centralized creation, policy enforcement, and life cycle control over customer-managed keys while abstracting the cryptographic primitives from application owners. Permissions to use a key should be decoupled from permissions to administer it, allowing strict separation of duties between security administrators who define policies and service principals that perform encrypt and decrypt operations. Effective access boundaries limit key usage to specific principals, workloads, or network locations, with conditional controls that bind usage to private endpoints or approved runtime identities. Auditors should expect to see explicit key policies or grants that enumerate allowed operations at a fine granularity, rejecting broad privileges that permit key modification, schedule deletion, or policy tampering. Envelope encryption, aliasing, and regional scoping are implementation details; the material point is that the organization can enumerate which principals may use which keys for which purposes and prove it with configuration and logs.

Secret stores exist to eliminate static credentials scattered across code repositories, container images, and build pipelines, replacing them with centrally stored values retrieved just in time. A mature pattern restricts read access to secrets by role and context, prohibits bulk export, and enforces transport over private service endpoints. Application retrieval should occur at runtime via short-lived tokens or instance identities, never through hard-coded strings or unprotected environment variables compiled into artifacts. Rotation features in secret stores should be enabled for any credential that a provider or database engine can refresh automatically, with version history retained to support safe cutovers and rollbacks. From an audit perspective, evidence of adoption includes deny rules that block plaintext secrets in code scans, pipeline policies that prevent publishing images with embedded credentials, and runbooks that document how applications refresh secrets without downtime.

Least-privilege principles must be expressed precisely for both keys and secrets, and they should be visible in policy definitions rather than implied by convention. Key usage roles should grant only the minimal cryptographic actions required by a workload, excluding administrative operations and cross-account grants unless explicitly justified. Secret access policies should scope read permissions to the exact path or namespace used by the service, deny wildcard patterns that invite abuse, and apply conditions that bind access to workload identity, environment, or network location. Strong boundaries also include permission ceilings, such as permission boundaries or service control policies, that prevent local administrators from escalating privileges to reach protected material. Auditors should sample policies for narrowly defined actions and resource ARNs or IDs, verify that denies are explicit where appropriate, and confirm documented exceptions reference a compensating control and an expiry.

Rotation is the operational test of whether secrets and keys are truly under control or merely cataloged. Keys used for data encryption should follow a rotation schedule appropriate to their sensitivity and regulatory requirements, with re-encryption plans documented for services that do not support transparent rotation. Secrets must rotate on a cadence that reflects their exposure risk, with higher frequency for credentials used in internet-facing paths or shared runtime environments. Healthy rotation is evidenced by automation: orchestrated cutovers that update consumers, track previous versions, and monitor for stale clients still attempting to use retired credentials. Auditors should inspect rotation events, confirm that version counters advance as expected, and verify that failed rotations trigger alerts and rollback procedures rather than leaving systems in a half-rotated, unpredictable state.

Usage logging converts policy intent into verifiable facts by recording every attempt to access a key or retrieve a secret, successful or not. KMS usage should be logged with the calling principal, key identifier, operation, source network, and outcome, enabling reconstruction of who decrypted what and when. Secret store access should capture the secret path, version, caller identity, and access method, and these logs must flow to a centralized sink with retention aligned to investigative needs. Correlating key and secret access with authentication and control-plane logs allows auditors to follow a chain from an administrator's policy change to an application's runtime decryption and any subsequent data-plane reads. The absence of these linkages is a critical gap because it obscures whether unexpected data access was enabled by configuration drift, credential abuse, or both.

Segmentation at the data plane means scoping access at the service boundary—bucket, container, database, queue—not merely at the network layer. Object stores should implement resource-level policies that default to private, block public ACLs, and require request conditions such as TLS enforcement, approved encryption keys, or specific virtual network origins. Databases need per-database or per-schema privileges with separate accounts for applications, administrators, and analytics jobs, along with client-side restrictions that confine connections to private endpoints. Container registries, message brokers, and analytics services should each have their own namespaces and roles, avoiding cross-service wildcards that grant broad read or write powers across multiple projects. The auditor's test is whether every data-holding resource demonstrates a least-privilege binding to exactly the workloads that require it and nothing more.

Modern application architectures complicate these protections by multiplying identities and execution contexts, but the principles remain the same. Containers and serverless functions should receive credentials dynamically through short-lived workload identities, injected at runtime via sidecars, identity providers, or platform metadata services rather than embedded in images. Build systems must never possess production secrets; instead, deployment pipelines should request temporary credentials at release time and pass them only to the target environment. Source repositories and artifact registries should be continuously scanned for accidental secret commits, with automatic revocation and rotation workflows triggered when findings occur. Auditors should validate that runtime identities map cleanly to service scopes, and that break-glass credentials exist but are vaulted, dual-controlled, and monitored for any access.

Cross-account and multi-region designs add governance challenges that are best addressed with explicit residency, replication, and sharing models for both keys and secrets. Keys often remain region-bound, so disaster recovery plans must specify how encrypted datasets are reprovisioned or re-encrypted when restored elsewhere, and whether bring-your-own-key or hold-your-own-key arrangements impose additional operational steps. Secret distribution should follow a hub-and-spoke pattern that publishes required versions to consuming accounts while preserving centralized control of source material, with replication integrity checks to prevent drift. Revocation needs to act as a kill switch across all replicas, ensuring that a compromised secret becomes unusable everywhere in minutes, not hours. An auditor should expect documented patterns for cross-tenant sharing, a registry of data-plane dependencies that names the exact keys and secrets each service consumes, and evidence that revocation, rotation, and recovery have been exercised under realistic conditions.

Evidence Locations: CSP Config State, Org Policies, SaaS Admin Exports

Audit evidence in the cloud must be precise, reproducible, and independently verifiable. Unlike traditional datacenter audits, where screenshots and manual notes once served as acceptable proof, cloud evidence now exists primarily as configuration data—structured, timestamped, and exportable directly from provider APIs or organizational management layers. The auditor's goal is to collect this evidence in a way that preserves provenance and traceability, allowing others to rerun the same queries and reach identical results. Every finding should rest on data that can be re-extracted, versioned, and correlated, not on ephemeral visual captures that cannot prove state integrity. Screenshots may assist in storytelling, but the authoritative record is the exported configuration snapshot.

The first tier of cloud evidence lies in the organization-level policies and guardrails that define how all underlying accounts operate. These are the rules of the environment—the Service Control Policies (SCPs), Azure Policy assignments, Google Organization Constraints, or equivalent global enforcements. They dictate allowable services, geographic restrictions, encryption mandates, and network rules across the enterprise. When auditors collect evidence here, they should export the full set of active policies directly from the management plane or governance console in a machine-readable format such as JSON or YAML. Each export should include metadata: timestamps, organization identifiers, and revision numbers. This provides provenance—the ability to prove that the exported file represents the exact state of policy enforcement at the time of audit. Without these exports, auditors must rely on trust statements or screenshots, which are insufficient for repeatable verification.

The second tier of evidence involves per-account or per-project configuration states. Every account or subscription in a cloud estate contains its own set of resources—networks, storage, compute instances, IAM roles, and service configurations—that must align with the baseline. Cloud providers offer multiple ways to extract this state: through configuration inventory services (such as AWS Config, Azure Resource Graph, or Google Cloud Asset Inventory) or via infrastructure-as-code repositories if the organization uses declarative templates for deployment. The key requirement is that these configurations be exportable in their entirety, producing a snapshot of actual deployed settings. Auditors should prefer exports that include resource identifiers, region, and timestamps, so configuration drift can be detected and evidence from different accounts can be compared side by side.

Logging and telemetry configurations form the third major evidence source. Because logs underpin accountability, verifying that control-plane, data-plane, and authentication logs are properly enabled and retained is a core audit objective. Evidence collection should therefore include the export of logging configuration states—such as which log types are active, where they are stored, how long they are retained, and what access controls govern them. Many providers allow configuration queries that return this information in structured form, allowing auditors to confirm whether log sinks are unified and whether retention meets policy. Provenance here means capturing both configuration and associated identifiers for the destination storage buckets or log analytics accounts, ensuring that retention claims can be independently validated.

SaaS environments require their own form of evidence collection, since the underlying infrastructure is fully managed by the provider. The most authoritative artifacts in these cases are administrative exports from the SaaS platform itself. Examples include audit event logs, access control lists, configuration policy reports, and security posture summaries. Nearly every enterprise SaaS provider—such as Microsoft 365, Salesforce, or ServiceNow—offers exportable admin reports that show user activity, sharing settings, and compliance configurations. Auditors should obtain these exports directly from the administrative interface or via API, not screenshots of the portal, and should confirm that timestamps, tenant IDs, and report generation metadata are included. This allows reproducibility: if an auditor or regulator later reruns the export with the same parameters, they should obtain matching data for the same time period.

Across all evidence categories, the principle of *exportable integrity* governs reliability. Each artifact must be retrievable from the source system using a documented, repeatable command or query. Cloud-native tools often record the request time and user identity associated with each export, forming a natural chain of custody. Auditors should ensure that exports are saved in immutable storage, versioned, and accompanied by hash values that verify no alteration after collection. Screenshots may still serve as helpful context—for example, showing the graphical control where a policy is toggled—but they should never replace the structured evidence itself. An export with cryptographic hashes, timestamps, and origin metadata always outweighs a static image in audit defensibility.

Evidence provenance also depends on context. An exported configuration file is only meaningful when tied to a specific scope—organization, account, region, or resource type. Auditors should annotate each artifact with its scope at the time of extraction and maintain a manifest of all collected evidence. This manifest should include the export command or API call used, the collector identity, the collection time, and the destination path where the evidence was stored. Maintaining this metadata allows independent reviewers to reproduce the collection process exactly. The audit's credibility depends as much on how evidence was obtained as on what it contains.

Consistency across accounts and tenants is another critical quality measure. The same export method should be applied uniformly across all environments in scope. If the audit relies on configuration inventories, every account should produce an inventory using identical parameters. Differences in data structure or missing fields can signal inconsistent tooling or partial collection. To address this, auditors should use centrally orchestrated collection processes, preferably through organization-level aggregation tools or automated compliance scripts. By normalizing evidence formats, the audit team can easily perform comparative analysis and detect deviations from baseline configurations.

Auditors should also verify that the organization maintains a routine export process independent of the audit cycle. Continuous evidence collection supports compliance monitoring and reduces audit preparation effort. For instance, nightly exports of resource configurations and policies can populate a compliance data lake, providing a near-real-time view of cloud posture. When auditors arrive, the organization can present versioned snapshots demonstrating how configurations evolved over time, not just a single point-in-time extract. This temporal evidence shows change control discipline and strengthens audit conclusions about operational consistency.

Conclusion

Mastering the principles outlined in this chapter is critical for ensuring that cloud and SaaS environments remain both operationally efficient and defensible under audit scrutiny. The move to shared infrastructure has not eliminated accountability—it has redistributed it. Security professionals must now demonstrate assurance through verifiable configuration states, enforceable policies, and measurable evidence rather than static controls. Understanding how those elements intersect across identity, data, and governance layers empowers auditors to assess risk with clarity and precision rather than assumption or abstraction.

This chapter reinforces the role of structured configuration management and telemetry as the foundation for trustworthy AI and cloud security operations. AI-driven analytics and automation depend on accurate, consistent data drawn from these very systems, making visibility and integrity of audit evidence a prerequisite for effective decision-making. By enforcing least privilege, hardening default configurations, and capturing immutable logs across the control and data planes, professionals establish a posture that supports not only compliance but also the resilience and transparency required in AI-enabled infrastructures.

With these foundations in place, auditors and security architects are better equipped to evaluate complex, multi-tenant ecosystems without losing sight of accountability. While technologies will evolve and new service abstractions will emerge, the strategic intent remains constant: every control must be both demonstrable and defensible. Auditing the cloud is therefore not merely a procedural task but also an essential discipline that validates trust in the digital systems that underpin modern enterprises and the intelligent capabilities built upon them.

Auditor Recommendations

1. **Clarify Audit Boundaries:** Establish a clear understanding of where provider responsibility ends and tenant responsibility begins across all cloud service models. Review shared responsibility documentation for IaaS, PaaS, and SaaS environments to identify which controls fall within the auditor's purview. This ensures that audit procedures focus only on evidence and configurations the organization can actually manage and verify.
2. **Verify Guardrail Enforcement:** Confirm that organization-level guardrails such as Service Control Policies, Azure Policies, or Organization Constraints are in place and actively enforced across all accounts. Evaluate how these guardrails restrict actions, enforce region or service limits, and prevent privilege escalation. Auditors should treat these as primary governance controls and test their effectiveness through configuration exports rather than visual confirmation.
3. **Assess Identity Inheritance:** Examine how permissions flow through the organization hierarchy, from management groups to individual workloads. Pay close attention to inherited permissions that may unintentionally broaden access beyond intended scopes. Validating the logic of inheritance and the presence of explicit denies ensures least privilege is enforced consistently throughout the cloud environment.
4. **Evaluate Baseline Consistency:** Confirm that network, storage, and compute configurations align with the organization's approved baseline standards. Use exported configuration states to compare settings such as encryption defaults, segmentation, and logging enablement across accounts. Detecting configuration drift early allows auditors to highlight systemic governance gaps before they escalate into compliance issues.
5. **Inspect Network Segmentation:** Verify that network architectures enforce a default-deny posture with controlled access between environments. Audit VPCs or VNets to ensure segmentation isolates sensitive workloads and prevents unnecessary public exposure. Auditors should also validate that any cross-account connectivity occurs through approved private links or gateways defined in policy.
6. **Validate Logging Coverage:** Ensure that logging is active and complete across all required planes—control, data, network, and authentication. Review configurations to confirm that all accounts and SaaS tenants forward logs to a centralized sink with defined retention and integrity controls. By validating logging coverage, auditors can confirm that the environment supports accountability and traceability.
7. **Confirm Retention and Integrity of Evidence:** Check that log and telemetry retention periods align with policy and regulatory requirements, and that archived data cannot be modified or deleted prematurely. Evaluate life cycle policies for completeness and immutability. Reliable retention guarantees that investigators and auditors can reconstruct events long after they occur.
8. **Audit Key and Secret Management Controls:** Review how encryption keys and credentials are stored, accessed, and rotated through cloud-native Key Management Services and secret stores. Verify separation of duties between administrators and key users, along with documented rotation policies. Auditors should expect evidence of automated key usage logging and periodic verification that credentials are not embedded in code or configuration files.

9. **Collect Exportable, Reproducible Evidence:** Require all audit evidence to be obtained as machine-readable exports from governance layers, configuration inventories, and SaaS administrative consoles. Avoid reliance on screenshots or informal attestations that cannot be independently verified. Structured exports with timestamps and identifiers provide defensible, repeatable proof of control effectiveness.
10. **Monitor for Multi-account Drift:** Evaluate whether all accounts and projects maintain alignment with centralized configurations for logging, baselines, and policies. Auditors should review automated compliance reports or periodic exports that detect deviations from standard configurations. Monitoring for drift ensures that organizational controls remain consistent even as environments scale or new services are deployed.

Chapter Questions

1. Which factor most directly defines what controls are auditable within a cloud tenant?
   - **A.** The shared responsibility boundaries and the tenant boundary
   - **B.** The provider's chosen hypervisor and hardware vendors
   - **C.** The number of regions the tenant operates in
   - **D.** The tenant's incident response playbooks

2. Which mechanism functions as an organization-level guardrail to constrain permissions across cloud accounts?
   - **A.** Local role assignments inside a single resource group
   - **B.** Service Control Policies or equivalent organization policies
   - **C.** Ad-hoc deny statements embedded in individual application code
   - **D.** VPC security groups configured per workload

3. What network baseline principle should govern inbound and outbound traffic across VPCs/VNets?
   - **A.** Allow all traffic within the tenant to minimize complexity
   - **B.** Permit public access if resources are tagged "public"
   - **C.** Enforce a default-deny posture with explicit, minimal allow rules
   - **D.** Rely on provider-managed DPI to implicitly block risky flows

4. Which storage baseline expectation best reduces accidental data exposure?
   - **A.** Storing access keys alongside objects for fast recovery
   - **B.** Enabling object versioning only in development environments
   - **C.** Relying on per-user ACLs without policies
   - **D.** Mandating encryption at rest by default and blocking public access unless explicitly approved

5. Which combination best represents the mandatory logging planes for comprehensive coverage?
   - **A.** Control plane, data plane, network plane, and authentication plane
   - **B.** Patch management, billing, compliance, and asset inventory
   - **C.** Application performance, synthetic monitoring, UX analytics, and tracing
   - **D.** Endpoint antivirus, EDR alerts, sandboxing, and email security

6. What is a common logging gap that undermines cross-tenant auditability?
   A. Over-collecting verbose debug logs from every microservice
   B. Misconfigured or disabled unified log sinks leading to per-account drift
   C. Retaining logs for seven years in cold storage
   D. Duplicating control-plane logs into multiple SIEMs

7. Where should application secrets be stored and retrieved from to avoid credential sprawl?
   A. Environment variables embedded in container images
   B. Plaintext files deployed with the application bundle
   C. A managed secret store with just-in-time retrieval at runtime
   D. Developer laptops during initial deployment

8. Which access model best reflects sound key governance for KMS-protected data?
   A. Granting all administrators full encrypt, decrypt, and key policy edit rights
   B. Allowing application owners to rotate and delete master keys directly
   C. Sharing a single cross-environment key for all workloads to simplify operations
   D. Separating key administration from key usage and scoping cryptographic actions to specific principals

9. What form of audit evidence carries the strongest provenance in cloud and SaaS environments?
   A. Machine-readable exports of configuration and policy state with timestamps and identifiers
   B. Annotated screenshots of portal pages
   C. Handwritten notes from operations staff
   D. Email confirmations from service owners

10. How should data-plane segmentation be expressed to prevent lateral access between services?
    A. By relying solely on tenant-wide network firewalls
    B. By scoping permissions at the resource boundary (e.g., bucket, container, and database) with least privilege
    C. By enabling public access temporarily during deployment windows
    D. By using a single admin role to manage all data services for consistency

10

Data Protection

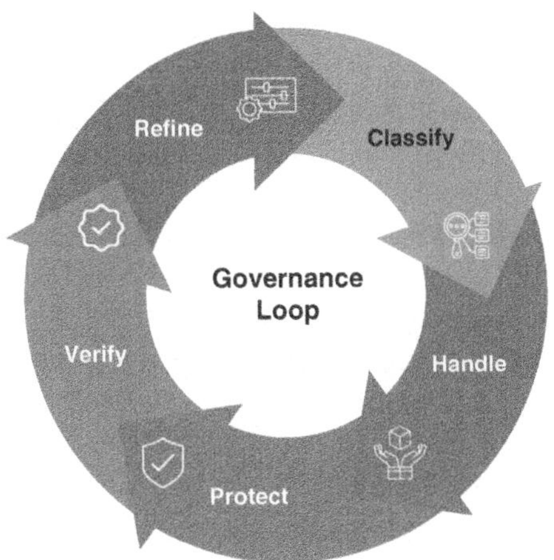

Data protection is the foundation of every credible cybersecurity and compliance program. Without disciplined control over how information is classified, stored, transmitted, and destroyed, even the most advanced technical defenses become unreliable. This chapter examines the practical systems that safeguard data integrity and confidentiality—from encryption and key management to tokenization, masking, and monitoring. Understanding these disciplines is essential to ensuring that sensitive assets remain protected across complex, hybrid environments where data is constantly moving between applications, users, and cloud services.

Modern organizations face an expanding landscape of data risk driven by cloud adoption, artificial intelligence, and continuous integration pipelines. Encryption, key management, and data loss prevention (DLP) controls now operate within automated ecosystems where governance must keep pace with speed and scale. By addressing how cryptographic keys are generated, rotated, and governed; how encryption operates in transit and at rest; and how exceptions are managed responsibly, this chapter provides a blueprint for building measurable assurance into systems that cannot rely on trust alone. The emphasis is on verifiable control—policies that can be tested, evidence that can be exported, and designs that hold up under audit.

From data classification to DLP events, every control described here connects back to risk management and regulatory accountability. The ability to trace information from creation through disposal, supported by auditable evidence and clear ownership, defines the maturity of an organization's data protection strategy. In an era where AI systems ingest vast amounts of sensitive data, the boundaries between privacy, compliance, and security are more intertwined than ever. By mastering the data protection principles and evidence practices covered in this chapter, auditors and security architects can ensure that both human and machine-driven processes operate within a framework of provable trust.

Data Classification and Handling Requirements

A data classification scheme translates abstract ideas about sensitivity into real, enforceable rules that govern how information is stored, transmitted, and destroyed. Each organization must decide how to categorize its information based on potential harm if that data were lost, stolen, or altered. Most classification systems use three or four levels—such as Public, Internal, Confidential, and Restricted—and each level comes with its own handling requirements. For example, Public data may be freely shared, while Restricted data may only be stored on encrypted systems with strict access controls. The purpose of classification is not to create paperwork but to establish predictable, auditable behaviors around information, ensuring that everyone—from IT administrators to business users—treats data according to its risk profile.

Once data is classified, specific storage requirements flow naturally from those categories. Restricted data must reside only in approved repositories, such as encrypted file servers, protected databases, or managed cloud services with customer-controlled keys. Confidential data might be stored in shared drives or collaboration tools, but only if they support encryption, version control, and access logging. Internal data can live in general-purpose systems, provided that authentication and basic monitoring are in place. Public data can be hosted with minimal restriction, but even then, organizations must ensure integrity controls to prevent tampering or defacement. For auditors, the key is to verify that each classification level has a defined storage standard and that systems enforce it through configurations, permissions, and encryption settings. Table 10.1 links each classification level to concrete handling rules and the specific evidence auditors will sample.

Transmission requirements apply the same logic to data in motion. Restricted or highly confidential data must always be transmitted using strong encryption protocols such as Transport Layer Security (TLS 1.2) or higher, VPN tunnels, or other managed secure channels. Sending such data by email or instant message without protection should be prohibited by policy and enforced by technical controls. Confidential or internal data may travel over standard encrypted channels, provided that the organization manages certificate validity and enforces secure configurations. Public data may be transmitted over ordinary channels, but auditors still verify that systems log and monitor transfers to detect misuse or data leakage. Each of these transmission rules should map directly back to classification policy, forming a consistent chain from policy language to technical enforcement.

Retention and disposal rules define how long data lives and what happens when it reaches the end of its useful life. Highly sensitive data is often kept only as long as legally or operationally required, then destroyed using secure methods such as cryptographic wiping, physical shredding, or managed data deletion jobs. Confidential data may follow longer retention cycles if tied to business records or compliance obligations. Public or low-impact data can typically be retained indefinitely, provided storage costs and data minimization goals are balanced. The important control is traceability—auditors should be able to connect a policy statement like "Restricted data

Table 10.1 Classification to handling and evidence traceability matrix.

Classification level	Storage requirements	Transmission requirements	Retention disposal	Primary evidence sources
Public	Approved general repositories with integrity controls	TLS for normal use with monitoring	Business defined retention with integrity checks	Repository configs and basic logs
Internal	Managed platforms with baseline encryption and access control	TLS with managed certificates and secure email routes	Retention per policy with scheduled deletion	Config exports and access logs
Confidential	Sanctioned stores with encryption at rest and role based access	Strong TLS with gateway enforcement and managed file transfer	Defined retention with deletion tickets and backup expiry	Key references KMS logs and deletion reports
Restricted	Approved repositories with customer managed keys and immutable logging	mTLS or approved VPN and pinned ciphers	Strict retention with crypto shred and destruction attestations	KMS HSM logs IAM grants and destruction records

retained for seven years" to documented backup settings, retention schedules, and evidence of deletion or destruction activities.

The scope of classification extends beyond where data is created to where it flows and where copies exist. Business processes often spread data across multiple systems—databases, data warehouses, analytics tools, and cloud storage buckets—and every copy inherits the same classification. An email attachment containing Restricted data does not lose its classification simply because it was sent. Auditors look for a data flow map or inventory that shows how each element of sensitive information moves through the environment. This mapping ensures that storage, transmission, and retention controls apply consistently across all systems that touch the data, not just the one where it originated.

To make classification practical, organizations must embed it in daily workflows. This can include metadata tags within files, classification fields in databases, or automated tools that detect and label content based on pattern matching or contextual analysis. Employees may also apply sensitivity labels manually when creating or sharing content. Automated tools and manual processes complement each other—automation catches what humans miss, while users provide context automation cannot infer. During audits, evidence of correct labeling is often found in file metadata, DLP logs, or collaboration platform settings that enforce classification labels automatically when users create or move data.

Each classification level must tie directly to specific control objectives. For instance, the policy for Restricted data might specify "encrypt at rest and in transit, enforce least-privilege access, monitor for exfiltration, and retain for seven years." Those objectives should then connect to actual system configurations and audit evidence, such as encryption key settings, IAM roles, and DLP incident reports. A traceability matrix is often used to show the link between classification level, control objective, and the evidence proving implementation. This traceability gives auditors confidence that the organization's written policy is not theoretical—it is operationalized in real systems and can be tested through configuration reviews or sampling.

No classification scheme is perfect, and exceptions are sometimes necessary. Legacy systems may not support encryption or labeling, and business operations may temporarily rely on insecure data flows while replacements are deployed. In these cases, organizations must document exceptions through a formal waiver process. Each waiver should describe the data affected, the risk accepted, compensating controls in place, and an expiration date for review. This ensures exceptions remain visible and controlled rather than becoming permanent gaps. Auditors typically check that exception logs are maintained, that management has approved them, and that compensating measures—like network isolation or enhanced monitoring—are functioning as described.

Encryption in Transit and at Rest

Encryption serves as the foundation of data protection, ensuring that information remains confidential and unaltered whether it is stored on a disk or moving across a network. In cybersecurity auditing, encryption is evaluated not only by its presence but by its completeness—known as coverage. Complete coverage means that all data assets, regardless of where they live or how they move, receive appropriate cryptographic protection aligned with their classification. Encryption is not a feature to check off a list; it is a control discipline that must extend uniformly across systems, databases, applications, and devices to eliminate weak links that attackers can exploit. The auditor's task is to determine whether encryption practices are comprehensive, consistent, and properly governed throughout the enterprise environment.

Encryption in transit focuses on safeguarding data as it moves between clients, servers, and services. Modern environments rely on TLS to protect network communications, with current standards mandating TLS 1.2 or higher and prohibiting outdated versions such as SSL or TLS 1.0/1.1. Proper cipher suite selection is critical—weak algorithms like RC4 or 3DES should be disabled in favor of strong, forward-secure ciphers such as AES-GCM with 256-bit keys and elliptic-curve key exchanges. Secure channels are required for web traffic (HTTPS), email transport (SMTPS, IMAPS), API calls, and service-to-service communication across internal microservices or hybrid clouds. Auditors assess this layer by reviewing configuration baselines, load balancer policies, and network security scans to verify that deprecated protocols are blocked and certificate management practices prevent expired or self-signed certificates from slipping into production.

Encryption at rest applies to data that resides on persistent media—disks, databases, storage buckets, and mobile devices. For enterprise storage, full-disk encryption (FDE) and volume-level encryption protect against physical theft or improper decommissioning, while database-level encryption secures individual columns or fields that contain sensitive identifiers, credentials, or financial information. In the cloud, services such as AWS KMS, Azure Key Vault, and Google Cloud KMS are commonly used to manage encryption keys centrally and enforce policy-based encryption across storage classes. Even virtual machine snapshots, data warehouses, and archival backups should employ encryption mechanisms, often using AES-256 as the standard. Auditors examine whether encryption keys are customer-managed or provider-managed, whether automatic encryption is enabled by default, and whether stored backups—especially older ones—adhere to the same encryption posture as production systems.

Coverage is the term used to describe how completely encryption has been implemented across all data states and assets. A system may advertise "encryption enabled," but if only some databases, volumes, or file shares are protected, coverage is incomplete. True coverage ensures that encryption spans endpoints, network traffic, cloud storage, and backup systems consistently, without leaving "blind spots" where plaintext data resides. Auditors verify this by examining architecture diagrams, key management logs, and configuration inventories to confirm that encryption is applied wherever classified data exists. They may also sample data flows to ensure encryption remains active not just at rest and in transit but also during processing in temporary caches or staging environments—places where organizations often overlook protection.

Backups and disaster recovery systems are common weak points in encryption coverage. Copies of sensitive data may be written to external media or cloud archives that lack equivalent encryption controls. Every backup set should be encrypted using either the same key hierarchy as production data or a separate managed key designated for long-term storage. Encryption should extend through the entire life cycle: from creation and storage to transport off-site and eventual deletion. Auditors typically request evidence such as encryption configuration files, key rotation reports, and backup logs showing that encryption jobs completed successfully. A single unencrypted backup tape or cloud export can undermine an otherwise secure environment, so ensuring parity of protection is critical to an audit's success.

Encryption governance ensures that these technical protections remain consistent, monitored, and updated. Governance begins with a documented encryption policy that specifies approved algorithms, key lengths, key management responsibilities, and rotation frequencies. It also defines where encryption is mandatory and where it may be optional based on data classification. Oversight typically falls under an information security committee or key management board, which maintains inventories of encryption keys, audits key custodianship, and reviews exceptions. Governance also includes monitoring compliance through automated scans, certificate expiration alerts, and periodic validation of encryption coverage across platforms. The goal is to make encryption not a one-time configuration but a sustained control maintained by policy and verification.

Exceptions to encryption requirements must be formally governed and strictly temporary. Legacy systems may lack native support for modern protocols, and high-performance workloads might resist encryption due to latency or throughput concerns. These scenarios should never be accepted silently. Each must be documented through a risk acceptance or waiver process that identifies the affected system, the data classification, and the compensating controls in place—such as network isolation, access restrictions, or encrypted front-end proxies. Every waiver must have an expiration date and a plan for remediation or upgrade. Auditors expect to see an approved exception register, signed by risk owners, and evidence that the system is under enhanced monitoring to offset the missing encryption layer.

Performance constraints are sometimes cited as reasons to avoid encryption, particularly in high-volume environments such as database clusters or file indexing systems. However, modern hardware acceleration and efficient cryptographic libraries make these concerns increasingly obsolete. When performance issues are legitimate, encryption can often be applied selectively—for example, encrypting specific columns in a database rather than entire tables. The principle remains the same: exceptions should be narrowly scoped and reviewed regularly. An audit should confirm that such performance-based exceptions are justified, documented, and aligned with business risk, not convenience.

Auditors assess the integration of encryption controls with other data protection mechanisms. Encryption must complement access controls, logging, and DLP rather than operate in isolation. For example, encrypted data should still generate access events, and DLP systems should recognize encrypted transfers without blocking legitimate traffic. A comprehensive encryption program achieves harmony between confidentiality and usability, protecting data across every layer of its life cycle. When encryption in transit, encryption at rest, and strong governance combine under full coverage, the result is a resilient and auditable defense against data compromise—one that balances technical rigor with operational reality.

Key Management: Generation, Rotation, Custody, and Separation of Duties

A mature key management program treats cryptographic keys as regulated assets with a defined life cycle that spans planning, generation, distribution, use, rotation, archival, and retirement. The organizing principle is governance metadata that travels with each key and makes decisions auditable at every step. At minimum, the record should capture business purpose, data classification served, accountable owner, algorithm and key length, approved usages, rotation interval, creation and expiration dates, custody model, and retirement strategy. It should also identify where the key is hosted, whether export is allowed, what wraps it in the hierarchy, and which systems are authorized to call it. Maintaining this inventory in a system of record—synchronized with identity, asset, and data catalogs—lets auditors trace a straight line from a protected dataset to the specific key material and the controls that govern its use.

Generation sets the tone for the entire life cycle because weak origins create strong liabilities. Keys should be created by approved mechanisms that provide demonstrable entropy and provenance, such as hardware security modules with certified random number generation or cloud key managers configured for non-exportable material. Generation ceremonies must be scripted, witnessed, and logged, with dual control for any action that could later enable export, wrapping key change, or administrative bypass. The metadata should record the generator, the environment and region, the initialization parameters, and the attestation artifacts proving the key was never exposed in plaintext. Where derivation is required, it should use vetted key derivation functions under policy, never ad hoc reuse or deterministic shortcuts that blur isolation between tenants, applications, or data sets.

Secure distribution is less about moving key bytes and more about tightly controlling where cryptographic operations may occur. Production keys should remain resident in hardened services, with applications invoking encrypt, decrypt, sign, or unwrap operations over authenticated APIs so that plaintext material never leaves a protected boundary. Envelope encryption enforces layered custody by using data encryption keys for bulk protection while key encryption keys or customer master keys perform wrapping, reducing the blast radius of rotation or compromise. Permissions must be least-privilege and purpose-bound, authorizing the exact operation and resource scope needed and applying conditions such as time limits, network location, and workload identity. The governance record should show which principals can use the key, how those grants were approved, and what compensating controls exist for high-risk capabilities such as decrypt or export. Table 10.2 specifies the minimum key metadata and the artifacts that make life cycle control auditable.

Rotation converts policy into recurring action and is the clearest measure of operational discipline. Intervals should reflect algorithm strength, regulatory expectations, and exposure, with short-lived data encryption keys, moderate cycles for database or storage service keys, and defined cadences for signing, sealing, and wrapping keys that balance risk with interoperability. Implementations should version keys rather than replace identifiers abruptly, supporting dual-key periods in which new writes use the latest version while reads honor the previous one until re-encryption completes. The inventory must record version lineage, rotation triggers—scheduled,

Table 10.2 Key governance metadata and life cycle controls.

Metadata field	Required content	Audit evidence	Control owner
Purpose	Business process and data class served	Key record with justification and approvals	Data owner
Owner	Named accountable custodian and backup	Access reviews and role assignments	Security governance
Algorithm Length	Approved algorithm and key size	Configuration export and policy reference	Crypto officer
Rotation Interval	Defined cadence and trigger types	Rotation logs and version lineage	Platform owner
Usage Restrictions	Allowed operations and resource scope	Key policy and effective grants	Security engineering
Custody Model	Separation of duties and quorum rules	SoD matrix and M of N event logs	Risk management
Retirement Plan	Disable destroy and archive steps	Destruction attestations and change tickets	Key management
Hosting Location	HSM or cloud KMS region and residency	Attestation reports and inventory map	Cloud platform

risk-driven, or incident-driven—and the scope of rekeying jobs so auditors can verify that old versions were retired cleanly. Evidence should include rotation run logs, key alias change histories, and exception tickets where re-encryption was deferred with documented risk acceptance.

Custody encompasses who can influence a key's life and how that influence is constrained to prevent unilateral control. Clear separation of duties is mandatory: requesters define the business need, approvers validate risk and alignment to policy, and operators execute changes within tightly bounded roles. No single individual should be able to generate, approve, and activate a production key, and policy administrators should not possess the ability to decrypt protected data. Roles such as security officer, crypto officer, and system administrator must be distinct, with dual control required for sensitive actions including deletion scheduling, export enablement, or policy downgrades. Periodic access reviews should reconcile authorized roles with current staffing and duties, removing privileges promptly when responsibilities change and documenting every variance as a time-boxed exception.

Recovery and escrow must be engineered without creating backdoors that undermine the assurance model. For data-at-rest keys, escrow can be achieved through secure backups of non-exportable keys wrapped under separate backup keys or through threshold schemes that require multiple custodians to reconstruct material. Authentication or code-signing private keys should not be escrowed in a form that enables impersonation; instead, recovery should favor reissuance under a new trust chain with explicit revocation of the old. Break-glass procedures must exist for urgent access, but they require multiparty approval, enhanced monitoring, and strict time limits, with post-event review to validate necessity and completeness. Regularly scheduled recovery drills should prove that escrowed material, backups, and documentation are sufficient to restore operations within stated objectives without violating separation of duties.

Audit trails are the connective tissue that demonstrate custody and change history beyond doubt. Every key-relevant event should produce tamper-evident records that capture who performed the action, what changed, when and where it occurred, and why it was authorized. High-value events include creation, import, policy modification, permission grant or revoke, version rotation, disablement, deletion scheduling, cancellation of deletion, export enablement, and any cryptographic operation performed on protected datasets. Logs must inherit time synchronization, integrity protection, and retention appropriate to the sensitivity of dependent data, and they should be aggregated for correlation and alerting on anomalies such as sudden spikes in decrypt requests. The governance record should reference these evidence sources directly so an auditor can sample end-to-end from business justification to the precise log lines proving compliant execution.

Archival and retirement are often where programs stumble, because inertia favors keeping old keys "just in case." Retirement should be a deliberate sequence: disable the key to stop new usage, complete re-encryption or resigning where needed, revoke residual permissions, wait out defined safety periods, and then destroy the material in a verifiable manner. Crypto-shredding is only credible if the destroyed key was indeed the sole means to decrypt the data, so inventories and wrapping chains must be accurate and complete. HSM zeroization, certificate revocation publication, and destruction attestations should be preserved alongside change approvals as part of the permanent audit package. Metadata should record the retirement rationale, affected systems, data disposition outcomes, and any dependencies that require deferred destruction under legal hold or regulatory retention.

Coverage is the systemic quality that ensures every place a protected dataset exists is governed by the correct key and policy. Each key record should map to specific assets, environments, regions, and workflows, including transient copies such as snapshots, exports, caches, and disaster recovery replicas. Development, testing, and training environments must never reuse production keys; they require separate hierarchies with clearly marked non-production policies and shortened lifetimes. Third-party platforms and software-as-a-service should be accounted for with customer-managed keys where feasible and with explicit documentation of provider-managed models where not, including the contractual controls that offset reduced custody. Routine reconciliations should compare the key inventory to data inventories and architecture diagrams, surfacing shadow keys or unprotected stores before they become audit findings.

Hardware/Cloud KMS/HSM Controls and Access Boundaries

Assurance expectations for hardware security modules and cloud key management services begin with a simple premise: the cryptographic boundary must be explicit, independently validated, and enforce separation between administrators, applications, and auditors. An HSM establishes a hardware-enforced boundary where private key material is generated and remains non-exportable, while a cloud KMS offers a service boundary that abstracts hardware but must still provide equivalent guarantees through attestation, configuration controls, and verifiable logs. Partitioning or tenancy constructs are expected to prevent one application, account, or tenant from affecting another, even when physical hardware is shared. The audit objective is to see those boundaries reflected in design documents, access models, and operational evidence rather than assumed from marketing claims, with clear statements of what is inside the cryptographic boundary and what is not.

Partitioning is the foundational control in appliance HSMs because it maps business and technical isolation to cryptographic isolation. Each partition or security domain should own its key hierarchy, policies, and operator roles, ensuring that compromise or misconfiguration in one partition cannot grant access to keys in another. Life cycle actions—generation, import, wrap, unwrap, disable, destroy—must be constrained to the partition that owns the material, and any cross-partition operation should require explicit, dual-controlled authorization. Auditors test the strength of partitioning by reviewing role assignments, access control lists, and command histories tied to each partition, and by validating that firmware and configuration attestations match approved versions across the modules that host those partitions.

Tenant isolation in cloud KMS follows the same goals but relies on logical boundaries backed by provider controls and certifications. Customer keys should be bound to a specific account, project, or subscription, with resource policies and identity-based access defining which principals may invoke cryptographic operations. Provider-managed hardware may be pooled, but cryptographic separation must prevent cross-tenant key discovery, side-channel leakage, or influence over another tenant's key state. Brief examples include using AWS KMS key policies to scope allowed principals and operations, Azure Key Vault access control to separate data-plane use from management-plane administration, or Google Cloud KMS service accounts that restrict encrypt and decrypt permissions to a defined workload identity, each combined with organization-level policies that deny broad grants by default.

Administrative models must embody least privilege and role separation so that no single person can create, approve, and operate on production keys. Distinct roles typically include security officer or crypto officer for policy and life cycle, system administrator for platform maintenance, and application owner for usage grants, with read-only audit roles separated from operational authority. In HSMs, these roles are enforced with tamper-responding devices, operator cards, and authentication factors; in cloud KMS, they are realized through identity and access management, service control policies, and conditional grants that bind permissions to context such as network location or workload identity. The expected evidence is a role matrix mapped to systems of record, change tickets showing multiparty approval, and periodic reviews that reconcile assigned roles with current duties.

Quorum controls—often expressed as M-of-N or dual control—are required for high-risk actions that could expose, disable, or destroy key material. Examples include enabling export on a non-exportable key, scheduling deletion on a root key, changing a wrapping key that protects many data keys, or downgrading a key's policy to allow broader access. An HSM typically enforces quorum with multiple operator credentials or smartcards presented at the device or via remote PIN entry, while cloud KMS achieves equivalent assurance with multi-approver workflows, just-in-time elevation, and break-glass processes that are heavily logged and time-bounded. Auditors should see configuration evidence that quorum is required for defined actions, along with logs that prove multiple distinct custodians were present for those events.

Approval workflows must translate policy into controlled, reviewable changes so that keys cannot silently drift into unsafe states. Requests to create keys, modify policies, grant new principals, or rotate versions should reference a business purpose, data classification, and risk assessment, then route to independent approvers before any operational step occurs. In cloud KMS, this is commonly implemented through change management systems that integrate with infrastructure-as-code pipelines and require pull-request approvals; in HSM environments, task orders and ceremony scripts document each step executed at the console. The audit trail should correlate the request, approvals, execution artifacts, and resulting configuration diffs, making it straightforward to reconstruct who did what, when, and why.

Access boundaries are enforced technically through a combination of resource policies, identity grants, network constraints, and service-level configurations that narrow where cryptographic operations are permitted. For KMS, resource policies can restrict decrypt operations to specific principals, VPC-bound endpoints, or trusted device states, while deny-by-default organization policies prevent wildcard grants and external account access. For HSMs, network segmentation, bastion patterns, and mutually authenticated management channels limit administrative reach, and application access occurs only through client libraries that never expose raw key material. Evidence includes effective policy documents, IAM role bindings, security group or firewall rules, and successful control tests that demonstrate a request from an unauthorized principal or network is rejected and logged.

Key-usage logging, attestation, and integrity monitoring provide the proof that access boundaries and administrative models are operating continuously. Every cryptographic operation—encrypt, decrypt, sign, verify, unwrap—should produce a tamper-evident record that includes caller identity, key identifier and version, operation type, request context, and outcome. Logs must be aggregated centrally, time-synchronized, and protected against alteration, with alerts for anomalous patterns such as sudden surges in decrypt calls, access from unexpected regions, or attempts to schedule key deletion. Attestation reports or device health signals for HSMs, and provider attestation or certificate of compliance for cloud KMS, should be retained with change records to prove that operations occurred on approved hardware and software baselines.

Life cycle assurance in these environments extends beyond creation and use to rotation, archival, and destruction with minimal blast radius. Envelope encryption patterns limit the scope of re-encryption by rotating data encryption keys under stable wrapping keys, while versioned keys allow reads with prior versions until rekeying completes. Deletion should be a staged process with disable, wait, and destroy steps, each requiring quorum and generating irreversible attestations, and recovery must rely on tested, access-controlled backups that do not undermine non-exportability. Auditors look for version lineage, rotation run books, deletion schedules with approvals, and restoration drills that validate recovery objectives without violating role separation or boundary controls.

Tokenization, Masking, and DLP Policy Design

Tokenization and masking are often grouped with encryption in casual conversation, but they solve different problems and carry different operational tradeoffs that matter deeply in audit. Encryption preserves the original data and relies on keys to render it unreadable, making it the right choice when the system must later recover exact values for business purposes. Tokenization substitutes sensitive values with nonsensitive surrogates drawn from a controlled vault, allowing applications to operate on references while the true data remains sequestered; the mapping is reversible only within the tokenization service. Masking alters the representation so that humans or noncritical systems see redacted or partially obscured data, often irreversibly for lower environments or screenshots. Choosing among these techniques depends on whether the consumer needs the exact original, a stable surrogate, or merely enough structure to validate formats or troubleshoot safely.

Analytics use cases highlight the distinctions clearly. When analysts need population-level trends without exposure to individual identifiers, tokenization with deterministic options can preserve joinability across datasets while keeping the vaulted originals out of the analytics platform. Irreversible masking is ideal for data science sandboxes and preproduction environments, where structural realism matters more than identity fidelity; masked values let pipelines run, dashboards render, and schema drift surface without risking leakage. Encryption still has a place in analytics, protecting staging zones, parquet files, and query traffic, but it does not by itself limit who can see plaintext once decrypted in the engine. A layered approach uses encryption for transport and storage, tokenization to restrict access to true values, and masking to minimize human exposure during exploratory work.

Operational support and customer service scenarios often demand context without full disclosure. Format-preserving masking allows agents to confirm a last four, a BIN range, or a postal code segment while preventing them from viewing the complete credential or personal detail. Tokenization can expose a stable token to ticketing and logging systems so that cases can be correlated over time without persisting sensitive content in chat transcripts or workflow notes. When escalation requires exact values—such as a payment gateway reconciliation—privileged tooling can retrieve the original from the vault under dual control, or a one-time reveal can be initiated through a supervised workflow. Encryption remains foundational for securing the systems that store tickets, recordings, and attachments, but the reduction of human-visible plaintext is delivered by masking and the segregation of crown-jewel values is delivered by tokenization.

Lower environments deserve special emphasis because they historically leak the most. Development, testing, and training systems should never receive live sensitive data in plaintext; irreversible masking or synthetic data generation is the default, and tokenization is used only when deterministic behavior is essential for functional testing. Build pipelines should enforce this policy by rejecting data imports that lack masking attestations and by scanning fixtures for forbidden patterns before deployment. Where limited realism is necessary—say, for fraud model validation—access to de-tokenization must be time-bound, logged, and tied to named service identities rather than generic accounts. Auditors expect to see environment-specific controls and evidence that production keys, vaults, and datasets are strictly segregated from non-production.

An auditable DLP policy starts with precise scope anchored to data classification and business process ownership. Scope must enumerate channels under control—endpoints, email, web gateways, file shares, collaboration suites, APIs, cloud storage, and data egress from analytics tools—and tie them to specific user populations and device states. Each scoped channel must declare where blocking is allowed, where only monitoring is permitted due to business continuity constraints, and how exceptions are requested and reviewed. Ownership is not an afterthought; data owners and control owners must be explicitly named, with responsibilities for tuning decisions, exception approvals, and incident response defined so that accountability is never ambiguous.

Patterns and classifiers are the heart of DLP and must combine signature techniques with context signals to reduce false positives. High-confidence detectors include exact data matching against hashed inventory sets, document fingerprinting for proprietary materials, and validated pattern-plus-checksum logic for identifiers like payment cards. Contextual features—business unit, application source, project tag, and recipient domain—help the engine treat the same string differently when it appears in a build log versus a finance export. Machine-learning or proximity-based classifiers can supplement but should not substitute for deterministic methods when regulatory identifiers are at stake. Auditable policy documents should map each classifier to the classifications it protects and articulate confidence thresholds that trigger different actions.

Actions must be explicitly defined and calibrated to risk and workflow impact. Typical actions include block, quarantine, encrypt-on-send, justify-and-allow with manager notification, or allow-but-log with elevated scrutiny for subsequent events. Policies should vary by channel and context, such that an external email with multiple high-confidence hits from a payroll export is blocked, whereas an internal share to a restricted team may be allowed with encryption and watermarking. User feedback loops—inline prompts, justification forms, and coaching messages—are as important as the technical block because they drive behavior change and provide auditable intent signals. Every action path must write durable events that capture who attempted what, which classifier fired, what decision the engine took, and what user justification, if any, was provided.

Tuning is a continuous control, not a one-time setup, and it requires a formal register that records changes and their rationale. The tuning and exception register should include the policy name, classifier revised, threshold adjustments, affected scope, data owner approval, expected impact on precision and recall, and review dates. Temporary suppressions for business deadlines or system migrations must carry expiry dates and compensating monitoring, ensuring that relaxed controls do not become permanent by neglect. Auditors will expect to sample this register, verify that approvals came from appropriate owners, and confirm that telemetry after the change matches the predicted impact rather than masking real leaks.

Effectiveness must be evidenced through a blend of quantitative metrics and qualitative review cycles. Quantitative signals include event volumes by channel, high-confidence versus low-confidence hit ratios, block rates, justify-and-allow frequencies, mean time to review incidents, and recurrence rates by user or department. Trend lines should demonstrate that precision improves over time while coverage remains broad, with outliers investigated rather than explained away. Qualitative oversight occurs in periodic reviews where data owners, security engineering, and operations examine representative incidents, assess user justifications, and decide whether classifiers or scopes need refinement. Meeting artifacts, action items, and subsequent metric movement form the auditable trail that DLP is being actively governed.

Integration with tokenization and masking completes the picture by shrinking the problem space that DLP must police. When sensitive fields are replaced by tokens upstream, fewer channels ever carry plaintext, leading to lower event volumes and higher signal-to-noise in what remains. Masked data reduces the need for broad exceptions in collaboration tools, enabling stricter DLP actions without breaking everyday work. The audit narrative should show that encryption protects storage and transport, tokenization minimizes where true values exist, masking limits human visibility, and DLP monitors and enforces policy at the edges—each control reinforcing the others so that lapses in one layer do not become catastrophic exposures.

Data Flow Mapping and High-risk Stores/Paths

Understanding how data moves through an organization is central to both effective security design and credible audit assurance. Every piece of information—whether a customer record, a source document, or a machine log—follows a life cycle that can be traced from its point of ingestion, through processing and storage, to sharing, backup, and eventual disposal. A data flow map makes that life cycle visible, identifying where sensitive data resides, how it travels, and where protection controls are applied. Without this visibility, security policies operate in abstraction, disconnected from the real systems and processes that handle the data every day. The goal for the author is to depict these flows comprehensively and trace them to responsible owners, classified data elements, and control mechanisms that demonstrate accountability and risk coverage.

Ingestion is the first critical stage and often the point of greatest diversity in data sources. Information may originate from customer portals, API integrations, IoT devices, third-party feeds, or internal batch uploads. Each source introduces its own handling rules, formats, and authentication methods. The author should illustrate how data enters the organization's environment, which systems act as the initial receivers, and what controls validate and sanitize inputs before they are accepted into trusted zones. Auditors look for evidence that ingress channels are identified and controlled—such as API gateways enforcing TLS, ingestion pipelines applying validation scripts, and credentialed service accounts limiting unauthorized submissions. The map should clearly show these entry points, linked to specific data owners and repositories.

Processing covers the transformation, enrichment, or aggregation of data once it has entered the organization's systems. At this stage, information may be decrypted, combined with internal datasets, or passed through analytics engines. Each processing system creates temporary storage, logs, and intermediate files that can become unintended exposure points if not properly secured. The author should guide readers to visualize how sensitive elements move between systems—especially across cloud environments or microservice boundaries—and which protections travel with them. Encryption-in-transit policies, workload identities, and tokenization boundaries should appear on the diagram. Auditors will expect to see process-level accountability: who owns the transformation scripts, which classifications apply to each intermediate dataset, and what evidence confirms that temporary files or logs are deleted when processing completes.

Storage represents the phase where data typically resides the longest, and thus where risk accumulates through concentration. High-risk stores are those that combine sensitive data volume, business criticality, and broad access—examples include customer master databases, document management platforms, and large cloud data lakes. The author should depict not only where data is stored but also how it is partitioned, encrypted, and governed. For each repository, indicate whether encryption at rest is enforced, which service or key protects it, and which roles or identities have access. Auditors will expect an inventory table that corresponds to the map, listing each storage node, its classification level, owning business unit, encryption coverage, and access control model. This inventory becomes a baseline artifact for continuous risk monitoring and audit review.

Sharing and backup extend data beyond its primary store, often to destinations with different protection postures. Internal sharing can include file synchronization, reporting extracts, or data replication to regional systems; external sharing may involve vendors, partners, or regulators. Backups replicate data for resiliency but also create duplicate exposure if encryption and retention policies are inconsistent. The author should make these flows explicit—showing outbound paths, transfer methods, and receiving systems. High-risk paths typically involve external or third-party hops, such as data exports to SaaS analytics providers or cloud-based archival systems. Auditors expect to see documentation proving that data classification and encryption requirements persist during transfers and that third-party contracts specify equivalent safeguards. The diagram should differentiate internal trusted zones from external or shared zones using clear visual cues.

Disposal is the final stage and a frequent weak link in data life cycle control. Secure deletion must be verifiable—whether through cryptographic key destruction, overwriting, or physical media shredding. The author should trace where and how data exits the environment, including automated retention policies, archive expiry jobs, or manual purge requests. If data flows into systems without defined disposal mechanisms, that gap represents residual risk. Auditors will request evidence such as deletion job logs, retention schedules, and attestations from system owners confirming that obsolete data is irrecoverable. The data flow map should therefore close the loop, showing the life cycle's end as clearly as its beginning.

High-risk nodes in a data flow are not always obvious from volume alone. Risk arises where concentration, exposure, and control weakness intersect. A small database containing executive credentials may pose greater danger than a massive anonymized data lake. The author should highlight criteria for identifying high-risk nodes: data concentration (how many sensitive records), exposure surface (number of users or systems with access), connectivity (number of downstream flows), and dependency on third parties or unmanaged endpoints. Each node should have a designated owner responsible for its classification and protective posture. Auditors will examine whether these high-risk areas receive enhanced monitoring, more frequent key rotations, and stricter change control, reflecting their criticality.

Third-party hops demand special scrutiny because data leaves the organization's direct control. The map should call out every external connection—API exchanges, cloud-to-cloud transfers, managed service integrations—and annotate them with contractual or technical safeguards. Examples include encryption requirements in vendor agreements, tokenization before transfer, or API gateways enforcing mTLS with certificate pinning. For each third-party path, auditors will look for evidence of data flow approval, due diligence, and monitoring. Vendor risk assessments, data processing addendums, and transfer logs form part of this evidentiary trail.

The artifacts auditors expect are both visual and documentary. A current data flow diagram should show systems, data classifications, directional flows, and control boundaries, with each node labeled by its owner and business function. Supporting artifacts include a data inventory listing all high-risk stores, a mapping of classification levels to applied controls, and a register of systems that process or transmit sensitive information. Each data store in the inventory should be linked to corresponding encryption, access, and retention controls, ensuring that every piece of sensitive data has a demonstrable protection chain. Version control over these diagrams and inventories is also critical; auditors often verify that updates reflect actual changes in architecture and that obsolete systems have been properly retired.

Evidence Locations: KMS/HSM Logs, Key Policies, DLP Events, and Configs

An auditor's assurance depends on verifiable, time-bounded evidence that cryptographic and data protection controls have operated continuously and as designed. The purpose of this section is to show how those proofs interrelate across systems—key management services, hardware security modules, encryption configurations, and DLP platforms—so that the chain of custody from policy to implementation is visible and defensible. Evidence must be exportable, tamper-evident, and anchored to system-generated timestamps within the defined audit period. Every log, configuration file, and ticket record should be able to answer who performed an action, what changed, when it occurred, and how it aligns with approved policy.

Key policies form the foundation of encryption evidence because they define how keys may be used, who may access them, and under what conditions. A complete record includes the key policy itself, its aliases, and the permission grants or access control lists that enforce role separation. Each key should reference its creation date, owner, algorithm, and rotation schedule. When rotation occurs, the policy's version history and alias changes provide chronological proof that new keys replaced old ones in accordance with defined intervals. These artifacts demonstrate intent—what the organization said it would do—and become the baseline for comparing actual key activity in subsequent logs. The auditor's first linkage is between the documented key policy and the operational evidence of use. The evidence chain in Table 10.3 shows how policy intent flows into operational logs and configuration artifacts across the audit window.

HSM and KMS audit logs provide the next layer of proof by showing every cryptographic operation and administrative action that occurred within the key management boundary. These logs should capture event type, actor identity, key ID or alias, operation performed (create, rotate, decrypt,

Table 10.3 Evidence chain for data protection controls.

Control area	Canonical artifact	Integrity requirement	Time bound	Example cross-link
Key policies	Policy text aliases and version history	Tamper evident export with hash	Full audit period plus retention	KMS usage logs
KMS HSM activity	Key operation and admin audit logs	Immutable ingest to SIEM with signature	Full audit period with clock sync	Change tickets
Storage encryption	Service configs and key references	Read only export from source of truth	Full audit period with updates	Key policy IDs
Backups	Job definitions and success logs with key IDs	Integrity checked archives and access logs	Retention schedule duration	Rotation records
DLP policy	Scopes classifiers actions and thresholds	Version controlled definition export	Policy review cadence	Tuning register
DLP incidents	Event exports with rule hits and outcomes	Write once storage with provenance	Incident life cycle duration	User justifications
Access control	Role bindings and grants for keys and stores	Read only directory export and attestations	Periodic access review window	SoD matrix
Attestation	Device and service health or compliance proof	Signed reports from provider or HSM	Per release or firmware cycle	Config baselines

disable, delete), timestamp, and result code. The relationship between key policies and HSM/KMS audit logs is direct: for each policy clause granting access or rotation rights, corresponding events must exist in the logs showing those actions executed by authorized roles only. Logs should be immutable within the system and exportable to a centralized security information and event management (SIEM) platform for retention and correlation. The exported versions must include digital signatures, checksums, or service attestations that ensure they have not been altered after generation.

Storage, database, and server encryption configurations are the physical realization of key policies. These artifacts prove that the encryption settings referenced in the policy are applied where data actually resides. Auditors should obtain configuration exports or screenshots showing that encryption-at-rest is enabled, keys are customer-managed or HSM-protected, and cipher suites meet the organization's cryptographic standard. Database configuration files or parameter groups often contain the linkage back to the key ID or alias, confirming that the same key policy governs both application and storage encryption. For virtualized or cloud systems, evidence may include service configuration manifests, infrastructure-as-code templates, and cloud provider encryption status reports. These records tie the logical controls of KMS/HSM to the tangible locations where data is stored.

Backups and archive encryption evidence extend the same principle to redundancy systems. Proof typically consists of backup job definitions, key identifiers associated with backup encryption, and successful job completion logs showing encryption active for every run. Because backup media can outlive production keys, retention schedules and key rotation logs must be correlated to ensure decryptability or planned crypto-shredding upon key retirement. Auditors often cross-reference backup configuration exports with KMS audit logs to confirm that encryption keys were available and in use at the time of backup creation. Any exception or skipped encryption step must be documented in ticketing systems, showing approval, compensating controls, and eventual remediation.

DLP systems produce a distinct but complementary class of evidence that demonstrates how data movement was monitored and controlled. Canonical artifacts include the DLP policy definitions—each mapping classification levels to detection rules, actions, and thresholds—and the event or incident exports that show those policies operating in practice. Event logs should include triggering rule identifiers, matched classifier types, user or system initiating the transfer, action taken (block, quarantine, allow), and timestamp. Over time, these records show control effectiveness through incident counts, false positive ratios, and resolution notes. The linkage to encryption and key management evidence lies in scope alignment: DLP rules protect the same data categories whose encryption policies are governed by KMS and HSM controls, confirming that the organization's protection strategy is consistent from prevention to detection.

Configuration repositories and change management systems are where intent meets accountability. Each key creation, policy update, encryption configuration change, or DLP rule modification must trace to an approved ticket with recorded justification, approvers, and timestamps. These records complete the provenance chain, proving that changes were not ad hoc but executed under governance. Modern organizations often integrate change management directly with version control systems, ensuring that configuration changes produce immutable commits tagged with ticket identifiers. During audit, reviewers should be able to traverse from a specific log entry—such as a key rotation event—to its corresponding change request, approval evidence, and policy update in version history.

To maintain evidentiary integrity, all of these sources must be time-synchronized and retained for at least the duration of the audit period plus any regulatory extension. Logs and exports should include cryptographic hashes or digital signatures, ensuring tamper detection if files are moved or archived. Where possible, evidence should originate from system-generated exports rather than manual screenshots to preserve authenticity. Storage locations for evidence—such as dedicated audit S3 buckets or write-once media—must enforce read-only access and capture access events for the evidence itself, preventing post-factum manipulation.

The relationships among these evidence sources form a continuous verification path. Key policies and aliases define expectations; HSM and KMS audit logs show actions taken under those expectations; encryption configurations in storage, databases, and servers demonstrate enforcement; DLP policies and incidents show detection of boundary violations; and ticketing systems document authorization and oversight. When stitched together chronologically, they form a tamper-evident narrative of how cryptographic and data protection controls were designed, applied, and maintained.

Auditors will assess not only the presence of these artifacts but their completeness and provenance. Each piece must stand on its own—containing timestamps, origin metadata, and digital integrity proofs—but also fit coherently into the larger chain of evidence. The ultimate assurance comes when every control decision, from key creation to data exfiltration prevention, can be traced through exportable, time-bound, and verifiable records that demonstrate the program's integrity over the entire audit window.

Conclusion

Mastering data protection principles is critical for ensuring that security controls translate into lasting assurance rather than isolated technical measures. Encryption, key management, and DLP controls only achieve their purpose when they are integrated into a coherent life cycle—one that classifies, tracks, and governs data from creation through destruction. This chapter reinforces that effective auditing depends not just on verifying individual configurations, but on confirming the continuity of protection across every system, workflow, and environment. When data handling and cryptographic governance align with business processes, security becomes measurable and defensible rather than assumed.

The role of auditors now extends into the architecture of trust that underpins AI-driven systems. Machine learning models, automated pipelines, and large-scale analytics rely on vast datasets that must remain traceable, protected, and compliant with regulatory expectations. The same principles that safeguard traditional data stores—controlled encryption, disciplined key management, precise DLP enforcement—are equally vital to maintaining confidentiality and integrity in AI ecosystems. With these controls, organizations can ensure that sensitive information fueling intelligent systems does not become a hidden liability within complex automation workflows.

While implementation details may vary across technologies and cloud providers, the strategic intent remains constant: to create verifiable assurance that data remains protected wherever it resides or moves. Auditors and security professionals who apply these principles establish not only compliance, but operational resilience—an auditable chain of custody that sustains stakeholder confidence. With these foundations in place, organizations can approach innovation, including AI adoption, from a position of governance rather than risk, demonstrating that strong data protection and agility can coexist in even the most dynamic digital environments.

Auditor Recommendations

1. **Establish Classification Traceability:** Build assurance by confirming that every data classification label leads directly to a defined control objective, an implemented safeguard, and verifiable evidence. Review whether these mappings are documented and current within data inventories. This ensures that classification schemes are not merely theoretical but also actively enforced and testable during audits.
2. **Validate Encryption Coverage:** Evaluate encryption in transit and at rest for completeness across production, backup, and temporary environments. Confirm that coverage includes every data state and that cryptographic configurations match policy requirements. Auditors should focus on identifying unencrypted "blind spots" where sensitive data could reside outside approved encryption boundaries.
3. **Assess Key Management Metadata:** Verify that each cryptographic key record contains complete metadata—purpose, owner, algorithm, rotation schedule, and retirement plan. Audit systems of record to confirm these details are accurate and align with the organization's governance standards. A well-maintained key inventory demonstrates control maturity and supports reliable evidence gathering.

4. **Confirm Separation of Duties in Key Operations:** Review key management roles to ensure that generation, approval, and activation are divided among distinct personnel. Require documentation proving that quorum or dual control applies to critical key actions such as export or destruction. This verification protects against unauthorized key manipulation and ensures the audit trail supports accountability.
5. **Evaluate HSM and KMS Access Boundaries:** Examine how access to hardware or cloud key management services is restricted and monitored. Validate tenant isolation, role enforcement, and policy-based approvals for sensitive life cycle actions. Auditors should collect evidence from policy exports and key-usage logs that demonstrate those boundaries are functioning as designed.
6. **Examine Tokenization and Masking Controls:** Assess how tokenization and masking reduce data exposure in analytics, support, and lower environments. Verify that reversible mappings are securely stored, access is logged, and irreversible masking is applied where possible. Effective review of these controls demonstrates that data minimization is operationalized, not just declared in policy.
7. **Review DLP Policy Governance:** Confirm that DLP policies define clear scopes, classifier rules, and approved actions supported by an exception register. Evaluate whether policy changes, tuning, and suppression decisions are logged with owner approval and expiration dates. Auditors should verify that incident metrics and review cycles demonstrate ongoing policy refinement and oversight.
8. **Audit Data Flow Diagrams for Completeness:** Require that data flow maps cover ingestion, processing, storage, sharing, and disposal stages, including third-party paths. Confirm that each node identifies data classification, system owner, and protective controls. A current and accurate flow map allows auditors to target testing on high-risk stores and external interfaces effectively.
9. **Scrutinize Exception Management:** Identify any systems operating outside full encryption or labeling requirements and verify that each exception is formally approved, time-bound, and compensated with documented safeguards. Confirm that reviews occur regularly and exceptions are tracked to closure. This approach ensures that deviations are managed transparently and remain within the organization's risk tolerance.
10. **Verify Evidence Integrity and Retention:** Ensure that all key management logs, encryption configurations, DLP events, and change records are collected in tamper-evident, time-synchronized repositories. Review retention practices to confirm evidence covers the entire audit period and includes cryptographic validation of integrity. Reliable, exportable evidence is the cornerstone of defensible auditing and regulatory confidence.

Chapter Questions

1. What is the primary objective of a data classification program in this chapter's context?
   - **A.** To translate sensitivity labels into enforceable storage, transmission, and disposal rules with auditable traceability
   - **B.** To standardize file naming conventions across repositories
   - **C.** To reduce infrastructure costs by deduplicating datasets
   - **D.** To prioritize application features in development backlogs

2. In the discussion of encryption, what does "coverage" most accurately refer to?
   - **A.** The number of cryptographic libraries deployed in production
   - **B.** The completeness of encryption across data in transit, at rest, backups, and intermediate caches
   - **C.** The variety of cipher suites enabled on web servers
   - **D.** The geographic spread of encrypted workloads

3. Which set best represents the minimum governance metadata required for each key?
   - **A.** Data owner, storage vendor, CPU architecture, and OS version
   - **B.** Ticket number, subnet, rack location, and SLA tier
   - **C.** Purpose, owner, algorithm/length, rotation interval, and retirement plan
   - **D.** Log retention period, proxy address, SOC shift schedule, and app uptime

4. Which practice best enforces separation of duties in key management operations?
   - **A.** Allowing senior admins to perform all tasks during maintenance windows
   - **B.** Using a single break-glass account for emergency generation and activation
   - **C.** Combining requester and approver roles but separating operator duties
   - **D.** Splitting requester, approver, and operator roles and requiring quorum for high-risk actions

5. For analytics on sensitive identifiers where joinability is needed without exposing originals, which control is most appropriate?
   - **A.** Deterministic tokenization with vaulted mappings
   - **B.** Irreversible masking of all fields prior to ingestion
   - **C.** Disk-only encryption with no changes to data representation
   - **D.** Manual redaction by analysts during query execution

6. What distinguishes an auditable DLP policy as described in this chapter?
   - **A.** A single global rule that blocks all external sharing
   - **B.** Defined scopes, patterns/classifiers, actions, and a tuning/exception register with approvals
   - **C.** Exclusive reliance on machine learning classifiers for detection
   - **D.** User-managed rules that can be edited without change control

7. When identifying high-risk nodes in data flow mapping, which criteria are emphasized?
   - **A.** Server age, CPU utilization, and storage vendor
   - **B.** Data freshness, dashboard popularity, and UI latency
   - **C.** Data concentration, exposure surface, connectivity, and third-party hops
   - **D.** Application programming language, code coverage, and build times

8. Which evidence most directly proves that HSM/KMS access boundaries are enforced?
   - **A.** Business continuity plans and disaster recovery playbooks
   - **B.** Endpoint antivirus logs and patch compliance summaries
   - **C.** Network throughput graphs and CDN hit ratios
   - **D.** Effective key/resource policies, precise grants, and key-usage audit logs with attestation

9. Which linkage best reflects the evidentiary chain from policy to implementation?
   A. Key policies/aliases/rotation logs → HSM/KMS audit logs → storage/db/server encryption configs → DLP policy definitions and incident exports → ticket/change systems
   B. DLP incidents → ticket/change systems → storage configs → key policies → KMS logs
   C. Storage configs → DLP incidents → key policies → KMS logs → tickets
   D. Ticket/change systems → storage configs → key policies → DLP incidents → KMS logs

10. What is the required stance for protecting backup and archive data?
    A. Encrypt production only, and rely on physical security for backups
    B. Use plaintext backups for faster recovery, then encrypt after restore
    C. Ensure backups are encrypted with managed keys, logged, and aligned to retention and rotation expectations
    D. Disable backup encryption during rotation windows to avoid failures

11

Logging, Monitoring, and Detection

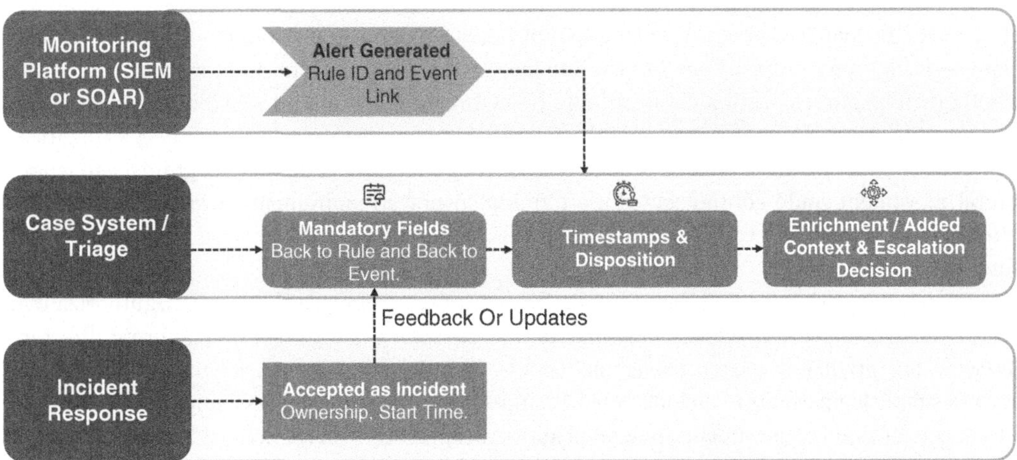

Effective security auditing depends on the ability to see, understand, and trust what systems are doing at every moment. Logging, monitoring, and detection form the evidentiary core of that visibility. They translate the billions of transactions, authentications, and data movements occurring across modern infrastructures into interpretable signals that auditors and defenders can evaluate. When governed properly, these signals become the factual backbone of risk assessments and compliance assurance. Without them, both operational detection and audit validation become guesswork—leaving organizations blind to misuse, misconfiguration, and emerging threats.

Modern enterprises operate in environments that are both distributed and dynamic—spanning on-premises systems, cloud services, and AI-driven analytics pipelines. Within this complexity, ensuring trustworthy telemetry, reliable log retention, and accurate detection content is vital not just for incident investigation but for organizational accountability. Effective monitoring requires balancing completeness with precision: knowing what to collect, how long to retain it, and how to interpret it without overwhelming teams or systems. This chapter's focus on coverage, integrity, tuning, and governance connects these operational practices directly to audit assurance, emphasizing that visibility itself is a controllable and measurable asset.

In an era where machine learning models and automated decision systems influence critical operations, auditable visibility becomes a cornerstone of AI security and governance. Understanding how telemetry gaps are identified, how detection rules evolve responsibly, and how evidence is preserved over time ensures that both human and algorithmic decisions can be verified. From ensuring log immutability and controlled access to validating triage workflows and escalation boundaries, this discipline underpins digital trust. The ability to demonstrate that detection systems are accurate, complete, and tamper-resistant is not merely a technical achievement—it is the foundation of credible assurance in a data-driven, AI-enabled enterprise.

Log Coverage Model: Sources, Depth, and Retention Targets

A well-defined log coverage model serves as the backbone of an organization's monitoring and detection capability. In cybersecurity auditing, it expresses not only what systems are being logged, but how deeply, for how long, and with what justification. A mature model begins with a mapping of coverage by source type—identity, endpoint, network, application, and cloud control or data planes—each representing a layer of visibility into system behavior. The auditor's task is to assess whether each source contributes meaningfully to threat detection and incident reconstruction, ensuring that no critical blind spots remain. For example, an organization may collect authentication events from Active Directory but overlook federated identity providers, creating a gap where lateral movement could go undetected. By framing coverage requirements through these source categories, auditors can evaluate the completeness and balance of monitoring efforts across the enterprise landscape.

Identity logs are often the first line of insight for auditors examining authentication, authorization, and privilege escalation activities. These include sources such as single sign-on platforms, directory services, and privileged access management tools. The depth of identity logging should extend beyond simple login events to include failed attempts, token issuance, role assignments, and session anomalies. In cloud environments, federated authentication between services adds another layer of complexity, where logs must capture both the control plane (who changed what) and the data plane (who accessed which resource). Depth in identity logging allows investigators to reconstruct user journeys with precision, an essential factor when assessing insider threats or policy violations.

Endpoint logs, encompassing workstations, servers, and mobile devices, provide visibility into what actions occur after access is granted. A robust log coverage model defines not only which endpoints are included but what level of telemetry is collected. For instance, simple antivirus alerts may reveal malware detections, but full endpoint detection and response (EDR) telemetry provides granular process creation, registry changes, and file modification data. The auditor examines whether endpoint coverage extends to high-risk assets and whether local logs are reliably forwarded to centralized systems. Sampling strategies can validate this, comparing device inventories against those actively sending logs. Gaps between intended and actual coverage often indicate onboarding or policy enforcement failures that need correction.

Network logs serve as the connective tissue between systems, enabling correlation of activities that cross trust boundaries. Firewalls, intrusion detection systems, and proxy servers each offer unique perspectives. However, an auditor must look beyond the existence of these logs to evaluate their depth—do they include both inbound and outbound flows, decrypted traffic metadata, and timestamps with sufficient precision? The inclusion of network telemetry from internal segmentation points, not just perimeter devices, is critical for detecting lateral movement and exfiltration. When auditors correlate firewall configurations with actual logging policies, discrepancies often emerge, such as dropped logs for specific interfaces or missing VLAN segments. These findings reveal how theoretical coverage diverges from operational reality.

Application logging defines how deeply business systems reveal operational events, user actions, and transaction flows. Inadequate application logs can render even the most advanced Security Information and Event Management (SIEM) tools blind to business-context anomalies. Auditors assess whether applications produce structured logs containing key fields—timestamps, user IDs, transaction identifiers, and error codes—necessary for root cause analysis. A mature log coverage model distinguishes between event categories, ensuring that security-relevant actions such as failed transactions, privilege escalations, or API abuse attempts are captured with sufficient granularity. Cloud-native and DevSecOps environments introduce continuous deployment pipelines where logging requirements must be built into container orchestration, code repositories, and API gateways to ensure coverage persists as systems evolve. See Table 11.1 for coverage by source depth and retention tier anchors the visibility model to specific evidence artifacts that prove completeness.

Cloud control and data plane logs occupy a unique place in modern coverage models. Control plane logs record administrative actions, such as provisioning resources or altering security groups, while data plane logs capture actual data access and usage. The auditor evaluates whether both planes are covered and properly retained according to risk. For instance, an organization may store AWS CloudTrail logs for only 30 days, which may meet operational needs but fail to support forensic requirements for regulatory inquiries. Proper segregation and retention of these logs—often across multiple accounts or tenants—must align with defined risk tiers. Incomplete or unretained logs in this domain can render entire incidents unverifiable, undermining compliance attestations.

Depth in a log coverage model refers not only to which event types are captured but also to which fields within those events are preserved. Field-level completeness determines whether an alert can be investigated or correlated with other data sources. For example, omitting source IP addresses or process hashes from an event schema limits correlation and increases investigation time. Auditors often review sample event payloads to verify schema completeness against vendor documentation or policy baselines. They also examine normalization pipelines, ensuring that critical fields are not stripped during ingestion or transformation. Inconsistent field capture across log sources introduces systemic risk to detection quality, particularly when analytics depend on specific identifiers to function correctly.

Table 11.1 Coverage by source depth and retention tier.

Source type	Key event examples	Required fields	Retention tier	Evidence artifact
Identity	Auth success fail role change	User ID Timestamp Source IP	High	Onboarding record and SIEM connector list
Endpoint	Process start file mod alert	Host ID Process hash Timestamp	High	Agent health report and ingestion metrics
Network	Flow allow deny proxy request	SRC IP DST ID Port Protocol	Medium	Firewall export and parser mapping
Application	Txn event error privilege change	User ID Txn id Status code	High	App logging config and sample payloads
Cloud control plane	Config change key action policy edit	Actor ID API call Resource ID	High	Object lock policy and audit export
Cloud data plane	Read write delete access	Principal Resource Operation	High	Access log export and retention policy

Retention targets translate coverage into temporal assurance—the ability to reconstruct events over time. Risk-tiered retention aligns storage duration with the criticality of systems and regulatory requirements. High-risk systems, such as domain controllers or financial applications, may warrant retention for one year or more, whereas lower-risk development environments might justify shorter periods. Auditors examine storage configurations, lifecycle policies, and cost optimization practices to ensure retention objectives are met without compromising compliance. Verifying retention is not merely a technical exercise; it is a governance control that ensures evidence integrity in the face of investigations or litigation.

Proving completeness of coverage requires reconciling two distinct data sets: the inventory of log-eligible assets and the onboarded sources within the monitoring platform. An auditor compares the configuration management database (CMDB), asset inventories, or cloud resource enumerations against actual ingestion metrics in the SIEM or data lake. This cross-check identifies "silent" assets—those that exist but are not sending logs—and validates that log collection agents are functioning correctly. Reports of source health, ingestion errors, and agent heartbeat failures become vital audit evidence. The presence of gaps is not inherently a failure; rather, the documentation of justified exclusions is what demonstrates governance maturity.

Exclusions should never be arbitrary. Each omission must be risk-assessed, justified, and formally documented. For example, a development test environment might be excluded due to isolation and data irrelevance, but the rationale should cite compensating controls such as restricted network access or periodic scanning. The auditor evaluates whether such exclusions follow an approval workflow, are periodically reviewed, and are transparently recorded in the organization's log coverage register. This record acts as a living document, evidencing both the scope of coverage and the reasoning behind deliberate limitations. When exclusions are ad hoc or undocumented, it signals a weakness in the control governance structure rather than a technical shortfall.

Integrity and Tamper Resistance

The credibility of any audit or investigation depends on the integrity of its underlying evidence. In cybersecurity auditing, logs serve as that evidence, documenting the chain of events that define system behavior and user actions. To be trustworthy, these records must not only exist but also remain unaltered from the moment they are written. Mechanisms that enforce immutability, ensure cryptographic integrity, and restrict access form the foundation of tamper-resistant logging. Without these safeguards, even the most comprehensive log coverage model collapses under the weight of doubt—because an altered record ceases to be evidence and becomes speculation. The auditor's role is to validate both the technical and procedural layers that uphold log trustworthiness, tracing how data is protected from its creation to its eventual archival.

Write-once storage, often implemented through append-only configurations, is a primary means of ensuring immutability. Once written, entries cannot be modified or deleted without leaving a detectable trace. In on-premises systems, this might be achieved through WORM (Write Once, Read Many) storage technologies or append-only filesystems. In cloud environments, similar properties can be configured using object-lock capabilities in services like AWS S3 or Azure Immutable Blobs. These mechanisms prevent retroactive alteration, ensuring that even privileged administrators cannot silently change historical data. The auditor reviews configuration baselines and platform policies to verify that immutability settings are enabled and enforced, and that retention periods are protected from reduction or deletion without explicit, logged authorization.

Cryptographic hashing and digital signing complement immutability by providing verifiable evidence that logs have not been altered. Each log file or event batch can be hashed using algorithms such as SHA-256, generating a unique digest that changes if even a single character in the source data is modified. In high-assurance environments, these hashes are chained together—each hash incorporating the previous one—to form an immutable sequence akin to a blockchain ledger. This provides mathematical proof that the sequence of log entries has not been tampered with. Auditors often request access to hash manifest files or signature verification reports, comparing them against known baselines to confirm the continued integrity of stored logs over time.

Time synchronization is another essential pillar of log integrity. Without consistent timestamps, correlating events across systems becomes unreliable and undermines forensic analysis. Network Time Protocol (NTP) or Precision Time Protocol (PTP) services ensure that devices record events in a synchronized temporal frame. Even small drifts between systems can distort the sequence of an attack narrative, obscuring causal relationships or falsely implicating legitimate users. An auditor examines time synchronization configurations, ensuring redundancy, authentication, and drift monitoring are in place. Validation often includes cross-checking event timestamps from multiple sources to confirm consistency within acceptable tolerances. The alignment of time across identity, network, and application logs is what transforms isolated entries into a coherent story.

Access control is the human counterpart to these technical safeguards. Log stores should be governed by strict least-privilege principles, allowing only designated security personnel to read or manage them. Write access should be system-generated only—never manual. Role-based access control (RBAC) or attribute-based models help enforce this separation, ensuring that administrators managing systems cannot also edit or purge logs of their own actions. Auditors review access control lists (ACLs), IAM policies, and directory group memberships to confirm these restrictions. They also examine the access logs of the log platform itself to verify that all viewing, copying, or export activities are monitored and attributable to named individuals.

Artifacts demonstrating these properties are essential for evidentiary confidence. For immutability, auditors may request configuration exports, retention policy documentation, or append-only proof reports generated by the storage platform. For cryptographic controls, they might inspect signed hash manifests or integrity validation reports showing verification success over time. Access control effectiveness can be demonstrated through access logs showing successful and denied attempts, administrative activity reports, and periodic access recertification records. Each artifact functions as a form of meta-evidence—proof that the integrity of the evidence itself is being guarded. Mature organizations maintain a chain-of-custody model for logs, documenting every stage from collection to archival.

Common pitfalls in maintaining log integrity often stem from convenience or oversight. Shared administrator credentials, for instance, obscure accountability and make it impossible to determine who accessed or altered logs. Mutable "hot" storage, where logs reside temporarily before archival, can be modified during the ingestion process if not properly controlled. Some teams unintentionally undermine immutability by storing logs on general-purpose file shares or systems where retention policies can be altered by local administrators. Others fail to segregate duties between system administrators and log custodians, creating opportunities for undetected tampering. Even automated processes, if misconfigured, can overwrite or truncate logs without proper auditing trails.

An auditor's evaluation of tamper resistance extends beyond verifying settings—it must assess resilience under realistic attack or error conditions. For example, if an attacker gains cloud administrative privileges, can they disable or delete logging before being detected? If local systems lose network connectivity, are their logs buffered securely until reconnected? Questions like these reveal whether integrity mechanisms are merely theoretical or truly operational. Periodic integrity testing, such as deliberately introducing a known hash mismatch to confirm detection, demonstrates control effectiveness in practice.

Detection Content Quality: Precision/Recall, Tuning, and Suppression

The effectiveness of a security monitoring program depends not just on the volume of logs collected, but on the quality of the detection logic applied to them. Detection content—rules, correlation searches, and analytics—forms the analytical brain of an SIEM or Security Analytics platform. An auditor evaluating detection quality must assess whether these rules accurately identify threats (precision), consistently capture relevant activity (recall), and evolve responsibly through versioning, testing, and documented approvals. Poorly designed or unmanaged detection content can create a false sense of coverage, where dashboards glow green even as genuine threats slip by undetected. Evaluating detection quality transforms an audit from a checklist exercise into an analysis of how well the organization's defenses actually think.

Precision refers to how often a detection rule's alerts are truly valid indicators of malicious or risky behavior. High precision minimizes false positives, reducing analyst fatigue and ensuring that response teams focus on meaningful alerts. Recall, on the other hand, measures how many real threats the detection rule captures compared to the total that occur. Striking a balance between precision and recall is a defining challenge for detection engineering. A rule that flags every failed login may have perfect recall but abysmal precision; one that triggers only on multiple failed logins from distinct locations may be more precise but could miss subtle credential attacks. In mature programs, quantitative tracking of rule performance—such as false positive rates, mean time to validate, and confirmed detection ratios—provides an empirical basis for tuning. Auditors review these metrics or their approximations, ensuring that rule adjustments are data-driven rather than anecdotal.

Tuning is the disciplined process of refining detection logic to maintain relevance and accuracy. As environments evolve, log formats change, new systems come online, and adversaries alter tactics; stale detections quickly lose effectiveness. Effective tuning follows a documented workflow: identification of noise or missed detections, hypothesis for change, test execution, peer review, and approval. Each step should generate durable records that explain why the rule changed and what result was achieved. Version control systems, whether embedded in the SIEM or managed through repositories such as Git, preserve diffs between rule versions, demonstrating traceability. Auditors examine these version histories and related change tickets to confirm that modifications were intentional, peer-reviewed, and authorized. The absence of this documentation often signals ad hoc rule management, where detection content drifts without accountability.

Rule testing represents the proving ground of detection quality. Before deployment, new or modified rules should be validated against representative data sets, ideally containing both benign and malicious examples. Automated test frameworks or replay environments allow analysts to measure detection accuracy, comparing expected versus actual outcomes. The auditor reviews these test results or sample logs demonstrating successful and failed triggers. Where feasible, testing extends beyond functionality to performance—ensuring rules execute efficiently without overloading the SIEM. Evidence of test results, along with test data retention and periodic retesting schedules, supports an auditor's conclusion that detection content is both technically sound and operationally sustainable.

Suppressions, or filters applied to detection rules, represent one of the most misunderstood and misused components of monitoring. When thoughtfully applied, suppressions eliminate noise from known, benign events that would otherwise overwhelm analysts. Acceptable suppressions are specific, narrowly scoped, and justified by documented context—such as excluding a trusted scanner IP, a known administrative script, or an expected service behavior. These suppressions should be time-bound or reviewed periodically to confirm continued validity. In contrast, blanket suppressions that broadly exclude entire subnets, event categories, or user groups can create dangerous blind spots. Such filters, often implemented in haste to quiet noisy alerts, effectively silence detection coverage in critical areas. Auditors differentiate between these by inspecting suppression definitions, reviewing their justifications, and verifying that approval workflows and expiration mechanisms are enforced.

To manage suppression responsibly, organizations maintain a suppression register—a centralized record listing all active suppressions, their scope, rationale, author, and review dates. This register functions as an accountability ledger for decisions that intentionally reduce visibility. During audits, this document provides immediate transparency into the trade-offs being made between signal and noise. When a suppression lacks justification or review history, it signals potential control weakness or operational fatigue. Mature teams integrate suppression management into their change control systems, ensuring that suppressions are governed with the same rigor as the detection rules themselves.

Durable evidence of detection content management is a hallmark of audit maturity. This includes rule version histories, diffs between iterations, approval records, and documented test results. For larger organizations, these artifacts are often stored in source control systems with tagging for release cycles or correlation with incident identifiers. Auditors use this evidence to reconstruct the evolution of critical detections—such as ransomware indicators or insider threat behaviors—over time. Such traceability demonstrates that the organization not only maintains its detection catalog but actively learns from operational feedback and adapts to new threat intelligence.

A common pitfall in detection content management is the lack of formal ownership. When responsibility for a rule set is distributed informally across analysts, quality degrades quickly. Rules may be modified directly in production without peer review, suppressions added ad hoc, and no reliable record kept of why or when changes occurred. Another issue arises when tuning focuses solely on reducing alert volume rather than improving analytical accuracy, leading to the silent erosion of visibility. Auditors flag these conditions as process deficiencies, emphasizing the need for designated rule owners, structured change control, and periodic content audits.

Detection quality must also be assessed in context with threat modeling and control coverage. A high-performing rule set should align with the organization's top risks, mapping to specific attack techniques or MITRE ATT&CK tactics. Auditors evaluate whether detection rules trace back to defined use cases—such as credential abuse, data exfiltration, or privilege escalation—and whether corresponding gaps are tracked in a backlog. The presence of a formal detection content lifecycle, complete with prioritization, testing, and retirement phases, indicates an organization that treats its detection logic as living intellectual property rather than static configuration.

Use-case Catalog and Ownership

A managed use-case catalog represents the organized backbone of a modern detection and monitoring program. Rather than existing as a loose collection of rules and correlation searches, the catalog functions as a structured inventory of every analytic, each tied to a defined purpose, owner,

Table 11.2 Managed use case catalog metadata fields.

Field name	Purpose	Primary evidence	Review cadence
Owner	Accountability for health and tuning	Access list or IAM group mapping	Quarterly
Objective	Operational outcome of the analytic	Rule description in repository	Semiannual
Mapped risks controls	Traceability to risk or control objective	Link to risk register reference	Quarterly
Required data sources	Dependencies that must be present	Ingestion report and source list	Monthly
Test status	Verification of function and accuracy	Test results and replay notes	Quarterly
Measurements	Alert rate and true false ratios	Metrics export from case system	Monthly
Version history link	Traceable change record	Commit log and rule diff	Semiannual
Approval status	Evidence of authorization	Change ticket and sign off	Per change
Retirement status	Disposition and rationale	Retirement record and date	Per change

and lifecycle. This catalog bridges the technical operation of detections with the strategic priorities of risk management, giving auditors and security leaders a single source of truth for what the organization is actively monitoring, why it matters, and how well it performs. Without a maintained catalog, detection logic drifts, redundant use-cases proliferate, and coverage gaps emerge silently. The auditor's task is to confirm that this catalog exists, that it is complete, and that its entries are governed by consistent metadata and lifecycle discipline. Table 11.2 standardized metadata ensures each analytic is owned tested measured and traceable to risk and control objectives.

At minimum, each use-case in the catalog must include clear and standardized metadata describing its purpose and accountability. The owner field identifies the individual or team responsible for maintaining the rule, including periodic reviews, tuning, and documentation. Ownership enforces accountability—ensuring that when an alert malfunctions or generates excessive noise, someone is both authorized and obligated to address it. The objective defines what the use-case is designed to detect, phrased in operationally meaningful language, such as "Detect unauthorized privilege escalation on Windows servers" or "Identify anomalous data egress from cloud storage." This articulation ties the rule to a tangible security outcome rather than abstract event patterns, providing clarity to both analysts and auditors assessing its relevance.

Each use-case should explicitly map to organizational risks, controls, or compliance requirements. This linkage grounds detection in business context rather than technical curiosity. For example, a use-case designed to detect suspicious administrative activity might map to the control "Privileged Access Monitoring" under ISO 27001 Annex A.9 or to a specific risk scenario in the enterprise risk register. By maintaining this mapping, organizations can demonstrate control coverage and traceability from audit frameworks to operational detections. Auditors often trace these links backward—starting with a defined risk or control objective and verifying that at least one active use-case supports it. Gaps in this mapping reveal unmonitored risks or outdated control assumptions that require remediation.

Required data sources form another critical piece of metadata. A use-case that depends on endpoint telemetry, identity logs, or specific API feeds must explicitly list them. This ensures that the rule's effectiveness can be verified against the log coverage model and alerts can be interpreted in context. If a required data source becomes unavailable—such as an endpoint agent being decommissioned or a cloud service changing its event schema—the catalog immediately shows which detections are impacted. Auditors compare these declared dependencies with ingestion reports to confirm operational continuity. The absence of such linkage often results in detections that exist in name only, unable to function as intended because their data inputs have silently disappeared.

Testing status and validation results ensure that use-cases are not theoretical. Each entry should document whether the detection has been tested, the date of the most recent test, and the outcome. This testing verifies not only that the rule fires as designed but also that alerts are actionable and appropriately prioritized. Test results—whether from simulated attacks, replayed logs, or sandbox environments—provide tangible assurance that the logic performs reliably. Mature programs store these results alongside versioned detection logic, allowing auditors to trace when and how the rule was last verified. A stale testing date or absent results indicates that a rule may have drifted from effectiveness, especially in fast-changing infrastructure environments.

Measurement metrics bring objectivity to detection performance. The catalog should include quantitative indicators such as alert volume, true positive rate, false positive rate, and mean time to validate. These measurements demonstrate whether the use-case delivers value or contributes to analyst overload. High false positive ratios may signal overly broad conditions, while a complete absence of alerts could suggest faulty logic or missing data. Auditors analyze these metrics across the catalog to assess overall detection health, ensuring that the monitoring program prioritizes quality over quantity. Trend data showing improvement in these ratios over time reflects a maturing detection engineering practice.

Lifecycle governance ensures that detections evolve responsibly from conception to retirement. Onboarding begins with proposal and design—when a new threat scenario or risk gap is identified. The proposed use-case is reviewed for alignment with organizational priorities, verified for available data sources, and approved before deployment. During the operational phase, periodic reviews—typically quarterly or semiannually—confirm that the detection remains relevant, effective, and free from redundant overlap. When a rule is replaced by a superior version or the associated risk is mitigated by architectural change, it enters retirement. Each transition—onboard, modify, retire—should generate a recorded change entry with date, rationale, and approver. These lifecycle records allow auditors to verify that detections are not created or deleted informally, preserving both transparency and institutional memory.

Change control for use-cases mirrors that of software development. Proposed edits to detection logic should pass through peer review and formal approval before being merged into production. The rationale for changes—such as noise reduction, data field updates, or logic refinement—must be documented directly within the catalog entry or linked change request. Versioning systems provide diffs between iterations, ensuring traceability of who changed what and why. Retirement decisions must be equally transparent, documenting whether the rule was superseded, deprecated due to system decommissioning, or retired after risk acceptance. This traceable chain of reasoning distinguishes a governed detection program from one driven by convenience or fatigue.

Cadence of review is another dimension of maturity. Leading organizations establish regular intervals—often aligned with audit or operational risk cycles—for catalog review meetings. During these sessions, rule owners present updates, discuss performance metrics, and propose additions or retirements. This governance cadence ensures continuous alignment between the catalog and the organization's evolving threat landscape. It also offers auditors a clear rhythm of evidence: meeting minutes, review logs, and signed approvals form a demonstrable pattern of oversight. Programs that neglect this cadence inevitably accumulate technical debt, with obsolete detections remaining active and relevant threats going unmonitored.

Alert Triage Interfaces and Escalation Paths

The alert triage process represents the critical decision point between detection and response—the juncture where monitoring transitions into incident management. For cybersecurity auditors, understanding how alerts are triaged, documented, and escalated is essential to evaluating both the efficiency and accountability of the organization's monitoring program. The focus is not on how incidents are remediated—that belongs to the realm of incident response—but on the structural and procedural integrity of the triage process itself. A mature triage function ensures that every alert follows a predictable, traceable path from generation to resolution, preserving the fidelity of information and the integrity of timing across systems.

Triage typically occurs within a defined platform boundary: either directly in the SIEM tool, in an integrated Security Orchestration, Automation, and Response (SOAR) platform, or within a dedicated case management system. The architecture often reflects the organization's maturity. Smaller teams may manage triage within the SIEM itself using built-in ticketing features, while larger enterprises rely on SOAR systems to orchestrate enrichment and workflow automation. The auditor must determine where the authoritative triage occurs—where analyst actions are first logged, where evidence is captured, and where decisions become part of the official record. This distinction is important, as multiple tools may display alerts, but only one should serve as the system of record for triage status, ownership, and handoff.

Each alert entering triage should contain a standardized set of mandatory fields to ensure completeness and facilitate analysis. These fields typically include alert ID, detection rule name, event timestamp, asset or user involved, severity rating, and data source identifiers. Additional metadata such as detection confidence, correlation ID, and enrichment summary provide necessary context for quick decision-making. The completeness of these fields determines whether analysts can act efficiently without repeatedly querying raw logs. Auditors examine whether these mandatory fields are enforced by the system or left to manual discretion, as missing or inconsistent data undermines traceability and complicates subsequent investigations.

During triage, analysts must add structured inputs that document their evaluation. Mandatory triage fields include the triage timestamp, analyst identifier, investigation notes, disposition code (such as "true positive," "false positive," or "informational"), and any escalation decision. These fields transform raw alerts into auditable records of human judgment. Time stamps are particularly important, marking the duration between alert generation and analyst review—one of the most telling indicators of monitoring responsiveness. A well-designed interface enforces these fields through templates or dropdowns, preventing incomplete handoffs or subjective note-taking. The auditor validates this enforcement by reviewing sample cases and ensuring no record proceeds through the workflow without required metadata.

Escalation to the incident response (IR) function must be governed by explicit and measurable criteria. Common escalation triggers include confirmed malicious activity, high-severity indicators such as data exfiltration or privilege misuse, or potential compromise of regulated data. The purpose of these criteria is not to script incident response playbooks but to establish consistent thresholds for when a triaged alert becomes a managed incident. Auditors assess whether these thresholds are documented, approved, and consistently applied across analysts and shifts. Ambiguity in escalation rules often leads to inconsistent decisions—some alerts escalated prematurely, others suppressed entirely—creating both operational inefficiency and audit exposure.

Handoff quality defines the boundary between triage and IR. A clean handoff ensures that when an incident is escalated, the receiving team inherits a complete, time-stamped, and context-rich record. The essential components of a quality handoff include a verified timestamp of escalation, enrichment details (such as resolved IPs, user attributes, or related events), and clear disposition codes reflecting triage conclusions. Each case must retain a direct link to its originating detection rule and the raw event(s) that triggered it, allowing IR analysts or auditors to trace evidence backward to its source. A mature environment embeds these relationships automatically, ensuring bidirectional traceability between the triage system, SIEM rule, and underlying log event.

Auditors often evaluate handoff quality by sampling closed cases and reconstructing the chain from detection to escalation. They confirm that timestamps follow a logical and continuous flow, that enrichment artifacts are attached or referenced, and that the escalation record includes sufficient metadata for IR to proceed without repeating triage steps. Missing timestamps, unpopulated disposition fields, or absent event links signal procedural weaknesses. These gaps do not merely slow response—they jeopardize evidentiary continuity, particularly in regulated environments where incident timelines must withstand external scrutiny.

In well-governed environments, escalation is not an informal conversation—it is a controlled workflow. When a case is promoted to IR, ownership formally transfers from the monitoring team to the response function, with a recorded acknowledgment in the case system. Automated notifications may trigger in parallel, updating dashboards and management reports. The transition is logged with date, time, and responsible personnel identifiers, creating a forensic-grade record of accountability. Auditors verify that these transitions are recorded automatically and not left to manual annotation, as human discretion often leads to inconsistent documentation or lost traceability.

Integration between triage platforms and IR case systems plays a decisive role in maintaining continuity. Bidirectional synchronization ensures that when IR analysts update an incident with root cause findings or remediation outcomes, those details flow back into the detection catalog and monitoring feedback loop. While the auditor does not evaluate IR playbooks, they do verify that such feedback mechanisms exist and function. This closed loop supports continuous improvement by allowing detection engineers to refine rules based on real-world incident learnings—a core indicator of detection program maturity.

Common pitfalls in triage and escalation governance include fragmented workflows, duplicate systems of record, and incomplete metadata capture. Some organizations rely on email or chat messages to escalate incidents, leaving no structured record in the case system. Others allow analysts to bypass required fields for convenience, eroding consistency and accountability. Weaknesses like these are easily exposed in audits when timelines cannot be reconstructed or when alerts appear resolved without documented analysis. Robust enforcement of mandatory fields, coupled with clear ownership and automated linkage between tools, mitigates these risks and strengthens the defensibility of the monitoring program.

A well-structured triage and escalation process demonstrates operational discipline, transparency, and reliability. For auditors, the presence of complete metadata, consistent escalation criteria, and preserved linkages between rule, alert, and case form the evidence of control effectiveness. When every alert's journey—from detection to resolution—can be retraced without ambiguity, the organization not only meets compliance requirements but achieves the operational clarity needed to respond with speed and confidence. The boundaries between triage and incident response become not points of friction, but proof of a seamless and trustworthy detection ecosystem.

Telemetry Gaps and Compensating Signals

Even the most sophisticated monitoring programs contain areas of incomplete visibility—telemetry gaps that emerge when expected event data is missing, delayed, or degraded. These blind spots threaten the reliability of a security monitoring program because they obscure the very evidence that detection systems depend on. For auditors, the existence of telemetry gaps does not automatically signify failure; what matters is how those gaps are identified, documented, and mitigated. A well-governed program treats telemetry visibility as a measurable control domain with explicit ownership, risk-based compensations, and closure tracking. The maturity of an organization's approach to these gaps often reflects the strength of its overall cybersecurity governance, distinguishing those that understand their weaknesses from those that only assume coverage.

The first step in managing telemetry health is discovering where the blind spots exist. This begins with asset-to-source reconciliation, comparing authoritative inventories—such as CMDBs, cloud resource inventories, or endpoint management systems—against the log sources actively feeding the SIEM or data lake. These reconciliations reveal coverage deltas between expected and onboarded assets. For example, if a company operates 12,000 servers but the SIEM reflects telemetry from only 11,100, auditors will immediately question the missing 900 endpoints. Automated reconciliation scripts or dashboards can flag such discrepancies daily, preventing slow drift in visibility. The audit inquiry centers on whether these reconciliations are institutionalized, tracked over time, and reviewed by accountable owners, rather than treated as occasional housekeeping tasks.

Failed collectors and broken ingestion pipelines form another frequent source of telemetry loss. A single malfunctioning log forwarder, expired certificate, or overloaded relay node can silently cut off entire categories of data. In large enterprises, a failed collector may affect thousands of downstream assets. Mature programs maintain health monitoring for all telemetry components, tracking heartbeat status, ingestion volumes, and latency metrics. Alerts for abnormal conditions—such as sudden volume drops or prolonged silence from critical agents—should automatically generate cases for remediation. Auditors validate whether this telemetry health monitoring exists and whether it is integrated into standard incident management processes. A failed collector that goes unnoticed for weeks indicates not just technical weakness but a breakdown in operational awareness.

License or storage limits present a subtler but equally dangerous form of data loss. SIEMs and cloud analytics platforms frequently cap daily ingestion volumes or total retention sizes, creating silent failure conditions once those limits are reached. When volume thresholds are exceeded, some systems drop events without warning or truncate fields to save space. Under financial pressure, organizations may intentionally throttle "less critical" log streams—often network or endpoint telemetry—without a documented risk assessment. From an audit perspective, these undocumented trade-offs constitute unacknowledged risk. A mature governance model addresses these limitations explicitly, performing impact assessments, obtaining management approval, and recording compensating measures for each intentional exclusion. This transparency turns resource constraints into managed risk rather than hidden failure.

When telemetry cannot be restored immediately, compensating signals serve as temporary substitutes to sustain partial visibility. Selecting these substitutes requires contextual judgment grounded in risk assessment. If endpoint telemetry is lost due to a malfunctioning EDR agent, network proxy, firewall, or DNS logs can provide alternative visibility into command-and-control activity. If cloud service audit logs are delayed or inaccessible, application or database audit logs may help reconstruct key user actions. The auditor evaluates whether these compensations are rationally chosen and documented, verifying that their coverage aligns with the risk associated with the missing data. A compensating signal should not be a superficial placeholder—it must provide a credible, measurable substitute that meaningfully supports threat detection until normal telemetry resumes.

However, compensating signals are never a permanent solution. They serve as temporary scaffolding to maintain visibility while the root issue is addressed. Effective governance mandates formal tracking of these compensations within a telemetry exception or visibility gap register. Each entry should specify the gap's origin, impacted assets, compensating signals in place, responsible owner, risk rating, and planned closure date. The register is reviewed on a defined cadence—often monthly or quarterly—by security operations leadership and audit stakeholders. Persistent entries that exceed their target resolution window are escalated, ensuring that "temporary" fixes do not become long-term complacency. During an audit, this register functions as a primary artifact of accountability, showing that the organization recognizes, manages, and actively works to eliminate its blind spots.

Root cause analysis transforms telemetry gap management from reactive maintenance to continuous improvement. Each discovered gap should trigger investigation into why it occurred—whether due to missing onboarding processes, outdated templates, or tooling incompatibilities. For instance, auditors often find that new virtual machines are spun up without log agents because the provisioning image was never updated. Corrective actions, such as embedding log collection agents into baseline templates or improving automation scripts, prevent recurrence. Documented lessons learned and systemic fixes demonstrate that the organization does more than patch symptoms—it strengthens its telemetry ecosystem. When these corrective actions are captured within a central knowledge base or change tracking system, auditors gain confidence in the durability of remediation.

Risk prioritization ensures that attention is focused where it matters most. A missing log source from a development test server may be acceptable, whereas telemetry loss from a domain controller, payment system, or privileged access management appliance represents a critical exposure. Mature organizations classify telemetry gaps by risk tier, linking them to affected business functions and regulatory obligations. These classifications dictate remediation timelines, funding prioritization, and escalation thresholds. Auditors assess whether these risk ratings align with the broader enterprise risk framework, verifying that telemetry loss is treated as a control deficiency, not a mere technical issue. When high-risk gaps persist without justification, it signals a governance lapse requiring management attention.

Metrics serve as the quantifiable pulse of telemetry health. Coverage percentage, ingestion latency, and mean time to restore visibility are measurable indicators of control performance. Organizations should define explicit targets, such as "95% of managed assets reporting active telemetry within the past 24 hours" or "no critical log source outages exceeding 48 hours." Regular reporting of these metrics—ideally through automated dashboards—demonstrates accountability and enables trend analysis. Auditors look for evidence that these metrics are tracked, reported to management, and used to drive continuous improvement. The absence of defined metrics often correlates with unrecognized or unmanaged data loss, reducing confidence in the overall detection program.

Evidence Locations: SIEM/Log Platform, Detection Repositories, and Tuning Records

For cybersecurity auditors, the strength of an audit finding lies not in the clarity of an assertion but in the integrity and provenance of the evidence that supports it. In the realm of logging and detection, this evidence must be both traceable and reproducible—able to withstand external scrutiny months or even years after the original assessment. Evidence does not reside in a single system; it exists as an interconnected web of artifacts spanning log ingestion, configuration management, detection repositories, and triage platforms. Understanding these relationships—and verifying that exportable, time-bounded snapshots exist for each—is essential to establishing audit defensibility. Screenshots and ad hoc screen captures are insufficient substitutes for structured, verifiable exports that carry metadata proving their origin, date, and completeness.

The first tier of canonical evidence resides within the source onboarding inventory—the authoritative list of log-producing systems, their configurations, and their ingestion status. This inventory links the organization's asset register to its log coverage model, identifying which endpoints, network devices, applications, and cloud services are actively sending telemetry. It should specify source identifiers, collection methods, and ownership. Auditors use this inventory as the starting point for reconciling expected versus actual log sources. Exportable evidence from this layer may include asset-to-log source correlation tables, onboarding forms, or data extraction from CMDBs. The goal is to obtain verifiable proof, in structured form, of what was intended to be collected and the date those intentions were last validated.

The second layer of evidence lies in the SIEM or log management platform itself, which operationalizes those onboarding definitions. This system contains the active configurations governing data ingestion, normalization, parsing, and retention. Key evidence includes configuration exports showing log source definitions, ingestion connectors, pipeline mappings, and retention settings. These exports serve as proof that logs not only exist but are being processed according to policy. For instance, auditors may examine exported lists of data connectors from the SIEM, comparing them to the onboarding inventory to confirm coverage alignment. Equally important are exports of retention configurations that demonstrate compliance with policy-mandated durations—such as 90-day hot storage and 1-year cold archive retention. These structured exports must include timestamps, ensuring auditors can confirm the period during which the configuration was valid.

Detection repositories form the next critical evidence layer, housing the analytic logic that transforms raw telemetry into actionable signals. In mature organizations, these repositories are maintained in version-controlled systems such as Git, with each rule treated as code. The repository captures rule content, metadata, change history, and approvals, providing auditors with proof of how detection content evolves over time. Exportable evidence includes branch snapshots, commit logs, and version diffs that show the precise logic changes between review cycles. This data should be captured in plain-text or structured export formats rather than through screenshots, preserving both readability and audit verifiability. Auditors focus on the linkage between the detection repository and the SIEM configuration—confirming that deployed rules in the SIEM correspond to those approved in the repository.

The tuning and suppression records provide the contextual glue connecting detection repositories to operational behavior. These records explain why a rule behaves the way it does in production, documenting noise reduction steps, exception handling, and risk-based justifications.

Evidence from this domain includes suppression registers, tuning rationale documents, and review logs demonstrating when changes were made and by whom. Each suppression or tuning decision must be traceable to a rule identifier in the repository and, ideally, reference corresponding test results or validation metrics. Exportable evidence here typically comes from structured reports or database dumps—showing current and historical suppression entries along with status fields such as "active," "expired," or "under review." Auditors prioritize such structured data because it can be analyzed for completeness and consistency, whereas screenshots or copied text cannot reliably demonstrate integrity.

Case management and triage systems form the operational endpoint of the evidence chain. They contain records of how detections were handled once triggered, including timestamps, analyst actions, dispositions, and escalation outcomes. These systems provide the behavioral proof that detection logic functions as intended. Exportable audit evidence includes case records filtered by time window, showing alert counts, true/false positive ratios, and escalation paths. These exports must include provenance fields—such as export timestamp, user performing the export, and applied filters—to ensure the snapshot represents a definitive state for the audited period. Auditors cross-reference these cases with detection rule identifiers, validating end-to-end traceability from log source through analytic logic to triage resolution. Table 11.3 links inventory configuration detection tuning and case outcomes with verifiable provenance and time bounds.

The relationships among these evidence layers form a chain of custody that mirrors the audit trail of the monitoring ecosystem. Source onboarding inventories establish what *should* be monitored. SIEM and log platform exports demonstrate what *is* being collected and retained. Detection repositories define *how* telemetry is analyzed. Tuning and suppression records explain *why* certain detections behave as observed. Finally, case system exports prove *what happened* operationally as a result. Auditors trace these relationships to ensure consistency—verifying, for example, that a tuned rule in the repository corresponds to the suppression records in the operational system and

Table 11.3 Evidence chain from source to case record.

Evidence layer	Exportable artifact	Provenance metadata	Period bound	Primary relationship
Source onboarding inventory	Asset to source table	Export timestamp and author	Scope dates	Maps assets to intended telemetry
SIEM configuration	Connector and parser export	System id and hash	Scope dates	Implements ingestion from inventory
Retention settings	Tier policy export	Export timestamp and storage class	Scope dates	Assures duration and immutability
Detection repository	Rule code and commit log	Commit id and author and date	Scope dates	Defines analytics deployed to SIEM
Tuning suppression records	Suppression register export	Change id and approver	Scope dates	Explains rule behavior in production
Case triage exports	Case list with dispositions	Exporter id and filter set	Scope dates	Proves operational handling of alerts

that alerts generated by that rule appear in triage exports for the appropriate period. Any break in these linkages undermines evidentiary integrity, signaling potential control failure or weak documentation practices.

Period bounds are an often-overlooked yet vital component of defensible evidence. Every export must clearly indicate the time frame it represents—whether configuration snapshots from March 2025, detection repository commits up to June 2025, or triage data covering Q3 2025. Without this temporal bounding, evidence loses its reliability, as auditors cannot confirm that it aligns with the scope period of the audit. Provenance metadata such as export timestamps, file hashes, and storage locations further reinforce authenticity. Organizations that automate periodic exports and preserve them in immutable storage demonstrate the highest level of evidentiary control, enabling future revalidation without reliance on volatile live systems.

Auditors emphasize exportable, structured snapshots over screenshots for both integrity and reproducibility. Screenshots may provide quick visual confirmation, but they lack embedded metadata, can be selectively framed, and are prone to accidental alteration. Exported data—whether in CSV, JSON, or XML format—can be independently parsed, validated, and compared against baselines. Where screenshots are unavoidable, such as for proprietary interfaces lacking export functionality, they should be supplemented with contextual metadata that identifies the system, timestamp, and user performing the capture. This approach transforms ephemeral visuals into traceable evidence suitable for formal assurance.

Conclusion

Mastering the principles of logging, monitoring, and detection is critical for transforming visibility into verifiable assurance. A well-designed telemetry architecture does more than collect data—it enforces accountability, enables accurate detection, and provides immutable evidence of system behavior. When auditors evaluate these mechanisms, they are assessing not just technical configurations but the organization's ability to prove its own trustworthiness. Every log, rule, and triage record forms part of an evidentiary chain that supports both operational defense and regulatory confidence.

This chapter reinforces the role of disciplined detection engineering and governance as the foundation of security assurance in AI-driven and cloud-centric environments. As automation accelerates decision-making, the integrity of the underlying data becomes inseparable from the integrity of the enterprise itself. Detection quality, tuning rationale, and audit-ready evidence repositories ensure that machine learning systems, orchestration tools, and security analytics operate transparently and accountably. Visibility, when properly governed, becomes the control of controls—the mechanism that validates whether every other safeguard is functioning as intended.

With these foundations in place, cybersecurity professionals are better equipped to balance operational agility with forensic reliability. The capability to trace events, verify authenticity, and demonstrate continuous coverage transforms monitoring from a reactive function into a proactive assurance discipline. While technologies will evolve, the strategic intent remains consistent across all architectures: to ensure that what occurs within the environment can be observed, trusted, and defended. The enduring lesson of this chapter is that true resilience begins with the ability to see—and to prove what was seen—beyond dispute.

Auditor Recommendations

1. **Define Log Coverage Expectations:** Establish a structured process for defining and verifying log coverage by source type, depth, and retention tier. Use reconciliations between asset inventories and onboarded sources to identify gaps and verify completeness. This approach ensures that visibility claims are based on measurable evidence rather than assumptions.
2. **Enforce Log Integrity Controls:** Require that immutability, hashing, and time synchronization controls are formally tested and evidenced. Confirm that storage platforms enforce write-once configurations and that access permissions reflect least-privilege principles. Validating these technical safeguards strengthens the credibility of audit evidence and ensures that logs remain tamper-resistant.
3. **Audit Detection Content Governance:** Verify that all detection logic is version-controlled and subject to documented approval and testing processes. Examine commit histories, rule diffs, and approval records to confirm a consistent workflow from design to deployment. Auditors should ensure detection content evolves under governance, not informal modification.
4. **Evaluate Detection Performance Metrics:** Review how precision, recall, and tuning cycles are measured and managed. Ensure that rule adjustments are data-driven and that false positive rates are tracked with supporting rationale for every tuning decision. By validating analytical accuracy, auditors can determine whether the detection environment effectively balances coverage and operational workload.
5. **Scrutinize Suppression Management:** Examine the suppression register to confirm that every exclusion has documented justification, approval, and expiration. Ensure reviews occur regularly and that blanket or indefinite suppressions are prohibited. Auditors must verify that suppression governance preserves monitoring effectiveness while controlling alert noise responsibly.
6. **Validate Use-case Catalog Maturity:** Confirm that each use-case entry includes defined ownership, mapped risks or controls, data source dependencies, and test status. Review version histories and change approvals to ensure updates follow a repeatable governance cadence. Auditors should treat the catalog as a key evidence artifact demonstrating structured detection lifecycle management.
7. **Assess Triage and Escalation Documentation:** Review triage records to ensure mandatory fields—timestamps, disposition codes, and escalation details—are consistently completed. Confirm that alerts link back to originating rules and data sources for full traceability. Reliable documentation provides auditors with confidence that handoffs between monitoring and incident response preserve evidentiary integrity.
8. **Monitor Telemetry Health Governance:** Evaluate how telemetry gaps are identified, logged, and tracked through closure. Require evidence of asset-to-source reconciliations, collector health metrics, and compensating signal documentation. Auditors should verify that visibility gaps are managed transparently as risk exceptions rather than silently accepted.
9. **Inspect Evidence Provenance and Export Controls:** Ensure all log, detection, and triage evidence is exportable, time-bounded, and stored with provenance metadata. Avoid reliance on screenshots or ad hoc samples that lack validation context. Auditors should demand structured, reproducible exports that can be independently verified over the audit period.

10. **Integrate Visibility into Audit Planning:** Incorporate telemetry coverage, detection governance, and evidence integrity as recurring components of annual audit plans. Prioritize periodic assessments of log integrity, coverage completeness, and use-case catalog accuracy. By embedding these reviews into audit cycles, auditors reinforce visibility as a measurable control that supports enterprise assurance.

Chapter Questions

1. What is the primary purpose of a log coverage model in a monitoring program?
   A. To optimize SIEM query performance
   B. To express required coverage by source and depth and tie it to retention targets
   C. To replace incident response procedures
   D. To eliminate the need for an asset inventory

2. What is the core security benefit of using write-once (immutability) controls for logs?
   A. Records cannot be altered or deleted without detection
   B. Log files are automatically compressed for storage efficiency
   C. Parsing becomes easier for analytics tools
   D. Administrators can edit events to correct errors

3. Why is consistent time synchronization across systems essential for log integrity?
   A. It reduces storage costs for hot and cold tiers
   B. It enables AI model training on historical data
   C. It simplifies retention policy management
   D. It ensures accurate event correlation and coherent timelines

4. Which statement best captures the relationship between precision and recall in detection rules?
   A. Precision measures the proportion of real threats captured
   B. Recall measures the rate of false positives
   C. Precision reduces false positives, while recall reflects the proportion of relevant threats detected
   D. Both metrics are optional because tuning eliminates error

5. Which characteristic defines an acceptable suppression in a detection program?
   A. A blanket filter excluding an entire subnet indefinitely
   B. A narrowly scoped, justified, time-bound exclusion with periodic review
   C. Disabling the rule in production during busy periods
   D. Ignoring noisy alerts until they stop firing

6. In a managed use-case catalog, which field most directly enforces accountability for a detection?
   A. Owner
   B. Objective
   C. Required data sources
   D. Measurements

7. Which triage artifact must be present to support high-quality handoff to incident response?
   - A. A color-coded dashboard view
   - B. An informal chat message notifying IR
   - C. Unstructured analyst notes without timestamps
   - D. Disposition codes with timestamps and links to the originating rule/event

8. Which method is used to identify telemetry gaps in coverage?
   - A. Conducting user satisfaction surveys
   - B. Relying on an annual policy review only
   - C. Asset-to-source reconciliation comparing inventories to onboarded sources
   - D. Capturing screenshots of SIEM dashboards

9. Which is an appropriate compensating signal when endpoint telemetry is temporarily unavailable?
   - A. Extending the log retention period
   - B. Using network proxy or DNS logs to observe command-and-control patterns
   - C. Disabling low-priority data sources system-wide
   - D. Waiting for the next quarterly review cycle

10. Where is change history for detection logic best evidenced for audit purposes?
    - A. SIEM retention settings export
    - B. Suppression register entries
    - C. Version control commit logs and rule diffs in the detection repository
    - D. Case/triage exports showing alert dispositions

12

Incident Response and Crisis Management

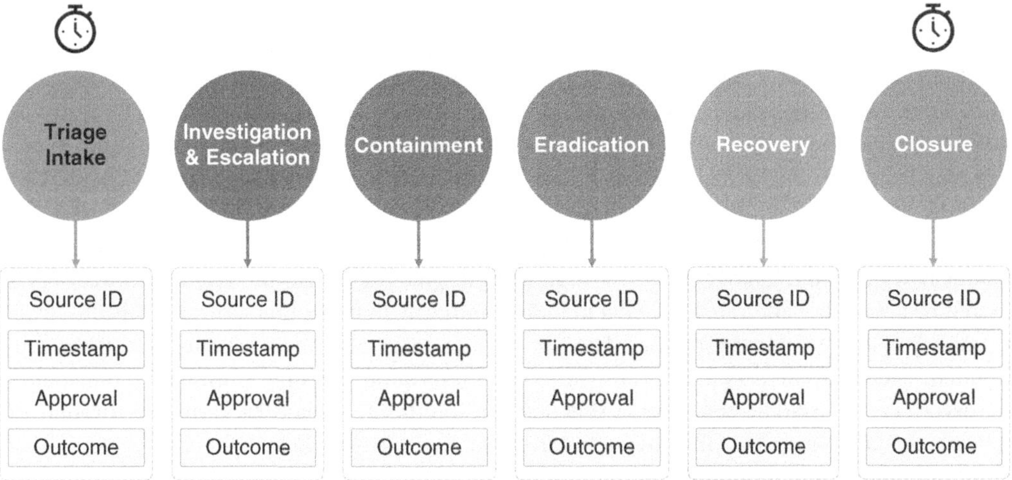

Incident response (IR) and crisis management form the true test of an organization's cybersecurity maturity. Technical controls may detect threats, but the ability to coordinate people, processes, and evidence under pressure determines whether damage is contained or magnified. This chapter examines how structured response models, disciplined documentation, and accountable decision-making transform chaos into control. By aligning incident operations with governance, risk, and compliance expectations, it demonstrates how auditors evaluate readiness not only through procedures on paper but through the traceability of every decision, action, and communication.

Effective IR is inseparable from business continuity and legal defensibility. The ability to preserve forensic integrity, meet disclosure obligations, and restore systems within defined recovery objectives is both a technical and regulatory imperative. Understanding how evidence flows—from detection and triage through containment, forensics, recovery, and lessons learned—reveals the interconnected nature of modern security architecture. Each function, from communications governance to backup readiness, becomes a point of audit assurance linking operational resilience to enterprise accountability.

As artificial intelligence, automation, and cloud orchestration accelerate response speed, they also introduce new dependencies and compliance risks. The principles presented here ground that complexity in structure and proof—emphasizing roles, artifacts, and verification over improvisation. For AI-enabled organizations, disciplined incident governance ensures that algorithmic actions, automated containment, and machine-generated evidence remain explainable and auditable. In this way, IR evolves from reactive firefighting into a measurable component of cybersecurity assurance, bridging operational execution with the trust demanded by regulators, customers, and the board.

IR Operating Model

An effective IR operating model defines not just how an organization reacts during a cybersecurity incident but also how accountability, authority, and documentation are governed throughout that process. It creates a disciplined chain of command that reduces confusion when systems fail, evidence disappears, and multiple stakeholders demand answers simultaneously. The structure must be documented in advance—often within an IR policy or charter—and should clearly outline who holds decision authority for containment, communication, and escalation. For auditors, this model provides the foundation for assessing whether the organization's response mechanisms are both repeatable and compliant with legal and regulatory obligations. A well-designed IR model serves as the operational backbone that transforms crisis into controlled execution, where every role, decision, and communication is auditable.

The incident commander acts as the central authority during response operations, ensuring that technical, legal, and executive teams move in unison. This role carries the highest level of operational responsibility and must have documented authority to make time-critical decisions, even when they disrupt standard processes. The commander declares incident severity, prioritizes containment over convenience, and ensures that communication remains controlled and evidence preserved. From an audit perspective, this position's authority should be verifiable through IR policies, escalation matrices, and after-action records. Auditors should look for clear evidence that the commander's actions are logged, that change management exceptions during an incident are tracked, and that post-incident reviews validate whether authority was exercised appropriately and within documented limits.

The communications lead manages the flow of information to internal and external audiences, preventing misinformation and speculation from escalating risk. This role translates technical updates into clear, fact-based reports for executives, employees, customers, and regulators. The communications process must be predefined: who can speak publicly, who approves messages, and how drafts are retained as part of the incident record. For auditors, communication controls are a critical verification point. They demonstrate whether an organization's statements were consistent with known facts and whether appropriate oversight—typically legal review—occurred before external disclosure. A mature IR program maintains a communications log, version control for public statements, and approval trails that auditors can inspect to ensure the organization adhered to its governance and compliance framework.

The forensics lead is responsible for establishing the factual narrative of what happened, how it occurred, and who was involved. This function coordinates evidence acquisition, analysis, and preservation—activities that carry both technical and legal weight. Proper chain-of-custody documentation, integrity verification (e.g., hash values), and secured evidence storage are mandatory to maintain admissibility and credibility of findings. From an auditor's standpoint, the forensics process is where technical rigor and procedural discipline must intersect. Auditors should confirm that evidence handling aligns with industry standards, that access is role-based and time-stamped, and that forensic activities are documented in a manner that can withstand regulatory or legal

Table 12.1 Decision rights by severity in the IR operating model.

Severity level	Incident commander authority	Actions requiring executive legal approval	Typical containment actions
Critical	Isolate network segments disable high risk identities initiate emergency changes	Public statement regulator notice revenue platform shutdown	Block malicious IPs revoke tokens quarantine endpoints
High	Authorize targeted host isolation suspend affected services approve temporary controls	Customer notification law enforcement engagement partner disclosure	Block domains disable compromised accounts restrict access
Medium	Direct local containment within business unit approve standard playbooks	Any action with broad customer impact or cross border data exposure	Reset credentials remove malicious tasks tighten firewall rules
Low	Oversee routine playbook execution coordinate verification	External messaging beyond standard advisories	Close phishing tickets enforce user resets update detection rules
Reserved Decisions	Not applicable	Extortion response regulator filings legal privilege directives	Not applicable

scrutiny. The absence of proper logging or tamper-proof evidence storage is a red flag indicating audit deficiencies in the organization's IR governance. Table 12.1 clarifies who may act at each severity and which decisions must escalate to executive and legal authority.

The legal and privacy advisors act as the interpretive layer between IR actions and the organization's legal or regulatory obligations. They guide the team on maintaining privilege, complying with privacy laws, and coordinating required notifications to affected parties or regulators. While they do not control technical actions, their input determines how documentation is phrased, how findings are shared, and when disclosure obligations are triggered. Auditors should evaluate whether counsel involvement is formally required at defined severity thresholds, whether privileged communications are segregated from general documentation, and whether privacy impact assessments are performed when personal or regulated data is involved. The presence of documented workflows showing how counsel influences incident handling demonstrates maturity and legal awareness—two essential audit criteria.

Decision rights form the structural backbone of an IR operating model. Each role must have clear boundaries for what it can decide independently, what requires concurrence, and what must escalate to executive or legal oversight. These thresholds often align with predefined severity levels, ranging from low-impact events contained at the departmental level to catastrophic breaches requiring board and regulator engagement. Auditors assess whether these decision matrices exist, are current, and are practiced through tabletop exercises or simulations. They also evaluate whether incidents of differing severity were handled in accordance with those rules. If decision rights are vague or inconsistently applied, auditors should flag it as a governance weakness, as it increases the likelihood of uncontrolled actions or delayed containment during real crises.

Documentation within the IR process must be both comprehensive and controlled, forming the evidentiary record for internal accountability, legal defense, and audit review. Every decision, system change, or data access event should be logged in a time-synchronized system of record. Logs must differentiate between observed facts, working hypotheses, and confirmed conclusions.

For auditing, this documentation becomes the audit trail—proof that decisions were based on verified data and approved processes. Auditors should check for the presence of immutable logs, standardized templates for situation reports, and version history for key documents. They should also ensure that retention policies align with legal hold requirements and that access to documentation repositories is limited to authorized personnel only.

Regulatory and contractual obligations shape not only *what* must be reported, but *when* and *how*. Many global privacy and breach laws impose strict time frames for notification, sometimes requiring regulatory disclosure within 72 hours of confirming an incident. The IR operating model must therefore define the trigger for "discovery," designate who has authority to initiate notification, and specify how counsel verifies completeness before submission. From an audit perspective, timeliness and procedural accuracy are primary indicators of compliance. Auditors should review whether regulatory notifications are logged, whether drafts were approved by legal before release, and whether decision rationales were recorded when choosing to delay or limit disclosure. Gaps here often reveal systemic weaknesses in regulatory readiness and communication governance.

Access control over evidence and sensitive data during response is another area with strong audit implications. The IR team operates under heightened privileges, often with access to confidential employee, customer, or operational data. Role-based access and just-in-time provisioning prevent unauthorized viewing or tampering. All forensic repositories, shared drives, and communication tools should maintain full access logs for audit inspection. In multinational organizations, evidence handling must also comply with cross-border data protection requirements, meaning forensic images or data sets may need to remain within specific jurisdictions. Auditors should examine whether technical and administrative safeguards are in place to prevent unlawful transfers or excessive data exposure, as these could constitute regulatory violations even during legitimate investigations.

After an incident, the same structure that enabled coordination becomes the foundation for organizational learning and assurance. A formal post-incident review should capture root causes, response effectiveness, and deviations from approved decision paths. The incident commander oversees this process, while legal, privacy, and forensics leads contribute their respective findings. The output is not only an internal improvement plan but an audit artifact demonstrating governance maturity. Auditors should expect to see evidence that lessons learned were logged, corrective actions assigned, and risk registers updated accordingly. A closed-loop process—where response outcomes inform control improvements—is the hallmark of a resilient and auditable IR program. Through this lens, IR becomes not merely a firefight but a continuous audit-driven feedback cycle strengthening the enterprise's overall security posture.

Detection Handoffs and Case Life Cycle (from Alert to Closure)

Every cybersecurity incident follows a predictable life cycle, transforming a raw alert into a verified case and ultimately a closed record of lessons learned. This life cycle ensures that each detection passes through a disciplined sequence of analysis, containment, and remediation, governed by both operational and audit controls. The goal is to standardize how alerts are assessed, escalated, and resolved—creating traceability from the first detection signal to the final recovery step. For auditors, the life cycle provides a structured map for evaluating whether incidents are handled consistently, efficiently, and in compliance with defined policies. A well-documented life cycle reduces ambiguity, enhances accountability, and preserves evidence necessary for both technical validation and regulatory assurance.

The process begins with triage intake, the first stage in which a detection signal—often generated by a SIEM, IDS, EDR, or threat intelligence feed—is reviewed for relevance and priority. Analysts perform initial validation, confirming whether the alert represents a true security event or a false positive. Required case fields at this stage include the detection source, timestamp, affected asset, detection rule ID, and analyst validation outcome. Time-based expectations, often captured in Service Level Agreements (SLAs), require acknowledgment of high-priority alerts within minutes or hours, depending on severity. From an audit standpoint, it is critical that every alert reviewed has a corresponding case record showing when it was received, who reviewed it, and what decision was made. This ensures visibility into the efficiency and consistency of the triage process. Table 12.2 aligns life cycle stages with mandatory case fields and SLA expectations that auditors will verify in the system of record.

Table 12.2 Case life cycle fields and time expectations.

Life cycle stage	Required case fields	Primary owner	Acknowledge SLA	Escalate SLA	Resolution SLA
Triage Intake	Detection source timestamp affected asset rule ID validation outcome	Tier 1 analyst	High priority within minutes medium within hours	Per severity matrix	Per severity matrix
Investigation Escalation	Incident type indicators scope affected systems data exposure status	Tier 2 analyst	Updates per bridge rhythm	When scope expands or critical assets implicated	Per severity matrix
Containment	Actions taken timestamps approvals rollback plan containment status	Incident commander	Immediate confirmation of actions	If containment fails or spreads	Until risk reduced to acceptable level
Eradication	Root cause method responsible team verification results	Forensics lead	Progress updates per plan	If reinfection detected or controls fail	Until threat neutralized and verified
Recovery	Restoration method validation checks readiness confirmation	DR lead	Status updates to command group	If RTO at risk or dependencies fail	Until services meet RTO and RPO targets
Closure	Root cause summary impact assessment corrective actions lessons learned	Incident commander	Final review scheduling	If required approvals missing	Closed after approvals and documentation complete

Once an alert is validated, it moves into the investigation and escalation stage, where analysts gather additional evidence and determine scope. Here, case fields expand to include incident type, threat actor indicators, affected systems, potential data exposure, and current containment status. Escalation paths are triggered based on predefined criteria—such as lateral movement detection or critical asset involvement—and each escalation must be timestamped and logged. Auditors should verify that escalation SLAs are met and that each handoff between analysts or teams is recorded in the system of record. Effective tracking of case assignments, investigation notes, and evidence links demonstrates operational maturity and provides proof of due diligence under security frameworks like ISO 27001 and NIST 800-61.

During containment, the priority shifts from analysis to action. Containment involves isolating affected systems, disabling compromised accounts, and blocking malicious IPs or domains to prevent further spread. At this stage, case records must show specific containment actions taken, their timestamps, approval authority, and any temporary workarounds implemented. These actions are often governed by decision rights documented in the IR playbook. Auditors should examine whether containment steps align with approved procedures, whether rollback plans exist for containment measures, and whether temporary controls were later removed or replaced by permanent ones. Each action taken should be recorded with enough granularity to reconstruct the event sequence—an essential requirement for both technical postmortem and external audit verification.

Following containment, the eradication stage focuses on removing the root cause of compromise. This can include deleting malicious files, patching vulnerabilities, resetting credentials, or removing unauthorized access routes. Case fields here must document the identified root cause, eradication method, responsible team, and verification results confirming that the threat has been neutralized. Time-based expectations ensure eradication occurs promptly to avoid reinfection or persistence. For auditors, eradication records demonstrate that the organization not only responded reactively but also remediated proactively. The presence of detailed evidence—such as logs of malware removal, configuration changes, or patch deployments—shows completeness and diligence in closing out technical risk. Lack of documentation or missing verification evidence is a red flag that remediation may have been partial or superficial.

The recovery stage transitions the organization from containment back to normal operations. Systems are restored from clean backups, configurations are validated, and service availability is confirmed. Required case fields at this stage typically include recovery start and completion times, system restoration method, validation checks performed, and confirmation of operational readiness. Recovery SLAs ensure critical systems return to production within acceptable downtime limits defined by business continuity plans. Auditors assess whether recovery timelines align with organizational recovery time objectives (RTOs) and whether the restored environment was verified free of compromise before reactivation. Proper documentation here bridges IR and business continuity auditing, demonstrating alignment between security and resilience functions.

Once the threat is neutralized and systems restored, the closure phase finalizes documentation and ensures all procedural, legal, and communication requirements have been fulfilled. This stage includes compiling an incident summary, mapping controls that failed or succeeded, and recording any regulatory notifications or customer disclosures made. Closure fields include root cause summary, impact assessment, corrective actions, and lessons learned. Closure SLAs ensure incidents do not remain in "pending" status indefinitely, and auditors should verify that every closed case has been formally reviewed and approved by the incident commander or designated authority. Closure validation provides auditors with assurance that IR cycles are finite, controlled, and measurable, preventing operational drift or data loss within case management systems.

Throughout each phase, time-based expectations provide measurable accountability. Acknowledgment SLAs define how quickly analysts must review new alerts; escalation SLAs define the maximum delay before involving higher-level responders; and resolution SLAs measure how long incidents remain open. These metrics are critical to both performance management and compliance auditing. Auditors should compare SLA targets against actual case timestamps within the incident management platform to determine adherence and identify patterns of delay. Deviations may indicate under-resourced teams, ineffective monitoring, or process breakdowns—all of which carry governance implications. A mature IR program uses these metrics not just to evaluate performance but also to inform continuous improvement and staffing models.

Every stage of the life cycle must be evidenced in a system of record, such as a Security Incident Management (SIM) or ticketing platform. Each case should include unique identifiers, cross-references to detection rules, related vulnerabilities, and evidence repositories. Actions, handoffs, and status changes must be logged automatically where possible, ensuring the audit trail cannot be modified without authorization. For auditors, this system of record is the single source of truth. It allows traceability from detection through to closure, proving that incidents were managed systematically rather than ad hoc. Reviewers should confirm that timestamps are synchronized, access controls are enforced, and case data retention meets policy and regulatory requirements. Without a reliable case management system, even the most sophisticated response plans risk collapsing under scrutiny.

The post-incident review and feedback loop close the life cycle, transforming reactive response into strategic improvement. Analysts, responders, and auditors collaborate to review performance, identify control gaps, and prioritize corrective actions. Audit teams should ensure that lessons learned are not only documented but also tracked to completion within risk registers or corrective action plans. This step converts operational evidence into governance insight—linking incident outcomes to enterprise risk posture. In a mature cybersecurity auditing environment, the case life cycle is not merely a process map but an accountability framework. It transforms every alert into an opportunity to demonstrate control effectiveness, reinforce regulatory readiness, and strengthen the organization's overall cyber resilience.

Forensics and Evidence Handling (Chain of Custody)

Digital forensics within IR must satisfy two parallel goals: produce reliable facts quickly enough to guide containment and recovery, and generate an evidentiary record that can withstand legal and regulatory scrutiny. Minimum expectations include isolating affected systems to prevent further alteration, acquiring defensible images, calculating and recording hash values, storing materials in controlled repositories, and maintaining complete access logs. These activities are not optional enhancements; they are the baseline for credibility in any post-incident investigation or audit. An auditor reviewing the program expects written procedures, trained personnel, and tooling that make these steps consistent, repeatable, and verifiable. Where process diverges from policy, auditors will look for documented rationale, approvals, and compensating controls that preserved evidentiary integrity despite operational constraints.

Isolation practices begin the moment an event is escalated to potential compromise, because evidence evaporates quickly when systems remain in normal operation. The priority is to stop ongoing alteration while preserving volatile data such as memory, running processes, and ephemeral network connections that can vanish as soon as a host is powered down or a service is restarted. Network-level isolation, host containment through endpoint controls, and credential revocation should be executed in a sequence that prevents the destruction of key artifacts, with every step timestamped and attributed to a specific operator. Analysts should avoid ad-hoc "fixes" like deleting files or uninstalling agents that disturb the scene before imaging occurs. Auditors will verify that responders followed a documented order of volatility, captured the rationale for any deviation, and recorded the precise commands or tooling used during isolation.

Imaging is the cornerstone of defensible analysis, requiring bit-for-bit acquisition of relevant storage while preventing write operations to the source media. Hardware or software write-blockers, forensic acquisition profiles for cloud volumes, and hypervisor or snapshot methods for virtual machines must be selected based on the platform and evidentiary need. Each acquisition must record device identifiers, logical and physical sizes, tool versions and parameters, operator identity, and start and end times so the process can be reproduced. In cloud and SaaS environments, responders often cannot access raw disks, so certified snapshot, export, or API-driven collection methods substitute for traditional imaging; the same documentation rigor still applies. Auditors examine whether imaging playbooks exist for on-premises, virtualized, containerized, and cloud workloads, and whether the chosen method preserved relevant metadata without altering the original evidence.

Hashing provides the mathematical proof that evidence has not changed from acquisition through analysis and archival. Minimum expectations include calculating cryptographic hash values—commonly SHA-256 or SHA-512—immediately after imaging, recording those values in the chain-of-custody record, and verifying them again whenever the evidence is accessed or transferred. Large evidence sets may be chunked with manifest files listing segment hashes to enable partial transfers without losing integrity assurances. Any reacquisition, recompression, or repackaging must include new hashes and a clear linkage back to the original values so auditors can trace lineage. During audits, mismatched or missing hash records are serious defects that undermine the credibility of conclusions and can call the entire investigation into question.

Secure storage transforms individual artifacts into a managed evidence library with predictable controls over confidentiality, integrity, and availability. Standard practice is to place master images and sensitive exports on encrypted, access-controlled repositories with immutability or write-once capabilities, while keeping working copies segregated in analysis sandboxes. Key management for at-rest encryption must be handled by dedicated custodians, and recovery procedures should be tested to ensure evidence remains readable years after collection. Physical evidence, such as removable media or seized devices, requires tamper-evident packaging, barcoding, environmental controls, and restricted, logged access. Auditors will check for documented retention policies aligned to legal holds, jurisdictional requirements, and contractual obligations, including procedures for evidence archival, retrieval, and end-of-life destruction with certificates of destruction.

Access logging underpins accountability by recording who touched what, when, why, and with which privileges. Least-privilege, role-based access control should limit visibility to assigned case personnel, with just-in-time elevation and time limits for administrative roles used during active investigations. Service accounts and automation must be uniquely attributable and prohibited from sharing credentials to preserve individual accountability. All evidence repositories, case management systems, and analysis workstations should forward detailed access and change events into centralized logging or a SIEM to prevent tampering and to enable correlation with incident timelines. Auditors will validate that access logs are complete, immutable for the required retention period, and routinely reviewed for anomalies, especially around high-profile cases or privileged data sets.

Chain-of-custody documentation is the formal record that tracks possession, control, and condition of each piece of evidence from collection to final disposition. A complete entry identifies the item with a unique evidence ID, describes the source system and acquisition method, lists associated hash values, and records each transfer with timestamps, custodians, and purpose of the handoff. Digital signatures or authenticated approvals should accompany custody changes, and timekeeping across systems must be synchronized so the record forms a coherent, defensible timeline. When evidence crosses organizational boundaries—to a forensic vendor, cloud provider, insurer, or external counsel—the custody record must capture contractual references, packaging or encryption details, and verification steps performed at receipt. Auditors expect to reconcile physical or logical inventory with chain-of-custody forms and flag any gaps, overwrites, or ambiguous sign-offs as control failures.

Analytical rigor requires that examiners work from verified copies to protect master images while enabling efficient tooling and collaboration. Analysts should document tool versions, configuration options, parsing scripts, and validation steps that confirm correct interpretation of file systems, logs, network captures, or cloud telemetry. Where tools recover artifacts differently, procedures should include cross-tool verification and peer review notes that explain discrepancies and justify analytical choices. Derived artifacts—timelines, decoded payloads, memory extracts, or de-obfuscated scripts—must reference their source evidence IDs and hashes so auditors can trace conclusions back to primary material. A defensible workflow reads like a laboratory notebook: complete, legible, and reproducible by an independent examiner following the same steps.

Working with third-party responders and external counsel introduces additional evidentiary and privacy risks that must be managed contractually and operationally. Statements of work and onboarding checklists should require adherence to the organization's evidence handling standards, specify data residency and cross-border transfer constraints, and mandate encryption, access logging, and timely return or destruction of materials. When legal privilege is asserted, deliverables intended for counsel should be segregated in privileged repositories with distinct access controls and labeling, ensuring operational reports do not inadvertently waive protections. Receiving parties must acknowledge custody with matching hashes and immediately report any packaging damage, media failure, or hash mismatch. Auditors evaluate whether vendor due diligence included evidence-handling capability reviews, whether transfers were recorded end-to-end, and whether privileged materials remained segregated throughout the engagement.

Modern environments demand specialized practices for ephemeral and platform-managed data that do not behave like traditional disks. Cloud control plane logs, serverless function traces, container runtime metadata, and SaaS audit logs often have short retention windows and must be exported quickly under preservation orders once an incident is suspected. Playbooks should define authenticated API collection methods, snapshot strategies for cloud volumes, and procedures for capturing volatile memory where feasible without destabilizing production systems. Each export must be hashed, labeled, and placed under custody like any other artifact, with clear mapping between provider-native identifiers and internal evidence IDs. Auditors will look for proof that retention risks were recognized, that preservation actions were timely, and that obtained datasets remained intact and attributable across tooling and storage transitions.

Closure of the forensic phase is not the end of accountability; it is the point where evidence stewardship transitions to long-term governance. The program should issue or release legal holds based on counsel's guidance, finalize inventory reconciliations, confirm that master images and logs reside in designated archival tiers, and ensure working copies are sanitized or destroyed according to policy. Any deviation during the investigation—missed hashes, tool failures, or custody exceptions—must be documented with impact assessment and compensating controls to preserve reliability of conclusions. Certificates of return or destruction from vendors and counsel should be attached to the custody record to complete the chain. Auditors reviewing the case expect to find a closed loop: every artifact tracked, every handoff evidenced, and every integrity check demonstrably satisfied from first capture to final disposition.

Communications and Regulatory Notifications

Effective communication during an incident is as critical as containment or forensics, because information—if mishandled—can magnify damage faster than any malware. A mature IR program therefore codifies its internal and external communication paths, using predefined templates, escalation charts, and approval flows to maintain consistency and compliance. These communication frameworks are designed to serve two masters: operational coordination and legal defensibility. Every message sent, from a 3 a.m. analyst update to a regulator filing, becomes part of the auditable record that proves the organization acted promptly, transparently, and responsibly. Auditors evaluating this domain focus on three key aspects: whether communication paths are documented, whether notifications follow defined triggers by regime, and whether artifacts exist demonstrating timeliness, accuracy, and completeness.

Internal communication paths begin with the incident commander and extend through the command bridge, IT operations, legal, communications, and executive leadership. A properly designed model defines who must be informed, in what order, and through which channel—secure chat, ticketing system, or executive briefing. Status updates must be factual, timestamped, and distributed through a system of record rather than informal channels. Typical internal templates include "initial alert notification," "incident update," and "containment confirmation," each specifying required fields such as severity level, affected assets, business impact, and next planned action. For auditors, these templates provide evidence that updates were standardized, reducing the risk of inconsistent or speculative statements. The audit trail should include timestamps for each communication, demonstrating adherence to internal Service Level Agreements (SLAs) for response coordination and executive engagement.

Executive communication represents the bridge between technical operations and strategic oversight. Executives require enough information to make timely decisions—such as invoking business continuity procedures or approving external disclosures—but not operational minutiae that can obscure key facts. The IR plan must identify who provides these briefings, their frequency, and the format. Typical artifacts include executive situation reports (SITREPs) summarizing scope, impact, and mitigation progress. Auditors should expect to see documented evidence that executives were informed within predefined time frames based on incident severity. Delays or inconsistencies in executive updates often signal governance gaps, especially if key business leaders were unaware of material incidents within required reporting windows.

Employee communications are equally important but must balance transparency with security. Internal notifications to staff may include directives such as changing passwords, halting specific workflows, or refraining from discussing the incident publicly. These notices should be approved by the incident commander and legal counsel to ensure accuracy and confidentiality. Templates for internal employee bulletins should include distribution lists, key instructions, version numbers, and approval timestamps. Auditors reviewing this area look for proof that staff notifications were distributed quickly and that messages did not leak sensitive data. Improper or delayed employee communication can result in inadvertent disclosure, rumor propagation, or policy violations that complicate the organization's regulatory posture.

External communications demand a higher level of control and oversight. These include notifications to customers, partners, insurers, law enforcement, and the general public. Each audience has different requirements for content, tone, and timing, but all external messages must pass through legal and executive approval before release. The communications lead typically maintains templates for customer notifications, public statements, and regulator filings, each version-controlled and mapped to specific jurisdictions. Audit evidence for external communication includes draft versions, approval logs, and delivery confirmations—such as regulator submission receipts or email dispatch records. These artifacts serve as proof that external communications were authorized, timely, and complete.

Regulatory notifications are governed by precise legal regimes, each with its own trigger thresholds and time frames. For example, the European Union's General Data Protection Regulation (GDPR) requires notification to supervisory authorities within 72 hours of becoming aware of a personal data breach. The U.S. Securities and Exchange Commission (SEC) expects prompt disclosure of material cybersecurity incidents affecting public companies. Sectoral laws like HIPAA or GLBA impose additional reporting duties for healthcare and financial entities. The IR plan must specify who determines when these thresholds are met, how counsel confirms materiality, and how the communications lead prepares draft filings. From an auditing perspective, the presence of a decision log showing when potential notification triggers were evaluated and who authorized the final determination is essential. Missing or incomplete logs raise questions about regulatory diligence.

The artifacts demonstrating timeliness are critical in proving compliance. These include detection-to-declaration timestamps, draft submission dates, regulator acknowledgment receipts, and correspondence logs showing interim updates or follow-up clarifications. A well-designed case management system links these artifacts directly to the master incident record, creating a timeline auditors can trace from breach discovery to final disclosure. Auditors will test whether notification deadlines were met and whether internal timekeeping systems are synchronized to prevent discrepancies. Even a small timing mismatch—such as conflicting timestamps between logs and reports—can create doubt about whether an organization truly acted within mandated windows.

Completeness of notification is another core audit dimension. Communications must include all required content elements—description of the incident, categories of data affected, potential impacts, mitigation measures, and contact points for further information. Templates for each regime should reflect statutory language to prevent omissions. Auditors reviewing regulator filings or customer notices will verify that all mandatory fields were included and that factual accuracy aligns with forensic findings. They will also evaluate whether follow-up notices were issued when new information emerged, a common requirement under evolving breach disclosure laws.

Legal and compliance oversight ensures that every communication—internal or external—passes through documented approval flows. A typical workflow routes drafts from technical or communications teams to legal counsel for privilege review, then to the incident commander for operational accuracy, and finally to an executive sponsor for sign-off. These steps should be logged in the system of record, with timestamps, names, and revision histories preserved. Auditors will look for evidence of proper sign-offs and confirm that only authorized individuals had publishing or submission rights. Lack of a formal approval trail represents a serious deficiency, as it undermines both governance and defensibility.

A mature program also maintains a communications playbook, which integrates messaging templates, regulatory matrices, contact lists, and notification triggers into a single reference. This playbook should be tested through tabletop exercises to confirm that responders can execute the communication sequence under pressure. It should define alternative communication methods in case corporate systems are compromised, ensuring continuity of messaging even during outages. Auditors will evaluate whether the playbook exists, whether it has been updated within the past year, and whether exercises produced documented improvements. The playbook itself becomes an auditable artifact demonstrating readiness for both crisis response and regulatory compliance.

Post-incident communication reviews complete the cycle by evaluating message accuracy, tone, and regulatory outcomes. This phase assesses whether statements matched later forensic conclusions and whether any retractions or clarifications were required. Audit teams use this review to identify systemic weaknesses—such as delays in legal review, inconsistent messaging across jurisdictions, or incomplete documentation. A strong communication governance framework ensures that every notification, from the first internal alert to the final regulator filing, is deliberate, traceable, and defensible. In the eyes of auditors, this level of documentation transforms communication from a potential liability into a demonstrable control of organizational maturity and regulatory trustworthiness.

Backup/Restore Readiness and BCP/DR Alignment (RTO/RPO)

IR, business continuity plan (BCP), and disaster recovery (DR) are often treated as separate disciplines, but in a mature cybersecurity program they form an integrated control ecosystem. Backup and restore readiness is the critical hinge between them—the mechanism that determines whether an organization can recover from destructive cyber incidents such as ransomware, insider sabotage, or cloud misconfiguration. Effective integration ensures that when IR initiates recovery, the organization already has verified, restorable data and tested continuity plans. For auditors, this integration is not theoretical; it must be observable through documented evidence of recovery point objectives (RPOs), recovery time objectives (RTOs), backup test results, and decision logs showing how gaps were handled. A well-designed program demonstrates that technical restoration capabilities directly support business continuity outcomes, bridging operational resilience with audit accountability.

Backups are the first line of defense against data loss, and their design determines the realism of recovery objectives. A comprehensive backup strategy should specify what data is included, how frequently it is captured, and where it is stored—onsite, offsite, or in the cloud. Backups should be immutable or protected from alteration, with encryption both in transit and at rest to prevent corruption or exfiltration. Audit evidence should include backup inventories listing covered systems, schedules, encryption status, and retention periods. From an auditor's viewpoint, completeness and integrity of these records demonstrate compliance with policy and standards such as ISO 27001 Annex A.12.3 or NIST SP 800-34. Missing systems, outdated retention schedules, or inconsistent encryption practices indicate a maturity gap that could render an otherwise solid IR plan ineffective when data must be restored under pressure.

Recovery time and recovery point objectives define the boundaries of acceptable disruption. RTO represents how quickly systems must be restored to avoid unacceptable business impact, while RPO defines how much data loss, measured in time, is tolerable between the last backup and the incident. Both are set collaboratively between business owners and IT, and they form part of the service-level framework auditors use to evaluate resilience. When IR activates recovery, responders rely on these metrics to determine whether restoring from backup is faster or safer than rebuilding systems from scratch. Auditors reviewing incidents should find evidence that

RTO/RPO values are documented, tested, and aligned with business criticality tiers. If recovery exceeded these thresholds, the audit trail must show who made the decision, what compensating actions were taken, and whether leadership formally accepted the deviation.

Restore testing converts backup strategy into proof of readiness. A backup that cannot be restored under realistic conditions is no control at all. Routine restore tests—performed quarterly or semiannually—validate that data can be recovered to a known-good state within RTO parameters. These tests should include not only file-level restores but also full-system rebuilds and application reinstalls to confirm dependencies are intact. Test evidence should include start and end times, system identifiers, success criteria, responsible personnel, and observed anomalies. Auditors verify that restore testing is performed regularly, that failed tests trigger remediation, and that corrective actions are documented and tracked to closure. A pattern of skipped or unsuccessful restore tests signals both operational risk and a lack of audit readiness.

Integration with BCP and DR ensures that backup and restore processes function within a broader recovery architecture. Business continuity focuses on sustaining critical services during disruption, while DR focuses on rebuilding technology assets afterward. The IR team triggers these disciplines when cyber incidents escalate beyond containment—such as widespread data encryption or data center loss. Coordination requires predefined communication paths, decision authority, and runbooks linking IR to DR activation procedures. Auditors examine whether IR plans reference BCP/DR activation criteria and whether continuity exercises include cyber incident scenarios. They also look for evidence that IR participation in DR exercises is documented, demonstrating operational alignment rather than siloed response.

Site failover simulations test the organization's ability to sustain operations if primary infrastructure becomes unavailable. These exercises may involve activating secondary data centers, cloud regions, or alternate work environments. Key artifacts include failover test plans, system readiness checklists, data synchronization reports, and debrief summaries. Measured outcomes should map back to RTO and RPO benchmarks, with results logged in a recovery validation report. Auditors expect to see that failover tests occur at least annually for critical systems and that lessons learned are documented with clear accountability for remediation. Incomplete or untested failover capabilities represent one of the most serious deficiencies in operational resilience audits, as they directly correlate with extended outage risk during real crises.

Decision logs are the connective tissue that ties testing, metrics, and recovery execution together. During both planned exercises and real incidents, decision logs capture who authorized specific recovery actions, when RTO/RPO thresholds were breached, and why alternative courses were chosen. These logs form a permanent record of judgment under stress, offering auditors transparency into how governance frameworks perform in practice. A mature organization uses structured decision templates—recording incident identifiers, system owners, impact assessments, and sign-offs from IR, DR, and executive stakeholders. Auditors reviewing these logs assess whether escalation followed policy, whether exceptions were documented, and whether deviations triggered root cause analyses or policy revisions.

Backup verification must extend beyond isolated tests to encompass ongoing monitoring and alerting. Automated reporting should confirm backup completion, replication status, storage health, and retention compliance. Failed or incomplete backups should trigger alerts requiring acknowledgment and resolution. Audit evidence may include daily backup dashboards, failure trend analyses, and SLA compliance summaries. Auditors should cross-check these metrics with incident records to ensure that systems affected by breaches had recent, verified backups. The absence of backup validation or evidence of ignored alerts reveals control breakdowns that could compound the impact of a major security event.

BCP and DR exercises provide the stage for integrating backup and restoration capabilities into real-world continuity scenarios. Tabletop exercises test decision-making and coordination, while live simulations test technology recovery in production-like conditions. A complete exercise record includes objectives, participants, timelines, observations, and improvement actions. Auditors look for evidence that exercises are scheduled, executed, and reviewed formally, with lessons integrated into updated recovery plans. They also examine whether exercise results demonstrate progressive improvement in meeting RTO/RPO targets. When objectives are repeatedly missed without corrective action, auditors view it as a systemic failure of governance, not merely a technical weakness.

When RTO or RPO targets are not met—either during an actual incident or a planned exercise—the organization must treat the deviation as an auditable event. A decision log should record when thresholds were exceeded, who made the call to accept or extend recovery times, and what risk acceptance or mitigation steps followed. Root cause analysis should determine whether failures stemmed from outdated assumptions, underfunded infrastructure, or process gaps. Auditors assess whether such deviations were escalated to executive or board-level risk committees and whether the results informed budget or control updates. In this way, unmet objectives become catalysts for continuous improvement rather than hidden failures.

Tabletop Exercises and Post-incident Learning

Tabletop exercises are the proving ground for an organization's IR and crisis management capability. They test readiness without the risk of operational disruption, allowing teams to rehearse coordination, decision-making, and communication under controlled conditions. A mature IR program integrates these exercises into its annual calendar with defined cadence—typically quarterly for high-impact functions and at least annually for enterprise-wide simulations. The exercises are scenario-driven, often based on realistic threats such as ransomware outbreaks, insider data theft, or cloud configuration compromise. For auditors, tabletop activities represent the living evidence that policies, playbooks, and procedures are not merely written artifacts but operationalized practices. The existence of formal exercise schedules, participation rosters, and documented outcomes demonstrates proactive governance and fulfills expectations under most cybersecurity frameworks.

Designing a tabletop exercise begins with setting clear, measurable objectives. Each exercise should focus on testing specific aspects of the IR plan: escalation protocols, communication flow, decision authority, evidence handling, or failover coordination. Scenarios must be relevant to the organization's environment, data sensitivity, and regulatory exposure. A ransomware scenario, for example, might test the intersection between IR, legal counsel, and DR teams. The scenario should include timed injects—new facts or complications—to evaluate how quickly participants adapt to changing information. Auditors reviewing exercise documentation expect to see written objectives, scenario outlines, expected learning outcomes, and roles assigned for facilitators, observers, and participants. Clear objectives ensure that exercises are not abstract discussions but structured rehearsals aligned with specific control validation goals.

Participation is another key area of audit focus. Exercises must include the full spectrum of stakeholders who would be involved in an actual incident: security operations, IT operations, legal and privacy counsel, communications, business leadership, and in some cases, third-party vendors or regulators. Attendance logs, sign-in sheets, or virtual participation records form part of the audit trail demonstrating engagement across all critical functions. Auditors look for evidence that senior leaders were present and that decisions during the exercise followed the same escalation and approval paths defined in policy. Consistent participation across departments reflects a culture of preparedness, while repeated absences or narrow participation indicate siloed operations and potential governance weaknesses.

Documentation of the exercise is as important as the exercise itself. Each session should produce a detailed record capturing the timeline of events, decisions made, communication exchanges, and areas of confusion or delay. Facilitators should maintain an observer log noting how closely participants followed the IR playbook, whether predefined roles were clear, and how decisions were justified. These records become permanent evidence that supports both internal audit and regulatory inquiries. Auditors reviewing these materials assess whether the organization has established a repeatable documentation template that includes exercise name, date, participants, objectives, observed outcomes, and improvement actions. Inconsistent or missing documentation suggests the exercise program lacks structure and accountability.

The cadence of tabletop exercises should match the organization's risk profile and complexity. High-risk sectors such as finance or healthcare often run targeted exercises quarterly, supplemented by cross-functional simulations annually. Critical infrastructure entities may also integrate exercises into national or sector-wide drills coordinated by regulators. Each event must be logged in a master exercise register showing date, scope, participants, and completion status. For auditors, the register demonstrates systematic planning rather than ad-hoc activity. They will check whether the cadence aligns with policy commitments, whether overdue exercises are justified, and whether results from previous sessions influenced subsequent ones. Cadence without continuity is a red flag—if lessons from prior exercises are not tested in later ones, organizational learning remains theoretical.

Objective evaluation of outcomes is where tabletop exercises transition from activity to assurance. After each simulation, a structured after-action review (AAR) should categorize observations into strengths, weaknesses, and improvement opportunities. Each finding must map to specific controls or processes, such as escalation timing, communication accuracy, or evidence handling protocols. Auditors reviewing AAR reports will expect a consistent scoring or rating system that enables trend analysis across multiple exercises. This trend data provides a longitudinal view of capability maturity and shows whether repeated issues are being addressed. Absence of measurable outcomes or reliance on narrative summaries without actionable metrics limits the auditability of the exercise program and diminishes its governance value.

The lessons learned process formalizes the translation of findings into lasting improvement. Each identified gap should result in a corrective action, assigned to a specific owner with a defined completion timeline. Actions might include updating the IR plan, revising escalation matrices, improving detection logic, or conducting additional training. The IR governance committee or risk management board typically tracks these actions to closure. From an audit perspective, this tracking mechanism is essential. Auditors will request evidence that corrective actions were logged, approved, and verified as implemented. They will also check whether lessons learned are prioritized based on risk impact, ensuring that critical issues receive immediate attention while lower-risk items are scheduled for future updates.

To ensure that lessons produce tangible change, organizations should link them directly to policy and control updates. If a tabletop exercise reveals confusion over decision authority, the IR charter should be revised. If recovery testing fails to meet RTO targets, the DR plan must be updated. These updates should be version-controlled, with approval and publication dates documented. Auditors assess whether plan revisions reference the specific exercise or incident that triggered them and whether affected stakeholders were notified. Traceability from exercise findings to policy changes provides strong evidence of continuous improvement—a key maturity indicator in both internal and external audits.

Timelines and ownership are crucial for maintaining accountability. Each improvement item should have a responsible individual or department, a target completion date, and defined verification criteria. These details belong in a remediation tracker reviewed periodically by the IR steering committee or risk management office. Auditors reviewing this tracker will test whether items were completed on schedule, whether delays were approved, and whether verification evidence—such as updated playbooks or system configurations—was retained. A robust tracking process transforms lessons learned from aspirational goals into auditable commitments that strengthen the organization's overall resilience.

Finally, mature programs incorporate feedback loops to measure whether implemented changes are effective. Subsequent tabletop exercises should deliberately retest previously identified weaknesses to validate improvement. Performance indicators—such as faster detection acknowledgment, reduced escalation time, or improved clarity in executive briefings—provide measurable evidence of progress. For auditors, these metrics demonstrate not only compliance but learning agility. When an organization can show, through data and documentation, that each exercise informs the next and that each lesson reshapes controls and culture, it proves that IR is not static procedure but an evolving discipline rooted in accountability and continuous improvement.

Evidence Locations: IR Plans, Case Systems, Forensic Repositories, and DR Reports

In cybersecurity auditing, the location and linkage of evidence determine whether an organization can prove what it claims to have done. The audit value of IR documentation lies not only in the content of individual records, but in the consistency and traceability across interconnected sources. Canonical evidence locations include four interdependent domains: the IR plan and its playbooks, the case management system, the forensic repository with custody logs, and the DR and BCP reports. Each domain captures a unique dimension of the incident life cycle—strategy, execution, technical proof, and recovery—and auditors must be able to follow the chain of evidence seamlessly among them. A mature organization treats these repositories as a coordinated evidence ecosystem, where provenance, timestamps, and cross-references form an unbroken record of operational truth.

The Incident Response Plan and Playbooks represent the highest-level evidence of intent and authority. They define roles, escalation triggers, decision rights, and required documentation throughout the response process. These plans serve as the reference against which auditors measure actual behavior recorded in the case management system. Version control is essential: auditors should find signed approval pages, change histories, and effective dates that demonstrate the plan was current during the incident being reviewed. Each playbook should contain embedded cross-references to related tools and repositories—for example, specifying which case management platform to use, where evidence is logged, and how DR coordination is activated. Exportable copies of the IR plan, accompanied by metadata such as approval timestamp and author, provide the starting point for any audit trail, confirming that responders operated under authorized and reviewed procedures. Table 12.3 maps the core evidence repositories to their provenance elements and the cross references that create a closed auditable chain.

Table 12.3 Evidence sources and cross-references.

Evidence source	Primary artifacts	Provenance elements	Cross-references
IR Plan and Playbooks	Roles escalation triggers decision matrices	Version control approvals effective date	Case system identifiers DR activation criteria
Case Management System	Incident IDs notes timestamps decisions	Time sync user attribution export logs	Forensic evidence IDs DR report links
Forensic Repository	Disk images logs memory dumps analysis outputs	Hash values custody entries storage location	Case IDs custody records
Chain of Custody Log	Transfer records signatures purpose of access	Timestamp integrity checks signatory identity	Evidence IDs repository locations
DR Reports	Restore logs failover results validation checklists	RTO RPO outcomes approval records	Case IDs decision logs
Communications Records	Internal updates customer notices regulator filings	Version history approvals send receipts	Case timeline legal references
Tabletop AARs	Objectives findings corrective actions	Attendance verification issue trackers	Updated playbooks policy revisions
Decision Logs	Threshold breaches approvals compensating actions	Author timestamps justification text	DR reports executive briefings
Backup Restore Test Records	Test plans outcomes anomalies	Start end times system identifiers responsible teams	DR readiness dashboards case references

The Case Management System serves as the operational ledger for all incident activity. Every alert, escalation, containment step, and closure action must be logged here, with timestamps synchronized to a trusted time source. Cases should contain structured fields—incident ID, severity, affected systems, assigned analysts, evidence links, and decision logs—and must reflect all major actions described in the playbooks. The system's design should enable exportable, time-bounded reports for each case, capturing the full chronology from detection to closure. From an auditor's perspective, this is where process meets proof: the IR plan tells what should happen, while the case system shows what actually did. The most mature environments maintain bidirectional cross-references: the case record links to the relevant forensic evidence IDs and recovery documentation, while those downstream artifacts reference the originating case number to preserve full provenance.

Forensic Repositories hold the technical backbone of the incident record. These repositories contain disk images, log archives, packet captures, and analytical outputs created during investigation. Each artifact should carry a unique evidence identifier, collection method, hash value, and storage location, forming a complete metadata record. Custody logs accompany every access or transfer, detailing who handled the evidence, when, and for what purpose. These repositories should be logically and physically secured, with write protections, access controls, and immutable audit trails. During audit reviews, evidence from forensic repositories must reconcile with case management entries—hash values should match, timestamps should align, and the number of collected artifacts should equal those listed in the case summary. Exportable evidence manifests or chain-of-custody reports allow auditors to verify that integrity and continuity were preserved from collection through analysis and eventual archival.

The Chain-of-Custody Logs act as the connective tissue between the case management and forensic systems. Each custody record should document ownership transfers between responders, vendors, counsel, or law enforcement. These logs must include incident IDs, evidence identifiers, hash validations, transfer methods, and authorization details. For auditors, custody logs are the definitive proof of integrity and provenance. Any missing handoff, inconsistent signature, or unverified hash constitutes a material weakness in evidence handling controls. Digital chain-of-custody systems that generate exportable, tamper-evident records provide the strongest assurance of compliance and enable fast validation during audits or legal inquiries. The relationship between the custody log and forensic repository must be one-to-one: every stored artifact should have a corresponding custody record with matching metadata and timestamps.

At the recovery and continuity layer, DR (DR) and BCP reports capture how the organization restored systems and validated readiness post-incident. These reports document recovery start and end times, system status, backup sources, RTO/RPO performance, and test results. Each DR record should include a direct reference to the associated IR case ID and to the decision log that approved restoration. Evidence artifacts in these reports include restore logs, failover test results, and post-recovery validation checklists. From an auditing perspective, these are the closing entries in the evidence chain—they demonstrate not only that the incident was contained and eradicated but also that the organization met its recovery commitments. Exportable, time-bounded DR reports provide auditors with objective evidence that recovery objectives were measured, achieved, or formally accepted when not met.

The relationships among these evidence domains form a closed, traceable circuit of proof. The IR plan defines how incidents must be documented; the case system captures the operational record of those actions; the forensic repository provides technical substantiation; and DR reports confirm restoration and continuity outcomes. Each domain references the next through identifiers and metadata, ensuring auditors can traverse the chain in either direction—from high-level governance down to raw technical evidence, or from a specific artifact back to the overarching plan. Provenance is maintained through consistent use of timestamps, version controls, and digital signatures. The organization's evidence model should allow any event to be exported as a self-contained package—containing the IR plan version in effect, the full case record, relevant forensic materials, and recovery documentation—preserving both integrity and temporal context.

From an auditing standpoint, exportability and time-boundedness are not conveniences—they are control requirements. Every evidence source must support authorized data extraction without altering the original records. Exportable data packages should include all contextual metadata necessary to verify authenticity: file hashes, system IDs, timestamps, and user actions. Time-bounded exports ensure that only information relevant to the incident window is shared, protecting privacy while preserving traceability. The ability to generate these exports quickly and completely is a primary indicator of evidence management maturity. If an organization cannot export a coherent, cross-referenced evidence set within a reasonable time frame, auditors interpret it as a deficiency in documentation governance or tool integration.

Finally, cross-references to related incidents create the longitudinal visibility that auditors and executives use to evaluate systemic risk. Each new case should link to prior events with similar root causes, affected systems, or control failures. These relationships enable aggregation of evidence across time, turning isolated incidents into trend data for continuous improvement. For example, repeated privilege escalation incidents might trace to the same unpatched system family, linking forensic records and DR recoveries across cases. Auditors reviewing such linkages verify that recurring issues are tracked, reported to governance committees, and addressed through measurable remediation. In this way, evidence locations and their interconnections serve not only as proof of past actions but also as the framework for forward-looking assurance. A complete, exportable, time-aligned evidence ecosystem—anchored by cross-references and maintained under strict provenance—is the hallmark of a resilient and auditable cybersecurity organization.

Conclusion

Mastering the disciplines of IR and crisis management is critical for ensuring that cybersecurity operations remain defensible, auditable, and aligned with enterprise governance. The ability to document every decision, action, and communication transforms response activities from reactive firefighting into structured, accountable processes. For auditors, this maturity is measured not by how quickly teams act, but by how consistently they adhere to defined authority, evidence handling, and reporting frameworks. This chapter reinforces that resilience is not built on improvisation but on repeatable, verifiable methods that withstand both technical scrutiny and regulatory review.

As AI systems increasingly participate in detection, triage, and containment, these governance foundations gain even greater importance. Algorithmic decision-making can accelerate response but also obscure accountability if not paired with traceable evidence and well-defined oversight. By embedding auditability into every phase—from alert validation to post-incident learning—security leaders ensure that AI-driven responses remain explainable and legally defensible. This alignment between human judgment, automated action, and audit control defines the next frontier of trustworthy cyber operations.

With these frameworks and expectations firmly in place, professionals are better equipped to evaluate not only whether incidents were resolved but also whether they were managed with integrity, precision, and compliance. Auditing IR in this way moves beyond measuring speed toward measuring governance maturity—the assurance that every response, every recovery, and every lesson learned contributes to a more accountable and resilient security posture. In a world where machine speed collides with human oversight, this balance between agility and assurance will define the credibility of tomorrow's cybersecurity programs.

Auditor Recommendations

1. **Validate Decision Authority:** Confirm that the organization's IR operating model clearly defines who can authorize containment, communication, and escalation at each severity level. Review documentation for evidence of approval matrices and written delegation of authority. This verification ensures that response actions were lawful, consistent, and properly governed.
2. **Assess Case Management Integrity:** Evaluate whether all incidents are logged, time-stamped, and cross-referenced within a single case management system. Check for exportable, time-bounded records that link case data to forensic evidence, communications, and DR reports. A reliable system of record is essential for audit traceability and regulatory defensibility.

3. **Verify Chain-of-custody Completeness:** Examine evidence repositories and custody logs to ensure every handoff—internal or external—is documented with identifiers, timestamps, and hash verifications. Confirm that access controls are role-based and time-limited, and that audit logs capture all evidence interactions. A continuous custody record is the cornerstone of credible forensic assurance.
4. **Review SLA Compliance Across the Case Life cycle:** Audit acknowledgment, escalation, and resolution times to ensure they align with defined service-level agreements (SLAs). Cross-check timestamps from detection to closure within the case system to identify bottlenecks or deviations. These time metrics provide measurable proof of operational discipline and responsiveness.
5. **Evaluate Backup and Restore Readiness Evidence:** Verify that backup inventories, restore test results, and site failover simulations are documented, approved, and retained. Ensure the organization tracks performance against RTO and RPO objectives, with deviations formally logged and justified. Reliable recovery records validate that resilience objectives are both defined and achievable.
6. **Inspect Communication Governance and Notification Controls:** Confirm that internal and external communications follow preapproved templates and documented approval paths. Review message logs for timestamped legal and executive sign-offs prior to regulatory or customer notifications. This oversight ensures consistency, prevents premature disclosures, and demonstrates procedural compliance.
7. **Audit Tabletop Exercise Documentation:** Check that each exercise includes defined objectives, attendance records, after-action reports, and assigned remediation owners. Ensure findings are tracked to completion and referenced in policy or playbook updates. Tabletop evidence demonstrates that preparedness is actively tested, measured, and improved.
8. **Trace Evidence Linkages Across Repositories:** Test whether incident cases, forensic data, and DR reports share consistent identifiers and metadata. Verify that cross-references are maintained and exportable, allowing auditors to reconstruct events without data loss. Robust linkage ensures the evidence ecosystem functions as a single, coherent record of truth.
9. **Examine Post-incident Review and Remediation Tracking:** Review after-action summaries and lessons-learned reports to ensure findings translate into documented corrective actions. Validate that owners, deadlines, and completion confirmations exist for every improvement item. Closed-loop remediation is a key indicator of continuous assurance and control maturity.
10. **Confirm Auditability of AI-driven Incident Response:** When automation or AI tools assist in detection or containment, confirm that all automated actions are logged, explainable, and mapped to human oversight. Verify that outputs from AI systems include timestamps and provenance data consistent with manual evidence. Maintaining transparency in machine-assisted decisions ensures auditability in modern, AI-enabled security operations.

Chapter Questions

1. What is the primary responsibility of the incident commander during a cybersecurity event?
   A. Draft all public statements for customers and media
   B. Determine which laws apply to the incident and prepare filings
   C. Coordinate the response, set severity, and authorize containment within guardrails
   D. Approve annual security budgets and tool purchases

2. Which practice most directly proves that digital evidence has not been altered between acquisition and analysis?
   - **A.** Capturing screenshots of system settings during imaging
   - **B.** Recording and reverifying cryptographic hash values at each handoff
   - **C.** Storing evidence on encrypted drives without additional metadata
   - **D.** Limiting access to evidence to the incident commander only

3. In an audit of incident records, which feature best demonstrates that the case management system is fit for purpose?
   - **A.** Free-text notes with optional timestamps for speed
   - **B.** A separate spreadsheet maintained by each responder team
   - **C.** Automatic deletion of low-severity cases after seven days
   - **D.** Exportable, time-bounded records with cross-references to forensic and DR artifacts

4. Which set best represents the time-based expectations used to measure handling of detections and cases?
   - **A.** Acknowledgment, escalation, and resolution SLAs
   - **B.** Budget approval, vendor onboarding, and procurement SLAs
   - **C.** Patch window, reboot window, and maintenance SLAs
   - **D.** Hiring pipeline, training schedule, and promotion SLAs

5. During containment, what documentation is essential to preserve auditability and investigative integrity?
   - **A.** Verbal approvals from executives captured in meeting minutes only
   - **B.** A summary statement that "containment completed successfully"
   - **C.** Specific containment actions with timestamps, responsible parties, and approval authority
   - **D.** A high-level diagram with proposed future improvements

6. When recovery objectives are missed during a failover exercise, what record should tie governance to restoration choices?
   - **A.** A marketing memo describing expected customer sentiment
   - **B.** A revised network diagram without timestamps
   - **C.** An informal email thread among responders
   - **D.** A structured decision log capturing threshold breaches, approvals, and compensating actions

7. Which control best governs the release of external customer or regulator communications during an incident?
   - **A.** Allowing analysts to post updates directly to speed responsiveness
   - **B.** Legal and executive approval using version-controlled templates and timestamped sign-offs
   - **C.** Auto-publishing detection alerts to a public status page
   - **D.** Leaving communications to third-party vendors to avoid conflicts of interest

8. What evidence shows that tabletop exercises drove real improvements rather than serving as discussion only?
   A. After-action reviews with corrective actions, assigned owners, and deadlines tracked to closure
   B. Calendar invites proving the meeting occurred
   C. A single slide deck summarizing talking points without follow-ups
   D. Anonymous participant feedback forms stored in a shared drive

9. Which relationship accurately characterizes the organization's evidence ecosystem for incident auditing?
   A. DR reports feed IR plans, which overwrite forensic records to save space
   B. Case management replaces the need for chain-of-custody tracking
   C. IR plans define expectations; case records log actions; forensic repositories supply technical proof with custody logs; DR reports confirm restoration
   D. Forensic repositories alone are sufficient to demonstrate compliance and governance

10. Why must AI-assisted containment and investigation be anchored in incident governance for audit purposes?
   A. Because automation eliminates the need for documentation and human review
   B. Because AI models always produce legally privileged work products
   C. Because automated tools guarantee accuracy without oversight
   D. Because explainability and traceable evidence are required to make automated actions defensible and compliant

13

Vulnerability Management and Pen Test Oversight

Vulnerability management and penetration testing oversight form the operational backbone of cybersecurity assurance. They transform abstract risk into measurable, testable evidence of control effectiveness. Understanding how assets are discovered, scanned, prioritized, and tested is essential to maintaining visibility in dynamic, hybrid environments where new systems appear as quickly as old ones are patched. The discipline described here turns technical scanning into governance—ensuring that every finding can be traced to an accountable owner, verified through remediation, and validated against defined service levels. This structured approach distinguishes organizations that merely identify weaknesses from those that can continuously prove they are being managed.

Modern enterprises cannot rely on severity scores alone to guide their response. Threat-informed prioritization models, such as those integrating Known Exploited Vulnerabilities (KEV) and exploit prediction data, allow teams to focus on what is actively being targeted, not just what looks dangerous on paper. Equally critical is the governance surrounding exceptions, risk acceptance, and testing independence. By establishing clear decision frameworks and evidentiary standards, organizations create an audit-ready posture—one where every deviation from policy has a documented rationale, expiry date, and compensating safeguard. This maturity reflects a shift from reactive patching toward accountable risk stewardship.

From continuous scanning to red-team validation, this chapter underscores how disciplined processes, transparent reporting, and cross-team accountability ensure that security improvements are both durable and verifiable. In an era where AI-driven automation accelerates change across infrastructure, maintaining this rigor is vital to prevent unseen drift and regression. The ability to demonstrate—through data, provenance, and repeatable testing—that vulnerabilities are discovered, prioritized, and resolved within defined tolerances is now a defining feature of cyber resilience. Governance over these activities is not simply a compliance necessity; it is the foundation of trustworthy digital operations.

Asset Coverage and Scan Cadence

A strong vulnerability management program begins with knowing exactly what needs to be protected. This means building a complete and accurate asset inventory that covers every host, container, application, database, and cloud resource in the environment. Auditors expect organizations to prove that this inventory represents all systems that could expose or store sensitive data. To achieve this, data is often pulled from multiple systems such as configuration management databases, endpoint management tools, cloud dashboards, and external discovery platforms. Each source contributes a piece of the overall picture. The key control for auditors is not simply having an inventory, but being able to demonstrate that every asset appearing in production, development, or testing is accounted for and mapped to an owner and risk category.

Asset reconciliation ensures that what exists in the network is also visible to scanning tools. This involves cross-checking scanner targets against inventory lists, network address ranges, and cloud account data. Any gaps—such as unmanaged hosts or unregistered subnets—represent potential blind spots. Mature programs implement automated processes to detect these discrepancies and generate alerts when new assets appear without being enrolled in scanning. For auditors, this reconciliation control is essential proof that the organization's scanning scope truly reflects its real-world environment, rather than an outdated or partial subset.

Once an organization understands its assets, it must decide how often and in what way to examine them for vulnerabilities. This decision depends heavily on risk tiering. Systems that are internet-facing or handle sensitive data, often called "crown-jewel" assets, require the most frequent and rigorous assessments. Lower-risk internal systems may be scanned less frequently, but still within defined intervals that reflect their exposure and criticality. The scan cadence must be documented, justified, and consistently followed over the audit period. Auditors typically request these schedules to confirm that frequency aligns with risk and that there is evidence of timely execution.

Discovery scans differ from assessment scans in both purpose and impact. A discovery scan is designed to identify what exists—what IPs are active, what services are running, and where changes have occurred since the last cycle. It answers the question, "What do we have?" rather than "What's wrong with it?" Discovery scanning is usually lightweight, frequent, and continuous. It often operates daily or even hourly in cloud environments where resources appear and disappear dynamically. The results feed the asset inventory and help ensure that no new devices, instances, or containers escape visibility.

Assessment scans, by contrast, evaluate the security posture of known assets. They are deeper, authenticated, and sometimes disruptive, using plugins or scripts to check configurations, missing patches, and software flaws. Because assessment scans can consume resources and risk causing instability, they are scheduled with greater care. Many organizations run authenticated scans

Table 13.1 Scan cadence by risk tier and asset class.

Asset class	Exposure tier	Discovery frequency	Assessment frequency	Justification evidence
Internet facing servers	High	Daily or continuous	Weekly	KEV or EPSS signal and public exposure
Customer facing applications	High	Daily	Weekly	Data sensitivity and business impact
Crown jewel systems	High	Continuous	Weekly	Board level risk and critical processes
Cloud workloads elastic	Medium	Hourly to daily	Biweekly	API inventory drift and short lived assets
Internal application servers	Medium	Daily	Monthly	Segmented network and reduced exposure
Workstations and endpoints	Low	Weekly	Monthly to quarterly	Enterprise patch cycle and user risk
Containers and images	Medium	Per build and admission	Per build and weekly runtime	Pipeline gates and registry scans
Partner connected services	High	Daily	Weekly	Third-party access paths and trust boundaries
Development and test environments	Low	Daily	Monthly	Segmentation evidence and non-production use
Network appliances and middleware	Medium	Weekly	Monthly	Change windows and stability constraints

weekly or monthly for high-risk systems and quarterly or semi-annually for lower-risk ones. This rhythm provides a balance between coverage and operational safety, giving auditors consistent data points without overwhelming teams or networks. Table 13.1 risk-based scan cadence aligns discovery and assessment frequency to exposure and evidence of impact.

The audit evidence for scan cadence is usually found in scan logs, reports, and change management tickets. Auditors look for timestamps showing that scans occurred as scheduled, with full completion and no unexplained gaps. They also verify that systems discovered between cycles are added to the next assessment run in a timely manner. Automated job scheduling and integration with continuous integration pipelines are viewed favorably, as they reduce reliance on manual scheduling and improve accountability.

Scoping decisions—what to include or exclude—must be documented clearly. For instance, an organization may justify excluding transient lab systems, encrypted storage volumes, or third-party managed services if they are covered elsewhere. However, each exclusion should have a defined rationale, risk acceptance, and compensating control. During audits, such documentation demonstrates that the organization made deliberate, risk-informed decisions rather than arbitrary omissions. Evidence such as approved scope change requests or sign-offs from system owners reinforces the control maturity.

Cloud and containerized environments add complexity because assets can be ephemeral. A virtual machine or container might exist for minutes and still introduce vulnerabilities during that time. Continuous discovery integrated with cloud APIs, orchestration platforms, and deployment pipelines helps close this gap. The goal is to align scanning cadence with asset life cycle speed—daily or even real-time in automated environments, compared to slower weekly or monthly cycles for traditional infrastructure. Auditors evaluate how effectively the scanning system adapts to these dynamics rather than adhering to static schedules.

Prioritization: KEV, EPSS, Exploitability, and Business Context

Once vulnerabilities are discovered and validated, the next critical step is determining which ones matter most and how quickly they must be addressed. Not every vulnerability is equal in its potential to cause harm, and a mature vulnerability management program distinguishes between theoretical risk and exploitable threat. This prioritization process blends several streams of intelligence: the inherent severity of a flaw as scored by the Common Vulnerability Scoring System (CVSS), real-world exploitation data from sources like CISA's KEV catalog, and predictive analytics such as the Exploit Prediction Scoring System (EPSS). By combining these inputs, organizations move from a purely technical rating toward a threat-informed risk ranking that better reflects real exposure. The audit expectation is that prioritization criteria are formalized, repeatable, and demonstrably applied across all systems rather than left to individual discretion.

CISA's KEV catalog identifies vulnerabilities actively exploited in the wild, providing authoritative evidence that attackers are targeting them. A vulnerability's inclusion in the KEV list effectively overrides its CVSS score—what matters most is that adversaries are using it now. When a system contains a KEV-listed flaw, remediation urgency becomes nonnegotiable. Many organizations set internal policies requiring immediate patching or compensating controls within days, not weeks. Auditors expect to see alignment between KEV publication and internal response, supported by change tickets or patch verification reports showing timely mitigation. Failure to demonstrate responsiveness to KEV advisories often indicates a reactive or immature program that treats vulnerability management as a technical chore rather than a business-critical defense.

The EPSS adds another dimension by estimating the likelihood that a vulnerability will be exploited in the near future. Unlike KEV, which reflects known activity, EPSS offers forward-looking probability based on data-driven modeling of exploit trends. By weighting vulnerabilities with high EPSS scores, teams can preemptively address issues most likely to attract attackers before public exploitation begins. Combining EPSS probability with CVSS impact allows for nuanced decision-making: a moderate-severity flaw with a 90% exploitation probability may deserve higher priority than a critical vulnerability with low exploit potential. Auditors often verify that this predictive intelligence is integrated into dashboards or ticketing logic and that remediation teams are trained to interpret it consistently. Table 13.2 prioritization blends severity exploitation signals exposure and business criticality into actionable order of work.

Table 13.2 Threat informed prioritization inputs and usage.

Input type	Description	How used in priority	Evidence artifact
CVSS	Impact and severity baseline	Initial severity band and SLA seed	Scanner export with CVE and score
KEV	Active exploitation indicator	Overrides severity to urgent	KEV snapshot with publication date
EPSS	Predicted exploitation likelihood	Boosts rank for likely abuse	EPSS score export for audit period

Input type	Description	How used in priority	Evidence artifact
Exposure context	Internet facing or internal or segmented	Adjusts SLA and urgency	Network diagrams and segmentation proof
Business criticality	Process and data sensitivity	Elevates priority for crown jewels	Asset classification in CMDB

Exploitability is not purely a statistical metric; it also depends on environmental factors. A remote code execution vulnerability on an exposed web server is far more urgent than the same flaw in an isolated lab network. Thus, exposure context—the system's network placement, authentication requirements, and reachable attack paths—plays a vital role in triage. Mature programs map vulnerabilities to attack surface categories such as internet-facing, partner-connected, or internal-only, and adjust remediation time frames accordingly. The auditor's focus is on whether this mapping is documented and evidence-backed. They will look for logic in how exposure drives priority and whether exceptions for isolated systems are justified through network segmentation evidence or compensating technical controls like intrusion prevention rules.

Beyond technical metrics, business context remains the decisive factor. A low-severity flaw on a system that supports payment processing or healthcare records can still represent material business risk. Effective vulnerability management ties each asset to business processes and data sensitivity levels so that vulnerability scores can be interpreted through an organizational lens. This linkage enables executives to understand vulnerability risk in terms of potential business disruption or regulatory exposure, not just technical scores. Auditors review these mappings during evidence collection, confirming that critical systems—sometimes called "crown jewels"—receive proportionally higher remediation priority, even if CVSS or EPSS metrics appear moderate.

Every prioritization decision must be documented, not just executed. Audit trails should show how risk ratings were determined, what data sources influenced them, and who approved exceptions or deferments. Mature programs maintain a decision register or tracking log where each vulnerability's treatment—remediate, accept, or mitigate—is recorded alongside justification and approval metadata. This documentation demonstrates control consistency and provides traceability during an audit or incident review. Without it, prioritization can appear arbitrary or ad hoc, undermining the credibility of the entire vulnerability management process.

Risk acceptance thresholds serve as formal boundaries for when known vulnerabilities may remain unpatched. These thresholds are typically tied to severity, exploitability, and business criticality—for example, critical and high vulnerabilities on internet-facing assets must be remediated within seven days, while lower-severity issues on isolated systems may be accepted for longer periods. However, each acceptance must be explicitly approved, time-boxed, and supported by compensating controls such as enhanced monitoring, intrusion detection tuning, or temporary access restrictions. Auditors expect to see these controls implemented and verified, not merely promised in documentation. Time-boxing ensures that accepted risk does not quietly become permanent risk.

Exception management forms the governance layer over prioritization. Some vulnerabilities cannot be remediated immediately because patches are unavailable, operational dependencies prevent change, or legacy systems require special handling. In these cases, an exception request must document the reason, residual risk, compensating control, and expiration date. Auditors will check that exceptions are reviewed regularly, reapproved if still valid, or closed once remediation becomes feasible. A strong governance process ensures exceptions remain the rare, managed outliers rather than a default pathway for inaction.

Remediation SLAs, Exceptions, and Risk Acceptance

A mature vulnerability management program establishes explicit service-level agreements (SLAs) that define how quickly vulnerabilities must be remediated once discovered. These timelines are typically stratified by both vulnerability severity and asset classification, ensuring that the most critical flaws on the most exposed systems receive the fastest attention. For instance, a critical vulnerability on an internet-facing application server might carry a seven-day SLA, while a medium-severity issue on an internal workstation might allow thirty days. These time frames are not arbitrary; they reflect organizational risk tolerance and are often aligned with industry standards or regulatory expectations. From an audit perspective, the presence of formally approved, risk-based SLAs demonstrates that the organization has operationalized vulnerability management into measurable, enforceable commitments rather than vague intentions.

Timeliness in remediation is measured through well-defined life cycle stages—assignment, start, and resolution. The "assignment" date reflects when responsibility for fixing a vulnerability is formally delegated to an accountable owner or team. The "start" date marks when remediation work begins, evidenced by change tickets, patch deployment plans, or configuration modification tasks. The "resolve" date captures when verification confirms that the vulnerability is no longer present, not simply when the patch was installed. Each stage creates audit evidence that progress was continuous, not deferred. Mature organizations automate these timestamps through integration between vulnerability scanners, ticketing systems, and configuration management tools, ensuring traceability without excessive manual reporting.

Consistency in SLA tracking is vital. If an organization defines a seven-day SLA for critical vulnerabilities, that countdown must start from a consistent trigger point—often the date of initial discovery or validation, not when a ticket is opened. Ambiguity in how time-to-remediate is calculated can invalidate audit metrics and obscure real performance trends. Auditors will often review multiple samples of closed vulnerabilities to test whether SLAs were measured uniformly and whether exceptions were formally recorded when deadlines were missed. When organizations can show reliable SLA adherence metrics and exception workflows, it signals strong governance maturity and a disciplined approach to cyber risk reduction.

Different asset classes require tailored SLA structures. Production servers, customer-facing applications, and cloud workloads demand aggressive timelines because their compromise could directly impact business continuity or data privacy. Development and testing environments may have slightly extended deadlines, provided they are properly segmented from production. Workstations and endpoints often fall under separate SLAs managed through enterprise patching programs. Auditors expect these variations to be documented, approved by governance authorities such as the CISO or Risk Committee, and consistently reflected in dashboards or performance reports. The key expectation is fairness and traceability—every asset type has a defined rule, and that rule is applied as written.

Exceptions and risk acceptance operate as safety valves within the SLA framework, allowing temporary deviation when remediation is infeasible. Common justifications include unavailable vendor patches, operational constraints that make immediate patching unsafe, or systems approaching decommission. However, exceptions cannot be open-ended. Each one must include a clear justification, a defined expiry date, and compensating controls to mitigate risk until remediation occurs. Typical compensating controls include network isolation, enhanced monitoring, temporary service restrictions, or intrusion prevention signatures. Auditors evaluate whether these controls were not only documented but also technically verified to be in place, ensuring that exceptions represent managed risk rather than neglect.

Governance of the exception process is critical. Formal approval workflows should identify who can authorize deviations from standard SLAs, usually involving the asset owner, the business risk manager, and the CISO or delegated authority. This multi-level approval structure prevents conflicts of interest where technical teams might otherwise self-approve exceptions for convenience. Audit evidence should include signed exception forms or digital approvals showing the decision chain, supporting rationale, and planned expiry. The approval log becomes a key artifact in demonstrating that risk acceptance is deliberate and accountable, not arbitrary or untracked.

Expiry management ensures that exceptions do not quietly become permanent. Each accepted risk or deferred vulnerability must have a defined review cycle—commonly every thirty, sixty, or ninety days, depending on the organization's risk appetite. During review, the responsible team reassesses whether remediation is now feasible, whether compensating controls remain effective, and whether the risk still aligns with business tolerance. Auditors look closely at this process, often selecting expired exceptions to confirm whether they were closed or reapproved properly. Failure to enforce expiry reviews is one of the most common weaknesses found in vulnerability management audits, as it allows temporary exceptions to accumulate and erode the control environment over time.

Risk acceptance differs subtly from an exception. While an exception temporarily delays remediation due to external constraints, risk acceptance is a formal decision to tolerate a vulnerability for a defined period because the residual risk is deemed acceptable. This decision must still pass through governance channels, supported by documented rationale such as low exploitability, strong compensating controls, or limited business impact. A mature program integrates these acceptances into the broader enterprise risk register for visibility, but the operational tracking of those items remains part of vulnerability management. Auditors expect each risk acceptance to include an expiration date and require formal revalidation before it continues.

Strong reporting ties these concepts together. Dashboards and audit reports should display metrics showing SLA compliance rates, counts of open and closed exceptions, and the age distribution of risk acceptances. This visibility allows leadership to assess whether the organization's remediation program is achieving its intended velocity and whether exceptions are being responsibly managed. Auditors often sample these reports against raw data to confirm integrity, ensuring that exceptions or accepted risks are not being used to artificially inflate SLA compliance figures. Transparency in these metrics fosters accountability and demonstrates that vulnerability management is embedded within the organization's overall risk governance model.

Validation of Fixes and Regression Controls

Proof of remediation begins with objective evidence that the vulnerable condition no longer exists on the affected asset, captured as close as possible to production state. The most authoritative artifact is a targeted, authenticated re-scan showing the vulnerability in a "not detected" status with matching asset identifiers, scan policies, and plugin versions recorded to avoid disputes about scope or false negatives. Configuration and state diffs complement re-scan evidence by demonstrating the precise change that removed risk, such as a patched package version, a disabled service, or a tightened access control entry, with cryptographic checksums or version numbers to anchor the record. Functional test results provide a third pillar by confirming the system still performs as intended after remediation, which reduces the temptation to roll back security changes under operational pressure. Auditors look for the triangulation of these artifact types because it proves not only that the signature disappeared but also that a deliberate control change occurred and left the service stable.

Authenticated re-scans have to be designed to resist common failure modes that create a false sense of closure. Credentials must grant sufficient privilege to query package managers, kernel modules, and configuration stores; otherwise, the tool may report "clean" simply because it could not see the vulnerable component. Timing matters as well: re-scans should be executed after change completion and service restarts but before the maintenance window closes, leaving room to remediate residual findings. Where vulnerabilities are detected across a fleet, sampling strategies are acceptable if they are statistically sound and tied to deployment rings or environment tiers, but critical, internet-exposed systems warrant one-for-one verification. Mature programs also annotate re-scan reports with the specific change request identifier to bind the evidence to the approved remediation plan.

Configuration and state diffs serve as durable, human-readable explanations of what changed and why it reduced risk. For package updates, evidence should show the vulnerable version number alongside the remediated version, ideally referencing vendor advisories that confirm fixed releases. For configuration hardening, before-and-after excerpts of policy files, registry keys, or infrastructure-as-code templates make the control shift explicit, with change history documenting who approved and executed the update. Service disablement and network segmentation require state validation beyond text diffs, such as port closure screenshots from authenticated scans, access attempts logged as denied, or micro-segmentation policy snapshots that limit east-west movement. These artifacts help establish that remediation was not cosmetic but rather enforced at the control layer relevant to the vulnerability.

Functional validation ensures the system remains fit for purpose after security work, because remediation that breaks business functions tends to be undone during off-hours firefighting. For applications, test suites covering the affected component should pass with the patched dependency, and any new security headers, cipher suites, or authentication flows should be exercised in staging and then verified in production using synthetic monitoring. For infrastructure, health checks and performance baselines should be compared pre- and post-patch, looking for regressions that could drive an untracked rollback. Where service owners operate change freezes, a minimal set of smoke tests must be defined in advance to shorten verification while preserving assurance. Capturing logs and metrics that corroborate healthy function strengthens the remediation record and deters undocumented reversions.

Preventing reintroduction relies on baseline enforcement so that patches and hardening are not one-time events but characteristics of the standard build. Golden images for servers, workstations, and container base layers should be updated promptly after remediation, signed, and distributed through the build pipeline to ensure downstream deployments inherit the fix rather than the prior vulnerable state. Infrastructure-as-code templates, configuration profiles, and policy definitions must be updated in source control with peer review to prevent drift between "golden" and "as built" configurations. Drift detection tools that continuously compare running state to declared baselines should alert when a package version or policy deviates from the approved standard. In audit terms, these controls demonstrate that remediation has been institutionalized, making backsliding an exception rather than the norm.

Continuous integration and delivery gates convert lessons from remediation into preventive controls within the software supply chain. Dependency scanning should block builds that reintroduce a vulnerable library version, with allowlists tightly scoped by package, version, and time-bound expiration to manage rare exceptions. Container image scanning must occur at both build and admission phases, ensuring that even if a vulnerable base slips through compilation, the runtime platform rejects the image until remediated. Policy-as-code in the pipeline should assert minimum baseline requirements such as compiler flags, transport encryption, and authentication libraries that were implicated in prior findings, shifting enforcement left. Evidence of these gates includes pipeline run logs, failed build records tied to specific vulnerability identifiers, and change approvals that document who authorized temporary bypasses and when they will be removed.

Partial fixes and compensating mitigations require careful framing to avoid overstating risk reduction. If a vendor patch addresses only certain versions or platforms, the evidence package must specify the remaining exposure and identify the assets still at risk, along with the planned timeline to complete full remediation. When immediate patching is infeasible, compensating controls such as virtual patching at a web application firewall, temporary network isolation, or tightened authentication policies can materially reduce exploitability, but they demand verification commensurate with a full fix. Artifacts might include firewall rule diffs showing blocked exploit paths, intrusion prevention signatures with hit counts confirming coverage, or access logs demonstrating enforced multifactor authentication. The record should explicitly label the status as "mitigated pending patch" with a review date to ensure compensations do not ossify.

Some vulnerabilities are classified as "won't fix" when the residual risk is accepted under governance and no further remediation is planned, but this status carries strict evidence and oversight obligations. The rationale must be precise, such as the feature being disabled by design, the vulnerable code path being unreachable due to architecture, or the asset being scheduled for imminent decommission with isolation controls in place. The approval trail should include the accountable business owner and security leadership, with the decision time-boxed and contingent on the continued effectiveness of specified controls. Technical evidence must substantiate the rationale; for example, packet captures and policy snapshots that prove the service is not externally reachable, or application telemetry showing the dangerous endpoint is not invoked. Without such corroboration, "won't fix" resembles convenience rather than risk management.

Verification does not end when a ticket closes; regression controls must monitor for the same class of weakness reappearing under new guises. Threat intelligence mappings that link vulnerabilities to underlying control failures help teams create recurring checks, such as enforcing secure defaults in new frameworks or banning deprecated cryptographic primitives across code repositories. Scheduled attestations that golden images still contain the fixed packages, combined with periodic out-of-band scanning from alternate tools, reduce single-tool blind spots that could mask recurrence. For third-party and managed services, contractually required attestation reports and coordinated re-scan windows establish shared accountability, especially where direct scanning is restricted. The audit trail should show that the organization learned from the initial incident and embedded safeguards that make recurrence less likely and faster to detect.

Penetration Testing Governance: Independence, Scope, and Reporting

Effective penetration testing governance begins with independence—the cornerstone of credible assurance. Auditors expect penetration testers to operate without conflicts of interest, meaning they must not assess systems or controls they helped design, configure, or maintain. This separation ensures objectivity and avoids the risk of self-review, which can bias results and undermine trust in the findings. Independence can be achieved through the use of third-party testing firms or by establishing internal red teams that report outside of normal IT or security operations, often directly to the CISO or Audit Committee. Auditors look for documented organizational charts, engagement contracts, or internal policy statements that clearly define independence boundaries and reporting lines. A mature organization demonstrates that penetration testing is not a self-graded exercise, but a disciplined, externalized validation of defenses.

Scoping is equally critical because it defines what will—and will not—be tested. Auditors expect scoping decisions to be explicitly risk-based and threat-informed, not merely constrained by convenience or available testing windows. A strong scoping process begins with a current asset inventory, business impact assessments, and an understanding of recent threat intelligence or incident trends. For example, if phishing and credential theft represent the primary attack vector in the threat landscape, scope should include user-facing authentication systems and email gateways. Similarly, if cloud misconfigurations are an emerging concern, testing must cover identity, storage, and API security in those environments. The test plan should explain how chosen targets represent realistic attack paths toward critical business assets, often called "crown jewels." Auditors will request this rationale to ensure that the organization's penetration tests reflect actual exposure, not a sanitized or low-risk subset.

Rules of engagement formalize how testing will occur and protect both the tester and the organization from unintended harm. These rules define approved testing windows, authorized IP ranges, methods to simulate social engineering, data handling expectations, and communication protocols in the event of service disruption or sensitive data discovery. For example, testers must know whether they are permitted to perform denial-of-service attempts, use live malware payloads, or escalate privileges within production systems. Auditors review signed engagement documents to verify that these boundaries were agreed upon in advance by all stakeholders, including legal, IT operations, and information security management. Properly structured rules of engagement demonstrate governance maturity and risk awareness—showing that penetration testing is controlled experimentation, not reckless intrusion.

Tester qualifications form another area of scrutiny. Penetration testing requires specialized technical skill and professional integrity. Auditors expect organizations to maintain evidence of tester competence, such as professional certifications (OSCP, GPEN, GXPN, CREST, or equivalent), background checks, and relevant experience in the technology domains being tested. For internal teams, training records and continuing education plans are used to show sustained proficiency. For third-party vendors, due diligence should include reviewing service organization controls (SOC 2) reports, insurance coverage, and confidentiality agreements. The goal is to demonstrate that those entrusted with simulated attacks have the skill, ethics, and oversight to conduct them responsibly. Auditors view qualification evidence as a safeguard equal in importance to technical accuracy.

Reporting is the tangible outcome of penetration testing, and auditors focus closely on its completeness and reproducibility. A high-quality penetration test report must contain, at minimum, a clear executive summary, detailed findings, exploit paths, data accessed, business impact, and reproducible steps for validation. Each finding should trace the sequence of attack vectors used, including screenshots, command outputs, or logs proving successful exploitation. Exploit paths should connect vulnerabilities to the business impact—such as how a misconfigured API led to exposure of sensitive data or unauthorized privilege escalation. The inclusion of reproducible steps ensures that remediation teams can verify and retest fixes confidently, while impact statements help executives prioritize remediation based on real operational risk.

Auditors also evaluate the traceability of findings to evidence. Reports should reference timestamps, target identifiers, and tool versions used during testing to support integrity. For each finding, there should be a severity rating, exploitability description, and recommended remediation action. Where applicable, screenshots or command outputs provide proof that the issue is not theoretical. The presence of a management response section in the report—summarizing how each issue will be addressed, accepted, or mitigated—demonstrates follow-through and accountability.

A consistent reporting template across multiple tests signals process maturity, allowing auditors to benchmark quality and completeness over time.

Transparency around scoping exclusions is equally vital. Not every system or environment can be tested, but auditors require clarity on what was left out and why. Management should document all exclusions in the test plan, citing reasons such as operational constraints, regulatory restrictions, or redundant coverage through other assessments. Each exclusion must include a compensating rationale—such as alternative testing methods, isolation controls, or planned future inclusion. Without this documentation, omissions appear arbitrary and can create audit findings related to incomplete coverage. Mature organizations maintain a record of cumulative exclusions over time, ensuring that the same high-risk systems are not perpetually deferred from testing cycles.

The governance process surrounding penetration testing should include oversight by a review board or risk committee. This group validates scoping logic, approves testing providers, and ensures that remediation progress from previous engagements has been verified. Auditors often examine minutes or approval records from these meetings as evidence that penetration testing is integrated into the broader assurance framework rather than treated as a standalone technical exercise. Such governance structures help institutionalize lessons learned, track systemic weaknesses, and ensure test results feed back into risk management and control improvement processes.

Independence must extend beyond execution into reporting and remediation follow-up. Test results should be submitted directly to management functions with audit oversight rather than to those responsible for system maintenance, preserving the integrity of the assessment. When internal teams perform tests, a peer-review mechanism or cross-team validation should confirm the accuracy and completeness of findings. Auditors look for this separation between tester and validator as proof that testing conclusions are unbiased. Together, independence, scope rigor, professional qualifications, and detailed, verifiable reporting create the evidentiary foundation of a trustworthy penetration testing program—one that withstands audit scrutiny and delivers meaningful, repeatable assurance to the organization's leadership.

Findings Life cycle and Cross-team Accountability

In a well-structured vulnerability management and audit environment, the life of a finding does not end when it is discovered—it begins there. Each identified issue, whether originating from automated scanners, penetration tests, code reviews, or configuration audits, must enter a centralized findings register that serves as the authoritative system of record. This register consolidates results from multiple tools and sources, translating raw technical data into standardized entries that can be tracked, prioritized, and governed through closure. The goal is not merely to store findings but to establish a single pane of truth where every vulnerability is visible, contextualized, and assigned an accountable owner. Auditors expect this register to demonstrate full traceability—from initial detection to final disposition—with timestamps, classification fields, and ownership metadata maintained accurately throughout its life cycle.

Deduplication is a critical control that maintains the integrity of this register. Because modern environments use overlapping scanners, red-team exercises, and external assessments, the same underlying weakness may surface multiple times under different identifiers. Without a normalization process, this duplication inflates metrics and obscures actual remediation progress. Mature programs employ correlation logic that matches findings by asset ID, vulnerability signature, plugin, or CVE number, while retaining references to their original source systems. Auditors look for evidence of such correlation processes, either through automated consolidation tooling or manual triage review, to confirm that metrics reflect distinct issues rather than redundant alerts. The deduplication process ensures that each unique risk receives one coordinated response, simplifying accountability and eliminating wasted effort.

Once a finding is validated and normalized, ownership assignment anchors accountability. Every record in the register must clearly identify a responsible individual or team, typically mapped through asset ownership hierarchies or application portfolios. Assignment triggers the opening of a remediation workflow, complete with severity rating, due date, and SLA alignment derived from the organization's risk-based remediation policy. In large enterprises, assignment often occurs automatically through integration with configuration management databases or tagging frameworks that link assets to business units. Auditors verify this chain by sampling findings and tracing ownership back to accountable managers, ensuring that no issue resides in an unowned or "orphaned" state. The presence of formal assignment logs and escalation paths for overdue items demonstrates that accountability is active, not theoretical.

Due dates transform accountability into measurable action. These deadlines are typically inherited from SLA policies by severity and exposure type, ensuring consistency across business units. A critical finding on an externally accessible application might require closure within seven days, whereas an internal low-risk configuration issue may allow thirty or sixty. When findings span multiple teams—such as security, operations, and application development—the assigned due date must reflect dependencies and coordination requirements. To avoid ambiguity, mature organizations document the start and stop criteria for these timers, specifying whether the clock begins at detection, validation, or ticket creation. Auditors often examine exception logs or SLA dashboards to confirm that overdue findings were either justified through approved extensions or escalated appropriately.

Integration with development and operations backlogs ensures findings are not treated as detached security artifacts but as work items embedded within existing delivery systems. For application vulnerabilities, the central register pushes issues into ticketing or Agile management tools such as Jira or Azure DevOps, aligning security remediation with normal sprint planning. Infrastructure findings may flow into IT service management queues managed through platforms like ServiceNow. This linkage enables security tasks to compete visibly with other operational priorities, ensuring resource allocation is transparent and measurable. Auditors expect reconciliation between the central register and these downstream systems, verifying that status updates—such as "in progress" or "completed"—synchronize automatically and that closed items in one system mirror verified closure in the other.

Validation of status changes is the cornerstone of findings life cycle governance. A finding should never move from "open" to "closed" based solely on self-attestation or ticket commentary. Closure requires objective evidence—re-scan results, configuration diffs, or test outcomes—validated by a control owner other than the implementer. "Mitigated" status indicates that compensating controls have reduced exploitability but not removed the underlying weakness, while "accepted" denotes formal risk tolerance approved through governance procedures. Auditors scrutinize whether these statuses are consistently defined and supported by documentation or artifacts. They will often request samples to confirm that evidence exists for each closure type and that no findings have been prematurely downgraded or mislabeled to improve compliance metrics.

To maintain life cycle discipline, periodic reconciliation cycles are conducted between the findings register and upstream data sources. This process detects drift where vulnerabilities reappear after being marked closed or where a scanner's latest results do not align with the register's status. Mature programs run automated reconciliations weekly or monthly, flagging discrepancies for review. These reconciliation reports form part of the audit evidence that life cycle controls are continuous, not event-based. In environments with continuous scanning or DevSecOps pipelines, reconciliation is near real-time, relying on APIs that update the register whenever a finding's state changes. The consistency of this feedback loop is a leading indicator of maturity and a focus area for auditors assessing the program's reliability.

Cross-team accountability is sustained through governance visibility. Dashboards and reports should make ownership, status, and timeliness transparent to all relevant stakeholders—from remediation teams to executive leadership. Weekly or monthly review meetings often include representatives from security, IT operations, application development, and risk management to discuss high-severity findings, recurring weaknesses, and overdue items. Escalation paths are predefined so that persistent delays or repeated exceptions are elevated to risk committees or audit oversight groups. Auditors look for evidence that these governance reviews occur regularly, with meeting minutes or action logs documenting follow-up. Such cross-functional participation demonstrates that vulnerability management is embedded in the organizational culture rather than siloed within security operations.

When a finding transitions toward closure, the final verification step ensures all linked tasks, dependencies, and compensations are complete. In complex environments, one vulnerability might trigger related configuration changes across multiple systems or applications; thus, closure validation should confirm that all affected assets are remediated, not just the initial target. For example, a vulnerable library version identified in one microservice may also exist in several others built from the same base image. Mature programs track these relationships through dependency mapping, ensuring that the closure of one finding cascades correctly. Auditors may test this control by tracing a closed vulnerability through related systems to confirm that systemic issues were fully addressed rather than patched in isolation.

Evidence Locations: Scanners, Ticketing, Exception Registers, and Pen Test Artifacts

Auditors assessing a vulnerability management or penetration testing program expect a clearly mapped ecosystem of evidence sources that collectively demonstrate the integrity, completeness, and timeliness of security activities. Each artifact must have identifiable provenance—where it originated, when it was produced, and how it ties to related records across systems. This chain of evidence enables "re-performance," meaning an auditor or third party could retrace the same workflow using the provided data and reach equivalent conclusions. Mature organizations therefore maintain an evidence model that links their configuration management database (CMDB), vulnerability scanners, prioritization inputs, remediation workflows, exception registers, and testing reports in a coherent, exportable structure. The objective is not simply to show that activities occurred, but that the relationships among them are logical, time-bounded, and independently verifiable.

The asset inventory or CMDB serves as the foundational proof source—the universe of items under governance. Every subsequent control activity references back to this inventory, whether by hostname, IP address, asset ID, or cloud resource identifier. Auditors view the CMDB as the "scope anchor," verifying that each scanned or tested system corresponds to a legitimate, owned, and classified asset. To ensure integrity, the CMDB must record asset attributes relevant to security governance such as business owner, environment (production, development, test), data classification,

Table 13.3 Evidence chain and cross reference map.

Artifact type	Key fields	Provenance	Cross-reference target	Time-bounded
CMDB export	Asset ID and owner and classification	System of record audit log	Discovery and assessment scope	Snapshot with timestamp
Discovery scan export	Asset ID and services and time	Scanner job metadata	CMDB entries and assessment jobs	Start and end times recorded
Assessment scan export	Asset ID and CVE and plugin version	Scanner policy and version	Remediation tickets and re scan	Scan window timestamp
Prioritization snapshot	KEV and EPSS and CVSS at decision	Threat intel feed source	Vulnerability record ID	Saved at triage time
Remediation ticket	Owner and due date and status	ITSM workflow logs	Assessment finding ID and change ID	Opened and closed timestamps
Change record	CR ID and approvers and window	Change control system	Remediation ticket and asset ID	Approved and implemented dates
Exception register	Justification and expiry and control	Governance approval trail	Finding ID and asset ID	Creation and review dates
Pen test SOW	Scope and rules and methods	Signed engagement doc	CMDB targets and report ID	Effective testing window
Pen test final report	Findings and exploit path and impact	Digital signature or hash	Findings register and tickets	Report delivery date
Re scan report	Not detected status and policy used	Scanner job metadata	Closed ticket and asset ID	Verification time after fix

and network segment. Evidence exports from the CMDB should include timestamps, asset life cycle status, and change history logs to demonstrate that coverage and scope remained accurate during the audit period. This inventory establishes the baseline against which discovery and assessment evidence are reconciled. Table 13.3 cross references artifacts with unique fields and timestamps enable reliable re performance of control activities.

Discovery and assessment scan exports are the next links in the chain. Discovery scans prove visibility—what assets and services were found—while assessment scans prove inspection—what vulnerabilities were detected and when. Each export must include asset identifiers, scan start and completion timestamps, tool name, version, and policy used. These attributes allow auditors to confirm coverage and repeatability, ruling out errors due to inconsistent configurations or outdated signatures. Discovery results are compared to the CMDB to confirm no unmanaged or unknown assets exist, while assessment outputs are validated against remediation records to confirm vulnerabilities were tracked through closure. Maintaining both raw scan data and filtered dashboards ensures transparency, as auditors may request unprocessed exports to verify that summarized reports have not omitted critical findings.

Prioritization inputs form the analytical bridge between discovery and remediation. Data such as CVSS base scores, CISA's KEV listings, and EPSS probabilities should be retained in exportable form, ideally embedded in or linked to each vulnerability record at the time of triage. This linkage allows auditors to reconstruct how severity and exploit likelihood influenced remediation priority and SLA assignment. Evidence may include downloaded KEV snapshots showing publication dates, EPSS datasets used for scoring at the time of analysis, and internal prioritization models that merge technical and business context. Because threat intelligence evolves, time-bounded exports are essential—auditors will look for evidence that the prioritization decisions were made based on data available during the audit period, not retroactively adjusted with newer feeds.

Remediation tickets and associated change records provide the operational proof that identified vulnerabilities were acted upon. These artifacts should contain references to the corresponding vulnerability IDs, remediation plans, patch versions, and closure evidence. For infrastructure changes, system logs and change control approvals validate that fixes were implemented through governed channels rather than ad hoc interventions. Integration between ticketing systems and vulnerability registers ensures synchronization of status—open, in progress, resolved, or verified closed. Auditors will cross-reference ticket closure timestamps against scan retest results to confirm that vulnerabilities were not prematurely marked as remediated. Each ticket should include clear ownership, due dates, and supporting attachments such as screenshots or scan excerpts, making it possible to reconstruct exactly how and when each issue was resolved.

Exception and risk-acceptance registers capture the cases where remediation could not or would not occur within defined SLAs. These records are essential to demonstrate controlled deviation from policy. Each entry must include the vulnerability or asset identifier, justification for the exception, risk owner approval, compensating controls, and an explicit expiry date. Evidence exports from these registers should also include review logs that show periodic reevaluation and renewal or closure of exceptions. Cross-references to remediation tickets or vulnerability IDs ensure traceability; auditors should be able to match an exception entry to the original finding and confirm that the issue was tracked continuously under governance. Registers that are exportable and version-controlled allow auditors to verify that no unauthorized exceptions were inserted or altered after the fact—a critical component of data integrity.

Penetration testing evidence constitutes the assurance overlay for the entire process. Statements of Work (SOWs) define test scope, objectives, and methodologies, while final reports provide the proof of execution and outcome. Each SOW must link back to the same asset inventory used for vulnerability management, confirming alignment between governance systems. Reports must contain detailed findings with timestamps, affected systems, exploit paths, and impact descriptions. Auditors expect to see that vulnerabilities identified during penetration testing were entered into the central findings register and linked to remediation tickets or risk-acceptance records, ensuring that they follow the same life cycle controls as scanner findings. Maintaining digital signatures or hashes of final reports helps prove provenance and assures that results have not been modified postdelivery.

Cross-referencing between these evidence sources is what makes an audit trail re-performable. Each artifact—whether a scan export, ticket, exception, or report—should contain unique identifiers and timestamps that allow it to be logically connected to others. For example, a vulnerability ID in a scanner export should appear in the prioritization log, the associated remediation ticket, and, if deferred, the exception register. When auditors can trace a single issue across this chain without ambiguity, they gain confidence that the organization's control environment is cohesive. Gaps in cross-referencing, on the other hand, indicate process fragmentation or data governance weaknesses. Mature organizations periodically test this linkage by randomly selecting findings and walking them through the entire life cycle to verify evidence consistency.

Time-boundedness of artifacts is another core expectation. Each dataset must reflect conditions as they existed during the audit period, not snapshots regenerated after the fact. For example, scan exports should show creation dates that align with patch cycles, and exception approvals should display the original approval and renewal timestamps. Version-controlled exports or immutable storage solutions provide strong assurance of data integrity. Auditors may request historical exports to validate that controls were consistently applied over time rather than reconstructed for inspection. Maintaining these records in exportable, machine-readable formats such as CSV or JSON allows for independent analysis and re-performance, fulfilling one of the key principles of auditability.

Provenance completes the picture—each artifact must demonstrate its origin and authenticity. This can be achieved through embedded metadata (user, timestamp, tool version), digital signatures, or storage within systems that enforce tamper-evident logging. Provenance assures auditors that evidence was generated by trusted sources and not retroactively altered. When combined with comprehensive cross-referencing, time-bounded exports, and clearly defined ownership of each dataset, provenance enables full traceability from initial detection to final verification. Together, these elements form the evidentiary backbone of vulnerability management governance, ensuring that every control action—whether scanning, prioritizing, remediating, or testing—can be independently verified and reproduced with confidence.

Conclusion

Mastering the governance of vulnerability management and penetration testing is critical for sustaining measurable assurance in complex, fast-moving digital ecosystems. The ability to connect asset discovery, prioritization, remediation, and verification under a unified control framework transforms reactive security into a disciplined, auditable process. These practices enable organizations to demonstrate—not merely claim—that security gaps are identified, contained, and validated through repeatable evidence. In regulated environments, such traceability defines the difference between operational competence and strategic accountability.

For AI-driven enterprises, this rigor becomes even more essential. Machine learning models, automated pipelines, and adaptive cloud systems expand the attack surface in ways traditional controls were never designed to handle. Continuous scanning, intelligent prioritization, and independence in testing help ensure that algorithmic systems, datasets, and underlying infrastructure remain defensible against both conventional exploits and AI-specific risks. By embedding governance and auditability into vulnerability processes, organizations strengthen trust in the data and automation that now drive decision-making at scale.

With these foundations in place, cybersecurity and audit professionals are better equipped to manage assurance across hybrid, cloud, and AI-enabled environments. The consistent application of SLAs, exception governance, evidence provenance, and independent validation reinforces a security culture grounded in proof, not perception. While tools and tactics will continue to evolve, the strategic intent remains constant—to ensure every vulnerability, whether human, technical, or systemic, is addressed through accountable, verifiable, and transparent governance.

Auditor Recommendations

1. **Verify Asset Completeness:** Establish a clear process for confirming that all assets within the audit scope are represented in the organization's inventory and scan coverage. Auditors should reconcile scanner targets against the CMDB or asset inventory to detect blind spots. This validation demonstrates whether the organization's vulnerability management truly reflects its operational footprint.

2. **Assess Scan Cadence Against Risk Tiers:** Evaluate whether scan frequencies are appropriately matched to the risk level of each asset class. High-risk or internet-facing systems should show evidence of more frequent discovery and assessment cycles than low-risk internal systems. Auditors should require documentation showing justification for scan intervals and the evidence supporting risk-based cadence decisions.
3. **Test the Integrity of Prioritization Models:** Examine how vulnerability severity, exploit intelligence, and business context are integrated into remediation prioritization. Auditors should verify that inputs like KEV and EPSS data are current and appropriately influence remediation timelines. This ensures that the organization's prioritization logic reflects real threat conditions rather than static technical ratings.
4. **Confirm SLA Enforcement Through Evidence:** Review remediation SLAs not as policy statements but as measurable, time-bound commitments supported by data. Auditors should sample tickets and verify timestamps for assignment, start, and closure to confirm that timelines are being tracked consistently. This approach validates operational discipline and distinguishes policy from performance.
5. **Scrutinize Exception and Risk Acceptance Governance:** Ensure exceptions and risk acceptances are formally approved, time-boxed, and supported by compensating controls. Auditors should verify that each exception includes an expiry date and review log demonstrating periodic reassessment. This oversight prevents accepted risks from persisting indefinitely without governance attention.
6. **Validate Remediation Through Technical Proof:** Require objective evidence such as authenticated re-scans, configuration diffs, or functional test results to verify closure. Auditors should not accept ticket closure alone as proof of remediation. Confirming technical validation ensures that vulnerabilities have been effectively eliminated and not just administratively resolved.
7. **Evaluate Independence in Penetration Testing:** Verify that penetration testers operate free from conflicts of interest and that reporting lines preserve objectivity. Auditors should confirm that testers are not evaluating systems they manage or maintain and that scope approval involves independent oversight. Independence ensures that test results can be trusted as unbiased evidence of control performance.
8. **Trace Findings Through the Full Life cycle:** Follow sample vulnerabilities from discovery to closure to confirm that records are centralized, deduplicated, and reconciled. Auditors should check that ownership, SLA tracking, and closure evidence exist for every stage of the life cycle. This process validates that the organization maintains accountability from detection to verified resolution.
9. **Inspect Evidence Provenance and Cross-referencing:** Review how the organization links scan exports, remediation tickets, exception registers, and penetration test reports. Auditors should expect time-stamped, exportable artifacts that can be independently re-performed. Provenance and cross-references confirm that evidence integrity is preserved and that the audit trail is complete.
10. **Evaluate Governance Visibility Across Teams:** Confirm that vulnerability management metrics, exceptions, and remediation progress are reviewed at governance meetings involving multiple departments. Auditors should examine meeting minutes or dashboards to ensure leadership oversight and cross-team accountability. This visibility demonstrates that vulnerability management is treated as a strategic risk process, not just a technical function.

Chapter Questions

1. Why should discovery scans be separated from assessment scans in a vulnerability program?
   - **A.** To optimize visibility while minimizing operational risk through lightweight discovery and scheduled, deeper assessments
   - **B.** To reduce the number of remediation tickets created by scanners
   - **C.** To comply with vendor licensing terms for multiple tools
   - **D.** To eliminate the need for maintaining an asset inventory

2. Which artifact provides the strongest proof that a vulnerability has been remediated?
   - **A.** A closed ticket in the ITSM system
   - **B.** An approved change request
   - **C.** An authenticated re-scan showing the issue is not detected on the asset
   - **D.** A verbal confirmation from the system owner

3. When a vulnerability appears in CISA's KEV list, how should it be handled?
   - **A.** Ignore the listing if the CVSS score is only medium
   - **B.** Prioritize immediate remediation regardless of the CVSS score
   - **C.** Schedule remediation for the next quarterly cycle
   - **D.** Accept the risk by default due to operational constraints

4. What is a required element of exception governance for deferred remediation?
   - **A.** A permanent approval with no review
   - **B.** A financial justification in lieu of controls
   - **C.** An exception with no named owner
   - **D.** A defined expiry date with compensating controls

5. Which timing trigger best supports consistent SLA measurement for remediation?
   - **A.** The date of initial discovery or validation of the finding
   - **B.** The date a change window first opens
   - **C.** The date a report is delivered to executives
   - **D.** The date a ticket is assigned to an engineer

6. Which control most effectively prevents reintroduction of a previously fixed vulnerability across deployments?
   - **A.** Sending an email reminder to operations staff
   - **B.** Documenting the fix in a shared wiki page
   - **C.** Updating golden images and baselines and enforcing them via CI/CD gates
   - **D.** Disabling monitoring to avoid false positives

7. Which statement best reflects auditor expectations for penetration testing independence?
   - **A.** Testers should report directly to system owners for rapid fixes
   - **B.** Testers may assess systems they maintain to speed scheduling
   - **C.** Testers should be embedded in the development team for convenience
   - **D.** Testers must operate without conflicts and not assess systems they built or manage

8. Which set of elements is considered minimum content for a high-quality penetration test report?
   - **A.** An executive summary only
   - **B.** A list of tools used without exploitation detail
   - **C.** Detailed findings, exploit paths, data accessed, business impact, and reproducible steps
   - **D.** Raw packet captures without narrative context

9. What is the primary purpose of deduplication in a central findings register?
   - **A.** To ensure one coordinated response per unique issue across sources
   - **B.** To inflate vulnerability counts to obtain more budget
   - **C.** To delay remediation by reducing visible workload
   - **D.** To remove evidence once a ticket is opened

10. Why is cross-referencing evidence sources with unique IDs and timestamps essential?
    - **A.** It enables automatic patch deployment without human review
    - **B.** It allows auditors to re-perform the control activities using time-bounded artifacts
    - **C.** It anonymizes assets to protect privacy during audits
    - **D.** It eliminates the need for remediation tickets or change records

14

Third-party and Supply-chain Security

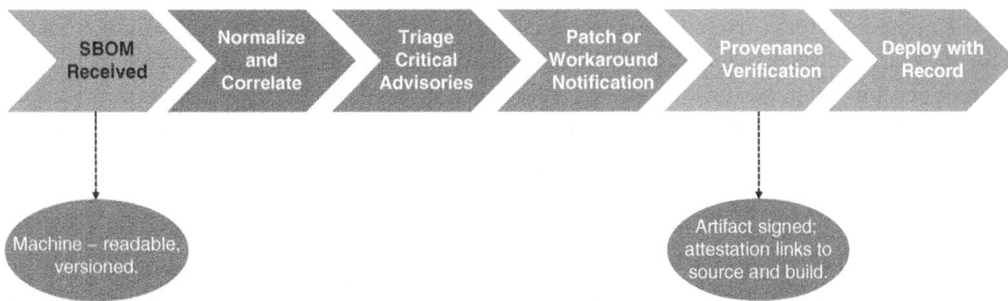

The integrity of an organization's security posture increasingly depends on the resilience of its third parties and suppliers. As enterprises adopt interconnected platforms, outsourced services, and AI-driven capabilities, the attack surface expands beyond what internal controls can contain. Breaches now often originate not from direct compromise, but from weak links in software supply chains or vendor ecosystems that lack transparency and accountability. Understanding how to evaluate, segment, and continuously monitor these external dependencies is essential to sustaining both operational resilience and regulatory trust in an era where assurance must extend across organizational boundaries.

Effective third-party and supply-chain security requires more than contract clauses or vendor scorecards—it demands a structured, evidence-based risk model. The discipline of cybersecurity auditing provides this structure by defining how vendors are classified, how diligence is scaled to risk, and how assurance artifacts substantiate ongoing performance. From risk tiering and contractual enforcement to continuous monitoring and software provenance, the principles covered here enable auditors to transform fragmented oversight into a cohesive control life cycle. This approach aligns with modern governance frameworks that expect demonstrable proof of risk management, not just procedural compliance.

As AI systems and automation increasingly rely on external APIs, pretrained models, and managed infrastructure, the importance of trustworthy supply chains becomes existential. The ability to verify provenance, enforce security obligations, and validate evidence through independent means defines whether an organization can maintain confidence in its digital ecosystem. By uniting procurement, legal, and technical oversight under a common auditable standard, the practices outlined in this chapter strengthen both security architecture and organizational credibility.

The result is a sustainable assurance framework—one capable of adapting to emerging risks without sacrificing transparency or speed.

Vendor Risk Segmentation and Due Diligence Depth

Vendor risk segmentation provides the organizing logic for third-party assurance, translating abstract concerns about "suppliers" into concrete tiers with clear expectations for diligence, contracting, and ongoing monitoring. An effective model starts by mapping each vendor to the business capabilities it enables and the failure modes that could materialize if that relationship degrades or is compromised. The segmentation scheme must be simple enough for procurement and business owners to apply consistently, yet nuanced enough to capture outsized risks introduced by data handling, integration points, and operational reliance. Treat segmentation as the backbone of the third-party program rather than an administrative label; it informs what evidence you require, how often you ask for it, and who must approve residual risk before the relationship proceeds. This approach aligns with the broader treatment of third-party and supply-chain Security as a core domain of cybersecurity auditing.

The four primary dimensions that determine tiering—criticality, data sensitivity, connectivity, and operational dependency—should be defined in measurable terms. Criticality looks beyond contract value to the business outcome at stake: revenue enablement, fiduciary reporting, safety-of-life, or compliance obligations. Data sensitivity should identify what the vendor can access, process, or store, distinguishing between public, internal, restricted, and regulated categories while noting whether exposure would create breach-notification duties. Connectivity captures the technical surface area between environments, including real-time integrations, access to administrative consoles, and any capability to move code or content into production systems. Operational dependency considers single-point-of-failure risk and practical substitutability, weighing time-to-restore with or without the vendor, concentration risk across the portfolio, and the existence of contractual continuity mechanisms.

To make these dimensions operational, establish a scoring rubric that converts qualitative inputs into tier thresholds, such as Tier 1 (critical), Tier 2 (high), Tier 3 (moderate), and Tier 4 (limited). Each dimension should carry calibrated weights so the model reflects your risk appetite; for example, administrative access into core infrastructure may outweigh moderate data sensitivity. The rubric should require evidence of the facts behind the score—architecture diagrams for connectivity, data flow maps for sensitivity, and business impact analyses for criticality—to reduce gaming or wishful thinking during intake. Document the thresholds, provide examples for common vendor types, and require a named owner to validate the tier when the relationship is created, with audit rights to review the rationale during engagement planning. A risk-based, framework-neutral posture ensures the rubric remains portable across regulations and sectors as the vendor landscape evolves.

Tiering directly governs diligence depth. For Tier 4 relationships, a streamlined review may focus on contractual representations and a lightweight questionnaire that confirms absence of sensitive data, no privileged connectivity, and a clear boundary between environments. For Tier 3, expand to third-party assurance artifacts such as SOC 2 Type II, ISO/IEC 27001 certificates, privacy program attestations, and summaries of business continuity testing, validating their scope and recency against the services consumed. Tier 2 vendors warrant corroborating evidence—such as targeted walkthroughs of incident response coordination, data retention practices tied to your record

Table 14.1 Vendor risk segmentation criteria matrix.

Dimension	Definition	Sample indicators	Tier impact
Criticality	Effect on business outcomes and obligations	Revenue enablement; safety of life; compliance drivers	High weight raises tier to critical
Data sensitivity	Exposure level of processed or stored data	Personal data; regulated records; trade secrets	Elevates tier when breach duties apply
Connectivity	Depth and privilege of integrations	Admin access; bidirectional sync; prod change paths	Increases tier due to rapid blast radius
Operational dependency	Single point of failure and substitutability	Long time to restore; concentration risk; no fallback	Drives tier to ensure continuity controls

schedules, and verification of roles with elevated access—often through a remote assessment. Tier 1 vendors merit enhanced diligence, potentially including onsite or virtual deep-dive reviews, tabletop exercises of joint incident scenarios, and contractual negotiation of audit rights, security SLAs, breach notification timelines, and explicit termination assistance to reduce exit risk. This progressive model mirrors the book's emphasis on evaluating third-party risk with practical, evidence-driven methods. Table 14.1 aligns vendor tiering to measurable risk drivers so diligence depth and monitoring cadence match real exposure.

Monitoring cadence should mirror the tier's inherent volatility and the speed with which risk can accumulate between checkpoints. Tier 1 vendors benefit from continuous signals—security incident notifications, SLA performance, change advisories for scope or subprocessor additions—supplemented by quarterly control discussions and an annual reassessment calibrated to the latest threat and compliance context. Tier 2 typically warrants semiannual touchpoints plus an annual controls refresh, while Tier 3 and Tier 4 may be reviewed annually or at contract renewal provided no triggers fire. Regardless of tier, define event-driven reviews for material changes, such as onboarding of new data elements, addition of privileged integrations, or the vendor's entry into regulatory scope that was previously out of play. Where feasible, integrate continuous control monitoring and automation to collect standardized attestations and artifacts at scale without sacrificing rigor.

Clear criteria mean little without clear ownership. Assign a business owner accountable for the relationship's value and a risk owner accountable for its security posture; in many organizations, the second role sits with a third-party risk function that partners closely with security, privacy, and legal. Procurement acts as the gateway, ensuring no commitments are executed until the tier is determined, diligence is commensurate with that tier, and any unresolved items are captured as risk exceptions with compensating measures or acceptance decisions. The model should specify who can approve residual risk by tier: operational management for Tier 3 and Tier 4, senior leadership for Tier 2, and executive or committee-level approval for Tier 1, with documented time-bound remediation plans. Embed these approvals into workflow so that purchase orders, access provisioning, and data exchanges cannot proceed until accountability and evidence thresholds are met.

Re-segmentation is essential because vendor relationships drift. Define explicit triggers that force a fresh tier decision: changes in scope or statement of work, introduction of new data classes or geographies, addition of network or admin-level connectivity, service outages that breach RTO/RPO commitments, and security or privacy incidents indicating control weakness. Treat contract renewals, major version releases, and vendor mergers or acquisitions as default triggers, since the underlying control environment or service design may have changed in ways that invalidate prior assumptions. Require the business owner to declare contemplated changes in advance through a change-control intake so the risk owner can evaluate impact and, if needed, pause expansion until diligence is updated. Establish a time-based floor as well—at least an annual re-segmentation for Tier 1 and Tier 2—so quiet drift does not accumulate beneath the radar.

Data sensitivity deserves special attention because it magnifies downstream obligations and the intensity of regulatory scrutiny. Elevate the tier when a vendor stores or processes personal data that carries breach-notification risk, sector-specific records that trigger supervisory expectations, or intellectual property that would materially harm competitiveness if exposed. Consider whether the vendor's role makes them a processor, a subprocessor, or an independent controller under applicable privacy regimes, because those distinctions shape contract clauses and monitoring scope. If sensitive data is present but connectivity is narrow and operational dependency is low, due diligence can still be deep—focusing on data life cycle rigor, encryption key governance, retention, and disposal—without overstating other dimensions. Conversely, even vendors with no sensitive data can land in a higher tier when privileged connectivity enables indirect access into critical environments, warranting oversight tilted toward change management discipline and access governance.

Connectivity signals how fast a risk can become an incident, so its treatment within tiering must be granular. Differentiate one-way data pushes from bidirectional syncs, user-level access from administrative or programmatic access, and preproduction connectivity from paths into production systems. A vendor with API-level integration to orchestrate workloads, elevate privileges, or modify configurations warrants a higher tier than a vendor that receives nightly files through a managed gateway. Document the integration topology and require disclosure of any fourth parties the vendor relies on to operate those connections, as this can surface hidden dependencies and points of failure. While the tiering model is not the place for tenant-level control prescriptions, it should unambiguously require evidence that connectivity is governed, logged, and constrained by design, and it should raise the diligence bar whenever that evidence is weak or fragmented.

Operational dependency wraps business impact, substitutability, and concentration risk into a single dimension that often separates a routine supplier from a critical partner. Map the workflows that would stall if the vendor falters and estimate the time-to-restore with and without them; the latter reveals whether you truly have an alternate path or whether "contingency" is a comforting fiction. Scan for concentration risk by looking horizontally across business units and regions: multiple teams may have converged on a single vendor, inflating systemic exposure even when each contract looks modest in isolation. Require continuity evidence proportionate to the tier—tested recovery objectives, escrow or exit strategies, and practical de-conversion plans—so the organization is not negotiating its way out of a corner during a crisis. A risk-based program will emphasize this dimension because it speaks directly to enterprise resilience and stakeholder expectations for reliable service.

A mature segmentation model extends to fourth-party visibility and contractual levers that keep the picture current. Require vendors—based on tier—to disclose material subprocessors, notify you before adding or changing them, and cascade comparable security and privacy obligations downstream. High-tier relationships should include rights to review downstream assurance artifacts and insist on timely remediation of findings that affect your data, connectivity, or continuity. Track concentration among fourth parties too; if dozens of your vendors depend on the same cloud region, payments processor, or identity provider, your aggregate risk may exceed what any single contract suggests. Use this visibility to challenge business continuity assumptions, refine tier thresholds for classes of vendors, and prioritize tabletop exercises where joint incident response will be essential to containing impact.

The ultimate test of segmentation is whether it improves decisions at speed—who you onboard, how you monitor, when you escalate, and what you are willing to accept. Calibrate the model with historical incident data and pilot it on upcoming procurements to check that tier assignments align with practitioner intuition and executive risk appetite. Publish a concise playbook that ties each tier to required artifacts, approval levels, and monitoring cadence; then train procurement, legal, and vendor managers to apply it consistently. Revisit the rubric at least annually to account for changes in the threat landscape, regulatory expectations, and your business model, retaining the risk-based, adaptable posture that keeps the program relevant as technologies and supplier ecosystems shift. This consistency with a risk-based, end-to-end auditing approach ensures vendor oversight remains practical, defensible, and aligned with enterprise objectives.

Contractual Security Clauses and Right-to-audit/Assurance Rights

The contract is the auditor's anchor point for verifying that security obligations move from aspiration to enforceable commitment. Every third-party engagement should begin with standardized language that sets minimum expectations for confidentiality, data protection, and compliance with relevant security frameworks. These baseline clauses do not replace due diligence; rather, they codify it. They ensure that risk management extends beyond trust in the vendor's representations and into binding terms that survive personnel changes, mergers, and operational disruptions. Strong contractual language clarifies what constitutes acceptable security posture, how obligations are measured, and what recourse the organization has when controls lapse or incidents occur. Without these provisions, even the most thorough precontract risk assessment can collapse into unenforceable goodwill when tested by a breach or a compliance audit.

The cornerstone clause is the explicit security requirements provision, which should require the vendor to maintain safeguards appropriate to the sensitivity and criticality of the data and services involved. This typically includes adherence to a recognized security framework, encryption of data at rest and in transit, access control principles such as least privilege, secure software development practices, and robust vulnerability and patch management processes. While the clause avoids dictating technology choices, it should compel the vendor to provide current documentation—such as SOC 2 reports, ISO certifications, or internal audit summaries—that demonstrates operational compliance. For high-tier vendors, the contract should also require participation in joint incident response exercises or periodic security reviews. These commitments transform abstract promises into measurable expectations that auditors can verify at renewal or during incident postmortems.

Breach notification clauses must eliminate ambiguity about timing, scope, and format of disclosure. A well-crafted provision requires vendors to notify the organization promptly—typically within 24 to 72 hours—of any event that compromises, or could reasonably be expected to compromise, confidentiality, integrity, or availability of data or systems within contractual scope. The clause should specify required details, such as nature of the incident, affected systems or data, containment measures, and steps taken toward remediation. Importantly, the notification obligation should extend to incidents involving subprocessors, ensuring visibility even when the initial exposure occurs beyond the vendor's direct control. For auditors, evidence of compliance with this clause includes incident reports, communication timelines, and post-incident reviews confirming that notification procedures were followed as written.

Subprocessor control clauses are increasingly vital in today's layered service ecosystems. Vendors frequently rely on cloud providers, managed service partners, and specialized technology subcontractors, each of which introduces its own risk surface. Contracts should mandate that vendors disclose all subprocessors with access to customer data or networks and require prior approval for any additions or changes. The clause must cascade key security obligations downstream, ensuring subprocessors are bound by equivalent confidentiality, data protection, and breach-notification terms. For critical relationships, the contract may include rights to review subprocessor assurance artifacts or conduct joint assessments. Auditors should look for documented evidence of subprocessor inventories, approval records, and periodic attestations that confirm compliance throughout the chain of custody.

Audit and assessment rights define the organization's authority to verify that the vendor's controls operate effectively over time. This clause should grant the customer the right to request relevant documentation, conduct remote or onsite assessments, or engage a qualified third-party auditor to perform reviews on its behalf. The provision should also specify reasonable notice periods and confidentiality protections for shared results, maintaining a balance between transparency and practicality. The right-to-audit clause deters complacency and signals to vendors that oversight is continuous, not ceremonial. Evidence of enforcement includes scheduled assessments at renewal checkpoints, tracked responses to findings, and remediation reports that demonstrate closure of identified gaps.

Data return and deletion clauses ensure that sensitive information does not linger in vendor systems after the relationship ends. The contract should require vendors to return all customer data in a specified format within a defined period, followed by verifiable deletion or destruction of all residual copies. This includes backups, logs, and replicas residing in disaster-recovery or archival environments. Auditors should expect to see certificates of destruction, secure transfer logs, and confirmation from the vendor's compliance or IT team that retention schedules have been executed. Periodic testing of data exit procedures, often during renewal or re-segmentation events, provides further assurance that the clause functions as intended rather than existing as a theoretical safeguard.

Exceptions to any standard clause must follow a formal risk acceptance process that documents the rationale, compensating controls, and expiration date. For instance, a vendor may resist granting direct audit rights due to multitenant architecture concerns; in such cases, equivalent transparency—such as providing independent assurance reports or audit summaries—should be approved as an exception only after risk evaluation. Each deviation should have a named owner, an expiration or review trigger, and explicit acknowledgment from senior management or the risk committee. Auditors reviewing vendor files should be able to trace these exceptions to approval records and verify that compensating measures remain valid at each renewal cycle.

Contracts are living instruments that require continuous enforcement. Renewal checkpoints provide opportunities to confirm whether clauses have been exercised or merely retained as placeholders. During each renewal, risk and procurement teams should verify that breach notifications, control assessments, and remediation plans from the prior term were delivered and closed. Penalties, such as withheld payments or service credits for missed security obligations, should be applied consistently to maintain credibility. Where the contract includes remediation commitments—such as specific time frames to patch vulnerabilities or address audit findings—evidence of timely completion should be captured in the vendor's performance file. These checkpoints create a measurable feedback loop that reinforces the connection between contractual terms and operational behavior.

Auditors should also evaluate the quality of the vendor's response history as an indicator of clause maturity. A vendor that consistently provides timely incident updates, accepts independent assessments without resistance, and proactively reports subprocessor changes demonstrates contractual alignment in practice. Conversely, repeated delays, vague responses, or failure to produce required documentation signal that the clauses exist only on paper. Over time, tracking these patterns supports tier reclassification or informs renewal decisions, ensuring that contractual commitments continue to reflect real-world performance. By embedding measurable, enforceable security clauses and maintaining disciplined oversight of their execution, organizations convert the contract from a static legal instrument into a dynamic tool of continuous assurance and risk control.

Assurance Artifacts: SOC Reports, SIG/CAIQ, and Certifications

Assurance artifacts provide the tangible evidence base for third-party oversight, translating vendor assertions about security into verifiable attestations. They act as the auditor's window into another organization's control environment, though each artifact carries inherent limitations that must be understood to avoid misplaced confidence. An effective auditor approaches these documents with skepticism balanced by technical literacy—recognizing what the artifact proves, what it omits, and where responsibility reverts to the organization consuming the service. The objective is not blind reliance but informed interpretation, ensuring the organization's own assurance conclusions remain defensible under scrutiny. Table 14.2 clarifies what common artifacts can support auditor reliance and where additional testing or controls are required.

System and Organization Control (SOC) reports are among the most relied-upon artifacts, particularly SOC 2 Type II for security, availability, processing integrity, confidentiality, and privacy principles. An SOC 2 Type II report provides independent attestation that a vendor's controls

Table 14.2 Assurance artifact reliance limits and auditor actions.

Artifact type	What it proves	What it cannot prove	Auditor action
SOC 2 Type II	Controls designed and operating during stated period	Customer specific control needs or config fit	Review scope and CUECs and record limits
SOC 1	Controls relevant to financial reporting only	Broader security posture or privacy coverage	Use only when financial processes are affected
SIG or CAIQ	Structured self-attestation against common controls	Independent verification or testing	Corroborate with third-party evidence
ISO IEC 27001	Presence of an audited ISMS	Granular control performance per service	Confirm scope statement and certificate validity
PCI DSS	Payment data protection at point in time	Enterprise-wide security assurance	Validate in scope systems and recency
FedRAMP authorization	Rigorous review for listed cloud service	Coverage outside authorized boundary	Map offering to your exact use case
Bridge letter	No material changes since report end date	Fresh control testing or new scope	Use only to cover short gaps

were designed and operated effectively over a defined period, typically six to twelve months. It can demonstrate that key safeguards—such as access controls, incident response, and change management—were tested by a qualified service auditor under AICPA standards. However, it cannot confirm that the vendor's controls meet your specific risk tolerance or configuration needs; it merely confirms their existence and operational effectiveness relative to their own control objectives. An SOC 1 report, conversely, focuses on controls relevant to financial reporting and is seldom appropriate for cybersecurity diligence except when evaluating vendors that impact accounting systems.

SOC reports also require careful handling of carve-outs and subservice organizations. A carve-out occurs when the primary vendor relies on another entity, such as a cloud provider or data center, whose controls are excluded from testing within the report. The absence of these controls introduces a blind spot that must be bridged through other assurance means, such as obtaining the subservice organization's own SOC 2 report or certifications. The inclusive method, where the primary vendor's auditor includes and tests subservice controls, provides greater transparency but is less common. Auditors must identify which model applies and document any residual exposure from untested dependencies. Overlooking carve-outs can result in unmitigated risk where critical hosting, identity, or storage functions reside outside the scope of attestation.

Complementary user-entity controls (CUECs) are another subtle but crucial limitation. These controls represent assumptions the vendor's auditor makes about what the customer organization must do for the vendor's controls to remain effective. For example, an SOC 2 report may assume that the customer enforces strong authentication for access to the vendor's portal or transmits data only through encrypted channels. If the customer fails to fulfill these user-side responsibilities, the overall control environment is weakened—even if the vendor's side performs flawlessly. Auditors must review CUECs in every report, identify those relevant to their environment, and ensure that internal controls exist to satisfy them. When gaps exist, the burden shifts back to the organization, and reliance on the vendor's attestation must be qualified accordingly.

Standardized security questionnaires like the Shared Assessments SIG (Standardized Information Gathering) and the Cloud Security Alliance CAIQ (Consensus Assessments Initiative Questionnaire) supplement SOC reports by filling in contextual gaps. These artifacts provide structured self-attestations aligned to common frameworks such as ISO 27001, NIST SP 800-53, or the Cloud Controls Matrix (CCM). They are valuable for mapping control coverage quickly and identifying areas requiring deeper inquiry, especially when no formal audit report exists. However, they are self-reported and therefore unverified unless independently validated or corroborated by other evidence. Their value lies in establishing a baseline for comparison and consistency across vendors, not in replacing third-party audits. When used properly, SIG and CAIQ responses serve as diagnostic tools—helping prioritize follow-up, not close the assurance loop.

Certifications such as ISO/IEC 27001, PCI DSS, or FedRAMP authorization can demonstrate that a vendor has undergone an external conformity assessment against defined security standards. ISO 27001 certification, for instance, validates that an information security management system (ISMS) is formally established and audited, but it does not attest to the detailed operational performance of individual controls. Likewise, PCI DSS compliance confirms adherence to payment-card data protection requirements at a point in time but may not cover the broader environment or new integrations. FedRAMP authorizations, while rigorous, apply only to specific service offerings and environments listed in the authorization package. Auditors must read the scope statements carefully to avoid over-reliance; certification boundaries often exclude critical subsystems, regions, or modules that directly affect your data.

Timeliness and period coverage determine the relevance of assurance artifacts. An SOC 2 report that ended twelve months ago offers diminishing value, as it reflects a control environment that may have changed substantially since. Ideally, artifacts should cover a period ending within the past six months for critical vendors, with rolling coverage for high-dependency relationships. If the vendor's reporting cycle lags, a bridge letter or interim update should be obtained to confirm no material control changes occurred since the audit period. Similar scrutiny applies to certifications: auditors should verify that certificates are active, current, and traceable to an accredited body. Expired or unverifiable certifications are red flags that the vendor's assurance program may not be maintained consistently.

When gaps or limitations are identified—whether from expired coverage, carve-outs, incomplete responses, or unfulfilled user-entity controls—they must be explicitly recorded in the auditor's workpapers and risk register. Each limitation should include a narrative of how the organization mitigates the associated uncertainty, whether through compensating controls, direct testing, or adjusted reliance levels. For example, if an SOC report excludes physical security due to a hosting carve-out, the auditor might obtain a separate data center attestation or accept residual risk after executive review. This documentation ensures transparency in reliance decisions and prevents unjustified assumptions of completeness.

Gap analysis transforms these artifacts from static documents into actionable insight. By comparing reported control coverage against internal security baselines or framework mappings, auditors can identify discrepancies that warrant further investigation. A vendor whose SOC 2 includes minimal logging controls, for instance, may still satisfy its attestation but fall short of the organization's continuous monitoring expectations. The analysis should record such differences, rate their materiality, and inform both contract negotiations and monitoring cadence. Mature programs automate portions of this comparison to streamline annual reassessment cycles while preserving auditor judgment for nuanced interpretation.

Reliance on assurance artifacts should never replace the auditor's obligation to exercise professional skepticism. These reports and certifications are indicators, not guarantees. Their purpose is to inform a risk-based conclusion, not to absolve the organization of responsibility for ongoing oversight. The auditor's role is to connect the evidence to business impact—to understand how the vendor's control assurances intersect with enterprise risk appetite, dependency level, and residual exposure. When assurance artifacts are read critically, validated for scope and timeliness, and integrated into a structured reliance model, they become a cornerstone of sustainable third-party assurance rather than a checkbox in the procurement file.

Continuous Monitoring: Questionnaires, Signals, and Triggers

Continuous monitoring transforms vendor risk management from a static exercise into a living process of observation and response. Once a vendor has passed initial due diligence, their risk profile does not remain frozen—technical, operational, and geopolitical conditions evolve constantly. Continuous monitoring ensures that new information, whether from formal updates or external signals, informs the organization's risk posture in near real time. It bridges the gap between annual assessments and day-to-day reality, providing early warnings when control environments drift, when financial or regulatory pressure mounts, or when new threats emerge. For cybersecurity auditors, this phase represents the difference between compliance-based oversight and true assurance rooted in vigilance.

Questionnaires remain a foundational tool but must be managed dynamically rather than archived after onboarding. Periodic questionnaires—issued quarterly or annually based on vendor tier—allow organizations to validate that security programs, incident response capabilities, and control frameworks remain current. They confirm whether the vendor has experienced material changes, such as leadership turnover, mergers, new subprocessors, or technology migrations that could alter risk. However, stale or incomplete questionnaires are one of the most common governance failures. When updates lapse, the vendor's file becomes misleadingly clean while the underlying risk profile may have shifted dramatically. Governance policies should define expiration thresholds—such as a maximum of twelve months without an updated attestation—and automatically trigger a re-segmentation or escalation if responses are overdue.

Beyond questionnaires, external signals now form a critical layer of continuous oversight. Security ratings platforms provide a quantitative lens on vendor hygiene, drawing on open-source intelligence, vulnerability scans, and incident reporting to generate comparative scores. These scores can highlight emerging risks such as unpatched systems, exposed credentials, or weak email security configurations. While ratings are imperfect and sometimes prone to false positives, their trend lines often reveal valuable patterns—particularly sudden declines that correlate with operational disruptions or loss of security maturity. Auditors should never treat ratings as authoritative but rather as directional input, prompting targeted inquiries or confirmation through the vendor's own disclosures.

Incident disclosures represent another vital signal, whether originating from the vendor directly or from public sources. Continuous monitoring should capture breach notifications, regulatory filings, and credible media reports involving vendors within scope. When an incident occurs, the monitoring function must assess whether the affected systems overlap with the organization's engagement and whether contractual breach notification clauses were honored. If the vendor fails to disclose an event that later becomes public, this is itself a significant signal of governance weakness and should trigger immediate escalation. Each incident, regardless of impact, becomes a test case for how the vendor's transparency and responsiveness align with contractual expectations and organizational risk tolerance.

Regulatory and sanctions checks ensure that vendors remain compliant with geopolitical and legal requirements that can shift abruptly. Automated screening against government sanction lists, export control restrictions, and adverse media databases protects the organization from inadvertently maintaining relationships with prohibited or high-risk entities. Continuous monitoring should also flag ownership or domicile changes, particularly those involving jurisdictions subject to new trade or privacy regulations. A vendor's sudden acquisition by a foreign entity, for example, could alter data residency obligations or introduce state-affiliated risk. Governance frameworks should specify escalation thresholds—for instance, any vendor appearing on a sanctions or denied-parties list triggers immediate suspension pending legal review.

Financial distress indicators are equally critical, especially for vendors that support mission-critical functions. Tools that track credit scores, bankruptcy filings, or payment delinquencies can reveal early signs of instability long before service disruption occurs. Continuous monitoring programs should integrate such signals, assigning higher weights to vendors where financial health directly correlates with operational continuity. When thresholds are crossed—such as a rapid credit downgrade or missed payroll disclosures—the vendor's tier should be reviewed and potentially elevated to ensure heightened oversight. Auditors must document both the trigger event and the subsequent actions taken, ensuring the rationale for reclassification or additional diligence is traceable.

Conflicting signals pose one of the most challenging governance problems. A vendor may self-attest to full compliance through questionnaires while external ratings or news sources suggest the opposite. In these cases, the monitoring process must include structured conflict resolution. Security and risk teams should convene to investigate discrepancies, validate data sources, and request clarification from the vendor. If contradictions persist, the vendor's risk tier should be temporarily elevated until the matter is resolved. Over time, recurring conflicts or poor responsiveness become indicators of deeper control immaturity and should be reflected in performance evaluations or contractual remediation plans.

Governance mechanisms ensure that continuous monitoring data remains credible and actionable. Each signal type—questionnaire responses, ratings, incident alerts, sanctions data, financial feeds—should have defined data owners, update frequencies, and review responsibilities. Automated platforms can aggregate these sources into dashboards, but human oversight remains essential to interpret context and determine materiality. Governance committees should meet at least quarterly to review high-severity alerts, overdue updates, and deviations from expected trends. Documented minutes and risk logs preserve an audit trail of decision-making, demonstrating that monitoring is not only performed but acted upon in accordance with policy.

Escalation thresholds must be codified so that response actions are consistent and proportional. Examples include automatic reassessment when a vendor's security rating drops by more than a defined percentage, when breach disclosures involve regulated data, or when financial distress indicators exceed a preset tolerance. Similarly, questionnaires that remain unanswered beyond their expiration window should trigger notifications to procurement and the business owner, potentially suspending new projects or payments until remediation occurs. These thresholds transform continuous monitoring from a passive observation process into a disciplined control system where predefined conditions initiate tangible action.

Continuous monitoring should feed directly into the vendor risk tiering model, ensuring that oversight intensity evolves with real-world performance. A vendor exhibiting stable signals and consistent transparency may gradually shift to a lower-risk tier, reducing administrative overhead. Conversely, a vendor with repeated missed attestations, declining security posture, or unreported incidents should escalate upward, increasing diligence depth and monitoring cadence. This dynamic linkage closes the feedback loop between monitoring and segmentation, keeping the program responsive and evidence-based. For cybersecurity auditors, this continuous motion of observation, verification, and recalibration represents the maturity frontier of third-party assurance—where vigilance, governance, and adaptation converge to safeguard the enterprise from supply chain uncertainty.

Software Supply Chain: SBOM, Dependency Risk, and Build Provenance

Software suppliers should be required to deliver continuous visibility into the components that make up their products, because assurance without transparency is wishful thinking. A Software Bill of Materials (SBOM) provides that visibility by enumerating libraries, transitive dependencies, versions, and licenses associated with each release that touches your environment. The SBOM must be machine-readable, versioned, and tied to a specific build or artifact identifier so auditors can reconcile what was purchased, what was deployed, and what is currently running. Timeliness matters as much as accuracy; SBOMs delivered months after release are historical curiosities, not assurance artifacts. The contract should specify delivery format, frequency aligned to releases and hotfixes, and notification obligations when the SBOM materially changes due to emergency patches or dependency substitutions that alter risk.

SBOMs alone do not confer security; they enable risk analysis that must be operationalized. The organization needs a standardized process to ingest supplier SBOMs into vulnerability management and governance systems that normalize naming, deduplicate components, and match versions to authoritative feeds. When suppliers provide vulnerability exploitability information, such as vulnerability exploitation status or equivalent assertions, those signals should be captured alongside the SBOM to support triage. Auditors should verify that supplier-provided identifiers map unambiguously to known components in internal inventories and that issues raised by SBOM analysis are tracked to closure through established remediation workflows. Where suppliers cannot produce SBOMs, an exception process should define temporary compensating controls and a clear timeline for full transparency.

Patch and notification obligations sit at the center of dependency risk because component weaknesses propagate through the supply chain with unsettling speed. Contracts should require suppliers to monitor authoritative vulnerability sources, identify affected components within their codebase, and publish impact assessments for each release they support. The obligation should include rapid notification to customers when newly disclosed vulnerabilities affect a shipped component, along with remediation plans, supported workarounds, and target timelines for fixed builds. Auditors should expect to see dated advisories, customer notification logs, and patch release notes that allow reconciliation of the supplier's claims with the versions in production. The absence of a disciplined notification process is itself a material risk, as it compresses customer response time exactly when speed matters most.

Triage expectations must be explicit so responses are repeatable rather than personality-driven. Critical vulnerabilities with confirmed exploitation or inclusion in authoritative exploited vulnerability catalogs should trigger an accelerated path that treats the supplier's patch as a security release, not a routine maintenance item. Medium-severity issues that lack exploitation evidence but affect internet-exposed components may still warrant expedited action based on asset criticality and threat context. Suppliers should commit to risk statements that classify each advisory's urgency and to providing clear, testable remediation steps, including configuration or feature flags when patches are not immediately available. Internally, those supplier statements must integrate with change risk assessments so that approvals, rollback plans, and post-deployment verification are commensurate with the vulnerability's potential business impact.

Build provenance provides the chain-of-custody assurance that the artifact you deploy is the artifact your supplier built and intended to distribute. At minimum, suppliers should sign release artifacts with verifiable keys and publish metadata that binds the signature to a specific source commit, build workflow, and dependency set. Reproducible builds strengthen assurance by enabling independent regeneration of the binary from source, reducing the chance that hidden steps, environment drift, or malicious tampering introduced differences. Where suppliers cannot support full reproducibility, auditors should look for intermediate attestations that record who built the software, when, using which reference inputs, and under what approvals. These provenance assurances are most valuable when they are consistent across releases and traceable in a form that can be verified without privileged access to the supplier's pipeline.

Signature verification and artifact attestation should be treated as operational controls rather than ceremonial gestures. Suppliers must rotate and protect signing keys, publish revocation procedures, and provide customers a reliable method for retrieving valid public keys and verifying signatures offline. Attestations that bind builds to source and dependency manifests should be immutable, timestamped, and linked to the SBOM so auditors can cross-check content and provenance as a single narrative. If a supplier reissues a build, the new artifact should carry distinct identifiers, updated signatures, and an amended SBOM that explains what changed and why. Ambiguity at this layer undermines rollback certainty and complicates incident response, where minutes often separate containment from crisis.

Supplier attestations are meaningful only when they map to internal control objectives that define acceptable risk. If an objective requires verified component transparency, then receiving an SBOM that omits transitive dependencies does not satisfy the control, regardless of supplier intent. If an objective requires authenticated provenance, a signature without a trustworthy key distribution path is insufficient because the trust anchor is missing. Auditors should design a reliance rubric that describes which supplier artifacts meet each objective, what supplemental evidence is necessary when artifacts are incomplete, and how to record residual assumptions. This translation layer keeps the program from drifting into paperwork compliance and ensures each supplier claim is weighed against the controls the organization must operate.

Dependency risk often hides in fourth-party layers where suppliers embed services or libraries outside their direct control. SBOMs and provenance statements should therefore disclose material upstream providers, including runtime images, package registries, and hosted services that influence build integrity. Auditors should verify that suppliers have their own intake controls for external packages, including verification of checksums, trusted sources, and version pinning to prevent unreviewed drift. When suppliers rely on managed services to distribute updates, the update channel itself becomes an object of assurance, and the supplier should attest to its integrity, authentication, and rollback safeguards. These disclosures allow customers to assess concentration risk and align continuity plans with real upstream dependencies rather than marketing diagrams.

Governance binds these practices into a sustainable operating model and avoids duplication with internal engineering procedures. Vendor management should set expectations for artifact cadence, acceptable reporting lags, and the minimum shelf life of security updates for supported versions, aligning them with internal patch windows and change freezes. Renewals are checkpoints to confirm that SBOM quality, notification performance, and provenance assertions met contractual targets and that deviations were corrected through measured penalties or remediation plans. Significant changes in a supplier's build infrastructure, acquisition of new upstream dependencies, or repeated delays in issuing critical fixes should trigger re-segmentation and heightened oversight. In this way, software supply chain evidence flows directly into tiering, monitoring, and risk acceptance, keeping the focus on verifiable assurances rather than promises about process.

Remediation and Offboarding/Exit Strategies

Remediation represents the most visible measure of a vendor's maturity: how effectively and transparently they correct identified weaknesses. Once an assessment, monitoring signal, or incident exposes a gap, the first task is assigning ownership. Each finding must have both a vendor owner—responsible for implementing the corrective action—and an internal risk owner—accountable for verifying adequacy and timing. Ownership ensures that remediation is not lost in the ambiguity between procurement, security, and operations. Clear designation within the vendor management system, combined with automated reminders and escalation paths, prevents findings from aging without closure. Every remediation plan should define the defect, corrective action, dependencies, responsible parties, and measurable evidence of completion, maintaining traceability from detection to verification.

Timelines for remediation must reflect the severity and potential business impact of the finding. Critical vulnerabilities or control failures that expose sensitive data, privileged access, or operational continuity require immediate containment and near-term resolution, often within days or weeks. Medium-severity findings may allow longer windows if compensating controls mitigate exposure, but they should still include specific deadlines rather than open-ended "next quarter" targets. Low-severity observations, such as documentation or procedural gaps, can align with regular vendor review cycles. Auditors must verify that remediation timelines are not only established but enforced; unaddressed critical findings signal governance breakdowns and justify reclassification of the vendor's risk tier. Tracking metrics such as average remediation duration, overdue findings, and closure verification rates provides management visibility into systemic weaknesses across the supply chain.

Verification closes the remediation loop. Completion is not confirmed merely because the vendor claims to have fixed an issue. Evidence must be reviewed by the internal risk function or an independent assessor to ensure the corrective action is both implemented and effective. For technical issues, verification may involve reexamining system configurations, reviewing updated audit reports, or validating that patches were deployed to all affected environments. For procedural or governance issues, auditors may request revised policies, training records, or control testing documentation. Verification should also assess whether the fix prevents recurrence—merely patching a symptom without addressing the root cause is insufficient. The verified closure record then becomes part of the vendor's performance history and informs future diligence depth.

Certain conditions may warrant escalation beyond routine remediation, including failure to meet remediation deadlines, repeated recurrence of similar findings, or lack of transparency during corrective actions. Escalation paths should be predefined and proportional, beginning with formal notices of noncompliance and progressing to executive review, contract amendment, or suspension of activities. Temporary suspension may occur when unresolved vulnerabilities pose immediate risk to confidentiality or availability, or when the vendor cannot provide assurance that their environment is secure following an incident. Termination becomes necessary when the vendor repeatedly breaches contractual obligations, fails to remediate critical weaknesses, or experiences sustained operational degradation that endangers business continuity. These thresholds should be codified in policy to prevent arbitrary decision-making under pressure.

Secure offboarding—or exit management—demands the same rigor as onboarding, yet it is often neglected until urgency forces improvisation. The first step is to preserve business continuity while orchestrating a controlled disengagement. Transition plans should designate backup suppliers or in-house capabilities capable of absorbing critical services. Key deliverables must be identified early: complete data extracts in agreed formats, final SBOMs or inventory lists, outstanding remediation evidence, and handover of documentation relevant to future audits or regulatory inquiries. A coordinated plan reduces the chaos of last-minute recovery and ensures continuity of operations without exposing data or access to unnecessary risk. Table 14.3 ensures a controlled vendor exit with verifiable evidence and clear ownership across security legal and operations.

Data return and destruction form the cornerstone of a secure exit. Vendors should be required to return all customer data within a defined window using approved transfer mechanisms and to provide written certification of complete data deletion once obligations are fulfilled. Certificates

Table 14.3 Offboarding evidence checklist and accountability.

Exit activity	Evidence artifact	Responsible party	Verification step
Data return	Final data extract receipt with hash	Vendor owner and legal	Reconcile format and hash to request
Data destruction	Certificate of deletion referencing systems	Vendor compliance	Validate backups and replicas included
Credential revocation	Account and key revocation log	Internal security operations	Confirm tokens and federation trusts removed
Access teardown	VPN and network rule removal record	Network team and vendor ops	Review change tickets and timestamps
Subprocessor termination	Written confirmation of downstream revocation	Vendor management	Match to subprocessor inventory
Escrow release	Escrow access confirmation or release notice	Legal and continuity owner	Open escrow package usability check
Transition support	Documented handover and dual run results	Business owner and vendor lead	Verify cutover results and rollback plan
Monitoring deactivation	Alert rule and watchlist removal record	TPRM and security monitoring	Confirm vendor no longer in dashboards
Final financial hold	Approval to release last payment after checks	Procurement and finance	Validate prerequisites satisfied

should reference specific systems, storage media, and backup repositories covered by the destruction event, signed by an authorized officer or compliance lead. Auditors should review these certificates and, when feasible, validate deletion through spot checks or attestation from subservice providers. Retained logs or forensic evidence required for legal or regulatory purposes must be documented and securely stored until expiration of retention requirements. The goal is a clean separation where no residual data or cryptographic material lingers outside the organization's control.

Credential revocation and access teardown are equally critical to preventing postcontract exposure. The organization must maintain a centralized inventory of vendor accounts, API keys, certificates, and shared secrets to enable immediate revocation upon termination. Vendors should be contractually obligated to confirm removal of all access to systems, portals, and data repositories, including those managed by subprocessors. Revocation events should be logged, timestamped, and validated by internal IT or security teams to ensure closure. This includes disabling VPN tunnels, revoking identity federation trust relationships, and invalidating tokens embedded in automation scripts or integrations. Delays in this process represent one of the most common vectors for post-offboarding breaches.

Escrow and continuity obligations come into play when vendors provide mission-critical technology or hold proprietary assets necessary for ongoing operations. Contracts should specify whether source code, encryption keys, or configuration files are to be placed in escrow with a trusted third party, to be released under defined conditions such as insolvency or sustained service interruption. During offboarding, these materials provide the foundation for rebuilding or transitioning services to alternate providers. Auditors should confirm escrow currency, validate release triggers, and verify that escrowed materials are complete and usable—not just symbolic placeholders. This practice reduces dependence on vendor goodwill and ensures recoverability under adverse conditions.

Transition risk management ensures that operations continue smoothly during vendor replacement or service migration. A detailed continuity plan should outline sequencing, testing, rollback options, and communication protocols among business owners, procurement, IT, and risk management teams. Dual-running arrangements, where both the outgoing and incoming vendors operate in parallel for a limited period, can minimize downtime and provide real-world validation of data integrity and performance. Internal teams should conduct focused risk assessments to identify residual vulnerabilities introduced by temporary overlap—such as data duplication or inconsistent access controls—and apply compensating measures until full cutover is achieved.

Governance during remediation and offboarding is the final guardrail that ensures closure activities meet both contractual and policy standards. Vendor management offices should maintain a formal checklist for exit activities, assign accountability for each task, and require sign-offs from security, legal, and operations before declaring the vendor relationship fully closed. Periodic audits should verify that terminated vendors no longer appear in access logs, payment systems, or data inventories. Lessons learned from each exit—particularly from difficult transitions—should feed into continuous improvement of onboarding templates, contract clauses, and risk tiering models. When remediation and offboarding are managed as deliberate, auditable processes rather than administrative afterthoughts, the organization achieves a complete life cycle of third-party control that extends from initial risk identification to secure disengagement without compromise.

Evidence Locations: Procurement/TPRM Systems, Contracts, and Assurance Repos

Evidence management is the connective tissue of third-party assurance, transforming individual risk activities into a defensible audit trail. In mature organizations, every piece of vendor-related evidence—from risk scoring to termination certificates—resides in a structured system of record with defined provenance, retrieval procedures, and retention boundaries. The goal is to enable independent re-performance of the entire assurance life cycle without reconstructing it from scattered emails or file shares. Auditors and examiners should be able to trace the lineage of a decision—why a vendor was classified at a certain tier, what diligence supported that decision, and how remediation or exit actions were executed—by reviewing time-bounded, exportable artifacts that document who collected them, when, and from where.

The procurement or enterprise resource planning (ERP) system typically anchors the vendor inventory, providing the authoritative list of suppliers and mapping each to its owning business unit, service category, and risk tier. This inventory serves as the entry point for any assurance review, linking contract identifiers, purchase order numbers, and system access requests to the vendors they support. Each record should include the vendor's unique ID, segmentation tier, and onboarding date, with change logs showing updates to tiering decisions or ownership transfers. Auditors rely on this system to confirm completeness—every active relationship must appear in the inventory—and accuracy—each entry must align with risk tiering criteria defined by policy. Without a reliable inventory baseline, no downstream evidence chain can be trusted.

Contracts and amendments form the second layer of proof, connecting commercial obligations with security and compliance expectations. These documents reside in a centralized contract management repository that interfaces with procurement systems. Each contract record should reference the vendor ID, include a searchable copy of executed agreements and subsequent amendments, and record key metadata such as effective dates, renewal terms, and security clause presence. When exceptions to standard clauses are approved, those approvals and compensating control justifications must be stored as attachments or linked records. Time-stamped approval workflows provide provenance showing who authorized deviations and when, establishing accountability. During audits, reviewers can reconcile these timestamps with risk tier changes or monitoring results to confirm that contract governance evolved appropriately with vendor risk.

Assurance repositories contain the heart of third-party evidence: diligence and monitoring artifacts. These include SOC reports, SIG or CAIQ questionnaires, ISO or PCI certifications, risk assessment notes, meeting minutes, and correspondence confirming remediation status. Each artifact should be linked to its corresponding vendor record and labeled with metadata indicating artifact type, coverage period, collection date, and collector identity. Version control ensures that only the most current attestation is used for evaluation while preserving historical copies for trend analysis. When auditors sample a vendor's file, they must be able to determine exactly when each artifact was obtained, who retrieved it, and which assurance conclusions were drawn from it. Properly configured repositories eliminate ambiguity between "when the vendor produced evidence" and "when the organization reviewed it," a distinction critical for compliance examinations.

Continuous monitoring outputs form the living feed of vendor assurance and must integrate with the assurance repository to maintain chronological integrity. These outputs include automated security ratings, regulatory watchlist hits, sanctions screening results, and incident alerts, along with corresponding analyst reviews or escalation notes. Systems should timestamp each signal's ingestion and each analyst's validation or commentary. When a trigger leads to reassessment or escalation, the evidence trail must show both the triggering data and the decision that followed. This structure allows auditors to reconstruct not just that monitoring occurred but how signals influenced oversight actions, closing the loop between passive observation and active risk management.

Remediation and exit records complete the life cycle. Once findings are identified, tracking systems should capture remediation plans, status updates, and closure evidence—such as patched version confirmations or verified policy updates—linked directly to the original assessment that generated the finding. Upon offboarding, secure exit documentation (data return certificates, credential revocation logs, destruction attestations, escrow verification, and transition plans) should be stored in the same repository under the vendor's profile. Each record should include submission and approval timestamps, along with digital signatures or user IDs of those performing and verifying the actions. This continuity ensures that every vendor's file tells a complete story from onboarding to offboarding, without detached evidence silos.

Relationships among these evidence sources must be bidirectional and navigable. A reviewer starting at the contract should be able to trace to its linked risk assessment and assurance artifacts, view monitoring signals that influenced renewal decisions, and confirm that all required offboarding documents are in place if the relationship has ended. Conversely, starting from a finding in a monitoring report, one should be able to navigate back to the specific contract clause it violated or to the vendor's last SOC report that failed to address the risk. Building and maintaining these relationships requires tight system integration between procurement, contract management, and third-party risk management (TPRM) platforms, often through APIs or data warehouses that synchronize vendor IDs and metadata daily.

Exportability is a defining characteristic of credible evidence systems. During audits or regulatory reviews, the organization must be able to produce a complete, time-bounded snapshot of all artifacts relevant to a specific vendor or reporting period. This export should include the artifact's filename, type, version, collection timestamp, and collector's identity to establish provenance. Each export event should itself be logged, recording who generated it and when, so that future reviewers can validate that evidence was not altered post hoc. Ideally, evidence exports are digitally signed or accompanied by checksum manifests that verify file integrity over time. These features provide the forensic assurance necessary for independent re-performance and regulatory defense.

Provenance and chain-of-custody controls ensure evidence credibility long after it is collected. Systems should automatically record metadata showing who uploaded or modified each artifact, with immutable audit logs capturing every access, download, or deletion event. Retention policies should align with both regulatory requirements and the life cycle of vendor relationships, preserving at least one full cycle beyond offboarding. When older evidence is purged, summary logs should remain to prove compliance with retention rules. The same rigor applied to production systems—versioning, access control, encryption, and integrity verification—must extend to evidence repositories, since they represent the organization's formal record of due diligence.

Governance over these interconnected evidence sources sustains reliability and readiness for scrutiny. The TPRM governance function should perform quarterly evidence completeness checks, sampling vendors across tiers to confirm that each phase of the life cycle—contract, assurance artifacts, monitoring results, and exit documentation—is properly linked and current. Findings from these meta-audits inform process improvements, such as automated reminders for expiring reports or mandatory upload steps at renewal. By institutionalizing this governance, the organization prevents the slow decay of data integrity that undermines assurance credibility. When evidence systems are treated as first-class assets, complete with provenance, linkage, and export controls, auditors gain a transparent, verifiable chain of proof capable of withstanding independent re-performance and external examination.

Conclusion

Mastering third-party and supply-chain assurance is critical for sustaining trust in complex, data-driven enterprises. The audit function must extend its scrutiny beyond internal controls to encompass the ecosystems that enable modern business operations. Each vendor, integrator, and software supplier represents both a dependency and a potential point of compromise. The discipline of verifying how these external entities handle data, maintain security controls, and respond to incidents defines the credibility of the enterprise itself. In this sense, third-party risk management is not a peripheral compliance activity—it is a central pillar of operational resilience and security governance.

This chapter reinforces the role of structured assurance in securing AI environments at scale. As organizations incorporate machine learning platforms, external APIs, and model-as-a-service providers, the traditional boundaries of control vanish. Auditors must therefore validate not only that suppliers are compliant, but that the chain of custody—from data sourcing to model deployment—remains verifiable and tamper-resistant. The frameworks, evidence models, and monitoring strategies discussed here provide the foundation for measuring that integrity. They ensure that risk decisions are grounded in evidence rather than assumptions, enabling leadership to maintain confidence in systems that depend on distributed, intelligent infrastructure.

With these foundations in place, professionals are better equipped to build adaptive, transparent, and defensible assurance programs that evolve with the threat landscape. While technologies and service models will continue to change, the strategic intent remains consistent: to maintain accountability across every entity that contributes to the organization's digital operations. Third-party and supply-chain security auditing unites governance, architecture, and continuous oversight into a single, traceable discipline—one that defines the organization's ability to withstand disruption without losing control of its obligations or its integrity.

Auditor Recommendations

1. **Validate Vendor Segmentation:** Confirm that vendor tiering decisions are supported by documented criteria such as criticality, data sensitivity, connectivity, and operational dependency. Review the scoring logic, ownership approvals, and re-segmentation triggers to ensure they are consistently applied. This practice allows auditors to verify that diligence depth and monitoring cadence truly align with each vendor's risk level.
2. **Assess Diligence Depth Alignment:** Evaluate whether the level of due diligence performed matches the assigned risk tier and business dependency. For critical suppliers, verify that evidence reviews, walkthroughs, and approval steps are conducted at the appropriate frequency and depth. Auditors should ensure that tiering outputs directly drive audit scope and monitoring intensity.
3. **Examine Contractual Control Enforcement:** Inspect vendor contracts to ensure essential clauses—security requirements, breach notification, subprocessor management, audit rights, and data return—are not only present but demonstrably enforced. Request proof of exercised audit rights, documented notifications, or data destruction certifications. Testing enforcement ensures contracts function as active control mechanisms rather than static legal formalities.
4. **Analyze Assurance Artifacts for Reliance Boundaries:** Review SOC reports, certifications, and standardized questionnaires critically to identify scope gaps, carve-outs, and complementary user-entity controls. Determine where those limitations transfer responsibility back to the organization's internal controls. Proper analysis prevents overreliance on external attestations and strengthens assurance judgments.
5. **Test Continuous Monitoring Governance:** Verify that ongoing monitoring includes multiple signal types—questionnaires, security ratings, incident disclosures, and financial indicators—and that these are reviewed on a defined schedule. Confirm escalation thresholds, analyst validation, and documentation of resulting actions such as tier adjustments or reassessments. Consistent governance ensures monitoring is actionable, not merely observational.
6. **Confirm Escalation and Trigger Effectiveness:** Review how alerts and events translate into formal escalations, reassessments, or suspensions. Examine sampled cases to ensure escalation paths followed policy-defined thresholds and that timing and approvals were recorded. This validation demonstrates whether the oversight program responds proportionally and consistently to emerging risks.
7. **Evaluate Supply Chain Transparency Evidence:** Examine the availability and quality of SBOMs, patch notifications, and provenance attestations provided by software suppliers. Confirm that these artifacts are versioned, signed, and reconciled with vulnerability data to support traceability. Testing transparency at this level validates the integrity of software components and supplier accountability.
8. **Audit Remediation Closure Processes:** Review how remediation findings are tracked from identification to verified completion, ensuring both vendor and internal ownership are documented. Check for supporting evidence—such as patched versions or updated procedures—and ensure overdue issues trigger escalation. Verified closure confirms that audits produce measurable security outcomes.

9. **Review Offboarding and Exit Controls:** Assess whether the vendor exit process includes verifiable evidence of data return or destruction, credential revocation, and subprocessor termination. Confirm that each step is documented, approved, and stored in the vendor's record. Auditing offboarding ensures the organization retains control of its data and systems after contractual relationships end.
10. **Verify Evidence Provenance and Re-performance Capability:** Ensure that all artifacts—contracts, assessments, monitoring outputs, and remediation records—are stored in a central repository with metadata showing who collected them, when, and from what source. Test that evidence exports are complete, time-bounded, and version-controlled. Provenance verification enables independent re-performance and strengthens the defensibility of the auditor's conclusions.

Chapter Questions

1. Which set best represents the primary dimensions used to segment vendor risk?
   A. Criticality, data sensitivity, connectivity, operational dependency
   B. Contract value, vendor headcount, marketing reach, brand reputation
   C. Programming language, code style, logo usage, office locations
   D. License type, server color, ad spend, website theme

2. What is the core purpose of a right-to-audit clause in vendor agreements?
   A. To guarantee service uptime through financial penalties
   B. To shift all incident liability to the vendor regardless of cause
   C. To provide authority to verify controls via documents or assessments over time
   D. To set pricing tiers based on security maturity

3. In an SOC 2 report, what do complementary user-entity controls (CUECs) primarily signify?
   A. Extra controls the vendor plans to add next year
   B. Controls the auditor tested at the vendor's subservice organizations
   C. Exceptions the service auditor carved out from scope
   D. Responsibilities the customer must operate for vendor controls to remain effective

4. When an SOC report uses a carve-out for a subservice organization, what should the auditor do to close the assurance gap?
   A. Accept the gap if the vendor is well-known in the market
   B. Obtain the subservice organization's attestation or equivalent evidence
   C. Reclassify the vendor to the lowest risk tier
   D. Skip testing until the next renewal period

5. What governance action should occur when vendor questionnaires become stale or overdue?
   A. Trigger escalation or re-segmentation and require updated attestations
   B. Archive the old questionnaire and wait for the next annual cycle
   C. Replace the questionnaire with a marketing case study
   D. Reduce the monitoring cadence to avoid alert fatigue

6. Which event most clearly meets escalation thresholds for immediate review or suspension consideration?
   A. A vendor's quarterly newsletter announcing a new feature
   B. A minor website typo reported by customers
   C. A single failed login attempt from an employee account
   D. Appearance on a sanctions or denied-parties list for the vendor entity

7. What is the primary value of a supplier-provided SBOM for the consuming organization?
   A. It eliminates the need for vulnerability management
   B. It replaces all contractual security clauses
   C. It enables component-level visibility to map vulnerabilities and manage dependency risk
   D. It guarantees no transitive dependencies are present

8. Which control most directly strengthens build provenance assurance from a supplier?
   A. Publishing a glossy product roadmap
   B. Signing release artifacts and providing attestation metadata linking to source and build inputs
   C. Using a popular programming language
   D. Allowing anonymous downloads of binaries

9. Which practice best verifies remediation closure for a high-severity vendor finding?
   A. Accepting a verbal confirmation from the vendor's account manager
   B. Waiting for the next annual SOC cycle to see if it appears
   C. Reviewing tangible evidence (e.g., patched versions, retested controls) validated by an internal verifier
   D. Downgrading the severity to avoid delays in operations

10. What evidence characteristic is essential to support independent re-performance during an audit of third-party oversight?
    A. Provenance metadata showing who collected each artifact, when, and from which source, with exportable, time-bounded records
    B. A single screenshot of the vendor's homepage
    C. An unsigned spreadsheet with mixed data from multiple vendors
    D. A private email chain stored in a personal mailbox

15

OT/ICS and Critical Infrastructure Audits

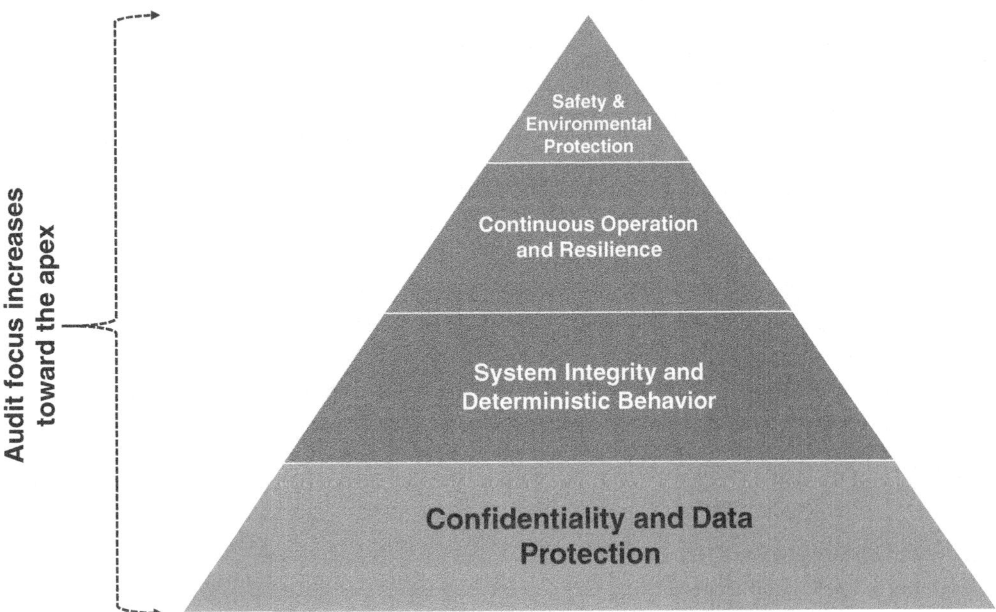

Operational technology and industrial control system (OT/ICS) environments represent the intersection of cybersecurity and physical safety—a domain where risk transcends data loss and enters the realm of human and environmental consequence. Understanding how auditors evaluate these systems is essential in order to maintain trust in critical infrastructure and ensure that digital assurance practices do not inadvertently disrupt the processes that keep societies functioning. Unlike traditional IT audits, where confidentiality dominates the conversation, OT auditing prioritizes safety, availability, and resilience. This chapter examines how these unique imperatives reshape control design, evidence collection, and risk evaluation across the industrial ecosystem.

From zoning and conduit architecture to allowlist enforcement, remote access governance, and change management discipline, this chapter explores how security assurance must adapt to legacy constraints and operational realities. It highlights the engineering logic behind network segmentation, the rigor required for compensating controls when patching is infeasible, and the delicate balance between continuous monitoring and process stability. These concepts form the basis of credible audit evidence—drawings, logs, and procedures that trace safety-critical decisions from design to operation. Each theme underscores the auditor's responsibility to confirm not just technical compliance but also the safe coexistence of cybersecurity with control system reliability.

In an era when cyber threats increasingly target infrastructure that underpins energy, transportation, and manufacturing, mastering OT/ICS auditing is indispensable to any advanced cybersecurity or AI-driven risk program. Modern AI security strategies depend on trustworthy operational data, stable physical processes, and resilient control networks—all of which rely on the sound governance and assurance practices defined here. By integrating regulatory frameworks such as NERC CIP, ISA/IEC 62443, and NIST guidance into field-tested auditing methods, this chapter bridges the gap between compliance, engineering, and risk management. The result is a practical framework for assessing and strengthening the cybersecurity foundations of the systems that power and protect modern life.

Safety and Availability Constraints (Risk Trade-offs)

Operational technology environments operate under a fundamentally different set of priorities than traditional IT systems. In industrial control systems, the first and most important obligation is to protect human life and maintain safe, stable operations. The processes managed by these systems—such as water purification, electrical distribution, or chemical refinement—can have immediate and severe consequences if interrupted or manipulated. A control failure can result not just in data loss, but in physical injury, environmental damage, or public harm. Because of this, decisions about risk in OT environments are dominated by safety and availability concerns, and auditors must understand that these priorities often outweigh confidentiality or even strict integrity requirements.

The emphasis on continuous operation shapes how cybersecurity controls are chosen, implemented, and evaluated. Many control systems run 24 hours a day, often for years, and cannot easily be rebooted, patched, or replaced without disrupting critical services. Stopping a turbine or disabling a process controller to install software updates could introduce more danger than leaving a known vulnerability unpatched. For this reason, compensating controls—such as strict network segmentation, access restrictions, or one-way data transfers—are often used in place of direct remediation. Auditors must recognize that this trade-off is not negligence but a deliberate, risk-informed decision grounded in operational safety.

These priorities also affect what counts as valid evidence during an audit. In a typical IT audit, evidence might include scan results, configuration baselines, or patch reports. In OT audits, however, evidence often takes the form of maintenance logs, system uptime reports, alarm and event records, or process control data that show consistent and safe operations. Auditors may rely more heavily on interviews with control engineers and review of change management documentation to understand how risk is managed without interrupting the system. The goal is not to prove absolute compliance with IT norms but to confirm that the organization's security posture effectively supports safe, reliable operation.

Availability, in this context, is more than just system uptime—it is the assurance that critical functions will continue uninterrupted to prevent hazardous conditions. For example, a power grid control center must maintain continuous command and monitoring capabilities even during cyber incidents. The failure of a single programmable logic controller might shut down an entire process line, creating cascading effects across a region. Therefore, redundancy, deterministic network design, and clearly defined failover procedures are all critical elements that auditors must verify. A well-audited OT system demonstrates resilience not by how quickly it shuts down in response to threats, but by how reliably it continues to operate under controlled and safe conditions.

Environmental impact is another factor that heavily influences OT risk decisions. A cybersecurity event in a water treatment plant or chemical facility can lead to contamination, pollution, or the release of hazardous materials. This potential harm requires auditors to view cybersecurity through a broader ethical lens—one that includes environmental stewardship and public trust. A well-designed control system balances safety interlocks, environmental protections, and cybersecurity safeguards so that no single layer undermines the others. When safety and cybersecurity intersect, the principle of "do no harm" becomes the guiding force for control evaluation.

Auditors must also recognize that traditional confidentiality-driven controls may not always apply or may need adaptation. Encryption and authentication, while important, can introduce latency that disrupts time-critical control signals. Continuous monitoring tools that perform active scanning or packet injection can overload fragile legacy devices. Instead, auditors should look for passive monitoring, network zoning, and whitelisting approaches that secure communications without impairing the deterministic timing essential for control logic. The success of these measures lies in their ability to integrate seamlessly into an environment where every millisecond and every command can affect physical safety.

Residual risk in OT/ICS systems must be described in a way different from in IT environments. It is not enough to quantify financial loss or downtime; the auditor must consider risks to life, safety, and public welfare. For example, leaving a system unpatched might carry a higher residual cyber risk, but applying that patch might risk system instability that endangers operators or damages equipment. The auditor's task is to assess whether the organization has documented, justified, and mitigated those risks appropriately. This includes verifying that operational procedures, training, and safety redundancies reduce the likelihood of catastrophic outcomes even if cyber defenses are compromised.

In many cases, OT environments rely on "defense in depth" that blends engineering and cybersecurity controls. Safety instrumented systems, for example, provide a last line of defense that operates independently from networked control systems. When auditors assess such environments, they must examine how cybersecurity safeguards complement—not conflict with—these safety systems. This requires coordination between IT security teams, control engineers, and safety officers. The audit must confirm that cyber measures enhance resilience without introducing unsafe dependencies or reducing operator awareness.

The auditor's role in OT and critical infrastructure environments is to evaluate whether the balance between safety, availability, and security is being responsibly managed. Every recommendation, every finding, and every control assessment must account for the physical realities of the environment. The highest standard of security in OT is not one that prevents every intrusion, but one that ensures safe, reliable, and continuous operation in the face of evolving threats. By internalizing this principle, auditors can move beyond checklists and begin to understand the true mission of OT cybersecurity—to protect people, the environment, and the essential services that society depends on.

Zones and Conduits: Network Segmentation for ICS

Network segmentation within industrial control systems is one of the most critical defenses against cascading cyber risk, forming the structural backbone of secure industrial architecture. The ISA/IEC 62443 framework formalized this concept through "zones" and "conduits," which separate and manage communications between logical or physical segments of the control environment. Each zone represents a collection of assets that share a similar security requirement, such as the corporate network, control network, or safety instrumented system. Conduits define and govern the communication pathways between those zones, applying security controls such as firewalls, data diodes, or protocol filters to enforce least privilege between systems. For auditors, understanding this zoning model is essential, as it provides both the foundation for assessing security posture and a roadmap for tracing the movement of data, commands, and trust within an operational environment.

The highest level of segregation typically exists between the corporate IT network and the industrial control system. The corporate network handles administrative functions—email, ERP, and business applications—while the control network manages real-time process operations. Between the two lies a demilitarized zone (DMZ), which acts as a controlled interface where limited data can be exchanged without allowing direct access to sensitive control assets. Within this DMZ, systems such as historians, patch management servers, and remote access gateways often reside, providing one-way or tightly filtered conduits for necessary data flow. A well-designed DMZ enforces unidirectional communication where possible, ensuring that business analytics can pull operational data safely without exposing the control layer to external influence or intrusion.

Deeper within the control environment, additional zones delineate specific operational layers. Level 3 often includes control servers, human–machine interfaces (HMIs), and engineering workstations responsible for coordinating supervisory functions. Level 2 typically hosts programmable logic controllers (PLCs) and distributed control system (DCS) components that execute commands in real time. Level 1 and Level 0 encompass sensors, actuators, and physical interfaces that interact directly with the process itself. Safety instrumented systems (SIS), while closely tied to these lower levels, are typically isolated into their own protected zone. Their mission—to prevent catastrophic events such as overpressure, chemical release, or equipment failure—requires independence from both IT and control logic. Auditors should verify that SIS components remain logically and physically segregated, with no uncontrolled conduits linking them to standard control or business networks. Table 15.1 summarizes common ICS zones conduits controls and evidentiary artifacts that support segmentation assurance.

Table 15.1 ICS zones and conduits overview.

Zone	Typical assets	Allowed protocols	Conduit control	Evidence artifacts
Corporate IT Zone	Email ERP analytics hosts	HTTPS SFTP	Firewall ACL review	Current network diagrams and rule exports
Industrial DMZ	Historians patch servers remote access brokers	HTTPS OPC UA SFTP	Firewall plus brokered services	DMZ build sheets and change tickets
Level 3 Control Zone	HMIs engineering workstations control servers	OPC UA vendor programming channels	Firewall with explicit permits	Annotated conduit diagrams and config baselines

Zone	Typical assets	Allowed protocols	Conduit control	Evidence artifacts
Level 2 Controller Zone	PLCs DCS controllers gateways	Modbus TCP DNP3 OPC UA	Protocol aware filtering	Rule comments with approver and date
Level 1 IO Field Devices	Sensors actuators IO racks	EtherNet IP Profinet vendor fieldbus	Switch ACLs and rate limits	Switch configs with signed reviews
Safety Instrumented System Zone	SIS logic solvers safety relays	Status only one way telemetry	Unidirectional gateway	Diode acceptance test records
External Vendor Access Path	Vendor laptops jump clients toolchains	RDP SSH file transfer as approved	Jump host with recording	PAM approvals and session logs
Enterprise Reporting Conduit	Historian replication to business side	One way data export	Data diode or broker	Export manifests and health alarms
Remote Monitoring Conduit	View only dashboards and alerts	HTTPS read only	Reverse proxy hardening	Access reviews and log samples
Emergency Engineering Conduit	Time bound programming access	Vendor channel as approved	Time boxed firewall rules	Auto removal evidence and tickets

When auditing network segmentation, evidence of proper zoning and conduit enforcement can take several forms. The most direct artifacts are network architecture diagrams, piping and instrumentation diagrams (P&IDs), and ISA/IEC-style zone-and-conduit drawings that visualize segmentation boundaries and communication flows. Supporting evidence includes firewall rule sets, router configurations, and access control lists (ACLs) that enforce the defined boundaries. Configuration management records, change tickets, and network topology maps generated from passive monitoring tools can further confirm whether the implemented architecture aligns with documented intent. In well maintained facilities, these artifacts should tell a consistent story: that traffic between zones is controlled, logged, and minimized, and that every conduit has a documented security purpose.

However, in many brownfield industrial plants—facilities that have evolved over decades—the reality often drifts away from the intended architecture. Over time, legacy systems, vendor maintenance links, and unplanned integrations erode segmentation boundaries. It is common to find firewalls with permissive rules created for temporary troubleshooting that were never removed, or "flat" networks where devices of multiple criticality levels share the same broadcast domain. In some cases, historian servers or remote access gateways are connected directly to control networks without passing through a DMZ. Such drift often occurs gradually, the byproduct of operational pressures to maintain uptime, support remote vendors, or retrofit aging equipment with modern interfaces. For auditors, recognizing these patterns of drift is key to identifying where real-world architecture diverges from policy.

Another frequent source of drift arises from poorly documented network changes and control system expansions. Many plants undergo iterative modernization efforts, adding new PLCs, controllers, or monitoring systems without comprehensive revalidation of the existing segmentation. As a result, new conduits may bypass established controls or share unmanaged switches with critical assets. Field engineers, under pressure to restore operations quickly, may create temporary connections that become permanent over time. Auditors should review not only current configurations but also historical change logs, seeking signs that network boundaries have evolved informally rather than through structured engineering review. Where evidence is incomplete, network traffic captures or passive asset discovery tools can help reconstruct the actual data flows and compare them to the documented design.

An effective audit also assesses the strength of conduits—not just their existence. Firewalls between zones should enforce rule sets based on specific protocols and destination ports, ideally allowing only required industrial traffic such as Modbus TCP or OPC UA between trusted endpoints. Remote access conduits should require multifactor authentication, encrypted tunnels, and clear time-bound authorizations. Where unidirectional gateways are deployed, auditors should confirm that physical enforcement mechanisms truly prevent reverse data flow. The quality of these conduits often determines whether a compromise in one zone can propagate laterally to others. Therefore, control over conduit configuration and change management represents one of the most important indicators of long-term cybersecurity maturity in industrial environments.

In modern ICS designs, zones and conduits are not static constructs but living entities that must evolve as operations and technologies change. Auditors should verify that organizations periodically review and validate their segmentation through network mapping, rule set audits, and configuration baselines. Evidence of a governance process—where engineering, IT, and cybersecurity teams jointly manage and approve changes—demonstrates that zoning is being maintained intentionally rather than reactively. The goal is not merely to document segmentation once, but to preserve it as a continuously enforced principle of operation. When managed properly, zones and conduits create both technical and organizational clarity, allowing complex systems to remain secure, stable, and resilient even as they age.

The auditor's evaluation of zones and conduits reveals far more than a network layout—it reflects the discipline of the organization's cybersecurity culture. A clearly defined and consistently enforced segmentation model signals that safety, reliability, and cybersecurity are being treated as integrated priorities. Conversely, unmonitored conduits, undocumented devices, and boundary erosion signal underlying weaknesses in governance and accountability. By tracing data pathways, verifying enforcement mechanisms, and identifying where architecture has drifted, auditors help operators restore the integrity of their defenses. Network segmentation, when properly implemented, is not simply a control—it is the architecture of trust upon which the safety and stability of critical infrastructure depend.

Allowlist/Whitelist Controls and Remote Access Methods

Positive security models—often called allowlisting—are the default posture for legacy or fragile industrial devices because they reduce system behavior to only what is explicitly known, tested, and required for safe operation. In control networks where timing, determinism, and reliability are paramount, a deny-by-default philosophy prevents the accidental introduction of new binaries, scripts, or network conversations that could destabilize logic execution or overwhelm limited resources. Many controllers and embedded operator stations cannot tolerate kernel hooks, frequent signature updates, or aggressive telemetry, making traditional endpoint tooling impractical or unsafe. Allowlisting sidesteps these constraints by enforcing a stable baseline and by treating any deviation as a fault condition to be investigated through established engineering change control.

For auditors, the key is to verify that the positive model is not aspirational but actively enforced through explicit rules, controlled exceptions, and evidence of operational discipline.

Application allowlisting on human–machine interfaces, engineering workstations, and server nodes works by permitting a precise set of executables, libraries, drivers, installers, and scripts based on cryptographic hashes, digital signatures, publisher rules, or path rules. Enforcement modes should progress from audit-only to full enforcement according to a documented plan, with rollback procedures and maintenance-window scheduling that reflect process safety constraints. Organizations that succeed here maintain "golden images," signed rule bundles, and checksum manifests tied to specific software baselines for each asset type and patch level. Changes to the allowlist are proposed through work orders, tested on offline or lab systems that mirror production, and promoted via controlled deployments with clear back-out criteria. Evidence that convinces an auditor includes exported allowlist rule sets, signature catalogs, image provenance records, change tickets linking approvals to specific hashes, and event logs showing attempted but blocked executions.

Network allowlisting complements application controls by restricting communications to specific protocol, port, and address tuples that map to defined conduits between zones. Rather than permitting broad ranges, well-engineered rule sets name the exact PLC subnets, historians, engineering jump hosts, and supporting services allowed to talk—and only over protocols required for the function, such as OPC UA, Modbus TCP, DNP3, or vendor-specific programming channels. Baselines are derived from passive traffic observation during steady-state operation and validated by control engineers to avoid blocking safety-critical interlocks or adding jitter to time-sensitive flows. The resulting firewall and switch ACLs are explicit, comment-rich, and version-controlled, with dormant "troubleshooting" rules eliminated after use. Artifacts that demonstrate rigor include zone-and-conduit diagrams, annotated firewall configurations, ACL diffs with reviewer sign-off, passive discovery reports used to justify permits, and logs that correlate allowed flows to approved conduits.

Operationalizing allowlists requires life cycle governance that treats rules as engineered products with owners, review cadences, and retirement plans. Every exception should have a defined start date, an expiry, a compensating control if the rule weakens segmentation, and a named asset custodian accountable for cleanup. Testing protocols need to prove that rule changes do not degrade controller scan times, HMI responsiveness, or SIS independence, and that rollback paths exist if performance or safety degrades. Mature programs maintain dependency maps that tie approved binaries and flows to a bill of materials for each asset, enabling rapid impact analysis when a component is updated or retired. Persuasive audit evidence includes governance charters, exception registers with aging metrics, pre-deployment test reports, performance baselines before and after changes, and periodic attestations from engineering leadership.

Remote access in industrial environments is constrained by design to preserve segmentation and to ensure that vendor or administrator activities are observable, accountable, and time-limited. Jump hosts—also known as bastions—located in the industrial DMZ broker all interactive access, forcing users to authenticate into a hardened, monitored system with preloaded toolchains rather than reaching control assets directly. Session policies restrict clipboard use, file transfer methods, and elevation, and they route command and desktop streams through recording and keystroke logging for later review. Administrators and vendors work "through" the jump host, not "around" it, and must align access with approved maintenance windows tied to specific work orders. Evidence that proves this model includes jump host hardening baselines, PAM or directory group membership reflecting role separation, session recording samples, keystroke hashes, and access reports mapped to ticket numbers.

Where access can be reduced to telemetry rather than control, unidirectional gateways—data diodes—provide physical assurance that information exits the control network without a return path. This architecture is well-suited for sending historian trends, alarms, or batch reports to business analytics while preventing inbound commands, malware callbacks, or credential replay. Diode deployments should include heartbeat and health monitoring, fail-safe behavior documentation, and periodic validation tests that demonstrate one-way physics using known-good procedures. Control consoles and programming workstations remain strictly on the protected side, eliminating the need to trust software policy alone for directionality. Auditable artifacts include installation diagrams showing fiber or optical isolation, device serials and firmware inventories, acceptance test records proving no reverse channel, alarm integrations for diode health, and an approved data export manifest listing allowed streams and schemas.

Time-boxed sessions enforce the principle that access exists only for as long as necessary to complete a defined task, and then is automatically revoked. Just-in-time workflows grant ephemeral entitlements via privileged access management, create temporary firewall rules with explicit expirations, and issue one-time credentials or certificates that cannot be reused. Break-glass processes are documented, tightly scoped, and regularly tested, with real-time notification to operations leadership when invoked. Enforcement is verified by demonstrating that expired rules truly disappear, that stale sessions are terminated, and that reentry requires a new approval linked to a maintenance record. Convincing artifacts include PAM approvals with start/stop timestamps, firewall rule histories showing creation and auto-removal, short-lived account audit trails, token issuance logs, and reconciled lists of open sessions against scheduled work.

Vendor access requires additional rigor because external parties may bring tools, drivers, and habits shaped by many customer environments. Strong programs insist that vendors use the site-provided jump host, operate within preapproved toolsets installed on that host, and avoid direct connectivity from vendor laptops to control networks. Any tool additions follow the same allowlist life cycle as internal software, with hashes, signatures, and rollback plans, and are removed after the engagement if not needed permanently. Contracts and scopes of work codify these expectations, including obligations to participate in session recording, abide by maintenance windows, and furnish named personnel lists. Evidence comprises vendor access rosters with role mapping, executed maintenance authorizations, toolchain allowlist exception records, post-maintenance summaries comparing planned and actual activities, and attestations that data handling mirrored site policy.

Oversight closes the loop by turning controls into measurable performance. Application and network allowlisting should generate telemetry for both allowed and blocked actions so that trends in denied executions, newly requested flows, and exception growth can be analyzed. Dashboards that highlight aged exceptions, dormant rules, and top blocked binaries help identify drift before it becomes systemic risk, while periodic "rule hygiene" reviews ensure the configuration remains minimal and comprehensible. Session recordings and jump host logs are sampled against a statistically valid plan, with focus on high-risk maintenance, first-time vendors, and emergency changes. Artifacts that satisfy assurance include SIEM use cases tied to allowlist events, review plans and sample results, exception aging reports with remediation notes, and evidence that findings drive timely rule cleanup.

Brownfield realities mean many endpoints cannot host agents or support modern enforcement features, but the positive model still applies when shifted to chokepoints and surrounding assets. For embedded devices, enforce allowlisting at the network layer, lock down the engineering workstation that programs them, and treat any required vendor console as a controlled, prehardened appliance. Where the environment cannot accommodate a desired control without jeopardizing process safety, document the rationale, apply layered compensating measures, and set a plan to revisit when technology or maintenance windows allow. Residual risk statements should connect each accepted exposure to specific compensating controls, review intervals, and safety considerations rather than vague intentions. The artifacts that demonstrate credibility here are explicit risk decisions signed by accountable owners, cross-references to compensating implementations, and evidence that reviews actually retire risks when conditions change.

Patch/Change Realities: Compensating Controls and Windows

In industrial control environments, the notion of timely patching—so foundational in IT security—often collides with the operational realities of continuous production. Many critical systems operate around the clock, supporting processes that cannot be safely stopped without days of preparation, resource coordination, and potential loss of production or service. Shutting down a refinery reactor, power generation turbine, or water treatment system simply to apply a software patch is not a trivial act—it can create safety hazards, environmental risks, or regulatory violations. For this reason, patch management in operational technology (OT) follows a fundamentally different tempo. The emphasis is not on immediacy but on predictability, stability, and safety, ensuring that no change, however small, introduces instability into systems where reliability is paramount.

This operational constraint makes compensating controls an essential component of OT cybersecurity. When a vulnerability cannot be remediated promptly through patching, the organization must demonstrate that alternate safeguards are in place to mitigate the exposure until the next scheduled maintenance window. Network isolation, application allowlisting, strict access control, and physical barriers often serve as these interim controls. The logic is simple but vital: if you cannot remove the vulnerability, you must reduce the avenues through which it could be exploited. For example, if a legacy control server cannot be patched, isolating it within a dedicated VLAN, restricting its communication to essential devices, and monitoring its network behavior continuously can achieve equivalent or greater risk reduction without compromising uptime.

Network segmentation plays a central role in this approach. Firewalls and data diodes between corporate, DMZ, and control zones can contain potential compromise and protect unpatched assets from direct exposure. Within the control network, device-level ACLs and one-way data flows further limit how vulnerabilities can be exploited. Auditors should evaluate not only the presence of these controls but also their enforcement rigor: whether the firewall rules are granular, whether exception requests are formally approved, and whether periodic reviews validate that temporary allowances are closed when no longer needed. Evidence of proper compensating control governance includes documented isolation diagrams, firewall configuration exports with annotated rule sets, and variance logs that link each exception to a specific, time-bound risk acceptance.

Application allowlisting offers another layer of defense, especially for fragile or unpatchable endpoints such as engineering workstations or legacy HMIs. By permitting only authorized binaries and scripts to execute, these systems remain protected even when known vulnerabilities exist in the operating system or installed software. An auditor should look for signed allowlist rule sets, configuration baselines, and change logs showing who authorized and tested modifications. In many mature facilities, these allowlist configurations are version-controlled and reviewed during each maintenance cycle. This demonstrates that while patching may be delayed, compensating controls are not static—they evolve in sync with operational and threat landscape changes. Table 15.2 maps deferred patch risks to rigorously governed compensating controls and audit evidence.

Table 15.2 Compensating controls when patching is deferred.

Compensating control	Risk addressed	Verification evidence	Review cadence
Network isolation	Exposure of vulnerable service	Firewall config export with approver	Monthly
Application allow listing	Unauthorized code execution	Allow list rule export with change ID	Per change
Jump host access control	Uncontrolled remote access	Session recordings and access reports	Per session
Unidirectional gateway	Inbound command injection	One way test record and device serials	Quarterly
Time boxed session	Privilege persistence after task	PAM approval with start stop timestamps	Per access
Variance approval record	Unmanaged patch deferral	Signed variance with expiry and owner	Weekly board review
Maintenance window schedule	Unsafe ad hoc change	Approved outage plan with test steps	Per window
Physical access restriction	Direct tampering of endpoint	Access logs and cabinet seals	Monthly
Network allow list tuning	Excess protocol exposure	Rule diffs with reviewer sign off	Per change
Enhanced monitoring	Silent exploitation attempt	SIEM use cases tied to blocked events	Monthly

Physical barriers also play a part in mitigating the risks of delayed patching. Locked cabinets, port-blocking devices, removable media restrictions, and supervised access to engineering stations all reduce the chance that an unpatched system could be tampered with directly. In high-sensitivity environments, portable media are subject to scanning or quarantine before entering the network, and maintenance laptops are pre-imaged from known baselines before being allowed on-site. These procedural and physical safeguards create a protective layer around vulnerable systems, ensuring that even human factors are accounted for. Evidence supporting these controls may include physical security logs, media scanning reports, and access authorization records tied to maintenance activities.

Maintenance windows are the linchpin that reconciles cybersecurity with production continuity. Unlike the ad hoc patch cycles common in IT, OT environments operate on carefully orchestrated maintenance schedules—sometimes quarterly, semiannual, or even annual—when systems can be safely powered down, validated, and brought back online. These windows are planned months in advance, aligning with operational, safety, and vendor availability constraints. During these periods, patches, firmware upgrades, and configuration updates are applied in a staged, test-driven manner. Auditors should expect to see maintenance window schedules, patch approval documentation, pre- and post-implementation test results, and change management tickets that reference both cybersecurity and process safety validation steps.

Variance approvals formalize the decision to defer a patch or system update beyond its typical window. These approvals should be risk-based and supported by documented justification, outlining both the technical reason for deferral and the compensating measures in place. A credible variance form specifies the affected asset, the known vulnerability, the risk rating, the next feasible patch opportunity, and the interim protections deployed. Senior engineering or cybersecurity leadership typically signs these documents, ensuring that deferrals are conscious, accountable decisions—not silent compromises. Evidence that supports this rigor includes completed variance forms, risk acceptance statements, and closure reports demonstrating that deferred actions were completed as planned during the next maintenance window.

The governance structure behind these controls is as critical as the controls themselves. A patch management board or change advisory committee—often including representatives from engineering, operations, and cybersecurity—should review open variances, track upcoming maintenance opportunities, and ensure compensating controls remain effective over time. The meeting minutes, risk dashboards, and aging reports of outstanding variances are valuable artifacts for auditors to assess whether this governance process is functioning effectively. The presence of expired variances or long-lived exceptions without review is a clear indicator of control weakness and should trigger follow-up inquiry.

Auditors should also evaluate how testing and validation are integrated into the change process. In OT, no patch should ever be applied directly to production without first being tested in a representative lab or staging environment. This is especially true for control logic or firmware updates, which can alter timing or command execution behavior. Supporting evidence may include lab test reports, rollback plans, simulation results, and engineering sign-off sheets. These demonstrate that the organization is not only managing change but also actively verifying that updates will not introduce unsafe conditions or downtime.

Patching in OT and critical infrastructure is not an act of neglect but an exercise in balance. The challenge lies in applying security enhancements without compromising the system's fundamental purpose—to operate safely and reliably. The auditor's responsibility is to ensure that this balance is being maintained transparently and with discipline. When patching is deferred, compensating controls must be robust, documented, and periodically tested. When maintenance windows occur, updates must be applied methodically and verified against safety requirements. The strength of an organization's OT cybersecurity posture is measured not by how quickly it patches, but by how responsibly it manages the inevitable delays.

Monitoring and Physical/Environmental Dependencies

Effective monitoring in industrial control environments spans three interrelated domains: the process itself, the alarm and event fabric that coordinates operator action, and the security telemetry that reveals adversary behavior without disrupting determinism. Process monitoring tracks variables such as flow, pressure, temperature, level, and valve positions against engineered ranges and safe operating limits, with trends stored in historians and routinely reviewed for drift, oscillation, or abnormal coupling between loops. Alarm systems convert deviations into operator prompts with priorities, limit settings, and suppression logic designed to surface only those conditions requiring timely intervention. Security telemetry adds a parallel layer—passive network monitoring, controller integrity checks, endpoint whitelisting events, and jump host session logs—that exposes unexpected communication paths or execution attempts. For the auditor, assurance depends on whether these three lenses present a coherent picture, with data lineage, time synchronization, and cross-correlation that can reconstruct what happened and why without guesswork.

A disciplined approach begins with well-defined points lists and alarm rationalization that assign purpose, priority, and response expectations to each annunciation. Auditors should expect to see evidence that alarm setpoints align with engineered safeties, including deadbands to prevent chatter and shelving rules that do not hide genuinely hazardous states. Process trends should demonstrate that control loops remain stable during normal load and during credible disturbances, and that operators can trace excursions to understood causes rather than opaque system behavior. Security monitoring must be tuned to industrial protocols and asset roles, using passive collection and protocol-aware inspection that will not inject latency into time-sensitive circuits. The connective tissue is time: synchronized clocks across HMIs, controllers, historians, and security sensors allow investigators to stitch together operator actions, interlocks, and network events with minute precision.

Security telemetry in OT favors passive collection and deterministic enforcement rather than aggressive probing. Network sensors at conduit boundaries should baseline normal protocol mixes, station addresses, and polling rates, alerting on new masters, unexpected broadcast storms, or programming mode transitions on controllers. Endpoint monitoring focuses on allowlist denials, driver changes, and configuration file integrity checks rather than heavyweight behavioral analytics that could degrade fragile hosts. Jump hosts and remote access brokers generate high-value records—authentication, privilege elevation, file transfer, and session recordings—that tie human activities to maintenance tickets and work orders. An auditor should validate that these sources feed a central repository with retention appropriate to incident timelines and regulatory expectations, and that alerting thresholds reflect both cyber risk and operational tolerance for noise.

Alarm system quality is a leading indicator of operational resilience, yet it is commonly undermined by nuisance annunciations and poor discipline. When every deviation produces a horn and banner, operators learn to acknowledge rather than investigate, creating the conditions for alarm fatigue where a real emergency is lost in the din. Auditors should sample alarm summary reports for standing alarms that persist across shifts, frequent repeats that indicate unaddressed root causes, and overuse of "shelve" or "suppress" functions without documented risk acceptance. Evidence of a healthy program includes alarm performance metrics, periodic reviews that retire stale points, and records showing that limit changes and alarm logic modifications follow change control with engineering sign-off. The test is pragmatic: does the alarm list teach operators something new and actionable, or does it reiterate what everyone ignores?

Process monitoring must extend beyond simple limit checks to embrace rate-of-change, boundary proximity, and correlation across related variables, because many unsafe evolutions are subtle until they are not. For example, a temperature trending toward a limit during a known start-up sequence may be acceptable, while the same slope at steady state suggests a failing cooling path or misconfigured controller tuning. Auditors should look for routines that compare present behavior to seasonally adjusted baselines, recent maintenance activities, and known transient patterns, rather than treating every deviation as equivalent. Controls engineers should be able to demonstrate how historian views and calculations support early detection, including dashboards that surface incipient faults rather than only hard trips. Where such analytics exist, assurance increases that operators will intervene before alarms cascade and overwhelm their capacity.

Physical and environmental systems interlock with cyber controls in ways that are often underappreciated until failure reveals the coupling. Power quality directly influences controller stability and network equipment behavior; brownouts, harmonics, or transfer events can produce recoveries that look like communication failures or malware to naïve analytics. Heating, ventilation, and air conditioning governs thermal margins for server rooms, switch cabinets, and motor control centers; a failed unit can silently degrade component reliability, introduce throttling, and increase error rates long before temperatures cross absolute limits. Safety instrumented systems operate on separate logic to arrest hazardous states, yet their diagnostic alarms and bypass indicators must be monitored by operations and security so that temporary maintenance modes do not become invisible permanent risk. The auditor's job is to confirm that environmental telemetry, power events, and safety statuses are ingested, time-aligned, and reviewed alongside process and security data.

Run-to-fail tolerances—an accepted maintenance strategy for certain noncritical assets—can erode assurance when their boundaries are vague or their telemetry is weak. If a device is permitted to operate until failure, monitoring must prove that its degradation cannot cascade into a loss of view, loss of control, or unexpected safety demand. Auditors should examine whether assets tagged for run-to-fail are truly isolated, whether spare strategies and switchover procedures are documented and practiced, and whether alarm thresholds reflect the residual risk. Evidence might include dependency maps showing that the failure does not take down shared switches or critical gateways, and test records that demonstrate switchover does not violate scan times or operator situational awareness. Without such guardrails, run-to-fail becomes an unbounded bet that operational luck will hold.

Alarm fatigue also intersects with run-to-fail when chronic device health alarms are normalized and left unresolved. A cooling fan warning in a control cabinet, a UPS battery degradation alert, or intermittent link flaps on a critical switch can become the soundtrack of the plant rather than triggers for action. Over time, operators and engineers may ignore or permanently shelve these signals, converting early-warning telemetry into background noise that masks the onset of genuine hazard. Auditors should request evidence of alarm rationalization for health and diagnostic points, sampling whether recurring health alarms generate work orders, root cause analysis, and closure. Where patterns show acknowledgement without remediation, the monitoring program is teaching the organization to look away at the very moment attention is required.

Assurance strengthens when monitoring functions are designed for cross-domain corroboration, not siloed interpretation. A spike in blocked execution events on an engineering workstation should be checked against maintenance windows, jump host sessions, and process variable stability to distinguish legitimate commissioning from malicious tooling. Power transfer logs, HVAC faults, and safety bypass records should be routinely correlated with cyber alarms to explain transient anomalies without defaulting to the simplest story. Auditors should verify that the organization rehearses these correlations through tabletop exercises and post-incident reviews, generating playbooks that encode data sources, time offsets, and expected patterns. The presence of consistent narratives that can be replayed from telemetry builds confidence that future investigations will be swift and decisive.

Monitoring must be governed like any engineered system, with owners, performance targets, and life cycle care. Point additions, alarm limit changes, and telemetry source onboarding should follow change control, including validation in a staging environment when feasible to avoid destabilizing production displays or SIEM pipelines. Metrics such as alarm rates per hour, ratio of priority alarms to total, mean time to acknowledge, blocked-execution trends, and percentage of time sources are in bypass create a quantitative pulse of system health. Auditors should look for evidence that these metrics drive action: backlog management, alarm redesign, network rule hygiene, or environmental maintenance. Where dashboards exist but drive no decisions, monitoring becomes theater; where dashboards change behavior, monitoring becomes assurance.

Regulatory and Standards Context

For auditors, the most consequential difference among OT regimes is whether the standard is regulatory with prescriptive obligations or voluntary with risk-based discretion. In regulatory contexts, scope and artifacts are defined by rule and enforced by an external body, so sufficiency is largely a matter of conformity and completeness; in voluntary models, sufficiency depends on defensible tailoring and risk rationale. This distinction reshapes testing depth: compliance audits often emphasize objective evidence for every required element, while risk-based assessments focus on whether controls, as implemented, are effective for the stated threats and consequences. The practical implication is that auditors must first anchor their scope to the governing regime, because that decision predetermines what is "in," what records must exist, and how findings translate into obligations, penalties, or improvement plans.

In the North American bulk electric system, NERC Critical Infrastructure Protection (CIP) standards establish mandatory requirements with material penalties for noncompliance, which drives a uniquely rigorous audit posture. Scoping hinges on the registered entity's functions and impact ratings for Bulk Electric System (BES) Cyber Systems, with explicit criteria determining which assets, networks, and processes fall within audit reach. Artifacts are extensive and standardized: documented procedures, implementation evidence, change and access records, logs, technical drawings, and attestations mapped requirement by requirement. Testing depth is granular and traceable, often following specific Reliability Standard Audit Worksheets or similar methods to verify not just that a control exists, but that it operated continuously and as stated over defined audit periods. The audit style is evidentiary and continuity-focused, favoring repeatable demonstrations over narrative justification.

NERC CIP also shapes how auditors examine segmentation, remote access, and vendor interactions, because several requirements prescribe outcomes and recordkeeping that exceed common IT expectations. Expect to validate Electronic Security Perimeters, Intermediate Systems, and protected interactive remote access through artifact trails that cover rule sets, session records, and configuration management with tight change control. Maintenance and patching are examined through defined processes and documented evaluations, including technical feasibility exceptions and risk justifications where strict timelines cannot be met. Personnel risk assessments, training, and access authorization are verified end to end, linking individuals to roles, privileges, and revocation records. The net effect is an audit rhythm oriented to completeness, traceability, and demonstrable operationalization of each requirement, rather than to generalized maturity narratives.

The NIST family provides a complementary, risk-based foundation that many OT organizations adapt for assurance without external enforcement, changing the auditor's emphasis from prescription to justification. NIST's approach centers on categorization, control selection and tailoring, documented implementation, and ongoing assessment, which requires auditors to test the coherence among the System Security Plan, assessment results, and Plans of Action and Milestones. Evidence strength is judged by whether risks are explicitly identified, controls are selected for those risks, and monitoring produces feedback that updates both posture and residual risk statements. In OT contexts, auditors should look for ICS-aware tailoring that explains where integrity and availability outweigh confidentiality, alongside rationale for compensating measures when patching or scanning would jeopardize safety. The quality of the risk narrative and the discipline of continuous monitoring become the primary assurance levers.

For industrial environments specifically, NIST guidance on control systems emphasizes passive discovery, segmentation, access minimization, and change discipline, which modifies how auditors test “coverage.” Rather than requesting invasive scans or proofs that would destabilize fragile assets, auditors evaluate whether the security architecture enforces least functionality through zones, conduits, and tightly scoped remote access. Testing depth focuses on evidence that controls are engineered to respect deterministic timing and fail-safe behaviors, including lab testing, staged rollouts, and rollback plans when changes could impact process safety. Strong programs show alignment between asset criticality, monitoring depth, and incident response playbooks that consider loss of view or loss of control scenarios. The result is an assurance model that privileges safe verifiability over exhaustive probing.

ISA/IEC 62443 reframes scoping and evidence around engineered systems rather than enterprise abstractions, which changes an auditor’s line of inquiry from “policies and endpoints” to “zones, conduits, and life cycle.” Scope begins with the Industrial Automation and Control System (IACS) boundary, decomposed into security zones with defined security levels and conduits that enforce interaction rules. Artifacts include zone-and-conduit drawings, requirement conformance specifications for components and systems, and test records demonstrating that implemented controls achieve the target security levels without undermining process constraints. Testing depth blends design review with implementation sampling: auditors confirm segmentation, verify allowlisted protocols and applications, and inspect interface hardening at the junctions between enterprise, DMZ, control, and safety domains. Assurance is strengthened when suppliers and integrators provide development life cycle evidence that aligns with the standard’s expectations.

A distinctive ISA/IEC implication for audits is the emphasis on supplier and integrator responsibilities across the system life cycle, which expands the artifact set beyond the operator’s internal records. Auditors should expect to see supplier development process evidence, component security specifications, and acceptance test results that demonstrate secure configuration and maintenance practices. Procurement and change processes are evaluated for how they encode security requirements into requests, contracts, and factory acceptance testing, ensuring that security is not retrofitted late in commissioning. Where certification or conformance claims exist, auditors validate scope, version, and applicability to the actual deployed configuration, not merely the product line. This supply-chain visibility provides assurance that systemic weaknesses are not imported through vendor defaults or undocumented features.

ISO/IEC information security management standards often appear in OT organizations as enterprise governance overlays, and their audit implications are chiefly about consistency and control of process rather than technical depth. When applied to operational environments, they drive evidence of risk management cadence, policy-to-control traceability, internal audit cycles, corrective actions, and leadership oversight. Auditors evaluate whether the management system binds engineering, operations, and cybersecurity into a single change and incident framework, including how exceptions are approved, tracked, and retired. While these standards do not prescribe the OT-specific technical controls, they require that such controls be systematically selected, measured, and improved. The presence of a coherent management system often predicts better documentation, cleaner handoffs between teams, and fewer ungoverned exceptions.

Across these regimes, scoping precision is the first audit milestone because it determines the boundary of evidence and the rules of engagement for testing. In electric sector compliance, scoping missteps can cascade into missed requirements and exposure to penalties; in risk-based frameworks, poor scoping produces hollow narratives where critical interfaces evade scrutiny. Effective auditors reconcile asset inventories, network drawings, safety system independence, and vendor access paths to confirm that declared scope matches operational reality. Artifacts that carry the most weight are those that tie design intent to operating evidence—change logs that match drawings, firewall exports that match conduit definitions, and maintenance records that match risk acceptances. This alignment anchors findings in facts rather than assumptions.

Evidence Locations: ICS Diagrams, Change Logs, Site Procedures, and Operator Logs

Canonical proof in operational technology environments rests on artifacts that are authoritative, time-bound, and attributable, allowing an independent party to reconstruct both the design intent and the operating reality. Auditors should insist on dated and signed materials, preserved in a controlled repository with clear version lineage, because the same document family—diagram, log, or procedure—may exist in multiple drafts or field-marked variants. Provenance matters as much as content: each item must indicate its system of record, the author or approver's role, and the conditions under which it was produced, whether during commissioning, outage testing, or routine operations. Assurance strengthens when these artifacts can be correlated across sources and timescales, forming a chain of evidence from engineering design through operational execution that supports independent re-performance without guesswork. The objective is not a pile of attachments but an integrated dossier that demonstrates what the plant is, what changed, who authorized it, and how it behaved.

P&IDs and industrial network/control diagrams are the structural backbone for scoping and verification, but their utility depends on fidelity to the as-built state. Auditors should expect to see zone-and-conduit overlays on control drawings, explicit identification of safety instrumented systems, and callouts for interlocks, fieldbuses, and vendor programming interfaces, each with drawing numbers, revisions, and approval signatures. Differences between "as-designed" and "as-found" must be reconciled through redlines or updated revisions, supported by site-verified markups from walkdowns or commissioning tests. When diagrams include title blocks with revision dates, drafter and approver names, and cross-references to work orders or management of change records, they become traceable anchors for subsequent evidence. Independent re-performance begins by following these drawings to confirm that physical assets, cabling, and logical trust boundaries align with the documented architecture. Table 15.3 shows how authoritative artifacts and metadata support independent re performance and provenance.

Table 15.3 Evidence traceability across OT artifacts.

Artifact type	Primary source of record	Required metadata	Typical cross reference	Re performance method
ICS network diagram	Controlled drawing repository	Revision ID date approver	Firewall export and change ID	Walkdown plus config compare
Piping and instrumentation diagram	Engineering document control	Drawing number revision stamp	Work order and MOC record	Field verification against tags
Management of Change record	Change management system	Unique change ID risk owner	Updated diagrams and configs	Sample end to end package

Artifact type	Primary source of record	Required metadata	Typical cross reference	Re performance method
SOP or site procedure	Operations document control	Effective date version approver	Operator logs and training record	Step comparison to actions
Operator shift log	Control room log system	Timestamp operator name supervisor	Affected assets and tickets	Timeline reconstruction
Alarm history report	Alarm management system	Priority setpoint change notes	Operator actions and limits	Performance metric sampling
Controller configuration export	Vendor approved export	Device ID firmware version hash	Approved logic package and MOC	Diff to prior baseline
Firewall rule export	Configuration repository	Rule set version reviewer date	Zone conduit diagram and ticket	Rule verification on device
Jump host session log	Access broker archive	User role start stop hash	Maintenance window and ticket	Playback and activity match
Traceability matrix	Audit workpapers	Artifact IDs source links owner	All above artifacts	Sampling and link validation

Management of Change and change control logs translate drawings into accountable action and are indispensable for proving that modifications were deliberate, reviewed, and safely executed. Complete records tie a unique change identifier to the affected assets, the engineering rationale, pre-implementation risk assessment, test plans, rollback criteria, and final validation results, all with dates and signatures from engineering and operations. Variance approvals for deferred patches or temporary bypasses should be adjacent to the change package, with explicit expiration dates and compensating controls to contain residual risk. Robust programs link each change to revised drawings, configuration exports, and operator notifications, creating a closed loop from decision to updated evidence. Auditors can re-perform by sampling a change, walking the linked artifacts, and verifying that the plant state now matches the approved intent.

Original Equipment Manufacturer guidance and site procedures or Standard Operating Procedures define the safe envelope of configuration and operation, and they provide the benchmark against which “correctness” is judged. OEM documents should be controlled copies with edition numbers, errata, and applicability to the installed firmware or hardware models, rather than generic marketing literature. Site procedures must show localization from OEM guidance—setpoints, maintenance intervals, and prohibited actions—approved by engineering leadership and operations management, with effective dates and periodic review stamps. Temporary procedures used during outages or commissioning need start and end dates, sign-offs, and evidence that they were withdrawn when conditions normalized. An auditor’s re-performance compares the configuration and operator actions observed in logs against the steps prescribed in these controlled documents to determine alignment.

Operator shift logs and alarm histories demonstrate how the system performed and how people responded, providing the behavioral complement to design and change records. High-quality logs record shift handovers, abnormal conditions, equipment status, bypasses, and maintenance activities with timestamps synchronized to plant time sources, plus the operator’s name or badge and supervisor countersignature when needed. Alarm histories should include priorities, acknowledgment times, shelving events, and any limit changes, enabling assessment of alarm discipline and identification of alarm fatigue patterns. When these records reference work orders or change identifiers, they become navigational beacons that help stitch the story of an event across systems. For re-performance, auditors correlate operator entries and alarm sequences with historian trends and security events to validate that responses followed approved procedures and produced the expected outcomes.

Configuration and state exports from control systems capture the authoritative technical truth at a point in time and are critical to validate that devices are configured as claimed. Useful exports include controller and safety logic, tag databases, HMI project files, engineering workstation allowlists, firmware inventories, historian point lists, network device configurations, and ACLs, each produced through read-only or vendor-approved methods to avoid altering state. Exports should be labeled with device identity, software versions, export tooling and options, and a cryptographic hash or checksum to attest integrity, stored in a versioned repository with access controls. Where direct exports are impossible, signed screenshots or vendor-generated reports must be accompanied by a method description and reviewer attestation to compensate for weaker provenance. Auditors re-perform by loading samples into vendor or lab tools, executing diff comparisons against prior baselines, and confirming that changes align with approved packages.

The most convincing assurance emerges when these sources are explicitly linked, creating a bidirectional map from design intent to operational evidence. A network diagram's conduit rules should point to firewall configuration exports and to a change ticket that introduced or modified them; the change ticket should reference updated drawings and operator notifications; the operator log should reflect the maintenance window and any transient alarms; the alarm history should show acknowledgment and recovery within expected limits; and a post-change configuration export should confirm steady-state conformance. This relational integrity can be formalized in a traceability matrix that lists artifact types, unique identifiers, dates, approvers, and cross-references, making sampling efficient and defensible. Such linkage not only streamlines audits but also enables the plant to self-diagnose drift before it becomes risk. Independent re-performance is then a matter of following the links rather than reconstructing context from memory.

Provenance and authenticity determine whether evidence is persuasive, so controls must make tampering or ambiguity improbable. Document control systems should enforce check-in/check-out with immutable version histories, electronic signatures bound to identities, and audit trails that show who viewed or modified each item and when. Time synchronization across HMIs, controllers, historians, and security tooling allows disparate logs to be aligned, preventing false narratives born of clock skew; evidence of NTP sources, offset monitoring, and drift alerts adds credibility. For digital artifacts, cryptographic hashes, export metadata, and repository checksums protect integrity; for paper or whiteboard markups, scan quality, witness countersignature, and "field-verified" stamps with dates and names provide site-verified authenticity. Auditors should prefer primary sources over derivative summaries, accepting screenshots only when accompanied by attestations and retrieval steps sufficient for replication.

Brownfield realities mean diagrams and inventories inevitably lag the plant, so reconciliation practices must convert discovery into durable truth. Periodic walkdowns, photographed cabinet interiors with asset tags, and passive network discovery snapshots should drive formal updates to drawings and inventories, each update tied to a change record and approver signature. Discrepancy logs should capture every mismatch between documents and reality, assign owners, and record closure dates, ensuring that "as-found" conditions become "as-built" documentation rather than lingering tribal knowledge. Where legacy systems cannot produce clean exports, site-verified narratives—maintenance worksheets, vendor service reports, and operator affidavits—fill gaps temporarily, but must carry expiry dates and plans to replace them with stronger evidence. Auditors gain confidence when they see this reconciliation cadence functioning and producing measurable reduction in discrepancies over time.

Independent re-performance depends on sampling strategies that start with artifacts and end with observable system behavior. An auditor may select a recent conduit rule change, retrieve the approved firewall export, verify the rule exists with correct parameters, correlate the maintenance window in operator logs, and examine alarm histories and process trends to confirm no unintended consequences occurred. For a controller logic update, the auditor can confirm the approved logic package, validate signatures and checksums, check operator notifications and bypass records, and compare pre- and post-implementation historian data for expected signatures, such as scan time stability or interlock behavior. Throughout, the presence of dated, signed artifacts with site-verified provenance reduces reliance on interviews and memory, converting assurance into a repeatable set of tests. When each step can be re-performed from controlled sources, confidence rises that the plant's documented posture matches its lived reality.

Conclusion

Mastering the principles of OT and ICS auditing is critical for professionals tasked with safeguarding systems that directly influence public safety, industrial reliability, and national resilience. The auditor's challenge is not simply to confirm the presence of controls, but to understand how those controls function under the constraints of continuous operation and physical consequence. By approaching assurance through the lens of engineered risk, cybersecurity professionals learn to evaluate not only digital defenses but also the interdependencies that define operational safety. This mindset elevates auditing from checklist compliance to a discipline rooted in system integrity and human protection.

While the technical specifics of segmentation, allowlisting, and compensating controls may differ across industries, the strategic intent remains consistent—to achieve security without compromising the mission of control systems. Effective auditors cultivate fluency in both engineering language and cybersecurity frameworks, allowing them to interpret evidence, validate safety assumptions, and identify risks that transcend traditional IT boundaries. Their insight connects network behavior with process dynamics, ensuring that findings are actionable, context-aware, and aligned with operational goals. This integration of technical accuracy and situational awareness defines excellence in OT assurance.

For AI and advanced analytics to operate safely within critical infrastructure, they must rely on trustworthy, resilient, and well-governed control environments. The lessons in this chapter reinforce that assurance is not a static artifact but a living system of oversight, one that blends engineering rigor with cybersecurity discipline. With these foundations in place, professionals are better equipped to evaluate AI-enabled operations, manage cyber-physical risk, and strengthen the resilience of the systems that sustain modern society.

Auditor Recommendations

1. **Prioritize Safety and Availability in Risk Assessment:** Treat human safety, environmental protection, and operational continuity as the foremost considerations in every OT audit. Recognize that traditional confidentiality-first approaches from IT environments do not directly apply when physical processes are at stake. Structure your audit questions and evidence expectations around how controls preserve stability and prevent unsafe states. This mindset ensures that cybersecurity remains a means to protect operations, not a disruption to them.
2. **Establish and Validate Network Segmentation Using Zones and Conduits:** Evaluate the control environment through the ISA/IEC zoning model, confirming that communication between IT, DMZ, control, and safety networks is intentionally restricted. Request current, dated network and control diagrams, and confirm their consistency with firewall configurations and routing rules. Identify drift patterns such as permissive firewall rules or undocumented connections that commonly appear in aging or brownfield facilities. Maintaining clear, enforceable segmentation is one of the strongest indicators of cyber maturity in industrial systems.
3. **Implement and Audit Positive Security Models Through Allowlisting:** Focus on allowlisting as a practical and safer control for legacy or fragile OT assets that cannot tolerate traditional endpoint agents or frequent patching. Verify that allowlist policies are explicitly defined, reviewed, and version-controlled, and that any exceptions are documented and time-bound. Assess whether event logs and rule updates are managed through a formal change control process to ensure accountability. A well-governed allowlist model demonstrates both operational discipline and technical control over system behavior.
4. **Constrain Remote Access Through Layered Oversight:** Require that all external and internal remote sessions pass through secured intermediaries such as jump hosts or unidirectional gateways. Validate that access is granted only during authorized maintenance windows and that all sessions are logged, monitored, and terminated automatically when tasks conclude. Confirm that vendors follow the same remote access pathways as internal personnel, with preapproved toolsets and just-in-time authorization. Tight control over remote access pathways significantly reduces exposure without disrupting necessary operational support.
5. **Audit Patch Management Through Compensating Controls:** When immediate patching is infeasible, verify that compensating safeguards such as isolation, allowlisting, and restricted connectivity are fully documented and regularly reviewed. Examine maintenance schedules to confirm that deferred updates are incorporated into planned outage cycles, with approvals justified through risk-based variance records. Review whether governance committees track open variances and verify closure once systems are safely updated. This structured approach ensures that patch deferrals are deliberate and temporary—not silent gaps in defense.
6. **Correlate Monitoring Data Across Process, Alarm, and Security Systems:** Evaluate how effectively the organization integrates process variables, alarm histories, and security telemetry to create a unified operational picture. Confirm that time synchronization across systems allows for accurate correlation of events and operator responses. Investigate signs of alarm fatigue or "run-to-fail" tolerances that can mask emerging risks. A mature monitoring program enables early detection of cyber-physical anomalies before they escalate into operational or safety incidents.

7. **Assess Physical and Environmental Interlocks in Security Assurance:** Verify that supporting infrastructure such as power systems, HVAC, and safety interlocks are monitored and governed alongside digital controls. Review logs or test records showing that environmental or utility events are captured within the same oversight framework as cybersecurity events. Ensure that safety system status, bypass conditions, and maintenance overrides are logged and reviewed regularly. Integrating physical dependencies into audit scope prevents narrow findings that miss real-world causes of operational disruption.
8. **Align Audit Scope and Depth with Governing Standards:** Identify whether the environment falls under prescriptive regulatory regimes like NERC CIP or voluntary frameworks such as ISA/IEC 62443 or NIST guidance, and adjust evidence expectations accordingly. In compliance-driven audits, emphasize completeness and continuity of required artifacts; in risk-based contexts, emphasize rationale, tailoring, and control effectiveness. Always verify that scope boundaries match the organization's operational footprint and connectivity realities. Clarity of scope ensures that assurance conclusions are defensible and appropriately scaled.
9. **Verify Traceability and Provenance of Audit Evidence:** Ensure that all key documents—network diagrams, change logs, SOPs, and configuration exports—are dated, signed, and stored in controlled repositories. Validate that each artifact has a clear origin, revision history, and site verification to confirm authenticity. Seek cross-references that tie changes to operational logs or alarms, forming a complete audit trail from design intent to execution. Evidence integrity and traceability are the foundation of credible and repeatable assurance.
10. **Foster Continuous Collaboration Between Engineering and Cybersecurity Teams:** Encourage structured engagement between control engineers, IT security personnel, and compliance staff throughout audit planning and execution. Promote shared vocabulary, joint walkthroughs of systems, and mutual review of findings to ensure recommendations respect both cybersecurity and process safety imperatives. Evaluate whether governance structures formally integrate these disciplines under change management and risk committees. Sustained collaboration bridges the cultural gap between safety and security, strengthening both without compromising either.

Chapter Questions

1. In OT/ICS audits, what primary concern should guide risk decisions and control evaluation?
   - **A.** Human safety, environmental protection, and continuous operation
   - **B.** Confidentiality of business data above all else
   - **C.** Rapid deployment of the latest security patches
   - **D.** User privacy and consent preferences

2. What is the principal role of an industrial DMZ between corporate IT and control networks?
   - **A.** Provide direct administrative access from corporate IT to PLCs
   - **B.** Broker limited, tightly filtered or one-way data exchange without exposing control assets
   - **C.** Increase bandwidth for analytics workloads traversing control networks
   - **D.** Host safety instrumented systems for faster response

3. Why are unidirectional gateways used at ICS boundaries?
   A. They enable bidirectional remote management of PLC firmware
   B. They replace the need for jump hosts by encrypting all traffic
   C. They provide physical assurance that data can flow out but not into the control network
   D. They accelerate historian queries by caching control data

4. Which evidence best demonstrates disciplined application allowlist governance on engineering workstations?
   A. A verbal statement from operations that only approved tools are used
   B. A monthly antivirus report showing zero detections
   C. A network diagram indicating the workstation's location
   D. Exported allowlist rule sets and signature catalogs tied to approved change tickets and rollback plans

5. When patching is infeasible during production, what auditor-validated action is most appropriate?
   A. Isolate the asset, restrict communications to essential conduits, enforce allowlisting, document a risk-based variance, and schedule remediation for a maintenance window
   B. Disable all alarms to avoid nuisance during production runs
   C. Permit vendor laptops to connect directly for ad hoc fixes
   D. Ignore the vulnerability until the next annual outage without documentation

6. What enables credible cross-correlation of process, alarm, and security telemetry during investigations?
   A. Daily operator briefings alone
   B. Time synchronization across HMIs, controllers, historians, and security sensors
   C. Higher polling rates on all PLCs
   D. Replacing passive monitoring with active probing

7. Which artifact relationship most strongly supports traceability from design intent to operating state?
   A. A single updated network drawing stored on a shared drive
   B. Unauthenticated screenshots of firewall GUIs
   C. Management of Change records linked to revised diagrams and post-change configuration exports
   D. A weekly email summary from the control room

8. What condition best characterizes alarm fatigue in control rooms?
   A. Operators silencing all alarms during night shifts
   B. Alarms configured only for informational notices
   C. Absence of any high-priority alarms for weeks
   D. Frequent nuisance annunciations leading operators to acknowledge rather than investigate

9. How should audit scope and testing depth be aligned when operating under a prescriptive regulatory regime such as NERC CIP?
   A. Anchor on completeness, continuity, and requirement-by-requirement evidence mapped to defined assets and periods
   B. Focus on informal narratives demonstrating good-faith efforts
   C. Defer to vendor attestations without independent sampling
   D. Prioritize experimental penetration testing against safety systems

10. Which approach best constrains remote vendor access to control assets?
   A. Allow VPN access directly to PLC subnets during emergencies
   B. Permit any remote session if antivirus is updated
   C. Require access through a hardened jump host in the industrial DMZ with session recording and just-in-time, time-boxed approvals
   D. Use email approvals to authorize shared admin passwords for short periods

16

Sector Overlays (Financial, Healthcare, Public)

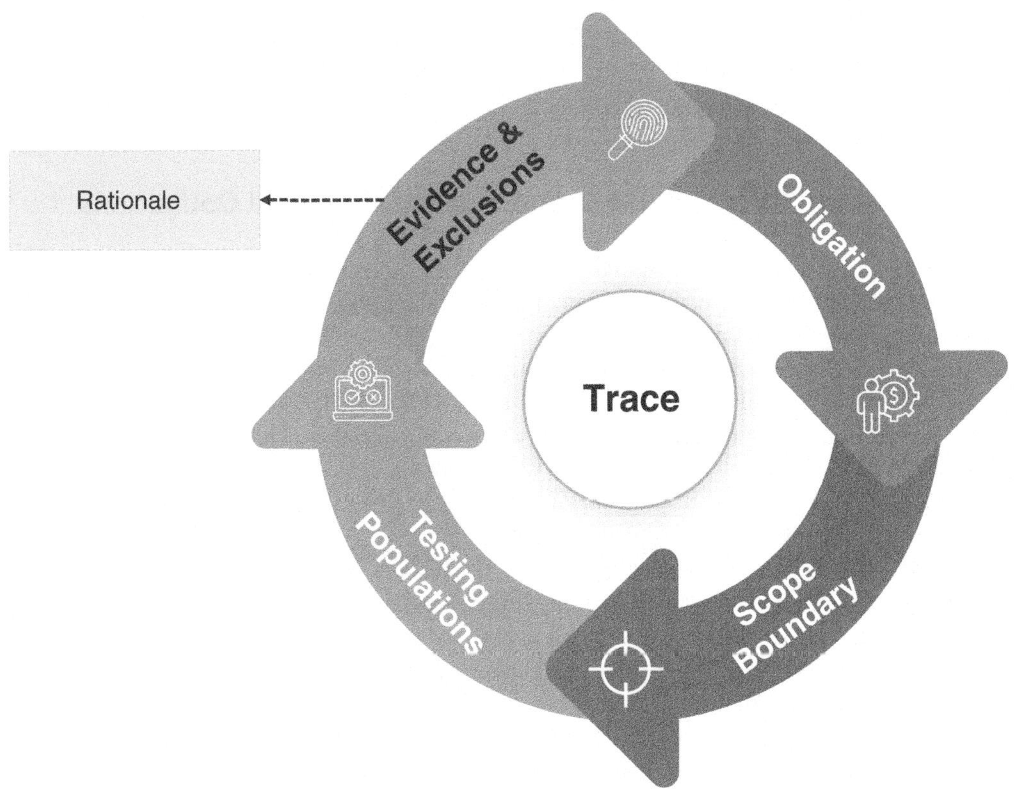

Sector overlays define how cybersecurity auditing adapts to the unique legal, operational, and evidentiary expectations of regulated industries. Financial services, healthcare, government, and payment systems each impose their own interpretations of risk and control assurance, transforming how auditors define scope, test effectiveness, and evaluate compliance. Understanding these overlays is essential to performing credible audits in environments governed by frameworks such as FFIEC, GLBA, HIPAA, HITRUST, FedRAMP, and PCI DSS. Each overlay translates general security principles into precise, enforceable obligations that dictate how systems are segmented, monitored, and authorized to operate.

Effective auditors learn to navigate these overlapping frameworks without losing sight of the common control foundation that underpins them. By recognizing where obligations converge and where they diverge, auditors can align evidence collection and testing approaches across multiple compliance programs. This discipline ensures that a single control—such as access management or encryption—can satisfy different regulatory expectations through sound documentation and traceable logic. The ability to reconcile conflicts, apply compensating controls, and maintain consistent conclusions across obligations reflects both technical skill and governance maturity.

In an era of AI-driven operations, multi-sector accountability becomes even more critical. Machine learning platforms may process financial data, patient records, or government information simultaneously, creating complex intersections of regulatory scope. Auditors must understand how authorization, segmentation, and continuous monitoring principles extend to these environments, ensuring that each dataset is protected according to its governing standard. From regulator workpapers and ATO packages to PCI ROCs and healthcare BAAs, this chapter emphasizes the auditor's role in linking evidence, context, and compliance into a coherent assurance narrative that withstands both regulatory and ethical scrutiny.

Overlay Scoping: Identifying In-scope Systems, Data, and Obligations

Sector overlays transform the way auditors define scope by beginning with regulatory and contractual obligations rather than technical boundaries. In cybersecurity auditing, scoping under an overlay is not just about identifying which servers, applications, or networks exist—it is about determining which systems and entities are legally responsible for compliance. A financial institution may have dozens of subsidiaries, but only those handling regulated financial data fall within scope for certain laws or frameworks. In healthcare, scoping must align with the covered entities and business associates defined under HIPAA, while in the public sector, the scoping process may focus on the agency, program, or grant recipient tied to a federal control baseline. Each overlay refines the boundary lines, ensuring the auditor evaluates only those systems that are directly accountable under the relevant obligations.

The essence of overlay scoping is traceability. Every inclusion or exclusion must be defensible, with a clear link from the obligation to the systems and data it governs. The process begins by mapping each requirement—such as safeguarding patient health records, protecting cardholder data, or securing taxpayer information—to the business processes that create or use that information. From there, auditors identify which systems, databases, and shared services store, process, or transmit the regulated data. Each decision must be explicitly documented, forming a transparent path from the original obligation to the technical scope and the populations selected for testing. This trace serves as both a scoping rationale and an audit artifact that demonstrates the integrity of the testing universe.

Scoping also requires auditors to interpret how data moves between entities, particularly when shared services are involved. In financial institutions, centralized IT or cloud environments may support both regulated and unregulated lines of business, blurring boundaries that auditors must untangle. Healthcare systems often share electronic medical record platforms across multiple clinics or partner organizations, meaning auditors must determine whether those shared platforms are in scope under the primary entity's compliance obligations. In the public sector, scoping decisions must consider interagency systems, third-party contractors, and grant-funded projects that might inherit federal control requirements. Each sector's overlay forces auditors to reconcile operational realities with legal definitions.

Auditors must also recognize that overlays narrow what counts as acceptable evidence. When obligations are rooted in regulation, the standard of proof is higher. Screenshots or verbal confirmations that might suffice in a general IT audit are rarely adequate under a regulatory overlay. Instead, auditors need formal system documentation, access control reports, encryption configurations, and change logs that directly support the scoping decisions. This evidence must be dated, authoritative, and tied to the specific systems identified as in scope. The overlay effectively filters out weak or generalized proof, demanding that every sample used in testing can be traced back to a clearly defined obligation.

A common mistake in overlay scoping is assuming that all systems within a network are automatically in scope. Effective scoping relies on identifying the "obligation boundary," not merely the network boundary. For instance, under the Payment Card Industry Data Security Standard (PCI DSS), only systems that store, process, or transmit cardholder data—or connect to those that do—fall within scope. Systems used solely for general business functions can be excluded if their isolation is proven through segmentation testing and access control validation. The same logic applies to healthcare, where systems without access to protected health information may be justifiably excluded if proper safeguards prevent data crossover. Each exclusion, however, must be backed by documented reasoning and verified evidence. Table 16.1 illustrates how auditors trace from obligation to scoping decisions to the exact populations used for testing with explicit exclusions and rationale.

Table 16.1 Obligation to scope to population trace matrix.

Artifact	Cadence	Source of truth	Linked document
Vulnerability scan results	Monthly	Scanning platform export	POA&M update entry
Control assessment updates	Quarterly	SCA team report	Security Assessment Report addendum
POA&M status and milestones	Monthly or as issues change	Official risk tracker	POA&M register
SSP revision log	Quarterly or upon major change	Configuration control record	System Security Plan
Asset inventory reconcile	Monthly	CMDB or inventory tool	Boundary and SSP annex
Boundary diagram verification	Quarterly or upon integration	Architecture repository	Authorized boundary record
eAuth assurance evidence	Quarterly or upon change	IdAM platform reports	eAuth determination
Configuration baseline drift report	Monthly	Configuration management tool	Baseline control record
Incident summary and lessons learned	Quarterly or after event	IR platform export	Closure evidence set

Overlay scoping also extends beyond data storage to include data influence. Systems that do not store regulated data but have administrative or network-level influence over in-scope systems must still be considered. For example, identity management servers, patch management systems, and monitoring platforms often exert control over regulated environments. Excluding them could create blind spots that undermine compliance. Auditors must evaluate how these supporting systems contribute to—or threaten—the confidentiality, integrity, and availability of the protected data. If their functions can affect compliance outcomes, they become part of the testing population.

In practice, the scoping process under sector overlays demands iterative refinement. Initial scoping decisions often reveal dependencies or interfaces that expand or contract the boundary. Auditors should revisit earlier assumptions as evidence is gathered, ensuring the chain from obligation to population remains intact. This continuous validation strengthens the audit's defensibility and prevents misalignment between the stated scope and the actual systems tested. In regulated sectors, a broken trace—where obligations cannot be clearly tied to the evidence population—can invalidate audit results and expose both the organization and auditor to compliance risk.

Overlay scoping reinforces the principle that precision is accountability. An auditor's credibility depends on being able to show that every testing population, sampling method, and evidence request originated from a well-defined obligation. This disciplined approach prevents scope creep, avoids wasted effort on irrelevant systems, and ensures the audit outcome is both accurate and regulator-ready. Whether in banking, healthcare, or government, overlay scoping transforms a complex compliance landscape into a structured, defendable framework for testing—one built on traceable logic, documented rationale, and verifiable control evidence.

Financial Services (FFIEC/GLBA): Controls Emphasis and Artifacts

In the financial sector, auditors must align their work with the FFIEC framework and the Gramm–Leach–Bliley Act Safeguards Rule, both of which emphasize strong governance, effective risk management, and documented control operation. Regulators expect to see a current, board-approved cybersecurity program supported by clear roles, oversight structures, and reporting mechanisms. Typical artifacts include risk assessments tied to business lines, data inventories, committee minutes, and approved policies. Evidence must be current and traceable, showing approval dates and management attestations that confirm accuracy and completeness. Supervisory guidance also shapes how deeply auditors sample, often requiring larger samples when prior issues, weak governance, or unclear documentation exist.

Access management receives heavy scrutiny because it protects customer information and system integrity. Regulators expect role-based access control documentation, privilege reviews, and evidence of proper provisioning and deprovisioning. Artifacts include user listings, approval workflows, authentication settings, and records of privileged access use. These must be recent, complete, and formally reviewed by business owners, not just IT staff. Samples often focus on privileged accounts and sensitive applications, with increased testing when automated tools or population completeness are in question. Evidence freshness is critical—access listings and review attestations should fall within the audit period and be supported by management certification.

Third-party risk management is another major focus because outsourcing never eliminates regulatory responsibility. Auditors must identify all vendors with access to customer or financial data and confirm that risk assessments, due diligence, and contracts meet regulatory standards.

Expected artifacts include vendor inventories, assurance reports, control questionnaires, and signed contracts with defined security clauses. Examiners often request monitoring reports, issue logs, and management attestations confirming data completeness. Sampling typically expands when vendor oversight relies solely on third-party attestations or when critical services depend on a small number of providers, creating concentrated operational risk.

Business continuity and resilience controls are examined for their ability to maintain critical operations during disruptions. Regulators require a current business impact analysis that defines recovery objectives and identifies key interdependencies. Auditors should collect plans, recovery runbooks, and recent exercise reports showing realistic testing and documented lessons learned. Freshness is proven through exercise logs, test results, and management sign-off on remediation tracking. Sampling depth often increases when shared services, cloud dependencies, or prior outage history exist, as regulators want proof that testing covered critical systems, vendors, and data recovery scenarios.

Governance under GLBA demands a risk-based security program that is approved and monitored by senior leadership. Auditors gather evidence showing that policies, standards, and controls are mapped directly to regulatory requirements and business risks. Typical artifacts include governance dashboards, risk and performance indicators, and board review materials. These must be recent, signed, and traceable to specific reporting cycles. Supervisory feedback often leads to deeper sampling of corrective actions, policy updates, and management review records to verify continuous oversight and accountability.

Change management and configuration controls are vital because configuration errors often lead to incidents. Required evidence includes change requests, approvals, risk assessments, deployment records, and baseline configurations for systems and networks. Fresh artifacts such as configuration exports and vulnerability scans must fall within the testing period. Regulators often expand sampling when institutions claim full automation or preventive design without independent validation. Management attestations confirming population completeness are expected for all configuration and change records.

Model risk management becomes important when automated decision tools influence credit, fraud, or monitoring outcomes. Regulators expect a current model inventory, validation reports, and documentation of ownership, purpose, and data lineage. Evidence should show performance tracking, recalibration, and any overrides. Because model accuracy can degrade quickly, auditors must ensure artifacts are recent and supported by attestations from model owners. Sampling increases when models affect regulatory reporting or when prior validations were insufficient.

Incident response and breach notification controls are also heavily reviewed. Auditors collect incident logs, escalation procedures, investigation reports, and communication templates to confirm readiness and regulatory compliance. Examiners expect recent incident summaries, root cause analyses, and management attestations showing that no material events were excluded. Evidence freshness is demonstrated through recent tabletop exercises and updated playbooks reflecting evolving threats. Sampling depth increases when institutions have repeated incidents or delayed notifications, signaling weaknesses in monitoring and response processes.

Across all control areas, success in financial-sector auditing depends on traceability, timeliness, and management accountability. Every artifact—whether an access list, recovery test, or vendor contract—must clearly connect to a regulatory obligation and fall within the audit's defined scope. Supervisory expectations push auditors toward precise, defensible testing that demonstrates full control operation during the period under review.

Healthcare (HIPAA/HITRUST): Safeguards, Mappings, and Evidence Nuances

Auditing in the healthcare sector requires mapping HIPAA's flexible safeguard requirements to the more prescriptive HITRUST CSF controls, creating a clear, testable structure for evaluating how protected health information (PHI) is handled. Every legal entity, application, and data store that creates, receives, maintains, or transmits PHI must be explicitly tied to the relevant safeguard category—administrative, physical, or technical—and documented within the defined certification boundary. HITRUST converts HIPAA's qualitative rules into measurable control objectives, allowing auditors to verify whether each safeguard is effectively implemented and continuously maintained. Change control becomes central to this process, as any modification to systems, configurations, or processes that could affect PHI must include evidence of risk review, testing, and documented approval before release. Each control and artifact must therefore trace directly from a HIPAA safeguard to the associated HITRUST requirement and the evidence used to validate compliance.

Administrative safeguards form the foundation of audit defensibility because they define how an organization manages risk, assigns responsibility, and enforces accountability. Auditors collect risk analyses that identify where PHI resides, assess threats and vulnerabilities, and describe remediation plans with assigned owners and due dates. Artifacts such as risk management plans, security policies, workforce training logs, and sanction procedures must be formally approved, version-controlled, and reviewed on a set cadence—typically annually or when major operational changes occur. A stale risk assessment or outdated training record can indicate systemic control breakdowns, prompting expanded testing. Management attestations play a critical role by confirming the completeness and accuracy of each artifact. The presence of signatures, timestamps, and distribution records demonstrates control maturity and establishes the evidence chain auditors need to rely on.

Technical safeguards represent the mechanisms that protect PHI at rest, in motion, and during processing. Auditors focus on access control, audit logging, data integrity, and encryption configurations to ensure confidentiality and traceability. Required artifacts include access control lists, identity provisioning records, authentication settings, encryption certificates, log management configurations, and system audit trail exports. Each artifact must be recent and reflect the production environment within the audit window. HITRUST requires proof that automated controls are monitored and validated, not simply configured once and forgotten. For example, user access listings should show last-login dates and be supported by quarterly review sign-offs, while key rotation and encryption settings must align with organizational policy. Sampling depth increases when evidence is incomplete, population boundaries are unclear, or logs lack sufficient detail to confirm full coverage of PHI systems.

Physical safeguards address how an organization prevents unauthorized physical access to areas or devices that handle PHI. In modern healthcare settings, this includes both traditional data centers and on-premises locations such as clinics, hospitals, and mobile workstations. Auditors review visitor logs, facility access badges, camera footage retention policies, and media disposal records to ensure physical protection aligns with documented procedures. Evidence must show that facility access is restricted to authorized personnel, that hardware and removable media are tracked throughout their life cycle, and that destroyed or repurposed equipment is verified as sanitized. Each record must be dated and signed, proving the action occurred during the audit period. Sampling often expands when physical and logical controls are not aligned, such as when facility access remains active for terminated employees or when disposal certificates cannot be traced to asset inventories.

Business Associate Agreements (BAAs) are another cornerstone of healthcare compliance, establishing contractual accountability for third parties that create, receive, or process PHI. Auditors gather signed BAAs, renewal records, and vendor inventories to confirm that each service provider with PHI access is covered by a valid agreement. These agreements must include clauses on security responsibilities, breach notification, and right-to-audit provisions. When a vendor maintains its own HITRUST certification, auditors may rely on that certification for certain control areas—but only if the certification's scope and boundaries precisely align with the PHI-related services in question. Evidence must confirm the currency and relevance of each vendor certification. Missing or outdated BAAs or certifications immediately trigger expanded testing and risk escalation, as they signal possible exposure to regulatory penalties.

Documentation rigor defines the difference between a compliant and a defensible audit. HIPAA requires covered entities and business associates to document all security activities, while HITRUST specifies the expected level of precision, completeness, and version control. Auditors expect evidence that is contemporaneous, signed, and formally approved within the audit window. Screenshots or informal confirmations are insufficient unless they are part of a validated workflow. Management attestations must explicitly confirm that evidence populations—such as user listings, system logs, and training completions—are accurate and complete. Sampling expands significantly when documentation lacks timestamps, when ownership is unclear, or when controls rely solely on verbal verification.

HITRUST certification boundaries also play a critical role in determining reliance and sampling depth. When organizations operate multiple environments or use shared services, auditors must confirm that the HITRUST certification boundary fully encompasses all systems handling PHI. A certification that excludes certain subsystems or interfaces cannot be relied upon for complete assurance. In those cases, auditors must perform independent testing or request supplemental evidence directly from the organization. Boundaries must be supported by architecture diagrams, inventory lists, and governance documentation that clearly show where PHI flows begin and end. This clarity prevents overreliance on certifications that only partially cover the environment.

Healthcare auditing under HIPAA and HITRUST ultimately revolves around demonstrating continuous, documented, and verifiable protection of PHI. Every safeguard—administrative, physical, or technical—must have supporting evidence that is both recent and traceable to an accountable owner. The best audits maintain a clear chain from regulatory obligation to control, from control to evidence, and from evidence to population sampling. Whether reviewing an access log, a disposal record, or a vendor contract, the auditor's goal is the same: to prove that PHI was protected consistently, that changes were properly controlled, and that every claim of compliance can be backed by fresh, defensible documentation.

Public Sector (FedRAMP, State/Local): Authorizations and Continuous Monitoring

Auditing in the public sector centers on the principle of authorization to operate (ATO)—a formal acceptance of risk by an authorizing official after reviewing documented security controls, assessments, and mitigations. Whether operating under FedRAMP for cloud environments or similar frameworks for state and local agencies, the ATO process transforms compliance into a continuous cycle of validation and accountability. Each system must maintain a defined security boundary, a current System Security Plan (SSP), and documented control implementations mapped to the appropriate NIST baseline. Auditors evaluate whether evidence supports that authorization conditions are still met, with particular attention to updates following configuration changes, new integrations, or significant incidents. The ATO is not a one-time milestone but an ongoing demonstration that security controls remain effective, current, and properly monitored.

Boundary definition is the foundation of every public sector audit, determining which components, networks, and data flows fall within authorization scope. Boundary diagrams illustrate system interconnections, shared services, and inherited controls, showing exactly where federal or state data crosses into external environments. These diagrams guide the auditor's understanding of where evidence should originate and which entities are responsible for maintaining it. For cloud providers and hybrid agencies, boundaries often overlap with external systems, requiring documentation of encryption, segmentation, and authentication mechanisms to confirm isolation. A clear and approved boundary ensures traceability between the SSP, test plans, and continuous monitoring outputs. When boundary documentation is incomplete or outdated, auditors expand sampling to confirm that all connected systems maintain the same level of protection required by the ATO.

Control inheritance is a defining feature of public sector compliance because many agencies and vendors rely on shared infrastructures. A system may inherit security controls from enterprise services such as identity management, network defense, or vulnerability management rather than implementing them independently. Auditors must verify that inherited controls are both operational and current, supported by evidence from the providing system's own ATO or authorization package. For example, a hosted application leveraging an agency's enterprise firewall inherits boundary protection controls but must still provide configuration details and monitoring results that confirm enforcement. Inherited control evidence must be referenced directly within the SSP and mapped to control identifiers, with timestamps showing alignment to the audit period. Missing or outdated inheritance documentation often triggers deeper review or revalidation of the parent system's control effectiveness.

Continuous monitoring transforms the ATO framework into a living compliance process. FedRAMP and state programs require systems to produce ongoing evidence—monthly vulnerability scans, quarterly control assessments, updated POA&Ms (Plans of Action and Milestones), and periodic SSP updates—to prove that controls remain effective over time. Auditors review scan reports, compare them against prior months, and validate that identified weaknesses have been properly tracked and remediated in the POA&M. The POA&M itself serves as both an audit artifact and a risk management tool, detailing open issues, severity, mitigation plans, and expected completion dates. Evidence freshness is critical; stale or missing updates often result in findings of noncompliance or increased sampling frequency. Auditors also ensure that control owners provide management attestations confirming the accuracy and completeness of monitoring data.

SSPs are the cornerstone documentation for public sector authorization and must remain current throughout the system life cycle. The SSP captures every implemented control, the responsible party, and the supporting evidence references. Auditors focus on whether the SSP accurately reflects the operational environment and whether recent changes—such as technology updates or new service integrations—are properly documented. Updates to the SSP should be performed at least quarterly or whenever major changes occur, supported by signed revision histories. When discrepancies exist between the SSP and observed configurations, auditors expand testing to confirm whether the system's authorization conditions are still valid. A well-maintained SSP allows seamless linkage between controls, test evidence, and continuous monitoring results, ensuring that compliance posture is both traceable and defensible.

Boundary diagrams, authentication methods, and Security Control Assessments (SCAs) heavily influence the type and cadence of evidence auditors require. Boundary diagrams dictate which networks and data paths must produce monitoring results, while eAuthentication (eAuth) requirements define identity assurance levels and corresponding evidence—such as multifactor authentication logs or credential issuance reports. SCAs determine testing depth and provide an independent verification of control performance, often driving quarterly evidence reviews and remediation tracking. Together, these elements create a structured rhythm for continuous monitoring: boundary verification ensures scoping accuracy, eAuth ensures user trustworthiness, and SCA findings drive control improvement cycles. Each contributes directly to the cadence of scans, patch reports, and status updates that auditors use to confirm the environment's ongoing authorization.

FedRAMP and state frameworks emphasize transparency and repeatability in evidence submission. Artifacts such as monthly vulnerability scans must show system-wide coverage, clear severity classification, and remediation validation. Quarterly assessments often include control testing summaries, SCA observation responses, and updated POA&Ms reflecting the most recent scan results. Continuous monitoring submissions must align with predefined schedules, and auditors review timeliness and completeness as part of compliance testing. Management attestations accompanying each submission confirm accountability for accuracy and closure of prior findings. When recurring evidence falls outside cadence or lacks linkage to corrective actions, auditors escalate findings as systemic monitoring failures, indicating potential risk to authorization status.

In the state and local context, continuous monitoring requirements may vary but follow the same core principles of accountability and traceability. Some programs rely on hybrid models combining federal NIST standards with state cybersecurity frameworks. Auditors review local equivalents of the SSP, POA&M, and vulnerability management plans, ensuring consistency with federal expectations. Boundary diagrams must still illustrate interconnections between state networks, service providers, and federal systems to confirm consistent data protection levels. Evidence cadence—monthly scans, quarterly reviews, and annual reauthorization—remains a best practice even when not explicitly mandated. The overarching goal is to maintain a transparent and verifiable record of ongoing control operation.

PCI DSS: Prescriptive Requirements and Segmentation/Scope Control

Auditing under the Payment Card Industry Data Security Standard (PCI DSS) demands a level of precision that few other frameworks require. Unlike principle-based standards such as HIPAA or ISO 27001, PCI is explicitly prescriptive—each control specifies exactly what must be implemented, tested, and documented. This specificity shifts the burden of compliance squarely onto scope definition and maintenance. The cardholder data environment (CDE) must be clearly identified, including all systems that store, process, or transmit cardholder data, as well as any system that can impact its security. Because every element within the CDE is in scope, organizations rely on rigorous segmentation and documentation to prove that unrelated systems are fully isolated. The accuracy of scope directly determines the accuracy of compliance findings, making scoping discipline the cornerstone of any PCI audit.

The first step in PCI scope control is defining the CDE boundary and verifying that no unaccounted connections or data paths exist. Auditors examine network architecture diagrams, firewall configurations, and routing tables to ensure segmentation controls effectively separate the CDE from other corporate networks. Any device, subnet, or service that touches or could impact the CDE's security must be explicitly documented. Network diagrams must be current, labeled, and validated against production environments. When diagrams are outdated or incomplete, auditors expand testing to uncover hidden dependencies. PCI's prescriptive design means that omissions, even if unintentional, can invalidate the compliance assertion. Scope clarity is not optional—it is a prerequisite for certification. Table 16.2 clarifies the core artifacts that prove disciplined PCI scope control and CDE isolation.

Segmentation testing is the most direct method for proving scope discipline. Auditors require evidence that systems outside the CDE cannot access or influence systems within it. This testing typically includes network scans, firewall rule reviews, and penetration tests targeting segmentation controls. Artifacts must demonstrate successful isolation—such as traceroute logs, blocked port scans, and results from third-party segmentation validation. Evidence freshness is crucial; tests must be conducted within the audit period and reflect the current state of the network. Weak segmentation results in "scope explosion," where entire environments become subject to PCI requirements, dramatically increasing testing effort and remediation cost. Maintaining and documenting clean segmentation boundaries protects both compliance standing and operational efficiency.

Data-flow diagrams provide another layer of assurance by visually linking systems, applications, and storage locations that handle cardholder data. These diagrams must show how data enters, moves through, and exits the environment, including encryption and decryption points. Auditors review these diagrams to ensure they align with network maps, asset inventories, and business

Table 16.2 PCI segmentation validation evidence pack.

Evidence item	Purpose	Freshness expectation	Placement in ROC or SAQ
Network segmentation test results	Prove isolation between CDE and out of scope zones	Within the current assessment window	Scope and segmentation section
Data flow diagram for card data	Show all card data paths and crypto points	Current and aligned to production design	Scoping and data flow section
Firewall rule reviews for CDE edges	Validate only approved paths reach the CDE	Reviewed during the audit period	Network security section
Privileged access inventory for CDE	Confirm control of admin influence over CDE	Export dated in period with owner sign off	Access management section
ASV external scan reports	Demonstrate external vulnerability management	Quarterly within period with pass status	Vulnerability management section
Internal scan and patch summaries	Show risk reduction inside segmented zones	Monthly or aligned to policy within period	Vulnerability management section
Penetration test with segmentation focus	Validate control efficacy under attack	Annual within period or after major change	Testing and results section
Change tickets impacting CDE boundary	Prove approved and recorded boundary changes	In period with approvals and deployment logs	Change management section

processes. Any inconsistency signals potential scoping gaps. Artifacts supporting these diagrams—such as data discovery scans or inventory tools—help confirm that no untracked repositories or legacy systems contain cardholder data. PCI's expectation of completeness means even one overlooked server or unmanaged endpoint can compromise compliance. Accurate, regularly updated data-flow documentation is therefore both a control requirement and an audit defense mechanism.

PCI also requires that connected-to or impacting systems be identified and justified. These systems may not store cardholder data directly but still influence CDE security—for example, directory servers, patch management systems, monitoring tools, or virtualization platforms. Auditors must verify that these systems are either within scope or demonstrably isolated through access restrictions, firewall rules, or VLAN configurations. Artifacts include configuration exports, access control matrices, and change management records confirming that no connectivity exists beyond documented, approved channels. The auditor's objective is to ensure that all influence paths are accounted for and properly secured. Failure to identify an impacting system can undermine the entire assessment and invalidate the Report on Compliance (ROC).

The prescriptive nature of PCI extends to evidence collection and reporting. Every control must be validated through specific artifacts, such as configuration files, logs, screenshots, or test results that correspond directly to PCI control requirements. Evidence must be dated within the audit period and include proof of the assessor's independent verification. The ROC or Self-assessment Questionnaire (SAQ) serves as the master reference, detailing which systems were tested, what evidence was reviewed, and how findings were resolved. Auditors use these documents to ensure alignment between the declared scope and the actual systems tested. Discrepancies between the ROC, SAQ, and supporting artifacts often trigger deeper investigation or conditional compliance.

Scope maintenance is not a one-time event but an ongoing operational practice. Organizations must continuously monitor network changes, firewall modifications, and asset deployments to ensure the CDE boundary remains intact. Auditors review change tickets, configuration management records, and access control updates to confirm that new systems have been properly classified and segmented. Routine validation activities—such as quarterly internal and external vulnerability scans and annual penetration testing—provide ongoing assurance that scope remains stable. Evidence freshness and traceability are key; every artifact must tie back to a defined system and a specific testing date. Consistent documentation ensures that compliance status can be defended at any point between formal assessments.

Alignment between network architecture, documentation, and attestation is critical for credibility. The ROC or SAQ must accurately represent the current environment, including scope diagrams, segmentation evidence, and data-flow mappings. Auditors confirm that all systems in the evidence set correspond to the CDE inventory and that exclusions are properly justified. Management sign-off on the ROC or SAQ attests that scope decisions are accurate and supported by factual evidence. This alignment prevents discrepancies between internal security operations and official compliance attestations—a common root cause of failed revalidations or post-breach compliance challenges.

Reconciling Conflicts: Precedence Rules and Documentation

Auditors frequently face situations where sector-specific requirements conflict with one another, forcing careful judgment and transparent documentation to preserve both compliance integrity and audit consistency. A healthcare organization processing payment transactions, for example, may find PCI DSS mandates more restrictive encryption requirements than those prescribed by

HIPAA or ISO 27001. In such cases, the auditor must apply a clear precedence logic that ensures the strictest applicable standard governs the control environment. The guiding principle is that when two or more obligations overlap, the higher or more prescriptive requirement prevails, provided it does not violate any legal or contractual condition. This approach maintains defensibility and creates consistency across audit engagements. All such decisions must be tied back to the organization's common control set, ensuring that each conclusion aligns with the universal framework established in Chapter 2.

Precedence logic begins with mapping each requirement to a shared control identifier within the organization's control catalog. Each control inherits its attributes—such as objective, test procedures, and evidence expectations—from this central reference, allowing auditors to trace any deviation to a documented decision. When a conflict arises, the auditor reviews the mapped controls side by side to determine which standard is more stringent or explicit in its requirements. For example, if PCI requires quarterly vulnerability scans while ISO calls for them "periodically," PCI's frequency takes precedence. By grounding these decisions in the common control set, auditors prevent scope drift and ensure consistent interpretation across business units, auditors, and reporting cycles. Documentation of the rationale, impact, and approval of each precedence decision becomes part of the permanent audit record.

Compensating controls play a key role in resolving conflicts where strict compliance with one framework may not be technically feasible without breaching another. These are alternative measures that achieve the same security intent as the original requirement. For instance, an organization might substitute a continuous vulnerability management process with automated scanning for PCI's quarterly scanning requirement, provided it offers equal or greater coverage and assurance. To be acceptable, compensating controls must be risk-assessed, formally approved, and tested for effectiveness. Auditors must document these controls in both the testing workpapers and the final report, clearly linking them to the corresponding requirement identifiers in the common control set. This ensures transparency and allows future assessors to evaluate the reasoning without reinterpreting historical decisions.

Documentation is the anchor that holds precedence decisions accountable. Every time a conflict is identified, the auditor must create an entry that records the specific standards involved, the sections in conflict, the decision made, and the justification for that decision. These entries should also include cross-references to impacted systems, evidence artifacts, and any related exceptions or compensating controls. The documentation should be reviewed and approved by the organization's compliance governance body—often the risk or audit committee—to confirm the decision aligns with enterprise policy and risk appetite. By embedding this process into the control life cycle, auditors create a living record of compliance logic that can withstand external scrutiny from regulators, assessors, and certification bodies.

Cross-sector conflicts often emerge when different frameworks prescribe divergent testing frequencies, evidence formats, or terminology. PCI's emphasis on prescriptive testing can clash with ISO 27001's flexible risk-based approach, or NIST's continuous monitoring cadence may differ from GLBA's annual review requirement. The auditor's responsibility is not to reconcile these frameworks philosophically but to document operationally how compliance will be maintained under all relevant standards. Using the common control set, auditors can define a unified cadence and evidence type that satisfies the strictest requirement while maintaining efficiency. This method avoids duplicative testing and ensures each standard's intent is honored without fragmenting the control environment.

When conflicts cannot be harmonized purely through precedence or compensation, auditors must escalate the issue through a defined governance process. This involves presenting the conflict, impact analysis, and recommended resolution to senior leadership or a cross-functional compliance council. The council's determination—supported by legal, technical, and risk management representatives—should be recorded in the control repository and reflected in future scoping or evidence collection procedures. Auditors should then update related control mappings, ensuring the chosen interpretation propagates through all affected frameworks and systems. This disciplined approach prevents one-off exceptions from eroding consistency across future audits.

Evidence linkage is critical when reconciling sector conflicts. Every control decision, whether based on precedence or compensation, must be supported by artifacts demonstrating its continued effectiveness. For example, if a PCI encryption control supersedes a less specific ISO control, the evidence—such as key management records, configuration exports, and encryption coverage reports—should be stored in a centralized evidence library tied to the shared control ID. This linkage allows auditors to demonstrate compliance across multiple frameworks with a single, validated set of artifacts. It also reinforces the "test once, satisfy many" philosophy that underpins mature compliance programs, reducing redundancy and improving audit efficiency.

Maintaining alignment with the common control set also ensures that conflicts are handled predictably over time. Each resolution becomes a reference case, guiding future auditors and minimizing interpretive differences. The control repository should include metadata such as precedence rationale, control equivalence notes, and accepted compensating measures, enabling auditors to quickly identify historical decisions and their outcomes. By treating each conflict as part of a structured knowledge base, organizations can strengthen the repeatability and scalability of their audit program. This systematic handling of conflicts turns what might otherwise be a source of inconsistency into an asset for continuous compliance improvement.

Auditors should also evaluate whether resolved conflicts introduce residual risk or create gaps in assurance coverage. Even when a higher standard is applied, operational constraints or resource limitations may prevent perfect implementation. The auditor's workpapers must note any residual exposure and link it to the enterprise risk register, ensuring management acknowledges and accepts it formally. This risk-based transparency aligns audit outcomes with organizational accountability, maintaining integrity while recognizing practical limitations. Each risk acceptance must be traceable to its related control, preserving audit defensibility.

Evidence Locations: Regulator-specific Workpapers, ATO Packages, ROC/SAQ

Evidence collection in sector-overlaid audits depends on knowing the canonical source for each obligation and maintaining an unbroken chain from requirement to artifact to the audited period. Canonical means the record of truth generated by the system of record or the formally approved governance process, not convenience screenshots or ad hoc exports. Auditors should treat each sector's repository as the anchor: regulator templates and exam workpapers in financial services, authorization packages and continuous monitoring submissions in the public sector, PCI's Report on Compliance or Self-Assessment Questionnaire in payments, and HIPAA/HITRUST risk analyses and Business Associate Agreements in healthcare. Each anchor must be supported by dated, version-controlled artifacts that prove when the control operated and who approved it. Cross-references to the common control set ensure the same artifact can satisfy multiple obligations without duplicative testing or inconsistent conclusions.

In financial services, the primary evidence containers are regulator-aligned templates and examination workpapers that mirror FFIEC handbooks and GLBA expectations. These workpapers typically compile board and committee packets, enterprise risk assessments, information security policies, and governance dashboards alongside access reviews, change tickets, and vendor files. The auditor's job is to ensure every item is contemporaneous with the period under review, bears clear authorship and approval, and maps to the specific control objective in the common control set. Where regulators have issued Matters Requiring Attention or supervisory letters, closure proofs and management attestations belong in the same workpaper chain to document remediation. The relationship is circular: governance artifacts justify control intent, operational artifacts prove execution, and regulator workpapers frame both in a format examiners can readily navigate.

Public-sector systems rely on authorization packages as the canonical container, with the SSP, Security Assessment Report, and Plan of Action and Milestones forming the core. Continuous monitoring submissions—monthly vulnerability scans, configuration baselines, inventory reconciliations, and quarterly assessment updates—extend this package with living evidence. Boundary diagrams and eAuthentication determinations set the scope and assurance levels, while SCAs provide independent test results that direct cadence and depth. Every submission must be time-stamped, tied to the approved boundary, and reconciled to the POA&M so remediation can be tracked end to end. For auditors, the linkage is explicit: the ATO package explains "what is authorized," the con-mon reports show "what is operating now," and both must agree with the control statements recorded in the common control set.

PCI environments center evidence on the Report on Compliance or the Self-Assessment Questionnaire, both of which are only as defensible as their supporting scope and segmentation proofs. Canonical proof includes current network and data-flow diagrams for the cardholder data environment, third-party Attestation of Compliance where reliance is claimed, quarterly ASV scans, annual penetration tests, and detailed segmentation test results. Configuration exports, key management records, and access listings must be dated within the assessment window and trace directly to in-scope systems. Because PCI is prescriptive, the ROC/SAQ must align exactly with the evidence set: if the document declares a segmented CDE, the segmentation test pack must prove isolation for every declared path. The common control set ties these PCI artifacts to parallel access, change, logging, and encryption controls used in other overlays, preserving a single interpretation of control effectiveness.

Healthcare evidence hinges on HIPAA's administrative, physical, and technical safeguards, expressed and measured through HITRUST's control statements when applicable. Canonical sources include risk analyses and risk management plans, workforce training records and sanction policies, system access logs and review attestations, encryption and key life cycle records, and incident documentation. Business Associate Agreements, with renewal logs and vendor risk assessments, are mandatory for any third party that creates, receives, or processes PHI. When reliance is placed on a vendor's HITRUST certification, scoping documents and the certification letter must demonstrate boundary alignment and currency. The mapping back to the common control set ensures that a single access review or encryption proof can support both HITRUST requirements and HIPAA safeguards without drifting into conflicting interpretations.

Across sectors, authoritative artifacts share common traits: they originate from the system of record, are approved through a documented governance path, and include immutable timestamps that fall within the audit period. Auditors should prioritize exports, signed reports, and workflow histories over screenshots, and prefer tool-native logs over manually compiled spreadsheets unless lineage is proven. Each artifact should carry metadata that identifies the control it supports, the population it came from, and the sampling method applied. Where automation generates evidence, re-performance or independent reconciliation validates population completeness.

By enforcing these traits, the audit file becomes reproducible, and conclusions remain stable under re-review or external examination.

Relating sector repositories is a matter of disciplined cross-referencing rather than duplication. A privileged access review can appear in financial regulator workpapers, substantiate PCI control testing for an impacting system, and support HIPAA/HITRUST technical safeguards if the same identity platform governs PHI access—provided the artifact is dated and the scope identifiers match. The ATO package's asset inventory can also resolve PCI scoping questions or healthcare data-flow uncertainties when the same shared services underpin multiple environments. Auditors should maintain a central index that maps each artifact's unique ID to all obligations it satisfies in the common control set. This architecture enables "test once, satisfy many" while preserving the strict sector-specific narratives expected by regulators and assessors.

Period alignment is the most common failure mode in multi-overlay audits, and it is preventable with explicit dating rules baked into evidence requests. Financial regulator workpapers should present the most recent two or three risk and board cycles within the window; ATO continuous monitoring must show monthly coverage without gaps; PCI scan and pen test artifacts must sit squarely inside the assessment period; HIPAA risk analyses and BAAs must be current as of the test date. Management representation letters should affirm population completeness for each repository, and change-control logs must explain mid-period deltas that could affect scope or control state. When artifacts disagree on timing, the earliest stale item sets the ceiling for assurance, and sampling depth should increase until freshness and traceability are restored.

Conclusion

Mastering the principles of sector overlays is critical for auditors who operate across environments governed by divergent yet overlapping regulatory frameworks. Whether examining a financial institution, healthcare provider, or public-sector system, the ability to interpret each sector's obligations while maintaining a unified control logic defines true audit maturity. Precision in scoping, evidence selection, and documentation allows auditors to navigate conflicting expectations without compromising rigor or traceability. These skills ensure that assurance activities remain defensible, repeatable, and aligned with both regulatory and operational realities.

The broader lesson of sector auditing lies in the discipline of harmonization. By grounding every control in a common framework and linking artifacts to clearly defined obligations, auditors preserve coherence across FedRAMP, HIPAA, PCI DSS, and other overlays. This approach transforms compliance from a fragmented checklist into a continuous system of accountability that adapts to evolving technology and governance requirements. While each sector enforces its own cadence and terminology, the strategic intent—to protect critical data and sustain trust through verifiable assurance—remains constant.

As AI systems become embedded within regulated infrastructures, the stakes of sector alignment grow exponentially. AI platforms that analyze financial transactions, patient data, or federal workloads inherit the obligations of every domain they touch. Professionals equipped with the methods outlined here can evaluate those environments with both technical precision and regulatory fluency. With these foundations in place, cybersecurity auditors are positioned not only to assess compliance but to safeguard the integrity, fairness, and resilience of intelligent systems operating at the heart of modern enterprise and government.

Auditor Recommendations

1. **Establish Clear Sector Boundaries:** Define precise system and data boundaries for every regulated environment under audit. Use authoritative documentation—such as boundary diagrams, asset inventories, and scoping justifications—to show how obligations shape what is in and out of scope. This clarity ensures that evidence aligns with the correct legal entities and control requirements. Properly documented boundaries also prevent redundant testing and enable traceable, defensible conclusions during regulator review.
2. **Prioritize Evidence Traceability:** Build a consistent chain linking each regulatory obligation to the scoping decision, control tested, and artifact reviewed. Require every piece of evidence to carry a date, source, and linkage to the control identifier in the common control set. This traceability demonstrates accountability and supports repeatable audits across different frameworks. Auditors who maintain complete evidence lineage reduce ambiguity, strengthen assurance quality, and simplify future revalidation efforts.
3. **Maintain Rigor in Documentation Currency:** Treat document freshness as a compliance control in itself. Risk analyses, SSPs, BAAs, and ROCs must be dated within the audit window and verified as the latest approved versions. Establish a recurring review schedule and obtain management attestations confirming accuracy and completeness. Outdated or undated documentation signals weak governance and invites expanded sampling or regulatory scrutiny.
4. **Apply the Strictest Requirement when Frameworks Overlap:** When sector obligations conflict, enforce the more prescriptive or restrictive standard. Use precedence logic grounded in the organization's common control set to justify the chosen interpretation and maintain consistency across future audits. Record each decision and its rationale within the control repository so it can be referenced in subsequent reviews. This approach ensures that multi-framework compliance remains coherent and defensible under examination.
5. **Validate Control Inheritance and Shared Services:** Verify that controls inherited from enterprise systems or third-party providers are active, current, and supported by up-to-date evidence. Review authorization packages, contractual clauses, and system reports to confirm that inherited controls remain effective across connected environments. Document these relationships in the audit file, mapping them directly to the parent system's ATO or certification boundary. This confirmation prevents reliance on stale or incomplete inherited assurances.
6. **Conduct Regular Segmentation and Scope Testing:** Use segmentation testing to confirm that systems outside regulated boundaries cannot access or influence in-scope environments. Collect traceroute results, blocked connection logs, and penetration test outcomes as proof of isolation. Perform these validations within each audit period and tie them directly to scoping documentation. Consistent testing ensures that scope remains contained and that segmentation continues to meet PCI and FedRAMP expectations.
7. **Align Evidence Repositories Across Frameworks:** Maintain sector-specific repositories—such as regulator workpapers, ATO packages, or ROC files—but map them through the common control set for cross-framework visibility. A single artifact, such as an access review or encryption record, should satisfy multiple obligations when scope and timing align. Use control identifiers and metadata tags to manage this linkage and prevent duplication. Alignment across repositories enhances efficiency and demonstrates integrated compliance management.
8. **Require Formal Management Attestations:** Strengthen audit credibility by obtaining written attestations from management confirming population completeness and evidence accuracy. Each attestation should reference the specific period, systems, and control areas under

review. Incorporate these statements into the audit record as verification that the organization acknowledges its representations. This practice reinforces accountability and reduces disputes about data integrity or evidence sufficiency.

9. **Monitor Continuous Authorization and Reporting Cadence:** For public-sector and FedRAMP environments, verify that continuous monitoring submissions—such as monthly scans, quarterly assessments, and POA&M updates—are timely and complete. Review historical submissions for gaps and ensure remediation activities align with documented milestones. Sampling should increase if evidence cadence slips or remediation timelines are missed. Consistent monitoring cadence validates that authorization remains active and that the control environment is continuously managed.
10. **Document Compensating Controls and Rationale Thoroughly:** When direct compliance with a requirement is not feasible, define compensating controls that achieve equivalent protection. Ensure these alternatives are risk-assessed, approved by governance leadership, and tested for effectiveness. Link each compensating measure to its corresponding control identifier and record the justification in audit workpapers. Thorough documentation of compensating logic preserves audit defensibility and demonstrates the organization's commitment to maintaining control assurance even under operational constraints.

Chapter Questions

1. What is the primary goal of sector overlay scoping for auditors?
   - **A.** To create a defensible trace from obligation to scope to testing populations
   - **B.** To standardize tool selection across audit teams
   - **C.** To minimize the number of artifacts collected
   - **D.** To eliminate the need for management attestations

2. In financial services oversight, which artifact most directly evidences governance by senior leadership?
   - **A.** Quarterly ASV scan reports
   - **B.** Governance committee charters and meeting minutes
   - **C.** PCI penetration test summaries
   - **D.** FedRAMP boundary diagrams

3. Within HIPAA/HITRUST, which mechanism contractually binds third parties that handle PHI?
   - **A.** Report on Compliance (ROC)
   - **B.** Plan of Action and Milestones (POA&M)
   - **C.** Business Associate Agreement (BAA)
   - **D.** Self-Assessment Questionnaire (SAQ)

4. Under public-sector authorizations, which recurring evidence best demonstrates ongoing vulnerability management?
   - **A.** Annual penetration tests with executive summaries
   - **B.** Semiannual incident tabletop exercise notes
   - **C.** Quarterly user access review sign-offs
   - **D.** Monthly vulnerability scans reconciled to POA&M updates

5. In PCI DSS assessments, which scope element must be precisely identified and isolated?
   A. The Cardholder Data Environment (CDE) with validated segmentation
   B. All enterprise endpoints regardless of connectivity
   C. Only internet-facing systems in production
   D. Development networks with no payment data

6. When sector requirements conflict (e.g., PCI vs. ISO), what should auditors do?
   A. Average the frequencies to find a middle ground
   B. Apply the stricter prescriptive requirement and document via the common control set
   C. Default to the most widely adopted framework
   D. Defer the decision to the vendor's assessor

7. How should auditors verify control inheritance for shared services?
   A. Assume effectiveness if previous audits were clean
   B. Rely on screenshots from the consuming system
   C. Confirm the parent system's authorization package and mapped evidence are current
   D. Accept verbal confirmation from the service owner

8. What defines evidence "freshness" across sector overlays?
   A. Artifacts accompanied by vendor logos
   B. Attachments that include screenshots only
   C. Documents stored in a centralized repository
   D. Artifacts dated within the audit period and linked to specific control identifiers

9. What is the chief purpose of segmentation testing in PCI scope control?
   A. Prove that out-of-scope systems cannot access or influence the CDE
   B. Speed up quarterly vulnerability scanning
   C. Replace the need for data-flow diagrams
   D. Reduce the frequency of ROC/SAQ submissions

10. How should sector-specific repositories relate to ensure consistency across obligations?
   A. Keep them isolated to preserve sector narratives
   B. Convert all artifacts into a single FedRAMP package
   C. Map artifacts through the common control set to enable "test once, satisfy many"
   D. Replace sector templates with internal spreadsheets only

17

Automation, Continuous Auditing, and Advanced Analytics

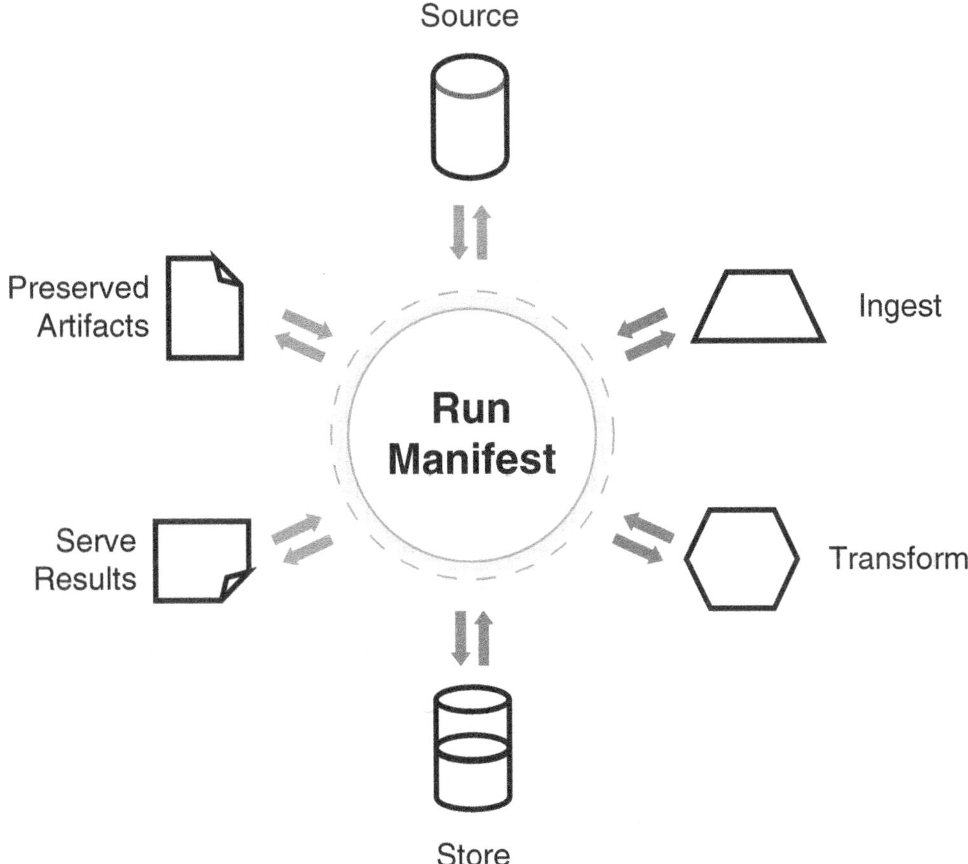

Automation, continuous auditing, and advanced analytics have reshaped how assurance is delivered in modern cybersecurity programs. What once relied on manual sampling and periodic reviews now demands scalable, data-driven verification that operates as continuously as the systems it monitors. Understanding how to design automated tests, manage assurance pipelines, and interpret analytical output is essential for auditors tasked with evaluating security in complex, adaptive environments. As organizations integrate artificial intelligence, cloud automation, and dynamic infrastructure, assurance must evolve from static evaluation toward continuous, evidence-based validation that can match the speed and volatility of digital operations.

Reliable automation does not emerge from technology alone—it depends on disciplined design, traceable data, and governance that preserves integrity across every stage of the assurance process. From defining control objectives and mapping automatable assertions to enforcing data lineage, version control, and change approvals, this chapter emphasizes how structure and transparency turn automation from a convenience into a trusted source of audit evidence. The same rigor that auditors apply to assessing security controls must be applied to the automation itself, ensuring that every result is explainable, repeatable, and defensible under scrutiny.

At its core, this chapter positions automation and analytics as strategic enablers of cyber risk management rather than mere efficiency tools. By applying continuous testing, variance analysis, and evidence preservation, auditors gain visibility that is both broader and timelier than any traditional approach could offer. These capabilities allow organizations to detect drift, confirm compliance, and respond to emerging threats with precision and confidence. In an era where AI-driven systems and automated defenses dominate security architecture, mastering automated assurance is no longer optional—it is a fundamental skill for maintaining trust, resilience, and accountability in cybersecurity governance.

Objectives and Scope of Automated Assurance

Automation in cybersecurity auditing begins with a clear understanding of *why* something should be automated before a single line of code or configuration is written. The objective is not to replace the professional judgment of the auditor but to strengthen it by extending the reach, accuracy, and consistency of assurance activities. Automation allows auditors to test more controls, more frequently, and across a broader environment than any manual approach could realistically achieve. It enables near-real-time insight into control performance, supports faster identification of anomalies, and drives down the cost of repetitive testing while improving the timeliness of findings. When applied with purpose and discipline, automation transforms the assurance process from episodic and reactive to continuous and proactive. But this transformation only succeeds when automation is built around well-defined control objectives, not simply because the technology exists.

Every automation effort should begin by articulating what specific risk or control objective is being tested and why it matters to the organization. This ensures that automation has a defensible rationale and measurable outcome. When that objective is clearly stated—such as verifying that configurations match approved baselines, that privileged accounts are regularly reviewed, or that logs are complete and tamper-free—the automation can be designed with precision and intent. Each automated check must tie directly to an auditable assertion so that its results are meaningful, interpretable, and repeatable. Without this direct mapping, the automation risks becoming little more than a data-driven curiosity, generating metrics that may look sophisticated but fail to strengthen assurance. The true value lies in producing results that an auditor can stand behind as reliable evidence of control effectiveness.

A recurring pitfall in automation design is starting from the tool instead of the objective. Many organizations adopt automated scripts or analytics platforms simply because they are available, hoping to uncover insights without defining the problem first. This "solution in search of a problem" approach often leads to redundant checks, irrelevant alerts, or inconsistent results that distract rather than inform. The proper path begins with identifying the assurance need—such as ensuring endpoint compliance or detecting configuration drift—and only then determining whether automation can meet that need better than manual review. By grounding automation in control objectives, auditors ensure that every line of code and every data query has a clear purpose tied to risk and compliance requirements. The goal is precision, not volume, of automation.

Certain classes of tests naturally lend themselves to automation and should be prioritized. Configuration and state checks are prime examples, as they involve comparing actual settings against known baselines—an exercise ideally suited to repeatable scripts. Data reconciliations, such as comparing HR records to access control systems or matching system inventories against procurement databases, are similarly well-suited because they follow deterministic logic. Variance tests, where expected outcomes are compared to observed results, also benefit from automation, allowing auditors to quickly surface exceptions for deeper analysis. These types of automated tests provide consistent, objective results that improve efficiency and allow the auditor to focus attention on interpreting patterns rather than manually collecting data. Automation in these areas amplifies human expertise rather than replacing it.

Despite its power, automation has natural boundaries that auditors must respect. Certain activities, particularly those involving qualitative assessment, contextual reasoning, or judgment, remain unsuitable for full automation. Evaluating whether a control design adequately mitigates risk, interpreting ambiguous or incomplete evidence, or assessing the cultural and behavioral dimensions of security all demand human insight. Automation can support these activities by collecting relevant data or flagging anomalies, but it cannot interpret organizational intent or risk tolerance. Auditors must remain the arbiters of meaning—ensuring that automated findings are properly contextualized within the broader risk landscape. Striking this balance preserves both audit credibility and professional value in a world increasingly driven by algorithms.

Defining the boundaries of what can and cannot be automated also safeguards the integrity of the assurance function. When automated routines are deployed within operational environments for continuous monitoring, there is a risk of blurring the distinction between audit oversight and management control. To maintain independence, auditors must clearly document the purpose, ownership, and governance of each automated routine, ensuring that audit tools remain under audit purview and not operational management. This transparency reinforces trust in the results and prevents potential conflicts of interest. Automated assurance must serve the third line of defense, not become an extension of the first.

Once the scope and boundaries are set, auditors must ensure that every automated check produces results that are transparent, reliable, and defensible. This begins with well-documented data inputs, clearly defined logic, and explicit decision thresholds. The results should be both reproducible and explainable—allowing any qualified professional to independently validate the same conclusion. Transparency in the design and logic of automation is critical; an auditor should be able to justify the reasoning behind every alert or exception generated. Automation that operates as a "black box" erodes confidence and undermines the very assurance it seeks to provide. Clarity, traceability, and repeatability are the hallmarks of credible automated testing.

Automation also revolutionizes how auditors approach sampling. Instead of testing a small, statistically representative subset of transactions, automation enables full-population testing—examining every instance within a defined scope. This leap in coverage increases assurance precision and reduces the likelihood of undetected control failures. Moreover, by embedding these routines within continuous auditing frameworks, auditors can monitor performance over time rather than in periodic snapshots. Exceptions can be identified and escalated within hours rather than months, fundamentally improving the speed and quality of risk response. The combination of continuous coverage and timeliness transforms assurance from a retrospective activity into an ongoing safeguard of trust.

Yet with increased frequency and reach comes greater responsibility. Automated assurance systems are not self-sustaining; they require ongoing validation, tuning, and governance. Changes in infrastructure, application updates, or shifts in data structures can silently break scripts or distort logic, producing inaccurate conclusions. Auditors must implement maintenance processes that periodically verify automation accuracy, update logic to align with new controls, and recalibrate thresholds as the environment evolves. In essence, every automated test becomes a control in its own right—requiring documentation, testing, and oversight to maintain reliability.

Data Sources and Pipelines (Lineage, Quality, and Access Controls)

An automated assurance system lives and dies by the integrity of its data pipeline. Everything the auditor concludes depends on whether the information feeding the analytics is accurate, complete, and trustworthy. Data typically enters the assurance pipeline through a combination of controlled interfaces: application programming interfaces (APIs), scheduled data exports, and log sinks that consolidate telemetry from systems, devices, and applications. Each method must be intentional and documented. APIs should use read-only tokens or service accounts with narrowly scoped permissions, ensuring that assurance processes observe but do not modify operational data. File exports must follow consistent naming conventions and include validation routines that confirm successful delivery. Log sinks—such as those feeding from SIEMs, cloud providers, or endpoint platforms—should timestamp events at collection and use encryption in transit to maintain confidentiality.

Once data enters the pipeline, its lineage becomes the most powerful safeguard of audit credibility. Lineage describes the path of data from its origin to its final analytical output, detailing every transformation, enrichment, and storage point along the way. In a well-designed assurance pipeline, lineage is automatically captured as metadata during each processing stage. For example, a configuration compliance job might record the API endpoint used, the time and version of the query, the transformation script applied, and the database table where results are stored. This end-to-end trace allows auditors to reproduce results and verify the integrity of intermediate steps. Without lineage, automated assurance is little more than a black box—efficient, perhaps, but unverifiable.

Maintaining visible lineage also reinforces independence and defensibility. Every pipeline component—source, transformation, and storage—must log who initiated the process, what logic was executed, and what data was produced. These records ensure that results can be reconstructed by an independent reviewer, not just the original automation engineer. By building this transparency into the architecture, the audit function creates a verifiable chain of custody for digital evidence. This becomes essential when audit findings are challenged, or when external assessors seek proof that analytics were performed objectively and reproducibly. Lineage is not optional documentation; it is the backbone of automated assurance trustworthiness. Table 17.1 summarizes intake paths and the specific metadata and checks that make lineage and quality defensible for audit purposes.

Data quality is equally critical. Even the most elegant analytics cannot compensate for flawed input. Assurance pipelines should implement baseline quality checks at ingestion and transformation stages to prevent contamination of results. Completeness checks verify that expected record counts or event volumes are present, ensuring full population coverage. Deduplication routines remove repeated entries created by retries, overlapping data pulls, or multiple collection agents. Timestamp validation confirms that events are chronologically sane, using consistent formats and

Table 17.1 Ingress methods and required metadata for lineage and quality.

Ingress type	Typical contents	Required auth	Lineage metadata	Quality checks
Read only API	Configs and states and events	Scoped token	Request params and response hash and record count	Completeness and deduplication and timestamp sanity
Scheduled export	Flat files and report extracts	Service account	File hash and generation time and source system	Row count match and schema conformance
Log sink	Telemetry and audit events	Mutual TLS	Producer id and topic and partition and offset	Loss detection and time normalization
Message queue	Change events and notifications	Client cert or token	Subscription id and sequence and ack id	Order guarantee and gap detection
Cloud inventory API	Assets and tags and states	Least privilege role	Query version and cursor and page count	Population reconciliation and null checks
Identity provider API	Users and groups and entitlements	Read only app reg	Endpoint version and scope and rate limit use	Join to HR roster and orphan detection

aligned time zones. If these controls are ignored, auditors risk basing conclusions on distorted timelines or incomplete populations—errors that can materially alter findings. Quality assurance at the data level ensures that every automated test starts from a foundation of reliability.

Beyond basic accuracy, quality controls should enforce schema consistency and field validation. Changes to data formats, such as renamed columns or altered value types, can quictly break downstream logic. Pipelines should monitor for unexpected schema drift and alert maintainers before anomalies propagate. Similarly, transformation scripts must validate that calculated fields fall within expected ranges—flagging missing, null, or malformed values that could mislead analytics. These mechanisms form the digital equivalent of audit sampling: small checks applied continuously to ensure the larger system behaves as designed. Over time, these embedded validations give auditors greater confidence that results remain accurate despite system updates or changing data sources.

Access control within the data pipeline is the final pillar of assurance integrity. Every component—from source connectors to transformation jobs to storage repositories—must enforce least privilege. Read-only service accounts should be isolated per source, and credentials must rotate regularly with logging of each use. Data stores should apply role-based access control (RBAC) so that only authorized personnel, such as the audit analytics team, can view or modify datasets. Segregation between development, testing, and production pipelines prevents accidental or unauthorized changes to live audit data. Multi-factor authentication, encryption at rest, and strict access logging further reduce the risk of tampering or unauthorized review.

Trustworthy results also require that access to pipeline metadata be controlled and independently reviewable. The very records that describe lineage and transformations must be protected from modification. Storing these logs in immutable or versioned storage ensures that no one can retroactively alter the evidence trail. Independent reviewers should be able to access lineage and quality reports without needing administrative privileges in the data platform itself.

This separation preserves the credibility of automated results while allowing oversight teams to verify their integrity. Transparency and immutability together make automated assurance auditable in its own right.

Another key consideration is data segregation by sensitivity and ownership. Assurance pipelines often integrate feeds from production systems, HR databases, or ticketing platforms—each with its own privacy and compliance obligations. Classifying data according to sensitivity determines the encryption requirements, retention schedules, and masking standards applied throughout the pipeline. Personally identifiable information (PII) or confidential business data should be tokenized or redacted where feasible, allowing analytics to proceed without exposing sensitive details. Proper data handling not only supports compliance but also demonstrates that automated assurance respects the same control principles it tests in others.

The final measure of an effective assurance pipeline is repeatability. Data intake, transformation, and validation processes must execute the same way every time, producing consistent results from identical inputs. Automated jobs should be versioned, time-stamped, and subject to change control procedures similar to software development. Each pipeline update should include a peer review and test run to confirm that quality checks and lineage tracking remain intact. Repeatability is what allows auditors to defend their conclusions over time, showing that the same logic, applied to the same data, produces the same outcome. In continuous auditing environments, this stability transforms daily data flows into defensible, evidence-based assurance.

Job Design and Governance (Change Control, Versioning, and Approvals)

Automated assurance jobs are, in essence, living audit procedures codified into software. Each one must begin with a precise specification that defines its purpose, inputs, logic, thresholds, and outputs. The specification acts as both design documentation and a contract of intent, describing exactly what the automation is expected to test, how it interprets data, and what constitutes a pass or fail condition. Inputs should be explicitly named and typed, referencing authoritative sources such as configuration baselines, asset inventories, or user directories. Logic and thresholds—whether a system is deemed compliant, a variance acceptable, or a metric within tolerance—must be clear enough for another auditor to reproduce the result without ambiguity. Outputs should include not just the raw results, but contextual metadata such as run identifiers, timestamps, record counts, and error summaries. This level of clarity ensures that automated assurance remains transparent, explainable, and defensible under scrutiny.

Version control is the cornerstone of automation governance. Every script, configuration file, query, and transformation rule must be managed in a source-controlled repository, with human-readable change histories that document who modified what and why. Using established version control systems, such as Git-based repositories, allows for branch isolation, peer review, and traceable merges. Versioning ensures that auditors can revert to any prior state of the job and reproduce historical results if needed. Equally important, configuration parameters—such as alert thresholds, time windows, or sampling rules—should be versioned alongside code. Without version alignment between logic and configuration, automation can drift silently, producing inconsistent results even though the underlying code has not changed. Maintaining this complete history forms the technical audit trail for the automation itself.

Change control governs how updates are designed, tested, and deployed, ensuring that automation evolves in a controlled manner rather than through ad hoc modifications. Each proposed change should include a description of its rationale, expected impact, and evidence of testing in a controlled environment. Before promotion to production, the change must undergo formal review and approval, ideally by both a technical peer and an independent audit lead who was not the author. This dual-approval model enforces separation of duties, preventing an individual from unilaterally altering an assurance process that affects audit results. Approved changes should follow structured deployment procedures—whether through continuous integration pipelines or manual promotion steps—with automated checks verifying successful implementation and rollback readiness.

Governance extends beyond the mechanics of change to the organizational framework that supports it. Every automated job must have an identified owner responsible for its ongoing maintenance, data quality, and performance. The ownership record should specify the job's purpose, scope, inputs, and dependencies, along with the associated stakeholders who consume its results. Jobs must also include defined schedules—daily, weekly, or event-driven—so that timing is consistent and predictable. Scheduling metadata should record start and completion times, run durations, and any deviations from the expected cadence. These details are vital not only for troubleshooting but also for demonstrating continuity of coverage when audit evidence is reviewed months or years later.

Failure management is another essential component of governance. Automated jobs should be designed with predictable failure behaviors rather than ad hoc reactions to errors. Each failure state—such as data unavailability, network timeouts, or unexpected schema changes—should trigger predefined responses. This typically includes configurable retry logic with exponential backoff to prevent system overload, alerting mechanisms that notify maintainers, and fail-safe termination if the integrity of results is in doubt. Jobs must never silently skip or truncate data, as that undermines the validity of assurance conclusions. Error-handling routines should capture sufficient diagnostic information for root cause analysis while avoiding sensitive data exposure. By treating failure handling as part of the design, not an afterthought, auditors ensure automation remains trustworthy under imperfect conditions.

Rollback capability is the final safeguard against automation drift. For every promoted change, there must be a documented procedure to revert the system to its previous stable version if defects or unintended outcomes are discovered. Rollbacks may involve redeploying prior code, restoring configurations from backups, or temporarily disabling a job while integrity checks are performed. These rollback plans should be tested periodically, just like disaster recovery procedures, to confirm they function as intended. Without tested rollback steps, a failed automation update can cascade across dependent jobs, producing misleading results or halting assurance coverage entirely. The ability to revert cleanly ensures that automation remains resilient even when change is frequent.

To prevent "silent drift"—the gradual misalignment of automated jobs from their intended behavior—auditors must establish periodic validation routines. This involves rerunning selected jobs with known input sets and comparing the output against baselines to confirm consistency. Discrepancies can reveal untracked changes in logic, configuration, or source data structure. Validation results should be logged and reviewed by the automation governance team as part of recurring quality assurance. Silent drift is one of the most insidious risks in automated assurance: results continue to appear normal, but their underlying assumptions have shifted. Regular validation acts as an early warning system, ensuring continued reliability.

Documentation serves as both evidence and education. Each job should have a concise but comprehensive record detailing its purpose, data sources, transformation logic, thresholds, owners, reviewers, and approval history. It should also describe the expected output, error-handling design, and rollback plan. This documentation must live alongside the job's code and configuration—preferably in the same version-controlled repository—so that reviewers can correlate logic, configuration, and governance metadata. When auditors or regulators examine how automated assurance operates, this documentation provides a transparent view into both design and oversight. It ensures that automation remains auditable, not just automated.

Promoting automation responsibly requires a mature operational mindset—one that mirrors traditional IT change management but applies it to the unique context of audit assurance. Changes must be traceable, reviews independent, and failures recoverable. Owners must be accountable for monitoring health, documenting updates, and ensuring that the system performs its function reliably. With disciplined job design, robust versioning, strict change control, and clear approvals, automated assurance remains both powerful and controlled. This governance framework transforms automation from a fragile experiment into a sustainable, defensible extension of professional auditing practice.

Automated Control Tests: Types, Frequencies, and Coverage Models

Automated control tests are the practical engines of continuous assurance, translating risk objectives into measurable, repeatable checks that operate at scale. These tests can be thought of as digital auditors that continuously examine evidence, compare it against expectations, and flag exceptions that demand attention. The most common forms include configuration conformance tests, drift detection routines, inventory reconciliations, and exception expiry checks. Each type of test plays a specific role within the overall assurance strategy, and their design must align with both the control's intent and its operational cadence. The frequency of testing—whether hourly, daily, or quarterly—is dictated by the volatility of the control domain and the risk appetite of the organization. High-risk, fast-changing systems warrant continuous or near-real-time testing, while stable, low-variance environments may only require periodic validation.

Configuration conformance tests are among the most widely deployed automated checks. They validate that system, network, and application settings match approved baselines, such as security hardening guides, benchmark configurations, or policy templates. These tests are well-suited for automation because configurations can be represented as structured data and compared mechanically against a standard. A configuration conformance test might verify that encryption is enabled on all storage volumes, that password policies meet minimum complexity requirements, or that firewalls enforce approved access rules. Frequency is determined by how often configurations are likely to change—daily in cloud deployments, weekly in infrastructure-as-code environments, or monthly in traditional data centers. Automated conformance tests are typically run after each deployment or configuration change, ensuring deviations are detected before they manifest as exploitable weaknesses.

Drift detection tests focus on identifying unauthorized or unexpected changes over time. While conformance checks look for compliance at a single point, drift detection compares successive states to detect movement away from a previously verified baseline. This is particularly important in environments where configurations are meant to be immutable, such as containerized workloads or managed infrastructure templates. A drift detection process might compare current firewall rules to last week's approved configuration, alerting if new ports have been opened or if rule order has changed. Because drift often signals control failure or unauthorized intervention, the testing frequency is typically high—ranging from hourly snapshots in critical systems to daily scans for general infrastructure. The faster an organization can detect drift, the smaller the potential exposure window.

Inventory reconciliations form another essential category of automated control testing. These routines validate that asset records, user lists, and system inventories are synchronized across authoritative sources. For example, an automated reconciliation might compare a cloud provider's list of virtual machines to the central asset register, or align HR records with active directory accounts to ensure terminated users have been deprovisioned. Reconciliations help auditors detect "shadow assets," orphaned accounts, and untracked systems that fall outside formal governance. Because data sources like HR systems and asset databases tend to update on predictable cycles, reconciliation tests often run daily or weekly, depending on how frequently the authoritative sources change. The more dynamic the environment, the more frequently reconciliations should occur to prevent blind spots in coverage.

Exception expiry checks close the loop on temporary control deviations. Organizations often allow exceptions—such as an unpatched system or a firewall rule extension—under controlled, time-bound conditions. Automated expiry tests monitor these exceptions to ensure they are either remediated or reapproved before deadlines lapse. These checks rely on structured exception registers that include approval metadata, risk classification, and expiration dates. Automated expiry reviews should run daily to catch exceptions nearing their due date and to generate escalation alerts for overdue items. This type of testing enforces discipline and prevents risk exceptions from becoming permanent, untracked vulnerabilities. It also provides auditors with a consistent view of exception management performance across the enterprise.

Determining the appropriate testing frequency for each control domain requires balancing coverage with operational feasibility. Risk and volatility are the key drivers. Controls that guard critical assets, like privileged identity systems or financial transaction gateways, demand frequent or even continuous validation. Conversely, low-risk controls, such as noncritical application patch levels, may be monitored weekly or monthly. Control cadence should also align with the underlying process cycle—for example, daily for user provisioning, quarterly for policy attestations, and continuously for security logging. By matching test frequency to the natural rhythm of change, auditors ensure that automation remains both efficient and relevant. Over-testing can generate noise and fatigue, while under-testing invites undetected risk exposure.

Coverage models define how much of the environment automated control testing touches. The ideal goal is population coverage—testing every applicable instance, transaction, or configuration within scope. Full coverage provides the strongest assurance but can be computationally intensive or unnecessary for lower-risk domains. In those cases, a risk-weighted subset model can be employed, prioritizing systems with higher data sensitivity, external exposure, or compliance requirements. For example, an organization might apply continuous monitoring to internet-facing servers but only weekly scans for internal development environments. The coverage model should always be transparent and justified by documented risk assessment, so that both management and auditors understand what is and is not under automated review.

New systems, applications, and services must be deliberately enrolled into automated control coverage to prevent blind spots. Onboarding processes should include an automation readiness assessment—verifying that the new system's data sources, APIs, and logs can be integrated into the assurance pipeline. Enrollment should occur as part of the deployment life cycle, not as a postlaunch activity. Each new system must be mapped to applicable control tests, with ownership assigned and baseline configurations captured before production release. Without this proactive enrollment, even the best automation framework can fall behind the pace of innovation, leaving portions of the environment unaudited. Regular reconciliation between asset inventories and test coverage reports helps identify any systems that have escaped automation.

Auditors must also consider how automated test results are aggregated and interpreted. The volume of continuous test data can be overwhelming unless structured dashboards and exception workflows are in place. Results should be tagged by control, system, and severity, enabling clear prioritization of findings. Automated tests that fail repeatedly without human review lose their assurance value; thus, governance must ensure that test failures trigger appropriate remediation or escalation. The combination of automated checks, calibrated frequencies, and risk-based coverage allows auditors to maintain visibility across dynamic technology landscapes while conserving resources for analytical interpretation.

Accuracy and Reliability: Ground-truthing, Thresholds, and Drift in Tests

Accuracy in automated assurance begins with disciplined ground-truthing that proves a job's logic detects what it claims to detect and ignores what it should ignore. The most direct method seeds known positives and known negatives into a controlled dataset, then verifies that the test flags the former and clears the latter without ambiguity. These seed cases should cover ordinary, edge, and adversarial scenarios, including boundary values, missing fields, and malformed timestamps that often appear in real data. Parallel runs against a manually validated "gold" sample provide an additional check, allowing auditors to compare machine outcomes to human determinations across identical inputs. When the automated result diverges from the adjudicated ground truth, the cause must be traced to logic, data quality, or threshold selection before promotion.

Independent cross-checks strengthen reliability by validating results through alternative evidence paths. A control that evaluates privileged access revocations, for example, can be corroborated by reconciling HR termination records to identity platform disablement events and ticket closure timestamps. Where feasible, the same assertion should be testable via two dissimilar mechanisms, such as querying authoritative APIs and separately parsing signed audit logs streamed to a trusted sink. Shadow-mode deployments—where the automated job runs without affecting escalation workflows—allow comparison against incumbent procedures until performance converges. These triangulations reduce the risk that a single faulty dependency or schema drift subtly corrupts outcomes without obvious failures.

Thresholds translate continuous measurements into discrete audit decisions and must be chosen with explicit articulation of error costs. A low variance tolerance might catch more true problems but can overwhelm responders with benign anomalies, while a higher threshold risks missing early indicators of control failure. Selection should be informed by empirical distributions from historical data, business risk appetite, and the operational capacity to investigate alerts, not by arbitrary round numbers. Precision, recall, and false discovery rate provide a common language for quantifying trade-offs, and confidence intervals around these metrics prevent overfitting to a single sample period. Documenting the rationale—including data windows, segments analyzed, and accepted residual risk—makes threshold choices defensible and repeatable.

Periodic reassessment is essential because systems, users, and attacker behaviors evolve, causing yesterday's optimal threshold to underperform today. Review cadences should align to control volatility: monthly for dynamic identity and cloud controls, quarterly for relatively stable baselines, and event-driven rechecks after major platform changes. Re-assessment should rerun the original ground-truth suite, incorporate fresh labeled cases from recent incidents, and test sensitivity to plausible data quality degradations such as partial outages or delayed feeds. Where performance degrades, structured experiments should evaluate candidate thresholds or alternate features before updating production logic. All changes to thresholds should follow the same approvals and rollback plans used for code changes to prevent untracked drift.

Capturing and analyzing error rates in production turns accuracy from a one-time exercise into an operating discipline. Every run should compute and store counts of positives, negatives, and exceptions, together with subsequent human adjudication where available, to estimate false positives and false negatives over time. When human triage resolves an alert as nonissue, the reason code—such as "expected maintenance," "known exception," or "stale asset record"—becomes training signal for rule refinement or data quality fixes. Control charts and stability metrics help detect sudden shifts in alert rates that may indicate upstream data drift or a broken connector rather than genuine risk changes. Persistent error patterns should trigger a root-cause review across logic, thresholds, and dependencies.

Drift management distinguishes between data drift, where input distributions change, and concept drift, where the relationship between inputs and control effectiveness shifts. Data drift appears as shifts in field cardinalities, missingness, or value ranges; monitoring should include automated schema checks, null-rate alarms, and percentile-based guards on key features. Concept drift emerges when the same indicator no longer predicts control failure—such as a new provisioning workflow altering the meaning of an "inactive" status—requiring a revisit of the assertion and its proxy signals. Drift detection should feed a playbook that prescribes validation steps, threshold stress tests, and stakeholder review to decide whether to recalibrate or redesign. Treating drift as an expected condition, not an anomaly, keeps automation aligned with living processes.

Robust documentation is the institutional memory that preserves reliability through personnel turnover and platform changes. For each automated test, the record must define the assertion, enumerate inputs and their authoritative sources, describe transformation logic, and state thresholds with rationales. It should include the ground-truth artifacts used in validation, error-rate dashboards referenced for ongoing monitoring, and known limitations such as populations temporarily excluded. Material changes—any modification that can affect a decision boundary, a data dependency, or the interpretation of results—require a dated changelog entry that links to approvals, test evidence, and rollback steps. This dossier forms audit evidence for the automation itself, enabling independent reproduction and review.

Confidence in correctness also depends on resilient failure behavior that protects result integrity under degraded conditions. When inputs are late, partial, or structurally inconsistent, the job should fail closed by withholding pass/fail judgments and emitting a data-quality exception with explicit diagnostics. Retries with bounded backoff prevent flapping during transient outages, while safeguards against silent truncation or opportunistic sampling avoid misleading "all clear" results. Where partial evidence can justify a limited assertion—for example, coverage for a subset of regions with complete data—the output must be clearly labeled to prevent overgeneralization. These patterns ensure that consumers never mistake absent evidence for evidence of absence.

To prevent confirmation bias, periodic "red team for rules" exercises should challenge core assumptions by simulating realistic but previously unseen edge cases. Engineers and auditors collaborate to craft novel seeds that mimic process changes, ambiguous states, and benign anomalies likely to confuse the current logic. The exercise evaluates whether thresholds and exception handling degrade gracefully, whether alerts remain interpretable, and whether documentation still reflects reality. Insights feed back into the test harness and ground-truth library, raising the floor for future validations. Over time, this adversarial posture makes the test suite a guardian against complacency as environments evolve.

Reliability improves when the pathway from detection to action is measured as rigorously as detection itself. Time-to-triage, rework rates after false alarms, and recurrence of the same exception category quantify the real-world cost of error and the sufficiency of thresholds. If responders routinely suppress alerts from a particular check, the signal-to-noise ratio is miscalibrated and demands threshold tuning or better contextual enrichment. Conversely, if post-incident reviews reveal missed opportunities where the test produced weak signals that were ignored, sensitivity may need to increase. Closing this loop transforms accuracy from a static property of code into a continuous quality attribute of the entire assurance process.

Evidence Preservation: Logs, Artifacts, and Reproducibility Standards

Evidence preservation is the foundation of credible automated assurance. Every automated control test, reconciliation job, or analytics routine produces evidence that must be retained in a structured, verifiable manner. This evidence encompasses not only the end results but also the data, logic, and context that produced them. At a minimum, auditors must preserve five categories of artifacts: raw data extracts from source systems, normalized tables after transformation, final result snapshots or reports, the code or query logic that generated those outputs, and any parameter or configuration files used during execution. Together, these components form the digital equivalent of audit working papers—capturing what was tested, how it was tested, and what the outcome was. Without such retention, automated assurance loses its defensibility, as results cannot be verified, re-created, or challenged with confidence.

Each preserved artifact must be tightly linked to a specific execution run through a consistent metadata structure. Every job should record a unique run identifier, along with the precise timestamps for start, completion, and duration. The outputs and logs associated with that run must be cryptographically hashed to detect tampering and to confirm that evidence has not been altered after generation. Metadata should also record the data sources accessed, their respective timestamps, record counts, and any transformation scripts or libraries invoked. This linkage allows an auditor to trace every piece of evidence back to its origin and verify that it corresponds to the environment and conditions under which it was produced. Properly indexed run metadata not only ensures reproducibility but also streamlines later audits or investigations when historical evidence must be retrieved.

Immutability is a nonnegotiable property of preserved evidence. Once artifacts are finalized and validated, they must be stored in a write-once, read-many (WORM) medium or an immutable storage bucket that enforces version retention and prevents deletion or modification. Retention policies should meet or exceed organizational audit record requirements, typically ranging from three to seven years depending on regulation and risk tolerance. Each record should include both human-readable and machine-verifiable manifests—files listing the included artifacts, their hashes, and their logical relationships. These manifests act as the notarized inventory of the run, ensuring that no artifact can be substituted or lost without detection. Access to preserved evidence must also be logged and periodically reviewed to confirm integrity and proper chain of custody.

Logs play a crucial role in preservation by capturing the operational context of each automated assurance run. Detailed execution logs should record system environment variables, command-line arguments, job steps, success and failure states, exception messages, and retry behaviors. These logs provide the narrative of execution—proof that the job performed as intended and that any failures were handled correctly. They also allow investigators to understand anomalies in output or deviations from normal performance. Structured logging formats, such as JSON or syslog-compatible output, facilitate both automated monitoring and long-term readability. Because logs often contain sensitive operational data, they must be secured with the same rigor as the audit evidence itself, encrypted both at rest and in transit.

To support full reproducibility, the computing environment used for the automated assurance job must also be captured. This includes versions of operating systems, programming languages, libraries, and dependencies. In modern environments, the most reliable method is containerization—preserving a container image that encapsulates the exact runtime environment. Alternatively, detailed environment manifests can be stored, listing library versions, compiler hashes, and configuration files. When an auditor or independent reviewer later reruns the job, these captured environments ensure that results are identical to the original, preventing discrepancies caused by library updates or dependency drift. Preserving the environment is the digital analog of freezing the audit conditions in time.

Result snapshots form the tangible output of assurance and must be preserved with both structure and clarity. These snapshots can take the form of summary tables, exception reports, or compliance dashboards exported at the end of each run. They should include all relevant metrics, such as population size, number of items tested, number of exceptions, and severity distributions. Each snapshot must also reference the version of the job logic that produced it and the associated run identifier, creating a closed loop between logic, data, and outcome. When results are later reviewed—by management, auditors, or regulators—the link between the snapshot and its underlying evidence allows them to verify that no post-processing or filtering has altered the original results.

Preservation standards must extend to documentation of logic and configuration. Every version of the query scripts, transformation rules, and parameter files must be archived along with the output they generated. This ensures that future reviewers can read and understand the specific logic applied to the data at the time of execution. Configuration files are particularly important because they often encode dynamic elements such as threshold values, time ranges, and exclusion rules that influence results. Retaining these files alongside the code creates an exact replay capability, allowing an independent auditor to replicate the test and compare outputs for consistency. When documentation is incomplete or decoupled from the preserved data, the ability to defend audit conclusions weakens significantly.

Reproducibility demands explicit linkage between all artifacts in the assurance process. The most effective method is a run manifest—a single, automatically generated record that lists every input, transformation, output, and supporting artifact with associated hashes and timestamps. The manifest should also include version tags for code repositories, container images, and configuration files. If a future reviewer needs to rerun the job, this manifest serves as the instruction manual and proof of authenticity. Automated validation routines should periodically verify that the manifest remains internally consistent by recalculating hashes and checking for missing files. In continuous auditing environments, manifest validation becomes part of the standard control set to ensure that long-term evidence remains intact and trustworthy.

Retention practices must also consider scalability and accessibility. Automated assurance pipelines can generate terabytes of logs and intermediate data over time, making selective retention essential. Policies should distinguish between transient data used for processing and durable evidence needed for audit defense. Compression, archival storage tiers, and life cycle management rules can reduce cost while maintaining accessibility for regulatory and internal reviews. Retrieval procedures should be tested periodically to confirm that stored evidence can be restored intact and interpreted correctly using the preserved environment specifications. Evidence that cannot be practically accessed is effectively lost, even if it exists physically.

Evidence preservation is not solely a technical exercise—it is a governance obligation. The preservation and reproducibility framework must be documented in policy and integrated into the organization's overall audit methodology. Responsibilities for evidence review, verification, and archival maintenance must be assigned, with periodic attestations confirming compliance with retention and immutability standards. Each preserved job should pass an independent reproducibility test at least annually, demonstrating that the outputs can be regenerated from preserved inputs, logic, and environments. This discipline ensures that automation in assurance remains transparent, defensible, and sustainable over time. In the end, evidence preservation is what transforms automated results from transient data into lasting, auditable proof of control performance.

Dashboards and Variance Analysis (Interpreting Results and Triggering Follow-ups)

Dashboards are the primary interface through which automated assurance results become actionable. They translate continuous testing data into clear, decision-oriented views that auditors, managers, and control owners can quickly interpret. A well-designed dashboard shows coverage percentages, drift trends, and exception aging in ways that make control performance instantly visible. Every dashboard element must show what scope it represents, when it was last refreshed, and how much of the total population was tested. A figure that simply says "95% compliant" without context is meaningless unless readers know what was measured and over what time period. Dashboards must help users distinguish between stable control health and emerging problems by emphasizing both trend direction and data completeness. As shown in Table 17.2, frequencies scale with risk while coverage shifts between full population and risk weighted subsets to keep signals actionable.

The first role of a dashboard is to summarize coverage. Coverage percentages show how much of the intended environment or control population is being monitored by automation. For example, a dashboard might display that 98% of servers are included in configuration compliance checks or that 90% of privileged accounts are covered in access reconciliations. These figures provide instant visibility into blind spots where automated testing has not yet been deployed. Coverage should always include both a percentage and a denominator—such as "180 out of 200 systems"—so the

Table 17.2 Automated test types with risk aligned frequencies and coverage models.

Test type	High-risk frequency	Medium-risk frequency	Low-risk frequency	Coverage model	Typical trigger
Configuration conformance	Per change or hourly	Daily	Weekly	Population where feasible	Fail rate above tolerance
Drift detection	Hourly	Daily	Every three days	Population for critical tiers	State change from last approved baseline
Inventory reconciliation	Daily	Weekly	Biweekly	Risk weighted subset	Mismatch between authoritative sources
Exception expiry	Daily	Daily	Weekly	Population of active exceptions	Items due within seven days or overdue

viewer can interpret its significance correctly. Where gaps exist, the dashboard should make them obvious enough to prompt immediate enrollment of missing systems or accounts.

Drift trends form the heartbeat of variance analysis. They illustrate how control performance changes over time and reveal whether exceptions are isolated or part of a growing pattern. A gradual upward drift in misconfigured endpoints, for example, may indicate weak change controls or inconsistent deployment scripts. By contrast, a sharp spike in exceptions after a single system patch may suggest a one-time disruption rather than systemic failure. Visualizing drift over days, weeks, or months allows auditors to see how quickly controls recover after exceptions are corrected, which in turn reflects process maturity. Dashboards should show both absolute counts of exceptions and the rate of change, helping teams differentiate between volume-driven spikes and genuine deterioration in control design or operation.

Exception aging metrics add a time dimension to control health. These measures show how long unresolved issues remain open, grouped by severity or risk category. A dashboard that shows dozens of high-risk exceptions older than 30 days sends a clear signal that remediation processes are stalled. Automated assurance gains credibility when it not only detects exceptions but also tracks whether they are being addressed in a timely way. Aging reports should display how many items fall into specific time brackets—such as less than 7 days, 8–30 days, or more than 30 days—and how these distributions change over time. When aging trends grow worse, they become leading indicators that governance or accountability mechanisms may be weakening.

Variance analysis ties the entire picture together by comparing observed results to expected baselines or tolerances. Each control area should have clearly defined benchmarks that represent normal operation. For instance, a configuration compliance rate of 97% might be acceptable for a development environment but insufficient for production systems. Variance analysis measures the deviation between current results and those expectations, highlighting where attention is required. Small, temporary variances may be benign, while sustained or widening gaps signal deeper issues. Dashboards that display variance as both percentage and historical trend make it easy for decision-makers to spot early warnings before control failures become incidents.

Once variances are detected, they must trigger defined follow-up actions. Automated systems can be configured to escalate issues that exceed thresholds, such as when coverage drops below 90% or exception aging surpasses a certain limit. Each trigger should initiate a documented response procedure that specifies who is notified, what investigation steps are taken, and how findings are tracked to closure. For example, a variance in configuration drift may trigger a manual review of affected systems, while repeated failures in log collection could launch a verification of data pipeline integrity. Triggers should balance sensitivity with practicality—too many alerts create fatigue, while too few allow problems to persist unnoticed.

Every follow-up must have a clear escalation path. When automated results show material deviations, those findings should flow to control owners first, then to management, and finally to audit leadership if resolution stalls. Escalation procedures must be written into governance documentation and periodically tested, just as incident response plans are. This ensures accountability for acting on automated findings rather than letting them accumulate without remediation. The chain of escalation also helps maintain independence, ensuring that the audit function retains oversight while operational teams perform corrective actions.

Dashboards also need to respect the boundary between ongoing monitoring and formal audit testing. Continuous monitoring reflects operational vigilance—tracking whether controls remain healthy between audits. Re-performing an audit test, by contrast, is a formal verification of control effectiveness that feeds into assurance conclusions. When variance triggers lead to additional tests, auditors must document whether these are follow-up validations or new audit procedures.

Blurring this line can create confusion about what constitutes official audit evidence versus routine monitoring data. Clear labeling within dashboards—such as "Operational Control Health" versus "Audit Test Result"—prevents misinterpretation.

Documentation is essential for interpreting dashboard data consistently. Every metric, threshold, and variance rule must have a defined source, calculation method, and rationale. This includes specifying how population counts are derived, how exceptions are classified, and how time frames are determined. The documentation should be accessible directly from the dashboard interface so users can trace what each metric means without guessing. Well-documented dashboards turn data into defensible evidence; poorly documented ones invite misinterpretation and erode confidence.

Finally, dashboards should be designed as living tools, not static reports. As automated assurance matures, new controls, systems, and data sources will be added. Dashboards must evolve in parallel, updating metrics, thresholds, and visualizations to reflect changes in scope and technology. Regular review cycles—ideally quarterly—ensure that dashboards remain aligned with audit objectives and risk priorities. By combining clear visualization, disciplined variance analysis, structured follow-ups, and transparent documentation, dashboards become more than status displays—they become trusted instruments of continuous assurance, guiding auditors and leaders alike toward timely, data-driven decisions.

Conclusion

Mastering the principles of automation, continuous auditing, and analytics-driven assurance is critical for maintaining trust in systems that now operate faster and change more dynamically than human oversight alone can manage. The modern auditor's role extends beyond verifying compliance—it now includes validating the reliability of automated evidence itself and ensuring that machine-driven processes uphold governance standards. When automation is built on sound objectives, transparent data lineage, and disciplined governance, it becomes an enduring safeguard rather than a source of unchecked complexity. These practices elevate assurance from a periodic activity to a continuous pillar of cyber risk management.

This chapter reinforces the role of automation as both a control and an audit instrument, especially in environments shaped by artificial intelligence, adaptive infrastructure, and real-time decision systems. By aligning automated tests with defined control objectives, maintaining versioned code and immutable evidence, and continuously evaluating accuracy through variance analysis, professionals create assurance frameworks that are both scalable and trustworthy. The rigor once reserved for manual audit testing must now be applied to the systems that perform those tests, ensuring that every automated result is explainable, repeatable, and defensible. In doing so, auditors preserve the core value of assurance even as its methods evolve.

With these foundations in place, cybersecurity auditors are better equipped to oversee AI-enabled enterprises where data, logic, and risk are constantly in motion. Automation and analytics do not replace the human element of assurance—they amplify it, allowing professionals to focus on interpretation, risk context, and strategic response. The future of cybersecurity auditing belongs to those who can bridge technology and judgment, pairing automation's precision with human discernment. By embracing these principles, auditors ensure that trust, transparency, and accountability remain central to every layer of intelligent, automated defense.

Auditor Recommendations

1. **Define Control Objectives Before Automating:** Establish a clear process for articulating control objectives before building or deploying automated assurance tools. Begin by identifying what risks the automation is meant to measure or mitigate, then design tests that align precisely with those objectives. This ensures automation supports valid assertions rather than creating unnecessary or misleading checks. Grounding automation in control intent prevents wasted effort and enhances audit defensibility.
2. **Design Robust Data Pipelines with Traceability:** Build assurance pipelines that document every data source, transformation, and output. Maintain metadata that records timestamps, record counts, and logic versions to provide complete lineage from input to result. When data lineage is transparent, auditors can trace findings back to their origin and validate both accuracy and scope. Traceability transforms automated results into reliable, reproducible evidence.
3. **Implement Continuous Quality Checks on Data Inputs:** Prioritize consistent validation of data completeness, accuracy, and integrity at every ingestion point. Incorporate checks for duplicate records, missing timestamps, or corrupted fields before data reaches analytical layers. Reliable automation depends on trusted inputs; even minor data flaws can cascade into material audit errors. A disciplined approach to input validation strengthens the credibility of automated assurance findings.
4. **Maintain Strict Version Control and Change Governance:** Treat automated jobs like production-grade audit assets requiring full version history and controlled promotion. Use code repositories and documented approval workflows to ensure transparency and accountability for every modification. Versioning both logic and configuration files prevents silent drift and enables rollback if results deviate unexpectedly. A rigorous governance process protects the integrity of automated assurance systems.
5. **Document Ownership, Scheduling, and Failure Behavior:** Assign clear ownership for each automated assurance job and record its expected frequency, inputs, and outputs. Define how failures are handled, including retry intervals, alert mechanisms, and escalation paths. Automation without defined failure behavior risks silent gaps in testing and delayed detection of breakdowns. Comprehensive documentation ensures operational continuity and accountability across the audit life cycle.
6. **Establish Calibration and Reassessment of Thresholds:** Regularly review and adjust the thresholds used in automated tests to reflect changing business risk and operational patterns. Compare current results to historical distributions and analyze false positive or negative rates to refine accuracy. Threshold drift is inevitable as systems evolve, so maintaining alignment ensures tests remain both relevant and reliable. Continuous calibration keeps automation tuned to real-world risk dynamics.
7. **Preserve All Evidence with Reproducibility in Mind:** Retain every element required to recreate a specific audit run, including raw data extracts, transformation scripts, configuration files, and output summaries. Store these artifacts in immutable repositories with run identifiers, timestamps, and cryptographic hashes. This practice enables independent re-execution of automated jobs, ensuring results can be verified years after their original run. Reproducibility safeguards the credibility of continuous assurance.

8. **Use Dashboards to Drive Insight, Not Just Reporting:** Design dashboards that translate automated results into meaningful decision signals rather than static metrics. Present coverage, exception trends, and drift analysis in context with population size and control scope. Well-structured dashboards support risk-based prioritization, helping audit teams focus on areas that truly warrant follow-up. The goal is actionable visibility, not data decoration.
9. **Define Escalation Paths for Automated Findings:** Create structured escalation procedures that specify how variance triggers and exception alerts are handled. Ensure alerts route to accountable control owners with clear expectations for triage and remediation time frames. Without defined escalation, automation becomes passive monitoring instead of an active assurance tool. Proper escalation transforms automated outputs into meaningful, managed actions.
10. **Validate and Re-verify Automation Regularly:** Schedule periodic reviews of all automated assurance components to confirm that logic, data, and results remain aligned with audit intent. Use controlled test data or cross-checks with independent sources to verify that automation continues to function as designed. Re-verification should include documentation updates and recalibration of any impacted metrics. This recurring discipline prevents degradation over time and maintains the reliability of automated audit assurance.

Chapter Questions

1. Why should control objectives be articulated before building automated assurance tests?
   - A. To maximize the number of dashboards created
   - B. To reduce compute costs during off-peak hours
   - C. To ensure tests map to specific risks and automatable assertions
   - D. To standardize color palettes across reports

2. Which ingestion design feature best prevents duplicate counts when a failed job is rerun?
   - A. Idempotent operations with durable checkpointing
   - B. Manual editing of CSV files before loading
   - C. Broad write permissions to source systems
   - D. Screen scraping from web consoles

3. What is the principal value of modeling pipeline transformations as a directed acyclic graph?
   - A. Increasing encryption key length by default
   - B. Accelerating dashboard rendering through caching
   - C. Compressing storage for raw extracts
   - D. Enabling end-to-end traceability and reproducible backtracking

4. Which automated test pattern best ensures temporary risk acceptances do not become permanent gaps?
   - A. Configuration conformance checks
   - B. Exception expiry checks
   - C. Inventory reconciliations
   - D. Drift detection routines

5. What should primarily inform the selection of alert thresholds for automated tests?
   A. Convenient round numbers that are easy to remember
   B. Vendor default settings applied universally
   C. Empirical data distributions, risk appetite, and response capacity
   D. Zero-tolerance values to eliminate false negatives

6. Which practice is essential for linking preserved artifacts to a specific execution run?
   A. Recording run identifiers, timestamps, and cryptographic hashes
   B. Deleting intermediate files weekly to save space
   C. Storing screenshots of dashboards only
   D. Using editable spreadsheets without version history

7. What governance boundary preserves audit independence when automation runs continuously in production?
   A. Allowing operational teams to change audit jobs without review
   B. Merging development and production pipelines for speed
   C. Disabling job logs to reduce noise
   D. Keeping audit oversight separate from operational ownership with documented purpose and approvals

8. When variance appears on dashboards, what should translate signals into concrete action?
   A. Changing widget colors to draw attention
   B. Predefined triggers mapped to playbooks and escalation paths
   C. Hiding denominators to simplify the view
   D. Waiting for the next quarterly audit cycle

9. In drift management, which statement best describes concept drift?
   A. Time-zone inconsistencies that skew timestamps
   B. Duplicate records introduced by overlapping collectors
   C. A shift in how inputs relate to the control outcome due to process changes
   D. Network retries causing temporary ingestion delays

10. How should new systems be onboarded to avoid blind spots in automated coverage?
   A. Perform an automation readiness assessment and enroll during the deployment life cycle
   B. Add them only after an incident proves they are risky
   C. Assume coverage once assets appear in inventory
   D. Monitor only internet-facing systems regardless of risk

18

AI Threat Modeling and Attack Surfaces

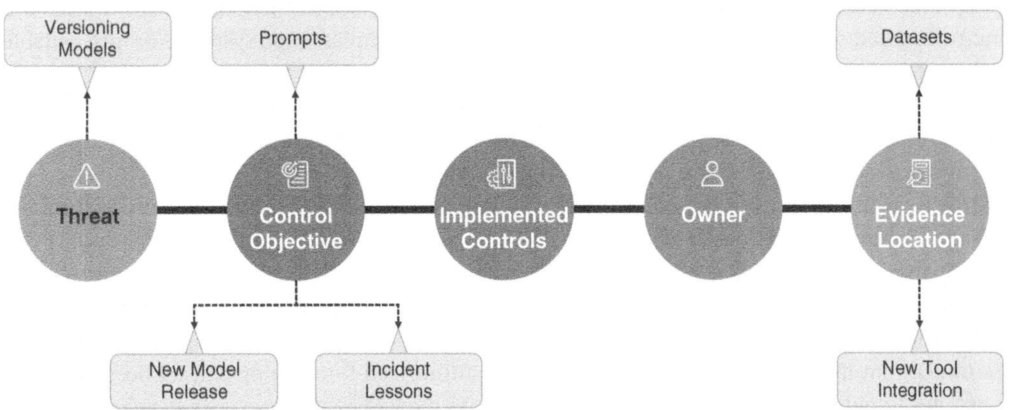

Artificial intelligence (AI) has redefined how organizations operate, but it has also reshaped how auditors must think about assurance, control, and accountability. The velocity of AI adoption—spanning models, datasets, prompts, and automated agents—demands a disciplined approach to understanding where risks emerge and how they can be mitigated within auditable boundaries. This chapter positions the auditor at the intersection of automation, analytics, and adaptive systems, equipping them to evaluate AI not as a black box but as an integrated, evolving ecosystem. Understanding this ecosystem is essential to maintaining trust, transparency, and regulatory compliance in environments where decisions are increasingly delegated to machine-driven logic.

From threat modeling to control design, AI auditing extends traditional assurance practices into domains where data, logic, and behavior are constantly in flux. This chapter examines how familiar frameworks can be adapted to map AI-specific attack surfaces—prompt injections, data poisoning, model theft, and misuse through integrations—and how these threats translate into measurable control objectives across identity, data protection, and behavioral safety. By emphasizing data integrity, traceability, and governance, it establishes a foundation for evidence-driven assurance that can withstand both adversarial pressure and operational change. This evolution is not about adding complexity but about preserving auditability in systems that learn and adapt faster than human oversight alone can match.

Ultimately, the principles presented here enable auditors to bring order and accountability to an inherently dynamic technology landscape. By connecting risk assessment, control validation, and traceable documentation into a single, coherent structure, AI assurance becomes a continuous practice rather than a static evaluation. The importance of this chapter lies in its synthesis—it bridges security engineering, governance, and ethics into a unified model of responsible oversight. In doing so, it prepares cybersecurity auditors to evaluate AI systems with the same rigor expected of any critical enterprise control, ensuring that innovation advances without eroding trust or compliance.

Scoping AI Assets: Models, Datasets, Prompts, Tools, and Agents

Defining the scope of AI assets is one of the most critical steps in auditing an AI-enabled environment. Unlike traditional systems that can be bounded by infrastructure or software versions, AI systems involve a network of interconnected components—each with its own role, owner, and risk profile. The boundary for assurance must include models and their versions, training and fine-tuning datasets, embeddings and vector stores, prompt templates and system prompts, callable tools and functions, and any agents or orchestrators that coordinate model interactions. It must also include all external and internal endpoints through which data or requests flow. Establishing this boundary early ensures that the audit remains grounded in a clear inventory of what is actually under review and what falls beyond the organization's direct control.

Models form the centerpiece of most AI systems, but they are not static assets. Each model version represents a distinct configuration that may respond differently to the same input. The auditor should confirm that every model in use is documented with its name, version, and source, whether it is an in-house build or a third-party offering. Ownership must be clearly assigned, and version control should be traceable from training to deployment. This traceability provides assurance that model drift, shadow versions, or unauthorized fine-tuning cannot occur without oversight. Equally important is verifying that access to model weights or parameters is controlled according to data classification policies, as these often embed sensitive intellectual property or proprietary data.

Datasets demand even more careful attention because they influence both accuracy and ethical risk. The auditor's role is to ensure that each dataset—training, validation, and testing—is properly cataloged with its origin, purpose, and sensitivity classification. Questions about consent, licensing, and regulatory compliance should be addressed during scoping, not as an afterthought. Data lineage must be preserved to demonstrate that datasets used for fine-tuning or retraining have not been contaminated by unauthorized or high-risk sources. A strong data governance framework supports these efforts, linking every dataset to its steward and to the models that depend on it.

Prompt templates and system prompts represent a new but equally important category of AI assets. In prompt-driven architectures, the behavior of a model is shaped as much by its prompts as by its weights. System prompts, in particular, define the model's role, tone, and constraints, and can inadvertently expose sensitive instructions if not secured. The auditor should verify that prompt libraries are version-controlled, documented, and subject to change management like any other code asset. This includes reviewing who can modify prompts, how revisions are tested, and whether prompt content aligns with the organization's acceptable use and data handling policies.

Embeddings and vector stores extend the model's memory and contextual understanding but also widen the attack surface. They may contain representations of sensitive data that could be reconstructed or inferred if improperly secured. During scoping, auditors should ensure that vector databases are treated as classified assets, complete with encryption, retention, and access control standards. Connections between models and vector stores must be mapped to clarify where data persists and under what trust boundaries it resides. This prevents hidden data flows that could undermine compliance or create leakage risks.

Tools and functions, often implemented as part of retrieval-augmented generation or function-calling frameworks, serve as extensions of the model's capabilities. Each tool introduces new dependencies and permissions that must be governed. The auditor should require documentation of every callable function the model can access—such as APIs for data retrieval, writing files, or executing code—and confirm that authorization is restricted by design. This scoping step is essential to prevent overprivileged or unmonitored tool usage, which could enable unauthorized data access or system manipulation through the AI layer.

Agents and orchestrators add yet another layer of complexity by managing multiple models, prompts, and tools dynamically. They may chain actions together or invoke external systems automatically. From an assurance perspective, this means each agent becomes a control plane requiring audit focus. Scoping should capture all agent configurations, their operating logic, and their dependency maps. The auditor must determine whether these orchestrators operate within approved trust boundaries and whether activity logs are maintained for traceability. Without clear accountability for these autonomous components, the organization risks losing visibility into decision-making chains.

Every AI asset must also be classified according to data sensitivity and ownership. This classification guides how information flows between components and defines which assets require encryption, isolation, or external oversight. For instance, a third-party model may reside outside the organization's direct trust boundary, yet still process sensitive prompts or outputs. Scoping must explicitly state these boundaries and document where first-party control ends and third-party responsibility begins. This clarity is foundational to both risk assessment and continuous assurance.

Threat Modeling Methods for AI Systems (STRIDE/ATT&CK Extensions)

Threat modeling remains one of the most effective ways to translate complex system design into actionable security insight. When applied to AI systems, however, traditional frameworks like STRIDE or MITRE ATT&CK require careful adaptation to capture new forms of risk unique to data-driven and prompt-mediated behavior. The goal is not to reinvent these proven methodologies but to extend them to account for the specific components that define AI functionality—data ingestion, prompt channels, retrieval paths, tool invocations, and output sinks. By weaving these dimensions into familiar analytical structures, auditors can systematically identify where AI systems are vulnerable to both adversarial exploitation and unintended operational failures.

Adapting STRIDE to AI begins with recognizing how each of its categories—Spoofing, Tampering, Repudiation, Information Disclosure, Denial of Service, and Elevation of Privilege—translates into the AI life cycle. For example, spoofing may involve impersonating a data source, a model endpoint, or even a user persona within a conversational interface. Tampering can include malicious data injection during training, prompt manipulation through crafted inputs, or unauthorized model fine-tuning. Each STRIDE dimension should be evaluated not only against static software assets but also against dynamic AI behaviors that evolve over time. The auditor should consider how model retraining, pipeline updates, and adaptive responses may introduce fresh vulnerabilities long after the initial deployment has been secured.

MITRE ATT&CK, while originally designed for enterprise threat tactics, provides an adaptable structure for understanding attacker behavior in AI contexts. By aligning model components and interaction points with ATT&CK techniques, auditors can better visualize the sequence of actions an adversary might take—from data poisoning to prompt injection to output manipulation. For example, "Initial Access" may map to an attacker gaining control over a dataset repository, while

"Execution" could represent unauthorized API calls through a model agent. This mapping encourages auditors to think in terms of adversary capability chains rather than isolated threats, helping identify where compensating controls or detection mechanisms must exist within the AI ecosystem.

A comprehensive AI threat model also requires mapping the full data journey—from ingestion to output. Data ingestion points are prime targets for tampering, whether through poisoned samples in training sets or manipulated retrieval data during inference. Prompt channels, including system prompts and user inputs, can be abused to bypass guardrails or extract sensitive information. Retrieval paths, such as those used in retrieval-augmented generation (RAG), may expose indirect data access if vector stores or APIs are insufficiently protected. Tool invocations extend these risks further, as a model granted access to external functions can be tricked into invoking them in harmful or unintended ways. Output sinks—dashboards, logs, or downstream systems—must also be modeled, since adversaries may seek to manipulate what the system communicates or trigger cascading effects through automated decision-making.

Capturing attacker goals and capabilities gives the model depth beyond simple control failure enumeration. The auditor should define what an attacker seeks to achieve—such as exfiltrating proprietary model weights, degrading accuracy, influencing recommendations, or manipulating an autonomous agent's behavior—and assess what level of access or expertise is required. This context allows the threat model to prioritize realistic attack paths instead of speculative ones. By framing threats around attacker intent and capability, auditors ensure that mitigations align with real-world risk tolerance rather than theoretical completeness.

Equally important are the preconditions that must exist for an attack or failure to occur. These might include the model's reliance on third-party APIs, exposure of prompt logs, or lack of input sanitization. By explicitly stating these preconditions, auditors can identify which design assumptions are most fragile. For instance, a system that assumes all data retrieved from a vector database is trustworthy effectively removes an entire defensive layer. Recognizing such implicit assumptions through threat modeling allows organizations to reinforce controls where they matter most.

Misuse and abuse cases extend this process by considering how legitimate features can be exploited for unintended purposes. An attacker may not need to breach the system if they can coerce it into harmful output using valid interfaces. Abuse cases could include crafting prompts that bypass content filters, manipulating ranking algorithms through adversarial inputs, or tricking a model into performing unauthorized tasks via indirect requests. Documenting these scenarios highlights the dual-use nature of AI capabilities and ensures the organization's ethical and operational safeguards evolve alongside its technical defenses.

A mature AI threat model also accounts for non-adversarial failure modes—scenarios where the system itself introduces risk without malicious intent. Hallucination is the most common example: a model may generate inaccurate or misleading content that causes financial, reputational, or safety consequences. Other failures may stem from concept drift, bias amplification, or data inconsistencies that emerge as inputs evolve. Including these within the same analytical structure as adversarial threats emphasizes that AI assurance is not solely about defending against attackers but also about maintaining reliability, integrity, and trustworthiness under normal operation.

Visualizing the relationships between threats, assets, and attack paths strengthens comprehension and traceability. For example, a data ingestion pipeline might map to specific STRIDE categories—tampering and information disclosure—while its corresponding ATT&CK mappings illustrate the tactics an adversary might use to poison or exfiltrate data. Linking these to the responsible owner, control domain, and data classification makes the model actionable for both engineers and auditors. Threat diagrams, whether node-based or flow-oriented, help maintain clarity as the number of AI components grows.

Core Attack Surfaces: Prompt Injection, Data Leakage, and Model Theft/Extraction

The primary attack surfaces in AI systems differ significantly from those in traditional applications because they revolve around how models interpret, transform, and expose information rather than how static code executes. For auditors, this distinction means that AI assurance must address threats that occur through language, data, and inference rather than only through network or host vulnerabilities. The most critical adversarial pathways—prompt injection, data leakage, and model theft or extraction—each exploit a unique layer of the AI system. Together, they define the boundaries where the system can be coerced, misled, or exfiltrated. Understanding these surfaces in detail allows auditors to link them to specific control families such as input/output filtering, authentication and authorization, rate limiting, and environment isolation, which collectively form the first line of defense against AI-specific attacks. Table 18.1 aligns each major attack surface with its enabling preconditions and the control families that most directly mitigate the associated risk.

Prompt injection represents the most visible and rapidly evolving threat. It occurs when an adversary embeds crafted instructions within input data or contextual information, effectively hijacking the model's decision process. Direct prompt injection involves an attacker sending a malicious instruction as part of a query—such as telling the model to ignore prior rules or disclose sensitive content. Indirect prompt injection is subtler, embedding the malicious text in external sources like retrieved web pages, documents, or vector database entries. When the model later retrieves or reads that poisoned content, it unknowingly executes the attacker's embedded instructions. Both forms depend on overly trusting the input channel or retrieval path, and both exploit the model's natural language flexibility. Effective countermeasures include strict input sanitization, context segregation, and filtering of retrieved data before it reaches the model's prompt assembly.

Sensitive data leakage is the second major attack surface and often arises as a secondary effect of prompt manipulation or inadequate output controls. When models are trained, fine-tuned, or contextualized with proprietary data, they may inadvertently memorize or reproduce elements of that data. Attackers exploit this by crafting prompts that induce the model to reveal internal

Table 18.1 Attack surfaces with preconditions and control families.

Attack surface	Example vector	Typical preconditions	Primary control families
Prompt injection direct	Adversarial user input overrides rules	Untrusted input channel and weak input validation	Input filtering and authz and isolation
Prompt injection indirect	Poisoned retrieved page or corpus entry	Untrusted retrieval path and weak provenance checks	Context sanitation and provenance and isolation
Sensitive output leakage	Coerced disclosure of secrets	Weak output filtering and poor data classification	Output filtering and data classification and isolation
Model extraction	High volume query harvesting	Unauthenticated endpoint and weak rate limits	Authz and rate limits and anomaly detection
Guardrail jailbreaks	Linguistic bypass of safety rules	Static prompts and limited response checks	Behavioral safety filters and layered review
Tool abuse via connectors	Coerced API call with elevated rights	Over broad token scopes and no consent	Least privilege and consent and segregation

information such as source code, customer records, or policy configurations. Leakage may also occur unintentionally through verbose system responses or logging practices that record generated content. Preconditions for leakage typically include weak data classification, insufficient output filtering, or lack of oversight on how model responses are consumed downstream. Controls in this domain should enforce data labeling, integrate content filtering at the output layer, and restrict model access to sensitive embeddings or retrieval sources through authentication and isolation mechanisms.

Model theft and extraction introduce a more insidious category of risk, where the attacker's goal is to reconstruct, replicate, or infer details about the underlying model itself. Model inversion techniques attempt to recover training data by analyzing outputs across multiple queries, while extraction attacks aim to clone the model's behavior by submitting large numbers of inputs and observing corresponding responses. These attacks undermine intellectual property, regulatory compliance, and even national security in high-value AI systems. Preconditions include unauthenticated or publicly accessible endpoints, absence of rate limits, and lack of monitoring for query patterns that indicate automated probing. The associated control families—authorization enforcement, rate limiting, anomaly detection, and network isolation—serve to make extraction attempts prohibitively expensive and traceable, thereby reducing the feasibility of large-scale theft.

A closely related surface involves jailbreaks, where an attacker bypasses model guardrails designed to prevent unsafe or unethical output. Jailbreaking techniques rely on exploiting linguistic creativity and context shaping, such as using metaphor, translation, or code formatting to disguise prohibited content requests. When combined with indirect prompt injection, jailbreaks can completely subvert safety policies and cause models to output instructions, credentials, or decision rationales that would otherwise remain protected. These attacks thrive in systems that rely solely on static system prompts or limited pattern-based filters. Auditors should look for layered defenses such as content moderation APIs, adaptive response filtering, and isolation of high-sensitivity prompt contexts to minimize exposure.

Many of these attacks share the same enabling conditions: untrusted content ingestion, overbroad tool permissions, and unauthenticated endpoints. Untrusted ingestion arises when AI systems automatically pull data from sources such as web crawlers, document repositories, or user uploads without validation or filtering. Overbroad permissions occur when models are granted unrestricted access to external tools or APIs—allowing an attacker, via prompt manipulation, to issue destructive or unauthorized commands. Unauthenticated endpoints represent perhaps the most direct vulnerability, permitting adversaries to interact with the model or its orchestrator without identification or rate control. Each of these preconditions expands the model's operational surface and should be minimized through rigorous architectural review and boundary enforcement.

Input and output filtering form the cornerstone of defensive design against these threats. Input filters validate and sanitize text before it becomes part of a model's prompt, removing embedded commands, special characters, or encoded payloads. Output filters serve as the final safety gate, scanning generated content for sensitive data, policy violations, or manipulative patterns before responses are displayed or logged. Authentication and authorization complement these controls by ensuring that only verified entities can submit or retrieve model queries, while rate limits deter automated probing and extraction. Environment isolation further strengthens assurance by segregating model instances, preventing one compromised workflow or tenant from affecting another.

From an auditing standpoint, each control family should map back to a specific surface and precondition. Input/output filtering aligns with prompt injection and leakage prevention, authorization and rate limiting address model theft and abuse, and isolation boundaries mitigate the cascading effects of any successful exploit. Continuous monitoring reinforces these safeguards by detecting abnormal usage patterns, such as repeated requests targeting the same model endpoint or unusual spikes in query complexity. While the technical mechanisms differ from traditional systems, the logic of layered defense remains the same: protect the data, restrict the interfaces, and limit the blast radius when something fails.

Data Integrity Risks: Poisoning, Backdoors, and Training Set Governance

Data integrity lies at the heart of AI system assurance because the trustworthiness of a model directly reflects the quality and control of the data used to build it. Unlike code, which can be reviewed line by line, data is often opaque, aggregated from many sources, and constantly evolving. This creates fertile ground for both accidental contamination and intentional manipulation. Accidental contamination occurs when flawed, mislabeled, or low-quality data enters a dataset through carelessness or process weakness. Adversarial poisoning, by contrast, is deliberate—the insertion of data crafted to distort a model's behavior or conceal malicious triggers. The auditor's challenge is to distinguish between these two origins of compromise and to verify that governance processes detect, trace, and remediate both with consistent rigor.

Data poisoning represents one of the most damaging integrity attacks because it targets the model's foundations rather than its surface behavior. Attackers may inject false samples during data collection, subtly altering the statistical distribution so the model learns harmful associations or incorrect classifications. In more sophisticated cases, poisoning may focus on high-value subsets—injecting adversarial examples that cause a model to fail under specific conditions, such as misclassifying particular inputs or leaking private data when triggered. Auditors should expect to see documented data acceptance criteria, automated validation checks, and anomaly detection at ingestion points to identify these deviations. The presence of multiparty review and reproducible sampling further strengthens assurance that datasets are not silently altered or manipulated before training.

Backdoors extend the poisoning concept by introducing hidden triggers that activate malicious behaviors under specific input conditions. A classic example involves inserting a pattern—such as a watermark, keyword, or image fragment—into training data so that, when it reappears in production, the model outputs a predefined response. These backdoors can persist across retraining cycles and may remain dormant until intentionally activated, making them difficult to detect through normal performance testing. Auditors should ensure that dataset inspection includes random sampling, trigger testing, and adversarial red-teaming focused on rare or edge-case inputs. Provenance records and data lineage are particularly valuable here, as they allow investigators to trace suspect samples back to their origin and confirm whether they were introduced intentionally or through oversight.

Distinguishing accidental contamination from deliberate poisoning requires attention to process signals more than technical artifacts. Accidental contamination often arises from inconsistent labeling, merging of incompatible datasets, or missing documentation of preprocessing steps. In such cases, the resulting performance degradation is typically diffuse rather than targeted. Adversarial poisoning, in contrast, tends to produce asymmetric effects—specific misclassifications, output biases, or reproducible anomalies that suggest deliberate intent. Auditors should therefore review governance artifacts such as dataset curation logs, contributor identities, and change histories to assess whether appropriate segregation of duties and review checkpoints exist. In strong governance environments, every data addition is traceable to an accountable owner

Table 18.2 Data integrity governance signals across dataset types.

Governance signal	Purpose	Applies to base training	Applies to finetunes	Applies to RAG corpora	Applies to evaluation sets
Dataset provenance	Prove origin and legitimacy	Yes	Yes	Yes	Yes
Label lineage	Trace who labeled and why	Yes	Yes	No	Yes
Reproducible snapshots	Freeze data for replay	Yes	Yes	Yes	Yes
Holdout management	Protect unbiased testing	Yes	Yes	No	Yes
Source authenticity checks	Detect poisoned sources	Yes	Yes	Yes	No
Trigger testing for backdoors	Probe hidden activations	Yes	Yes	Yes	No

and justified by clear inclusion criteria. Table 18.2 highlights which governance signals must be applied consistently across base training finetunes RAG corpora and evaluation sets to sustain data integrity.

Dataset provenance forms the first and most important signal of integrity. Provenance documentation should specify source systems, collection methods, and licensing terms, as well as the transformations applied to convert raw data into usable training form. A reliable provenance trail allows an auditor to determine whether the organization collected data ethically, maintained consent records where required, and avoided scraping or third-party sources that might embed toxic or malicious samples. Complementing provenance is label lineage—the record of how labels were created, reviewed, and revised. Because labeling errors can act as unintentional poisoning, maintaining a verifiable lineage across curators and revisions provides assurance that ground truth remains stable and defensible.

Holdout datasets provide another critical governance control, serving as unbiased benchmarks for evaluating model generalization and detecting hidden contamination. By isolating a subset of data from all training and tuning activities, auditors can help ensure that model performance metrics are not inflated by inadvertent data reuse. Unexpected degradation on holdouts may signal poisoning, data leakage between splits, or conceptual drift. The auditor should confirm that holdouts are managed under strict access controls, refreshed periodically to reflect domain evolution, and retained in immutable storage for reproducibility. Reproducible data snapshots—frozen versions of datasets tied to model releases—further strengthen assurance by ensuring that every training run can be independently reconstructed and verified.

As AI systems evolve through fine-tuning, retrieval-augmented generation (RAG), and continuous evaluation, integrity controls must scale beyond a single static training set. Fine-tuning introduces new data drawn from user feedback, specialized corpora, or domain updates, any of which can carry fresh contamination risks. Governance policies should therefore extend provenance tracking and validation pipelines to these incremental updates. In RAG architectures, where models retrieve data dynamically from vector stores or document indexes, the integrity of the underlying corpus becomes equally vital. Auditors should expect version-controlled corpora, periodic cleansing procedures, and source authenticity checks that mirror those applied to the original training data. Evaluation sets, often overlooked, also require stewardship to ensure that metrics are meaningful and not gamed through selective sampling or overfitting.

Integrity assurance at scale depends on consistency, not complexity. Each control—provenance, curation lineage, holdouts, and snapshot reproducibility—must apply uniformly across the AI life cycle. The same principles that govern the base model should extend to fine-tunes, contextual retrieval layers, and evaluation frameworks. This uniformity enables traceability across all derivatives of a model and allows auditors to confirm that every decision, retraining, or corpus update inherits the same integrity expectations. By requiring these controls to be enforced through governance rather than ad hoc engineering, organizations ensure that data integrity remains a continuous property of the system rather than a one-time certification event.

Abuse Paths via Integrations: Plugins, Connectors, and Tool Invocation

Integrations are among the most powerful yet perilous components of modern AI ecosystems. Plugins, enterprise connectors, and callable tools enable models to move from generating text to performing real-world actions, transforming passive reasoning systems into active agents. This capability also introduces new abuse paths that adversaries can exploit for token exfiltration, unauthorized operations, or lateral movement across integrated environments. For auditors, these integration points redefine the boundary of AI assurance: the system's risk no longer ends where the model stops speaking but extends wherever its outputs can trigger an action. Understanding how integrations expand the attack surface is essential to designing controls that maintain the principle of least privilege and ensure that the AI's reach remains both intentional and bounded.

Plugins and connectors are inherently powerful because they act as translators between the model's intent and operational systems. When a model calls a plugin or connector, it often gains indirect access to enterprise resources such as databases, ticketing systems, messaging platforms, or file repositories. If the AI layer or its prompts can be manipulated, an attacker may coerce it into issuing legitimate but malicious commands—downloading sensitive files, deleting records, or escalating privileges within an external application. Token exfiltration becomes a prime concern in such scenarios, as authentication secrets used by plugins may be exposed in prompts, logs, or debug outputs. The auditor should expect that every plugin or connector maintains isolated credentials, never reuses tokens across systems, and enforces time-bound, least-privilege access scopes aligned with its functional purpose.

Callable functions and tool invocations amplify these risks by bridging inference and execution environments. A model configured to invoke a "create user," "send email," or "query database" function can become an unintentional conduit for privilege escalation if input validation and context filtering are weak. Attackers may embed malicious commands within prompt text, convincing the model to execute a legitimate API call on their behalf. Because these functions often run under elevated permissions, such misuse can yield results equivalent to insider-level compromise. The appropriate assurance response is architectural: restrict callable tools to clearly defined scopes, require explicit confirmation or consent for sensitive actions, and isolate the model's execution context so that even successful injection attempts cannot cascade into unrestricted operations.

Lateral movement through integrations occurs when a compromised AI workflow becomes a launch point for attacks against adjacent systems. Once an adversary manipulates a model connected to multiple tools, they can pivot across applications by chaining legitimate connector calls—retrieving data from one source, modifying records in another, and transmitting the results outward. In a complex enterprise, these connections may traverse boundaries between cloud tenants, data classifications, or business functions. The auditor's task is to verify that each integration is mapped to its trust domain, that cross-domain data flows are justified, and that permissions cannot be inherited across connectors. Network segmentation, role-based authorization, and compartmentalized tokens serve as guardrails that prevent a single compromised integration from escalating into systemic exposure.

Least privilege remains the guiding principle for every integration. Each plugin, connector, or callable function should request only the minimal permissions necessary to perform its specific task, and auditors should confirm that these permissions are periodically reviewed for necessity and expiration. Broad-scoped tokens—especially those granting administrative or write access—must be replaced with granular, single-purpose credentials. Auditors should pay special attention to environments where developers or end users can install or authorize plugins themselves, as this decentralization often bypasses enterprise oversight and introduces unvetted code paths into critical systems.

Explicit consent mechanisms represent another essential safeguard for high-risk actions. When a model attempts to perform an operation that can alter data, send communications, or invoke external APIs, users or system controllers should be prompted for confirmation. Consent may be enforced interactively or through policy gating based on risk level, but it must always be explicit. This requirement serves both technical and ethical functions—it ensures accountability for automated actions and prevents silent misuse of trusted integrations. The auditor should verify that consent workflows exist for sensitive functions and that their design prevents preapproval or prompt manipulation that could circumvent user awareness.

Separation between untrusted content and tool invocation is perhaps the most overlooked but vital element of AI integration governance. The same text that models interpret as prompts often contains user-provided or retrieved data. If that content is not clearly segregated from command channels, malicious instructions can piggyback into the model's reasoning and cause it to activate tools unintentionally. Proper design enforces strict contextual boundaries: untrusted content is processed for interpretation only, never for direct execution, and all invocations must pass through a controlled, validated layer before reaching connected systems. Auditors should confirm that such boundaries exist and that the AI cannot transform arbitrary input into active commands without oversight.

The governance challenge expands as the number of integrations grows. Each new connector or plugin increases complexity and multiplies the risk of privilege overlap, token reuse, or blind trust. A mature organization will maintain a central inventory of approved integrations, documenting their owners, permission scopes, and associated risk tiers. Periodic reviews should ensure that deprecated or unused connectors are revoked and that no tool operates outside its intended business context. Continuous visibility into how integrations are used allows auditors to detect anomalies—such as excessive invocation rates or cross-domain data flows—that may indicate abuse or policy violations.

Control Objectives and Risk Acceptance Criteria for AI Systems

Establishing clear control objectives and measurable risk acceptance criteria is essential for translating complex AI threats into actionable governance practices. Unlike conventional systems, AI platforms interact with dynamic inputs, probabilistic outputs, and contextual reasoning, which means that risks must be managed through both traditional security domains and AI-specific behaviors. Effective control objectives span five dimensions—identity, data protection, behavioral safety, tool governance, and exposure management—each of which defines how the organization will prevent, detect, and tolerate risk in alignment with business priorities. The objective is not to eliminate uncertainty but to define acceptable thresholds and ensure that mitigation strategies align with operational realities and organizational risk appetite.

Identity controls form the foundation of AI assurance, governing who and what can interact with the model. Auditors should confirm that all user and system identities—human, service, or agent—are authenticated through strong, centralized mechanisms that enforce least privilege. Control objectives in this area focus on ensuring that every interaction can be attributed to a verified entity and that all model calls are traceable through audit logs. Acceptance criteria might specify, for example, that 100% of production AI endpoints require token-based authentication, or that no privileged action may be invoked without multifactor validation. The business tolerance for anonymous access should be explicitly documented and justified by operational need. In most environments, unverified identity access to AI endpoints represents an unacceptable residual risk due to its potential for data exfiltration or abuse.

Data protection objectives aim to safeguard both the training assets that shape the model and the information it processes during inference. Controls should ensure that sensitive or classified data cannot be ingested, retrieved, or exposed beyond defined trust boundaries. For auditors, this means validating encryption at rest and in transit, confirming isolation between datasets, and verifying that output filtering prevents disclosure of restricted information. Risk acceptance criteria may include measurable leakage thresholds, such as "zero tolerance for PII exposure in model outputs" or "less than one percent of retrieval results may include data classified above the model's clearance level." These thresholds translate abstract privacy goals into verifiable metrics that can be tested during assurance reviews.

Behavioral safety controls focus on constraining what the model is allowed to say, do, or infer. The goal is to prevent harmful, biased, or unauthorized behaviors that might arise from prompt injection, hallucination, or adversarial manipulation. Control objectives here should include blocking defined classes of disallowed actions—such as executing code, generating credentials, or producing regulated content—and maintaining observable safeguards for harmful language and misinformation. Acceptance criteria could define quantitative boundaries, for example, "ninety-five percent coverage of known abuse patterns in behavioral filters" or "zero-tolerance for high-severity unsafe output in operational environments." These thresholds allow auditors to measure whether behavioral controls are both comprehensive and effective, rather than relying solely on qualitative assurances.

Tool governance represents one of the most critical emerging control domains for AI systems that can call external functions, plugins, or connectors. Objectives must ensure that tool invocation occurs only within approved workflows, under the explicit consent of authorized entities, and with scoped permissions that prevent lateral escalation. Auditors should verify that every tool is registered, risk-rated, and tied to an owner responsible for permission reviews. Acceptance criteria may include "no tool operates without explicit approval in the enterprise registry," "all high-risk actions require user consent," or "token scopes for callable tools cannot exceed read-only access except where formally justified." These measurable standards help contain the blast radius of compromised or manipulated AI-driven actions.

Exposure and rate limit management serve as technical enforcers of resilience against abuse and model extraction. Control objectives in this domain define how frequently an entity may query the model, how much data can be retrieved per session, and how anomalies in access patterns are detected and handled. Auditors should ensure that rate limits exist for both authenticated and unauthenticated users, that automated detection monitors for volumetric abuse, and that thresholds are tied to business impact rather than arbitrary numbers. Acceptance criteria might specify "maximum of 500 requests per minute per token," "automatic throttling after repeated failed input validation attempts," or "real-time alerting for more than 5× normal request rate." These metrics transform exposure management from a reactive control to a proactive assurance mechanism.

Each control objective must also be anchored to the organization's business impact thresholds and risk tolerance statements. For instance, a customer-facing chatbot may tolerate limited response variability but zero tolerance for privacy violations, whereas an internal data science model may accept slightly higher leakage risk in exchange for operational efficiency. Auditors should confirm that risk owners have formally defined these boundaries and that acceptance criteria are aligned with both regulatory requirements and the organization's enterprise risk management framework. This ensures that AI governance remains consistent with broader business strategy rather than existing as a separate, uncoordinated discipline.

It is also vital to express acceptance criteria in measurable terms that can be validated during periodic reviews. Abstract goals such as "minimize data leakage" or "maintain user safety" are insufficient; instead, criteria must be quantifiable, such as "block 100% of known disallowed actions," "maintain less than 0.1% false negative rate in content filtering," or "detect 90% of abnormal query bursts within 30 seconds." These measurable thresholds allow auditors and operators to assess effectiveness objectively and to recalibrate controls as the threat landscape evolves. Measurability transforms governance from policy intent into actionable accountability.

While continuous testing and automation enhance these controls, their specific implementation belongs in the operational layer rather than the policy layer. The auditor's concern is that the control objectives and risk acceptance criteria exist, are documented, and are defensible against business impact. This structured translation—from threat awareness to measurable control expectation—ensures that AI systems remain governable even as they evolve. By defining identity assurance, data protection, behavioral safety, tool governance, and exposure management with explicit acceptance metrics, organizations create a transparent and repeatable basis for evaluating AI risk posture. This discipline gives executives confidence that AI systems operate not in an uncontrolled gray zone, but within well-defined parameters that align technical safeguards with the enterprise's overall risk appetite.

Documentation and Traceability: from Threat to Control to Evidence

Effective AI assurance depends on the organization's ability to demonstrate a complete and traceable link between identified risks and the controls that mitigate them. This "threat-to-control-to-evidence" chain forms the backbone of accountability for AI systems, ensuring that every documented risk corresponds to specific control objectives, that each control has an assigned owner, and that all supporting evidence can be readily located and verified. For auditors, this chain is not just an administrative exercise but a validation of operational maturity. Without it, even well-designed safeguards cannot be proven effective or repeatable. Traceability transforms AI risk management from a collection of policies into a verifiable system of record that can withstand regulatory, legal, and organizational scrutiny.

The traceability chain begins with the threat model, which captures how adversaries, failures, or environmental factors could compromise the AI system's confidentiality, integrity, or availability. Each documented threat—whether prompt injection, data leakage, model inversion, or poisoning—must map directly to one or more control objectives that articulate how the organization intends to prevent or mitigate it. This linkage should be explicit and recorded in a unified repository, such as

Table 18.3 Traceability chain elements and update triggers.

Chain element	Required contents	Owner role	Evidence location example	Update triggers
Threat entry	Scenario and impact and preconditions	Risk analyst	Threat register item	New model release
Control objective	Desired risk outcome and scope	Control architect	Control catalog record	New tool integration
Implemented control	Technical or procedural safeguard	System owner	Config baseline or policy file	Incident lessons learned
Version record models prompts datasets	Identifiers and dates and lineage	Model owner	Version index or manifest	Dataset refresh
Evidence artifact	Logs or reviews or test results	Control operator	Evidence repo path	Control change
Risk register cross reference	Link to enterprise risk item	Risk manager	ERM system entry	Severity re rating

an AI assurance register or a structured risk management platform. The purpose is to ensure that no threat exists without a corresponding control objective, and no control is implemented without a clearly defined risk justification. This alignment provides auditors with a clear pathway to trace the rationale behind every safeguard. Table 18.3 provides a concise mapping from threat to control to evidence with clear ownership and triggers that drive timely documentation updates.

Each control objective must, in turn, link to the actual implemented controls—technical, procedural, or organizational—that fulfill it. These may include input validation mechanisms, model access restrictions, prompt filtering, data provenance tracking, or authorization policies. For each implemented control, ownership must be unambiguous. The control owner is responsible not only for execution and maintenance but also for ensuring that the control's evidence artifacts remain current and accessible. Clear delineation of ownership prevents accountability gaps and ensures continuity when systems evolve or personnel change. Auditors should verify that control ownership is assigned at both the functional and operational levels, tying individual accountability to enterprise oversight.

Evidence location is the next critical component of the traceability chain. Every control must point to the records, reports, or logs that substantiate its operation. These may include configuration baselines, access control records, red team results, or periodic model output reviews. Evidence should be cataloged with unique identifiers and stored in repositories that enforce access control and versioning. The auditor's task is to confirm that evidence exists, that it aligns with the stated control objective, and that it can be independently verified if sampled. While detailed sampling and evidence validation methods are governed elsewhere, auditors should still ensure that the traceability structure allows quick navigation from threat to control to proof without ambiguity or manual reconstruction.

Versioning represents a particularly important requirement for AI systems because of their dynamic nature. Models, prompts, datasets, and integrations change frequently, and without version control, traceability quickly deteriorates. Every version of a model or prompt should maintain its own threat mapping, control implementation list, and evidence references. When a new model version is released or a dataset is updated, the traceability record must automatically branch or update to reflect the new state. This ensures that controls remain relevant to the specific configuration under audit rather than referring to obsolete baselines. Datasets and vector stores likewise require version tracking, documenting not only content changes but also updates to labeling, preprocessing, and curation lineage.

Update triggers define when traceability documentation must be reviewed and refreshed. The most common triggers include the release of a new model or fine-tune, integration of a new plugin or tool, identification of a novel threat pattern, or post-incident lessons learned. Each trigger should prompt a formal reassessment of the associated control mappings and evidence references. Auditors should confirm that the organization has a documented process for initiating these updates, assigning responsibility for validation, and closing the loop through change control. This structured update cadence prevents the AI assurance record from becoming static while ensuring that reactive updates are captured with the same rigor as planned revisions.

Cross-referencing with the enterprise risk register ensures alignment between AI-specific threats and broader organizational risk management. Each AI threat entry should reference its corresponding risk register item, including severity, impact rating, and mitigation status. Conversely, risks recorded in the enterprise register that involve AI should link back to the detailed threat documentation maintained by the AI assurance team. This bidirectional linkage promotes transparency and allows leadership to assess aggregate risk posture without duplicating assessments across silos. For auditors, these references demonstrate that AI risks are integrated into the same governance fabric as all other business-critical risks.

The documentation framework must also support traceability across organizational layers—connecting technical controls to governance oversight. Control owners should document not only how controls function but also how their effectiveness is measured over time. Metrics, testing schedules, and key performance indicators may be referenced at a high level within the traceability chain, with the detailed testing procedures governed separately. This ensures that the documentation remains concise, readable, and sustainable without sacrificing depth or auditability.

Maintaining a single, authoritative traceability register prevents fragmentation, where different teams maintain overlapping or inconsistent documentation. Each entry—threat, control objective, control implementation, owner, evidence reference, and version—should be recorded in a structured format capable of supporting change history, search, and audit queries. The system should allow auditors to answer critical questions immediately: What threat does this control mitigate? Who owns it? What evidence supports it? When was it last reviewed? The ability to answer these questions with confidence defines a mature AI assurance program.

In an environment where AI systems evolve rapidly, traceability is the foundation of sustainable assurance. It provides a living, transparent chain that demonstrates not only that risks are known and managed, but that the organization can prove it. By linking every threat to its control, every control to its owner, and every owner to verifiable evidence—with versioning and update triggers clearly defined—auditors ensure that AI governance remains both accountable and adaptive. This disciplined approach allows organizations to manage the velocity of AI change without losing the integrity of their risk management process.

Conclusion

Mastering the principles outlined in this chapter is critical for ensuring that AI-driven environments remain secure, reliable, and auditable as they evolve. The convergence of automation, analytics, and adaptive intelligence requires auditors to think beyond static controls and embrace a mindset grounded in continuous assurance. By translating emerging threats into measurable objectives and maintaining transparent chains of evidence, cybersecurity auditors position themselves as essential stewards of accountability in systems that learn and act autonomously. Their expertise becomes the anchor that keeps innovation aligned with governance, ethics, and organizational trust.

This chapter reinforces the role of structured control design and risk acceptance as the backbone of AI assurance. Whether addressing prompt manipulation, data integrity, or model misuse, auditors must ensure that every safeguard is tied to a defined threat and supported by verifiable evidence. The real strength of an AI assurance program lies not only in its technical controls but also in the traceability that links intent, implementation, and oversight. Such rigor transforms security from a defensive posture into a proactive discipline—one capable of detecting, adapting to, and mitigating risk at machine speed without sacrificing human judgment.

With these foundations in place, professionals are better equipped to audit AI systems with both precision and confidence. The frameworks and methods explored here elevate assurance beyond compliance checklists, establishing a living system of governance that evolves alongside the technology it protects. While implementation details may vary across organizations, the strategic intent remains consistent: to create verifiable, trustworthy, and responsibly governed AI systems. By embedding these practices into audit processes, cybersecurity professionals help ensure that the promise of AI is realized safely, ethically, and within the boundaries of sound risk management.

Auditor Recommendations

1. **Define Asset Boundaries Clearly:** Establish a structured process for mapping every AI component—models, datasets, prompts, tools, and agents—within your audit scope. Ensure each asset is assigned an owner, classification, and trust boundary to maintain accountability and prevent gaps in assurance. Treat these boundaries as living records that evolve alongside model updates and system integrations. This clarity enables auditors to focus testing and validation where risk is most concentrated.
2. **Adapt Threat Modeling to AI Contexts:** Incorporate AI-specific dimensions into familiar methodologies such as STRIDE or MITRE ATT&CK to account for prompt channels, retrieval paths, and output sinks. Capture attacker goals, preconditions, and failure modes, including non-adversarial risks such as hallucination or bias amplification. Use these structured models to align threat intelligence with the AI life cycle rather than traditional infrastructure. This ensures that audits remain relevant as model behavior evolves dynamically.
3. **Prioritize Review of Core Attack Surfaces:** Focus audit efforts on the most exploited AI pathways—prompt injection, data leakage, and model extraction. Validate that input and output filtering, authentication, rate limits, and environment isolation are applied consistently across interfaces. Pay particular attention to indirect prompt channels and overbroad tool permissions, as these frequently bypass conventional safeguards. A disciplined focus on these attack surfaces enhances both control coverage and audit efficiency.
4. **Strengthen Data Integrity Governance:** Implement rigorous controls over dataset provenance, labeling lineage, and version management. Require documentation of data sources, transformations, and holdout procedures to differentiate accidental contamination from intentional poisoning or backdoors. Verify that every dataset, fine-tune corpus, and retrieval source maintains reproducible snapshots and traceable ownership. Strong governance here reinforces every other assurance function in the AI life cycle.

5. **Enforce Least Privilege Across Integrations:** Ensure all plugins, connectors, and callable tools operate under tightly scoped permissions aligned with business necessity. Validate that no shared tokens or excessive scopes allow unintended data access or cross-system actions. Require explicit consent for high-risk operations and verify that untrusted content cannot directly trigger tool execution. This disciplined enforcement minimizes the blast radius of any compromised integration.
6. **Translate Risks into Measurable Control Objectives:** Convert identified AI threats into explicit, testable control statements covering identity, data protection, behavior safety, tool governance, and rate limiting. Define measurable acceptance criteria, such as blocked action classes or maximum tolerated leakage risk, to establish clear performance expectations. Align these metrics with business impact and risk tolerance to ensure that governance reflects both compliance and practicality. This translation transforms threat awareness into actionable assurance.
7. **Maintain Continuous Traceability:** Require a single documentation chain that links each threat to its control objectives, implemented safeguards, responsible owners, and supporting evidence. Integrate versioning for models, prompts, and datasets so that traceability remains intact through updates and retraining. Define triggers for documentation refresh, such as model releases, tool integrations, or post-incident findings. A traceable lineage of decisions and evidence strengthens audit defensibility and organizational accountability.
8. **Integrate AI Risks with Enterprise Risk Registers:** Ensure that AI-specific threats and mitigation measures feed into the organization's broader risk management framework. Cross-reference each AI control to enterprise-level risks and document its current effectiveness status. This linkage promotes transparency between technical assurance and executive oversight. Embedding AI risk within enterprise governance prevents it from becoming an isolated compliance exercise.
9. **Audit for Evidence Quality, Not Quantity:** Focus on the integrity, relevance, and accessibility of evidence supporting AI controls rather than collecting excessive data. Confirm that evidence repositories enforce version control and ownership while maintaining sufficient granularity for verification. Assess whether evidence actually demonstrates control effectiveness under real conditions. This approach keeps audits efficient while maintaining the rigor expected in high-assurance environments.
10. **Reinforce Accountability Through Governance Culture:** Promote a culture where every stakeholder—from model developers to compliance officers—understands their role in AI assurance. Require clear ownership of each control, explicit responsibility for updates, and cross-functional collaboration during risk reviews. Auditors should advocate for this governance mindset as part of their reporting and recommendations. A culture of accountability ensures that AI assurance remains sustainable long after individual audits conclude.

Chapter Questions

1. Which primary objective justifies establishing a precise AI asset boundary for assurance?
   A. To accelerate model inference performance
   B. To consolidate deployment mechanics into one environment
   C. To enumerate models, datasets, prompts, tools, agents, and endpoints with owners, classifications, and trust boundaries
   D. To align DevOps pipelines with marketing timelines

2. When extending familiar threat modeling methods to AI contexts, what must be explicitly represented to capture AI-specific risks?
   - **A.** Only network perimeters and host configurations
   - **B.** Data ingestion, prompt channels, retrieval paths, tool invocations, and output sinks
   - **C.** Hyperparameter search spaces and loss curves
   - **D.** Physical data center rack layouts

3. Which option best characterizes indirect prompt injection?
   - **A.** The model emits lengthy outputs due to poorly tuned temperature settings
   - **B.** A user directly instructs the model to ignore prior rules
   - **C.** A developer modifies a system prompt during deployment rollback
   - **D.** Malicious instructions are embedded in external content that the system retrieves and incorporates into the prompt context

4. Which precondition most commonly enables model extraction and large-scale abuse attempts?
   - **A.** Unauthenticated or broadly exposed endpoints
   - **B.** Strict rate limits on every API token
   - **C.** Immutable holdout datasets for evaluation only
   - **D.** Isolated vector stores with per-tenant keys

5. Which governance signal most directly establishes the origin and legitimacy of training data?
   - **A.** Dataset provenance
   - **B.** Hyperparameter tuning logs
   - **C.** UI wireframes for labeling tools
   - **D.** CPU utilization records during training

6. For integrations that allow tool invocation, which control most effectively limits the blast radius if the model is manipulated?
   - **A.** Expanding token scopes to reduce user prompts
   - **B.** Centralizing a single token for all connectors
   - **C.** Enforcing least-privilege, narrowly scoped credentials per tool
   - **D.** Disabling audit logging to minimize latency

7. Which control objective most directly addresses preventing high-volume cloning or model extraction via excessive queries?
   - **A.** Identity assurance and role definitions
   - **B.** Behavioral safety and content policy checks
   - **C.** Tool governance with consent prompts
   - **D.** Exposure and rate-limit management

8. Which of the following is a valid example of measurable risk acceptance criteria for data protection?
   - **A.** "Minimize sensitive data exposure wherever possible."
   - **B.** "Zero tolerance for PII exposure in model outputs."
   - **C.** "Outputs should generally be safe for most users."
   - **D.** "Reduce leakage to an acceptable level."

9. What requirement keeps the threat-to-control-to-evidence chain accurate as models and prompts evolve?
   A. Quarterly design thinking workshops
   B. Centralized UI/UX pattern libraries
   C. Versioning for models, prompts, and datasets within the traceability register
   D. Fixed annual release cycles

10. Which event should trigger an immediate review and refresh of traceability mappings and evidence links?
   A. Annual budget approval
   B. Integration of a new plugin or connector
   C. Cosmetic changes to the web UI
   D. HVAC maintenance in the primary data center

19

Secure MLOps and Model/Endpoint Controls

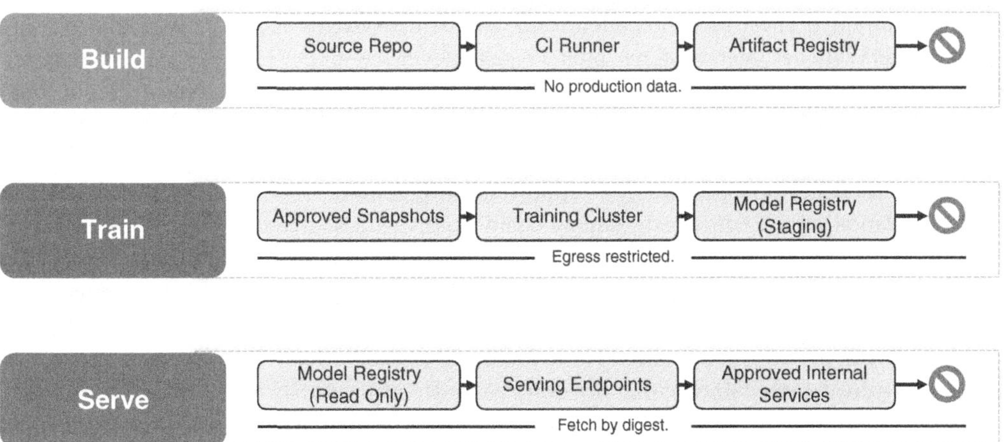

Automation, continuous auditing, and advanced analytics are transforming how cybersecurity assurance is performed. Traditional audit cycles that relied on static evidence and periodic testing can no longer keep pace with the velocity of change in modern digital ecosystems. Machine learning pipelines, automated controls, and real-time telemetry now allow auditors to evaluate compliance and security posture continuously, rather than retroactively. Understanding how to design, monitor, and validate these automated systems is essential to ensuring that efficiency gains do not come at the cost of control, transparency, or trust.

As organizations increasingly integrate artificial intelligence and machine learning into their operations, the boundaries between software assurance, data governance, and risk management begin to blur. This chapter examines how automated control environments, model validation procedures, and provenance tracking form the foundation of trustworthy AI systems. By exploring key elements such as supply chain integrity, environment hardening, and data lineage, it establishes the mechanisms auditors use to verify that automation enhances—not undermines—accountability. Through this lens, automation becomes not a replacement for professional judgment, but a force multiplier for it.

For cybersecurity leaders, these topics are central to building resilient AI security architectures that meet both regulatory and ethical expectations. Continuous auditing provides early detection of deviations, while analytics-driven oversight offers a proactive view of operational and compliance risk. The result is a governance model capable of adapting to high-speed change while preserving the evidence trail that underpins assurance. In an era where decisions are increasingly delegated to algorithms, mastering these disciplines ensures that control remains in human hands—even when much of the work is performed by machines.

Supply Chain Integrity: Artifacts, Registries, Signing, and Provenance

The machine learning supply chain introduces an intricate web of dependencies that extends far beyond traditional software development. Instead of a single, linear build pipeline, modern ML systems rely on a sequence of interconnected components—source code, datasets, engineered features, model binaries, container images, and inference environments—that each contribute to the final product. These elements often reside in distinct systems such as source control platforms, dataset registries, feature stores, model registries, and container repositories. Each transfer between systems represents a potential point of risk, where data integrity, authenticity, or version control could fail. From an auditing perspective, maintaining supply chain integrity requires that every artifact is uniquely identifiable, fully traceable, and supported by immutable evidence linking it to its creator, source inputs, and approved configuration.

The foundation of any trustworthy supply chain begins with source code management. Every change to the codebase must be tracked through a version control system that records the author, timestamp, commit identifier, and description of modifications. Build systems should automatically capture the branch, repository, and dependency versions used in each build process, ensuring that reproducibility is possible at any time. These build records collectively form the earliest layer of provenance—documented lineage that ties every compiled artifact to its origin. Once an artifact is produced, it should be cryptographically signed by the build system using a secure, managed identity. The resulting signature acts as a digital fingerprint that allows auditors and downstream systems to confirm that the artifact is genuine, untampered, and produced under approved conditions.

Datasets form the most volatile and high-risk layer in the ML supply chain because they directly shape model performance and bias. Without careful control, data can drift, become corrupted, or lose its documented origin. For every dataset used in model training or validation, a registry entry should capture the dataset identifier, version number, schema, storage location, and hash digest of its contents. It should also record metadata such as the data source, collection method, time period covered, and any preprocessing steps or filters applied. These records must include the identity of the curator and approver, along with timestamps for each action. A dataset registry serves as the auditor's anchor—allowing them to verify not only what data was used but also whether it was properly authorized, reproducible, and consistent with governance policies.

Feature stores extend this traceability by documenting the transformations applied to datasets before model training. Each feature definition should include its name, the computation logic or script reference, the upstream datasets and their versions, and any transformation parameters used. When a feature set is generated, its metadata should record the processing job that produced it, the execution time, and the validation results that confirm no data leakage or corruption occurred. By maintaining parity between training and inference feature versions, organizations can avoid one of the most common integrity failures in ML operations—mismatched features between environments. Continuous auditing tools can automatically cross-check feature versions across production and training pipelines, providing near-real-time assurance that the same logic and data lineage are consistently applied. Table 19.1 lists the minimum provenance and verification data that must be captured for each ML artifact to support end-to-end audit traceability.

Table 19.1 Minimum auditable provenance fields across ML artifacts.

Artifact	Registry location	Immutable ID	Required inputs recorded	Builder identity attested	Signature verified
Source code	Repository URL	Commit hash	Dependencies and config recorded	Build service identity	Yes
Dataset snapshot	Data registry	Snapshot digest	Source and transform lineage recorded	Curator identity	Yes
Feature set	Feature store	Feature version ID	Upstream datasets and code refs recorded	Pipeline job identity	Yes
Training run	Experiment tracker	Run ID	Datasets features hyperparameters recorded	Trainer service identity	Yes
Model weights	Model registry	Artifact digest	Linked to training run ID	Signing identity	Yes
Preprocessing bundle	Artifact registry	Bundle digest	Linked to code commit and schema	Build service identity	Yes
Container image	Container registry	Image digest	Base image and SBOM recorded	Builder signing identity	Yes
Deployment manifest	Config registry	Manifest digest	Model image config checksums recorded	Release approver identity	Yes

The model training stage generates several critical artifacts that must be governed with equal precision. Each training run should automatically log the code commit used, the dataset and feature versions, the hyperparameters selected, and the computing environment in which the training occurred. The resulting artifacts—model weights, configuration files, and evaluation metrics—must each be recorded with immutable digests and linked back to the run that produced them. This creates a complete lineage from input to output that can be independently validated. For auditors, the ability to replay or reproduce a training event is a key test of supply chain maturity. If a model version cannot be reconstructed from its recorded lineage, it suggests weak controls or missing evidence within the organization's Machine Learning Operations (MLOps) framework.

The model registry functions as both a historical record and a policy enforcement checkpoint. It must store every model version with detailed metadata linking it to its source code, datasets, features, and training configurations. The registry should include validation metrics, approval records, and the identities of reviewers who authorized its release. Automated controls should evaluate the completeness of provenance before a model is marked as "approved for deployment." If any signature, dataset version, or lineage element is missing, the system should block promotion until all compliance criteria are met. This dual role—archiving and gatekeeping—ensures that every deployed model is both auditable and trustworthy, reducing the likelihood of shadow models or unverified updates slipping into production.

Container images and inference environments represent the final layer of the ML supply chain, where all previous artifacts converge into an operational state. Each container or deployment package must be built from version-pinned base images, explicit dependency manifests, and verified model binaries. Build pipelines should produce cryptographically signed container images whose digests are published to a secure registry. Deployment manifests must reference these digests directly, avoiding mutable tags that can be overwritten. Runtime verification tools should continuously check that running containers match their signed digests, alerting auditors to any drift or substitution. This ensures that the deployed inference environment exactly matches the approved configuration, closing the loop on supply chain transparency.

Underlying all of these components is the concept of provenance—the detailed documentation of what was built, how it was built, and by whom. Provenance records should be machine-readable and structured in a consistent schema, capturing the build environment, configuration parameters, inputs, outputs, and digital signatures. These records form a chain of custody that links every artifact from data collection through deployment. When stored in immutable object storage or append-only logs, they create a permanent, tamper-resistant audit trail. Automated verification processes can continuously scan these records to confirm that each artifact in use aligns with an approved provenance chain, giving auditors high-confidence evidence without relying solely on manual review.

Digital signing and verification complete the system of trust by turning provenance from an informational asset into a security control. Each build system, data curation process, or pipeline job should sign its outputs using managed keys that are rotated regularly and stored in secure cryptographic modules. Verification of these signatures should occur at multiple stages—during build completion, registry admission, deployment approval, and runtime monitoring. This layered validation ensures that even if one control fails, other checkpoints will detect tampering or unauthorized substitution. For continuous auditing programs, these automated integrity checks form the backbone of real-time assurance, allowing auditors to see not only whether artifacts are compliant now but also whether they have remained compliant throughout their life cycle.

In mature MLOps environments, the combination of immutable registries, signed artifacts, structured provenance, and automated verification transforms supply chain integrity from a reactive exercise into a continuous control. Auditors can trace the full lineage of any model version within seconds, identify anomalies or missing signatures automatically, and provide evidence-based assurance to management and regulators. By enforcing these practices—careful tracking of artifacts, verifiable provenance, and end-to-end cryptographic integrity—organizations create an auditable foundation for trustworthy, explainable, and secure machine learning operations.

Environment Hardening: Build/Train/Serve Isolation and Access Boundaries

Environment hardening in machine learning operations begins with one fundamental principle—separation. The build, training, and serving environments must be isolated from one another to reduce risk and make auditing simpler. Each environment handles different types of data, code, and permissions, so mixing them creates unnecessary exposure. The build environment turns source code into deployable artifacts; the training environment uses approved data to create models; and the serving environment runs those models in production. When these stages are kept separate—with distinct networks, accounts, and credentials—any compromise or error is contained within its boundary instead of cascading across the entire pipeline.

The build environment should be the most controlled from a supply chain perspective. It compiles source code, packages dependencies, and creates versioned artifacts that flow into downstream environments. For security, builds should happen in isolated projects or accounts that have no access to production data or services. Continuous integration runners should use minimal privileges, pulling dependencies only from verified repositories and writing outputs to secured artifact registries. Secrets, such as signing keys, must never be stored directly on build servers. Instead, use a secure key management system to issue short-lived credentials during the build process. This prevents leaked credentials from granting long-term access and ensures every signing operation can be audited.

Training environments require a different kind of protection because they interact with sensitive data and generate valuable model artifacts. Each training job should run in its own isolated workspace—ideally a temporary cluster or container that is destroyed once the job completes. Training nodes should have read-only access to approved datasets and write-only access to the designated model registry. They should not be able to access source repositories, production databases, or external internet destinations unless specifically required. Enforcing this isolation means that even if a training node is compromised, it cannot move laterally or exfiltrate data. In most cloud environments, this isolation can be achieved by assigning separate projects, VPCs, or subnets for training workloads, with strict network rules and private service endpoints for data access.

The serving environment—the layer that hosts models in production—is where isolation and access control must be the tightest. Serving systems should only fetch preapproved, signed model artifacts from the registry and should never be able to modify or upload them. They must operate with read-only credentials and have no connection to the training infrastructure or raw datasets. Secrets used by production endpoints, such as API keys or service tokens, should be injected dynamically at runtime using a secure secrets management service. Outbound network traffic should be restricted to only the destinations absolutely required for model inference, such as a database or telemetry service. By narrowing this environment's permissions and communication paths, organizations can minimize damage if a serving node is breached.

GPU and accelerator pools introduce their own challenges. Because they often share physical hardware across workloads, they can become attack surfaces for data leakage or resource abuse. Organizations should dedicate GPU clusters to specific environments or projects when possible, rather than allowing multiple teams to share the same hardware. If sharing is unavoidable, use strict workload isolation features—such as hardware partitioning, container isolation, and scheduler-level quotas—to prevent one job from accessing another's memory or processes. The firmware and drivers that control these accelerators should be patched frequently and validated through secure boot to prevent exploitation of low-level vulnerabilities. Logging GPU allocations and monitoring utilization can help auditors detect suspicious or unauthorized workloads. Table 19.2 summarizes strict isolation controls that bound data access registry rights network paths and secret usage for each life cycle stage.

Table 19.2 Build train serve isolation and access boundaries.

Environment	Data store access	Model registry rights	Network egress	Secrets handling
Build	No production data	Write to artifact registry only	Restricted to registries and mirrors	HSM backed short lived tokens
Train	Read approved snapshots only	Write new versions to staging only	Blocked to internet allow listed services only	Injected at runtime rotated
Serve	No raw datasets read only model pull	Read only fetch by digest	Allow listed internal services only	Sealed storage runtime injection

Access to data and model artifacts across all environments must follow the principle of least privilege. Every user, service, or automated job should have only the permissions it needs—no more, no less. Training jobs should only be able to read approved datasets and write to controlled output locations, while build servers should only access code repositories and artifact registries. Access to model registries should be divided between "writers," who can upload new versions, and "readers," who can deploy or test them. Restricting write access sharply reduces the risk of tampering or accidental overwrites. All access events should be logged, timestamped, and reviewed through automated alerting systems to ensure no unauthorized use occurs.

Egress restrictions are another critical control that reinforces isolation. Training and serving environments should have tightly limited outbound network access to prevent exfiltration of proprietary data or model weights. For example, training nodes should not be able to reach the public internet unless connecting through approved proxies or gateways. Similarly, serving systems should be allowed to communicate only with internal services that are explicitly listed in policy. By enforcing these egress boundaries at both the network and identity layers, auditors can confirm that each environment communicates only with trusted systems, creating a transparent and controllable flow of information.

In multi-tenant clusters—where multiple teams or projects share infrastructure—guardrails are essential to prevent one tenant from affecting another. Each tenant should run in its own namespace or virtual project with isolated compute, storage, and identity boundaries. Resource quotas must prevent a single user or job from consuming all available compute or storage, which can lead to denial-of-service or budget overruns. Monitoring and logging should capture per-tenant activity to ensure accountability. Auditors reviewing these environments should look for clearly defined policies separating tenants and automated mechanisms that enforce them.

Data Governance and Lineage: Datasets, Features, Labels, and PII Handling

Strong data governance is the backbone of any reliable and auditable machine learning operation. Every dataset used for model development should have a clearly documented lineage—from its raw form through each transformation and curation stage until it becomes a finalized training, validation, or test set. Without this traceability, it becomes nearly impossible for auditors to verify what data influenced a model's behavior or whether it complied with applicable privacy, quality, and consent requirements. Governance is not only about access control; it's about ensuring that every copy, transformation, and subset of data can be tied back to an immutable source, with the evidence to prove it.

The life cycle of a dataset typically begins with raw data ingestion. This raw tier represents the first copy of information as received from its original source, such as transaction logs, sensor feeds, or user-submitted content. From here, the data moves into a curated tier, where it is cleaned, normalized, and enriched under controlled processes. Each transformation—filtering, aggregation, or anonymization—must be versioned and recorded with metadata identifying who performed it, when, and using which code or configuration. Auditors reviewing these records should be able to reconstruct the entire path from the curated dataset back to the raw source. Only once data has passed through this controlled curation process should it be promoted into the training, validation, or test tiers, where it becomes part of the model's official dataset lineage.

Version control for datasets is essential to maintain both reproducibility and accountability. Every dataset used in model development should have a unique version identifier—typically a hash or digest derived from its exact contents. When even a single record changes, the resulting dataset must generate a new identifier, ensuring that model retraining on updated data can be tracked precisely. This versioning discipline extends to metadata as well, such as schema definitions and preprocessing scripts. An auditor should be able to see not only which dataset version was used in training but also what schema, transformation code, and validation checks were active at that moment. Such precision is the difference between a defensible, well-governed ML environment and an unverifiable "black box" pipeline.

Feature stores carry this lineage forward by serving as the record of how data fields are transformed into machine learning inputs. Each feature should be stored with metadata describing its definition, source datasets, transformation logic, and valid time windows. The feature store should maintain versioned histories so that auditors can verify which feature versions were used in specific training runs or production deployments. Access controls must be applied at the feature level to ensure that sensitive or restricted data—such as Personally identifiable information (PII)-derived attributes—cannot be unintentionally exposed through downstream pipelines. Durable links between datasets, features, and models form the connective tissue that lets an auditor move in either direction: from model to data, or from data to all the models it influenced.

Labeling processes introduce another layer of governance complexity. High-quality labeling requires more than just annotation; it demands measurable consistency and oversight. Inter-rater reliability checks help confirm that multiple annotators are applying labels consistently, revealing areas where definitions or taxonomies may be ambiguous. Over time, label taxonomies often evolve—especially in domains like threat detection, where new categories emerge. To prevent label drift, organizations must version their labeling schemas and record when each model was trained against a particular version. These records give auditors and data scientists the ability to identify whether differences in model performance stem from evolving data or shifting label definitions.

PII handling is one of the most critical and legally sensitive aspects of data governance. The principle of minimization applies across all stages of the data life cycle—only collect and retain the fields absolutely necessary for model performance and auditing. During data curation, PII should be stripped, masked, or tokenized as early as possible, with raw copies isolated in secure vaults accessible only to authorized personnel. If certain identifiers must persist for linkage or deduplication, they should be pseudonymized with irreversible mappings stored under separate encryption keys. Auditors should be able to confirm that each environment—raw, curated, and training—enforces retention and access rules aligned with data protection requirements, ensuring PII does not linger beyond its justified purpose.

Retention and replication controls ensure that data copies remain governed even as they move across environments. Every time a dataset is duplicated, exported, or cached, the system should inherit the same retention rules and access restrictions as the source. Automated policies can flag or quarantine datasets that violate these inheritance rules, ensuring no unmanaged data copies exist in staging or personal workspaces. When data reaches the end of its retention period, its removal must be logged and verifiable. These deletion records are a crucial form of audit evidence, demonstrating that the organization is enforcing data life cycle policies rather than merely declaring them.

Durable identifiers and immutable links across datasets, features, labels, and models make end-to-end traceability possible. A model's registry entry should reference the exact dataset and feature versions used, while each dataset entry should point to the upstream raw data and transformations that created it. This interconnected metadata graph allows auditors to trace a model's behavior back to a precise data snapshot—down to the specific records and transformations that produced it. The same graph supports forward tracing as well, helping organizations understand which models or services depend on a particular data asset before making changes. In regulated industries, this traceability provides both compliance assurance and operational confidence that models behave as expected under controlled, repeatable conditions.

Training and Validation Governance: Reproducibility, Metrics, and Bias Checks

Governance over the training and validation phases of machine learning is what ensures a model is not just functional, but defensible. In practical terms, "reproducibility" means that another engineer, auditor, or automated system could rerun the training process using the same inputs and configurations and obtain an identical—or statistically equivalent—result. Achieving this standard requires more than saving code; it demands precise control over the training environment, from random seed initialization to library versions and data snapshots. Each experiment must be conducted under deterministic conditions so that any differences in outcomes reflect deliberate changes, not environmental noise. For auditors, reproducibility is the cornerstone of trust: without it, no model's behavior can be confidently verified or explained.

Seed management is one of the most overlooked elements of reproducibility. Random seeds are used to initialize data shuffling, parameter weights, and algorithmic sampling in most training frameworks. If seeds are not fixed and recorded, even the same code and data can produce different models. Proper governance requires pipelines to explicitly set random seeds for every stage of training, from data loaders to model initialization. The selected seeds should be logged in the experiment metadata so that anyone reviewing the run can replicate the process exactly. Combined with pinned library versions—ensuring that the same frameworks, compilers, and dependency packages are used—this eliminates the subtle variability that often undermines reproducibility in practice.

Pinned libraries and deterministic pipelines are equally vital. Machine learning frameworks and hardware acceleration libraries change frequently, and even minor version updates can alter numerical precision or randomization behavior. By freezing dependencies and documenting their versions, organizations can recreate a consistent computational environment across retraining cycles. Deterministic pipelines, meanwhile, ensure that data transformations, feature generation, and batch processing follow the same order and logic every time. These pipelines should be automated, version-controlled, and tested to verify that identical inputs yield identical outputs. In an audit context, this means that if a model's performance shifts, investigators can trace the cause to an intentional parameter or data change rather than undetected drift in tooling.

Every experiment and training run should produce a detailed record that captures the conditions under which the model was built. These experiment logs must include dataset versions, feature set identifiers, hyperparameters, algorithmic configurations, and training duration. They should also record environmental details such as the computer hardware, framework versions, and any distributed training settings. Critically, all metrics collected during training—loss curves, accuracy scores, confusion matrices, and validation statistics—should be stored alongside the run metadata. These records form the evidentiary backbone for auditors who must later verify that a model was trained according to documented procedures and that its reported performance is genuine.

Performance acceptance gates are another pillar of training governance. Each model must meet predefined thresholds for key metrics before it can advance toward deployment. These gates are not generic release checks; they are domain-specific standards that reflect real operational expectations. For instance, a fraud detection model might require a minimum precision or false positive rate, while a classification model for malware detection might emphasize recall. These thresholds should be documented in policy and reviewed periodically by both technical and compliance stakeholders. Automated validation pipelines can enforce these gates by halting promotion of models that fail to meet the established criteria, providing a transparent and consistent decision trail.

Bias and fairness checks form the ethical and regulatory counterpart to performance testing. While the definition of "bias" depends on context, every organization should implement at least baseline fairness evaluations appropriate to its data domain. This might include measuring performance across different demographic segments, input distributions, or contextual conditions. For cybersecurity models, for example, it may involve verifying that the detection rate remains consistent across different network types, user roles, or device classes. Bias checks should be conducted automatically during validation, with results logged as part of the experiment record. If material discrepancies are found, retraining with balanced data or adjusted loss weighting should be documented as part of corrective action.

Documenting fairness evaluations also means defining acceptable deviation ranges and establishing who has authority to approve exceptions. Governance frameworks should require sign-off from both the model owner and an independent reviewer—typically from a compliance or risk function—before deploying any model that exhibits known disparities. This double sign-off creates an auditable accountability trail, showing that bias was not ignored but evaluated and accepted within reason. These records, when tied back to specific dataset versions and labeling definitions, help ensure that decisions are explainable and defensible to both internal and external stakeholders.

Validation must also encompass monitoring for drift between training and test data distributions. Even when a model passes initial bias checks, shifts in data patterns over time can reintroduce imbalance or degrade performance. Automated drift detection tools should be configured to alert when input features or prediction distributions deviate from training baselines beyond defined thresholds. This ensures that governance does not end at model approval but continues into the operational life cycle. An auditor reviewing these alerts should see clear evidence of response—either retraining, recalibration, or documented risk acceptance—to confirm that fairness and accuracy remain continuously managed.

Deployment Controls: Approvals, Canary/Rollback, and Version Pinning

Moving a model from testing to production requires a deliberate, auditable process designed to prevent errors and unauthorized changes. Each promotion—from development to staging, and finally to production—must pass through an approval chain that verifies both technical integrity and policy compliance. A model is not just approved because it performs well; it must also come from a trusted build, be signed with verified credentials, and demonstrate full compatibility with the systems it interacts with. To keep the process objective, approvals should follow a two-person rule: the model owner initiates the release, and an independent reviewer—often from risk, governance, or quality assurance—confirms that all checks and documentation meet requirements. This shared responsibility ensures transparency and eliminates the possibility of a single engineer quietly pushing unverified models into service.

Compatibility checks form the backbone of technical validation during deployment. Before a model reaches staging, automated tests should verify that its input and output schemas align with those expected by the feature store and client applications. For example, if a feature has been renamed or its data type changed, the system must block promotion until the mismatch is corrected.

Table 19.3 Model promotion gates and rollback triggers.

Stage	Gate check	Pass criteria	Evidence captured	Fail-safe action
Staging admission	Schema and contract validation	All feature and client contracts pass	Validation report and signer record	Reject promotion
Shadow evaluation	Live traffic mirror comparison	Divergence within tolerated bounds	Shadow metrics and diff logs	Disable shadow
Canary step one	Low traffic slice health	SLOs and core metrics meet thresholds	Canary dashboard snapshot and approval	Auto rollback to prior digest
Canary expansion	Multi window cohort stability	Metrics sustained across patterns	Approval record with window details	Halt and revert to stable
Production steady state	Version pinning and signature checks	All digests and signatures verified	Manifest and signature logs	Rollback on violation

Likewise, downstream systems must confirm that response formats, latency thresholds, and error codes match their integration contracts. These checks prevent the most common deployment failures—such as incompatible data formats or missing features—from slipping into production. By codifying compatibility rules into automated validators, organizations can catch schema and interface issues early, long before end users are affected. Table 19.3 aligns promotion decisions with objective gates captured evidence and predefined rollback actions to contain deployment risk.

Each artifact involved in deployment must also be cryptographically verified. The model file, preprocessing code, and container image should all be digitally signed by the trusted build system, with signatures validated automatically before deployment. Unsigned or untrusted artifacts should be rejected outright. This cryptographic proof ensures that the deployed model has not been tampered with since it was built and that it originates from a known, secure pipeline. Even the deployment manifest—the file that defines which model version to run—should be signed and stored immutably. In combination, these measures make it possible to prove, at any later date, exactly what code and data were deployed and by whom.

Version pinning is another essential practice that prevents accidental or malicious model swaps. Instead of using floating tags like "latest" or "stable," all model references must point to immutable digests or version identifiers. This applies not only to the model itself but also to related elements like preprocessing scripts, configuration files, and threshold values. Pinning ensures that a production deployment always runs the exact same versions that were validated in testing. If an issue arises, engineers and auditors can quickly reproduce the state of the system and roll back to a known good configuration. Without strict version pinning, even a small registry update could silently alter model behavior, creating inconsistencies that are nearly impossible to trace.

Once a model passes approvals, it enters controlled rollout phases designed to reduce risk. The first stage is often "shadow mode," where the new model runs in parallel with the current production model but does not influence live outcomes. It processes real traffic and logs predictions for comparison, allowing teams to evaluate performance under authentic conditions. Metrics such as accuracy, latency, and stability are compared to the production baseline, and discrepancies trigger further analysis. Shadow testing helps identify issues that might not appear during offline validation—such as unexpected feature values or production-specific timing effects—without any impact on users.

If shadow testing is successful, the next step is a canary release. In this approach, a small percentage of real traffic—often 1–5%—is routed to the new model, while the majority continues to use the current one. Automated monitors continuously track key performance indicators like latency, error rates, and model accuracy. If any of these metrics exceed predefined thresholds, the system automatically reverts to the previous model version. Canary deployments offer a safe way to observe how the model behaves in a live environment, while still providing an immediate rollback path if something goes wrong. The process should run long enough to capture natural fluctuations in workload and data patterns, ensuring results are representative.

A/B testing extends this concept by focusing on statistically valid comparisons between model versions. Users or requests are split into separate groups—one using the current model, the other using the new version—with consistent assignment to maintain fairness. The results are evaluated based on defined success metrics such as detection rates, false positives, or user satisfaction scores. This testing method is especially useful when teams need to compare trade-offs, such as precision versus recall, or assess whether a new model improves long-term outcomes. As with other rollout types, all experiment parameters, test durations, and evaluation criteria should be recorded for audit and repeatability.

Rollback procedures are the safety net of any responsible ML deployment. Rollbacks should be automated and reversible within minutes, allowing the system to return to the last known stable state without manual intervention. When a rollback occurs, the event must be logged with the reason, time, and identity of the approver. Because all artifacts and configurations are version-pinned, the rollback process can simply redeploy the previously approved digest, ensuring consistency and integrity. Having these rollback mechanisms pretested and ready prevents prolonged outages or data corruption if a new model performs unexpectedly once live traffic reaches it.

Endpoint and Inference Protections: AuthN/AuthZ, Rate Limits, and Abuse Guards

Inference endpoints represent the public face of an organization's machine learning system, and therefore they must be treated with the same rigor as any critical production service. These endpoints translate model predictions into business actions, often in real time, and are a high-value target for both misuse and attack. Protecting them begins with strong authentication and authorization—controls that determine who can access the endpoint, under what conditions, and for what purpose. Each tenant, client, or service account should have its own identity, with scoped permissions that restrict access to only the specific models or APIs it requires. Endpoints should never accept anonymous or unverified requests, even in testing, as this opens the door to data scraping, model theft, or uncontrolled consumption of compute resources.

Authentication should rely on modern, verifiable mechanisms such as signed tokens, mutual TLS, or workload identities issued by a trusted provider. These credentials must be short-lived and auditable, making it possible to tie every inference request back to a known entity. Authorization policies then enforce what each caller can do—whether they can query a single model, access batch endpoints, or request explanations. Granular authorization, such as model-level or route-level controls, prevents users from invoking models they are not approved to use. Tenant isolation is also critical: one customer's data or request metadata must never be visible or inferable by another. This isolation can be enforced through unique virtual endpoints, separate API keys, or distinct routing namespaces for each tenant's traffic.

Network-level protections reinforce authentication by limiting exposure. Inference services should be deployed within private networks or behind controlled gateways, with public access mediated through API management layers or reverse proxies. Firewalls and service meshes can enforce allowlists for ingress, ensuring that only approved front-end systems or tenants can reach inference nodes. Outbound traffic must also be controlled; inference servers should not have unrestricted internet access, which prevents model outputs or data from being exfiltrated to unmonitored destinations. Combined, these network boundaries keep the inference infrastructure compact, defensible, and auditable—qualities essential for regulated or multi-tenant environments.

Governance at the endpoint layer includes managing how often and how heavily clients can query models. Rate limiting and quota enforcement prevent abuse, denial of service, or runaway consumption of shared compute. Each tenant or API key should have defined limits on request frequency, payload size, and concurrent sessions. Enforcement should happen close to the network edge to conserve compute cycles for legitimate traffic. Similarly, maximum payload sizes should be defined to prevent overly large or malformed inputs that can degrade performance or trigger failures in preprocessing routines. If inference involves structured or untrusted user input, input validation must occur before the request is passed to the model, ensuring it meets expected formats and length constraints.

Output controls are just as important as input filtering. Depending on the model's purpose, responses may need to be sanitized or redacted before returning to the caller. For example, classification APIs should strip internal confidence scores if those values could reveal model internals, while generative or text-based systems may require automated content filters to block sensitive, unsafe, or disallowed outputs. Output limits—such as maximum token counts or truncation rules—protect both users and infrastructure from excessive or unintended responses. These safeguards help ensure that even under heavy or unpredictable workloads, inference behavior remains stable, compliant, and appropriate to the organization's operational standards.

Abuse and safety guardrails are essential for protecting both the system and its users from malicious or unintended use. Prompt filtering can detect and block queries that attempt to extract confidential data, bypass policy, or trigger harmful model behaviors. In applications that handle sensitive information—like personally identifiable data or internal content—automatic redaction or masking should occur before requests reach the model. For models with tool-use or code-execution capabilities, strict invocation constraints are mandatory; the system must whitelist approved tools, limit execution scope, and monitor for disallowed actions such as file access or external network calls. These restrictions reduce the likelihood that an inference endpoint becomes a vector for lateral movement or data exposure.

While robust logging supports accountability, it must balance visibility with privacy. Inference logs should capture key metadata—caller identity, request timestamp, model version, and response status—without storing full payloads or prompts unless explicitly authorized. For cases requiring deeper traceability, logs can reference hashed or tokenized representations of inputs so that investigations can occur without revealing sensitive content. Audit systems should be able to reconstruct event sequences using these identifiers, confirming who invoked which model and when. Retention periods for inference logs must align with organizational and regulatory policies, ensuring that information persists long enough for auditing while minimizing unnecessary data exposure.

Segregation of Duties and Operator Roles in MLOps

Effective segregation of duties (SoD) is a cornerstone of trustworthy machine learning operations. In an MLOps environment, where automated systems build, train, evaluate, and deploy models continuously, the risk of self-approval or concealed manipulation increases if clear role boundaries are not in place. SoD ensures that no single individual or process can control an entire model's life cycle—from raw data ingestion to production deployment—without independent oversight. Rather than relying on broad ethical expectations, these controls must be rooted in operational design: defined roles, enforceable permissions, and traceable records that link every action to a verified identity.

The data curator is responsible for sourcing, cleansing, and maintaining datasets used in training and validation. This role ensures that datasets are complete, compliant, and properly versioned but should not have the ability to approve model deployments or modify live systems. The curator's authority is limited to the raw and curated data tiers, allowing the audit trail to clearly show who handled each dataset version. A properly designed system prevents data curators from altering model registries or accessing production environments, which ensures that any data tampering or labeling errors are caught through independent validation rather than propagated directly into production.

The model trainer operates within the boundaries of defined datasets, transforming curated inputs into trained models. Trainers initiate jobs, select algorithm configurations, and tune hyperparameters, but they should not control data sourcing or have authority to deploy models beyond staging. Their credentials should permit write access to the training environment and model registry for storing new artifacts but exclude privileges to promote those artifacts to production. This separation prevents a single operator from training a model on manipulated data and immediately promoting it without review. Training logs, model signatures, and job metadata provide auditors with immutable evidence linking every model version to the responsible trainer and the approved data versions.

The model evaluator provides an independent review of model performance, reproducibility, and fairness before deployment. Evaluators validate results against defined metrics and bias thresholds, confirm that provenance records are complete, and document their sign-off as part of the promotion workflow. Crucially, evaluators must not be able to retrain models, modify datasets, or alter artifacts in registries. Their role is analytical, not operational. Evaluation reports and approvals become auditable artifacts that link specific model versions to explicit acceptance criteria. If an evaluator and a trainer were the same individual, the control loop would collapse, allowing unverified models to pass without oversight—an unacceptable risk in any regulated or safety-critical domain.

The deployer or approver role represents the final gate between validation and production. This individual or automated control must verify signatures, confirm compatibility with feature store schemas, and ensure that deployment manifests match the versions reviewed during evaluation. The deployer should have read access to registries and production systems but no ability to modify datasets, retrain models, or alter evaluation results. Approvers typically work in coordination with governance or compliance functions to document formal promotion records, which serve as evidence of independent review. This separation ensures that deployment decisions are auditable and reversible, with clear accountability for who authorized each release.

The platform operator maintains the underlying MLOps infrastructure—pipelines, registries, compute clusters, and secret management systems. While this role requires broad system-level access, it should not include rights to manipulate data, train models, or approve deployments. Platform operators focus on stability, performance, and patching, not on business or analytical decisions. Their actions, such as creating service accounts or updating configurations, must be logged in real time with immutable audit entries. Separation between the operator and deployer roles prevents a single person from having control over both the runtime environment and the release process, which would otherwise create opportunities for undetected tampering or post-deployment modification.

Conflicts of interest arise when an individual holds overlapping roles that compromise independence. The most critical conflicts to avoid include allowing the same person to both prepare training data and approve deployments, granting one account full access to both secret stores and model registries, or enabling developers to modify audit logs or provenance records. In well-structured environments, these conflicts are addressed through fine-grained identity and access management, enforced by automated policy rather than manual review. Role-based and attribute-based access controls ensure that cross-role privileges cannot coexist without formal justification. If a temporary escalation is necessary—for example, to troubleshoot a failed deployment—it must be time-boxed, logged, and reviewed by an independent approver afterward.

Temporary privilege escalation is sometimes unavoidable in continuous delivery systems, but it must always be transparent. Privileged access management (PAM) tools can enforce automatic expiry on elevated roles, requiring operators to request just-in-time access that expires after a short window. Every elevation should generate a record capturing who requested it, the reason, the duration, and what actions were performed during that period. These logs provide auditors with the means to confirm that elevated rights were used appropriately and that privileges returned to their normal state once the issue was resolved. Without such controls, even a well-intentioned engineer could inadvertently leave backdoors or overexposed credentials in the environment.

Segregation of duties ultimately produces a verifiable map of accountability across the MLOps life cycle. Each role—curator, trainer, evaluator, deployer, and operator—should have its own identity, permissions, and logging scope, all reflected in the system's auditable artifacts. Approval records show who authorized what; role mappings demonstrate how privileges are separated; and access logs confirm that actions were executed by the correct entities. These artifacts together provide tangible proof that SoD exists not as an abstract ethical guideline but as a technical control. When enforced systematically, they prevent self-review, detect privilege overlap, and ensure that no single person can compromise the integrity of the machine learning supply chain.

Conclusion

Automation and continuous auditing redefine how cybersecurity assurance is achieved in intelligent, data-driven environments. The principles explored throughout this chapter demonstrate that trust in machine learning and AI-enabled systems cannot rely on manual inspection or one-time reviews. Assurance must be embedded into the pipeline itself—through verifiable provenance, controlled environments, and measurable governance. Mastering these disciplines allows auditors to transform oversight from a reactive exercise into a living system of controls that validates every stage of the AI life cycle.

This chapter reinforces the role of continuous validation and advanced analytics in securing AI ecosystems at scale. By ensuring that data, models, and infrastructure operate under transparent, verifiable conditions, organizations can achieve both compliance and resilience in an era defined by automation. When applied correctly, these controls do more than satisfy auditors—they build confidence across stakeholders who must trust that automated decisions remain explainable, accountable, and aligned with ethical and regulatory expectations.

With these foundations in place, professionals are better equipped to oversee complex, automated architectures without losing sight of human accountability. Continuous auditing is not simply a technical shift; it represents an evolution in assurance philosophy—one that treats automation as both a risk vector and a governance instrument. By embedding integrity, traceability, and controlled autonomy into every layer of the AI pipeline, cybersecurity auditors strengthen the very systems that increasingly shape modern digital operations.

Auditor Recommendations

1. **Enforce Life Cycle Segregation:** Establish a clear process for separating build, training, and serving environments within your audit scope. Each stage should maintain distinct permissions, identities, and data access boundaries to prevent cross-contamination and unauthorized promotion of models. Review access policies and network configurations to ensure that no individual or system can control all three phases simultaneously. This segregation not only supports operational security but also enables auditors to trace accountability at every point in the model life cycle.
2. **Validate Provenance and Signing Controls:** Prioritize consistent verification of artifact provenance and cryptographic signatures across all ML components. Confirm that each dataset, model binary, and container image is traceable to its approved source, with signed attestations that link it to a controlled build pipeline. During audits, require evidence of signature validation at deployment checkpoints to prevent unverified artifacts from entering production. Such validation ensures the integrity and authenticity of every asset within the AI supply chain.
3. **Assess Data Lineage and Retention Practices:** Evaluate whether dataset versioning, lineage tracking, and PII minimization are being consistently enforced. Auditors should confirm that each data transformation—from raw ingestion through curated and training sets—is recorded and linked to immutable identifiers. Review how retention and deletion policies are implemented across environments to verify compliance with privacy requirements. Effective lineage management allows auditors to reconstruct the full history of data use behind any model decision.
4. **Require Reproducibility Evidence:** Insist that all training and validation processes produce reproducible results as a condition for model acceptance. This includes confirming fixed random seeds, pinned dependencies, and deterministic pipeline configurations. Audit teams should verify that experiment records capture the full set of environmental parameters, datasets, and metrics required for replication. Reproducibility transforms model validation from a matter of trust into a verifiable control.
5. **Set Explicit Validation and Bias Gates:** Establish measurable acceptance criteria for model performance and fairness before promotion. These criteria should include defined thresholds for accuracy, drift, and bias indicators appropriate to the organization's domain. Require independent reviewer sign-off for any model that approaches or exceeds these limits, and document rationale for exceptions. Embedding these gates into the audit process ensures consistency between ethical expectations and operational practices.
6. **Verify Deployment Approval Workflows:** Audit the end-to-end approval chain for model promotion to ensure it reflects proper segregation of duties. Confirm that approvals involve both technical validation and independent governance oversight, with immutable records of who authorized each release. Review compatibility and schema checks to ensure that deployed models align with feature store contracts and client interfaces. This disciplined approach prevents unauthorized or unvetted models from reaching production systems.
7. **Evaluate Inference Endpoint Protections:** Examine the controls that protect inference endpoints against misuse or overexposure. Verify that strong authentication, granular authorization, and tenant isolation are implemented to safeguard against data leakage or model abuse. Assess rate limiting, payload size restrictions, and input/output filtering as part of the audit scope to confirm that the environment enforces responsible use. Endpoint governance provides measurable assurance that deployed models operate within approved boundaries.

8. **Audit Operator Role Boundaries:** Confirm that MLOps roles such as data curator, trainer, evaluator, deployer, and platform operator remain distinct in both policy and practice. Review access logs and privilege assignments to ensure no single user holds overlapping authorities that enable self-review or unsupervised model promotion. Document how temporary escalations are time-bound, approved, and fully logged for post-event review. Role integrity reinforces accountability and minimizes insider risk within automated environments.
9. **Examine Continuous Auditing Mechanisms:** Evaluate whether continuous monitoring and automated validation controls are integrated into the ML life cycle. These systems should verify artifact integrity, model performance, and configuration drift in near real time, generating evidence suitable for audit review. Focus on how the organization converts automated findings into durable audit artifacts rather than transient alerts. Continuous auditing ensures that compliance and risk oversight remain synchronized with rapid deployment cycles.
10. **Integrate Audit Evidence with Governance Systems:** Require that all key artifacts—approvals, lineage records, experiment logs, and access mappings—are systematically linked to the organization's governance framework. Ensure that each piece of evidence can be traced to a responsible role and a verifiable event within the pipeline. Encourage standardized metadata and logging formats to simplify cross-domain review and reporting. This integration transforms auditing from a periodic exercise into a continuous component of operational governance.

Chapter Questions

1. What is the primary purpose of provenance records in the ML supply chain?
   A. Detect latency spikes during inference
   B. Compress model binaries to reduce storage
   C. Reconstruct who built each artifact, from which inputs, and with which configurations
   D. Enable A/B routing across multiple model versions

2. Which control most effectively prevents unvetted model swaps at deployment?
   A. Strict version pinning using immutable digests for models, images, and configs
   B. Autoscaling policies on serving clusters
   C. Blue/green releases that reference the "latest" tag
   D. Longer inference timeouts during rollout

3. Why should the serving environment have read-only access to the model registry?
   A. To speed up artifact downloads via client-side caching
   B. To enable self-training directly on production endpoints
   C. To allow on-host edits of model weights if needed
   D. To prevent tampering or unauthorized uploads from production systems

4. Which scenario most clearly violates segregation of duties in MLOps?
   A. A platform operator rotating cluster nodes without model registry write access
   B. The same individual preparing training data and approving production deployment
   C. An evaluator reviewing validation metrics and bias checks
   D. A deployer validating signatures but lacking dataset curation rights

5. Which combination is essential for practical reproducibility of model training?
   - A. Adding more GPUs and memory to the training cluster
   - B. Enabling canary rollout prior to staging
   - C. Fixed random seeds, pinned libraries, and deterministic pipelines
   - D. Using larger batch sizes to stabilize gradients

6. What is the safest first exposure pattern for a new model with zero user impact?
   - A. Shadow mode on mirrored production traffic
   - B. Full cutover to the new model during low traffic
   - C. Immediate 50/50 A/B split across all users
   - D. Blue/green database migration alongside deployment

7. What is the primary reason to restrict egress from training nodes?
   - A. Reduce storage costs for experiment artifacts
   - B. Improve convergence speed during optimization
   - C. Allow flexible package installation from any source
   - D. Prevent exfiltration of datasets and model artifacts

8. Which endpoint protection best enforces tenant boundaries?
   - A. Shared API keys across multiple clients
   - B. Per-tenant identities and authorization scopes with isolated routing namespaces
   - C. Public, unauthenticated access with IP allowlists
   - D. Encrypting and storing full prompts in logs indefinitely

9. Which metadata must be validated before promoting a model artifact?
   - A. Cryptographic signature from a trusted build and a matching registry digest
   - B. Alignment with the product team's UI theme
   - C. Presence of a marketing tag in the registry entry
   - D. Inclusion of a README file in the repository

10. Which practice ensures a model can be traced back to its exact data snapshot?
   - A. Performing regular backups of the data lake
   - B. Applying differential privacy to training data
   - C. Using durable identifiers that link the model to specific dataset and feature versions and transformations
   - D. Having labels applied only by subject-matter experts

20

AI Monitoring and Incident Response

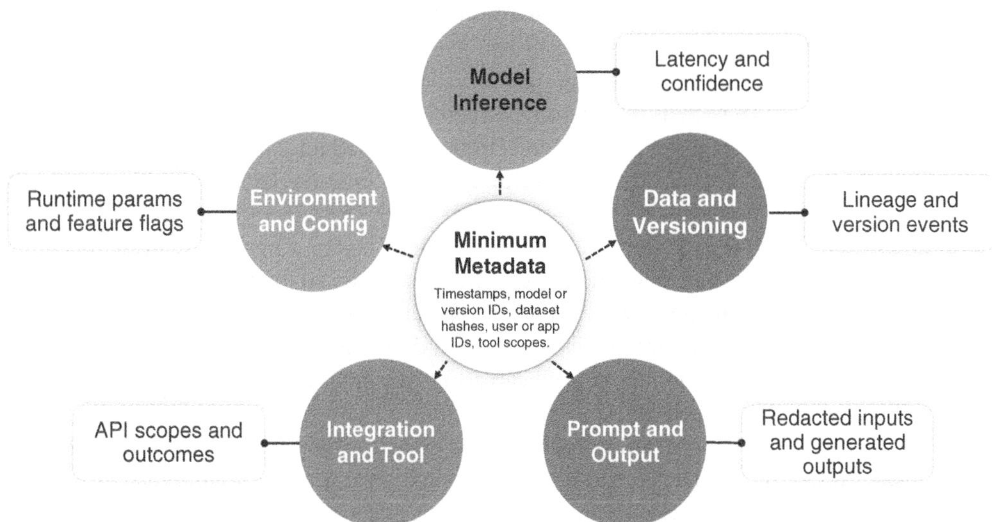

Artificial intelligence (AI) has redefined both the scope and the speed of modern cybersecurity operations, bringing new efficiencies—and new risks—to the enterprise landscape. As AI systems become integral to detection, decision-making, and automation, auditors must learn to assess not just algorithms but the operational frameworks that govern them. Monitoring, containment, and forensic readiness are no longer peripheral capabilities; they are essential components of trustworthy AI assurance. Understanding how to evaluate these mechanisms equips auditors to verify that AI-driven environments remain safe, explainable, and accountable under real-world conditions.

From continuous monitoring for model drift and abuse detection to structured triage, evidence handling, and escalation across enterprise boundaries, this chapter examines how organizations maintain control when AI systems fail or behave unpredictably. It emphasizes the need for auditable telemetry, well-defined containment mechanisms, and disciplined coordination between AI assurance and traditional incident response teams. The discussion bridges technical controls—such as kill switches, feature flags, and data provenance tracking—with governance expectations that ensure every response action can be traced, verified, and improved upon.

Ultimately, this chapter reinforces that resilience in AI-enabled environments is not achieved through prevention alone but through prepared, evidence-driven recovery. The ability to reconstruct, contain, and learn from AI incidents defines organizational maturity in an era where automated decisions can have material, ethical, or legal consequences. For cybersecurity auditors, mastering these disciplines means moving beyond compliance checklists toward a holistic assurance model—one that treats AI behavior, governance, and response capability as inseparable elements of enterprise risk management.

Monitoring Objectives: Drift, Performance Degradation, and Safety/Abuse Signals

Monitoring in AI systems must begin with clear, measurable objectives that define exactly what must be detected, how quickly it must be identified, and why it matters to the organization. The goal is not to "watch everything," but to establish a disciplined set of detection priorities that directly protect business value, compliance posture, and user trust. These objectives must explicitly outline the phenomena to be tracked—such as model drift, data drift, and safety or abuse violations—and pair each one with concrete detection thresholds and latency expectations. For example, a well-formed monitoring objective might state: "Detect a five percent shift in input data distribution within fifteen minutes," or "Quarantine any model response that exceeds toxicity thresholds within two seconds of generation." Each objective must tie back to a defined business impact, ensuring that alerts trigger meaningful action rather than adding to operational noise. Without this alignment, monitoring becomes a reactive data exercise rather than a proactive risk management process.

Performance drift is often the first indicator that an AI system's outputs are no longer aligned with its intended performance standards. Drift can occur gradually, as model weights become misaligned with changing real-world data, or abruptly, after an untested code change, a corrupted dataset, or a new integration. Detecting performance drift requires continuous comparison between real-time results and expected baselines established during model validation. Key metrics may include accuracy, latency, rejection rate, retrieval hit rate, or other indicators that reflect the quality of the system's decision-making. For example, if a fraud detection model begins approving transactions that historically would have been flagged, the system must alert operators before the issue leads to financial losses or reputational harm. Monitoring for performance drift ensures that degradation is detected at the earliest possible stage, allowing corrective measures—such as retraining, rollback, or tuning—to be implemented before user experience or compliance obligations are compromised.

Data drift represents one of the most persistent and subtle risks in AI operations. It refers to the change in statistical or semantic characteristics of the data the model receives, which can cause output behavior to shift unexpectedly. These changes might result from user behavior trends, seasonal cycles, the introduction of new data sources, or adversarial manipulation. Monitoring for data drift involves comparing new data inputs to historical norms using statistical distribution tests, similarity scoring, or embedding-based distance measures. The objective is to determine whether the data feeding the model still reflects the environment it was trained for. For instance, an AI trained on medical data from one region might start seeing patient patterns from another region, causing predictions to deviate from expected baselines. By defining clear data drift thresholds—such as an allowable variance in data distributions or embedding centroids—organizations can decide when to escalate for investigation or retraining.

Safety and abuse monitoring form the third core pillar of AI oversight. These systems aim to identify when an AI model is being misused, manipulated, or generating harmful content.

Abuse may stem from malicious users attempting prompt injection, data poisoning, or other adversarial attacks designed to subvert the model's guardrails. Safety violations, by contrast, often occur when the model itself generates biased, toxic, or confidential outputs. Effective monitoring solutions deploy layered safety filters that continuously scan for red flags in both user inputs and model outputs, testing for harmful topics, discriminatory language, or policy violations. When such events are detected, automated workflows must trigger response actions such as quarantining the output, restricting the session, or escalating to human review. The objective is to maintain both user safety and organizational compliance, ensuring that harmful incidents are addressed within seconds—not hours—of detection. Table 20.1 links detection targets to thresholds latency and actions so auditors can evaluate objective alignment with business risk.

Defining monitoring thresholds and latency targets is crucial to transforming detection into response capability. Latency refers to the time between the occurrence of an issue and the system's recognition of it, while thresholds define the sensitivity level for what constitutes an anomaly. These parameters must balance responsiveness with operational practicality. For high-risk applications—such as autonomous vehicles, financial transaction systems, or medical diagnostics—the acceptable latency for detection may be measured in milliseconds or seconds. Lower-risk systems, such as internal analytics tools, may tolerate longer intervals. Similarly, thresholds must be calibrated to minimize both false positives and false negatives. Setting thresholds too tightly can overwhelm teams with alerts, while setting them too loosely can allow critical issues to slip through unnoticed. Continuous tuning of these thresholds, based on live performance data, ensures that monitoring remains reliable and adaptive.

Table 20.1 Monitoring objectives and actions.

Detection target	Threshold example	Detection latency target	Primary action	Business risk mitigated
Model performance drift	Accuracy drop over 3 points	15 minutes	Alert and throttle responses	Customer trust erosion
Data drift	Embedding centroid divergence over threshold T	15 minutes	Tighten retrieval and escalate review	Misclassification and bias
Safety violation output	Toxicity score above policy limit	2 seconds	Quarantine response and notify reviewer	Regulatory exposure
Prompt injection attempt	Guardrail breach detected by policy rules	2 seconds	Block request and flag account	Tool abuse and data leakage
Integration failure	Tool call error rate above baseline	5 minutes	Disable tool via feature flag	Unauthorized action propagation
Latency anomaly	P95 latency above SLO for 3 windows	10 minutes	Enter safe mode with reduced features	Availability and SLA breach
Retrieval quality drop	RAG hit rate decrease over 10 percent	30 minutes	Increase retrieval strictness and refresh index	Hallucination risk
Moderation trigger spike	Safety filter activations spike above norm	5 minutes	Activate safe mode and sample outputs	Harmful content spread

Every monitoring objective should trace back to a defined business or regulatory outcome. This alignment converts technical indicators into actionable governance data. For example, a performance decline of 2% might not trigger alarm in an experimental system but could be unacceptable in a production environment tied to customer-facing services. Similarly, a minor increase in response latency might have no business impact in an internal report generator but could be critical in real-time fraud detection. By explicitly connecting metrics to business impact—such as customer satisfaction, compliance adherence, or revenue protection—organizations ensure that monitoring data drives intelligent prioritization. This linkage also helps auditors and executives interpret monitoring results in the context of strategic risk rather than isolated technical metrics.

Adaptability is another key objective of modern AI monitoring. AI systems evolve continuously as they ingest new data, face changing user behaviors, or integrate additional model components. Static thresholds and rigid detection rules can quickly become obsolete, creating blind spots or generating unnecessary noise. Adaptive monitoring frameworks incorporate feedback loops that adjust parameters based on historical patterns, known incident responses, and evolving baselines. For instance, after several months of consistent model behavior, a drift detector might automatically tighten sensitivity around known weak points. Conversely, if false positives increase, the system can recalibrate tolerance levels without requiring manual intervention. This adaptive capability ensures monitoring remains relevant, scalable, and efficient as both the model and its operating environment mature.

Abuse and misuse detection must extend beyond end-user behavior to include insider and operational risks. A common oversight occurs when internal staff unintentionally deploy models trained on unapproved datasets, misconfigure inference environments, or bypass moderation tools for testing convenience. These actions can introduce compliance exposure or safety vulnerabilities, even in trusted environments. Therefore, monitoring must also encompass version control, deployment integrity, and configuration tracking to ensure that models remain compliant with organizational and regulatory requirements. Establishing audit logs for model deployments, configuration changes, and access events allows organizations to verify that monitoring objectives are being applied consistently across the AI life cycle.

Signal Design and Coverage: Model, Data, Prompt, and Integration Telemetry

Effective AI monitoring and incident response depend on comprehensive telemetry design—one that captures model behavior, data transformations, user interactions, and integration flows with sufficient fidelity to reconstruct events. Unlike traditional systems, AI environments produce multidimensional signals that extend beyond infrastructure metrics. They require coordinated telemetry across multiple planes: model inference metrics, dataset and version changes, prompt and response logs, and external integration or tool activity. Each plane provides a distinct layer of evidence, and only together can they deliver the full context necessary for auditability and root-cause analysis. The objective is not to collect everything indiscriminately, but to design telemetry signals that are rich enough to explain *why* a behavior occurred, not just *that* it occurred.

The model telemetry plane focuses on the performance and internal health of the AI model during inference. Metrics in this plane include model version identifiers, latency, confidence scores, and anomaly indicators such as temperature spikes or token-level instability. Collecting this data enables teams to differentiate between model logic failures and upstream or downstream integration issues. For example, if latency increases but accuracy metrics remain stable, the issue may lie in infrastructure load rather than model drift. Conversely, consistent confidence degradation may indicate subtle corruption in model parameters or a training data regression. Each inference event should be tagged with a timestamp, model identifier, and execution environment reference to enable later cross-correlation with other system logs.

Dataset and version telemetry track the provenance and evolution of data that shapes model behavior. Every dataset used for training, fine-tuning, or retraining should be versioned with immutable identifiers such as dataset hashes or unique commit references. These identifiers ensure that auditors can verify which data the model relied on at any point in time and whether unapproved data sources were introduced. This level of transparency is crucial when investigating whether a drift or bias issue originated from data contamination, incomplete updates, or unauthorized modifications. Additionally, telemetry should log dataset lineage events—such as ingestion timestamps, preprocessing transformations, and schema changes—so the sequence of data evolution can be fully reconstructed during incident reviews or post-mortems.

Prompt and output telemetry serve as the behavioral evidence layer of AI oversight. This plane captures the exact inputs the system received and the outputs it produced, enabling reconstruction of model behavior during user interactions. Because prompt and output logs may contain sensitive or personal data, they must be appropriately redacted, tokenized, or pseudonymized before storage or export. The purpose of this telemetry is not to surveil users, but to allow analysts and auditors to reproduce anomalous outputs, evaluate potential prompt injections, and confirm whether safeguards operated as expected. Each logged event should include metadata such as timestamps, model or service version, user or application ID, and redaction status. For high-risk environments, replayable traces of prompts and responses—securely stored and access-controlled—allow for controlled forensic analysis without exposing original content. Table 20.2 specifies the minimum vendor neutral metadata needed to reconstruct events across telemetry planes.

Integration and tool telemetry extend visibility into the operational ecosystem that surrounds the AI model. AI systems rarely operate in isolation; they are typically embedded in workflows that invoke APIs, orchestrate tool calls, or interface with external data systems. Logging these interactions provides critical insight into whether an incident stemmed from model logic, tool misuse, or an integration fault. For example, an AI assistant that triggers a downstream automation tool could execute an unauthorized action if telemetry fails to capture the scope or permissions of that call. Telemetry in this layer should record tool identifiers, function scopes, execution outcomes, and contextual metadata—such as the originating user ID or session token—to enable

Table 20.2 Telemetry coverage and minimum metadata.

Telemetry plane	Core signals captured	Required metadata fields	Primary audit use
Model inference	Latency and confidence and refusal rate	Timestamps and model IDs and version IDs	Correlate behavior to specific builds
Data and versioning	Dataset lineage and version events	Dataset hashes and ingestion times	Verify provenance and integrity
Prompt and output	Redacted inputs and generated outputs	Timestamps and user IDs and app IDs	Reproduce behavior with privacy controls
Integration and tool	API call scopes and outcomes	Tool IDs and execution results	Trace cross system effects
Environment and config	Runtime params and feature flags	Config snapshot IDs and env refs	Confirm settings at time of incident

complete reconstruction of cross-system activities. This audit trail ensures that human actions, AI reasoning, and system integrations are traceable as a single, coherent chain.

Designing effective telemetry requires balancing completeness with privacy, cost, and security. Overcollection creates noise and increases exposure risk, while undercollection leaves critical blind spots that impede investigation. The minimum metadata needed for auditability should include timestamps, model and version IDs, dataset hashes, user or application identifiers, and tool or integration scopes. Timestamps establish event chronology; model and version IDs allow correlation with deployment pipelines; dataset hashes ensure data integrity verification; and user or app IDs attribute actions to specific entities. Tool scopes provide visibility into external calls, helping identify whether a misconfiguration or overprivileged function contributed to an incident. These metadata fields together form a minimal, vendor-neutral foundation for reconstructing the timeline and causal chain of AI-related events.

The interplay among telemetry planes is what makes them powerful for incident reconstruction. Consider a scenario where an AI system begins generating incorrect or harmful outputs. Model telemetry may show that accuracy metrics dropped shortly after a new version deployment. Dataset telemetry could reveal that a new dataset hash appeared in the training pipeline around the same time. Prompt logs might show that user queries contained previously unseen patterns. Integration telemetry could confirm that a downstream content moderation API was temporarily unavailable. Only by correlating these signals can investigators establish whether the issue stemmed from faulty data, model regression, or external dependency failure. Thus, telemetry must be structured not as isolated data streams, but as synchronized evidence channels that tell a unified operational story.

Equally important is ensuring that telemetry itself is tamper-evident and verifiable. Logs should be cryptographically signed or stored in append-only systems to prevent retroactive manipulation. Each telemetry record must maintain integrity across its life cycle, from collection through retention and audit review. Auditors rely on this chain of trust to validate the authenticity of evidence and confirm that monitoring controls are functioning as designed. Implementing these safeguards ensures that AI telemetry not only enables detection and analysis but also upholds the legal and regulatory standards required for defensible auditing and reporting.

Containment Mechanisms: Kill Switches, Safe Modes, and Feature Flags

Containment mechanisms are the emergency brakes of AI systems—purpose-built tools that allow teams to halt, limit, or reconfigure system behavior when an incident threatens safety, compliance, or operational integrity. Unlike traditional IT systems, where downtime may simply inconvenience users, AI systems can cause real harm if left running under compromised conditions. A well-designed containment strategy therefore blends immediacy, precision, and accountability. The three foundational components of this strategy—kill switches, safe modes, and feature flags—offer escalating levels of control, from total shutdown to selective restriction. Each must be engineered for rapid activation, transparent governance, and auditable proof of who acted, when, and why.

A kill switch represents the ultimate containment control: an authoritative, immediate stop to model execution or AI-driven decision-making. Its purpose is to terminate the system's activity when continued operation would cause unacceptable risk, such as generating harmful outputs, violating data privacy laws, or amplifying a security breach. Kill switches must be accessible only to a limited and pre-authorized group, typically composed of security operations, compliance officers, or designated incident commanders. These individuals must be authenticated through multifactor authorization before activation. The kill switch's action must occur in seconds—ideally within one to five seconds of invocation—to prevent further propagation of harm. Systems should be designed to gracefully degrade or freeze active processes, ensuring that all outputs, caches, and logs are preserved for investigation. Because a kill switch can disrupt business continuity, its use requires precise documentation and predefined approval protocols that demonstrate necessity, proportionality, and oversight.

A safe mode serves as the next layer of containment, providing a degraded but controlled operational state that prioritizes safety and stability over performance or completeness. When safe mode is engaged, the AI system continues operating under restricted parameters—for example, disabling high-risk features like tool access, external data retrieval, or self-learning updates—while maintaining essential functions. This mode is especially valuable when the root cause of an incident is still being investigated but a full shutdown would be too disruptive. Safe modes can also automatically activate in response to specific triggers, such as sustained drift beyond acceptable thresholds, repeated safety filter violations, or abnormal request volumes. In practice, this might mean reverting a chatbot to a static FAQ database, reducing model temperature, or disabling integrations until integrity checks pass. While safe mode activation should ideally occur within minutes, the more critical requirement is that its transition and operational limits are transparent, logged, and reversible only through approved workflows.

Feature flags represent the most granular and flexible containment mechanism, allowing specific components, features, or integrations to be selectively enabled or disabled without redeploying the system. They are essential for testing, progressive rollouts, and rapid mitigation of discovered vulnerabilities. For example, if an AI assistant's image-generation feature begins producing noncompliant content, engineers can disable that feature flag instantly while keeping text-based responses active. Effective feature flag design incorporates both operational agility and risk governance: only authorized personnel may toggle production flags, and each change must create a clear audit record that links the decision to a responsible individual and supporting rationale. While feature flags are typically invoked by engineers or site reliability teams, they must also integrate into incident command structures so that decision-making authority remains traceable.

Speed is the defining characteristic of containment. Kill switches must act within seconds, safe modes within minutes, and feature flag adjustments within minutes to hours depending on the scope of the issue. Latency in containment directly correlates with potential damage: the longer a compromised AI continues to operate, the more data it can leak, the more users it can misinform, or the more systems it can affect. Therefore, containment mechanisms should be designed as preapproved, low-friction actions that can be executed immediately, with subsequent approvals occurring after stabilization rather than before. Incident runbooks should clearly outline who has the authority to invoke each control, under what conditions, and what the communication sequence must be once the mechanism is activated.

Containment actions carry significant evidentiary and governance implications. Every activation—whether a kill switch, safe mode transition, or feature flag toggle—must generate a tamper-evident audit trail. This includes timestamps, user or role identifiers, system state snapshots, and the explicit reason for activation. Post-incident, auditors should be able to reconstruct the full decision chain: who approved the containment action, what evidence justified it, when it was executed, and how it was rolled back. Rollback proof, in particular, ensures that restoration occurred in a controlled, validated manner rather than through ad-hoc intervention. These records not only preserve accountability but also serve as compliance evidence for regulators or third-party auditors, demonstrating that containment controls were implemented responsibly and effectively.

Governance around containment must integrate with the organization's incident command and communication framework, ensuring consistent response and escalation. While the operational trigger for a containment action might come from engineers or automated systems, the oversight must remain with the incident response leadership defined in Chapter 12. Clear communication channels—between AI operations, cybersecurity, compliance, and executive leadership—ensure that decisions are transparent, coordinated, and properly logged. For example, when a kill switch is triggered, the incident commander must notify affected business units, initiate postmortem procedures, and engage legal or regulatory liaisons if the event meets disclosure thresholds.

From an architectural standpoint, containment mechanisms should be tested regularly through simulated exercises. These "fire drills" verify that kill switches operate under realistic latency, that safe modes preserve essential functions, and that feature flag toggles propagate as expected across distributed systems. Such tests validate both the technical and human components of containment—ensuring teams know how to execute under pressure and that systems perform reliably when urgency is highest. These exercises also expose dependencies and bottlenecks that can be refined before a real incident occurs.

AI Incident Triage and Classification (Boundaries with Enterprise IR)

AI incident triage begins with a clear understanding of what differentiates an "AI incident" from a traditional IT or cybersecurity event. While enterprise incident response typically focuses on compromised systems, unauthorized access, or service outages, AI incidents center on the *behavior* and *outputs* of intelligent systems. An AI incident occurs when a model behaves in a way that violates safety expectations, privacy requirements, or ethical boundaries—even if no explicit security control was breached. Typical triggers include harmful or biased outputs, data leakage through model responses, tool or integration misuse, model integrity compromise, or evidence of adversarial manipulation such as prompt injection or data poisoning. These incidents are unique because their impact often originates from the model's learned behavior, not from an external intrusion. Identifying and classifying such events quickly is essential to prevent reputational, regulatory, or operational damage.

An AI incident can manifest across multiple layers of the ecosystem. At the user-facing level, incidents might involve a chatbot producing offensive, biased, or dangerous recommendations. At the data layer, leakage could occur when the model unintentionally reveals sensitive training data or confidential input information in its responses. At the system level, an attacker may exploit tool integration to perform unauthorized actions through natural language instructions. Finally, at the integrity level, incidents may arise from model corruption—such as tampered weights, poisoned datasets, or unauthorized fine-tuning that alters model behavior. By defining these categories clearly, organizations can establish thresholds for escalation and assign ownership between AI assurance teams and enterprise security functions.

The severity taxonomy for AI incidents should be structured around business impact, safety risk, and containment complexity rather than purely technical indicators. A critical severity event represents a direct and ongoing risk to human safety, data confidentiality, or regulatory compliance—for example, an AI system exposing personal health information or producing self-directed harmful instructions. A high severity event may involve harmful but limited exposure, such as offensive or biased outputs reaching a public audience or an AI-powered automation triggering an incorrect action in a connected system. Medium severity covers incidents that indicate model degradation or potential misuse but with controlled exposure—such as recurring prompt injection attempts that the system successfully neutralizes. Low severity incidents typically include early warnings or internal anomalies that do not yet affect users but warrant monitoring or minor remediation. Classifying incidents this way ensures proportional response effort, resource allocation, and documentation rigor.

Triage serves as the bridge between detection and response, transforming raw telemetry into structured understanding. The AI assurance team must validate the initial signal—such as a flagged prompt, performance anomaly, or drift alert—and assess whether it meets the threshold for incident designation. Triage requires correlating multiple sources of telemetry: model inference logs, dataset hashes, integration calls, and user identifiers. The goal is to determine scope and credibility—whether the anomaly is an isolated error, a systemic model failure, or an active attack. At this stage, the team also estimates the blast radius: how many users, transactions, or systems could be affected if the issue persists. A clear blast radius estimate helps prioritize response urgency and coordinate escalation with enterprise incident response teams.

During triage, AI assurance teams must package three primary categories of information for handoff to enterprise IR: signals, artifacts, and contextual metadata. Signals are the triggering indicators—logs, metrics, or events—that first revealed the anomaly. Artifacts include concrete evidence such as redacted prompt-output pairs, dataset identifiers, or configuration snapshots. Contextual metadata provides the narrative glue, outlining when and how the anomaly occurred, what containment actions (if any) have been applied, and what dependencies or integrations might be affected. Together, these elements allow enterprise IR teams to evaluate whether the event extends beyond AI behavior into infrastructure or security domains. This structured handoff ensures that investigations are continuous rather than duplicated or fragmented between teams.

Boundaries between AI incident response and enterprise IR must be explicitly defined to avoid confusion during high-pressure events. The AI assurance lane owns all incidents rooted in model logic, training data integrity, and behavioral safeguards. This includes managing containment actions such as kill switches, safe mode activation, or model rollback, as well as maintaining audit trails of prompts, responses, and model versioning. The enterprise IR lane, on the other hand, assumes control when the incident crosses into infrastructure compromise, unauthorized access, or regulatory exposure. For instance, if a prompt injection allows a user to extract credentials from a downstream system, the AI team addresses the behavioral vulnerability while enterprise IR handles the data breach investigation, external communications, and remediation of access controls.

Maintaining this separation of responsibilities avoids redundancy and accelerates coordinated response. The AI assurance team focuses on technical root cause analysis—determining whether the failure stemmed from model misalignment, drift, or data contamination—while enterprise IR manages cross-functional coordination, legal obligations, and stakeholder communication. Each team must maintain continuous bidirectional visibility: AI responders must inform enterprise IR when containment actions are taken, and enterprise IR must loop back any broader system findings that could affect future model behavior. Shared tools such as incident management platforms or ticketing systems can synchronize this visibility while preserving role-based access to sensitive AI logs or artifacts.

The triage process also serves a preventive function by improving the organization's future readiness. Every AI incident investigation contributes to refining detection thresholds, improving safety filters, and adjusting model retraining protocols. Documenting triage logic—what signals were prioritized, what evidence proved decisive, and how false positives were eliminated—creates institutional knowledge that sharpens future detection and response. Post-incident reviews (PIRs) should ensure that lessons learned feed directly into monitoring configuration, containment triggers, and model governance policies, strengthening the entire assurance framework over time.

Timeliness and precision are essential qualities of effective AI triage. Incidents involving model outputs or data exposure evolve quickly, and delayed classification can multiply harm before containment begins. To counter this, AI teams must operate with preapproved criteria for declaring incidents, allowing them to act decisively without waiting for executive sign-off. Enterprise IR, meanwhile, must trust those declarations and be prepared to integrate AI-specific data into their existing playbooks for communication, escalation, and regulatory reporting. This partnership ensures that when an AI system crosses the line from anomaly to active risk, the organization responds with clarity, speed, and authority.

Forensics and Evidence Handling for AI Incidents (Repro Inputs/Outputs, Snapshots)

AI forensics demands a level of precision and reproducibility that goes beyond traditional digital investigation. When an AI system behaves unpredictably, produces harmful outputs, or leaks data, the investigation's credibility hinges on the ability to reconstruct *exactly* what occurred. This reconstruction requires not only preserved logs and configuration states but also the specific model version, input data, and contextual parameters that influenced the output. The goal is to make AI incidents auditable in the same way network or endpoint incidents are—grounded in verifiable, immutable evidence. However, because AI systems involve stochastic processes, dynamic models, and ephemeral states, forensic handling must account for unique volatility and nondeterminism. Effective evidence protocols ensure that even fleeting or probabilistic model behaviors can be explained, documented, and reproduced to the greatest extent technically possible. Table 20.3 outlines the evidence set and controls required to preserve replayable context for AI incident investigations.

The cornerstone of AI forensics is input and output preservation, particularly the exact prompts or data inputs that triggered an anomalous behavior. These inputs must be captured in their original form, redacted according to privacy and sensitivity rules, and stored securely in immutable evidence repositories. Redaction standards should ensure that personally identifiable information (PII), proprietary data, or sensitive content are replaced with consistent placeholders without altering the prompt's operational meaning. Outputs must be preserved in parallel, maintaining the original format and metadata such as timestamps, model name, temperature setting, and token count. The combination of prompt and response forms the minimal reproducibility artifact necessary to replay the incident. Forensic teams must treat these pairs as privileged evidence, maintaining access logs and encryption throughout their life cycle to meet both compliance and ethical obligations.

Every preserved record must also include model and version identifiers to ensure reproducibility. Even minor model updates—such as patch-level fine-tuning or embedding refreshes—can materially alter behavior. Capturing version strings, commit hashes, or container image digests allows investigators to correlate observed outputs to the exact build used at the time of the incident. When model deployments occur via CI/CD pipelines, forensic protocols should automatically snapshot and tag the active version upon incident flagging. This ensures that, even if new versions are released later, the forensic process can replay the original state in a controlled environment. Without this metadata, investigators risk confusing later behavior with historical conditions, undermining the validity of root cause analysis and audit reports.

Table 20.3 Forensic artifacts and replay readiness.

Artifact	Contents	Preservation method	Chain of custody controls	Replay relevance
Redacted prompt output pairs	Original inputs and outputs with sensitive data masked	Immutable evidence store with access logs	Hash values and signed entries	Core basis for reproduction
Model and version identifiers	Model name and version and commit reference	Automatic snapshot on incident flag	Timestamped linkage to deployments	Maps outputs to exact build
Configuration snapshot	Temperature and top p and safety limits	Config export at incident time	Role-based access and change history	Explains behavior boundaries
Vector store snapshot	Relevant indices and embeddings at time of event	Checkpoint to durable storage	Recorded handoff with verifier	Recreates retrieval context
Ephemeral cache dump	Session memory and recent context tokens	Immediate write to disk on trigger	Sealed archive with integrity checks	Restores short term state
Random seed and sampling params	Seed and sampling strategy used	Log capture during inference	Protected metadata registry	Enables deterministic replay where possible
Tool call trace	Scopes and parameters and results	Wrapper logging around calls	Correlated IDs across systems	Rebuilds end to end action chain
Deployment image digest	Container image or package digest	Registry reference with digest pinning	Audit trail of pulls and promotions	Locks environment for replay

Configuration snapshots provide the operational context necessary to interpret model behavior accurately. These include runtime settings such as temperature, top-p values, safety thresholds, prompt templates, and integration parameters. Configuration drift is a common culprit in AI anomalies—particularly when experimental settings or feature flags are inadvertently promoted into production. Capturing configuration data alongside version identifiers enables forensic analysts to determine whether the incident stemmed from a code-level defect, a tuning misconfiguration, or a data-dependent behavior. In distributed systems, configuration snapshots should also include environmental variables, dependency versions, and hardware specifications to ensure full reproducibility of inference conditions.

AI forensics must extend beyond the model to cover external tool and integration telemetry, especially for systems with tool-augmented or retrieval-augmented capabilities. Every external call—such as a database query, API invocation, or knowledge retrieval—must be logged with its parameters, execution timestamp, and return status. This evidence establishes whether an error or misuse originated inside the model or from a downstream dependency. For example, if an AI agent executed a harmful file operation, investigators must determine whether the command was generated by the model or misinterpreted by the integration layer. Capturing external tool call parameters allows for complete reconstruction of the event chain, clarifying responsibility and guiding both containment and remediation efforts.

A particularly challenging aspect of AI evidence handling involves volatile assets, including ephemeral model weights, in-memory vector stores, and transient caches. These elements can change within seconds as the model learns, updates embeddings, or stores session context. To maintain forensic integrity, systems must be designed to capture *state snapshots* automatically when anomalies or containment triggers occur. This may include serializing temporary model weights, exporting cache contents, or capturing vector indices before memory resets. Because these artifacts often reside in volatile storage, rapid preservation workflows—such as automated write-to-disk or checkpointing—are critical. Chain of custody protocols should specify exactly who initiates these captures, how they are secured, and how evidence integrity is validated afterward. Logs should document hash values, storage locations, and handoff timestamps, ensuring traceability across all handlers.

Establishing a chain of custody for AI incident evidence mirrors traditional digital forensics but must account for the higher volume and dynamic nature of machine learning assets. Each artifact—whether a prompt, model checkpoint, or system snapshot—must be assigned a unique identifier and tracked through a custody register that records every access, transfer, or modification. Cryptographic hashing of each file ensures that any alteration is detectable, while timestamped entries document the sequence of custody. For organizations under regulatory or contractual oversight, preserving this integrity not only strengthens internal investigations but also provides defensible documentation for external audits or legal inquiries. Without chain of custody assurance, evidence risks being dismissed as unreliable or tampered.

Reproducibility in AI investigations requires careful management of determinism and seed constraints. Many AI systems rely on randomization in token sampling, reinforcement learning policies, or gradient updates. To enable faithful replays, forensic protocols must capture the random seed or sampling configuration used during inference whenever possible. While full determinism may not always be achievable—particularly with nondeterministic hardware or distributed inference systems—capturing these parameters narrows the variability window and allows investigators to approximate original outcomes. Replay attempts should be documented in structured logs that describe the environment, parameters, and outcomes, including whether the behavior could be reproduced exactly or only probabilistically. This transparency helps future auditors and stakeholders understand the confidence level associated with forensic conclusions.

Documentation of replay attempts serves as both technical record and accountability proof. Each replay should note the environment used (e.g., container hash, hardware type), the model and dataset versions, and the input-output pair being tested. Investigators must log whether each replay produced consistent behavior, partial matches, or divergent results. Where behavior differs, analysts should annotate possible causes—such as stochastic inference, time-sensitive data access, or changed dependencies. This practice transforms raw forensic work into a reliable narrative that demonstrates methodical analysis rather than subjective interpretation. Replay documentation also supports audit trails for future training adjustments, model validation, or policy revisions.

Because AI incidents often intersect technical, ethical, and legal domains, evidence handling must also respect privacy, compliance, and retention boundaries. Redacted evidence sets should be used for internal analysis, while unredacted originals must be stored under restricted access for legal review. Retention periods must comply with corporate data policies and applicable regulations such as GDPR or HIPAA, balancing investigative needs with privacy obligations. Secure deletion policies should be enforced once evidence no longer serves active or legal purposes. This disciplined approach ensures that forensic evidence serves its investigative purpose without creating new compliance risks.

Third-party AI Services: Assurance, Terms/Controls, and Escalation Paths

When AI systems rely on third-party services—whether for inference, fine-tuning, or tool integration—the monitoring and incident response landscape changes significantly. Control over infrastructure, telemetry, and runtime configurations shifts partially or entirely to the provider, introducing new dependencies into the assurance chain. In these scenarios, the organization no longer maintains full technical visibility into the AI's internal processes but must instead operate through the contractual, operational, and evidentiary guarantees made by the vendor. This dynamic demands a structured approach to assurance that combines continuous monitoring of what can be observed directly with rigorous evaluation of what must be trusted indirectly through attestations, logs, or contractual commitments. Effective third-party AI oversight ensures that even without full control, the organization can still detect, respond to, and escalate incidents with speed and accountability.

The first key difference in monitoring third-party AI services lies in telemetry availability and ownership. Providers often limit access to raw inference logs, system metrics, or infrastructure-level events due to multi-tenant security constraints or proprietary architectures. As a result, internal monitoring teams must rely on higher-level signals such as API response metadata, latency trends, and content safety indicators exposed through the provider's dashboards or APIs. This limitation means that anomaly detection often becomes a matter of interpreting *symptoms*—unexpected outputs, changes in model behavior, or abnormal response times—rather than inspecting underlying causes directly. To mitigate blind spots, organizations should implement wrapper logging around provider endpoints, capturing request and response payloads, timestamps, and correlation identifiers at the application layer. This local telemetry provides an independent audit trail that complements whatever visibility the third-party platform grants.

Incident handling also changes fundamentally when inference or tool execution runs on external services. When an incident arises—such as a harmful output, data exposure, or model malfunction—the internal team cannot directly isolate or halt the offending system. Instead, containment and remediation must occur through escalation to the vendor's support or trust and safety channels. The contract with the provider therefore becomes a functional component of the incident response plan. Clauses must specify the expected notice window for security or operational incidents, the escalation contact methods (such as 24/7 hotlines or dedicated portals), and the time frame for initial response. Mature contracts include explicit Service Level Objectives (SLOs) for incident response, defining how quickly the vendor must confirm acknowledgment, initiate containment, and provide status updates. In critical-use contexts—such as healthcare, finance, or public services—organizations should negotiate faster acknowledgment times and direct communication channels to avoid being caught in standard support queues during emergencies.

Data governance introduces another layer of complexity. Third-party AI providers typically define strict data use terms that govern how customer inputs, outputs, and derived metadata are stored, analyzed, or reused. These terms determine what forensic evidence can be preserved, how long logs are retained, and whether redacted or full copies of data can be requested for investigation. Some providers prohibit storing or retrieving raw prompt content, while others allow enterprise customers to request retrieval of anonymized logs under confidentiality. AI auditors and compliance officers must be intimately familiar with these policies to avoid evidence loss during incident handling. Contracts should explicitly require providers to retain inference logs and configuration snapshots for a defined minimum period—often 30 to 90 days—to ensure traceability during investigations. In cases involving potential regulatory exposure, data retention and retrieval terms must also align with the organization's legal hold and chain of custody procedures.

When investigating incidents involving third-party AI, organizations must carefully separate what can be validated internally from what must rely on provider attestations. Direct validation is possible for local elements such as API request and response logs, wrapper telemetry, input-output preservation, and downstream integration behavior. These locally observable artifacts allow internal teams to reconstruct what the organization's systems *sent to* and *received from* the external model. However, deeper layers—such as how the provider processed the data, what intermediate models or prompts were used, or how responses were filtered—remain opaque. In these cases, investigators must depend on provider attestations, audit reports (such as SOC 2 or ISO 27001 certifications), or third-party validation of the provider's controls. Effective governance requires maintaining both forms of assurance in parallel: validating what can be measured internally, and confirming that the rest is covered by the provider's certified control environment.

Contractual assurances serve as the backbone of third-party AI incident management. Well-structured contracts specify not only the provider's security standards but also the transparency obligations that come into play during incidents. These may include requirements to notify customers within a set number of hours following detection of a breach, commitments to share root cause analysis reports, and rights to participate in joint incident reviews. For enterprise-grade AI integrations, contracts should also define emergency suspension rights—granting the customer authority to disable integrations or revoke tokens unilaterally if the service behaves dangerously or noncompliantly. Without these provisions, organizations risk being unable to act quickly in high-severity scenarios where the provider holds operational control of the system.

The escalation path for third-party AI incidents should mirror the organization's internal incident response structure but with defined external interfaces. The first responder—often a monitoring or operations engineer—identifies an anomaly and escalates it to the AI assurance lead. If the issue appears rooted in the third-party platform, the AI lead coordinates with enterprise IR and immediately notifies the provider using predefined contacts. Communication must be clear and traceable: initial escalation to the vendor should include timestamped incident summaries, example payloads (appropriately redacted), observed impact scope, and relevant correlation identifiers. From there, the vendor's response timeline determines how the organization proceeds with internal containment and user notifications. Enterprise IR should remain engaged throughout to ensure that legal, compliance, and public communication functions align with contractual and regulatory obligations.

In practice, incident evidence handling with external AI providers is often constrained by what the provider is willing or able to disclose. Some may share diagnostic information such as response IDs or safety filter activations but not raw inference logs. Others may require nondisclosure agreements or legal requests before releasing deeper forensic artifacts. To ensure readiness, organizations should maintain internal playbooks that define alternative evidence sources—such as network traffic logs, application telemetry, or user reports—to compensate for unavailable provider data. Additionally, escalation procedures should outline fallback steps if the provider is unresponsive, including isolating dependent workflows, disabling integrations, and invoking contractual dispute mechanisms when service-level obligations are breached.

The boundaries between AI assurance and enterprise incident response remain the same in principle, even when the AI component is outsourced. The AI assurance team handles immediate triage, validation, and evidence collection, while enterprise IR leads escalation, communication, and cross-system containment. The difference is that part of the "response environment" now resides outside organizational control. Accordingly, both teams must understand the limitations of their visibility and the handoff expectations with external providers. This relationship depends on well-defined contracts, tested communication channels, and mutual trust in each party's responsibilities during high-severity events.

Post-incident Learning: Control Updates, Model Retraining, and Governance Cadence

Post-incident learning transforms a reactive event into a proactive improvement cycle. In AI assurance, every incident—whether minor or severe—offers a unique opportunity to strengthen system resilience and governance maturity. Because AI failures often arise from complex, interdependent causes, the response cannot stop at containment. The true value lies in the translation of findings into durable design, monitoring, and policy improvements that prevent recurrence. This process bridges technical recovery with organizational learning, ensuring that the same conditions that led to an incident cannot quietly rebuild themselves in future versions. Effective post-incident governance transforms anomalies into intelligence, feeding directly into model refinement, detection systems, and operational safeguards.

One of the most immediate post-incident actions involves updating prompts, filters, and inference parameters. Many AI safety or performance issues emerge from poorly constrained prompts, inadequate content filters, or misaligned model parameters. Once the incident is resolved, teams should review the exact input and output context to identify where existing controls failed. This could lead to refining prompt templates to close loopholes, strengthening keyword or embedding-based toxicity filters, or tightening inference temperature and response length limits. If the incident was triggered by a particular prompt injection or pattern of abuse, those signatures should be codified as new detection rules within safety or monitoring systems. Prompt and filter updates should be tracked as configuration changes with full version control, ensuring they can be audited and reverted if future conflicts arise.

Beyond immediate control refinements, findings often point to new detection signals or adjusted thresholds in the monitoring layer. For example, if a model's harmful behavior was preceded by subtle changes in data distribution or user input style, those indicators should become explicit telemetry signals. New thresholds may be introduced for response latency anomalies, spike detection on moderation triggers, or shifts in model confidence levels. Each adjustment should be grounded in data—measured from post-incident replay or historical baselines—to avoid overcorrection that leads to false positives. Adding these enhanced signals creates an ever-tighter feedback loop between detection and prevention, gradually evolving the monitoring framework toward predictive rather than reactive capability.

A recurring outcome of PIR involves model retraining or rollback decisions. When evidence shows that a model's weights or fine-tuning data caused or contributed to the failure, retraining may be necessary to realign the system's behavior with intended policies. Retraining decisions must consider both technical feasibility and business continuity—balancing the cost of revalidation against the risk of continued exposure. In cases where retraining is too slow or uncertain, an immediate rollback to a previously verified model version provides a safer, temporary control. To make these transitions defensible, organizations must maintain a clear lineage of model versions, training data hashes, and deployment timestamps. The forensic evidence collected during the incident investigation guides whether retraining or rollback is warranted, ensuring decisions are evidence-based rather than speculative.

In some scenarios, removal or restriction of risky tools and integrations may represent the most effective corrective action. If an external API, plugin, or retrieval tool consistently introduces vulnerabilities or operational instability, the PIR should question its continued use. Disabling or sandboxing these components may reduce capability but enhances reliability and trust. For instance, if a retrieval-augmented system frequently surfaces disallowed or unverified documents, isolating that integration until its content moderation improves can prevent recurrence. These decisions should be recorded within governance systems as risk exceptions or design changes, ensuring both transparency and traceability for future audits.

The formal mechanism for embedding lessons learned is the PIR, sometimes called a "blameless postmortem." The PIR must focus not on fault assignment but on identifying systemic weaknesses—technical, procedural, or governance-related—that allowed the issue to occur. It should include representatives from AI assurance, security, operations, compliance, and, where applicable, vendor partners. Each PIR produces a detailed report summarizing root cause analysis, contributing factors, timeline reconstruction, and recommended control improvements. These reports should be archived in a searchable repository to support pattern analysis across multiple incidents over time. The objective is to institutionalize collective memory so that individual lessons evolve into organizational knowledge.

To ensure post-incident insights lead to actual change, organizations must establish a governance cadence that ties PIR findings directly into operational backlogs and release cycles. Control updates, new detection logic, and retraining tasks should be entered into the engineering backlog, prioritized based on residual risk and user impact. Governance bodies—such as the AI Risk Council or Model Oversight Committee—should review these items in regular intervals, typically monthly or quarterly, to verify implementation progress. This cadence guarantees that lessons learned translate into measurable updates before the next model release or major deployment. The same body should validate that recommended controls were implemented, tested, and shown effective, closing the feedback loop between discovery and assurance.

Effectiveness checks are the next layer of accountability. After implementing corrective actions, teams must validate whether the change eliminated or mitigated the original failure condition. This validation can include A/B testing of the new filters, regression testing of retrained models, or simulation of prior incident triggers to confirm they no longer succeed. Where monitoring signals were added or thresholds adjusted, synthetic incident injection—controlled replay of the original failure scenario—serves as a litmus test for readiness. This concept ties directly into the continuous testing and assurance principles outlined in Chapter 17, where automated red-teaming, drift simulation, and filter stress testing ensure sustained protection. Effective governance requires that these validation results be documented, reviewed, and integrated into audit trails to demonstrate continuous improvement.

In complex AI ecosystems, post-incident learning must extend beyond the technical domain into policy and governance refinement. Each major event tests the adequacy of escalation procedures, vendor communication protocols, and containment authorities. If an incident exposed confusion over who could activate a kill switch or request provider logs, those gaps must be codified into updated playbooks and contractual clauses. Similarly, repeated incidents of similar nature—such as recurring data drift or toxicity spikes—may signal deeper governance issues requiring policy intervention. Embedding these governance adjustments into standard operating procedures ensures that cultural learning complements technical improvement, reinforcing resilience across both human and system dimensions.

Conclusion

Mastering the disciplines of AI monitoring and incident response is critical for maintaining trust, accountability, and resilience in intelligent systems. As organizations deploy AI models across sensitive and high-impact domains, the ability to detect drift, contain errant behavior, and preserve forensic integrity becomes as essential as traditional vulnerability management. These functions extend the auditor's oversight from infrastructure controls into the cognitive layer of enterprise risk—where logic, data, and ethics intersect. The professional auditor's role evolves here from reactive observer to active validator of AI reliability, ensuring systems operate within defined safety and compliance boundaries.

This chapter reinforces the role of structured assurance frameworks in securing AI environments at scale. Effective incident response for AI is not built on intuition but on repeatable evidence handling, transparent governance, and predefined containment authority. The tools and telemetry that underpin these activities must be as auditable as the models themselves, allowing every critical decision—from kill switch activation to retraining justification—to be reconstructed and defended. In this ecosystem, accountability is not a single control but a continuous process that binds technical design to organizational governance.

With these foundations in place, cybersecurity and audit professionals are better equipped to transform AI risk into a managed, measurable discipline. While the underlying technologies will continue to evolve, the strategic intent remains consistent: to ensure AI behaves predictably, operates ethically, and can recover gracefully from failure. Embedding these practices into enterprise audit programs ensures that assurance keeps pace with innovation—providing confidence not just in what AI can do, but in how securely and responsibly it does it.

Auditor Recommendations

1. **Define Monitoring Objectives Clearly**: Establish a clear process for defining what your AI monitoring program must detect, and within what time frames or thresholds. Align each objective—such as detecting model drift, data drift, or safety violations—to a measurable business or compliance risk. This precision ensures that detection metrics support meaningful oversight rather than generic activity tracking. By formalizing objectives in measurable terms, auditors can validate whether monitoring systems deliver the assurance they are intended to provide.
2. **Strengthen Telemetry Design for Auditability**: Prioritize consistent and comprehensive telemetry across model, data, and integration layers. Ensure that every inference, dataset version, and tool call generates the minimum metadata—timestamps, model IDs, dataset hashes, and user identifiers—needed to reconstruct events accurately. Strong telemetry coverage transforms otherwise opaque AI behavior into auditable evidence. Auditors should verify that these telemetry structures are tamper-evident and aligned with retention and privacy requirements.
3. **Establish Tested Containment Controls**: Develop and validate containment mechanisms—such as kill switches, safe modes, and feature flags—that can be invoked rapidly during AI incidents. Each mechanism should have predefined authority boundaries, activation latency goals, and audit logging requirements. Auditors should confirm that these controls

are not theoretical but exercised through regular simulations and verified for both speed and integrity. A well-tested containment framework prevents escalation and ensures accountable decision-making during crises.

4. **Differentiate AI Incidents from Traditional Events**: Define what constitutes an AI-specific incident and the thresholds for escalation to enterprise incident response. Establish criteria for recognizing harmful outputs, prompt abuse, or data leakage as distinct from infrastructure failures. During audits, assess whether triage processes capture AI-specific signals and clearly delineate responsibilities between AI assurance and enterprise IR teams. This clarity ensures faster containment and prevents overlapping or contradictory investigations.
5. **Preserve Reproducibility in Evidence Handling**: Enforce the preservation of reproducible artifacts for every AI incident, including redacted inputs, outputs, configuration snapshots, and model version identifiers. Require that all volatile assets—such as vector stores or ephemeral caches—are captured when anomalies are detected. Auditors should validate that forensic processes maintain a verifiable chain of custody, complete with timestamped evidence and replay documentation. This rigor ensures that post-incident investigations meet both technical and regulatory standards.
6. **Formalize Vendor and Third-party Escalation Paths**: Integrate contractual obligations and escalation procedures for AI incidents that involve external service providers. Ensure that service-level agreements specify notification timelines, evidence-sharing commitments, and access to relevant logs. Auditors must verify that escalation channels are tested and that provider attestations can be trusted where direct validation is impossible. This oversight ensures continuity of governance even when systems or models operate outside internal control boundaries.
7. **Apply Post-incident Learning to Governance Cycles**: Treat every AI incident as a source of organizational intelligence. Require PIRs that document findings, control updates, and retraining or rollback decisions. Auditors should confirm that lessons learned are integrated into risk registers, backlog prioritization, and future testing cycles. Embedding continuous learning into governance cadence ensures that improvements are systemic rather than situational.
8. **Validate Model Retraining and Rollback Decisions**: Establish documented criteria for when retraining, rollback, or tool removal is justified following an incident. These criteria should rely on objective evidence such as telemetry signals, model drift measurements, or confirmed bias indicators. Auditors should verify that all retraining events are versioned, peer-reviewed, and tested before redeployment. This practice ensures that corrective actions enhance reliability rather than introducing new uncertainty.
9. **Ensure Transparency in Audit Trails**: Require that every containment, escalation, and recovery action leaves a complete, immutable audit trail. Each record must include who approved the action, when it occurred, what evidence supported it, and how rollback was executed. Auditors should regularly test these trails for completeness and verify their linkage across AI assurance and enterprise IR systems. Transparent auditability transforms incident response into a defensible and accountable process.
10. **Promote Continuous Testing and Assurance Readiness**: Incorporate ongoing testing of detection thresholds, containment mechanisms, and governance controls as part of the organization's assurance cadence. Encourage teams to perform controlled simulations of past incidents to verify that monitoring and recovery processes remain effective. Auditors should assess whether test outcomes are documented and used to refine controls before the next release cycle. Sustained readiness is the hallmark of mature AI assurance—where resilience is continuously demonstrated, not merely declared.

Chapter Questions

1. What is the primary purpose of defining explicit AI monitoring objectives with thresholds and latency targets?
   A. To align detection with business and compliance risk and enable decisive escalation
   B. To maximize data collection regardless of operational value
   C. To replace all SIEM use cases with model-centric monitoring
   D. To guarantee zero false positives through strict rules

2. Which metadata set best supports auditable AI telemetry across model, data, prompt, and integration planes?
   A. Team org charts, office location, deployment owner initials
   B. Debug stack traces, container logs, kernel version notes
   C. Marketing campaign ID, billing code, API rate-limit tier
   D. Timestamps, model/version IDs, dataset hashes, user/app IDs, and tool scopes

3. What operational change does "safe mode" introduce during containment?
   A. A permanent shutdown of all AI services until full revalidation is complete
   B. Unrestricted operation while extra logging runs in the background
   C. Degraded but safer behavior that disables high-risk features while maintaining essential function
   D. Automatic retraining on the latest data to restore normal behavior

4. During AI incident triage, what information must be packaged for enterprise IR handoff?
   A. Marketing statements, public FAQs, and brand talking points
   B. Signals, relevant artifacts (e.g., redacted I/O, configs), and an estimated blast radius
   C. Source code for all AI components and vendor proprietary models
   D. A complete rebuild pipeline for every historical model version

5. Which evidence set is most critical to reproducibly replay an AI incident?
   A. Preserved prompts/outputs (redacted), model/version identifiers, and configuration snapshots
   B. Only network perimeter logs from the same time window
   C. A nightly database backup from a nearby date
   D. A summary email describing the anomalous behavior

6. In third-party AI incidents where inference runs on an external platform, which response path is typically required?
   A. Immediate internal redeployment to a local model without notification
   B. Waiting for the model to self-correct under normal traffic
   C. Escalation to the provider via contractual notice windows and agreed SLOs
   D. A universal shutdown of all enterprise systems unrelated to AI

7. What parameter most directly supports deterministic replays in AI forensics when feasible?
   A. The random seed or sampling configuration used at inference time
   B. The user interface theme active during the session
   C. The server's disk quota configuration
   D. The public IP allowlist for outbound connections

8. Which governance action best ensures post-incident learning results in durable change before the next release?
   A. Writing a lessons-learned memo and archiving it for future reference
   B. Scheduling a retrospective after the next quarterly planning cycle
   C. Relying on individual engineer judgment to implement fixes ad hoc
   D. Prioritizing PIR findings into the backlog with effectiveness checks tied to release gates

9. What is the principal assurance benefit of production feature flags in AI systems?
   A. They permanently remove unsafe capabilities from the product
   B. They enable selective disablement of risky functions with auditable toggles and rapid rollback
   C. They increase throughput by bypassing moderation for trusted users
   D. They encrypt all datasets at rest regardless of platform support

10. Why is integration/tool telemetry essential alongside model and prompt logs?
   A. It replaces the need for prompt redaction by capturing raw content only
   B. It proves the provider's SOC 2 scope without further validation
   C. It eliminates the need for chain of custody on other artifacts
   D. It records external calls and parameters, enabling end-to-end reconstruction of cross-system actions

21

Audit Reporting and Executive Communication

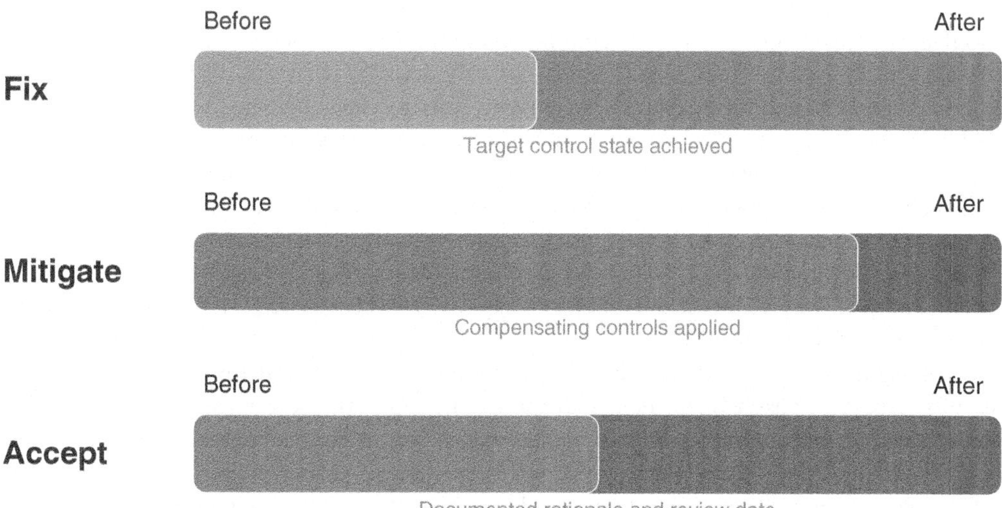

Effective audit reporting is where technical assurance becomes organizational decision-making. A finding that is meticulously gathered but poorly communicated loses its power to drive change, while a well-structured report can clarify priorities across business, compliance, and security leadership. This chapter examines how structured findings, severity calibration, and traceable evidence connect to residual risk and management accountability. Understanding these elements is essential to transforming audit work from documentation into actionable insight—linking assurance outcomes directly to enterprise risk management and governance oversight.

Modern cybersecurity programs operate at a scale and complexity that demand disciplined communication between auditors and executives. From the structure of individual findings to the framing of Board-level summaries, clarity and consistency determine whether audit results strengthen governance or simply add noise. This chapter emphasizes the mechanics of traceability, severity and materiality standards, recommendation quality, and management response design—ensuring that audit conclusions withstand scrutiny and inspire credible remediation. By standardizing these practices, organizations can ensure that every report tells a verifiable story about control effectiveness, business impact, and leadership accountability.

In an era where AI-driven systems, cloud ecosystems, and regulatory expectations evolve rapidly, the ability to communicate risk precisely has never been more critical. Audit reports that translate control evidence into business risk—supported by data-driven trends, calibrated metrics, and well-governed issue registers—allow executives to make confident, defensible decisions. This chapter reinforces that audit reporting is not a final administrative step but a strategic function of cyber risk governance. Through strong reporting discipline, auditors enable organizations to see, measure, and act on risk in a way that aligns security assurance with the speed and complexity of today's digital enterprise.

Report Structure and Traceability

A well-constructed audit report is the culmination of disciplined evidence gathering, structured analysis, and transparent reasoning. It must not only describe what was tested and discovered but also demonstrate how the auditor's conclusions were reached and why those conclusions are reliable. Every finding should follow a consistent framework that connects observations to the evidence that supports them, and ultimately to the conclusions and recommendations that follow. The standard format—observation, criteria, condition, cause, effect or risk, recommendation, and management response—creates both logical flow and defensibility. Each component must tie back to supporting documentation so an independent reviewer can trace the entire chain of reasoning without ambiguity. This level of traceability transforms the report from a static document into a fully auditable artifact in itself.

The observation serves as the logical entry point for every finding, defining the specific control area, process, or asset under review. It frames the intent of the control and establishes its role in achieving governance, risk, or compliance objectives. The auditor's language should be clear, specific, and aligned with the organization's terminology—using precise names for systems, applications, and procedures rather than broad generalizations. A well-written observation gives the reader immediate clarity about what was examined and why it matters, ensuring the issue is relevant and framed within the correct business context. Without this anchoring statement, even accurate findings risk being misunderstood or minimized by nontechnical audiences. Table 21.1 outlines the required finding components and the traceability references that allow an independent reviewer to re-perform conclusions.

Criteria outline the expectations or authoritative standards that define proper control performance. These may derive from internal policies, regulatory requirements, or recognized frameworks such as NIST, ISO, or COBIT. The key is specificity: the report should reference the exact clause, section, or statement that establishes the benchmark for compliance. Clear criteria are what make an audit finding objective rather than subjective; they demonstrate that the auditor is evaluating against an accepted yardstick, not personal opinion. By grounding findings in explicit criteria, the report strengthens its legitimacy and helps management see how each issue connects to their own obligations and policies.

The condition describes what was actually found during testing and should represent the factual reality observed. It must be verifiable, time-bounded, and free from interpretation. Each statement of fact should correspond to identified evidence—such as configuration files, screenshots, transaction logs, or tickets—stored in the workpapers. The report should reference the evidence location and sample details but avoid reproducing lengthy test procedures that belong in technical documentation. The goal is to provide enough clarity that a reviewer can independently re-perform the

Table 21.1 Standard finding components and traceability references.

Component	Purpose	Required references
Observation	Define control context and objective	Control ID slash system name slash process map
Criteria	State authoritative requirement	Policy section ID slash regulation clause slash framework control
Condition	Describe tested result and scope	Workpaper tab ID slash population ID slash sample IDs
Cause	Explain why the gap exists	Interview notes ID slash workflow evidence ID
Effect Risk	Translate gap to exposure	Risk rating reference slash impact pathway notes
Recommendation	Specify target control state	Success criteria list slash verification plan ID
Management Response	Commit to action and ownership	Owner name role slash due date slash resource plan
Traceability	Enable re performance	Evidence file path slash artifact hash or timestamp
Scope Limitation	Disclose assurance boundaries	Excluded systems list slash period covered details
Third-party Reliance	Identify reliance on external attestations	SOC report ref slash vendor attestation link

test and reach the same result. When conditions are written precisely, they stand as an objective record of what occurred within the scope of the audit.

The cause portion of the finding explains why the condition exists and, more importantly, what underlying issue led to it. Causes might include gaps in process design, lack of automation, unclear ownership, insufficient resources, or conflicting priorities between security and operations. The auditor must base the cause on data, not speculation, often corroborated through interviews or consistent patterns observed in testing. A credible cause statement transforms a simple observation into an opportunity for systemic improvement. By diagnosing the real driver behind the issue, the audit report helps the organization address root problems rather than repeatedly patching surface symptoms.

The effect—or risk—articulates why the condition matters. This is the bridge between technical detail and business consequence. A well-written effect section translates the control deficiency into potential impact areas such as financial exposure, data compromise, operational disruption, or reputational harm. It should also describe the likelihood of occurrence and any mitigating factors that reduce the risk. Using clear, professional language avoids both understatement and exaggeration. Readers should walk away with a realistic understanding of what is at stake if the issue remains unresolved. Connecting technical findings to business risk reinforces the value of the audit and helps leaders prioritize remediation efforts.

The recommendation section is where analysis becomes action. It should propose a path to achieve compliance or reduce risk, aligning with the criteria while remaining flexible enough for management to choose the implementation method. Strong recommendations are specific, actionable, and measurable—for example, "Implement automated review of privileged account changes and retain approval logs for one year" rather than "Improve user access controls." When appropriate, the auditor should acknowledge compensating controls that partially address the risk, clarifying whether they are temporary or permanent measures. Well-crafted recommendations empower management to make informed, timely decisions and create a foundation for meaningful follow-up testing.

The management response closes the loop between assurance and accountability. It documents whether management agrees with the finding, outlines their remediation plan, identifies responsible parties, and provides target completion dates. The response should be sufficiently detailed to allow future validation, not a generic statement of intent. If management disagrees, their rationale must be captured for transparency, along with any risk acceptance decision. Strong audit programs insist on clarity here, as vague or deferred responses weaken the entire assurance process. When handled properly, the management response transforms findings from passive observations into actionable commitments that can be tracked to closure.

Traceability is what gives the audit report its evidentiary strength. Each finding must be linked to the specific workpapers, datasets, and evidence that support it. A consistent indexing system and disciplined cross-referencing allow an independent reviewer to follow the logic without external explanation. The report should make it possible to locate the relevant population, re-select the same samples, and verify the same artifacts that informed the auditor's conclusion. This traceability also protects the audit function when questions arise later, demonstrating that every statement in the report is grounded in tangible, retrievable evidence.

Scope limitations and third-party reliance are vital disclosures that define the boundaries of assurance. If certain systems, geographies, or time periods were excluded, or if the audit relied on information from external sources such as SOC 2 reports or managed service attestations, these facts must be clearly stated. Readers must understand what was and was not examined so they do not assume coverage that does not exist. Disclosing limitations is a sign of professional integrity, not weakness—it ensures that the assurance provided is accurately understood and prevents future disputes over audit scope or responsibility.

Language precision is equally critical in maintaining report credibility. The writing should clearly separate fact from interpretation. Factual statements use phrases such as "testing confirmed" or "evidence indicates," while interpretive judgments use conditional phrasing like "this increases the risk that" or "this may result in." Maintaining this distinction ensures the report remains objective and balanced. Overstating certainty where evidence does not support it can undermine trust, just as hedging on clear findings can make the audit appear timid or inconclusive. Consistency of tone across all findings reflects professionalism and enhances the readability of the report for both technical and nontechnical audiences.

When structured properly, the audit report becomes far more than a list of deficiencies—it becomes a decision-making instrument for executives and stakeholders. By showing clear traceability from evidence to conclusion, it builds confidence that findings are accurate and actionable. It demonstrates that the audit process was thorough, independent, and methodical. For the reader, the report's structure provides a clear line of sight from observed facts to business impact to recommended action. For the auditor, it provides defensibility, consistency, and a repeatable framework for assurance. This disciplined approach to structure and traceability is the hallmark of credible cybersecurity auditing and the foundation of lasting trust in the audit function.

Severity, Materiality, and Residual Risk

A disciplined audit program relies on consistent, well-defined severity and materiality ratings to ensure that findings are interpreted and prioritized uniformly across engagements. These ratings form the bridge between technical control deficiencies and business decision-making, translating audit results into language executives can use to allocate resources and assess enterprise risk posture. To achieve this, the audit team must adopt a clearly defined framework that ties severity and materiality directly to measurable factors—specifically, business impact, likelihood of occurrence, and the overall strength of the control environment. This structure prevents subjective judgments from diluting audit credibility and promotes comparability between different reports, functions, and audit cycles.

Severity reflects the degree of risk posed by a control deficiency and should be calibrated according to the potential impact on confidentiality, integrity, availability, compliance, and reputation. A consistent severity scale—typically low, moderate, high, and critical—anchors discussions in quantifiable terms. For instance, a control gap exposing sensitive data may rate as high severity if it could result in a regulatory breach or public disclosure, whereas the same issue within a sandboxed environment might be considered moderate. Severity should not hinge solely on the number of items affected but on the realistic business consequences if the control were to fail. This approach aligns audit conclusions with enterprise risk management practices and keeps reporting relevant to senior leadership.

Materiality complements severity by considering the scope and magnitude of the issue in the context of the organization's operations. It examines how significant the deficiency is relative to total transactions, users, assets, or business value exposed. In other words, while severity focuses on potential impact per incident, materiality focuses on aggregate exposure. For example, a single misconfigured server holding noncritical data may represent a moderate severity issue but low materiality; conversely, a systemic process flaw affecting thousands of privileged accounts might constitute high materiality even if the immediate impact has not yet occurred. Defining these thresholds in policy ensures that auditors apply materiality consistently rather than allowing engagement teams to improvise case by case.

Likelihood is the third variable that shapes both severity and materiality ratings. It represents the probability that a control weakness could be exploited or cause failure under normal operating conditions. The likelihood assessment should account for existing compensating controls, environmental maturity, and threat exposure. When assessing likelihood, auditors must balance technical evidence with contextual judgment—an unpatched vulnerability in an isolated network may present a lower likelihood than the same vulnerability on an Internet-facing system. Documenting the rationale behind likelihood assessments in the workpapers reinforces transparency and allows peer reviewers to understand how each rating was derived. Table 21.2 provides a normalized rubric to apply consistent severity and materiality ratings across engagements.

Consistency across engagements is critical. Even well-designed rating systems lose value if different auditors apply them differently. Establishing a rating calibration process—often through periodic team reviews or risk rating committees—helps maintain uniform interpretation of severity and materiality criteria. These calibration exercises should use anonymized examples from recent audits to discuss edge cases, refine definitions, and confirm that ratings align with the organization's overall risk tolerance. The objective is not to enforce identical outcomes but

Table 21.2 Severity and materiality calibration factors.

Rating level	Business impact	Likelihood	Control environment signal
Low	Limited operational effect with minimal exposure	Unlikely based on threat and isolation	Mature controls with consistent monitoring
Moderate	Noticeable disruption or contained data exposure	Plausible with known vectors	Controls operate but have gaps
High	Significant disruption or regulated data risk	Likely given exposure and threat	Controls inconsistent or partially effective
Critical	Enterprise level impact or regulatory failure	Imminent or actively observed	Controls ineffective or absent

to ensure similar risks receive similar treatment, regardless of who conducted the engagement. Over time, this consistency strengthens the credibility of audit results and builds trust among executives and board members who rely on them.

Residual risk represents the level of exposure that remains after mitigating factors or compensating controls have been considered. Every audit finding should clearly distinguish between inherent risk (the risk before controls) and residual risk (the risk after controls). This differentiation allows stakeholders to understand how much protection currently exists and how much risk persists despite mitigation. When partial remediation has occurred or compensating controls reduce the likelihood or impact, auditors must explicitly state "before" and "after" residual risk levels. Doing so communicates that the condition still poses a measurable risk, even if reduced, and provides a transparent record of progress without overstating assurance.

Compensating controls deserve careful handling in severity assessment. They may reduce residual risk but do not erase the underlying deficiency. For example, if a segregation-of-duties conflict exists in an application but management reviews transactions daily for anomalies, the review is compensating—but not equivalent to redesigning the control. The report should reflect this nuance by showing reduced residual risk while acknowledging that inherent risk remains higher than desired. Avoid re-arguing design adequacy within the report itself; design discussions belong in the workpapers. The report's purpose is to state the condition, document the impact, and present the final risk level after mitigation, not to reopen engineering debates.

Residual risk statements must also align with management's stated risk appetite. When management accepts a certain level of residual exposure, that acceptance should be documented, justified, and consistent with enterprise policy. If the auditor believes residual risk remains above tolerance, the report should clearly note this variance, ensuring decision-makers are aware that acceptance carries implications beyond technical closure. This transparency is essential for board-level governance, where the distinction between "resolved" and "risk accepted" drives oversight and accountability.

A well-designed severity and materiality model enhances comparability not only within one audit cycle but across time. When prior-year findings are revisited, consistent definitions allow auditors to measure improvement meaningfully and evaluate whether risk reduction initiatives are effective. Overly fluid rating criteria make year-over-year progress impossible to quantify and erode confidence in trend analysis. Therefore, once definitions are approved, they should remain stable for multiple audit periods, with changes applied only through formal policy revision and communicated to all auditors.

Calibration, documentation, and communication together ensure that the rating system serves its purpose—clarity and consistency. Each severity and materiality rating must be defensible through evidence, contextual reasoning, and adherence to established scales. Residual risk, meanwhile, provides the essential "after picture" that allows leadership to prioritize investment and track improvement. When these elements work together, audit reports evolve from simple lists of findings into analytical tools that guide resource allocation, strategic planning, and risk-informed governance. A consistent, transparent approach to severity, materiality, and residual risk turns the audit function into a trusted interpreter of enterprise risk rather than a mere observer of compliance.

Recommendation Craft: Actionable Owners, Timelines, and Success Criteria

The quality of an audit report often hinges on the clarity and practicality of its recommendations. Even the most accurate finding loses value if the resulting recommendation is vague, lacks ownership, or cannot be verified for completion. A well-crafted recommendation transforms an audit observation into a plan of action by identifying the accountable owner, the intended outcome, the milestones and dependencies that shape delivery, and the success criteria that define when the issue is truly resolved. Every recommendation must therefore be outcome-based, specific, and measurable. It must describe what will change, who will ensure it happens, and how success will be evidenced—not merely express a desire for improvement.

Each recommendation begins with ownership. An accountable owner must be named by role, not by department or collective entity. Ambiguous phrases like "management should ensure" or "the team should address" diffuse responsibility and reduce accountability. Instead, ownership should point to the person or position with both the authority and resources to implement the remediation—typically a control owner, system manager, or executive sponsor. Clear ownership also enables effective follow-up; auditors and governance committees can verify progress and escalate when deadlines slip. Accountability transforms a recommendation from a suggestion into a commitment, making it actionable and traceable across audit cycles.

Outcome-based language defines the "what" and the "why" of remediation. A strong recommendation states the end condition the organization must achieve, not just the action to take. For example, instead of "Enhance access controls for privileged users," a better statement would be "Restrict privileged accounts to unique credentials with documented approval and monitoring of all administrative actions." The latter example defines a tangible control state that can be tested. Recommendations should avoid vague verbs such as *improve*, *enhance*, or *strengthen*, unless followed by measurable objectives. Each phrase in the recommendation should lead to a testable outcome—something an auditor can later verify through evidence rather than interpretation.

Every recommendation must also include realistic timelines and milestones. The audit report should record both the planned completion date and key progress points that allow interim validation. A complex system redesign may require multiple phases—such as requirements gathering, pilot testing, and final deployment—and each milestone should have a corresponding target date. This helps management allocate resources effectively and allows the audit team to conduct meaningful follow-ups instead of waiting for an undefined "future completion." Timelines must balance urgency with feasibility; overly aggressive dates encourage superficial fixes, while indefinite ones invite stagnation. The schedule should reflect the nature of the risk and its proximity to regulatory or business deadlines.

Dependencies are another crucial component of recommendation craft. Many control deficiencies cannot be corrected in isolation—they depend on technology upgrades, third-party deliverables, staffing changes, or cross-departmental coordination. These dependencies should be explicitly documented so that delays can be anticipated and monitored. For instance, if remediation requires a system vendor patch or policy revision approval, those external factors must be listed in the management response. Documenting dependencies not only clarifies implementation risk but also helps governance bodies track systemic bottlenecks across multiple findings, improving overall risk management maturity.

Success criteria define how closure will be demonstrated. They answer the essential question: *what evidence will prove this issue is fixed?* Success criteria should describe observable outcomes such as "audit logs demonstrate enforcement of new approval workflow for 90 days," "updated configuration baselines are in effect and tested," or "new policy revisions are published and acknowledged by all affected users." Without these indicators, remediation verification becomes subjective and inconsistent. Success criteria should be designed collaboratively with management to ensure feasibility and alignment with operational realities. In essence, they convert a recommendation from a theoretical statement into a testable hypothesis that can be validated objectively.

A mature audit program distinguishes among three remediation pathways—fix, mitigate, and risk acceptance—and articulates which one applies to each finding. A "fix" means the underlying control weakness will be corrected so that the risk is fully addressed. A "mitigate" pathway applies when partial remediation or compensating controls can reduce exposure to an acceptable level but do not resolve the root cause. "Risk accept" means management formally acknowledges the remaining exposure and decides not to act further. The chosen pathway must be justified and consistent with the organization's risk appetite. The auditor's role is to confirm that the chosen approach aligns with documented policies and that any accepted risk has been approved by an appropriate authority.

Recommendations should also describe the expected end state of risk reduction, not just the task to be performed. For instance, "Deploy endpoint encryption on all laptops" is an action; "All company laptops are encrypted using FIPS 140-2 validated algorithms and enforce centralized key escrow" is an outcome. The difference lies in verifiability—auditors can test the second statement but can only observe activity for the first. This precision in language makes progress measurable and creates a clear standard for closure testing. The report's purpose is not to list to-do items but to define target control states that can be independently confirmed through evidence.

Avoiding ambiguous verbs is more than a writing preference—it is a control discipline. Terms like *optimize*, *review*, or *enhance* imply good intent but fail to define what completion looks like. Each verb in the recommendation should represent an observable change: *implement*, *establish*, *restrict*, *monitor*, or *document* all imply measurable results. The audit team should review all recommendations before finalizing the report to ensure the language meets this testability standard. If a recommendation cannot be validated objectively, it must be rewritten until the end state is clear enough for re-performance.

When crafted effectively, recommendations become operational roadmaps that drive meaningful remediation and accountability. They transform audit reports from diagnostic documents into governance tools. Executives and audit committees can then prioritize based on impact, track progress with confidence, and verify closure through evidence rather than assurances. The value of the audit function lies not just in identifying weaknesses but also in enabling sustainable improvement—and that begins with precise, actionable, and measurable recommendations. By defining ownership, timelines, dependencies, and success criteria, auditors ensure that every recommendation can withstand scrutiny, deliver tangible results, and contribute to a stronger, more resilient control environment.

Management Responses and Commitments

An effective management response is more than a courtesy note or an acknowledgment of findings—it is a formal commitment that links assurance to accountability. A response that lacks clarity, timing, or ownership undermines the entire purpose of audit reporting. For a management response to be acceptable, it must clearly articulate the planned corrective or mitigating action, the resources allocated to execute it, and the specific time frame within which it will be completed. It must also state how the organization intends to treat the underlying risk—whether by accepting it, mitigating it, transferring it, or fixing it outright. The response serves as the organization's official position on the issue, and it must be specific enough to support tracking, validation, and escalation when commitments are not met.

Time-bounded actions are the first hallmark of an acceptable management response. Every remediation plan must specify a realistic completion date and, where appropriate, interim milestones. These milestones allow auditors, governance bodies, and risk owners to monitor progress and detect delays early. Generic timelines such as "to be completed as soon as possible" or "planned for the next quarter" provide no accountability and should not be accepted. The timing must align with the risk severity—high-risk issues demand rapid mitigation or interim controls, while lower-risk items may allow longer windows for sustainable implementation. A credible response demonstrates that management has assessed urgency and built a plan proportionate to exposure.

Resourcing is the second critical component of a complete management response. A plan without adequate personnel, funding, or technical support is merely aspirational. Management must identify whether remediation will use existing resources or require new investment, and confirm that approvals are secured. The audit report should document these commitments so that resource constraints do not become the silent reason for missed deadlines. When resourcing gaps exist, they should be transparently stated, along with any compensating actions—such as partial control deployment or enhanced monitoring—that will temporarily reduce risk until full remediation can occur. This level of candor enables governance bodies to assess whether plans are feasible or require executive intervention.

Interim risk treatments bridge the gap between discovery and resolution. For high-severity findings, waiting until full remediation is complete may leave the organization exposed for months. Management should describe specific interim measures—such as manual reviews, access restrictions, or compensating technical controls—that will remain in place until the permanent fix is verified. These temporary controls must be measurable and monitored, not merely declared. The presence of interim mitigation indicates that management is managing risk actively rather than passively accepting exposure. Audit teams should confirm that these temporary measures are indeed functioning and that their expiration or replacement is clearly defined in the plan.

Every management response must declare its stance on the risk treatment strategy. The options—accept, mitigate, transfer, or fix—define how management intends to handle the exposure. A "fix" eliminates the root cause and restores the control to its intended design. A "mitigate" approach reduces risk to an acceptable level through alternative or partial controls. "Transfer" may apply to outsourced or insured risks where responsibility is shifted to another party. "Accept" represents conscious acknowledgment that the residual risk will remain, typically due to cost, practicality, or strategic reasons. The chosen stance must be explicit, justified, and consistent with the organization's documented risk appetite. Ambiguity here leads to confusion during follow-up and weakens overall governance.

When management opts for risk acceptance or exceptions, formal documentation becomes essential. Each acceptance must include a written rationale that explains why the risk will remain and how the decision aligns with tolerance thresholds. Acceptance should never be implied by inaction or expired deadlines—it must be a deliberate decision recorded through the appropriate governance channel. The documentation should specify who approved the acceptance, the residual risk level at the time of decision, and any conditions that would trigger re-evaluation, such as changes in threat landscape or regulatory obligations. These details establish transparency and accountability, ensuring that risk acceptance is a managed process rather than a convenient default.

Exception handling follows a similar logic but typically involves time-limited deviations from policy or control design. When exceptions are granted, they must include an expiry date, review cadence, and justification that articulates the business necessity and compensating safeguards in place. For example, management may request an exception to delay encryption rollout pending system upgrades, provided data is stored within restricted network segments and monitored for unauthorized access. Each exception should automatically trigger re-evaluation at expiry to determine whether extension, closure, or conversion to full risk acceptance is appropriate. This cyclical review process ensures that temporary exceptions do not quietly become permanent vulnerabilities.

Consistency in documenting management responses builds institutional memory and enables effective tracking of commitments. Each response should reference the related finding identifier, risk owner, and the intended verification evidence for closure. Without this linkage, follow-up testing becomes cumbersome and dependent on informal communication. Although detailed issue tracking belongs to a separate register process, the initial report must still provide enough information for continuity between audit documentation and future validation. The goal is not to replicate a project management plan but to ensure that each finding leaves behind a clear, auditable trail of responsibility and action.

Auditors must exercise professional judgment in assessing whether a management response is adequate. A response that merely acknowledges the issue or offers a generic commitment to "review the process" does not constitute an acceptable remediation plan. Similarly, responses that defer accountability or rely on unapproved future initiatives lack credibility. When responses are insufficient, auditors should return them for revision before finalizing the report. This review step reinforces quality standards and signals to the organization that audit closure is contingent on substantive, testable commitments.

Follow-through transforms commitments into results. Once responses are accepted, the responsibility shifts to governance functions and management oversight teams to track implementation, verify closure, and reassess any accepted risks. Periodic status updates and validation testing ensure that commitments do not fade into administrative backlog. When management delivers on time-bound, resourced, and clearly justified responses, the audit process evolves from a compliance exercise into an engine of continuous improvement. Ultimately, the discipline of well-structured management responses strengthens accountability, reduces residual risk, and demonstrates to executives and regulators that the organization treats assurance as an ongoing responsibility, not a one-time event.

Trend and Benchmark Views

Trend views are valuable only when they illuminate reality rather than decorate a narrative. Presenting quarter-over-quarter results must start with methodological transparency: define what was measured, how it was calculated, and which datasets were included or excluded during the period. The audience should understand whether movements reflect genuine risk reduction or artifacts of timing, sampling, and scope boundaries. Trend narratives should stick to assurance outcomes—what testing revealed and what changed in risk exposure—and avoid drifting into operational storytelling that the underlying data cannot support. By treating the trend section as an evidence-based explanation rather than marketing, the report preserves credibility and gives leadership the context required to act wisely.

Normalization is the antidote to scope bias. If one quarter includes three business units and the next includes five, raw counts of findings cannot be compared without adjustment. Use denominator-aware metrics such as findings per one hundred controls tested, repeat-rate per control family assessed, or coverage-adjusted defect rates tied to the size of the in-scope population. Disclose any change in sampling strategy, evidence thresholds, or inclusion criteria that could shift the baseline, and annotate trend graphics accordingly so the reader does not mistake a methodology change for improved control health. Normalization is not statistical theater; it is the minimum needed to ensure that quarter-over-quarter comparisons say something true.

Cycle time to close is a core assurance metric because it measures the organization's ability to convert findings into resolved risk. Define it precisely from the date the report is issued to the date independent validation confirms closure, not the date management marks the ticket "complete." Segment the metric by treatment path—fix, mitigate, or risk accept—because each carries different effort and evidence requirements, and aggregate figures can hide material delays in true remediation. Aging buckets, such as less than 90 days, 90–180 days, and greater than 180 days, reveal whether backlog is decaying or ossifying. Avoid incentives that reward premature closure or superficial fixes; the point is durable risk reduction, not speed for its own sake.

Repeat finding rate is the clearest signal of whether remediation is addressing root causes or merely symptoms. To present it properly, map findings across periods using stable identifiers tied to the control objective, not just ticket numbers that change with tooling. Distinguish direct recurrences from thematic repeats where different systems exhibit the same underlying cause, and show both counts and proportions relative to controls tested. Provide lineage notes where a control was redesigned; a recurrence after design change is more serious than a repeat caused by deferred rollout. When repeat rates decline, explain the mechanism—governance changes, tooling upgrades, or clarified ownership—so leadership understands which interventions are actually working.

Control health indicators are most meaningful when anchored to a common control set rather than shifting local taxonomies. Tie reporting to the organization's approved control library—grouped by families such as access management, change, logging and monitoring, vulnerability handling, and data protection—and evaluate each family against consistent effectiveness criteria. Display coverage alongside performance: a family with few findings but minimal testing coverage is not healthy; it is unexamined. Where scoring is used, describe the rubric explicitly—evidence sufficiency, design adequacy, and operating effectiveness—and keep weights stable over time so the index remains comparable. The aim is to show whether foundational controls are maturing, not to invent composite numbers that obscure reality.

Visualization choices shape interpretation and must be handled conservatively. Use stable time windows and avoid smoothing techniques that mask seasonality unless you disclose the method and show the unsmoothed view somewhere in the materials. Annotate trend breaks for significant events, such as the addition of a new business line, migration to a new ticketing platform, or adoption of a revised sampling strategy. Keep axes consistent across quarters so that apparent improvements are not artifacts of rescaling, and resist stacking unlike metrics on a single chart where units and meanings differ. Readers should be able to glance at a figure and understand both trajectory and context without decoding design tricks.

External benchmarks can help leadership calibrate performance, but they require disciplined restraint. Only compare against cohorts with comparable scope, method, and maturity, and document those attributes so the audience knows what is—and is not—being held equal. If your program tests operating effectiveness while the benchmark reflects policy conformance, label the inference limit plainly; the figures are not commensurate and should not drive targets. Provide ranges or percentiles rather than single-point comparisons to avoid false precision, and avoid reputational league tables that encourage gaming rather than improvement. Benchmarks are a compass, not a scoreboard, and their role is to frame questions, not to declare victory.

Keep assurance metrics distinct from operational key performance indicators (KPIs) to prevent category errors. Assurance metrics include things like control defect density by family, cycle time to validated closure, repeat finding rates, and coverage against the common control set. Operational KPIs measure run-state performance such as patch deployment velocity, mean time to detect, mean time to contain, or help desk resolution times. Both are valuable, but they answer different questions: one tests whether controls are designed and operating effectively; the other tracks whether operations are meeting service goals. Blending them in a single chart invites misinterpretation and can obscure whether improvements stem from stronger controls or simply faster operations.

Quarter-over-quarter trend reviews should emphasize longitudinal insight rather than quarterly theatrics. Use rolling four-quarter windows to smooth one-off spikes and reinforce program direction, and pair quantitative trends with short, evidence-grounded narratives that explain the drivers of change. Guard against Goodhart's law by periodically testing whether any metric is being optimized at the expense of real control effectiveness, and retire or adjust measures that begin to invite gaming. Maintain a light but explicit data-governance protocol around metric definitions, source systems, and calculation logic so that the trend pack is reproducible and defensible. When trend and benchmark views are constructed with this discipline, they become an early-warning system for control drift and a reliable guide for investment, not just a colorful appendix.

Board/Audit Committee Briefing Formats

Board and Audit Committee briefings demand precision, restraint, and a structured flow that keeps leaders operating at the right altitude. The purpose is not to recite audit mechanics or parade tool screenshots, but to convey the assurance message in business terms—what was tested, what was found, what risk remains, and what decisions are required to manage that risk. A disciplined narrative structure ensures the briefing informs governance without overwhelming it. Every presentation should follow a simple, consistent pattern: **scope tested → key findings → residual risk → business impact → decisions requested**. This formula transforms technical reports into executive intelligence, allowing the Board to understand the "so what" without descending into operational minutiae.

The first element—**scope tested**—anchors the discussion. It defines which business units, systems, and risk domains were covered in the audit cycle, along with any exclusions or scope limitations. This clarity sets the boundaries for what the findings represent and prevents overgeneralization. For example, if only one regional data center was tested, that distinction must be clear before the findings are discussed. The scope statement should fit on a single slide or paragraph and use organizational terms familiar to executives, not internal audit jargon. The goal is to establish where assurance has been applied so the Board can immediately see how it maps to strategic priorities, regulatory exposures, or emerging risks.

Next, the **key findings** summarize what matters most. These should represent clusters or themes, not an itemized list of every control gap. Typically, three to five consolidated findings convey the majority of residual risk in a way that leadership can absorb and debate. Each finding should include a brief description of the issue, its root cause category, and its current remediation trajectory. Avoid technical phrasing such as "unencrypted traffic over port 1433"; instead, translate to business relevance, such as "unencrypted database connections expose customer data in transit." The aim is to tell a risk story, not a configuration story. Supporting detail belongs in appendices or pre-reads for those who want depth after the meeting.

The **residual risk** portion links the audit findings to the organization's risk appetite. This section should describe what risk remains after current controls, interim mitigations, or partial remediations have been applied. Use consistent severity scales and color codes—such as red for high, amber for moderate, and green for low—so executives can instantly interpret exposure. Where compensating controls exist, acknowledge them while clarifying that they reduce but do not eliminate risk. The residual risk discussion should directly reference enterprise risk categories—data privacy, regulatory compliance, operational continuity, financial reporting integrity—so the Board can see how these technical gaps map to business governance responsibilities.

Business impact gives the findings economic and strategic context. Here the focus shifts from control design to enterprise consequence: what would happen if the identified risk materialized? The discussion should estimate plausible outcomes such as financial loss, reputational damage, legal exposure, or regulatory penalties, keeping the emphasis on business disruption rather than control failure. Avoid speculative worst-case narratives; base statements on reasonable scenarios informed by evidence and threat modeling. The Board needs to understand not just the technical problem but the organizational exposure it represents—how a system issue could affect customers, compliance posture, or brand trust. This helps translate security findings into decisions that align with enterprise priorities.

The briefing must culminate in **decisions requested**—specific actions the Board or Audit Committee is being asked to approve, endorse, or note. These might include additional funding for remediation, acceleration of a security program, approval of a revised policy, or formal acceptance of residual risk. Each decision should be framed as a clear choice with stated implications. For example: "Approve $1.2 million to modernize endpoint detection to close high residual risk in threat response," or "Accept remaining risk of legacy system exposure pending 2026 platform replacement." Explicit decision framing reinforces governance accountability and prevents meetings from ending with nods of concern but no actionable direction.

Visuals are the language of executive comprehension, and they must reinforce—not replace—the narrative. **Issue heatmaps** are ideal for showing the distribution of residual risk across domains, business units, or control families. Use consistent scoring rubrics and color scales quarter to quarter so trends are meaningful. **Trajectory charts** can illustrate whether overall control maturity, finding counts, or closure rates are improving or stagnating, providing a sense of momentum. Keep charts simple: two or three metrics per visual, minimal labels, and clear legends. The goal is to communicate trend and proportion, not precise numerical values. Complex or overly technical visuals may satisfy analytical curiosity but distract from strategic insight.

Maintaining the Board at the correct altitude requires editorial discipline. Executives and directors should not be briefed on testing tools, ticketing systems, or detailed methodologies. Their role is to evaluate risk exposure, resource sufficiency, and alignment with enterprise risk appetite—not to adjudicate control design. Technical annexes can be supplied as reference material, but the live briefing should stay focused on implications, trends, and decisions. In effect, the auditor acts as an interpreter between the language of control assurance and the language of governance.

The Board should leave the session knowing what risks exist, how management plans to address them, and what commitments require oversight—not which scripts or utilities were used in testing.

Board and Audit Committee briefings must also align with the organization's established communication rhythm. The briefing package should be concise—typically ten to twelve slides or a five-page memo—and include an executive summary, key visuals, and decision points. Each session should reinforce continuity by referencing prior-cycle results and demonstrating progress or regression against commitments. This cadence builds narrative consistency over time, allowing directors to see how the organization's control environment is evolving rather than treating each meeting as an isolated event.

Briefings must respect the boundaries of related disciplines. Incident response playbooks, crisis communications protocols, and media handling belong to operational leadership and are discussed in dedicated forums, not within the audit reporting cycle. When major findings intersect with those areas—for example, systemic weaknesses that could impair incident handling—the briefing should acknowledge the dependency but defer tactical detail to the relevant function. This separation keeps the Board's attention on assurance implications while ensuring other governance structures retain ownership of execution.

Issue Register Governance and Closure Validation

An effective issue register is the backbone of audit follow-through. It converts individual findings into a structured, trackable system of record that governs remediation, acceptance, and validation. The register must function as a *single source of truth*—the authoritative repository against which all progress, accountability, and closure are measured. Fragmented spreadsheets or departmental trackers inevitably lead to inconsistencies, missed deadlines, and unverified closures. A properly governed issue register maintains integrity through standardized fields, disciplined ownership, and clear linkages to supporting evidence. It ensures that every open risk remains visible, every commitment is documented, and every closure can be independently verified.

Each entry in the issue register must include a unique identifier that follows a consistent naming convention—typically reflecting year, audit engagement, and sequential numbering. This ID becomes the permanent reference point across all related communications, reports, and assurance activities. The register should also capture key metadata: issue title, severity and materiality ratings, accountable owner, business unit, due date, and current status. These attributes create a uniform view across all findings, allowing management to filter, prioritize, and analyze systemic risk patterns. Without such structure, data aggregation becomes unreliable, and leadership loses the ability to see how individual findings aggregate into enterprise risk trends.

Severity and materiality within the register must mirror the same definitions used in audit reporting. This alignment ensures that governance decisions are consistent regardless of whether a finding is viewed in isolation or as part of broader analytics. When severity or residual risk ratings change over time—because of remediation progress or environmental shifts—the register should record the date and rationale for the update. Historical traceability matters: regulators and internal reviewers often ask not only what the risk is today but how it evolved. Capturing these rating changes builds an audit trail of risk treatment decisions and provides insight into organizational learning over time. Table 21.3 standardizes status meanings and the evidence required to validate closure while clarifying residual risk posture.

Table 21.3 Issue status definitions and closure evidence requirements.

Status	Operational definition	Required evidence	Residual risk treatment
Open	Finding logged and ownership assigned no action started	Register entry with owner and due date	Inherent risk unchanged
In Progress	Remediation underway with approved plan	Project plan ID slash milestone tracking proof	Inherent risk pending mitigation
Mitigated	Compensating control reduces exposure interim only	Compensating control evidence with start date	Residual risk reduced but present
Awaiting Validation	Remediation implemented pending independent check	Implementation artifacts and change record	Residual risk pending confirmation
Closed	Independent validation confirms effective control	Dated validation artifacts and re test results	Residual risk addressed per criteria
Accepted	Formal approval to retain exposure with rationale	Approval record and next review date	Residual risk owned and monitored

Ownership is the cornerstone of accountability. Each issue must have a named owner, not a department or team. The owner should be the individual with authority to allocate resources and make risk treatment decisions, typically a control owner, process manager, or executive sponsor. Secondary fields may record contributors or implementers, but accountability must reside with a single, identifiable person. This structure prevents "shared responsibility" from becoming "shared neglect." Regular ownership validation—especially during reorganizations or role changes—ensures continuity and avoids orphaned issues lingering in the system.

The issue register must define and enforce consistent status categories. Common life cycle stages include *open*, *in progress*, *mitigated*, *awaiting validation*, *closed*, and *accepted*. Each status must have an operational definition tied to evidence and governance action. For example, "mitigated" means compensating controls or partial remediation have reduced risk to an acceptable interim level but permanent fixes are incomplete. "Closed" means full remediation has been completed, verified, and independently validated with dated evidence. "Accepted" means management has formally acknowledged residual risk and documented rationale and approval consistent with risk appetite. Without standardized meanings, status labels lose integrity and obscure real exposure.

Independent closure validation is nonnegotiable. Closure cannot rely solely on management assertion or screenshots provided by the control owner. The audit or risk assurance function must verify remediation through review of evidence, interviews, or targeted retesting. The validation process must produce dated artifacts that demonstrate the control is operating as intended—such as configuration exports, access logs, or transaction samples showing the new process in action. These artifacts should be attached or linked directly to the register entry, ensuring that each closure is fully supported and re-performable. Closure validation not only protects the credibility of audit outcomes but also provides tangible proof for regulators and external auditors who may rely on the internal audit's work.

Evidence linkage is what distinguishes a living issue register from a simple task tracker. Every entry should reference the source workpaper from which the issue originated and the location of closure evidence. When validation confirms successful remediation, the corresponding evidence should be uploaded or cited by exact file path or repository link. If evidence resides in a restricted system due to confidentiality, a summary record should still exist in the register to preserve traceability. The goal is to ensure that any reviewer—internal or external—can follow the chain from finding to fix and confirm closure without manual hunting or dependence on tribal knowledge.

Governance over the register itself must be structured and transparent. A designated owner—typically the Chief Audit Executive or Head of Risk Assurance—should maintain version control, oversee data quality, and ensure timely updates. Governance reviews should occur at defined intervals, such as monthly management meetings or quarterly risk committee sessions, to verify the accuracy of statuses, due dates, and ownership. Escalation thresholds should also be established: for example, any high-severity issue past due by more than thirty days automatically escalates to senior leadership review. These procedural controls preserve the integrity of the register as a reliable management tool rather than an administrative afterthought.

Time-bound commitments are essential for momentum. Each entry must carry a due date aligned with the issue's severity and complexity. Extensions should be rare and must include justification and approval from appropriate governance levels. When due dates change, the register must retain a record of the original and revised dates to show accountability over time. These data points also feed trend analysis—helping the audit function measure remediation velocity, average closure cycle time, and backlog age. By analyzing this information, leadership can identify chronic bottlenecks, systemic dependencies, or resource constraints that impede control improvement.

Risk acceptance and exceptions documented within the register must meet the same standards as in formal audit responses: rationale, approver, residual risk rating, and review cadence. Accepted risks should not disappear from the register; instead, they remain visible with next review dates clearly listed. This practice ensures that acceptance decisions are periodically revisited, especially when business conditions, regulations, or technologies change. A well-governed register treats risk acceptance as a living decision that can expire, not as a one-time escape clause.

Unresolved issues and accepted risks must link seamlessly into the next **assurance plan**, creating continuity between audit cycles. Open or high-risk items should automatically populate the risk universe for consideration in future planning, ensuring the next year's audit scope addresses persistent or deferred exposures. This linkage prevents recurrences from being forgotten and integrates issue management directly into the broader assurance life cycle. The mechanics of planning belong to later discussion, but the principle is simple: what remains open today informs what must be tested tomorrow.

Conclusion

Mastering the principles of audit reporting and executive communication is critical for transforming assurance work into strategic value. Technical accuracy alone cannot influence decision-making unless it is framed through structured findings, consistent severity ratings, and traceable evidence that withstands independent scrutiny. The disciplined approach to documenting, rating, and validating issues establishes not only audit credibility but also organizational accountability. When reports connect findings to measurable residual risk and business impact, they shift security assurance from a compliance exercise to a driver of informed governance.

This chapter reinforces the role of clarity, traceability, and governance alignment in securing AI-enabled and data-driven enterprises at scale. As automated systems, predictive analytics, and machine learning models increasingly define operational resilience, audit reporting must evolve to express risk in terms that integrate both human oversight and algorithmic control. Consistent reporting frameworks and well-governed issue registers give leadership a coherent view of exposure across traditional infrastructure and intelligent platforms alike. These practices ensure that emerging risks—from AI bias to autonomous decision faults—are evaluated through the same disciplined lens that governs cybersecurity assurance today.

With these foundations in place, professionals are better equipped to guide organizations through complex risk landscapes with precision and transparency. Effective audit communication not only closes findings but also strengthens trust among executives, regulators, and technical teams who depend on the audit function for unbiased insight. While tools and technologies will continue to evolve, the strategic intent remains constant: to provide reliable, actionable assurance that aligns security risk management with organizational objectives. By upholding these standards, cybersecurity auditors become essential interpreters between evidence and enterprise—bridging the technical and strategic dimensions of modern security governance.

Auditor Recommendations

1. **Enforce Structured Reporting:** Establish a clear process for structuring audit findings using standardized components such as observation, criteria, condition, cause, effect, recommendation, and management response. This consistent structure enables traceability between evidence and conclusions, ensuring that reports are both defensible and reproducible. A disciplined format strengthens audit credibility and allows independent reviewers to re-perform conclusions without relying on subjective interpretation.
2. **Prioritize Rating Consistency:** Apply defined severity and materiality scales uniformly across all engagements to maintain comparability and transparency. Calibrate these ratings using objective factors such as business impact, likelihood, and control environment maturity rather than auditor preference. Consistency in rating methodology builds trust among executives and regulators who rely on audit results for risk-based decision-making.
3. **Document Residual Risk Transparently:** Require every finding to include a statement of residual risk—explicitly describing the remaining exposure after compensating controls or partial remediation. This "before and after" clarity helps leadership understand not just what was fixed, but what risk persists. Transparent residual risk documentation turns audit reports into tools for informed governance rather than simple compliance checklists.
4. **Craft Actionable Recommendations:** Write outcome-based recommendations that define measurable success criteria and name accountable owners. Avoid vague terms like *enhance* or *improve*; instead, describe specific, testable end states that can be independently validated. Strong recommendations make remediation progress auditable, transforming findings into practical roadmaps for lasting control improvement.
5. **Require Substantive Management Responses:** Insist that management responses include concrete commitments—time-bound milestones, assigned resources, and interim mitigation steps when full remediation is delayed. A well-formed response must also declare a clear stance on risk treatment: fix, mitigate, transfer, or accept. This level of precision ensures that management accountability extends beyond acknowledgment to measurable follow-through.
6. **Govern the Issue Register as a Living System:** Maintain a single source of truth for all audit findings that includes unique identifiers, ownership, due dates, severity, and closure evidence links. Define what "closed," "mitigated," and "accepted" mean, and enforce independent validation before status changes occur. A disciplined register prevents issue fatigue, supports accurate analytics, and ensures no risk quietly disappears from oversight.

7. **Use Trends to Drive Insight, Not Optics:** Track metrics such as cycle time to close, repeat finding rates, and control health scores, but normalize for scope and testing coverage. Present trends with clear caveats about methodology and data limits to prevent narrative manipulation. The objective is learning and improvement, not producing artificially positive charts that obscure reality.
8. **Brief Executives at the Right Altitude:** Structure Board and Audit Committee communications around scope, key findings, residual risk, business impact, and decisions requested. Use clean visuals—such as heatmaps and trajectory charts—to convey risk concentration and movement over time. Keep discussions focused on implications and governance actions, avoiding tool-level or procedural details that dilute strategic attention.
9. **Validate Closure with Evidence:** Require that every issue closure be supported by dated, verifiable artifacts that demonstrate control operation, not merely implementation. Independent retesting by audit or assurance staff should confirm that the fix is complete and effective. This practice protects audit integrity, ensures sustainable remediation, and provides defensible documentation for regulators and external assessors.
10. **Integrate Open Risks into Future Planning:** Carry forward unresolved or accepted risks into the next assurance plan to ensure continuity of oversight. Link issue register data directly to audit scoping decisions, prioritizing areas where remediation delays or repeat findings persist. By embedding lessons learned into planning, audit programs evolve continuously and align testing resources with the organization's most pressing residual risks.

Chapter Questions

1. Which component of a structured finding establishes the objective standard against which the control is evaluated?
   A. Observation
   B. Criteria
   C. Condition
   D. Effect/Risk

2. Which recommendation phrasing best aligns with outcome-based, testable end states?
   A. "Enhance identity governance across applications."
   B. "Improve server hardening where feasible."
   C. "Review privileged access quarterly."
   D. "Restrict privileged accounts to unique credentials with logged approvals and monitored administrative actions."

3. When should "before/after" residual risk statements be explicitly documented?
   A. Only after full remediation is complete
   B. Only for low-severity findings
   C. When compensating controls or partial remediation are applied
   D. At the auditor's discretion if space permits

4. Which sequence reflects the recommended flow for Board/Audit Committee briefings?
   - **A.** Scope tested → Key findings → Residual risk → Business impact → Decisions requested
   - **B.** Key findings → Tools used → Test scripts → Decisions requested → Business impact
   - **C.** Business impact → Residual risk → Tools used → Scope tested → Decisions requested
   - **D.** Decisions requested → Scope tested → Key findings → Test procedures → Business impact

5. What is the primary method to prevent trend views from "gaming the narrative"?
   - **A.** Compare raw finding counts quarter to quarter
   - **B.** Normalize metrics for scope, coverage, and sampling changes
   - **C.** Focus exclusively on severity ratings
   - **D.** Include screenshots of every tool used

6. In the issue register, what distinguishes a status of "closed" from "mitigated"?
   - **A.** Owner signed off that work is done
   - **B.** Ticket is marked complete in the tracking system
   - **C.** A compensating control reduces exposure temporarily
   - **D.** Independent validation confirms remediation with dated evidence artifacts

7. Which element is required for an acceptable management response?
   - **A.** Acknowledgment of the finding without dates
   - **B.** Time-bound actions, identified resources, and a clear risk treatment stance
   - **C.** Inclusion of vendor marketing materials
   - **D.** A promise to "monitor" the situation

8. What is the recommended practice when using external benchmarks in audit reporting?
   - **A.** Compare against any published industry average
   - **B.** Only compare against internal historical data
   - **C.** Use cohorts with comparable scope and method, and label inference limits
   - **D.** Rely on league tables to rank security performance

9. How should repeat finding rate be measured to reflect true recurrence?
   - **A.** By matching ticket numbers across quarters
   - **B.** By mapping to stable identifiers tied to the control objective
   - **C.** By tracking changes in staffing levels
   - **D.** By correlating to quarterly budget variances

10. Which request appropriately belongs in the "decisions requested" portion of a Board briefing?
    - **A.** Selecting a specific EDR product SKU
    - **B.** Approving funding or policy changes to address high residual risk
    - **C.** Choosing the sample methodology for the next audit
    - **D.** Reviewing the detailed test scripts used by auditors

22

Annual Audit Planning and Capability Development

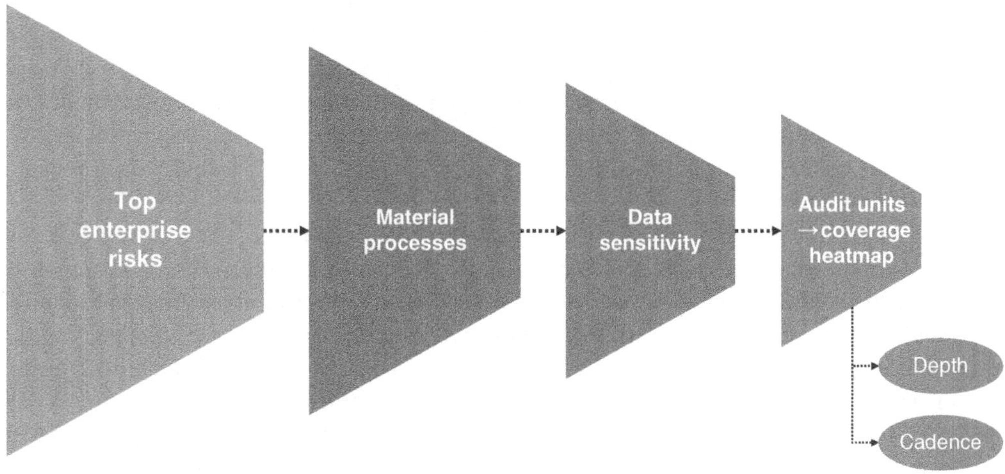

Annual audit planning is where the discipline of cybersecurity assurance transforms from isolated engagements into a coherent, risk-aligned strategy. Effective planning ensures that coverage, depth, and frequency of audits mirror the organization's true risk landscape—not just its compliance obligations. By connecting enterprise risks, control maturity, and resource capabilities, the planning process converts abstract risk statements into actionable assurance activities. This alignment is critical for organizations that must demonstrate not only control effectiveness but also agility in responding to a rapidly shifting threat environment shaped by digital transformation and AI integration.

Sustained audit capability depends on more than scheduling—it relies on people, tools, and disciplined change management. From skill mapping and specialist sourcing to analytics enablement and evidence governance, a modern audit function must balance technical depth with operational efficiency. Automation, data-driven testing, and intelligent analytics expand coverage but also demand strong control over provenance, independence, and access. By integrating these elements into a unified planning framework, this chapter underscores how thoughtful design and resourcing transform the audit program from a compliance mechanism into a predictive, value-generating function.

Equally important is the ability to adapt. Emerging risks, regulatory changes, and organizational shifts require an audit plan that evolves without losing structure or accountability. Through defined triggers, quality assurance mechanisms, and maturity road maps, this chapter demonstrates how an audit program remains resilient—able to recalibrate priorities while preserving consistency and trust. In an era where AI-driven systems, cloud ecosystems, and digital interdependencies redefine assurance boundaries, mastering the art of annual audit planning is what separates a reactive audit function from one that truly strengthens enterprise governance and risk confidence.

Risk-based Coverage Model

A risk-based coverage model transforms the abstract world of enterprise risk into a practical audit plan that can be scheduled, funded, and executed. It begins with understanding what truly matters—where the organization could be most harmed and how those risks intersect with business processes and data. Every enterprise has a handful of processes that are mission-critical and a limited number of data classes that, if compromised, could cause significant damage. By mapping those priorities against the systems, vendors, and control owners that support them, the auditor begins to see a landscape of "audit units." These units form the building blocks of coverage, allowing risks to be visualized, prioritized, and sequenced across the audit year through a clear, data-driven heatmap.

Turning high-level risk into actionable audit scope requires discipline. For each top risk, the auditor identifies which business processes carry that risk forward and where it materializes within technology or data flows. For example, a risk such as unauthorized access may span identity governance, privileged access tools, and sensitive data repositories. Each of these becomes a logical unit with its own entry and exit points. The goal is to avoid both overlap and omission—ensuring every critical process and dataset has a home in the plan, but nothing is reviewed twice unless risk justifies it. This structure not only strengthens coverage but also makes the plan defensible when presented to the audit committee or regulators. Table 22.1 illustrates how impact level maturity and prior results drive planned depth and cadence for representative audit units.

Table 22.1 Coverage decision matrix for risk-based planning.

Audit unit	Impact level	Control maturity	Prior findings	Planned depth	Cadence
Identity governance	High	Immature	Repeat	Design plus effectiveness	Semiannual
Payment processing	High	Maturing	Some	Design plus effectiveness	Annual
Cloud platform	Medium	Maturing	None	Design focus	Annual
OT ICS network	High	Immature	Repeat	Design plus effectiveness	Semiannual
AI model governance	High	Immature	Some	Design plus effectiveness	Annual
Endpoint configuration	Medium	Mature	None	Design focus	Biennial
Vendor risk management	Medium	Maturing	Some	Targeted effectiveness	Annual
Data loss prevention	High	Maturing	Some	Design plus effectiveness	Annual

Audit unit	Impact level	Control maturity	Prior findings	Planned depth	Cadence
Change management	Medium	Maturing	Repeat	Targeted effectiveness	Annual
Backups and recovery	Medium	Mature	None	Design focus	Biennial

Materiality is a guiding principle in shaping those units. A process that handles customer payment data or regulated health information deserves different attention than one that manages marketing metrics or employee schedules. By linking each audit unit to its process criticality and data sensitivity, the model helps determine both the attention it deserves and the kind of assurance work required. This mapping also clarifies ownership. Business and IT leaders can see precisely where their domain fits within the broader risk picture, promoting accountability and collaboration rather than resistance when the auditors arrive.

Once the scope is defined, the next decision is depth. Every domain can be tested at multiple layers—design adequacy, operating effectiveness, or both. Design adequacy answers whether the control is conceptually sound, while operating effectiveness determines if it actually works in daily practice. High-risk areas, or those with immature or untested controls, demand both layers of assurance. Areas with strong performance histories and mature automation may need only design verification or selective spot checks. This balance conserves audit resources while maintaining integrity in coverage, focusing attention where assurance value is greatest.

Depth also evolves over time. When an organization demonstrates control stability and good self-reporting, the auditor can gradually reduce testing intensity and reallocate time to new or changing risks. Conversely, when findings accumulate or remediation lags, that same area deserves deeper and more frequent examination. A mature audit function treats depth as a dynamic lever—not a fixed rule—to ensure that each hour spent auditing contributes to measurable risk reduction.

Cadence, or audit frequency, should never be driven solely by tradition. Annual reviews may be suitable for some domains, but others move faster than that rhythm can accommodate. Systems that handle financial transactions, manage privileged access, or rely on third-party integrations often change too rapidly for long gaps in assurance. In those cases, a semiannual or rolling review may be warranted. Meanwhile, stable processes with minimal change and strong continuous monitoring can be revisited less often. The key is to match the audit's timing to the pace of risk, not the page of the calendar.

A well-constructed coverage heatmap ties these ideas together. Along one axis, it lists processes, systems, or control domains. Along the other, it displays risk levels, data sensitivity, and control maturity. Color shading then communicates where assurance will be deepest and most frequent. This visualization is far more than a graphic—it is a management tool that aligns limited audit resources with the organization's true risk profile. When leadership asks why one area was prioritized over another, the heatmap provides an immediate, data-based answer.

The weight of data classification within this model cannot be overstated. Sensitive or regulated data elevates every associated process. Even a moderate-likelihood event can become high-risk when it involves personal health information or intellectual property. The coverage model must therefore integrate the enterprise's data classification scheme directly into the prioritization logic, ensuring sensitive information automatically receives proportionate scrutiny. Over time, this approach drives cultural awareness: protecting high-value data becomes an enterprise habit, not merely an audit checkbox.

Control maturity serves as another essential calibration point. Mature domains with automated enforcement and strong monitoring may need less manual testing, but they should still be observed periodically to confirm that automation continues to function as intended. Immature areas, by contrast, benefit from more granular testing and a stronger focus on design soundness and accountability. Maturity ratings are not static—they should be reevaluated whenever ownership changes, tools are replaced, or the environment undergoes significant transformation.

Historical findings give the plan its memory. Unresolved or repeat issues raise both depth and frequency requirements until sustained remediation is proven. Compensating controls and temporary waivers should be tracked with explicit expiry dates and reassessed to ensure they remain valid. In this way, the coverage model not only drives future audits but also reinforces accountability for past performance. Audit becomes a feedback loop—each year's results sharpen the next year's priorities.

Inputs to the Plan

An effective annual audit plan is not drawn from intuition or habit—it is built from evidence. The process begins with gathering inputs that reflect how the organization's risk landscape has evolved since the last cycle. Four categories of information consistently shape the audit universe: recent incidents and near misses, performance metrics and trend data, business and IT strategy shifts, and regulatory or compliance changes on the horizon. Each input influences not just what is audited but also when, how deeply, and with what priority. The strength of the plan lies in its traceability—every inclusion or exclusion must connect back to one of these tangible inputs, leaving a clear record of why decisions were made.

Incident data is often the most immediate and persuasive input. Security events, operational outages, or data breaches reveal weaknesses that policy documents and risk registers can miss. A single high-impact incident, such as a ransomware infection or insider misuse, can instantly reorder audit priorities for the coming year. Even near misses—events that did not escalate due to luck or rapid containment—deserve equal weight because they often highlight systemic vulnerabilities. When incorporated into the planning process, each incident must be analyzed for root cause and mapped to the control domains it implicates. If the issue originated in change management, identity governance, or patch discipline, those areas earn earlier or deeper coverage. This traceability ensures that lessons from the past year become action for the next.

Metrics and trend data serve as the plan's memory, revealing where the control environment is improving and where it is stalling. Common metrics include repeat findings, remediation closure timelines, policy exception rates, and control uptime or performance data. For example, an increase in repeat findings suggests that prior audits failed to produce sustained remediation, warranting expanded depth or frequency in that area. Slow closure SLAs indicate that management ownership may be unclear or that resourcing is inadequate, which in turn may justify a governance-focused audit or escalation to the audit committee. When trend data is integrated into planning dashboards, it turns qualitative observations into quantitative evidence. The model then becomes predictive—areas that show declining performance can be scheduled for earlier engagement rather than waiting for failure to confirm risk. Table 22.2 links canonical inputs to specific plan decisions and records the traceable documentation required for governance.

Table 22.2 Planning inputs to plan decisions traceability log.

Input type	Example signal	Plan decision affected	Plan change type	Documentation element
Incident	High impact event	Scope plus depth	Create ad hoc review	Rationale and approval record
Near miss	Contained attempt	Depth	Increase depth	Assumptions noted
Trend metric	Spike in repeat findings	Depth plus cadence	Advance timing	Rationale recorded
Trend metric	Slow closure SLA	Cadence	Advance timing	Escalation note
Strategy shift	Cloud migration announced	Scope	Add unit	Assumptions noted
Strategy shift	AI service launch	Scope plus depth	Add unit and increase depth	Rationale recorded
Regulatory deadline	New privacy law deadline	Cadence	Advance timing	Applicability statement
Architecture shift	Zero trust rollout	Scope plus depth	Expand unit	Rationale recorded
Corporate action	Acquisition signed	Scope plus cadence	Add unit and advance timing	Approval record
Corporate action	Divestiture planned	Scope	Remove unit with rationale	Exclusions noted

Business and IT strategy shifts reshape the audit landscape even when no incident has occurred. New cloud migrations, mergers, or digital product launches change the organization's control dependencies and therefore the assurance priorities. Similarly, a strategic pivot—such as moving from on-premises infrastructure to a hybrid environment—introduces different control layers and vendor risks that must be reflected in the plan. The auditor's task is to align coverage with strategic direction so that assurance keeps pace with change. This often requires reviewing business road maps and technology portfolios to anticipate where controls are being stretched or where governance frameworks may lag. Each strategy-driven scope addition should be documented with a clear rationale linking it to the strategic initiative, ensuring leadership understands that audit attention follows transformation.

Regulatory and compliance developments are another critical planning input, particularly in industries with evolving privacy, security, and reporting obligations. Upcoming deadlines for new frameworks, such as updates to NIST, ISO 27001, or emerging privacy regulations, often dictate both the timing and the focus of audits. For example, a pending data protection regulation might prompt an accelerated audit of consent management or data retention practices to validate readiness. When regulators or external assessors announce heightened expectations in specific areas—third-party risk management, AI model governance, or incident reporting—the plan should explicitly reflect those requirements. Traceability here means documenting which regulations influenced scope, what assumptions were made about applicability, and how the audit schedule aligns with compliance milestones.

Each of these input types—incidents, metrics, strategic changes, and regulatory deadlines—has a unique impact on scope and timing, but their true value comes from integration. When viewed together, they create a holistic understanding of the organization's operational reality. An area that scores high on all four inputs—say, a newly cloud-migrated financial system that suffered a recent outage, shows unresolved findings, and faces new compliance scrutiny—would naturally rise to the top of the plan. Conversely, a mature and stable domain showing consistent metrics, no incidents, and minimal regulatory change can justifiably move to a longer audit cadence. The key is that each decision can be explained in terms of input weight rather than subjective judgment.

Traceability is the organizing principle that turns these data points into defensible planning logic. For every audit unit, the plan should record which inputs influenced its inclusion, what assumptions were made about risk drivers, and why certain areas were excluded or deferred. This documentation is not mere bureaucracy—it preserves the rationale behind professional judgment, ensuring the plan can withstand scrutiny from boards, regulators, or peer reviewers. It also provides continuity across audit years, enabling future teams to understand the reasoning behind coverage changes. A traceable plan demonstrates that assurance is not reactive, but intentional and data-informed.

Documentation also requires transparency about exclusions. If a known risk area is omitted due to limited resources, overlapping coverage from another function, or management-led assurance activities, that rationale must be explicitly captured. Doing so not only protects the audit function from future criticism but also provides management a clear picture of residual risk acceptance. Exclusions, when documented thoughtfully, can actually enhance credibility by showing that prioritization decisions were deliberate, not accidental. This disciplined approach encourages constructive dialogue about resourcing and risk appetite rather than finger-pointing after the fact.

Resource and Skill Planning

A well-crafted audit plan is only as strong as the team executing it. Once risks, scope, and timing have been defined, the next step is to align people and skills to those priorities. This process begins by translating planned audit units into the technical and domain expertise required to assess them effectively. A review of cloud infrastructure demands a different skill set than one focused on industrial control systems or artificial intelligence governance. Mapping these skills to the plan ensures that every engagement is staffed by auditors who understand both the technology and the business context it supports. Without this mapping, even the best-designed coverage model risks producing shallow or misdirected assurance.

The skill inventory typically starts with foundational capabilities—general IT audit proficiency, risk assessment, and control design evaluation. On top of these, specialized competencies are layered according to the year's focus areas. If the plan includes audits of multicloud deployments or infrastructure as code pipelines, expertise in cloud security architecture and DevSecOps practices becomes essential. If operational technology environments are in scope, auditors must understand OT/ICS protocols, segmentation models, and the nuances of safety-integrated control systems. Similarly, audits involving machine learning models or generative AI governance require familiarity with model life cycle controls, data provenance, and bias mitigation frameworks. This explicit linkage between audit topics and skill requirements forms the backbone of resourcing strategy.

Once the necessary skill domains are identified, the auditor-in-charge determines whether those competencies exist internally or must be sourced externally. Internal staff may handle recurring domains where institutional knowledge and independence are strong, while co-sourced specialists can supplement in areas where deep technical understanding is critical but rarely needed year-round. For instance, penetration testing of OT environments or validation of AI model governance may justify temporary external support. However, co-sourcing must always be balanced with independence safeguards. External contributors should report functionally to the audit leadership, not to the management teams whose work they are assessing, and their scope must be clearly documented to prevent conflicts of interest or over-reliance.

Independence in staffing extends beyond reporting structure—it encompasses mindset. Auditors embedded within technical teams or seconded from operations can inadvertently lose objectivity if their prior design decisions are under review. Clear role boundaries, rotation schedules, and conflict declarations help maintain credibility. Similarly, when external experts are engaged, their deliverables should be reviewed by internal audit leadership to ensure conclusions align with audit methodology and professional standards. Independence is not a matter of distrust; it is the mechanism that preserves confidence in audit findings, particularly when specialized work requires collaboration with those being audited.

Resource planning also involves building a deliberate development road map for the audit staff. Technical environments evolve faster than most certification cycles, so continuous learning is not optional. Each auditor's annual performance plan should align with the skills forecasted in the audit plan itself. If upcoming work includes container security or identity federation, targeted training in Kubernetes security or IAM frameworks can be scheduled months in advance. Formal credentials—such as CISA, CISSP, CISM, or cloud platform certifications—should complement, not replace, hands-on training and peer learning. Encouraging rotation between technology domains, inviting guest instructors from engineering or threat intelligence teams, and supporting participation in professional forums all contribute to a richer capability baseline.

Team composition should strike a balance between generalists and specialists. Generalists bring adaptability, context awareness, and cross-domain pattern recognition; specialists bring depth, precision, and technical authority. A strong audit function blends both, pairing generalists as engagement leads with subject-matter experts who focus on control testing or data analysis. This pairing model ensures that complex findings are both technically sound and communicated in a language that executives understand. As technologies like AI, edge computing, and zero-trust architectures continue to reshape the landscape, maintaining this mix becomes a strategic necessity rather than a luxury.

Beyond skill matching, capacity planning must include contingencies for the unexpected. No annual plan survives contact with reality unaltered. Breaches, regulatory inquiries, or leadership directives can generate urgent assurance needs that fall outside the scheduled plan. Mature audit functions reserve a defined percentage of capacity—often between 10 and 20%—for ad hoc reviews or incident-driven engagements. This buffer prevents disruption to core coverage while preserving the ability to respond when the organization most needs assurance. Documenting how this contingency capacity is calculated and managed demonstrates foresight and operational resilience.

When contingency work does arise, having flexible staffing models pays dividends. Cross-trained auditors who can shift between domains without steep learning curves enable rapid response. Maintaining standing agreements with trusted co-sourcing partners allows specialized expertise to be engaged quickly under preapproved terms. Likewise, retaining knowledge repositories—such as prior workpapers, checklists, and evidence templates—reduces ramp-up time for unexpected reviews. Resource planning is not just about headcount; it is about designing a system that can scale and pivot without sacrificing rigor.

Training plans must evolve in parallel with this operational flexibility. Beyond certifications and classroom learning, simulation exercises and "audit war games" can build readiness for unpredictable scenarios. Running mock investigations of a cloud misconfiguration or a data exfiltration attempt gives auditors the muscle memory needed to perform under pressure. These experiences deepen technical understanding while reinforcing procedural discipline. They also strengthen coordination between audit, incident response, and compliance teams, which is crucial when assurance work overlaps with active response operations.

Finally, every resource and skill decision should be documented as part of the planning record. The audit plan should list key skill requirements for each engagement, identify how those needs will be met, and note any assumptions or dependencies. If specialist support is contingent on budget approval or vendor availability, that dependency should be transparent. Documenting this mapping provides traceability for stakeholders and sets expectations for the audit committee regarding staffing sufficiency. It also signals maturity: a function that plans for expertise as carefully as it plans for risk coverage demonstrates it understands that people—not just procedures—are the foundation of effective assurance.

Tooling and Data Enablement

Executing a modern audit plan requires more than skilled professionals—it demands a reliable digital backbone that supports efficiency, consistency, and defensibility. The foundation of that backbone is a well-integrated toolchain that manages the entire audit life cycle, from planning to reporting. At minimum, the audit function must maintain a governance, risk, and compliance (GRC) platform or equivalent workpaper management system, a secure evidence repository, well-defined data access pathways, and an analytics environment capable of processing both structured and unstructured data. These tools collectively enable the team to deliver coverage at scale, maintain control over audit artifacts, and produce insights that transcend manual review.

The GRC or workpaper system serves as the central command center for the audit plan. It houses the universe of audit entities, the annual schedule, risk assessments, and engagement-level workpapers. A mature GRC system ensures every audit is traceable—from initial scoping decisions through testing, findings, and remediation verification. It standardizes templates, enforces workflow approvals, and provides dashboards for leadership oversight. When properly configured, it also establishes a single source of truth for risk coverage, allowing auditors to link each engagement directly to enterprise risks and regulatory obligations. The goal is not simply digitization but governance—ensuring that every audit activity has an auditable trail of what was tested, who performed it, and what evidence supports the conclusion.

The evidence repository complements the GRC system by serving as the controlled environment for all supporting artifacts—logs, screenshots, extracts, reports, and correspondence. Security and integrity are paramount here. Access should be role-based, following the principle of least privilege so that auditors can view only what pertains to their engagements. Every upload or modification must be time-stamped and linked to a user identity to preserve provenance. Retention schedules should align with internal policy and regulatory requirements, typically maintaining evidence for multiple audit cycles while ensuring secure disposal when retention periods expire. Encryption at rest and in transit is mandatory, and multifactor authentication should protect all repository access. These measures safeguard not just the confidentiality of audit materials but the credibility of audit results.

Data access pathways define how auditors obtain the information necessary for testing and analytics. Ad hoc file transfers and unsecured exports are unacceptable in a mature environment. Instead, controlled data ingestion processes should be defined, specifying approved connectors, staging zones, and anonymization standards where sensitive personal or operational data is involved. Auditors must have read-only access wherever possible to prevent unintended data modification, and their activity within data systems should be logged. For cloud-based systems, service account credentials should be segregated from operational accounts and rotated according to enterprise identity management policy. Clear documentation of these pathways ensures transparency to data owners and supports compliance with privacy and data-handling regulations.

The analytics platform extends the reach of the audit function by transforming raw data into meaningful assurance evidence. It may take the form of a dedicated analytics server, a cloud-hosted environment, or a federated platform shared with enterprise data teams. Regardless of architecture, it must support secure ingestion, reproducible queries, and controlled outputs. Auditors rely on these tools to identify patterns, anomalies, or control deviations that would be impractical to detect manually. Examples include continuous monitoring of privileged access activity, transaction anomaly detection, or log correlation to verify segregation-of-duties compliance. Every analytic routine should be version-controlled, peer-reviewed, and documented to ensure repeatability and transparency. Governance of automation jobs and continuous scripts, however, is covered separately in Chapter 17; this section focuses solely on the enabling platforms and data infrastructure supporting those processes.

Access control is a recurring theme across the toolchain, and for good reason. The audit function often holds privileged visibility into sensitive operational data, from financial records to security configurations. Without strict access boundaries, the very tools designed to protect the organization could become vectors of risk. Implementing granular permissions within the GRC system, enforcing data classification tagging in the repository, and maintaining independent access reviews are essential. Each tool should feed access logs into the organization's broader monitoring framework so that anomalous activity—such as bulk downloads or unauthorized sharing—can be detected promptly. Independence also applies at the tool level; management personnel whose operations are under audit should never administer the systems housing audit evidence or results.

Retention and provenance requirements complete the picture of data enablement. Every piece of audit evidence, from SQL queries to screenshots, must carry context: who obtained it, when, from what source, and under which control conditions. Metadata that captures this information should be embedded automatically wherever possible. Retention schedules must distinguish between working papers, final reports, and transitory materials, ensuring that records are neither deleted prematurely nor stored indefinitely. When the retention period ends, destruction should be documented, and media sanitized according to recognized standards. Provenance tracking, in turn, ensures that evidence remains trustworthy even years later—particularly important for audits supporting regulatory certifications or litigation defense.

Integration among these tools is vital. A disconnected toolchain leads to versioning errors, lost evidence, and fragmented audit trails. The GRC platform should link directly to the evidence repository and analytics outputs, allowing a reviewer to trace every finding from data source to conclusion without leaving the system. Similarly, evidence metadata should flow automatically into workpaper references to reduce manual errors. Where integration requires APIs or middleware, change management controls must apply to ensure connections remain secure and functional after updates. The result is a seamless, end-to-end ecosystem that supports audit execution with minimal administrative friction.

The choice of tooling also influences team culture. Efficient systems allow auditors to focus on analysis rather than document wrangling. A mature digital environment encourages curiosity—auditors can explore data confidently, knowing controls are in place to protect integrity. At the same time, it promotes consistency: every engagement follows the same process, uses the same templates, and generates evidence of the same quality. This consistency builds trust with management and regulators alike. Over time, it also enables trend analysis across audits, revealing systemic issues that would otherwise remain hidden.

As audit functions adopt more automation and data-driven methods, the governance of those automation routines must remain distinct from the infrastructure that supports them. While analytics platforms host scripts and dashboards, the design, testing, and control of automation jobs fall under the broader topic of automation governance, discussed in Chapter 17. Here, the focus is on readiness—ensuring the team has the secure tools, clean data, and reliable access needed to perform high-quality audits today while preparing for greater automation tomorrow. A sound toolchain, properly governed, transforms the audit function from a reactive compliance mechanism into a proactive, data-empowered partner in organizational assurance.

Mid-year Replan Triggers and Change Control

An annual audit plan is never static; it is a snapshot of risk at a particular moment in time. As the year unfolds, business conditions, technology landscapes, and regulatory expectations inevitably evolve. To remain credible, the audit function must establish clear triggers and disciplined processes for revisiting and updating the plan mid-year. This ensures that audit coverage stays aligned with actual enterprise risk rather than the assumptions that existed when the plan was first approved. A mature replanning process blends agility with control—quick enough to react to emerging threats, yet formal enough to maintain governance and transparency.

The first category of replan triggers arises from material security or operational incidents. A major data breach, system outage, or insider misuse event can instantly reshape the risk profile of a domain and warrant immediate assurance attention. Even when management leads the post-incident investigation, the audit function has a duty to independently assess the adequacy of controls, root-cause analysis, and remediation follow-through. These situations often result in ad hoc or expedited audits that supplement the existing plan. To prevent over-reaction, the audit charter should define thresholds for when an incident justifies plan modification—typically tied to financial impact, regulatory exposure, or strategic relevance. Below those thresholds, incident learnings can inform future scoping rather than immediate reallocation.

Regulatory or legal developments are the second major replan driver. New privacy laws, sector-specific mandates, or enforcement actions can quickly render an existing plan obsolete. For example, if a new state privacy regulation introduces expanded consumer data rights or reporting obligations, previously lower-priority audits of data inventory and consent mechanisms may need to move forward in the calendar. Likewise, emerging cybersecurity requirements for critical infrastructure can shift focus toward operational technology or supplier assurance. The audit team must maintain active horizon scanning for upcoming compliance changes and document when such developments trigger re-prioritization. Doing so not only aligns coverage with regulatory timelines but also demonstrates to oversight bodies that audit decisions are grounded in external context, not arbitrary preference.

Architecture shifts and strategic technology transformations are another form of trigger. Cloud migrations, implementation of zero-trust architectures, or adoption of AI-driven analytics can introduce entirely new risk domains. These changes often occur mid-year, outside the original planning horizon. When they do, the audit function should perform a structured impact analysis to determine whether the change constitutes a new audit unit, an expansion of existing scope, or simply an adjustment to timing. Because architecture transformations usually unfold over multiple quarters, maintaining flexibility is essential; a partial audit early in the program may transition into a full design and effectiveness review once deployment stabilizes. Explicit documentation of this staged approach helps manage stakeholder expectations and preserves the integrity of coverage reporting.

Corporate actions—acquisitions, divestitures, or mergers—represent some of the most disruptive replan triggers. The integration of a newly acquired entity introduces unfamiliar systems, control cultures, and inherited risks that the original plan could not anticipate. Conversely, divestitures may remove entire segments of previously planned work. Each event demands rapid assessment of risk exposure, resource implications, and timing adjustments. The audit team must determine whether to perform pre-integration due diligence reviews, parallel control testing, or post-integration assurance depending on transaction timelines. Because such events can materially alter enterprise risk, escalation to the Audit Committee is typically required before modifying the approved plan.

A lightweight yet controlled change process is essential to manage these triggers without devolving into ad hoc decision-making. Every proposed plan adjustment should begin with an impact analysis that evaluates how the change affects coverage, resource allocation, and risk balance across domains. This analysis should be concise—typically one or two pages—summarizing the rationale, the affected audit units, and the proposed timing adjustments. Once drafted, it should be reviewed by the Chief Audit Executive or equivalent authority, who determines whether formal Audit Committee approval is required based on predefined thresholds. Material additions, deletions, or re-prioritizations generally require committee approval, while minor timing shifts can be approved internally.

The concept of version control, though often associated with software, applies equally to audit planning. Every approved modification must generate a new, versioned copy of the plan with an effective date and record of approvals. Versioning ensures that historical context is preserved—stakeholders can see how and why the plan evolved over the year. This also supports annual reporting, allowing the audit function to distinguish between planned and unplanned work when explaining deviations from the original schedule. Maintaining a single authoritative plan repository, typically within the GRC system, prevents confusion and ensures everyone is working from the same version of truth.

Escalation thresholds should be explicitly defined within the audit methodology. A plan change that shifts more than a certain percentage of total hours, adds or removes entire audit domains, or alters coverage of top enterprise risks should trigger formal Audit Committee notification. Likewise, any adjustment resulting from an external regulator's directive must be disclosed, regardless of scope size. These thresholds create transparency and prevent the perception of arbitrary mid-year pivots. By codifying escalation rules, the audit function protects its independence and builds trust with governance bodies, demonstrating that replanning is driven by objective criteria rather than convenience or pressure.

Carry-over engagements and deferrals must also be documented within the replanning framework. When an engagement cannot be completed due to resourcing constraints, environmental dependencies, or management unavailability, it should be reclassified rather than quietly dropped. The new plan should clearly indicate whether the work is deferred to the next cycle, replaced by alternative coverage, or canceled with rationale. Documenting these decisions ensures continuity and accountability. It also allows the audit committee to evaluate whether recurring deferrals indicate structural capacity issues or shifting organizational priorities that require attention.

Quality Assurance and External Review

A mature cybersecurity audit program must hold itself to the same standards of rigor and accountability that it demands of others. Quality assurance is the mechanism that ensures this discipline—verifying that audit work is consistent, conclusions are defensible, and the overall methodology remains fit for purpose as the environment evolves. A strong QA framework does not merely look backward at finished reports; it continuously tests the health of the audit function itself. It provides leadership with confidence that every engagement, regardless of who performed it, reflects the same professional standards, analytical depth, and ethical integrity expected from a world-class audit organization.

At the heart of any QA program lies the principle of consistency. Different teams or regional offices may execute audits across varied technologies and business lines, yet their work should converge on the same quality benchmarks. To achieve this, periodic workpaper reviews are conducted to assess documentation completeness, testing sufficiency, and the clarity of evidence-to-conclusion linkages. These reviews validate that conclusions are supported by verifiable data and that risk ratings—whether "high," "medium," or "low"—are applied uniformly across the function. Random sampling of completed audits can help detect drift in methodology or interpretation, while targeted reviews of complex engagements, such as cloud architecture or OT/ICS controls, confirm that specialist work still aligns with enterprise standards.

Quality assurance must also address the calibration of judgment. Even with standardized templates and procedures, human interpretation introduces variation. One auditor's "significant deficiency" might be another's "moderate gap" without shared benchmarks. Rating consistency checks mitigate this by comparing findings across engagements and examining how similar control failures are categorized. Calibration sessions, where audit leads jointly review anonymized cases, can surface biases and align thresholds for materiality and residual risk. The goal is not to eliminate individual judgment but to ensure that judgment operates within predictable, documented parameters. When management or regulators read two audit reports from different teams, they should see consistent logic, terminology, and proportionality in conclusions.

A well-governed QA program must include a structured process for periodic internal assessments. These reviews examine adherence to the audit methodology, compliance with professional standards, and the effectiveness of supervisory review layers. Internal QA teams operate independently from engagement execution and report directly to the Chief Audit Executive or equivalent leader to preserve objectivity. Their work focuses on whether established policies—such as scoping documentation, evidence retention, and sign-off protocols—are being followed in practice. Findings from internal QA assessments should be formalized, tracked, and subject to the same closure discipline as operational audit issues. By treating QA results as actionable improvement items, the audit function demonstrates continuous self-accountability.

External or peer reviews extend quality assurance beyond the organization's own perspective. Engaging external auditors or participating in peer review programs allows the function to benchmark itself against industry standards and leading practices. These reviews typically occur on a recurring cycle—every three to five years—and assess the adequacy of the audit methodology, staffing competence, and governance alignment. External reviewers can identify blind spots that internal teams may miss, such as over-reliance on manual testing, insufficient data analytics, or lagging adoption of risk-based approaches. More importantly, an independent opinion provides the audit committee and executive leadership with assurance that the function remains credible and compliant with professional expectations.

The feedback loop from QA and external review into the broader audit ecosystem is where real improvement occurs. Results from quality assessments should directly inform training priorities, methodology updates, and tool enhancements. If repeated QA findings show inconsistent evidence quality in cloud audits, targeted training in cloud control testing becomes a development requirement. If external reviewers highlight deficiencies in analytics governance, the audit methodology should be revised to codify stronger validation or version control requirements. These feedback loops prevent the QA function from becoming a static checkpoint; instead, it becomes an engine for institutional learning and maturity.

QA insights should also inform the periodic refresh of audit templates, checklists, and guidance materials. As audit teams experiment with new tools or testing techniques, lessons learned should be harvested and codified into standard workpapers or reference guides. This approach promotes efficiency while preserving flexibility—teams can innovate locally, but successful methods are quickly shared globally. Maintaining this balance between standardization and adaptability is one of the hallmarks of a high-performing audit function. It ensures that innovation strengthens quality rather than fragmenting it.

While ethics and independence are foundational to quality, those themes remain governed separately under the professional standards and are discussed comprehensively in Chapter 5. Within the QA context, independence primarily means ensuring reviewers do not assess work in which they participated and that feedback mechanisms encourage transparency without fear of reprisal. Constructive critique must be seen as a path to excellence, not as punishment. When auditors trust the QA process, they engage more openly, share challenges, and adopt corrective actions willingly. This culture of improvement sustains quality far more effectively than compliance enforcement alone.

Modern QA programs also leverage technology to enhance consistency and insight. Automated sampling tools can select engagements for review based on risk factors or randomly within defined strata. Analytics dashboards can track recurring QA findings across teams, spotlighting where targeted coaching or process refinement is needed. Integration of QA metrics into performance management ensures that individual accountability aligns with collective quality goals. Over time, the accumulation of QA data provides a valuable trend line—showing how the function's maturity progresses and where future investments in training or tooling will yield the greatest return.

Documentation and transparency complete the quality assurance framework. Every QA review, whether internal or external, must produce a formal report that captures scope, criteria, findings, and management responses. These reports should be retained according to evidence policies and summarized for the audit committee to demonstrate oversight of the function itself. Tracking corrective actions to closure closes the loop and ensures that lessons are not lost between review cycles. By institutionalizing this documentation, the audit function builds a continuous record of improvement, which becomes a powerful narrative of accountability and growth.

Maturity Road map and Outcome Measures

An effective cybersecurity audit program does not merely execute annual plans—it evolves deliberately through a defined maturity road map. A 1–3 year road map provides the structure for this evolution, transforming the audit function from a compliance-driven activity into a strategic value partner. The road map articulates clear milestones across people, process, and technology dimensions, allowing progress to be measured in tangible outcomes rather than good intentions.

Table 22.3 Maturity road map milestones and outcome measures.

Year	Milestone	Target metric	Stakeholder value signal	Method to verify
Year 1	Increase coverage breadth	Top risks covered 90	Higher exec satisfaction	Dashboard review
Year 1	Reduce cycle time	Fieldwork days down 10	Improved audit predictability	QA sampling
Year 2	Expand automation use	Audits with analytics 60	Stronger insight delivery	Tool utilization log
Year 2	Lower repeat findings	Repeat down 25	Visible risk reduction	Issue trending report
Year 3	Continuous monitoring uplift	Key domains monitored	Timely risk signals	Analytics runbook
Year 3	Method calibration strength	Consistent ratings	Greater trust in severity	QA rating study

Its purpose is not perfection but direction—to ensure each audit cycle moves the function closer to a more integrated, efficient, and insightful state of practice. Table 22.3 presents a three year progression of milestones targets and verification methods tied to stakeholder value.

The starting point for any road map is an honest assessment of current capability. Using frameworks such as internal maturity models or established standards for assurance functions, the audit team identifies where it stands on dimensions like risk alignment, automation, analytics integration, and stakeholder engagement. This baseline establishes the "as-is" condition and clarifies what the "to-be" state looks like in one, two, and three years. Milestones might include increasing coverage breadth across critical systems, introducing automated evidence collection, shortening audit cycle times, or reducing repeat findings by a specified percentage. Each milestone must be specific, measurable, and achievable within the planning horizon—vague aspirations cannot drive improvement.

Coverage breadth represents one of the first and most visible maturity levers. In year one, the road map may focus on ensuring all top enterprise risks and data classes are represented within the audit universe. By year two, emphasis might shift toward cross-domain reviews that assess control interactions between IT, security, and business operations. By year three, the function could target full coverage across digital transformation initiatives such as cloud, AI, or OT environments, ensuring that assurance keeps pace with innovation. Tracking progress requires quantifiable indicators—percentage of risk domains covered, proportion of systems tested, or number of business processes assessed against defined control frameworks.

Automation adoption is another cornerstone of the road map. Initial goals often focus on integrating analytics tools into manual processes—replacing sample-based testing with data-driven review of entire populations. In subsequent years, automation can expand to continuous monitoring scripts, exception dashboards, and AI-assisted evidence validation. The road map should specify adoption metrics such as percentage of audits leveraging automated controls testing, number of analytics routines operationalized, or reduction in manual data-handling time. These milestones align directly with efficiency and assurance quality, enabling the audit team to provide faster insights without compromising rigor.

Cycle time targets bring operational discipline to the maturity journey. Shorter audit cycles indicate not only efficiency but responsiveness—evidence that the function can deliver assurance at the speed of risk. The road map might set phased targets: for example, a 10% reduction in average fieldwork duration in year one, a 20% reduction in year two through workflow automation, and full real-time status dashboards by year three. These targets drive internal process improvements such as streamlined documentation templates, better resource scheduling, and automated report generation. Over time, improved cycle times build stakeholder trust by demonstrating that the audit function can meet business tempo without sacrificing depth or quality.

Reducing repeat findings is a powerful indicator of control maturity and audit effectiveness. The road map should include explicit targets—perhaps a 25% reduction in repeated deficiencies by year two—supported by initiatives such as enhanced root cause analysis, improved issue tracking, and follow-up audits that measure sustained remediation. Achieving these outcomes demonstrates that the audit function's work is driving genuine organizational improvement rather than simply identifying recurring weaknesses. It also allows audit leadership to quantify value in terms that resonate with executives: fewer unresolved risks, more predictable control environments, and stronger governance assurance.

To ensure these milestones remain meaningful, outcome metrics must connect directly to stakeholder value. Executive satisfaction, measured through postaudit surveys or annual stakeholder interviews, gauges how well the audit function's insights support decision-making and strategic alignment. Audit predictability—how closely execution aligns with planned scope, timing, and communication—reflects operational reliability, a key aspect of trust with management. Risk reduction signals, such as declining severity in enterprise risk ratings or improvements in control self-assessment scores, offer tangible proof that audit work is improving the organization's security posture. Each metric must be defined with clear collection methods, ownership, and reporting cadence to maintain accountability.

Stakeholder feedback should not be treated as a formality but as a guiding compass for road map evolution. Regular feedback sessions with executives, the audit committee, and process owners help calibrate focus areas and identify where audit insights deliver the greatest perceived value. If leadership consistently praises risk communication but cites delays in reporting, the road map should prioritize timeliness improvements. If business units express appreciation for collaborative findings workshops, expanding that practice could become a formal milestone. Over time, these feedback loops make the road map more than a technical artifact—they turn it into a living agreement between the audit function and its stakeholders about what "value" truly means.

Linking the road map to annual planning closes the maturity loop. Each year's audit plan should explicitly reference the road map deltas—the specific areas where the function aims to advance capability. For instance, if the road map calls for expanding analytics coverage from 30% to 60% of engagements, the next plan should show which audits will adopt those tools. If automation adoption or cycle time improvements are behind schedule, the plan should allocate time for process optimization or targeted training. This integration ensures that maturity development is not a side project but a central component of how the function operates and measures success.

Transparency in measuring outcomes reinforces accountability. Dashboards summarizing road map progress, such as trend lines for repeat findings, automation utilization, and stakeholder satisfaction scores, should be shared regularly with leadership. Visualizing this data highlights both achievements and areas needing additional investment. It also sends a clear message: the audit function measures its own performance with the same discipline it applies to the organization it audits. This culture of measurement and self-improvement differentiates mature audit teams from merely compliant ones.

Conclusion

Mastering the discipline of annual audit planning elevates cybersecurity assurance from a reactive compliance exercise to a proactive instrument of governance. When risk coverage, resource allocation, and quality controls are thoughtfully aligned, the audit function becomes a living system that mirrors the organization's evolving threat surface. This capability allows leadership to see not just where risks exist, but how effectively they are being managed—and how quickly the enterprise can adapt when circumstances change. Strategic planning is therefore not administrative overhead; it is the foundation of trust between auditors, executives, and regulators.

For AI-driven and digitally transformed enterprises, this rigor becomes even more vital. Automated systems, cloud-native architectures, and machine learning models introduce risks that shift faster than traditional audit cycles. A mature planning framework—with defined triggers, skilled teams, and data-enabled tooling—gives the audit function the agility to pursue emerging risks without sacrificing consistency or independence. It reinforces the auditor's role as both a guardian of integrity and an advisor on responsible AI assurance, where ethics, transparency, and control design converge.

With these foundations in place, cybersecurity auditors are better equipped to deliver measurable value: reducing uncertainty, accelerating readiness, and strengthening confidence in the organization's defense posture. Each plan revision, quality review, and maturity milestone adds resilience to the system as a whole. While technologies and frameworks will continue to evolve, the principles of structured, risk-based planning remain constant—the anchor that ensures assurance keeps pace with innovation and continues to protect the enterprise in an increasingly intelligent and interconnected world.

Auditor Recommendations

1. **Build a Structured Risk-based Coverage Model:** Establish a clear process for translating enterprise risks, material processes, and sensitive data classes into defined audit units. Use coverage heatmaps to visualize where assurance is most needed, ensuring each unit has an appropriate depth and frequency based on control maturity and prior results. This structured model allows your audit program to remain risk-driven, traceable, and defensible in executive and regulatory discussions.
2. **Align Audit Depth and Cadence to Control Maturity:** Avoid relying solely on uniform annual coverage schedules that ignore risk variability. Instead, adjust audit depth and timing based on control reliability, environmental change, and historical performance. High-risk or immature areas should receive both design and effectiveness testing, while mature, well-performing domains may focus on design validation. This approach ensures resources are applied proportionally to risk exposure.
3. **Integrate Incident and Trend Data into Planning:** Incorporate lessons from recent incidents, near misses, and performance metrics—such as repeat findings or closure delays—into your annual planning process. Use this data to prioritize areas requiring deeper review or earlier reengagement. Treat these inputs as leading indicators of where systemic issues persist, converting operational evidence into actionable audit direction.

4. **Balance Internal Expertise with Specialist Support:** Map each planned engagement to the skills it requires, such as cloud, DevSecOps, OT/ICS, or AI auditing capabilities. Determine where internal auditors can lead and where co-sourced experts are needed, maintaining strict independence safeguards. This balance ensures technical accuracy while preserving credibility and control over the assurance narrative.
5. **Invest in Continuous Team Development:** Create an intentional training and credentialing road map aligned with upcoming audit priorities. Encourage auditors to pursue advanced certifications, attend specialized workshops, and engage in cross-domain learning between IT, operations, and data analytics. Strengthening technical depth before engagements begin ensures the team delivers higher-quality assessments and more insightful recommendations.
6. **Establish Robust Tooling and Evidence Governance:** Maintain a minimum toolchain consisting of a GRC or workpaper system, secure evidence repository, and controlled data access pathways. Define clear access, retention, and provenance standards to protect audit integrity and confidentiality. Properly governed tools not only enhance efficiency but also ensure audit artifacts withstand scrutiny during reviews or investigations.
7. **Implement Defined Triggers for Mid-year Replanning:** Create explicit criteria for when the annual plan must be revisited—such as major incidents, new regulatory requirements, architectural shifts, or corporate acquisitions. Establish a lightweight but disciplined change control process with documented impact analyses, versioned plan updates, and clear escalation thresholds. This ensures agility without compromising governance or transparency.
8. **Embed Quality Assurance as a Continuous Function:** Develop a formal QA program that periodically reviews workpapers, tests rating consistency, and benchmarks adherence to the audit methodology. Include periodic peer or external reviews to validate methodological soundness and identify improvement opportunities. Treat QA results as living feedback that shapes training priorities, tool updates, and methodology refinements.
9. **Measure Maturity Progress Through Defined Outcomes:** Use a structured road map with clear milestones—such as increased automation use, reduced repeat findings, or improved cycle times—to assess progress over a one to three years horizon. Tie outcome measures to stakeholder value indicators like executive satisfaction, audit predictability, and measurable risk reduction. This outcome-based approach transforms the audit function from reactive assurance to strategic enablement.
10. **Maintain Agility Without Losing Discipline:** Design your audit program to adapt to emerging risks while preserving methodological consistency and independence. Use version control, documentation, and escalation protocols to ensure transparency when priorities shift midstream. A disciplined but flexible structure allows the audit function to stay aligned with evolving enterprise strategy and technology trends while maintaining professional rigor.

Chapter Questions

1. Which outcome best describes the purpose of a coverage heatmap in risk-based planning?
   A. Listing every control mapped to a single policy
   B. Ranking auditors by productivity across engagements
   C. Visualizing prioritized audit units derived from enterprise risks, material processes, and sensitive data classes
   D. Tracking training hours and certifications by team member

2. What should primarily determine audit cadence for each domain?
   A. The number of active projects in the PMO
   B. The size of last year's audit report
   C. The total number of controls in the library
   D. Risk velocity, business change, and control durability

3. Which set represents canonical inputs that shape the annual audit plan?
   A. Travel budgets, remote-work policies, and office seating charts
   B. Recent incidents/near misses, trend metrics, strategy shifts, and upcoming regulatory deadlines
   C. Social media analytics, marketing conversions, and brand mentions
   D. Laptop refresh schedules, printer inventory, and cafeteria vendor contracts

4. Which independence safeguard is essential when using co-sourced specialists?
   A. External specialists report functionally to audit leadership rather than management being audited
   B. Audited managers preapprove all specialist workpapers before testing
   C. Specialists administer the evidence repository to speed uploads
   D. Specialists publish final ratings without internal review

5. Which minimum toolchain best enables execution of the plan?
   A. Shared email folders, spreadsheets, and chat logs
   B. Ticketing portal, HR system, and presentation software
   C. GRC/workpaper system, secure evidence repository, controlled data access pathways, and analytics platform
   D. Finance ledger, expense tracker, and travel booking site

6. What is a cornerstone of lightweight change control for mid-year plan updates?
   A. Skipping documentation to accelerate decisions
   B. Maintaining a versioned plan with effective dates and approval records
   C. Allowing any auditor to reprioritize items informally
   D. Collapsing all changes into the next annual cycle

7. Which scenario most clearly warrants a mid-year replan?
   A. A routine vendor patch delivered on schedule
   B. A minor UI change to an internal dashboard
   C. A team offsite moved to a later month
   D. A material incident, a new law with near-term deadlines, a major architecture shift, or an acquisition/divestiture

8. What is the primary purpose of rating consistency checks in the QA program?
   - **A.** Calibrating severity so similar control failures receive comparable ratings across teams
   - **B.** Reducing the word count of executive summaries
   - **C.** Replacing peer review with automated grammar checks
   - **D.** Ensuring all findings default to "medium"

9. Which outcome measures most directly tie the maturity road map to stakeholder value?
   - **A.** Number of meetings per audit and average email response time
   - **B.** Executive satisfaction, audit predictability, and risk-reduction signals alongside milestones like automation adoption and fewer repeat findings
   - **C.** Count of slide templates and graphics used per report
   - **D.** Volume of internal newsletters sent by the audit team

10. What is the primary reason to reserve contingency capacity in the annual plan?
    - **A.** To maintain agility for ad hoc reviews or incident-driven work without disrupting core coverage
    - **B.** To reduce the number of planned audits regardless of risk
    - **C.** To eliminate the need for replanning triggers altogether
    - **D.** To allow management to reassign auditors freely during peak periods

Chapter Answers

These are the answers for the chapter quizzes.

Chapter 1

1. Correct Answer: C. To provide independent assurance on control design and operating effectiveness. Explanation: The third line's mandate is to deliver objective assurance rather than operate or oversee controls. This preserves independence from the first and second lines.

2. Correct Answer: A. Unimpeded access to systems, records, personnel, and time-bound escalation to the audit committee. Explanation: Credible assurance depends on comprehensive access and clear escalation when access is obstructed. The charter must codify these rights to make independence actionable.

3. Correct Answer: D. Advisory input cannot later be self-reviewed by those who designed the control. Explanation: Self-review is a primary threat to independence when auditors later assess work they helped design. Safeguards such as recusal or separate reviewers are required to avoid this conflict.

4. Correct Answer: B. Concise quarterly updates with off-cycle notification for material issues. Explanation: The board needs a disciplined cadence for oversight and the ability to hear about material risks promptly. This balance supports challenge and direction without operational micromanagement.

5. Correct Answer: C. Objective, verifiable criteria traceable to policy and mapped to procedures. Explanation: Standards must be testable and connected upward to policy and downward to procedures and evidence. Vague or static requirements provide little assurance value.

6. Correct Answer: A. Unique ID, objective, owner/operator, frequency, evidence location, and linked risks. Explanation: These fields enable traceability, accountability, and efficient evidence retrieval for assurance. They also support risk-based planning by linking controls to the risks they mitigate.

7. Correct Answer: D. Unique ID, risk statement, owner, likelihood/impact, inherent/residual ratings, linked controls, last review date. Explanation: This metadata makes the register decision-ready and aligns accountability with authority. It also supports reassessment as circumstances evolve.

8. Correct Answer: B. Use defined change triggers so risk or control updates prompt reassessment of linked records. Explanation: Synchronization requires governance mechanics, not ad hoc updates. Triggers and version history keep coverage aligned with changing exposure.

9. Correct Answer: C. Explicit expiry dates with renewals requiring fresh justification and risk reassessment. Explanation: Time-bound approvals prevent exception sprawl and normalize reassessment. Auto-renewals undermine governance discipline and obscure residual risk.

10. Correct Answer: A. Plan read-only or cloned data access and use metadata, sampling, or attestations to preserve evidence sufficiency. Explanation: These approaches respect privilege and privacy while maintaining reasonable assurance. They align with audit's need for sufficient, appropriate evidence without disrupting operations.

Chapter 2

1. Correct Answer: A. To anchor conclusions to explicit criteria and align with management's assertions. Explanation: Frameworks provide the yardstick for assurance and tie testing to what management claims about the environment. This keeps conclusions comparable, defensible, and free of personal preferences.

2. Correct Answer: B. Evaluating whether the chosen criteria are suitable for the subject matter. Explanation: Suitability requires criteria to be relevant, complete, measurable, and neutral for the objectives at hand. Auditors assess this before designing procedures to ensure a defensible engagement.

3. Correct Answer: C. To harmonize overlapping requirements into single canonical controls mapped across regimes. Explanation: A common control set eliminates duplication by mapping multiple framework requirements to one authoritative control statement. This enables consistent ownership, evidence, and reuse across obligations.

4. Correct Answer: D. The framework name and version with the exact source control reference ID. Explanation: Precise source references are essential to prove how a common control satisfies external requirements. This metadata underpins reliable traceability and reporting by framework.

5. Correct Answer: A. To prevent auditors from opining on components not intended to be in scope. Explanation: Clear boundaries avoid unintended coverage of entities, systems, or data flows and ensure evidence collection aligns with the assertion. This discipline is vital in complex environments with shared services and shadow IT.

6. Correct Answer: B. Demonstrating objective-level alignment that achieves the same risk outcome. Explanation: Equivalency is about intent, not identical wording, and must meet the same assurance strength. Sufficiency is then judged by rigor, frequency, and evidence.

7. Correct Answer: C. Log the gap with justification, identify affected requirements, and plan remediation or risk acceptance. Explanation: Residual gaps are governance items that require transparent documentation and accountable treatment. They show where enhancements or accepted risks remain.

8. Correct Answer: D. Freshness rules, provenance documentation, and versioning with change history. Explanation: These governance elements keep evidence current, reproducible, and tamper-evident for reuse across audits. They also support consistent linkage to the common control set.

9. Correct Answer: A. They specify customer responsibilities that must be implemented for the provider's controls to be effective. Explanation: CUECs define what the user entity must do to complete the control objective when relying on a provider's SOC report. Without implementing CUECs, reliance becomes conditional or invalid.

10. Correct Answer: B. Formal exception documentation with rationale, risk impact, governance approval, and an expiration or review date. Explanation: Deviations must be justified, time-bound, and approved at the proper level to prevent permanent workarounds. This ensures compensating controls deliver equivalent protection and remain under oversight.

Chapter 3

1. Correct Answer: C. Threat → Vulnerability → Scenario → Impact. Explanation: This sequence ties an actor or condition to a weakness, then to a credible path to loss, and finally to business consequences. It provides a disciplined, auditable chain from cause to effect.

2. Correct Answer: D. Business context including process criticality, data sensitivity, and legal exposure. Explanation: Materiality in security is contextual and must reflect what actually matters to the enterprise. Aligning thresholds to business drivers prevents misprioritization of low-impact technical issues.

3. Correct Answer: B. They block or constrain actions before harm and are judged by universal, consistent enforcement. Explanation: Preventive controls aim to eliminate or reduce the opportunity for exploitation, so enforceability and coverage are key assurance criteria. Their effectiveness is measured by resistance to bypass and consistency under load.

4. Correct Answer: A. System-generated logs that are time-stamped, tamper-evident, and reproducible. Explanation: Such artifacts provide the most durable, re-performable evidence of control operation. They minimize reliance on human memory and reduce the risk of post hoc alteration.

5. Correct Answer: C. When the decision can be expressed as deterministic policy using attributes available at enforcement time. Explanation: Deterministic, attribute-driven decisions scale reliably and reduce discretion-driven error. Continuous enforcement narrows exposure windows in high-velocity environments.

6. Correct Answer: B. When event frequency is low, potential impact is bounded, and human judgment adds value. Explanation: In these cases, manual review can be efficient and appropriately risk-aligned. The key is strong documentation, competency, and defined cadence to keep the control reliable.

7. Correct Answer: A. Risk → Control Objective → Control Owner → Evidence Location. Explanation: This chain anchors why a control exists, what it intends to achieve, who is accountable, and where proof resides. Each link must be explicit and durable to support assurance work over time.

8. Correct Answer: D. "Reviewed for alignment with access governance policy; design appears consistent pending implementation verification." Explanation: The phrasing provides advisory input without assuming ownership or granting approval. It preserves independence by avoiding prescriptive configuration details.

9. Correct Answer: C. Documented impact assessment linking the change to affected control objectives and updates to relevant registers. Explanation: Governance requires that changes be evaluated for their effect on control intent and risk coverage. Traceable updates to risk and control records demonstrate disciplined oversight.

10. Correct Answer: A. Approval history, RACI, effective dates, versioning, and resolvable links to procedures and evidence with stable IDs. Explanation: These elements create a trustworthy, time-anchored record that auditors can follow and re-perform. Stable identifiers and version history prevent ambiguity as teams and tools change.

Chapter 4

1. Correct Answer: C. Provenance. Explanation: Provenance records the lineage of evidence from original capture through each transformation, tool, and location. This traceability allows reviewers to reproduce the pipeline and confirm that meaning and integrity were preserved.

2. Correct Answer: C. Generating and validating a cryptographic hash at transfer. Explanation: Hash validation provides a tamper-evident check that the artifact remains unchanged across handoffs. It complements timestamps and handler records to demonstrate unbroken integrity.

3. Correct Answer: A. Export from the system of record using documented queries and reconcile counts to authoritative totals. Explanation: Pulling from the authoritative source with documented logic and reconciliation proves both origin and completeness. This method is reproducible and minimizes disputes about scope or omissions.

4. Correct Answer: B. When distinct subgroups exhibit different characteristics or risk profiles. Explanation: Stratification ensures each meaningful segment is adequately represented, improving coverage and efficiency. It targets variability that random sampling might underrepresent.

5. Correct Answer: D. Adjusting selection probabilities based on inherent or residual risk. Explanation: Risk-weighted sampling concentrates testing where failure would have the greatest impact, aligning effort with exposure. The weighting rationale must be documented to remain defensible.

6. Correct Answer: B. Whether the control functioned consistently over the defined period. Explanation: Operating effectiveness focuses on execution over time—frequency, timing, roles, and evidence of performance. A control can be well-designed yet ineffective if it is skipped or performed late.

7. Correct Answer: D. When inspection cannot determine if the control would reach the correct decision from the same inputs. Explanation: Re-performance independently applies the documented rules to original inputs to verify the outcome. It resolves ambiguity about actual decision logic or thresholds.

8. Correct Answer: C. Validating that input datasets are complete and accurate. Explanation: Full-population tests only deliver reliable assurance if the underlying data reflect the true universe. Otherwise, comprehensive analytics can provide false confidence.

9. Correct Answer: A. Verify the legacy control up to the cut-over date and the successor control immediately after, confirming continuous coverage. Explanation: Dual verification prevents a gap in control coverage during transition. Evidence should anchor the exact cut-over date and show both sides operated as intended.

10. Correct Answer: B. Documented, reproducible steps and preserved artifacts that enable an independent reviewer to re-perform the test and reach the same conclusion. Explanation: Reviewability hinges on another qualified professional being able to follow the same procedures and evidence to the same result. Clear steps, identifiers, and preserved scripts or queries make that possible.

Chapter 5

1. Correct Answer: A. A neutral posture that withholds judgment until sufficient, appropriate evidence is gathered. Explanation: Professional skepticism is a disciplined neutrality toward claims until evidence supports a conclusion. It is distinct from cynicism or deference and resists premature closure.

2. Correct Answer: C. Self-review threat. Explanation: Assessing work you previously designed or configured creates a direct conflict because you would be reviewing your own prior judgments. This undermines independence in both fact and appearance.

3. Correct Answer: C. Preserving images with tamper-evident controls and documented chain of custody in an authorized lab. Explanation: Highly sensitive artifacts require controlled handling that ensures integrity and traceability. Tamper-evident storage and chain-of-custody documentation satisfy those requirements.

4. Correct Answer: B. Pressure to alter conclusions without evidence. Explanation: Requests to change ratings based on optics rather than new, probative evidence indicate influence rather than factual dispute. Such pressure should be declined and documented through governance channels.

5. Correct Answer: D. When access is restricted or evidence defects are material to reliance and scope expansion is impractical. Explanation: A qualification is warranted when a limitation materially affects assurance and cannot be resolved within the engagement. It transparently communicates residual uncertainty to readers.

6. Correct Answer: A. Recording applied criteria, alternatives considered and rejected, rationale for the decision, and reviewer sign-offs with dated cross-references. Explanation: Comprehensive, dated documentation allows another qualified auditor to reconstruct the reasoning path. Cross-references tie judgments to specific evidence and approvals.

7. Correct Answer: A. Restate criteria and reestimate severity from scratch after initial fieldwork using only current evidence. Explanation: Reanchoring interrupts the influence of prior conclusions by forcing evaluation against present facts. This practice reduces the risk of carrying forward outdated judgments.

8. Correct Answer: C. Using dedicated individual accounts with multifactor authentication and time-bound, task-specific permissions. Explanation: Least privilege requires identifiable, constrained access aligned to specific tasks and durations. Shared or overly broad rights create accountability gaps and unnecessary exposure.

9. Correct Answer: D. Record each delay with its impact and escalate through governance when patterns persist. Explanation: Contemporaneous documentation and formal escalation convert logistical friction into a traceable governance issue. This preserves evidence sufficiency and the audit's independence.

10. Correct Answer: B. Perform alternative procedures that corroborate the same assertion via independent sources such as endpoint artifacts or change records. Explanation: Alternative procedures test the same control outcome using different, independent evidence when primary sources are unavailable or unreliable. This maintains assurance quality without introducing new scope.

Chapter 6

1. Correct Answer: C. Authoritative events from HRIS and contractor systems. Explanation: These systems are the sources of truth for workforce status and drive joiner, mover, and leaver events. Aligning access timing to these events ensures accounts reflect real employment changes and reduces ghost or stale access.

2. Correct Answer: B. FIDO2/WebAuthn security keys or platform passkeys. Explanation: These methods are phishing-resistant and bind authentication to the device and origin. They provide stronger assurance than OTPs delivered over vulnerable channels like SMS or email.

3. Correct Answer: C. Token lifetimes and signature validation parameters. Explanation: Federation trust is enforced through how tokens are issued, signed, validated, and expired. Properly configured token policies and signature verification determine what assertions are accepted across boundaries.

4. Correct Answer: D. Triggering real-time alerts on use, conducting immediate post-use review, and rotating credentials. Explanation: Break-glass accounts must be tightly controlled, monitored, and reset after any use to prevent persistence of risk. This preserves emergency capability without creating a shadow access path.

5. Correct Answer: A. Reduce standing privilege by granting time-bound rights tied to an approved purpose. Explanation: Just-in-time elevation issues only the minimum necessary access for a limited duration and revokes it automatically. This sharply lowers exposure to misuse and lateral movement.

6. Correct Answer: B. Vaulting credentials and enforcing rotation or short-lived tokens. Explanation: Nonhuman identities cannot use interactive MFA, so assurance relies on secret minimization, secure storage, and frequent rotation. Vault integration and ephemeral credentials reduce the risk of long-lived compromise.

7. Correct Answer: C. Session recordings or command transcripts linked to approved tickets. Explanation: This creates a verifiable chain from request to execution, showing what was done, by whom, and under what authorization. Such artifacts provide the strongest basis for accountability and forensic review.

8. Correct Answer: D. Maintaining an explicit mapping of canonical HRIS IDs to each system's account identifiers. Explanation: Consistent identifier mapping allows reliable joins across HRIS, IdP, PAM, and target logs despite naming variations. It prevents false correlations and supports reproducible audit evidence.

9. Correct Answer: A. Adjust challenges based on contextual risk while minimizing user friction. Explanation: Risk-based access evaluates signals like device posture, location, and behavior to trigger step-up challenges only when warranted. This preserves usability for low-risk activity while strengthening defenses for high-risk events.

10. Correct Answer: B. Automatic rotation or invalidation of the credential before any future issuance. Explanation: Rotation at check-in ensures that previously issued secrets are unusable, eliminating reuse risk. It is a core assurance behavior of PAM vaulting and check-out workflows.

Chapter 7

1. Correct Answer: C. Comparing routing tables and ACL exports to approved zone diagrams. Explanation: Validating segmentation requires matching the implemented paths and rules to the intended zone relationships. Routing and ACL evidence reveal real traffic permissions, exposing drift that diagrams alone cannot show.

2. Correct Answer: A. Deny-by-default on inter-zone traffic with narrowly scoped allow rules. Explanation: A default-deny posture enforces least privilege and prevents unintended pathways between zones. Narrow allow rules ensure only justified, documented flows are permitted.

3. Correct Answer: C. Preventing data exfiltration and command-and-control communications. Explanation: Egress controls limit where internal systems can connect, cutting off common exfiltration and C2 paths. By restricting outbound destinations, they reduce the blast radius of compromises.

4. Correct Answer: B. Per-application access decisions based on identity and device posture. Explanation: ZTNA/SASE grants access to specific applications contingent on who the user is and the health of the device. This contrasts with legacy VPNs that often provide broad network reach once a tunnel is established.

5. Correct Answer: B. Allow only explicitly approved cloud services to go direct, with the rest enforced through inspection. Explanation: Selective split tunneling preserves performance benefits while keeping most traffic under policy enforcement. This approach reduces blind spots that full split tunnels can introduce.

6. Correct Answer: A. Constrain outbound IP/port rules to match approved domains and services enforced by DNS/proxy. Explanation: Aligning firewall egress with DNS/proxy policies closes gaps where direct-by-IP connections could bypass domain-based controls. Coordinated rules ensure all layers enforce the same intent.

7. Correct Answer: D. It returns a harmless internal address for blocked domains to expose and monitor attempted misuse. Explanation: Sinkholing prevents resolution from reaching malicious infrastructure while generating observable events. Security teams can detect and investigate those attempts using the sinkhole telemetry.

8. Correct Answer: C. Timely signature and feed updates with alert disposition and tuning records. Explanation: Fresh detection content paired with documented triage and tuning shows a living control that adapts to threats. Disposition evidence proves alerts drive investigation and improvement, not just noise.

9. Correct Answer: A. Serving as a validated, known-good reference for a specific deployment to support compliance checks and drift detection. Explanation: Golden configurations provide the benchmark against which running configs are compared for variance. They encapsulate both baseline hardening and site-specific requirements.

10. Correct Answer: D. Correlating multiple identifiers (hostname, management IP, serial/device ID) and maintaining a cross-system mapping. Explanation: No single identifier is reliable across all data sources and time. A reconciled mapping ensures inventory, configuration, and telemetry refer to the same physical or virtual device.

Chapter 8

1. Correct Answer: A. Automatic, versioned enforcement of rules and approvals. Explanation: Encoding governance as policy in code makes controls enforceable by machines and reviewable like any other change. This creates durable, auditable records of what rules were active and who approved modifications.

2. Correct Answer: B. Software Composition Analysis (SCA). Explanation: SCA maps included components and cross-references them with known vulnerabilities to expose inherited risk. It targets third-party packages, manifests, and images rather than custom source code.

3. Correct Answer: C. Whether runtime behavior and controls work under real request–response conditions. Explanation: DAST exercises running services to surface issues that only appear at execution time, such as misconfigured headers or broken auth flows. It complements static checks by validating the deployed configuration behaves as intended.

4. Correct Answer: D. At the API gateway or service mesh before requests reach services. Explanation: Centralized enforcement ensures consistent token verification and coarse access control across all services. It reduces reliance on disparate application implementations and provides uniform telemetry and rejection behavior.

5. Correct Answer: A. Ensuring payloads conform to defined contracts and rejecting malformed data early. Explanation: Schema validation guards the contract boundary, preventing malformed or unexpected inputs from reaching business logic. Enforcing schemas at gateways or service boundaries reduces attack surface and brittle client behavior.

6. Correct Answer: C. Controlling request volume per identity and returning HTTP 429 when thresholds are exceeded. Explanation: Rate limits and quotas protect availability and upstream dependencies by throttling abusive or accidental surges. Clear 429 responses and keyed metrics provide operational proof that limits are active.

7. Correct Answer: B. "Plan"/diff outputs comparing desired IaC state to live resources, plus policy evaluation reports. Explanation: Drift detection evidence ties the declared baseline to what actually exists, exposing out-of-band changes. Policy reports classify violations so owners can remediate or document approved exceptions.

8. Correct Answer: D. Authors propose changes; designated code owners approve; limited deployment identities apply to production. Explanation: This model separates design, approval, and execution, preventing unilateral production changes. Automation accounts are scoped to deploy but cannot modify governance without review.

9. Correct Answer: A. Commit or tag → build artifact digest → deployment ticket and approval records. Explanation: This linkage forms a verifiable chain of custody from source to production, including who approved the change. It enables auditors and responders to identify exactly what code and configuration were shipped.

10. Correct Answer: C. VCS/repo metadata → CI logs/artifacts → artifact registry digests → gateway/policy repos → change tickets. Explanation: These systems provide the canonical hop-to-hop lineage needed to reconstruct any production state. Each step references the previous with hashes, digests, or IDs, producing immutable, reviewable evidence.

Chapter 9

1. Correct Answer: A. The shared responsibility boundaries and the tenant boundary. Explanation: Audit scope in cloud hinges on what the customer actually controls, which is defined by shared responsibility and the tenant's boundary. These determine which configurations, identities, and logs can be tested directly versus validated via provider assurance.

2. Correct Answer: B. Service Control Policies or equivalent organization policies. Explanation: Organization-level guardrails like SCPs and organization policies impose permission ceilings across accounts to prevent privilege escalation. They filter allowable actions regardless of local role assignments, enforcing least privilege at scale.

3. Correct Answer: C. Enforce a default-deny posture with explicit, minimal allow rules. Explanation: Baseline network segmentation requires explicit allowances and blocks all other flows to reduce unintended exposure. This principle applies across VPCs/VNets using security groups, firewall rules, and controlled endpoints.

4. Correct Answer: D. Mandating encryption at rest by default and blocking public access unless explicitly approved. Explanation: Default encryption and prohibiting public access are core storage baselines that address common breach patterns. Exceptions should be documented and controlled to avoid accidental exposure.

5. Correct Answer: A. Control plane, data plane, network plane, and authentication plane. Explanation: Comprehensive visibility requires management actions, resource interactions, traffic telemetry, and identity events. Together these planes provide end-to-end traceability for audit and forensics.

6. Correct Answer: B. Misconfigured or disabled unified log sinks leading to per-account drift. Explanation: When centralized sinks are absent or broken, logs fragment across accounts and regions, creating blind spots. This drift prevents consistent retention and cross-tenant correlation.

7. Correct Answer: C. A managed secret store with just-in-time retrieval at runtime. Explanation: Central secret stores eliminate hard-coded credentials and support controlled, auditable access with rotation. Runtime retrieval ties access to workload identity and context, reducing sprawl and exposure.

8. Correct Answer: D. Separating key administration from key usage and scoping cryptographic actions to specific principals. Explanation: Strong KMS governance enforces separation of duties and narrowly scoped permissions for encrypt/decrypt operations. Administrative capabilities like policy edits and deletion should be restricted to distinct roles.

9. Correct Answer: A. Machine-readable exports of configuration and policy state with timestamps and identifiers. Explanation: Exportable, reproducible snapshots provide provenance and allow independent verification, far surpassing screenshots. They enable consistent comparisons across tenants and over time.

10. Correct Answer: B. By scoping permissions at the resource boundary (e.g., bucket, container, database) with least privilege. Explanation: Data-plane segmentation binds access to specific service scopes, preventing broad cross-service permissions. This approach complements network controls and restricts lateral movement within data services.

Chapter 10

1. Correct Answer: A. To translate sensitivity labels into enforceable storage, transmission, and disposal rules with auditable traceability. Explanation: Classification exists to drive concrete handling behaviors and to create a traceable line from policy to technical controls and evidence. This ensures consistent, testable protection across systems rather than ad hoc user decisions.

2. Correct Answer: B. The completeness of encryption across data in transit, at rest, backups, and intermediate caches. Explanation: Coverage addresses whether encryption is applied uniformly to all assets and data states, not just select components. Auditors look for gaps like unencrypted backups or staging areas that break that continuity.

3. Correct Answer: C. Purpose, owner, algorithm/length, rotation interval, and retirement plan. Explanation: These metadata elements form the minimum governance record that allows life cycle decisions to be audited. Without them, rotation, custody, and retirement cannot be proven or managed consistently.

4. Correct Answer: D. Splitting requester, approver, and operator roles and requiring quorum for high-risk actions. Explanation: Separation of duties prevents unilateral control over key material and is reinforced by M-of-N or dual control for sensitive operations. This structure reduces insider risk and creates verifiable approval trails.

5. Correct Answer: A. Deterministic tokenization with vaulted mappings. Explanation: Deterministic tokens preserve joinability for analytics while keeping originals sequestered in a controlled vault. Masking or disk-only encryption either breaks joins or fails to limit plaintext exposure inside the analytics engine.

6. Correct Answer: B. Defined scopes, patterns/classifiers, actions, and a tuning/exception register with approvals. Explanation: An auditable DLP program ties detection logic to channels

and data classes, prescribes actions, and records tuning and exceptions with owner approval. This produces measurable outcomes and traceable governance.

7. Correct Answer: C. Data concentration, exposure surface, connectivity, and third-party hops. Explanation: High-risk nodes emerge where sensitive volume meets broad access and complex interconnections, especially across external paths. These criteria focus attention on the most consequential points in the flow.

8. Correct Answer: D. Effective key/resource policies, precise grants, and key-usage audit logs with attestation. Explanation: Policies and grants define who can perform which cryptographic operations, and usage logs provide tamper-evident proof they occurred as authorized. Attestation ties activity to approved hardware/service baselines.

9. Correct Answer: A. Key policies/aliases/rotation logs → HSM/KMS audit logs → storage/db/server encryption configs → DLP policy definitions and incident exports → ticket/change systems. Explanation: This sequence reflects intent (policies), execution (key activity), enforcement at data stores, detection at boundaries, and governance approvals. It creates a coherent, time-bound narrative from design to operation.

10. Correct Answer: C. Ensure backups are encrypted with managed keys, logged, and aligned to retention and rotation expectations. Explanation: Backups must match production protection to avoid becoming the weakest link, with evidence that encryption and key availability are maintained. Retention and rotation alignment ensures decryptability when needed or crypto-shredding when data expires.

Chapter 11

1. Correct Answer: B. To express required coverage by source and depth and tie it to retention targets. Explanation: The coverage model defines which sources and fields are collected and connects them to risk-based retention, ensuring measurable visibility. It enables auditors to verify completeness through reconciliations and documented exclusions.

2. Correct Answer: A. Records cannot be altered or deleted without detection. Explanation: Immutability and append-only controls provide tamper resistance, often strengthened with hashing or signing. These properties preserve evidentiary value over the full life cycle of the logs.

3. Correct Answer: D. It ensures accurate event correlation and coherent timelines. Explanation: Synchronized clocks allow investigators to align events across identity, endpoint, network, and application sources. Even minor drift can distort sequences and undermine forensic credibility.

4. Correct Answer: C. Precision reduces false positives, while recall reflects the proportion of relevant threats detected. Explanation: Effective tuning aims to balance analyst workload (precision) with detection coverage (recall). Measuring both guides data-driven improvements to rule logic.

5. Correct Answer: B. A narrowly scoped, justified, time-bound exclusion with periodic review. Explanation: Acceptable suppressions are specific, documented, and reviewed to prevent permanent blind spots. Blanket or indefinite filters create unmanaged risk and erode visibility.

6. Correct Answer: A. Owner. Explanation: Named ownership assigns responsibility for maintenance, tuning, and periodic review of the analytic. This accountability ensures timely action when performance degrades or context changes.

7. Correct Answer: D. Disposition codes with timestamps and links to the originating rule/event. Explanation: Structured handoff data preserves traceability from alert generation through escalation. These artifacts support forensic timelines and prevent re-triage by the response team.

8. Correct Answer: C. Asset-to-source reconciliation comparing inventories to onboarded sources. Explanation: Reconciliation exposes coverage deltas between expected and actual telemetry. It is a primary control for detecting silent failures or onboarding gaps.

9. Correct Answer: B. Using network proxy or DNS logs to observe command-and-control patterns. Explanation: Compensating signals provide temporary visibility aligned to the risk created by the outage. Network-level telemetry can approximate lost endpoint insight until full coverage is restored.

10. Correct Answer: C. Version control commit logs and rule diffs in the detection repository. Explanation: Treating detections as code enables auditable change history with diffs, approvals, and provenance. These artifacts demonstrate intentional evolution of detection content.

Chapter 12

1. Correct Answer: C. Coordinate the response, set severity, and authorize containment within guardrails. Explanation: The incident commander is the single point of operational authority, orchestrating responders, declaring severity, and authorizing containment within predefined limits. This role ensures speed without sacrificing governance or evidence preservation.

2. Correct Answer: B. Recording and reverifying cryptographic hash values at each handoff. Explanation: Hash verification provides mathematical assurance that evidence remains unchanged across collection, transfer, and analysis. Rechecking hashes at custody transitions preserves provenance and legal defensibility.

3. Correct Answer: D. Exportable, time-bounded records with cross-references to forensic and DR artifacts. Explanation: Audit-ready case systems produce coherent, time-scoped packages that link actions to evidence and recovery outcomes. Exportability with cross-references enables independent verification without altering source data.

4. Correct Answer: A. Acknowledgment, escalation, and resolution SLAs. Explanation: These SLAs quantify responsiveness from alert intake through case closure and are central to life cycle accountability. Auditors compare actual timestamps to these targets to assess performance and process health.

5. Correct Answer: C. Specific containment actions with timestamps, responsible parties, and approval authority. Explanation: Granular documentation allows reconstruction of events and confirms actions were authorized and sequenced correctly. This record also protects forensic integrity by showing what changed and when.

6. Correct Answer: D. A structured decision log capturing threshold breaches, approvals, and compensating actions. Explanation: Decision logs connect governance to real-time choices when RTO/RPO targets are missed, documenting risk acceptance or remediation. They provide auditable rationale and accountability for deviations.

7. Correct Answer: B. Legal and executive approval using version-controlled templates and time-stamped sign-offs. Explanation: External messaging must be accurate, consistent, and compliant, which requires formal review and authorized release. Version control and approvals create a defensible trail of what was said and why.

8. Correct Answer: A. After-action reviews with corrective actions, assigned owners, and deadlines tracked to closure. Explanation: Actionable AARs convert observations into measurable improvements and demonstrate continuous assurance. Ownership and timelines ensure lessons translate into policy or control changes.

9. Correct Answer: C. IR plans define expectations; case records log actions; forensic repositories supply technical proof with custody logs; DR reports confirm restoration. Explanation: This end-to-end linkage creates a closed, traceable circuit of evidence with provenance at each step. Cross-references and timestamps enable auditors to validate integrity and outcomes.

10. Correct Answer: D. Because explainability and traceable evidence are required to make automated actions defensible and compliant. Explanation: AI can accelerate response, but without governance, its decisions may lack accountability and legal standing. Documented oversight and evidentiary trails keep automation auditable and aligned with compliance.

Chapter 13

1. Correct Answer: A. To optimize visibility while minimizing operational risk through lightweight discovery and scheduled, deeper assessments. Explanation: Separating discovery and assessment allows frequent, low-impact discovery to keep coverage current while reserving authenticated, deeper checks for planned windows. This structure preserves visibility and reduces operational disruption.

2. Correct Answer: C. An authenticated re-scan showing the issue is not detected on the asset. Explanation: Authenticated re-scans directly verify that the vulnerable condition no longer exists under real configurations. They provide stronger assurance than tickets or approvals, which only indicate intent or process.

3. Correct Answer: B. Prioritize immediate remediation regardless of the CVSS score. Explanation: KEV denotes active exploitation in the wild, elevating urgency beyond static severity scores. Treating KEV items with top priority aligns response with real attacker behavior.

4. Correct Answer: D. A defined expiry date with compensating controls. Explanation: Exceptions must be time-boxed and paired with controls that reduce exposure during the deferral period. This prevents "temporary" exceptions from becoming unbounded risk.

5. Correct Answer: A. The date of initial discovery or validation of the finding. Explanation: Using a consistent, earliest trigger removes ambiguity and ensures comparable SLA metrics across teams. Later triggers can mask true time-to-remediate performance.

6. Correct Answer: C. Updating golden images and baselines and enforcing them via CI/CD gates. Explanation: Embedding fixes into golden images and pipeline gates ensures future builds inherit the remediation and blocks regressions. This institutionalizes the fix across deployments.

7. Correct Answer: D. Testers must operate without conflicts and not assess systems they built or manage. Explanation: Independence avoids self-review and preserves the credibility of findings. Reporting outside operations further reinforces objectivity.

8. Correct Answer: C. Detailed findings, exploit paths, data accessed, business impact, and reproducible steps. Explanation: These elements allow remediation teams to validate issues and understand impact while enabling repeatable verification. They also provide auditors with traceable, evidence-backed narratives.

9. Correct Answer: A. To ensure one coordinated response per unique issue across sources. Explanation: Deduplication prevents inflated metrics and fragmented efforts when multiple tools report the same weakness. It streamlines ownership and accelerates effective remediation.

10. Correct Answer: B. It allows auditors to re-perform the control activities using time-bounded artifacts. Explanation: Unique IDs and timestamps create a verifiable chain across CMDB, scans, tickets, exceptions, and reports. This provenance enables independent confirmation of the organization's control actions.

Chapter 14

1. Correct Answer: A. Criticality, data sensitivity, connectivity, operational dependency. Explanation: These dimensions drive tiering decisions that determine diligence depth and monitoring cadence. They reflect business impact, data exposure, integration surface, and reliance, which are central to the chapter's risk model.

2. Correct Answer: C. To provide authority to verify controls via documents or assessments over time. Explanation: Right-to-audit clauses operationalize oversight by enabling document requests and assessments beyond onboarding. This converts contractual promises into verifiable, ongoing assurance.

3. Correct Answer: D. Responsibilities the customer must operate for vendor controls to remain effective. Explanation: CUECs shift part of the control burden back to the auditee, requiring internal controls that complement the vendor's environment. Failure to implement them weakens overall assurance even if the vendor's controls are effective.

4. Correct Answer: B. Obtain the subservice organization's attestation or equivalent evidence. Explanation: Carve-outs create blind spots that must be bridged with additional artifacts from the subservice provider. This preserves end-to-end assurance across dependencies in the service chain.

5. Correct Answer: A. Trigger escalation or re-segmentation and require updated attestations. Explanation: Stale questionnaires undermine continuous monitoring and must prompt action to refresh evidence. Governance links overdue updates to tier changes or escalations to keep oversight current.

6. Correct Answer: D. Appearance on a sanctions or denied-parties list for the vendor entity. Explanation: Sanctions hits are high-severity triggers that warrant immediate suspension review and legal involvement. They represent nontechnical but critical risk conditions defined in continuous monitoring thresholds.

7. Correct Answer: C. It enables component-level visibility to map vulnerabilities and manage dependency risk. Explanation: SBOMs provide the inventory necessary to correlate components with disclosures and prioritize remediation. They are the basis for timely triage when suppliers report vulnerable dependencies.

8. Correct Answer: B. Signing release artifacts and providing attestation metadata linking to source and build inputs. Explanation: Digital signatures and attestations bind binaries to a specific source and workflow, strengthening chain-of-custody. This supports verification that deployed artifacts are authentic and intended.

9. Correct Answer: C. Reviewing tangible evidence (e.g., patched versions, retested controls) validated by an internal verifier. Explanation: Verified, objective evidence closes the loop and demonstrates that corrective actions are effective, not just claimed. Internal validation adds independence and reliability to the closure decision.

10. Correct Answer: A. Provenance metadata showing who collected each artifact, when, and from which source, with exportable, time-bounded records. Explanation: Provenance and exportability enable independent re-performance by external reviewers. Time-bounded artifacts and version control preserve the integrity of the assurance trail.

Chapter 15

1. Correct Answer: A. Human safety, environmental protection, and continuous operation. Explanation: OT/ICS risk decisions prioritize preventing physical harm and maintaining stable processes over traditional confidentiality-first approaches. Controls are evaluated on how they reduce credible physical hazards while sustaining safe operation.

2. Correct Answer: B. Broker limited, tightly filtered or one-way data exchange without exposing control assets. Explanation: The industrial DMZ is a controlled intermediary that enables necessary data flows without permitting direct access to sensitive control networks. This design reduces attack paths while supporting business and monitoring needs.

3. Correct Answer: C. They provide physical assurance that data can flow out but not into the control network. Explanation: Unidirectional gateways (data diodes) enforce one-way physics, allowing telemetry to leave the control side while blocking inbound commands or callbacks. This materially reduces risk without adding latency to control loops.

4. Correct Answer: D. Exported allowlist rule sets and signature catalogs tied to approved change tickets and rollback plans. Explanation: Disciplined allowlisting is evidenced by version-controlled rule bundles linked to formal change control and tested rollback paths. Such artifacts demonstrate enforcement, accountability, and safe operational practice.

5. Correct Answer: A. Isolate the asset, restrict communications to essential conduits, enforce allowlisting, document a risk-based variance, and schedule remediation for a maintenance window. Explanation: When patching must be deferred, rigorously governed compensating controls and documented variances keep risk managed until planned outages. This approach ensures deferrals are temporary, justified, and tracked to closure.

6. Correct Answer: B. Time synchronization across HMIs, controllers, historians, and security sensors. Explanation: Aligning clocks enables investigators to stitch together events across domains with precision, turning disparate records into a coherent narrative. Without synchronization, correlations can be misleading or impossible.

7. Correct Answer: C. Management of Change records linked to revised diagrams and post-change configuration exports. Explanation: Management of Change ties authorization and risk assessment to actual technical state, while updated drawings and exports prove what was implemented. This chain of evidence enables independent re-performance and verification.

8. Correct Answer: D. Frequent nuisance annunciations leading operators to acknowledge rather than investigate. Explanation: Alarm fatigue occurs when excessive or poorly tuned alarms condition staff to clear alerts without analysis, eroding operational awareness. Rationalization and performance metrics are required to restore alarm effectiveness.

9. Correct Answer: A. Anchor on completeness, continuity, and requirement-by-requirement evidence mapped to defined assets and periods. Explanation: Prescriptive regimes emphasize exhaustive, traceable proof that each requirement operated as stated throughout the audit window. The audit posture favors standardized artifacts and continuity over narrative discretion.

10. Correct Answer: C. Require access through a hardened jump host in the industrial DMZ with session recording and just-in-time, time-boxed approvals. Explanation: Jump hosts centralize control, monitoring, and recording while preventing direct reach into control networks. Time-boxed, just-in-time entitlements ensure access exists only for specific, approved tasks.

Chapter 16

1. Correct Answer: A. To create a defensible trace from obligation to scope to testing populations. Explanation: Overlay scoping demands a clear chain from the governing obligation to what is in scope and the populations tested. This traceability makes the audit reproducible and defensible under regulatory review.

2. Correct Answer: B. Governance committee charters and meeting minutes. Explanation: These artifacts directly demonstrate board and senior leadership oversight, a central emphasis area under FFIEC/GLBA. They show how risk and control performance are reviewed and acted upon at the governance level.

3. Correct Answer: C. Business Associate Agreement (BAA). Explanation: BAAs are the canonical contractual instruments binding third parties to HIPAA/HITRUST obligations for PHI. They define security responsibilities, notification timelines, and audit rights needed for assurance.

4. Correct Answer: D. Monthly vulnerability scans reconciled to POA&M updates. Explanation: Continuous monitoring under public-sector authorizations requires routine scans tied to POA&M remediation tracking. This pairing proves both detection and active risk reduction over time.

5. Correct Answer: A. The Cardholder Data Environment (CDE) with validated segmentation. Explanation: PCI's prescriptive scope hinges on precise CDE identification and isolation to prevent "scope explosion." Validated segmentation evidence proves unrelated systems cannot impact the CDE.

6. Correct Answer: B. Apply the stricter prescriptive requirement and document via the common control set. Explanation: Precedence logic requires selecting the most stringent applicable control and recording the rationale for consistency. Mapping through the common control set preserves alignment across frameworks.

7. Correct Answer: C. Confirm the parent system's authorization package and mapped evidence are current. Explanation: Control inheritance is only reliable when the provider's ATO/certification and evidence remain current and properly mapped. This verification prevents reliance on stale or incomplete inherited controls.

8. Correct Answer: D. Artifacts dated within the audit period and linked to specific control identifiers. Explanation: Freshness and traceability ensure evidence represents the environment actually tested and supports the correct control. Undated or unlinked artifacts weaken assurance and trigger expanded sampling.

9. Correct Answer: A. Prove that out-of-scope systems cannot access or influence the CDE. Explanation: Segmentation testing directly validates isolation, the core safeguard keeping PCI scope contained. Without it, connected systems become in scope, inflating assessment size and risk.

10. Correct Answer: C. Map artifacts through the common control set to enable "test once, satisfy many." Explanation: Cross-mapping preserves sector-specific narratives while eliminating duplicate testing. The common control set aligns artifacts to multiple obligations consistently.

Chapter 17

1. Correct Answer: C. To ensure tests map to specific risks and automatable assertions. Explanation: Defining control objectives first ensures automation serves a validated assurance purpose, not tool-driven curiosity. This mapping makes results interpretable as audit evidence tied to risk.

2. Correct Answer: A. Idempotent operations with durable checkpointing. Explanation: Idempotency and checkpoints allow safe reprocessing without inflating counts or creating duplicates. They also enable precise recovery from failures at known high-water marks.

3. Correct Answer: D. Enabling end-to-end traceability and reproducible backtracking. Explanation: A directed acyclic graph records each transformation and dependency, allowing reviewers to trace outputs to exact inputs and logic versions. This structure underpins reproducibility and independent validation.

4. Correct Answer: B. Exception expiry checks. Explanation: Expiry checks monitor time-bound exceptions and trigger action before approvals lapse. They prevent temporary deviations from silently becoming permanent control gaps.

5. Correct Answer: C. Empirical data distributions, risk appetite, and response capacity. Explanation: Thresholds should reflect historical behavior, business tolerance, and team bandwidth to investigate alerts. Arbitrary or universal settings either overwhelm responders or miss meaningful signals.

6. Correct Answer: A. Recording run identifiers, timestamps, and cryptographic hashes. Explanation: These linkages prove which artifacts belong to which execution and detect post-run tampering. They are foundational for reproducibility and chain-of-custody.

7. Correct Answer: D. Keeping audit oversight separate from operational ownership with documented purpose and approvals. Explanation: Separation of duties and explicit governance prevent uncontrolled changes to assurance logic by first-line teams. This preserves independence and credibility of automated results.

8. Correct Answer: B. Predefined triggers mapped to playbooks and escalation paths. Explanation: Triggers convert variance into consistent follow-ups with assigned owners and time expectations. This approach avoids alert fatigue and ensures exceptions drive action.

9. Correct Answer: C. A shift in how inputs relate to the control outcome due to process changes. Explanation: Concept drift means the same indicators no longer predict control effectiveness because the underlying process or meaning changed. It requires recalibration or redesign of the test logic.

10. Correct Answer: A. Perform an automation readiness assessment and enroll during the deployment life cycle. Explanation: Onboarding as part of release ensures data feeds, APIs, and mappings are in place before go-live. This practice prevents unaudited systems from creating blind spots.

Chapter 18

1. Correct Answer: C. To enumerate models, datasets, prompts, tools, agents, and endpoints with owners, classifications, and trust boundaries. Explanation: A precise asset boundary turns a complex AI system into an auditable set of accountable components. This enables targeted control testing and eliminates blind spots caused by ambiguous ownership or undefined trust zones.

2. Correct Answer: B. Data ingestion, prompt channels, retrieval paths, tool invocations, and output sinks. Explanation: These elements define how inputs become context and how outputs can cause downstream effects, which is where AI-specific threats arise. Modeling them ensures traditional frameworks capture the full AI interaction surface.

3. Correct Answer: D. Malicious instructions are embedded in external content that the system retrieves and incorporates into the prompt context. Explanation: Indirect injection exploits trusted retrieval paths or corpora so harmful instructions arrive via context rather than direct user input. This makes detection harder and elevates the need for context filtering and provenance checks.

4. Correct Answer: A. Unauthenticated or broadly exposed endpoints. Explanation: Open endpoints allow automated probing at scale, enabling extraction and abuse without attribution. Strong authentication is a prerequisite for effective throttling and monitoring.

5. Correct Answer: A. Dataset provenance. Explanation: Provenance ties each sample to its source and collection method, enabling validation of legitimacy and licensing. It is the keystone for distinguishing accidental contamination from deliberate poisoning.

6. Correct Answer: C. Enforcing least-privilege, narrowly scoped credentials per tool. Explanation: Tight scoping confines what any coerced tool call can accomplish, reducing lateral movement and data exposure. Per-tool credentials also prevent token reuse across systems.

7. Correct Answer: D. Exposure and rate-limit management. Explanation: Controlling query volume and access patterns directly counters automation-driven cloning attempts. These limits make extraction costly and more detectable.

8. Correct Answer: B. "Zero tolerance for PII exposure in model outputs." Explanation: Acceptance criteria must be specific and testable to guide assurance activities. A zero-tolerance statement for PII exposure is measurable and aligns with clear business and regulatory expectations.

9. Correct Answer: C. Versioning for models, prompts, and datasets within the traceability register. Explanation: Versioning preserves the integrity of links from threat to control to evidence as configurations change. Without it, audits can reference outdated baselines and lose accountability.

10. Correct Answer: B. Integration of a new plugin or connector. Explanation: New integrations alter trust boundaries, permissions, and data flows, requiring immediate documentation updates. Prompt refresh ensures controls and evidence remain aligned with the expanded attack surface.

Chapter 19

1. Correct Answer: C. Reconstruct who built each artifact, from which inputs, and with which configurations. Explanation: Provenance provides an auditable chain of custody that ties artifacts to builders, inputs, and settings. This traceability enables auditors to verify integrity and accountability across the ML supply chain.

2. Correct Answer: A. Strict version pinning using immutable digests for models, images, and configs. Explanation: Pinning to content digests prevents mutable tags from silently changing deployed behavior. It ensures the running state matches the validated artifacts and can be reliably rolled back.

3. Correct Answer: D. To prevent tampering or unauthorized uploads from production systems. Explanation: Read-only access limits the blast radius if a serving node is compromised, blocking registry modification. This preserves the integrity of approved artifacts and the audit trail.

4. Correct Answer: B. The same individual preparing training data and approving production deployment. Explanation: Combining data curation and final approval collapses independent review and enables self-promotion. Proper SoD requires separate roles to detect errors or manipulation before release.

5. Correct Answer: C. Fixed random seeds, pinned libraries, and deterministic pipelines. Explanation: These controls eliminate nondeterministic variability so reruns yield identical or statistically equivalent results. They also allow auditors to attribute performance changes to intentional modifications rather than environmental drift.

6. Correct Answer: A. Shadow mode on mirrored production traffic. Explanation: Shadowing exercises the candidate model under real conditions without affecting user outcomes. It surfaces incompatibilities and performance gaps safely before any traffic is routed to the new model.

7. Correct Answer: D. Prevent exfiltration of datasets and model artifacts. Explanation: Egress restrictions stop compromised jobs from sending sensitive data or weights to untrusted destinations. They reinforce isolation of the training environment and protect high-value assets.

8. Correct Answer: B. Per-tenant identities and authorization scopes with isolated routing namespaces. Explanation: Dedicated identities and namespace isolation ensure one tenant's requests and metadata cannot be accessed by another. This approach enforces clean separation and auditable access control at the endpoint layer.

9. Correct Answer: A. Cryptographic signature from a trusted build and a matching registry digest. Explanation: Signature verification and digest matching confirm the artifact's authenticity and immutability. They are core gates that block untrusted or altered artifacts from promotion.

10. Correct Answer: C. Using durable identifiers that link the model to specific dataset and feature versions and transformations. Explanation: Durable IDs and immutable links enable precise backward tracing from a deployed model to the exact data snapshot. This satisfies audit requirements for accountability and reproducibility.

Chapter 20

1. Correct Answer: A. To align detection with business and compliance risk and enable decisive escalation. Explanation: Clear objectives with thresholds and latency tie monitoring to real impact, ensuring alerts are actionable rather than noisy. This structure empowers auditors to verify that detection leads to timely containment and governance decisions.

2. Correct Answer: D. Timestamps, model/version IDs, dataset hashes, user/app IDs, and tool scopes. Explanation: This minimal, vendor-neutral set enables correlation across telemetry planes and supports defensible reconstruction. Each field anchors chronology, provenance, attribution, and integration context for audits.

3. Correct Answer: C. Degraded but safer behavior that disables high-risk features while maintaining essential function. Explanation: Safe mode prioritizes safety and stability by restricting risky capabilities without a full shutdown. It preserves essential service while investigation and remediation proceed.

4. Correct Answer: B. Signals, relevant artifacts (e.g., redacted I/O and configs), and an estimated blast radius. Explanation: This package lets enterprise IR assess scope, impact, and dependencies without duplicating AI-specific analysis. It cleanly separates AI assurance responsibilities from broader corporate response playbooks.

5. Correct Answer: A. Preserved prompts/outputs (redacted), model/version identifiers, and configuration snapshots. Explanation: These artifacts form the reproducibility core for replaying the incident in a controlled environment. They allow investigators to test hypotheses about behavior under the original conditions.

6. Correct Answer: C. Escalation to the provider via contractual notice windows and agreed SLOs. Explanation: When control resides with the vendor, containment and remediation depend on contractual escalation routes and timelines. Internal teams coordinate evidence and communication while the provider executes platform-level actions.

7. Correct Answer: A. The random seed or sampling configuration used at inference time. Explanation: Capturing seed and sampling parameters reduces nondeterminism, improving the fidelity of replay attempts. It narrows variability so analysts can compare outcomes meaningfully.

8. Correct Answer: D. Prioritizing PIR findings into the backlog with effectiveness checks tied to release gates. Explanation: Binding lessons learned to backlog prioritization and validation ensures changes land before the next deployment. This cadence turns insights into measurable improvements rather than shelfware.

9. Correct Answer: B. They enable selective disablement of risky functions with auditable toggles and rapid rollback. Explanation: Feature flags provide fine-grained, accountable control to mitigate issues without redeploys. Audit trails on toggles support governance and incident reconstruction.

10. Correct Answer: D. It records external calls and parameters, enabling end-to-end reconstruction of cross-system actions. Explanation: Many AI failures involve downstream tools or APIs, so capturing scopes, parameters, and outcomes is essential. This telemetry links model behavior to external effects for full causal analysis.

Chapter 21

1. Correct Answer: B. Criteria. Explanation: Criteria define the authoritative requirement or standard that the control must meet, anchoring objectivity in the finding. By stating precise clauses or policy references, auditors separate fact from interpretation and enable defensible judgments.

2. Correct Answer: D. "Restrict privileged accounts to unique credentials with logged approvals and monitored administrative actions." Explanation: This phrasing specifies a verifiable end state that can be tested through evidence and monitoring. It avoids vague verbs and sets clear success criteria for closure validation.

3. Correct Answer: C. When compensating controls or partial remediation are applied. Explanation: "Before/after" statements clarify how mitigation changes risk without implying full resolution. They communicate remaining exposure transparently and prevent overstatement of control efficacy.

4. Correct Answer: A. Scope tested → Key findings → Residual risk → Business impact → Decisions requested. Explanation: This flow keeps the Board at the right altitude by defining boundaries, surfacing themes, quantifying remaining risk, linking to impact, and closing with explicit choices. It avoids tool detail and methodology digressions that dilute governance focus.

5. Correct Answer: B. Normalize metrics for scope, coverage, and sampling changes. Explanation: Normalization prevents misleading trends caused by shifting baselines or expanded testing footprints. It ensures that observed movement reflects true control health rather than measurement artifacts.

6. Correct Answer: D. Independent validation confirms remediation with dated evidence artifacts. Explanation: "Closed" requires third-party verification that the control now operates as intended, supported by retained artifacts. "Mitigated" indicates temporary risk reduction through compensating measures, not full resolution.

7. Correct Answer: B. Time-bound actions, identified resources, and a clear risk treatment stance. Explanation: Acceptable responses must commit to a schedule, specify resourcing, and declare whether the risk will be fixed, mitigated, transferred, or accepted. Mere acknowledgment or vague monitoring promises do not create accountability.

8. Correct Answer: C. Use cohorts with comparable scope and method, and label inference limits. Explanation: Benchmarks are meaningful only when methodologies align; otherwise comparisons are misleading. Stating limitations preserves integrity and prevents false precision in executive decisions.

9. Correct Answer: B. By mapping to stable identifiers tied to the control objective. Explanation: Control-objective lineage distinguishes true recurrences from ticket renumbering or cosmetic changes. This method highlights whether root causes persist across systems or periods.

10. Correct Answer: B. Approving funding or policy changes to address high residual risk. Explanation: Decision requests should present clear governance choices that alter risk posture, such as funding, policy updates, or risk acceptance. Tool selection and test design are operational matters and fall below Board-level decision altitude.

Chapter 22

1. Correct Answer: C. Visualizing prioritized audit units derived from enterprise risks, material processes, and sensitive data classes. Explanation: The coverage heatmap converts abstract risk inputs into a clear picture of where assurance should focus and at what intensity. This prioritization makes the plan defensible and aligned with business impact.

2. Correct Answer: D. Risk velocity, business change, and control durability. Explanation: Cadence should match how quickly the risk surface moves and how stable controls remain, not a fixed calendar. Aligning frequency to these factors keeps assurance relevant and timely.

3. Correct Answer: B. Recent incidents/near misses, trend metrics, strategy shifts, and upcoming regulatory deadlines. Explanation: These inputs provide traceable evidence that directly informs scope, depth, and timing decisions. Using them embeds operational reality and compliance expectations into the plan.

4. Correct Answer: A. External specialists report functionally to audit leadership rather than management being audited. Explanation: This safeguard preserves independence and ensures conclusions remain under the audit function's governance. It prevents conflicts of interest while still leveraging deep technical expertise.

5. Correct Answer: C. GRC/workpaper system, secure evidence repository, controlled data access pathways, and analytics platform. Explanation: This minimum toolchain governs workpapers, protects evidence with access, retention, and provenance controls, and enables data-driven testing. Together, it forms the backbone for efficient, defensible execution.

6. Correct Answer: B. Maintaining a versioned plan with effective dates and approval records. Explanation: Version control creates transparency and a traceable history of changes, preserving governance while enabling agility. It ensures stakeholders understand why priorities shifted and who approved the updates.

7. Correct Answer: D. A material incident, a new law with near-term deadlines, a major architecture shift, or an acquisition/divestiture. Explanation: These events materially alter enterprise risk and justify re-prioritizing coverage mid-year. Lesser operational changes do not typically meet the threshold for plan modification.

8. Correct Answer: A. Calibrating severity so similar control failures receive comparable ratings across teams. Explanation: Rating consistency checks align judgment to common thresholds, making results comparable across engagements. This supports uniform remediation expectations and strengthens credibility.

9. Correct Answer: B. Executive satisfaction, audit predictability, and risk-reduction signals alongside milestones like automation adoption and fewer repeat findings. Explanation: These measures tie capability gains to outcomes stakeholders value: reliability, insight, and reduced residual risk. They also make roadmap progress visible and actionable over 1–3 years.

10. Correct Answer: A. To maintain agility for ad hoc reviews or incident-driven work without disrupting core coverage. Explanation: Reserving capacity ensures the audit function can respond quickly to emergent needs while protecting planned engagements. This balance preserves both responsiveness and coverage integrity.

Glossary

Acceptance criteria The specific, pre-agreed conditions a control, process, or piece of evidence must meet to be considered sufficient for the audit objective. Defining these upfront reduces scope creep and debate during fieldwork. Clear criteria also support consistent ratings across engagements.

Advocacy threat A threat to auditor independence that arises when the auditor appears to promote or defend management's position. This can bias judgments about control design or effectiveness. Auditors should avoid roles or actions that put them in the position of arguing for the auditee.

Alternative procedures Substitute tests performed when preferred evidence is unavailable or incomplete. Examples include re-performance in place of missing logs or corroborating through third-party confirmations. Auditors must document why the alternative is appropriate and how it attains the same assurance.

Analytics-assisted testing The use of data analysis to enhance coverage, precision, or efficiency of audit tests. Techniques range from simple filters and joins to statistical sampling and anomaly detection. Auditors should validate data lineage and quality to ensure conclusions remain reliable.

Anchoring bias A cognitive bias where initial information (the "anchor") unduly influences later judgments. In audits, early narratives or prior ratings can skew risk assessments and findings. Mitigate it by independently reviewing evidence and using structured decision checklists.

Audit charter The formal document that establishes the audit function's purpose, authority, and responsibility. It confirms access rights to records and personnel and defines reporting lines to preserve independence. A current, approved charter anchors the legitimacy of every engagement.

Audit committee A governing body (often of the board) that oversees financial and nonfinancial assurance activities, including cybersecurity audits. It approves plans, reviews significant findings, and monitors management remediation. Direct communication with the committee strengthens independence and impact.

Audit units The discrete organizational areas, systems, or processes selected as the scope of an engagement. Defining audit units helps size effort, assign risk ratings, and track coverage over time. Clear unit boundaries reduce overlap and gaps across the audit plan.

Automated assurance The continuous or event-driven evaluation of controls using scripts, rules, or monitoring tools. It can expand coverage and detect deviations faster than periodic manual testing. Auditors should validate data sources and logic to rely on these results.

Bridge letter A short attestation from a service provider covering the gap between the end date of its last assurance report and your reliance date. It typically states whether any material changes occurred during the gap period. Auditors use it to maintain reliance while awaiting the next full report.

CAIQ The Consensus Assessments Initiative Questionnaire is a standardized set of cloud security due-diligence questions from the Cloud Security Alliance. Auditors use it to evaluate third-party cloud providers consistently and map responses to control requirements. It streamlines evidence collection and comparison across vendors.

Carve-out method A reporting approach where a primary service auditor excludes a subservice organization's controls from the scope of the report. Users are expected to evaluate the carved-out entity separately, often via additional assurance or complementary controls. Auditors must assess whether reliance is still appropriate given the carve-out.

Chain of custody The documented trail showing who collected, handled, transferred, and stored evidence from creation to archive. Maintaining this chain supports authenticity and admissibility, especially for logs and forensic artifacts. Breaks in custody reduce the reliability of conclusions.

Common control set A harmonized group of controls used across multiple standards or business units to avoid duplication. Auditors leverage it to test once and satisfy many requirements via cross-mapping. It improves consistency of ratings and reduces audit fatigue.

Compensating controls Alternative controls that mitigate risk when a primary control is missing or infeasible. They should address the same objective and provide comparable assurance. Auditors evaluate their design, operation, and documented rationale to accept them.

Complementary user-entity controls (CUECs) Controls at the customer that a service provider assumes will be in place for its own controls to operate effectively. Auditors must verify that relevant CUECs are designed and implemented at the user organization. Failure to meet CUECs can invalidate reliance on the provider's report.

Completeness The attribute that all relevant transactions, events, or assets are fully captured in the population under audit. Auditors test completeness to ensure sampling and analytics aren't biased by omissions. It often requires reconciling to an external system of record.

Configuration conformance The degree to which systems match an approved baseline or standard. Auditors compare effective settings to the baseline to identify drift and control gaps. Consistent conformance supports reliable security posture and repeatable operations.

Confirmation bias A cognitive bias where evidence that confirms an initial belief is favored over contradictory data. In audits, it can lead to overlooking exceptions or alternative explanations. Structured workpapers and peer review help counter this bias.

Control maturity A staged view of how well a control is designed, implemented, and optimized over time. Auditors use maturity criteria to contextualize findings and guide remediation roadmaps. Higher maturity usually correlates with lower residual risk and fewer repeat findings.

Control objective The specific outcome a control is intended to achieve, such as restricting access to authorized users or preserving log integrity. Clear objectives let auditors test whether the control actually mitigates the targeted risk. They also enable consistent mapping across frameworks and reports.

Control owner The person or role accountable for designing, operating, and maintaining a control. Auditors confirm the owner's responsibilities, authority, and evidence practices. Strong ownership reduces gaps, accelerates remediation, and improves repeatability.

Cross-framework traceability The documented linkage that shows how one control maps to equivalent requirements in other standards. Auditors use these mappings to "test once, satisfy many" and to explain scope coverage. Good traceability lowers audit fatigue and helps reconcile differing terminology.

Cryptographic hashing A one-way mathematical function that converts data into a fixed-length digest. Auditors rely on hashes to verify evidence integrity, detect tampering, and support chain-of-custody. Hashes must be generated with approved algorithms and recorded alongside the artifact.

Design adequacy An assessment of whether a control's design, on paper, can reasonably achieve its objective given the risk. Auditors review policies, procedures, roles, and configurations before testing operation. If design is inadequate, operating effectiveness tests will not yield meaningful assurance.

DevSecOps An operating model that integrates security controls into development and operations workflows. For auditors, it shifts evidence from point-in-time sign-offs to continuous artifacts (e.g., pipeline gates and IaC scans). The focus is on control design in the pipeline and the reliability of automated checks.

Digital signing The use of asymmetric cryptography to bind a signer's identity to data and prove integrity. Auditors verify signatures on binaries, documents, and configurations to ensure authenticity. Proper key management and timestamping strengthen evidentiary value.

Evidence location The authoritative place where audit evidence resides (e.g., ticketing system, log archive, and GRC tool). Auditors document locations to ensure repeatability and facilitate re-performance. Centralized, indexed locations reduce retrieval time and loss risk.

Evidence persistence The retention of audit-relevant artifacts for a defined period in reliable storage. Auditors check that retention policies align with regulatory or engagement needs. Persistence supports re-performance, dispute resolution, and longitudinal analysis.

Evidence pointer A precise reference (link, ID, or path) that directs reviewers to the exact artifact used to support a test step or conclusion. Strong pointers make workpapers traceable and speed peer review. They also reduce rework when evidence must be re-performed or refreshed.

Evidence preservation The set of controls that ensures collected evidence remains intact, accessible, and unaltered for the required retention period. Auditors look for immutable storage, access controls, and documented retention schedules. Preservation enables dispute resolution and follow-on audits.

Evidence repository The structured store (system or folder hierarchy) used to collect and organize engagement evidence. Auditors evaluate access controls, versioning, and metadata to maintain integrity and traceability. Well-governed repositories streamline reviews and peer quality checks.

Exception aging A metric that tracks how long identified exceptions or issues remain open. Auditors use it to assess remediation discipline and management attention. Long aging often signals resource constraints or weak ownership.

Exception handling The standardized process for logging, triaging, risk-rating, approving, and remediating control failures or deviations. Auditors evaluate whether exceptions receive timely analysis and appropriate compensating measures. Mature handling prevents recurring findings and controls drift.

Exception register The authoritative log of active exceptions, including risk, owner, due date, and status. Auditors reconcile this register against findings and waiver systems to confirm completeness. A well-maintained register supports reporting and escalation.

Exception sprawl The unchecked growth of waivers and deviations that gradually erode baseline controls. Auditors flag sprawl when exceptions lack expiry, review, or compensating controls. Containing sprawl requires governance, metrics, and periodic cleanup.

Familiarity threat An independence risk that arises when long relationships or close ties with the auditee bias judgment. Rotation, second-partner review, and strict role boundaries help mitigate it. Auditors should disclose potential threats and document safeguards.

FedRAMP authorization A formal approval for U.S. federal agencies to use a cloud service that meets defined security requirements. Auditors review the underlying SSP, POA&M, and assessment artifacts for reliance. Understanding inheritance and boundary scope is key when mapping to enterprise controls.

Findings register The central log of audit issues with severity, root cause, owner, and target date. Auditors use it to track remediation and analyze trends like repeat findings. Clear definitions and consistent ratings improve comparability across engagements.

Full-population testing Testing that evaluates every item in a defined population rather than a sample. It's powerful when data is structured and tooling can automate checks, but auditors must validate completeness and accuracy first. Use it to reduce sampling risk and increase assurance.

Gap analysis A structured comparison between current control state and required criteria (standard, policy, or risk objective). Auditors document gaps, assess risk impact, and prioritize remediation actions. It helps plan scope, timelines, and resource needs.

Governance, Risk, and Compliance (GRC) An integrated approach and tooling that aligns governance objectives, risk management, and compliance activities. Auditors rely on GRC systems for control inventories, workflows, and evidence tracking. Strong GRC integration improves traceability and reporting consistency.

Independence in fact and appearance The requirement that auditors are both actually unbiased and perceived as unbiased by stakeholders. It covers relationships, roles, and incentives that could impair objectivity. Documenting safeguards and disclosures preserves trust in the audit's conclusions.

Independent re-performance The auditor's direct execution of a control or calculation to verify results without relying on management's output. It provides high assurance when inputs and criteria are well defined. Clear workpapers must show steps taken and evidence used.

Inherited controls Controls operated by another party (e.g., a cloud provider) that reduce the customer's control burden. Auditors evaluate the provider's assurance reports and the customer's complementary responsibilities. Proper inheritance mapping prevents control gaps and double-testing.

Intimidation threat A threat to independence that arises when auditors feel pressured by management or leadership. It can suppress candid findings or soften ratings. Escalation channels and governance support help auditors maintain objectivity.

ISO/IEC 27001 An international standard for establishing, implementing, maintaining, and continually improving an ISMS. Auditors assess conformity against the standard's requirements and Annex A controls. Certification evidence can inform, but not replace, control testing in other frameworks.

Issue register The authoritative log of audit findings with severity, owners, milestones, and closure dates. Auditors use it to monitor remediation progress and analyze trends like repeat issues. Consistent status definitions enable accurate reporting to the audit committee.

Least privilege The principle of granting only the minimum access required to perform a role or task. Auditors test for excessive entitlements, privilege creep, and weak reviews. Strong provisioning and periodic recertifications reduce breach impact and audit exceptions.

Legal hold A directive to preserve potentially relevant information for litigation or investigation. Auditors verify that scope, custodians, and systems are covered and that deletions are suspended. Effective holds protect evidence integrity and reduce spoliation risk.

Look-back procedures Retroactive testing to verify whether a control operated effectively over a prior period, often when evidence was missing at the time. Auditors recreate or reexamine transactions and logs to validate conclusions. Proper scoping and documented criteria prevent hindsight bias.

Management assertion A formal statement from management claiming that controls are designed and operating effectively or that statements are accurate. Auditors evaluate this assertion against evidence and criteria. Clear, bounded assertions help align scope and responsibility.

Management attestations Periodic confirmations by management that required controls, reviews, or reconciliations occurred as stated. Auditors test the basis and supporting evidence for these attestations. Weak or boilerplate attestations signal potential control design gaps.

Management participation threat An independence risk that arises when auditors take on decision-making or operational roles for the auditee. This blurs the line between assurance and management responsibility. Auditors must avoid designing or operating controls they later assess.

Management response The documented action plan and risk acknowledgment that management provides for each finding. Auditors assess whether responses are specific, time-bound, and risk-proportionate. Vague responses or shifting dates often lead to repeat findings.

Mapping rules The documented logic for aligning one control or requirement to equivalent items in other frameworks. Auditors rely on these rules to ensure consistent cross-framework traceability. Transparent mappings reduce duplication and support "test once, use many."

Materiality The threshold at which a control failure or misstatement would influence stakeholder decisions. Auditors calibrate testing depth and reporting based on materiality. Right-sizing materiality avoids trivial findings while ensuring significant risks are addressed.

Materiality thresholds Quantitative or qualitative cutoffs used to operationalize materiality for testing and reporting. Auditors define these up front and apply them consistently across samples and exceptions. Clear thresholds support defensible ratings and reduce debate.

Model risk The possibility that decisions based on models (e.g., scoring, forecasting, and detection) are flawed due to bad design, data, or governance. Auditors evaluate model documentation, validation, and change control. Strong governance and monitoring mitigate bias and drift.

Operating effectiveness Evidence that a well-designed control actually performed as intended over the period under review. Auditors sample transactions, inspect artifacts, and re-perform steps to confirm operation. Failures here outweigh design strength and drive findings.

Organization policies The formal rules and standards that define required security behaviors and configurations across the enterprise. Auditors test alignment between actual practices and these policies, noting exceptions and waivers. Strong policy governance enables consistent criteria for design and operating effectiveness.

PCI DSS A prescriptive standard for protecting cardholder data across people, process, and technology. Auditors assess scoping, segmentation, and evidence against PCI requirements and reporting forms (e.g., ROC and SAQ). Properly defined CDE boundaries reduce testing noise and improve assurance.

Peer review A quality control step where another auditor evaluates workpapers, methods, and conclusions. It helps catch logic gaps, bias, or insufficient evidence before reporting. Regular peer review raises consistency and strengthens defensibility of findings.

Period coverage The specific timeframe over which controls are asserted and tested (e.g., 1/1–12/31). Auditors confirm that evidence and samples fall within this window and that any gaps are addressed with bridge letters or alternative procedures. Clear coverage avoids reliance errors.

Plan of action and milestones (POA&M) A structured remediation plan listing findings, actions, owners, and target dates. Auditors review POA&M quality and progress to judge management's remediation discipline. Weak POA&Ms correlate with repeat findings and extended risk exposure.

Policy as code The practice of encoding policy requirements into machine-enforceable rules within pipelines and platforms. For auditors, it provides evidence artifacts (e.g., gate logs) that are repeatable and tamper-evident. Reviews focus on rule provenance, scope, and exception handling.

Policy debt The accumulation of outdated, inconsistent, or unenforced policies that no longer reflect reality. Auditors flag policy debt when it drives frequent exceptions or compensating controls. Reducing debt improves clarity, compliance, and testing efficiency.

Population definition The precise description of the full set of items subject to a test (e.g., all privileged accounts in scope). Auditors document sources, filters, and reconciliation steps to ensure completeness and accuracy. A sound definition underpins valid sampling and analytics.

Portfolio evidence pack A curated set of reusable artifacts that satisfy common control requirements across engagements. Auditors leverage this pack to accelerate planning and reduce duplicate requests. Governance and versioning are essential so evidence remains current and trustworthy.

Privileged access management (PAM) Processes and tools that control, monitor, and audit elevated access. Auditors evaluate provisioning, session recording, break-glass procedures, and periodic reviews. Effective PAM limits blast radius and reduces high-severity access findings.

Professional skepticism A questioning mindset that expects errors or bias and seeks corroborating evidence. Auditors apply it by challenging management narratives, testing assumptions, and tracing to source records. It guards against overreliance on prior ratings or persuasive anecdotes.

Provenance The documented origin and custody of an artifact, showing where it came from and how it was transformed. Auditors review provenance to trust automation outputs, analytics, and imported evidence. Clear lineage reduces disputes and enables confident re-performance.

Qualified conclusion An audit opinion or finding that contains a limitation or exception affecting scope or assurance. Auditors use qualified language when evidence is insufficient, scope is restricted, or deviations are material but not pervasive. The qualification must state what was affected and why.

Rating calibration A deliberate process to align severity and confidence ratings across auditors and engagements. Calibration sessions compare sample findings against shared criteria and exemplars. This improves consistency, reduces bias, and strengthens committee reporting.

Rating consistency The degree to which similar issues receive similar ratings across time and teams. Auditors check consistency with playbooks, peer review, and periodic back-testing. High consistency builds stakeholder trust and supports trend analysis.

Re-performance Independently executing a control or calculation to verify the result without relying on management's evidence alone. It provides strong assurance when inputs and criteria are well documented. Workpapers should show exact steps, parameters, and outputs.

Report on compliance (ROC) The formal assessment report for PCI DSS that documents scope, testing, and results. Auditors examine the ROC to understand segmentation, evidence sufficiency, and residual gaps. Users rely on it alongside SAQs and AOCs to judge compliance posture.

Residual risk The level of risk remaining after controls and mitigations are applied. Auditors assess whether residual risk aligns with the stated risk appetite and materiality thresholds. Clear articulation of residuals helps prioritize remediation and acceptance decisions.

Right-to-audit A contractual clause allowing customers or regulators to examine a provider's controls and evidence. Auditors confirm the clause's scope, notice period, and cooperation requirements. Strong language facilitates timely access and reduces reliance uncertainty.

Risk acceptance A documented decision by management to tolerate a known risk within defined limits. Auditors verify that acceptance criteria, duration, and compensating controls are explicit and approved at the right level. Time-bound reviews prevent quiet, indefinite rollovers.

Risk appetite The amount and type of risk an organization is willing to accept in pursuit of its objectives. Auditors use it to calibrate materiality, scope, and the severity of findings. Misalignment between appetite and actual residual risk is a key governance red flag.

Risk-based assurance An audit planning approach that allocates effort to areas of highest inherent and residual risk. It prioritizes controls with the greatest impact on objectives and materiality. Clear risk rationales in the plan support stakeholder buy-in and defend testing depth.

Risk register The centralized log of identified risks, their owners, treatments, and status. Auditors test that entries are current, consistently rated, and connected to control objectives. Cross-checking the register against incidents and exceptions validates completeness.

SDLC governance The policies and checkpoints that control how software moves from idea to production. Auditors look for defined gates (requirements, testing, segregation of duties) and reliable evidence artifacts from the pipeline. Strong governance reduces change-related findings and drift.

Second-partner review An independent quality check by a senior auditor not involved in fieldwork. It challenges assumptions, tests traceability, and validates conclusions before issuance. Regular use improves consistency and reduces rework after committee review.

Security control assessment (SCA) A structured evaluation of security controls against defined criteria, common in public-sector programs. Auditors verify test plans, evidence sufficiency, and scoring discipline. SCAs inform ATO decisions and continuous monitoring priorities.

Security information and event management (SIEM) A system that aggregates and analyzes logs for detection, investigation, and reporting. For auditors, it is an evidence source for coverage, retention, and alert-handling workflows. Testing focuses on log completeness, integrity, and response documentation.

Security ratings Externally generated scores that estimate an organization's security posture using observable signals. Auditors treat them as supplementary indicators, not a substitute for control testing. Discrepancies between ratings and internal evidence can reveal blind spots.

Segregation of duties The separation of critical tasks so no single person can both perform and conceal an error or abuse. Auditors test approval flows, access combinations, and break-glass oversight. Compensating controls are required when strict separation isn't feasible.

Shared responsibility model A delineation of which security and compliance tasks are handled by a service provider versus the customer. Auditors trace responsibilities to specific controls, evidence, and CUECs. Clear assignments prevent gaps when relying on third-party environments.

SOC 2 Type II An attestation report that evaluates the design and operating effectiveness of a service organization's controls over a defined period (e.g., 6–12 months). Auditors use it to assess ongoing control performance across the Trust Services Criteria. Pay attention to scope, CUECs, subservice carve-outs, and exceptions.

Software composition analysis (SCA) A control process that inventories third-party and open-source components to identify vulnerabilities and license risks. For auditors, SCA outputs are evidence of SBOM coverage, alert handling, and remediation timelines. Effectiveness hinges on complete dependency discovery and governance.

Statement of applicability A document that lists applicable controls, exclusions, and justifications—commonly used in ISO/IEC 27001 contexts. Auditors rely on it to determine which controls should be tested and why others are out of scope. Clear rationale improves traceability and defensibility.

Stratified sampling A sampling method that divides a population into homogeneous subgroups (strata) and samples each group. Auditors use it to improve precision and ensure representation of higher-risk strata. Proper stratum definitions and weights are essential for valid conclusions.

Structural independence The organizational design that ensures the audit function reports to a level capable of acting on findings (e.g., board or audit committee). Auditors assess reporting lines and charter language to confirm independence. Strong structure protects objectivity and credibility.

Subservice organization A third party that performs some processes on behalf of a service organization, affecting control objectives. Auditors evaluate whether controls are carved out or included and what user responsibilities (CUECs) apply. Misunderstanding this boundary can lead to reliance gaps.

Suitability of criteria The appropriateness, completeness, and relevance of the benchmarks used to evaluate controls or assertions. Auditors must confirm criteria are available, objective, and measurable. Weak criteria undermine conclusions, regardless of evidence volume.

System of record The authoritative source system for a specific data set or process (e.g., HRIS for workforce identity). Auditors reconcile populations to the system of record to test completeness and accuracy. Changes to this designation should be documented and approved.

Systematic sampling Selecting items from a population at regular intervals after a random start. Auditors use it for efficiency when populations are ordered without bias. Care is needed to avoid periodicity that could skew results.

Index